THE UNIVERSITY OF
WINCHESTER

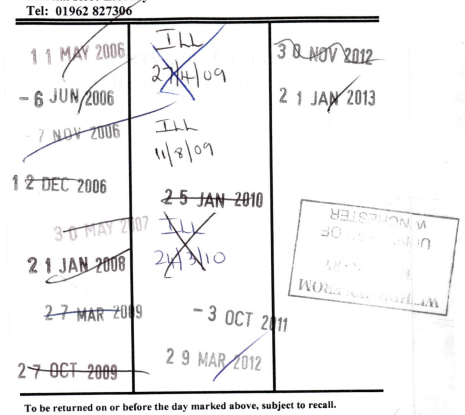

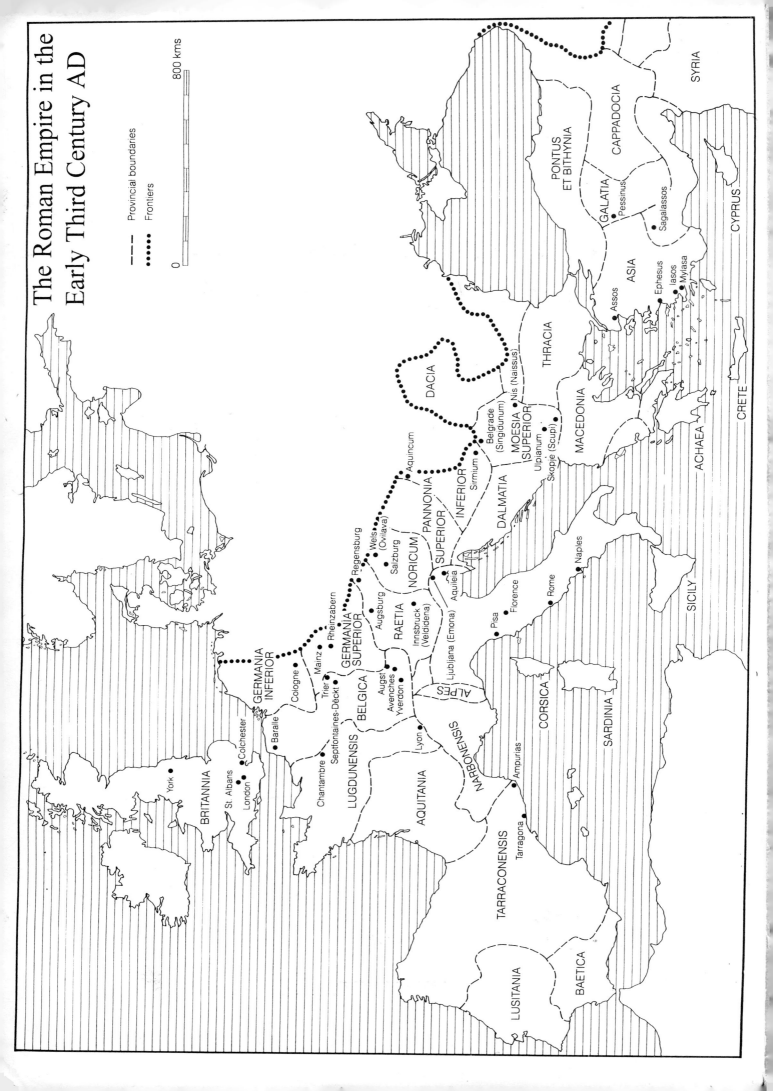

The Roman Empire in the Early Third Century AD

Provincial boundaries
Frontiers

800 kms
0

SYRIA

CYPRUS

CRETE

ACHAEA

SICILY

CAPPADOCIA

PONTUS ET BITHYNIA

GALATIA

Pessinus

Sagalassos

ASIA

Ephesus
Iasos
Mylasa

Assos

THRACIA

MACEDONIA

DACIA

Nis (Naissus)

Belgrade (Singidunum)

MOESIA SUPERIOR

Ulpianum

Skopje (Scupi)

Sirmium

DALMATIA

PANNONIA INFERIOR

Aquincum

PANNONIA SUPERIOR

Regensburg

Wels (Ovilava)

Salzburg

NORICUM

Aquileia

Naples

Rome

Florence

Pisa

RAETIA

Augsburg

Innsbruck (Veldidena)

Ljubljana (Emona)

ALPES

CORSICA

SARDINIA

GERMANIA INFERIOR

Cologne

Mainz

Trier

Rheinzabern

GERMANIA SUPERIOR

BELGICA

Augst

Avenches

Yverdon

Septfontaines-Déckt

Chantambre

Baralle

Lyon

LUGDUNENSIS

AQUITANIA

NARBONENSIS

Ampurias

TARRACONENSIS

Tarragona

York

BRITANNIA

St. Albans

London

Colchester

LUSITANIA

BAETICA

Burial, Society and Context in the Roman World

Edited by

John Pearce, Martin Millett and Manuela Struck

Oxbow Books

Published by
Oxbow Books, Park End Place, Oxford OX1 1HN

ISBN 1 84217 034 1

A CIP record of this book is available from the British Library

This book is available direct from
Oxbow Books, Park End Place, Oxford OX1 1HN
(Phone: 01865-241249; Fax: 01865-794449)

and

The David Brown Book Company
PO Box 511, Oakville, CT 06779, USA
(Phone: 860-945-9329; Fax 860-945-9468)

and

from our website

www.oxbowbooks.com

*Cover: A stele from South Shields, executed in Palmyrene style.
The burial monument of Victor, a trooper of an auxiliary cavalry unit,
the first* ala Asturum *(RIB 1064: CSIR i. I 248).
Photo by Martin Millett.*

Printed in Great Britain at
The Short Run Press
Exeter

Contents

The dead in the landscape

Burial and ethnicity

Society, religion and burial in late Roman Britain and Italy

Preface

Martin Millett

The papers presented in this volume are the product of a symposium held under the aegis of the Research Centre for Roman Provincial Archaeology at the University of Durham between 18th and 20th April 1997. The impetus for the meeting came from John Pearce, then a Ph.D. student at Durham. His objectives are elaborated in the Introduction (below) but these should be understood against the background of the study of burial practices within Roman archaeology in Britain. Here, in contrast to other parts of Europe (especially in the German-speaking world) there has been remarkably little general interest in broader aspects of interpretation of burials.

Although a large number of cemeteries have been explored in Roman Britain they have never been seen as central to the study of the province. A narrowly defined 'historical' tradition of studying the Roman provinces had an almost exclusive hold on British academia until the 1980s. For scholars in this tradition, inscribed tombstones had some importance as sources for prosopography or for the study of military dispositions but otherwise burials seem to have remained irrelevant (cf. Frere 1967). However excavations were uncovering burials and museums came to be filled with the better preserved objects that were often found with the bodies. Objects from cemeteries were accumulated during the urban expansion of the nineteenth and early twentieth centuries in towns like Colchester and thus came to form the core of museum collections (e.g. May 1930). These collections contained well-preserved artefacts and were therefore key sources for those producing artefact typologies (e.g. Hull 1958). These works generally treated the objects independently of their contexts and in many museums it is now almost impossible to reconstruct grave groups. Although some archaeologists sought to use burial assemblages to answer broader archaeological questions (e.g. Hawkes and Dunning 1931), burials and grave goods were rarely the centre of attention in the study of Roman Britain. In works of synthesis about individual sites, the cemeteries were most often of interest only in as a means of defining the occupied areas. The exceptions were confined to those sites which had produced an exceptional range of material (e.g. RCHME 1962). Similarly, as there was little interest in the people themselves, the bodies excavated with the objects were only rarely studied and published.

From the 1970s attitudes began to change as the study of Roman provincial archaeology in Britain broadened its approach. Major cemetery excavations were increasingly undertaken within the 'Rescue Archaeology' boom and a minority of those working on these sites began to ask what information cemeteries could contribute to our wider understanding (e.g. Clarke 1975). As the intellectual climate changed two trends can be detected. First, there was a tendency amongst British archaeologists to explore a variety of ways in which the excavated information could be used for a better understanding of the past. Second, some of those working on Roman Britain began to seek ideas and methods from other branches of archaeology – from both Romanists working in other countries and specialists studying other periods. Against this background those with an interest in burials began to develop more varied approaches to their material.

The fruits of this were seen first in the volume edited by Richard Reece and published in 1977 under the title *Burial in the Roman World*. This was the product of a seminar held at the Institute of Archaeology in London in 1974. A further conference was held at New College in Oxford in 1981 but only Reece's paper, provocatively entitled 'Bones, bodies and dis-ease' was published in 1982. During this period there was a renewed interest in burial studies, with even the suggested formation of a burial studies group. This activity was marked by on at least two successful PhD projects which sought to explore the subject further (R.F.J. Jones (1983) and R. Philpott (1991)). Others began ambitious projects, including large-scale data-bases which were never completed.

Despite this activity and the gradual process of publishing the major cemetery excavations of this era (Lankhills, Poundbury, Cirencester, King Harry Lane), burial studies still did not find a central place in Roman archaeology in Britain. Nevertheless, as those of us who were taught by Richard Reece took up teaching posts the subject achieved a higher profile within University courses. At the same time developing contacts with those interested in studying burials on the continent resulted in the growth of a small, informal network of scholars across Europe. This group came together formally in Mainz in 1991 for a seminar which resulted in the publication of an important set of papers edited by Manuela Struck in 1993. Those attending the meeting from Britain were excited and encouraged by the dynamism of the ideas and the enthusiasm of those working on the subject. Further volumes have been produced from conferences in Tours in 1992 (Ferdière 1993) and Xanten in 1995 (Fasold et al. 1998) and the proceedings of a conference in Rome in 1998 will be published shortly (*Culto dei morti ...* forthcoming).

The Durham meeting on which this book is based was in many senses a follow up to that held in Mainz. John Pearce worked with Manuela Struck to construct the programme which addressed ideas seen as particularly relevant to current debates in Roman archaeology. They put together an excellent programme although in the way of these things, a number of the papers addressed questions different to those raised in the introductory paper. Different national traditions of study, the varying types of information available and individuals with divergent ideas led to an exciting and varied weekend. Whatever other impression one came away with, it was clear that burial studies had broad relevance to a variety of aspects of Roman provincial archaeology across Europe. In putting together this publication we have decided to take a liberal line in allowing the contributors to explore the aspects of the subject they chose. Whilst this has arguably produced a more diverse volume than might have been desired we believe it illustrates the richness and diversity of current studies of Roman burial practice. We hope that some of these papers will inform and stimulate those working on Roman Britain to take cemetery sites more seriously. Equally, we believe that all those working on burials across the empire will benefit from a publication which explores different approaches to the wide diversity of available data.

This volume has been put together largely through the hard work of my co-editors who also undertook most of the work of organising the seminar. The meeting was hosted at the Department of Archaeology in Durham thanks to the good offices of Professor Anthony Harding, the then Head of Department. Travel costs for the speakers

were partly met thanks to grants from the Cramp Fund of the Department of Archaeology, Durham University, the British Academy and the Society for the Promotion of Roman Studies. Through Hilary Bowler, St Cuthbert's Society accommodated and fed participants; speakers were also provided with hospitality by members of the Department of Archaeology. Post-graduates of the Department of Archaeology helped to ensure the smooth running of the conference, and friends and colleagues from Durham, Oxford and elsewhere have subsequently assisted in the translation of papers and abstracts. To all these we express our warmest thanks.

Bibliography

Clarke, G. 1975. Population movements and late Roman cemeteries. *World Archaeology*, 7: 46–56

Culto dei morti... (forthcoming) *Culto dei morti e costumi funerari romani. Roma, Italia settentrionale e province nord-occidentali dalla tarda Repubblica alla prima età imperiale.* Proceedings of conference, Deutsches Archäologisches Institut, Rome 1998

Fasold, P. *et al.* (eds) 1998. *Bestattungssitte und kulturelle Identität. Grabanlagen und Grabbeigaben der frühen römischen Kaiserzeit in Italien und den Nordwest-Provinzen.* Xantener Berichte, 7, Cologne: Rheinland-Verlag

Ferdière, A. ed. 1993. *Monde des morts, monde des vivants en Gaule rurale.* Tours: Université de Tours.

Frere, S. S. 1967. *Britannia: a history of Roman Britain (1st ed.).* London: Routledge and Kegan Paul

Hawkes, C. F. C. and Dunning, G. 1930. The Belgae of Gaul and Britain. *Archaeological Journal*, 87: 150–335

Hull, M. R. 1958. *Roman Colchester.* Society of Antiquaries Research Report, 20, London: Society of Antiquaries

Jones, R.F.J. 1983. *Cemeteries and Burial Practice in the Western Provinces of the Roman Empire.* Unpublished Ph.D. thesis, London University

May, T. 1930. *Catalogue of the Roman Pottery in Colchester and Essex Museum.* Cambridge: Cambridge University Press / Colchester Corporation

Philpott, R. 1991. *Burial Practices in Roman Britain. A survey of grave treatment and furnishing A.D. 43–410.* BAR British Series, 219, Oxford: BAR

Reece, R. ed, 1977. *Burial in the Roman World.* CBA Research Reports, 22, London: CBA

Reece, R. 1982. Bones, bodies and dis-ease. *Oxford Journal of Archaeology*, 1/3: 347–58

RCHME 1962. *Royal Commission on Historical Monuments: Eburacum: Roman York.* London: HMSO

Struck, M. (ed.) 1993. *Römerzeitliche Gräber als Quellen zur Religion, Bevölkerungsstruktur und Sozialgeschichte.* Mainz: Johannes Gutenberg Institut für Vor- und Frühgeschichte

Abstracts, Zusammenfassungen, Résumés

1. Burial, society and context in the provincial Roman world

J. Pearce

This paper argues for the application of wider developments in the archaeological study of mortuary practice to the interpretation of burial practice in the Roman, especially the provincial Roman, world. Particular consideration is given to current approaches to the reconstruction of cultural identity and social status from burial evidence, which are argued to take insufficient account of the transformation of the identity of the deceased in burial ritual, a transformation dependent on culturally specific constructions of death and burial. An archaeological framework for establishing the context of burial is considered, based on comparing burial with other types of archaeological evidence. Such a framework suggests lines of enquiry which may strengthen current approaches to Roman period burial evidence and expand the scope of analysis. Given the wealth of archaeological evidence from cemeteries, settlements and votive sites, the Roman period offers an especially rich opportunity for putting burial in context.

Dieser Beitrag plädiert dafür, einen weiteren Blickwinkel bei der archäologischen Erforschung von Grabsitten zu berücksichtigen, um zur Interpretation dieser Sitten in der Römischen Welt und speziell in den Provinzen zu gelangen. Besondere Aufmerksamkeit erfahren die aktuellen Versuche, kulturelle Identität und sozialen Status mit Hilfe der Funde und Befunde aus den Gräbern zu rekonstruieren, da der Transformation der Identität des Verstorbenen – eine Transformation, die von kulturspezifischen Konzepten zu Tod und Begräbnis abhängt – m.E. nicht genügend Rechnung getragen wird. Es wird vorgeschlagen, aus dem Vergleich von Gräbern mit anderen Fundgattungen einen archäologischen Rahmen zu erarbeiten, der den jeweiligen Kontext, in dem Gräber verstanden werden sollten, darstellt. Aus diesem Rahmen ergeben sich dann Fragen, die die aktuellen Untersuchungsansätze zu römerzeitlichen Gräbern unterstützen und vorhandene Fragestellungen erweitern. Mit dem Reichtum an archäologischem Material aus Gräberfeldern, Siedlungen und Opferplätzen bietet die römische Periode eine besonders gute Möglichkeit, Gräber im Kontext zu sehen.

Cet article propose d'appliquer des développements générales dans l'étude archéologique des pratiques mortuaires à l'interprétation des pratiques funéraires du monde romain, et plus particulièrement les provinces. Nous donnons une attention particulière aux approches actuelles de l'identité culturelle et de la position sociale à travers les sépultures, qui ne prennent pas suffisamment en compte la transformation spécifique à la culture que subit l'identité du défunt pendant les rites funéraires, une transformation qui dépend à la fois de la mort et de l'enterrement. Une telle structure, établissant le contexte de l'enterrement, fondée sur une comparaison entre les sépultures et les autres découvertes archéologiques, ouvre une voie de recherches qui peut renforcer l'étude des enterrements de l'ère romaine, ainsi qu'étendre le champ de l'analyse. Etant donné la richesse des témoignages archéologiques des cimetières, des habitations et des dépôts votifs, la période romaine nous offre une occasion particulièrement riche pour situer l'enterrement dans son contexte.

2. Ritual, sequence, and structure in Late Iron Age mortuary practices in north-west Europe

A. Fitzpatrick

Many recent analyses of the Late Iron Age have concentrated on the role of 'romanisation' as a stimulus to change. Burials have been regarded as sensitive indexes of how local elites responded to 'Rome'. The mortuary rituals enacted at three Late Iron Age sites in north-western Europe are examined here; Acy-Romance in France, Clemency in Luxembourg and Westhampnett in Great Britain. All three sites were in use during the century preceding the Roman conquests. The analyses and publication of these sites reveal diverse and complex local beliefs, something of which can be recovered archaeologically but which, as yet, have not been incorporated satisfactorily into ideas of 'romanisation'. While the mortuary rituals at all three sites display differing responses to Roman influences, they do share similarities. The rituals enacted in the sacred spaces involved the deliberate destruction of people, animals and worldly goods to allow their transference to the gods as metaphysical essences. The sacred spaces were also microcosms of the living world where the mourners renegotiated their emotions and relations with the living and the dead, the dead, and their gods. The complexity and diversity of these rituals have been overshadowed by the concentration on 'romanisation before the conquest.' One of the challenges to students of 'romanisation' is how to incorporate this heterogeneity within a concept that, whether by accident or design, can become a concept of homogeneity.

Viele kürzlich durchgeführte Studien haben sich auf die Rolle der Romanisation als Auslöser für Veränderungen konzentriert. Gräber wurden dabei als sensibler Indikator für die Reaktion lokaler Eliten auf ‚Rom' angesehen. An dieser Stelle werden die Grabsitten, gebräuchlich an drei späteisenzeitlichen Fundorten in Nordwesteuropa, untersucht: Acy-Romance in

Frankreich, Clemency in Luxembourg und Westhampnett in Großbritannien. Alle drei Gräberfelder wurden während des letzten Jahrhunderts vor der römischen Okkupation benutzt. Die Untersuchung und Publikation dieser Plätze veranschaulicht die Verschiedenheit und Komplexität der örtlichen Bestattungsbräuche, die sich zum Teil archäologisch nachweisen lassen, aber noch nicht zufriedenstellend in unser Konzept von Romanisation integriert sind. Obwohl der Totenbrauch an den drei Plätzen unterschiedliche Reaktionen auf römische Einflüsse zeigt, weist er trotzdem Ähnlichkeiten auf. Rituale, die innerhalb geheiligter Bereiche ausgeführt wurden, beinhalteten die Zerstörung von Menschen, Tieren und weltlichen Gütern, um deren Transport zu den Göttern in Form metaphysischer Essenzen zu ermöglichen. Die geheiligten Bereiche waren außerdem Mikrokosmen der dieseitigen Welt, in denen die Trauernden ihre Emotionen und ihr Verhältnis zu den Lebenden, Verstorbenen und Göttern neu definieren konnten. Die Komplexität und Vielfältigkeit dieser Rituale wurde aufgrund unserer Konzentration auf die Frage der ,Romanisation vor der Eroberung' nicht genügend beachtet. Eine der Herausforderungen für die ,Romanisations'-Forscher, ist deswegen die Frage, wie diese Heterogenität mit einem Konzept vereinbart werden kann, das – aus Zufall oder mit Bedacht – ein Konzept von Homogenität darstellt.

Plusieurs analyses récentes de l'Age de fer tardif se sont concentrées sur le rôle de la 'romanisation' comme stimulus des changements. On a considéré les sépultures comme des indices sensibles de la façon dont ont réagi les élites régionales envers Rome. Nous examinons ici les rites mortuaires qui ont eu lieu sur trois sites de l'Age de fer tardif du nord-ouest de l'Europe: Acy-Romance en France, Clemency au Luxembourg et Westhampnett en Grande Bretagne. Ces trois sites ont été utilisés pendant le siècle précédant les conquêtes romaines.

Leurs analyses et leur publication révèlent des croyances diverses et complexes. On peut en retrouver une partie à travers l'archéologie, mais jusqu'à maintenant on ne les a pas situées de façon satisfaisante en rapport aux idées sur la 'romanisation'. Tandis que les rites mortuaires de ces trois sites montrent des réactions différentes face aux influences romaines, ils partagent aussi certaines similitudes. Les rituels qui avaient lieu dans les espaces sacrés impliquaient la destruction délibérée de personnes, d'animaux et de biens matériels afin de les faire passer aux dieux en tant qu'essences métaphysiques. Les espaces sacrés étaient des microcosmes du monde vivant où les alliés du défunt renégociaient leurs émotions et leurs relations entre les vivants, les morts et leurs dieux. La concentration sur la 'romanisation avant la conquête' a éclipsé la complexité et la variété de ces rituels. L'un des défis des chercheurs sur la 'romanisation' consiste à intégrer cette hétérogènéité dans un concept qui devient parfois, soit par hasard, soit à dessein, un concept d'homogénéité.

3. Reconstructing funerary rituals: the evidence of ustrina *and related archaeological structures*

M. Polfer

This paper deals with several categories of archaeological features occurring in provincial Roman funerary contexts, cremation areas, postholes, single pyre debris pits and other pits filled with cremated material. The available evidence is discussed in the first part of the paper, while the second part focuses on the analytical potential of these features for future research into provincial Roman burial practice. It is argued that these features deserve as much attention as the graves themselves, as they allow us to appreciate stages and aspects of the funerary process that cannot be observed through graves alone. In the final part of the paper, this argument is illustrated with the results of the case-study of the cemetery of Septfontaines-Dëckt (Luxembourg). Here it has for the first time been possible to compare the objects from graves with those from the pyre site. The study shows that the objects encountered in graves are not representative – in terms of neither function nor quantity nor quality – of all the objects involved in the funerary process.

Der Beitrag behandelt fünf Kategorien archäologischer Strukturen, die in provinzialrömischen Gräberfeldern angetroffen werden können: Ustrinen und Pfostenlöcher sowie Aschen-, Abraum- und Opfergruben. Im ersten Teil des Beitrags werden wichtige Befunde vorgestellt, im zweiten Teil wird das Erkenntnispotential dieser Befundkategorien für die zukünftige Gräberforschung diskutiert. Ihre Untersuchung verdient die gleiche Aufmerksamkeit wie diejenige der Gräber selbst, da wir durch sie Etappen und Aspekte des Bestattungsprozesses fassen können, die in den Gräbern weitgehend ausgeblendet sind. Im letzten Teil des Beitrags wird dies verdeutlicht anhand einiger Resultate einer Studie zum provinzialrömischen Brandgräberfeld von Septfontaines-Dëckt (Luxemburg), wo erstmals eine vergleichende Analyse der Grabinventare und des Material eines zentralen Verbrennungsplatzes möglich war. Die Studie belegt eindeutig, dass Grabinventare a priori – weder in funtionaler noch in qualitativer oder quantitativer Hinsicht – als representativ gelten können für die Gesamtheit aller in den Bestattungsprozess implizierten Gegenstände.

Cet article porte sur différentes catégories de structures archéologiques observables en contexte funéraire provincial romain: aires de crémation, trous de poteaux, fosses à cendre, fosses dépotoirs, fosses à offrandes. La documentation archéologique disponible est presentée dans la première partie, dans la seconde partie le potentiel de ces structures pour l'étude future des rites funéraires est discuté. L'auteur soutient la thèse que leur étude mérite la même attention que celle des tombes elles-mêmes, puisque ces structures nous permettent d'approcher des étapes et des aspects du processus funéraire qui nous échappent dans l'étude des seules tombes. Dans la dernière partie de la contribution, cette thèse est illustrée par quelques résultats de l'étude de la nécropole à incinération gallo-romaine de Septfontaines-Dëckt (Luxembourg), où il a été pour la première fois possible de confronter le matériel issu des tombes à celui provenant d'une aire de crémation centrale. Cette étude montre e.a. que les inventaires secondaires ne sont pas représentatifs – ni en termes de fonction, ni en termes de quantité ou de qualité – pour l'ensemble des objets intervenant au cours du processus funéraire.

4. Phoenix rising: aspects of cremation in Roman Britain

J. McKinley

The common, though perhaps understandable 'short-hand' use of imprecise and potentially misleading terminology – cremation and subsequent burial frequently being considered or referred to as synonymous – implicitly discards many hours of activity; preparation of the pyre and the corpse, the cremation, the collection and burial of the cremated remains and the subsequent clearing-up processes. All of these activities may potentially be deduced from the analysis of the archaeological remains. It is the intention of this paper to focus on three specific types of cremation-related deposits, and by using examples from a number of Romano-British rural and urban cemeteries, to illustrate the potential for the recovery of data of a form which may increase our understanding of the whole mortuary practice of cremation, not just the burial.

Wir bedienen uns einer unpräzisen und möglicherweise irreführenden Terminologie, die eine Identität von Verbrennung und nachfolgender Beisetzung impliziert. Dies ist durchaus verständlich, führt aber dazu, dass stundenlange Handlungen, wie die Vorbereitung des Scheiterhaufens und des Leichnams, die Einäscherung, das Aussammeln des Leichenbrandes, die Beisetzung der verbrannten Überreste und die abschließenden Aufräumarbeiten, ignoriert werden. Es ist theoretisch möglich, alle diese Aktivitäten aus der Analyse von archäologischem Material und Befund abzuleiten. Ziel dieses Beitrages ist es, sich auf drei Typen von Deponierungen, die im Zusammenhang mit Brandgräbern stehen, zu konzentrieren und Beispiele für sie aus einer Reihe romano-britischer Gräberfelder von ländlichen und städtischen Siedlungen vorzuführen. Auf diese Weise sollen die Möglichkeiten illustriert werden, Befunde zu erkennen, die unser Verständnis des gesamten Grabbrauches, und nicht nur der Grablege verbessern können.

L'usage répandu d'une terminologie imprécise et trompeuse peut se comprendre – les mots 'cremation' et 'burial' sont souvent considérés comme synonymes – mais cet usage abandonne tacitement beaucoup d'heures d'activité: la préparation du bûcher et du cadavre, l'incinération, le ramassage et l'enterrement des restes incinérés et le nettoyage qui s'en suit. En principe, nous pouvons déduire toutes ces activités de l'analyse des restes archéologiques. Cet article se concentre sur trois types de dépôts relatifs au processus de l'incinération. Il a pour but de montrer qu'il est possible d'obtenir un type de données qui peut améliorer notre compréhension de toutes les pratiques mortuaires, et pas seulement de la sépulture, à partir d'exemples tirés de plusieurs cimetières romano-britanniques ruraux et urbains.

5. Functional and conceptual archaeobotanical data from Roman cremations

A. Kreuz

Archaeobotanical investigations of Roman period burials and related contexts pose the question of whether it is possible to establish culturally determined changes in burial ritual with the help of plant remains (seeds, fruits, wood etc.). We propose to divide the plants attested according to their use or type and to distinguish functional from conceptual data for the purposes of interpretation. On this basis the paper will discuss what indications for ritual and for everyday life can be obtained from both these groups of data.

Archäobotanische Untersuchungen römerzeitlicher Bestattungen und begleitender Befunde führen zu der Frage, ob es möglich ist, kulturell bedingte Veränderungen der Grabsitten mit Hilfe der pflanzlichen Überreste (Samen, Früchte, Holz uzw.) festzustellen. Es wird vorgeschlagen, die nachgewiesenen Pflanzenarten in Nutzungs- oder Wuchsgruppen zu gliedern und

für die Interpretation funktionale von konzeptionellen Daten zu unterscheiden. Dabei wird diskutiert, welche Hinweise zu Ritual und weltlichem Alltag aus diesen beiden Datengruppen zu erzielen sind.

L'examen archéobotanique des sépultures et des structures connexes de l'époque romaine conduit à la question s'il est possible de constater à partir des restes des plantes (semences / graines, fruit, bois etc.) des modifications d'origine culturelle au sein des rites funéraires. Nous proposons de diviser les plantes identifiées en groupes, d'une part selon leur utilisation et d'autre part selon leur croissance, et de distinguer lors de l'interprétation les données fonctionelles des données conceptionelles. Il sera ensuite discuté quels indices ces deux groupes de données peuvent nous livrer pour le rituel funéraire et pour la vie quotidienne.

6. Pottery assemblages in Gallo-Roman cemeteries

M. Tuffreau-Libre

Cemeteries have always been an important source of information for pottery specialists and it was not until pottery from settlements and workshops began to be studied systematically that an alternative picture of Gallo-Roman pottery gradually emerged. Once the regional repertoires were better known and better dated, it was clear that burial material posed a number of problems. There seemed to be a complete chronological disparity between the dates derived from funerary contexts and those from settlements. There was therefore a need to reconsider ceramic assemblages from burials, taking into account their specific nature. This study tries to redefine the characteristics of pottery assemblages in burials, to establish more precisely what information they provide and their limitations. It also presents a case study of the material from the cemetery of Baralle in northern France. In conclusion it is clear that the study of pottery from burial sites has much to offer for ritual, social and economic studies but great care must be taken over its chronological interpretation.

Gräberfelder waren immer eine bedeutende Quellengattung für Keramikspezialisten. Viele chronologische Typologien basieren ausschließlich auf dem Material dieser Fundortart. Erst als begonnen wurde, die Keramik aus Siedlungen und Werkstätten zu untersuchen, entstand langsam ein alternatives Bild der gallo-römischen Keramik. Sobald die regionalen Keramikrepertoires besser bekannt und datiert waren, wurde klar, dass das Material aus Gräbern eine Reihe von Problemen aufwirft. Letztere betreffen sowohl die Chronologie als auch die Zusammensetzung der Keramikinventare, die jetzt erneut und auf andere Art analysiert werden müssen, wobei ihrem besonderen Charakter Rechnung zu tragen ist. Dieser Beitrag versucht, die Eigenarten von keramischen Grabinventaren neu zu definieren und die Art der Informationen, mit denen sie uns versorgen, sowie deren Beschränkungen genauer zu bestimmen. Der Beitrag dient außerdem als Fallstudie einer Nekropole, nämlich der von Baralle in Nordgallien. Am Ende wird klar, dass das Studium von Keramik aus ländlichen Bestattungsplätzen einen großen Beitrag bei der Erforschung von Religion, sozialen und ökonomischen Verhältnissen leistet, man bei chronologischen Schlüssen jedoch Vorsicht walten lassen muss.

Les nécropoles ont toujours été une source de renseignements importantes pour les céramologues. De nombreuses chrono-typologies générales ont été construites à partir de ces découvertes. Avec le progrès des études systematiques de céramiques issues d' habitats et d' ateliers s'est dessinée une autre image. Les répertoires régionaux étant mieux connus et datés, les matériels funéraires sont apparus en décalage, tant au niveau des datations que de la composition des assemblages. Il a donc fallu reconsidérer autrement les ensembles des nécropoles, en tenant compte de leurs spécificités. L'article publié ici tente de redéfinir les caractéristiques des ensembles de céramiques funéraires, de cerner plus précisément les renseignements qu'ils nous apportent et leurs limites. Il présente aussi un exemple d'étude de nécropole, celle de Baralle, située dans le Nord de la Gaule. En conclusion, il est clair que l'étude de la céramique en milieu funéraire apporte beaucoup pour les études religieuses, sociales et économiques, mais qu'il faut rester prudent dans les interprétations chronologiques.

7. Mors immatura *in the Roman World – a Mirror of Society and Tradition*

S. Martin-Kilcher

In the category of 'special burials' four groups can also be particularly distinguished in the Roman period, (1) children who died before, during or shortly after birth, (2) children and juveniles and, in many cultures, unmarried or childless adults, (3) women who died in childbirth and (4) the 'bad death'. This paper investigates young girls of the second group, those deceased who were so particularly furnished with *crepundia* (various personal amulets), dolls and / or miniature vessels. It can be shown that these categories of grave goods are related to a non-attained wedding. A comparison of the grave furnishing of Roman and Germanic children shows deep differences in mentality which are expressed in the different representation of social status.

Unter den Sonderbestattungen sind auch in römischer Zeit insbesondere vier Gruppen zu unterscheiden: (1) um den Geburtstermin verstorbene Kinder; (2) Kinder und Jugendliche, in manchen Kulturen auch unverheiratet oder kinderlos verstorbene Erwachsene; (3) im Kindbett verstorbene Frauen und (4) infolge eines 'schrecklichen' Todes Verstorbene. Der Beitrag untersucht junge Mädchen der zweiten Gruppe, und zwar speziell mit Crepundia (div. persönliche Amulette), mit Puppen bzw. mit Miniaturgeschirr ausgestattete Verstorbene. Es kann gezeigt werden, dass diese Beigabenkategorien mit dem nicht erreichten Hochzeitsfest zu verbinden sind. Ein Vergleich mit der Grabausstattung römischer und germanischer Kinder zeigt tiefe Unterschiede der Mentalität, die sich in der unterschiedlichen Darstellung der gesellschaftlichen Stellung ausdrücken.

Parmi les sépultures à caractère particulier on peut discerner quatre groupes: (1) enfants morts au stade périnatal; (2) enfants et jeunes individus – dans différentes cultures également des célibataires et des adultes sans déscendance-; (3) femmes mortes en couches et (4) 'mort brutale'. L'article examine un groupe de jeunes filles avec un mobilier funéraire spécial, composé de crepundia (div. amulets personnels), avec poupée(s) et/ou vases miniatures. On peut mettre en évidence que ces catégories de mobilier sont à lier avec des individus n'étant pas parvenus au mariage. La comparaison du mobilier funéraire d'enfants romains

et germaniques met en évidence une profonde différence des mentalités s'exprimant dans une différente représentation de la position sociale.

8. *Portrait figures on sepulchral altars of Roman* liberti: *evidence of Romanization or assimilation of attributes characterizing higher social strata?*

D. Dexheimer

The decoration on some funerary altars of the first and early second century AD in Upper Italy includes realistic depictions, among which portrait figures are particularly striking. The persons mentioned in the inscriptions bear a close relation to those depicted; in seven of nine cases, they are identical with the donors who were still living when the altars were built. For the sides of the altars the commissioners chose portrait figures of which the prototypes can be found on statues raised in public spaces. The right to have statues erected in public places was considered a high honour and a necessary pre-condition was the membership of a higher *ordo*, which implied the status of free citizen birth. Freedmen, or, for example, veterans were not allowed to sponsor the making of such statues as they did not fulfil these prerequisites. In eight of the nine examples examined, the donors of altars with portrait figures on their sides were members of lower status groups, i.e. slaves, *liberti*, and veterans. By choosing such ornament, the donors, although not allowed to erect such statues in public, expressed both their desire for social acceptance and their readiness to adapt to their Roman cultural milieu by adopting common forms of artistic expression.

Das Bildprogramm oberitalienischer Grabaltäre des 1. und frühen 2. Jahrhunderts umfasst realistische Darstellungen, unter denen Porträtfiguren besonders auffallen. Die Personen, die in den Inschriften genannt werden, stehen in engem Verhältnis zu den Dargestellten: In sieben von neun Fällen sind sie identisch mit den Spendern, die zur Bauzeit des Altars noch am Leben waren. Für die Darstellungen an den Altarseiten wählten die Auftraggeber Porträtfiguren, deren Prototypen sich an Statuen auf öffentlichen Plätzen finden. Das Recht, auf öffentlichen Plätzen Statuen zu errichten, wurde als große Ehre und notwendige Voraussetzung für die Zugehörigkeit zu einer höheren *ordo* angesehen, die den Status der freien Geburt implizierte. Freigelassenen oder beispielsweise Veteranen war es nicht erlaubt, Statuen zu finanzieren, da sie diese Voraussetzung nicht erfüllten. In acht der neun untersuchten Fälle handelt es sich bei den Spendern der Altäre mit seitlichen Porträtfiguren um Angehörige niederer Klassen, z. B. Sklaven, Freigelassene und Veteranen. Durch die Wahl dieses Motivs drückten die Spender, denen das Aufstellen solcher Statuen auf öffentlichen Plätzen untersagt war, ihr Verlangen nach gesellschaftlicher Anerkennung und ihre Bereitschaft, sich der römischen Kultur anzupassen, aus, denn sie bedienten sich bewusst eines gängigen künstlerischen Repertoire.

La décoration, en Italie septentrionale, de quelques autels funéraires du Ier et du IIe siècle de notre ère comprend des représentations réalistes, dont des personnages figurés qui sont particulièrement frappants. Les personnes dont les inscriptions font mention ont un rapport étroit avec celles représentées; dans sept sur neuf cas, ils sont identiques aux donateurs qui étaient toujours vivants lors de la construction des autels. Pour les côtés des autels les donateurs ont choisi des personnages figurés dont on peut trouver les prototypes parmi les statues dressées aux espaces publics. On considérait le droit de se faire dresser une statue aux espaces publiques comme un grand honneur et il fallait appartenir à un *ordo* supérieur, qui laisse supposer qu'il s'agissait de citoyen libre de naissance. Les *liberti*, ou, par exemple, les vétérans ne pouvaient pas commander de telles statues parce qu'ils ne remplissaient pas ces conditions. Dans huit sur neuf exemples examinés, les donateurs de ces autels avec des personnages figurés latéraux appartenaient à des groupes d'une position inférieure, c'est-à-dire les esclaves, les *liberti* et les vétérans. Le choix d'une telle décoration de la part des donateurs qui ne pouvaient pas se faire dresser des statues dans un espace public exprime bien le désir d'approbation sociale et le fait qu'ils étaient prêts de s'adapter à leur milieu culturel romain en adoptant des formes courantes d'expression artistique.

9. High status burial in Roman Britain (1st–3rd cent. AD) – Potential of interpretation

M. Struck

This article concentrates on the following three questions: 1. To what extent is status in life reflected in the burial rite? 2. Do Romano-British high status burials show patterns in distribution, chronology and burial rite? 3. Do the results of burial analysis contribute to our understanding of the social structure of Roman Britain? Nine main types of high status burials were distinguished from Britain. Their geographical distribution, chronology and social environment (especially the associated settlement types) demonstrate, once again, the different developments in south-east Britain, the military zones and the rest of the province.

Der folgende Beitrag konzentriert sich auf drei Fragen: 1. In wieweit lässt sich Status im Leben auch im Totenbrauch erkennen? 2. Zeigen romano-britische Élitegräber Regelhaftigkeiten in Verteilung, Chronologie und Bestattungssitte? 3. Tragen die erzielten Resultate zu unserem Verständnis der Gesellschaftsstruktur des römischen Britanniens bei? Neun Typen von Élitegräbern konnten für Britannien unterschieden werden. Ihre geographische Verbreitung, Chronologie und ihr soziales Umfeld (besonders im Hinblick auf die zugehörigen Siedlungstypen) demonstrieren erneut die Unterschiede zwischen dem Südosten, den Militärzonen und der restlichen Provinz.

Cet article se concentre sur les trois questions suivantes: 1. Dans quelle mesure le statut social est-il reflété dans les rites funéraires? 2. Peut-on isoler des caratéristiques particulières concernant la répartition géographique, la chronologie ou le rite funéraire parmi les sépultures de notables romano-britanniques? 3. Les résultats de l'analyse des sépultures contribuent-ils à notre compréhension de la structure sociale de la Bretagne romaine? Nous avons distingué neuf types principaux de sépulture de notables en Bretagne. La répartition géographique, la chronologie et l'environnement social (surtout les types d'habitation liés aux sépultures) montrent encore une fois les développements différents entre le sud-est, les zones militaires et le reste de la province.

10. Funerary rites in Verulamium during the early Roman period

R. Niblett

In the first half of the first century AD burial rites at Verulamium show evidence for complex and prolonged rituals, including both inhumations and cremations. Burials were frequently contained within, or were aligned on, rectilinear, ditched enclosures. There is some evidence to suggest that central burials within the enclosures were afforded special rites which resulted in the deposition of burnt pyre debris with the burial. These rituals had largely died out by the early second century, although there is evidence for the careful siting of cemeteries in the second and third centuries.

In der ersten Hälfte des 1. Jahrhunderts n. Chr. können für Verulamium komplizierte und langwierige Bestattungssitten rekonstruiert werden, die sowohl die Körper- als auch die Brandbeisetzung beinhalteten. Gräber lagen häufig in Grabengevierten oder waren an diesen ausgerichtet. Für die Zentralbestattungen in den Grabeneinfriedungen scheinen besondere Rituale ausgeführt worden zu sein, die das Deponieren der Scheiterhaufenreste mit sich brachten. Diese Bräuche wurden bis zum frühen 2. Jahrhundert aufgegeben, obwohl es auch für das 2. und 3. Jahrhundert Hinweise auf sorgfältig angelegte Gräberfelder gibt.

Pendant la première moîtié du premier siècle après J.-C. les rites funéraires à Verulamium témoignent de rituels complexes et étendus qui comprennent des inhumations et des incinérations. Souvent les sépultures se trouvaient à l'intérieur d'enclos rectangulaires entourés de fossés ou alignées sur eux. Il y a beaucoup d'évidences pour penser que la sépulture centrale avec l'enclos était en lien avec des rites spéciaux consistant à déposer les restes brûlées de bûcher dans la sépulture. Ces rituels avaient totalement disparus avant le début du deuxième siècle, quoique l'emplacement des cimetières témoigne d'un choix soigneux aux deuxième et troisième siècles.

11. Biology and burial practices from the end of the 1st century AD to the beginning of the 5th century AD: the rural cemetery of Chantambre (Essonne, France)

P. Murail and L. Girard

The Gallo-Roman rural cemetery of Chantambre (Essonne, France) was in continual use from the end of the first century to the beginning of the fifth century AD. Its complete excavation has uncovered almost 500 funerary structures. Rites of cremation and inhumation co-existed during the initial phase of use, inhumation becoming the exclusive rite thereafter. A global analysis including archaeological data and the study of skeletal remains has demonstrated that burial practices were linked to age and sex. Some burial practices also evolved over time, demonstrated by the early abandonment of cremation, the increasing rarity of grave goods and change in the spatial organisation of the tombs. Other practices however persisted, for example the inhumation of neonates in ceramic containers and other burial types. Anthropological data together with archaeological data provide evidence of a strong homogeneity in the population and a broad stability over time. The transition between the Early and the Late Empire seems to be very progressive, without radical change.

Das gallo-römische Gräberfeld von Chantambre (Dép. Essonne, Frankreich) wurde vom Ende des 1. bis zum Beginn des 5. Jahrhunderts n. Chr. kontinuierlich belegt. Die Ausgrabung, die den Bestattungsplatz vollständig erfasste, erbrachte fast 500 Grabanlagen. Während der ersten Nutzungsphase wurde sowohl brand- als auch körperbestattet, später löste die Sitte der Körperbestattung den Kremationsritus ab. Die Auswertung des archäologischen und anthropologischen Materials ergab, dass die Bestattungssitten von Alter und Geschlecht abhingen. Eine chronologische Entwicklung innerhalb des Grabbrauchs zeigt sich in der oben erwähnten frühzeitigen Aufgabe des Brandritus, der Abnahme der Grabbeigaben und den Änderungen in der räumlichen Verteilung der Gräber. Andere Sitten dagegen überdauerten, wie z. B. die Körperbestattung für Neugeborene in Keramikbehältern, und andere Bestattungsarten. Die anthropologischen und archäologischen Daten sprechen für eine äußerst homogene und konservative Bevölkerung. Der Übergang von der Älteren zur Jüngeren Kaiserzeit vollzog sich ohne dramatischen Bruch.

La nécropole rurale gallo-romaine de Chantambre (Essonne) est un espace funéraire utilisé en continu de la fin du Ier siècle au début du Ve siècle apr. J.-C., dont la fouille exhaustive a livré près de 500 structures funéraires. Les rites de l'incinération et de l'inhumation coexistent au début de l'utilisation du site, l'inhumation devenant le rite exclusif par la suite. Cet article a pour objectif de révéler certains aspects de la palethnologie funéraire et de la biologie de cette population à partir d'une analyse globale incluant les données archéologiques et l'analyse des vestiges osseux. La structure par âge et par sexe de la population archéologique est assimilable à celle d'une population 'naturelle', pouvant correspondre à l'ensemble d'une population vivante d'effectif estimé entre 50 et 80 personnes. Des pratiques funéraires liées à l'âge ont pu être mises en évidence, différenciant trois groupes (nouveau-nés, enfants et adultes – adolescents). Certaines pratiques funéraires évoluent au cours du temps, de manière progressive. Les analyses métriques, morphologiques et paléopathologiques ont apporté, outre des indications descriptives, des éléments en faveur d'une forte homogénéité de la population tout au long de l'utilisation de l'espace funéraire. L'ensemble de ces données semble démontrer une transition entre le Haut et le Bas Empire très progressive, sans changement brutal.

12. A Roman cemetery in the eastern Civitas Treverorum. Preliminary report on the excavations at Wadern-Oberlöstern in Northwest Saarland (Germany)

A. Abegg-Wigg

Excavations took place in the Roman cemetery at Wadern-Oberlöstern from 1991 to 1996. A consideration of the internal structure of this complex reveals a remarkable co-existence of various grave forms and structures connected with rituals conducted at or near the graves both during and after the burial itself. Apart from funerary structures such as tumuli with a rectangular surrounding wall, a burial enclosure and a stone cist, there are also simple cremations together with 'ritual' pits, ash and ceramic deposits. Selected features are studied in detail in order to see to what extent this heterogenous rural cemetery is an expression of individual statements and communal traditions, as well as whether it reveals a discourse between native and intrusive (Italic, South Gallic) rites.

Die Betrachtung der internen Struktur des von 1991 bis 1996 ausgegrabenen römerzeitlichen Gräberfeldes von Wadern-Oberlöstern zeigt ein eindrucksvolles Nebeneinander verschiedener Grabformen und Einrichtungen, die im Zusammenhang mit rituellen Handlungen am Grab oder in der Nähe des Grabes während und nach der Bestattung stehen. Neben monumentalen Grabbauten wie durch quadratische Mauern eingefriedeten Grabhügeln, einem 'Grabbezirk' und einer Aschenkiste fanden sich einfache Erdgräber sowie sog. Aschengruben, Ascheschüttungen und Deponierungen von Gefäßen. Anhand ausgewählter Befunde wird näher untersucht, inwiefern sich in diesem vielseitigen ländlichen Gräberbezirk individuelle Äußerungen, durch die Gemeinschaft geprägte Traditionen bzw. eine Auseinandersetzung zwischen einheimischem und fremdem (z.B. italisch, südgallisch) Grabbrauchtum zeigen.

La nécropole de Wadern-Oberlöstern a été fouillée de 1991 à 1996. L'organisation interne de ce complexe démontre une coexistence remarquable de plusieurs types de sépulture et de structures en liaison avec les rituels qui avaient lieu pendant et après l'enterrement lui-même. A part des structures funéraires, un tumulus entouré d'un mur rectangulaire, un enclos funéraire et un 'ciste' en pierre, il y a aussi de simples incinérations, de fosses rituelles et des dépôts de charbon et de céramique. L'étude détaillée des certains prélèvements nous permettra d'établir dans quelle mesure cette nécropole rurale hétérogène est structurée selon des sentiments individuels et des traditions collectives, et dans quelle mesure on y trouve un dialogue entre les rites autochtones et allochtones (par exemple italiques, gaulois du sud).

13. An elite funerary enclosure in the centre of the villa of Biberist-Spitalhof (Switzerland) – a case study

C. Schucany

The funerary enclosure with *bustum*, sited at the centre of the Gallo-Roman villa of Biberist-Spitalhof and dated to the third quarter of the second century AD, has yielded evidence which has allowed the burial rite to be reconstructed, from the cremation and burial of the deceased to later offerings and finally to the desecration of the tomb. The dead, a 50 year old man, a baby and, as the grave goods suggest, probably also a woman, were provided with a complete set of vessels for their future life. This corresponds well to traditional Gallic burial custom.

Die inmitten der römischen Villa von Biberist-Spitalhof angelegte und ins 3. Viertel des 2. Jahrhunderts n.Chr. zu datierende Grabanlage, ein *bustum*, ermöglicht die Rekonstruktion der Beigabesitte und des Begräbnisritus von der Kremation über die Beisetzung der Toten, später dargebrachten Opfer bis zur Aufhebung der Grabstätte, vermutlich infolge eines Besitzerwechsels. Den Toten – ein ca. 50 jähriger Mann, ein Säugling sowie aufgrund der persönlichen Beigaben eine Frau – hatte man ganz gemäss der gallischen Tradition einen ausserordentlich reichen, sorgfältig zusammengestellten Haushalt für ihr zukünftiges Leben mitgegeben.

L'enclos funéraire avec un *bustum*, situé au centre de la villa gallo-romaine de Biberist-Spitalhof et daté du 3e quart du 2e siècle apr. J.-C., a livré des données pour la restitution des rîtes funéraires: de la crémation et de l'enterrement des décédés aux offrandes postérieures jusqu' à la désécration de la tombe. Les morts – un homme de 50 ans, un bébé et probablement une femme selon son équipement personnel, ont reçu un assortiment complet de vaisselle pour leur future vie, ce qui correspond bien à la coutume traditionnelle gauloise.

14. Putting the dead in their place: burial location in Roman Britain

S. Esmonde Cleary

Romano-British burials come from a wide range of contexts, of which conventional cemeteries are but one, and these contexts can be used to tell us much about how the dead were viewed by the living. Categorisation by site-type remains of use; with significant differences in burial location between the towns, military sites, villas, other rural sites. It is also clear that cross-type analyses have much to offer, e.g. infant burial, body-part burial, ?murder and sacrifice. Recurrent patterns of burial locations can be noted: formal cemeteries and smaller grave-yards, 'backland' burial, ditches and other boundaries, wet places. By the fourth century human burial in a grave in a cemetery had become one option in a wider range of contexts of ritual deposition, and human remains had become one of a wider range of material which might be ritually deposited. The dead much concerned the living.

Romano-britische Gräber sind von völlig verschiedenen Fundplatztypen bekannt, unter denen konventionelle Gräber-felder nur einen Teil darstellen. Die unterschiedlichen Orte, an denen Gräber angetroffen werden, können Auskunft darüber geben, welches Verhältnis die Lebenden zu den Toten hatten. Die Kategorisierung von Fundplatztypen ist von Nutzen; die Platzwahl für die Anlage von Gräbern unterscheidet sich wesentlich bei Städten, militärischen Anlagen, *villae rusticae* und anderen ländlichen Siedlungen. Auch die Untersuchung einzelner Gräbertypen, z. B. Kindergräber, Bestattungen von Körperteilen, Mord (?) und Opfer, bringt interessante Ergebnisse. Regelhafte Muster bei der Platzwahl für Gräber können beobachtet werden: formale Gräberfelder und kleinere Bestattungsplätze, Bestattungen in den rückwärtigen Teilen von Siedlungen, in Gräben und anderen Einfriedungen, an nassen Plätzen. In Gräberfeldern des 4. Jahrhunderts stellte eine Beisetzung im Grab nur eine Möglichkeit in einer ganzen Bandbreite ritueller Deponierungen dar, und menschliche Überreste bildeten nur einen Teil des Materials, das vielleicht rituell deponiert worden war. Tote waren äußerst präsent im Bewusstsein der Lebenden.

Les sépultures de la Bretagne romaine ne proviennent pas seulement des cimetières, mais d'une grande variété de contextes, qui enseignent sur la manière donts les vivants voyaient les morts. Classer les sépultures selon le type de site reste utile, avec des différences significatives entre les villes, les sites militaires, les villas et les autres sites ruraux. Il est aussi évident que des analyses croisées de certains types de sépultures, par exemple celle du nourrisson, ou l'enterrement de certaines parties du corps, le meutre (?) et le sacrifice, à travers les contextes différentes, ont beaucoup à nous offrir. Nous pouvons noter des emplacements répétés des sépultures, aux cimetières officiels ou plus petits, au fond des habitations, aux fossés et aux autres limites et aux endroits humides. Au IVe siècle enterrer un individu dans une sépulture à l'intérieur d'un cimetière n'était qu'un choix parmi plusieurs contextes de dépôt rituel, et les restes humaines qu'un type de matériel qu'on déposait d'un façon rituel. Les morts intéressaient beaucoup les vivants.

15. Continuity of Prehistoric Burial Sites in the Roman Landscape of Sandy Flanders

F. Vermeulen and J. Bourgeois

Due to a recent boom of remote sensing and excavation information in north-western Belgium, new avenues of thought have become available concerning the pre- and protohistoric landscape of sandy Flanders. An as yet unexploited theme in this regional research by the University of Ghent is the persistence of burial places and connected sacred areas into the Roman period. Did the rural tombs of earlier occupants of the land preserve their role as topographic and cultural markers of the landscape? Were such cemeteries crucial in attaching rights to the land through the presence of the dead or of the ancestors of the indigenous population? Is there an observable breach in the attitude towards the ancient cemeteries as a result of the Romanisation of the region? These and other questions fundamental to our understanding of the cultural and ideological landscape in Roman times will dominate our discussion of the archaeological evidence available.

Infolge des kürzlichen Booms in der geophysikalischen Erkennung von Fundstellen und Informationen aus Ausgrabungen in Nordwestbelgien konnten neue Denkansätze zur prä- und protohistorischen Landschaft Flanderns entwickelt werden. Ein noch nicht beachteter Problemkreis in dieser regionalen Untersuchung der Universität Gent ist die Kontinuität von Bestattungsplätzen und damit in Verbindung stehenden heiligen Bezirken in römischer Zeit. Fungierten im ländlichen Milieu die Gräber der Landbesitzer als topographische und kulturelle Markierungen? Waren solche Gräberfelder wichtig, um durch die Präsenz der Verstorbenen oder Vorfahren der einheimischen Bevölkerung das Recht auf das Land zu manifestieren? Lässt sich als Folge der Romanisierung des Landes ein Bruch im Verhältnis zu den Grabstätten der Vorfahren beobachten? Diese und weitere Fragen, die in unserem Verständnis der kulturellen und ideologischen Landschaft große Bedeutung besitzen, stehen im Vordergrund der folgenden Diskussion des archäologischen Materials.

Les récentes découvertes dues à la prospection aérienne et aux fouilles dans la Belgique du nord-ouest ont ouvert de nouvelles perspectives sur notre compréhension du paysage pré- et protohistorique dans la Flandre sablonneuse. Le thème de la persistance des places d'ensevelissement et des lieux sacrés connexes est encore totalement nouveau et inexploité dans la recherche régionale qu'effectue l'Université de Gand. Les tombes et nécropoles ont-elles longtemps conservé leur rôle de marqueur topographique et culturel dans ce paysage? Doit-on assigner à ces cimetières une place fondamentale dans la mise en place des droits territoriaux, par le biais de la présence de morts ou de celle d'ancêtres des populations indigènes? Peut-on observer une rupture dans l'attitude envers la présence de monuments funéraires avec l'arrivée des Romains dans notre pays? Partant du matériel disponible, ces questions fondamentales pour notre compréhension du paysage culturel et idéologique à l'époque romaine fonderont notre discussion.

16. The living and the dead: approaches to landscape around Lyons

L. Tranoy

The study of the funerary spaces of the colony of Lugdunum reveals varied mortuary practices. Mausolea, similar to Italian models, were constructed along the roads. Elsewhere groups of modest, often intercutting burials, developed. These burial areas stretched across a territory which falls completely outside the regulation of the urban framework. In certain suburbs the concept of a 'world of the dead' is quite relative, since without any strict demarcation tombs occurred side by side with all the activities generated by city life that took place beyond the strictly urban limit. At Lyons the increasing number of excavations in areas on the margins of the (Roman) town has brought to light an indiscriminate mix of burials and all types of occupation which surround the town, workshops of artisans, warehouses and houses. If in some cases burials were made in the ruins of a home or workshop, elsewhere dating evidence proves that burials took place in very close proximity to warehouses or workshops in use, or even dwellings.

Die Untersuchung der Gräberfelder und Bestattungsplätze der *colonia* Lugdunum führt uns eine ganze Bandbreite an Grabsitten vor Augen. Mausoleen, ähnlich den italienischen Vorbildern, wurden entlang der Straßen errichtet. An anderen Stellen entstanden Gruppen einfacher, sich vielfach überschneidender Gräber. Diese Gräberareale erstrecken sich über ein Territorium, das sich außerhalb der Bestimmungen der urbanen Organisation befand. In bestimmten Vorstädten war das Konzept der ‚Welt der Toten' ziemlich relativiert: Ohne klare Abgrenzung erscheinen Gräber Seite an Seite mit allen Äußerungen städtischen Lebens, das sich außerhalb der offiziellen Stadtgrenze abspielt. In Lyon hat die Intensivierung der Ausgrabungen in den Außenbezirken der Stadt deutlich gemacht, wie vermischt Gräber und suburbane Besiedlungsspuren, nämlich Werkstätten von Handwerkern, Lagerhäuser und Häuser, vorliegen. Während in einigen Fällen Bestattungen in den Ruinen von Werkstätten und Wohnhäusern liegen, beweist das datierende Material an anderer Stelle, dass die Lager, Werkstätten und sogar Wohnhäuser, in deren direkter Nachbarschaft sich die Gräber befanden, noch in Gebrauch waren.

L'étude des espaces funéraires de la colonie de Lugdunum met en évidence des pratiques variées. Des mausolées, semblables aux modèles italiens, sont construits le long des voies. Ailleurs, se développent des ensembles de sépultures modestes et souvent enchevêtrées. Ces zones sépulcrales s'étendent sur un territoire qui échappe totalement au schéma urbain régulateur. Dans certains faubourgs, la notion de 'monde des morts' est bien relative, puisque les tombes côtoient, sans délimitation stricte, toutes les activités qu'engendre la vie citadine et qui se déploient au-delà de la limite strictement urbaine. A Lyon, la multiplication des fouilles dans les quartiers périphériques a mis en évidence une véritable promiscuité entre les sépultures et toutes sortes d'occupations qui encerclent l'agglomération: ateliers d'artisans, entrepôts, maisons. Si, dans certains cas, les tombes s'installent dans les ruines d'un habitat ou d'un atelier, ailleurs la chronologie

prouve que les enterrements se pratiquaient au voisinage très proche d'entrepôts ou d'ateliers en activité, voire d'habitations.

17. Burial in Asia Minor during the imperial period, with particular reference to Cilicia and Cappadocia

M. Spanu

The Roman conquest of Anatolia, concluded under Vespasian, was not able to efface all cultural differences among the several provinces. Many local aspects (like some languages) disappeared, but specific traditions survived. Above all, this may be found in religion, where epigraphic and archaeological sources illustrate all through the imperial period many regional deities' names, rituals and cults. Of course 'Romanisation' also influenced local societies, but within the long tradition of urban living this process occurred in a different way to the western provinces. For a better understanding of 'Romanisation' in Anatolia the evidence from cemeteries would be very important but in spite of many artistic and architectural studies of monumental tombs we have very few data from archaeological excavations. Starting from this general view, this paper offers some consideration of cemeteries in Asia Minor, bringing together the few pieces of evidence from burials and other funerary contexts.

Die römische Eroberung Anatoliens, die unter Vespasian abgeschlossen war, konnte nicht alle kulturellen Unterschiede zwischen den einzelnen Provinzen verwischen. Viele lokale Eigenarten verschwanden zwar (wie einige Sprachen), aber eine Reihe spezieller Traditionen überlebte. Vor allem ist dies im Bereich der Religion zu beobachten, wo epigraphische und archäologische Quellen durch die ganze Kaiserzeit hindurch die Namen regionaler Gottheiten, regionale Rituale und Kulte belegen. Mit Sicherheit beeinflusste die Romanisierung auch die örtlichen Gesellschaftsformen. Vor dem Hintergrund der langen Tradition urbaner Kultur vollzog sich dieser Prozess jedoch in einer anderen Art als in den westlichen Provinzen. Zum besseren Verständnis der Romanisierung Anatoliens wäre das Material aus den Gräberfeldern von großer Bedeutung. Aber obwohl viele kunsthistorische und architektonische Studien zu monumentalen Grabmälern vorliegen, gibt es nur wenige Publikationen zu archäologischen Ausgrabungen. Von diesem Ausgangspunkt aus stellt der Beitrag einige Überlegungen zu den Gräberfeldern in Kleinasien vor, indem die wenigen Informationen von Gräbern und anderen funerären Befunden zusammen analysiert werden.

La conquête romaine de l'Anatolie, qui s'acheva sous Vespasien, ne pouvait pas effacer toutes les différences culturelles au sein des provinces. Beaucoup d'aspects des cultures locales, comme par exemple quelques langues, ont disparu, mais des traditions particulières ont survécu. Parmi elles beaucoup se retrouve dans le domaine religieux: l'épigraphie et l'archéologie illustrent pendant toute l'époque impériale des noms des dieux régionaux, des rituels et des cultes. La 'Romanisation' a bien sûr influencé les sociétés locales, mais à cause de la longue tradition de vie urbaine le processus s'est déroulé différemment que pour les provinces occidentales. Pour mieux comprendre la 'Romanisation' en Anatolie les témoignages des nécropoles devraient être très importantes, mais malgré plusieurs études de l'art et de l'architecture des tombes monumentales, très peu de données des fouilles archéologiques sont à notre disposition. A partir de cette perspective, cet article propose quelques réflexions sur les nécropoles de l'Asie Mineure, en rassemblant les quelques témoignages et les données des sépultures et des autres contextes funéraires.

18. Early Roman graves in southern Bavaria: a review

P. Fasold

The Augustan and Claudian period burials of north Raetia and north-west Noricum are the focus of this investigation. With their help this paper attempts as its main aim to classify the ethnic composition of the population of the province, in order also to shed light on the Romanisation process in this region. It should first be emphasised that burials and settlements of the late Celtic population are currently undetectable. Since the region north of the Alps was evidently to a large extent unpopulated, prior to the Roman occupation, the population of the province was predominantly composed of new settlers. On the basis of the grave furnishing and constructions we may suppose migrants to have come from strongly Romanised areas of Upper Italy and Gaul, as well as from Germania Libera and Noricum. Above all however an inner-Alpine-Raetian component of the early settlers is to be stressed. Since the areas along the valley of the Etsch were already under Cisalpine Celtic influence, the Celtic survivals in north Raetia are therefore to be traced back less to indigenous Vindelican traditions than to the Celtic traditions of the Po valley. The co-existence of different burial customs shows clearly how heterogeneous was the composition of the population of north Raetia in the first century.

Im Mittelpunkt dieser Untersuchung stehen die augusteisch-claudischen Bestattungen Nordrätiens und Nordwest-Norikums. Mit ihrer Hilfe soll vor allem versucht werden, die ethnische Zusammensetzung der Provinzbevölkerung aufzuschlüsseln, um damit auch den Romanisierungsprozess in dieser Landschaft zu beleuchten. Zuerst ist festzuhalten, daß Gräber und Siedlungen einer spätkeltischen Bevölkerung bislang nicht nachweisbar sind. Da die Region nördlich der Alpen vor der römischen Okkupation offenbar weitgehend unbewohnt war, setzte sich die Provinzbevölkerung vorwiegend aus Neusiedlern zusammen. Auf Grund von Grabausstattung und -anlage sind Zuwanderer aus stark romanisierten Gebieten Oberitaliens und Galliens ebenso zu vermuten, wie aus der Germania Libera und aus Norikum. Vor allem aber ist ein inneralpin-rätischer Anteil der frühen Ansiedler hervorzuheben. Da die Gebiete entlang des Etschtals schon in spätrepublikanischer Zeit unter oberitalisch-gallischem Einfluss standen, sind keltische Relikte in Nordrätien deshalb weniger auf einheimisch-vindelikische, als auf gallisch-padanische Traditionen zurückzuführen. Das Nebeneinander verschiedenster Grabbräuche macht damit deutlich, wie heterogen die Bevölkerung Nordrätiens im ersten Jahrhundert zusammengesetzt war.

Au centre de cet enquête se trouvent les sépultures d'époque augustéenne et claudienne du nord de la Rhétie et du nord-ouest de Noricum. En se servant de ces témoignages, cet article vise à classer la composition ethnique de la population de la province, pour éclairer aussi le processus de Romanisation dans cette région. Nous devons d'abord souligner que jusqu'à maintenant on n'a pas pu trouver les sépultures et les habitations de la population celtique. Vu que la région au nord des Alpes fût en grande partie non peuplée avant l'occupation romaine, la population de la province se composait surtout de nouveaux colonisateurs. De l'étude du mobilier et des structures funéraires nous pouvons supposer que les nouveaux arrivés venaient des régions fortement romanisées de l'Italie septentrionale et de la Gaule, aussi bien que de Germania Libera et de Noricum. Avant tout cependant on doit insister sur la composante alpine et rhétienne de ces premiers colonisateurs. Vu que les régions le long de la vallée de l'Etsch étaient déjà à l'époque tardo-républicaine sous l'influence de l'Italie du nord gauloise, les survivances celtiques remontent donc moins aux traditions autochtones vindeliques qu'aux traditions celtiques du Pô. La co-existence d'usages funéraires différents montre nettement comme la composition de la population de la Rhétie du nord était hétérogène pendant le premier siècle de notre ère.

19. Early Roman graves in Cologne

M. Riedel

A section of the cemetery situated outside the north-western corner of Roman Cologne reveals well the mixing of Roman and indigenous burial rites. Approximately a quarter of these burials are inhumations, a very high proportion for the early Roman period in the Rhineland. This non-Roman burial rite may be connected to the immigration of a Gallic population, such as the Remi from northern Gaul. The inhumations demonstrate a number of peculiarities. The prone position of some burials, which also occurs elsewhere along the north-west frontier of the Roman empire, probably has a ritual explanation, perhaps for the protection of the living from the evil powers surrounding the buried dead. Holes in the skulls and in bones from limb extremities may rather be explained as fatal injuries suffered, for instance, during the revolt of the Batavii in 70 AD. Numerous inhumations carelessly buried complete the picture of a cemetery in which predominantly socially marginal groups like the poor, criminals, victims of epidemic and war, but probably also unromanised members of the native population, were buried. The skeleton of a ritually slain horse may belong to the burial of an individual from Germania Libera.

Ein Ausschnitt des römischen Friedhofs vor der Nordwestecke des römischen Köln läßt die Vermischung römischer und einheimischer Grabsitten gut erkennen. Rund ein Viertel dieser Gräber des späten 1. Jahrhunderts n.Chr. sind Körper-bestattungen, in dieser Frühzeit ein sehr hoher Anteil im Rheinland. Diese nichtrömische Bestattungssitte hängt vielleicht auch mit der Einwanderung gallischer Bevölkerung, etwa der nordgallischen Remer zusammen. Diese Körperbestattungen weisen eine Reihe von Besonderheiten auf. Die hier wie auch entlang der nordwestlichen Reichsgrenze auftretende Bauchlage ist wahrscheinlich rituell zu verstehen, vielleicht zum Schutz der Lebenden vor den bösen Kräften um den Bestatteten. Einige Löcher an Schädeln und Extremitäten sind wohl eher als tötliche Kriegsverletzungen etwa vom Batavér-Aufstand 70 n. Chr. zu erklären. Zahlreiche unsorgfältig ausgeführte Bestattungen ergänzen das Bild eines Friedhofs, in dem überwiegend gesellschaftliche Randgruppen wie Arme, Verbrecher, Kriegs- und Epidemieopfer, aber wohl auch nicht romanisierte Einheimische bestattet wurden. Das Skelett eines rituell getöten Pferdes könnte zur Bestattung eines Germanen aus der Germania Libera gehören.

Une partie de la nécropole qui se trouve à l'extérieur du coin nord-ouest de Cologne romaine montre bien le mélange des rites funéraires autochtones et romains. Les inhumations constituent environ un quart des sépultures, une proportion très élevée pour le haut empire en Rhénanie. Ce rite non-romain est peut-être lié à l'immigration d'une population gauloise, par exemple les Rèmes du nord de la Gaule. Ces inhumations ont un certain nombre de particularités. L'enterrement de certains individus sur le ventre, que l'on retrouve ailleurs le long de la frontière nord-ouest de l'empire, est peut-être un rituel pour protéger les vivants contre les pouvoirs mauvais qui entourent les morts ensevelis. Les trous dans les crânes et les extrémités des os des membres s'expliquent plutôt comme le résultat de blessures mortelles subies pendant la révolte des bataves de 70 après J.-C.. De nombreuses inhumations ensevelies avec peu de soin confirment l'idée qu'on se servait de cette nécropole pour enterrer les groupes marginaux, les pauvres, les criminels, les victimes de l'épidémie et de la guerre, mais aussi la partie non-romanisée de la population autochtone. Le squelette d'un cheval tué au cours d'un rituel appartenait peut-être à la sépulture d'un individu provenant de Germania Libera.

20. Connection between funerary rites and ethnic groups in the cemeteries of north-eastern Pannonia

J. Topál

In the last 30 years of Roman provincial research certain researchers have argued that indigenous and foreign components of the population in the province of Pannonia can be identified in both the cemetery and settlement record, while others have argued that such a distinction cannot be made, especially in the late Roman period. This paper will therefore deal with some aspects of the ethnic components reflected in the funerary rituals of this area. Tombstone depictions, epitaphs and burial rites and objects of personal equipment allow us to outline ethnic relations in the early Roman period. Certain funerary practices and objects of equipment or jewellery can be ascribed to separate ethnic traditions. While the gradual Celticization of the whole Carpathian region took place by the end of the 3rd century BC, nevertheless signs of survival of autochthonous Illyrian-Pannonian funeral traditions can be traced. Onomastic and sculptural evidence also suggest that Celtic culture in Pannonia does not derive solely from the Norican-Alpine civilization. In this territory at least three ethnic components merged: the autochthonous population, the Celtic Eravisci who arrived in the late La Tène period and the incoming groups of south-western Celtic tribes (presumably Boii and Taurisci) at the turn of the first century AD.

In den letzten 30 Jahren provinzialrömischer Forschung haben sich einige Kollegen dafür ausgesprochen, dass sich die einheimischen und fremden Bevölkerungsanteile in der Provinz Pannonia sowohl in den Gräberfeldern als auch in den Siedlungen identifizieren lassen. Andere haben diese Unterscheidungsmöglichkeit bestritten, speziell für die spätrömische Periode. Dieser Beitrag wird sich deshalb mit einigen Aspekten ethnischer Bestandteile befassen, wie sie sich in den Grabbräuchen dieser Gegend widerspiegeln. Bildliche Darstellungen und Inschriften auf Grabsteinen sowie Bestattungssitten und persönliche Gegenstände erlauben es uns, Rückschlüsse auf verschiedene Kulturen in der frührömischen Periode zu ziehen.

Bestimmte Grabsitten, Gebrauchsgegenstände und Schmuck können unterschiedlichen ethnischen Traditionen zugeschrieben werden. Obwohl die Keltisierung des gesamten Karpathenbeckens bis zum Ende des 3. Jahrhunderts v. Chr. abgeschlossen war, lassen sich Anzeichen für ein Überleben autochthoner illyrisch-pannonischer Bestattungspraktiken erkennen. Onomastik und Skulptur sprechen außerdem dafür, dass die keltische Kultur in Pannonien nicht allein aus der norisch-alpinen Zivilisation hervorgegangen ist. In diesem Gebiet vermischten sich mindestens drei kulturelle Komponenten: die autochthone Population, die keltischen *Eravisci*, die in der späten La Tène-Zeit immigrierten, und einwandernde Gruppen südwest-keltischer Stämme (wahrscheinlich *Boii* und *Taurisci*) von der Wende zum 1. Jahrhundert n. Chr.

Pendant les 30 dernières années de recherches sur les provinces romaines certains chercheurs ont avancé qu'on peut identifier des éléments indigènes et étrangers parmi la population de la province de Pannonie grâce aux études de cimetières et d'habitations, tandis que d'autres chercheurs ne reconnaissent pas une telle distinction, surtout à l'époque romaine tardive. Cet article traite donc de quelques aspects des éléments ethniques reflétant les rituels funéraires de la région. Les représentations funéraires, les épitaphes, les rites funéraires et le mobilier personnel nous permettent d'exposer dans ses lignes générales les relations ethniques du début de la période romaine. Nous pouvons attribuer certaines pratiques funéraires, objets du mobilier et bijoux aux traditions ethniques particulières. Bien que la 'Celticization' graduelle de toute la région carpathienne a eu lieu à la fin du 3e siècle avant J.-C., néanmoins on peut distinguer des vestiges des traditions funéraires illyro-pannoniennes autochtones. Les témoignages onomastiques et sculpturelles suggèrent que la culture celtique de Pannonie n'a pas ses origines seulement dans la civilisation norico-alpine. Dans ce territoire au total trois éléments ethniques se sont intégrés: la population autochtone, les Eravisques celtiques qui sont arrivés à la La Tène tardive et les groupes immigrantes des tribus celtiques du sud-ouest (on pense aux Boii et Taurisci) au début du 1er siècle après J.-C..

21. Romanization and ethnic elements in burial practice in the southern part of Pannonia Inferior and Moesia Superior

A. Jovanovic

This paper discusses the graves from cemeteries in the Roman provinces of Pannonia Inferior and Moesia Superior, dating from the beginning of the 1st century AD to the middle 3rd century AD. The main classification is made according to the origin of the grave-form. Thus the basic division is: Roman grave-forms; intrusive grave-forms of non-Roman origin; and autochthonous grave-forms. Graves have been classified into these groups on the basis of an analysis of the following elements, manner of burial, grave-form, grave-goods, chronology, distribution, origin and ethno-cultural traits.

Dieser Beitrag behandelt die Gräber der Gräberfelder in den römischen Provinzen Pannonia Inferior und Moesia Superior, und zwar vom Beginn des 1. bis zur Mitte des 3. Jahrhunderts. Der kulturelle Ursprung der Grab- und Bestattungsformen führt zu einer ersten Einteilung der Gräber. Drei Gruppen von Grab- und Bestattungsformen ergeben sich: römische, fremde mit nichtrömischem Ursprung und autochthone, wobei Bestattungsart, Grabform, Beigaben, Chronologie, Verbreitung, Ursprung und ethno-kulturelle Besonderheiten die Kriterien darstellten.

Cet article examine les sépultures des cimetières des provinces de Pannonia Inferior et Moesia Superior du commencement du 1er siècle après J.-C. jusqu'au milieu du 3e siècle après J.-C.. Les types de sépulture sont classées surtout selon leur origine. Nous pouvons identifier des types de sépultures d'origine romaine, d'origine non-romaine du dehors et d'origine autochtone. Nous avons classé les sépultures selon ces groupes d'après l'analyse des éléments suivants, le mode de sépulture, la forme, le mobilier, la chronologie, la distribution, l'origine et les traits ethno-culturels.

22. *Putting Late Roman Burial Practice (from Britain) in Context*

L. Quensel-von-Kalben

This paper argues for a more holistic approach to cemetery studies for a better understanding of the social dimensions of mortuary behaviour. The repertoire for the detection of patterns of social behaviour is currently rather limited. Multivariate quantitative methods, as applied in this study, are thought to be promising for the future. The burial furniture and treatment of the dead at eight Late Roman cemeteries from south and east Britain are compared. Age and gender as well as differences in status, probably the most basic social dimensions, are analysed separately for each cemetery and then compared with each other. Is there any ordering principle behind the different types of cemeteries? With all the limitations of such a preliminary analysis, the writer believes that while chronological and regional trends are not, religion and the connection to an urban or rural background are of major importance in the structuring of Late Roman cemeteries in Britain.

Bisherige Analysen von Gräberfeldern haben zumeist eine begrenzte Fundgruppe oder einem speziellen Bestattungsritus gegolten. In diesem Aufsatz wird hingegen ein holistischerer Ansatz vertreten, um die soziale Dimension von Bestattungsverhalten zu ermitteln. Ein solcher Ansatz läßt sich z.Z. vermutlich nur mit Hilfe von multivariaten quantitativen Verfahren durchführen, wie in dieser Studie versucht. Eine Stichprobe von acht spätrömischen Gräberfelder aus dem Osten und Süden Englands wurde in Hinblick auf Bestattungsweisen und Grabbeigaben untersucht. Zu Beginn wurden die Gräberfelder separat auf Unterschiede in der Behandlung von Alter, Geschlecht und sozialem Status/Reichtum analysiert. In einem zweiten Schritt wurde die Behandlung dieser sozialen Dimensionen auf den Gräberfeldern verglichen. Lassen sich die resultierenden Gräberfeld"typen" durch ein Ordnungsprinzip erklären? Bei allen Interpretationsschwierigkeiten, mit denen eine vorläufige Untersuchung wie die vorliegende zu kämpfen hat, hält der Autor religiöse und siedlungsgeographische Unterschiede für zentrale Faktoren der Typbildung. Chronologische und regionale Faktoren scheinen dagegen – überraschenderweise – als Erklärungsmodelle auszuscheiden.

Cet article propose une façon plus holistique d'étudier les cimetières pour mieux comprendre les dimensions sociales du comportement funéraire. Nous ne disposons pour ce moment que d'un répertoire assez limité pour déceler les types de comportement social. Les méthodes quantitatives à variables multiples que l'on utilise pour cette étude s'annoncent prometteuses pour l'avenir. Nous comparons le mobilier et les usages funéraires de huit cimetières du sud et de l'est d'Angleterre. L'âge, le sexe ainsi que les différences de statut social, les dimensions sociales les plus fondamentales, sont d'abord analysés séparément pour chaque cimetière, puis comparés avec les autres. Existe-t-il une principe qui gouverne les différentes 'types' de cimetière? Malgré les limitations d'une analyse préliminaire, l'auteur pense que sont significatives la réligion et une contexte urbaine où rurale. Les différences chronologiques où régionales sont peu importantes.

23. *Gender imbalances in Romano-British cemetery populations: a re-evaluation of the evidence*

C. Davison

A study of 2,476 definitely sexed burials from 25 Romano-British cemeteries found a significant male bias in many larger urban sites. Such a bias was not mirrored in rural areas. Limitations in sources of data meant that it was not possible to examine chronological or regional variation within this pattern. The following hypotheses to explain this bias were proposed and examined, that it was the result of an influx of men into urban centres for military or economic reasons, of differential female infanticide, of flaws in analysis of skeletal material or of the separation of male and female burials within cemeteries. In the context of recent archaeological emphasis on the influence of the civilian population on urban development, it was felt that the cultural separation of the male and female dead might provide a more credible explanation. It is argued that less spatially dominant female interment areas might reflect the disenfranchisement of women within a new urban gender hierarchy.

Die Untersuchung von 2 476 Bestattungen, die aus 25 romanobritischen Gräberfeldern stammen und deren Geschlecht mit Sicherheit bestimmt werden konnte, ergab für Städte einen signifikanten Überhang auf Seite der Männer. Dieses Ungleichgewicht wurde für ländliche Bestattungsplätze nicht festgestellt. Die eingeschränkte Quellenlage erlaubte keine Analyse chronologischer und regionaler Abweichungen. Folgende Hypothesen zur Erklärung der ungleichen Verteilung wurden vorgestellt und untersucht: Sie war Resultat des Zuzugs von Männern in die urbanen Zentren aus militärischen und wirtschaftlichen Gründen; sie war Folge des Tötens von weiblichen Neugeborenen; sie geht auf einen Fehler bei der Geschlechtsbestimmung zurück; sie indiziert die Existenz geschlechtsspezifischer Areale innerhalb der Gräberfelder. Da von archäologischer Seite seit kurzem der Einfluss der Zivilbevölkerung bei der Entwicklung der Städte betont wird, erscheint die räumliche Trennung von männlichen und weiblichen Verstorbenen als Erklärung am wahrscheinlichsten. Weniger ausgedehnte weibliche Bestattungsareale könnten die Entrechtung von Frauen innerhalb der neuen Geschlechtshierarchie der Städte widerspiegeln.

L'étude dans 25 cimetières romano-britanniques de 2,476 sépultures, dont le sexe est définitivement établi, prouve la tendance vers une sur-représenatation de la population mâle dans plusieurs sites urbains. Nous n'avons pas trouvé une telle tendance en examinant les cimetières ruraux. Les données sont trop limitées pour examiner une variation chronologique ou régionale de cette tendance. Notre recherche nous a amèné à formuler les hypothèses suivantes pour expliquer cette tendance: l'afflux des hommes aux centres urbains pour des raisons militaires ou économiques; un infanticide disproportionné du sexe féminin; des erreurs d'analyse des squelettes; la séparation des sépultures des hommes et des femmes dans les cimetières. Il nous a semblé que l'étude de la séparation culturelle des hommes et des femmes morts constitue une piste intéressante dans cette perspective, vu la récente insistance de l'étude archéologique sur l'influence de la population civile au développement urbain. Le fait que les zones funéraires des femmes sont moins dominantes sur un plan spatial permet d'établir peut-être le manque de pouvoir des femmes dans l'hiérarchie sexuelle urbaine nouvelle.

24. Glass goods as grave furniture and ornaments in the catacombs of Rome: some examples

P. De Santis

The form of the catacomb burials – *loculi* excavated in tufa, sealed with bricks or marble slabs – has preserved objects fixed in the mortar which sealed the grave or cemented into the small recesses excavated in tufa. Such funerary furniture, outside the grave, is still visible in cemeteries with intact *loculi* which escaped the systematic plundering of the seventeenth and eighteenth centuries in particular. Any interpretation should be based on the two concepts of 'ornament' (*arredo*) and 'furniture' (*corredo*); in the catacombs, personal items and grave furniture intended as an offering to the dead person coincide with the grave ornaments, as they too are placed outside the grave, sometimes with a specific decorative function. Two cemetery regions were chosen as samples for this study because of their very good state of preservation and because they can be set against a sound and well defined chronological background. They are the lower floor of the catacomb of Pamphilus, along the via Salaria *vetus*, and a small gallery in the so-called 'regione delle cattedre' in the *Maius* cemetery on the via Nomentana. The analysis of glass vessels has led us to widen the interpretation of their function. When found intact, vessels can be related to the rite of the *refrigerium* and to the ritual of sprinkling perfumes near the grave and inside it. The fixing to the exterior of the tomb of a piece of broken glass, the commercial value of which in antiquity must be stressed, can be related to the wish to secure the grave from anonymity and to highlight its inviolability.

Der Typ der Katakombengräber, *loculi* bzw. Grabnischen, die in Tuffsteinwände eingetieft und mit Ziegeln zugemauert oder Marmorplatten verschlossen sind, hat zur Erhaltung von Objekten geführt, die in den Mörtel beim Verschließen des Grabes gesteckt oder in kleinen aus dem Tuff gehauenen Nischen mit Zement befestigt wurden. Diese Beigaben außerhalb des Grabes sind noch in Arealen von Nekropolen mit intakten *loculi* sichtbar, die von den systematischen Plünderungen hauptsächlich während des 17. und 18. Jahrhunderts verschont geblieben sind. Die beiden Konzepte von Grabschmuck (*arredo*) und Grabbeigabe (*corredo*) müssen bei jeder Interpretation berücksichtigt werden. In den Katakomben können Gegenstände des persönlichen Besitzes des Toten sowie Opfergaben an den Verstorbenen zusammenfallen mit dem Grabschmuck, da sie

ebenfalls außerhalb des eigentlichen Grabes plaziert wurden, manchmal auch auf dekorative Weise. Zwei Regionen von Gräberfeldern wurden als Beispiele gewählt, weil sie besonders gut erhalten und datierbar sind. Es handelt sich zum einen um das untere Geschoss der Pamphilus-Katakombe an der via *Salaria vetus*, zum anderen um eine kleine Gallerie, *regione delle cattedre* genannt, in der *Maius*-Nekropole an der via *Nomentana*. Die Analyse der Glasgegenstände hat zu einer erweiterten Interpretation ihrer Funktion geführt. In intaktem Zustand gefunden, können diese Objekte im Zusammenhang mit dem Ritus des *refrigium* und des Versprengens von Wohlgerüchen am oder im Grab gestanden haben. Einzementiert oder in den Mörtel gesteckte Bruchstücke von Glas, dessen kommerzieller Wert in der Antike unterstrichen werden muss, kann dagegen den Wunsch ausdrücken, das Grab vor Anonymität zu schützen und seine Unverletzlichkeit zu betonen.

La tipologia delle sepolture che caratterizza i contesti catacombali, loculi scavati nelle pareti di tufo e sigillati con laterizi o lastre marmoree, ha permesso di conservare gli oggetti affissi nella malta di chiusura del sepolcro o cementati in piccole nicchie scavate nel tufo. Questo corredo funerario, esterno alla tomba, è ancora visibile nelle aree cimiteriali che presentano loculi intatti, non violati dalle sistematiche opere di spoliazione compiute soprattutto nel XVII e XVIII secolo. I due concetti di *arredo* e *corredo* sono da porre alla base di ogni approccio interpretativo; negli insediamenti cimiteriali ipogei il corredo personale e il corredo posto come offerta al defunto coincidono con l'arredo della tomba in quanto sono collocati al suo esterno, a volte anche con una specifica funzione decorativa. Come campione d'indagine sono state scelte due regioni cimiteriali; esse sono adatte allo scopo per il loro ottimo stato di conservazione e perché inquadrate entro limiti cronologici ben definiti. Si tratta del piano inferiore della catacomba di Panfilo, sulla via Salaria *vetus*, e di una piccola galleria della cosiddetta 'regione delle cattedre' nel cimitero *Maius* sulla via Nomentana. L'analisi dei materiali vitrei a disposizione ha portato a diversificare le interpretazioni sulle loro funzioni. Quando si trovano integri essi sono da mettere in relazione con i rituali del *refrigerium* e dello spargimento di sostanze odorose presso il sepolcro e al suo interno. L'affissione di frammenti vitrei, di cui è da sottolineare il valore commerciale nell'antichità, è invece da connettere con la volontà di riscattare la sepoltura dall'anonimato e di ribadirne l'inviolabilità.

25. Clothing in burial practice in Italy in the early Christian period

R. Martorelli

The evidence of ancient writers and of the Church Fathers shows that notwithstanding the exhortation to simplicity both in life and in death, the first Christians were accustomed to bury their relatives by wrapping their bodies not only in a simple linen shroud but also in rich clothing. Archaeological discoveries today supply evidence of many textile remains, coloured and decorated with gold thread, belonging to the clothes in which the deceased were inhumed. The scarcity of such evidence depends on both the perishable nature of this material and the fashion of the period. The catacomb paintings show a very simple dress type, comprising mainly tunic, *pallium*, *dalmaticum* and cloak, while metal dress accessories, which are normally preserved archaeologically, are lacking. This investigation again confirms that the custom of grave furnishing does not disappear in the early Christian period.

Die schriftliche Überlieferung der antiken Autoren und der Kirchenväter belegt, dass trotz des Gebots der Einfachheit im Leben wie im Tode die ersten Christen ihre Verwandten nicht nur in einfache Leinentücher, sondern auch in wertvolle Kleidungsstücke einzuschlagen pflegten. Durch archäologische Funde sind uns heute viele Textilreste bekannt, und zwar farbige und mit Goldfäden durchwirkte, die von den Kleidern, in denen die Verstorbenen beigesetzt wurden, stammen. Die Seltenheit solcher Funde beruht zum einen auf der Vergänglichkeit des Materials und zum anderen auf der damaligen Mode. Die Malereien in den Katakomben zeigen einen sehr einfachen Trachttyp, der hauptsächlich aus Tunika, *pallium*, *dalmaticum* und Mantel bestand, während archäologisch erkennbare metallene Asseçoirs fehlten. Diese Untersuchung bestätigt erneut, dass die Sitte der Grabbeigaben in frühchristlicher Zeit nicht verschwand.

Le testimonianze degli antichi scrittori e dei Padri della Chiesa attestano che, nonostante l'esortazione alla semplicità nella vita come nella morte, i primi cristiani usavano dare sepoltura ai loro congiunti, non solo avvolgendo i corpi in un semplice lenzuolo di lino, ma anche in ricchi abiti. I rinvenimenti archeologici, infatti, documentano oggi molti resti di tessuti, colorati ed ornati di fili d'oro, pertinenti delle vesti con cui i defunti erano stati inumati. La scarsità dei residui dipende sia dalla natura del materiale, di per sé deperibile, sia dalla moda dell'epoca. Le pitture delle catacombe mostrano un tipo di abbigliamento molto semplice, costituito prevalentemente da tunica, pallio, dalmatica e mantellina, mentre scarseggiano gli accessori metallici, che di norma si conservano nei secoli. Le indagini confermano sempre di più che l'uso del corredo funebre non scompare in epoca paleocristiana.

26. Amulet and burials in Late Antiquity: some examples from Roman cemeteries

D. Nuzzo

The presence of superstition and magical practices in Late Antiquity is widely attested alongside the spread of Christianity: several documents record the condemnation of such superstitions by both the imperial authorities and the Church. The connection between superstition and burial practices is clearly documented by inscriptions and magic signs with obvious apotropaic value engraved outside some tombs in Roman cemeteries. A set of objects, fixed in the closing mortar of the *loculi*, with possible apotropaic value, can be considered as amulets of the dead and of the tomb, defenders of their integrity (bells, appliqués with the image of Medusa's head, masks, nails, semi-precious stones and animal teeth). Condemnation by the ecclesiastical authorities was not sufficient to eliminate the more deep-rooted superstitions, those connected not to official religion but to personal – and ancestral – piety. Different symbols and different traditions of pagan and Jewish origin coexisted with Christian traditions and symbolism to protect the dead and their tomb from evil forces and from whosoever would profane them. The mixture of different cultures and *mentalités*, and particularly the persistence of pagan symbols seems to demonstrate that from the fourth century, to be Christian in Rome did not imply necessarily a radical refusal of tradition, especially if connected with the sphere of magic.

Aberglaube und Magie sind ein hinlänglich belegtes Phänomen in der Spätantike, das parallel zur Verbreitung des Christentums verfolgt werden kann: Zahlreiche Dokumente berichten davon, dass sowohl die kaiserlichen Autoritäten als auch die Kirche solchen Aberglauben verdammten. Die Verbindung zwischen Aberglauben und Bestattungssitte ist deutlich bezeugt durch Inschriften und magische Zeichen von offensichtlich apotropäischem Charakter, die außen an einigen Grabstätten in stadtrömischen Nekropolen angebracht worden sind. Einsatz von Objekten, die beim Verschließen der *loculi* in den Mörtel gedrückt wurden und wohl apotropäische Funktion besaßen, kann als Amulette des Verstorbenen und des Grabes, als Behüter von deren Unverletzlichkeit (Glocken, Appliken mit Medusakopfbildern, Masken, Nägel, Halbedelsteine, Tierzähne) verstanden werden. Der Tadel der kirchlichen Autoritäten genügte nicht, um den tiefer verwurzelten Aberglauben auszurotten, der seinen Ursprung nicht in der offiziellen Religion, sondern in persönlicher und althergebrachter Frömmigkeit hatte. Ganz unterschiedliche Symbole und verschiedene Traditionen heidnischen und jüdischen Ursprungs bestanden neben christlichen Traditionen und Symbolen mit der Aufgabe, die Toten und ihre Gräber von bösen Mächten oder wem auch immer, der sie entweihen wollte, zu schützen. Die Mischung verschiedener Kulturen und Mentalitäten, und speziell das Weiterleben heidnischer Symbole, scheint zu demonstrieren, dass Christsein in Rom seit dem 4. Jahrhundert nicht unbedingt eine radikale Ablehnung der Tradition bedeutete, und dies besonders im Bereich der Magie.

La presenza di superstizioni e pratiche magiche in età tardoantica, in concomitanza quindi con la progressiva affermazione del cristianesimo, è ampiamente documentata dalle testimonianze scritte, che ne registrano la condanna sia da parte dell'autorità imperiale sia da parte della Chiesa. Il rapporto esistente tra pratiche superstiziose e sepoltura è con evidenza documentato da alcune iscrizioni e dalla presenza di segni magici con chiaro valore apotropaico incisi all'esterno di alcune sepolture dei cimiteri romani. Una serie di oggetti, fissati nella calce di chiusura dei loculi, ai quali può essere attribuito valore apotropaico, possono essere considerati amuleti del defunto e della tomba, difensori della loro integrità (campanelli, appliques con l'immagine della testa di Medusa, maschere, chiodi, pietre semipreziose, denti di animali). La condanna delle autorità ecclesiastiche non fu sufficiente ad eliminare le forme di superstizione più radicate, quelle legate non alle forme della religione ufficiale, ma alla religiosità personale e, insieme, ancestrale. Diversi simboli e tradizioni, di matrice pagana e giudaica, coesistono dunque con espressioni della fede cristiana allo scopo di proteggere il defunto e la sua sepoltura dalle forze del male e, soprattutto, da quanti volessero violarla. La mescolanza di diverse culture e mentalità e in particolare la persistenza dei simboli pagani sembrano dimostrare come a Roma a partire dal IV secolo l'appartenenza alla comunità cristiana non implichi necessariamente il rifiuto radicale della tradizione, soprattutto se legata alla sfera del magico.

27. Funerary equipment from the circiforme basilica by the Via Ardeatina, Rome

P. Del Moro

In 1991 an early Christian basilica of the *circiforme* style was located on the Via Ardeatina, in the *suburbium* of Rome. The archaeological excavations were focused on the north-eastern end of the basilica, a portion of the portico and a mausoleum, all of which were preserved at foundation level. The floor levels were occupied by graves of the 'pozzetto' type with one or more levels; the only monumental grave, with a sarcophagus, lay in the middle of the exedra, and was surrounded by five graves which must have contained sarcophagi. The basilica complex was used as a cemetery from the mid fourth to the mid fifth century and was reoccupied in the sixth to seventh centuries. The topographical, architectonic and archaeological data seem to confirm the hypothetical identification as the basilica founded by Pope Mark (336), recorded in late Antique and early medieval sources. The analysis of the graves and of the grave goods (relatively scarce and comprising above all coins and objects for personal use) shows a homogeneous social group of low status from whom the dead who occupied the group of privileged graves in the exedra are differentiated.

1991 wurde eine frühchristliche Basilika vom 'circiforme' Typ in der Via Ardeatina, im *suburbium* von Rom, lokalisiert. Die archäologischen Ausgrabungen konzentrierten sich auf das Nordostende der Basilika, einen Teil der Portikus und ein Mausoleum. Die Bauten sind in Fundamenthöhe erhalten, in die Böden sind ein oder mehrere Lagen von Gräbern vom 'pozzetto' Typ eingetieft. Das einzige monumentale Grab, das mit einem Sarkophag ausgestattet ist, befindet sich im Zentrum der Exhedra und ist von fünf Gräbern umgeben, die ursprünglich wohl auch Sarkophage beinhaltet haben müssen. Von der Mitte des 4. bis zur Mitte des 5. Jahrhunderts wurde die Basilika als Bestattungsplatz benutzt und im 6. und 7. Jahrhundert wiederaufgesucht. Topographie, Architektur und archäologische Funde sprechen für eine (hypothetische) Identifizierung des Baus mit der Basilika, deren Errichtung unter Papst Markus für das Jahr 336 durch spätantike und hochmittelalterliche Quellen überliefert ist. Die Auswertung von Grabanlagen und –beigaben (wenige und hauptsächlich aus Münzen und Gegenständen des persönlichen Besitzes bestehend) sprechen für eine homogene Bevölkerung der unteren sozialen Schichten, von denen sich die Toten aus den priviligierten Gräbern in der Exhedra unterscheiden.

Nel 1991 è stata individuata presso la via Ardeatina, nel suburbio di Roma, una basilica paleocristiana del tipo *circiforme*. Gli scavi archeologici hanno interessato il settore terminale nord-est della basilica, parte del portico ed un mausoleo, conservati a livello di fondazione, con i piani pavimentali occupati da tombe del tipo 'a pozzetto', ad uno o più livelli; l'unica tomba monumentale, con sarcofago, è posta al centro dell'esedra, ed ha intorno cinque tombe che dovevano contenere sarcofagi. Il complesso è stato utilizzato come cimitero dalla metà del IV alla metà del V secolo, con rioccupazioni nel VI–VII secolo. I dati topografici, architettonici ed archeologici sembrano confermare l'ipotetico riconoscimento nella basilica fondata da

papa Marco (336), ricordata da fonti tardoantiche ed altomedioevali. L'analisi delle tombe e dei corredi (poco diffusi e costituiti soprattutto da monete e da oggetti di uso personale) indica una composizione sociale omogenea e non elevata, dalla quale si differenziano i defunti che hanno occupato il gruppo di tombe privilegiate nell'esedra.

28. *Intra-mural burials at Rome between the 5th and the 7th centuries AD*

R. Meneghini and R. Santangeli Valenzani

The introduction of burials into towns is one of the most obvious indicators of change between the ancient and medieval city. The first stage of research aimed to locate all the attestations of burials datable to the early medieval period found within the walled circuit, both in recent excavations and in documentation from older excavations. On this basis this study intends to establish, first of all, the chronology of the phenomenon, the juridical and institutional context in which it took place and its significance for the history of 'mentalités' and funerary customs, and secondly to use these data to reconstruct the urban and social landscapes of Rome in the first centuries of the early medieval period.

Das Verlegen von Grabstätten in das Innere der Städte ist eines der deutlichsten Anzeichen des Wechsels von der antiken zur mittelalterlichen Stadt. Den Beginn der Untersuchung bildet die Erfassung aller Beispiele für Gräber innerhalb der Stadtmauern, die ins Frühe Mittelalter datieren. Moderne und Dokumentationen älterer Ausgrabungen werden dabei berücksichtigt. An erster Stelle soll so die Chronologie des Phänomens präzisiert und der rechtlich-institutionelle Hintergrund sowie die Bedeutung, die diese Neuerung für Geistesgeschichte und Grabsitten hatten, erhellt werden. An zweiter Stelle geht es um die Rekonstruktion der städtischen und sozialen Landschaft Roms während der ersten Jahrhunderte des Frühen Mittelalters mit Hilfe dieses Material.

L'introduzione delle sepolture nella città costituisce uno dei più evidenti segni del cambiamento tra la città antica e la città medievale. Partendo da una ricerca tendente a individuare, negli scavi recenti e nella documentazione relativa ai vecchi scavi, tutte le attestazioni di sepolture rinvenute all'interno della cerchia delle mura databili all'altomedioevo, questo studio si propone di precisare, innanzitutto, la cronologia del fenomeno, la cornice giuridico-istituzionale in cui ha avuto luogo e il suo significato per la storia della mentalità e dei costumi funerari e, in secondo luogo, di utilizzare questi dati per una ricostruzione del paesaggio urbano e del paesaggio sociale della Roma dei primi secoli dell'altomedioevo.

List of Contributors

DR ANGELIKA ABEGG-WIGG
Institut für Ur- und Frühgeschichte der Christian-Albrechts-
Universität
24098 Kiel
Germany
abegg@ufg.uni-kiel.de

DR JEAN BOURGEOIS
Department of Archaeology
Ghent University
Blandijnberg 2
9000 Gent
Belgium
Jean.Bourgeois@rug.ac.be

CLIVE DAVISON
Rêve de la Mer
Clos des Mielles
Rue de Carteret
Castel
Guernsey GY5 7XB
UK
clive_davison@hotmail.com

DR MARIA PAOLA DEL MORO
Viale dell' Umanesimo 12
00144 Rome
Italy
c/o gianluca.delmoro@tiscalinet.it

DR PAOLA DE SANTIS
Via Toscanini 24
70126 Bari
Italy
p.desantis@dscc.uniba.it

DR DAGMAR DEXHEIMER
Clemens-August Str. 69
53115 Bonn
Germany
Dagmar.Dexheimer@t-online.de

DR SIMON ESMONDE CLEARY
Dept. of Ancient History and Archaeology
Edgbaston
Birmingham B15 2TT
UK
a.s.esmonde_cleary@bham.ac.uk

DR PETER FASOLD
Museum für Vor- und Frühgeschichte
Archäologisches Museum
Karmelitergasse 1
60311 Frankfurt am Main
Germany

DR ANDREW FITZPATRICK
Wessex Archaeology
Portway House, Old Sarum Park
Salisbury SP4 6EB
UK
a.fitzpatrick@wessexarch.co.uk

LOUIS GIRARD
169 Avenue Renaudin
92100 Clamart
France

DR ALEKSANDAR JOVANOVIC
Faculty of Philosophy
Centre for Archaeological Research
11000 Belgrade
Cika Ljubina 18–20
Yugoslavia

DR ANGELA KREUZ
Kommission für Archäologische Landesforschung in Hessen
Schloß Biebrich / Ostflügel
65203 Wiesbaden
Germany
idkal@wiesbaden-online.de

PROF. STEFANIE MARTIN-KILCHER
Universität Bern
Institut für Ur- und Frühgeschichte
und Archäologie der Römischen Provinzen
Bernastraße 15A
3005 Bern
Switzerland
stefanie.martin-kilcher@sfu.unibe.ch

DR ROSSANA MARTORELLI
Dipartimento di Scienze Archeologiche e Storico-Artistiche
Università degli Studi di Cagliari
Cittadella dei Musei
Piazza Arsenale, 1
09100 Cagliari
Italy

JACQUELINE MCKINLEY
Wessex Archaeology
Portway House, Old Sarum Park
Salisbury SP4 6EB
UK
j.mckinley@wessexarch.co.uk

DR ROBERTO MENEGHINI
Mercati Traianei, 94
Via IV Novembre
00186 Rome
Italy

PROF. MARTIN MILLETT
Department of Archaeology
University of Southampton
Highfield
Southampton SO17 1BJ
UK
Martin.Millett@soton.ac.uk

DR PASCAL MURAIL
UMR 5809
Laboratoire d'Anthropologie des Populations du Passé
Université Bordeaux 1 Avenue des Facultés
33 405 Talence cedex
France
p.murail@anthropologie.u-bordeaux.fr

ROSALIND NIBLETT
Kyngston House
Inkerman Rd
St Albans
Herts AL1 3BB
UK
rniblett@compuserve.com

DR DONATELLA NUZZO
Corso Trieste 128
00198 Rome
Italy
d.nuzzo@dscc.uniba.it

DR JOHN PEARCE
Centre for the Study of Ancient Documents
67 St Giles
Oxford OX1 4TD
UK
john.pearce@lithum.ox.ac.uk

DR MICHEL POLFER
Séminaire d'Etudes Anciennes (Semant)
Centre Universitaire de Luxembourg
162A, Avenue de la Faïencerie
1511 Luxembourg
polfermichel@netscape.net

LUCAS QUENSEL-VON-KALBEN
Kummerfelder Str. 1
25494 Borstel – Hohenraden
Germany

DR RICHARD REECE
The Apple Loft
The Waterloo
Cirencester
Gloucestershire GL7 2PU
UK
Richard@reece100.freeserve.co.uk

DR MATTHIAS RIEDEL
Römisch-Germanisches Museum
Roncalliplatz 4
50667 Köln
Germany

DR RICCARDO SANTANGELI VALENZANI
Mercati Traianei, 94
Via IV Novembre
00186 Rome
Italy
santangeli@katamail.com

DR CATY SCHUCANY
Kantonsarchäologie
Werkhofstr. 55
4500 Solothurn
Switzerland

DR MARCELLO SPANU
Dipartimento di scienze del mondo antico
Università della Tuscia
Via S. Camillo de Lellis
01100 Viterbo
Italy

DR MANUELA STRUCK
59, Kidderminster Rd
Bewdley
Worcestershire DY12 1BU
UK
struck@lineone.net

DR JUDIT TOPÁL
Budapest III 1031
Záhony u. 4
Budapest Történeti Múzeum, Aquincumi Múzeum
Hungary

DR LAURENCE TRANOY
Université de la Rochelle
Faculté des Langues, Arts, et Sciences Humaines
23, avenue Albert Enstein
17071 La Rochelle Cedex 9
France
ltranoy@univ-lr.fr

DR MARIE TUFFREAU-LIBRE
CNRS Centre de Céramologie Gallo-Romaine
Palais St Vaast
Rue Paul Doumer
62000 Arras
France

DR FRANK VERMEULEN
Department of Archaeology
Ghent University
Blandijnberg 2
9000 Gent
Belgium
Frank.Vermeulen@rug.ac.be

1. Burial, society and context in the provincial Roman World

John Pearce

Introduction

The archaeological evidence for burial practice has always been central to the reconstruction of both prehistoric and early medieval societies, but has remained less integral to the study of the Roman world. Wider developments in the archaeological interpretation of mortuary practice have also had relatively little influence. In syntheses of the archaeology of Roman Britain and other provinces, burial has often been excluded from the main political or military narratives, and considered primarily within descriptive accounts of 'day-to-day' provincial life (Millett this volume). Only at certain points, usually 'transition' periods, is burial evidence more central to such narratives, for example as a marker of the movement of peoples in the immediate pre-Roman period in north-western Europe and for the arrival of Germanic incomers in the late Roman period. The identification of popular conversion to Christianity has also been debated on the basis of late Roman burial practices. The emphasis on specific historical questions has however been a distraction from exploring the relationship between burial and society over the longer term.

Recent perspectives on the archaeology of the Roman provinces provide a context for rejuvenating the study of burial and demand that we examine some of the concepts used in the analysis of burial practice. A number of objections have been raised to the studies which displaced from centre stage political and military narratives in favour of social and economic processes, especially that of Romanisation (e.g. Blagg and Millett 1990; Brandt and Slofstra 1983; Millett 1990). Both the term 'Romanisation' and the emphasis on mapping the spread of 'Romanitas' have been argued to produce a one-directional historical narrative (Barrett 1997). A more diverse range of response to the material manifestations of Roman power have been envisaged, not precluding emulation but also allowing for resistance (Hingley 1997; Webster 1996) and selective appropriation related to local social formations (e.g. Terrenato 1998). In short a process of 'Romanisation' cannot be taken for granted as given or normative. Instead our aim is to understand how 'Roman' material forms were adopted in different contexts, including burial. Economic and social changes did not take place in a vacuum but developed with and through change in ritual, belief and ideology (e.g. Metzler *et al.* 1995; Roymans 1996; Woolf 1998). Emphasis on the ideological component of 'Romanisation' has stimulated a revival in interest in the spheres traditionally seen as pertaining to ideology, such as religion and burial (e.g. Freeman 1993). It is thus a fruitful time to re-evaluate the use of burial evidence for Roman societies.

Just as the size of the Roman world defies feasible synthesis of all the various aspects of burial practice (Morris 1992: 206), so it also resists any critique which attempts to cover all relevant source materials and possible topics of discussion. The influence of the 'intellectualist' approach is clear in the attempts to identify through burial evidence either Roman and native belief systems or, in the later imperial period, adherence to Christian afterlife beliefs. Ian Morris (1987; 1992) has criticised this approach to burial in the Greco-Roman world for examining burial practice only as evidence for afterlife beliefs and for a one-dimensional interpretation of funerary symbolism as such evidence. Given Morris' extended criticism this approach is not examined further here. Also excepted from consideration here are three broad sources of evidence. Literary evidence for attitudes towards death and the dead from the Roman world is remarkably diverse but has been used to reconstruct a composite picture of Roman funerary rituals and attitudes to the dead ignoring spatial and chronological diversity (e.g. Toynbee 1971). More closely focused studies of the literary evidence will inevitably produce a fragmented account which is biased to Rome and Italy, although patchy evidence does exist from elsewhere, for example pre-Roman and Roman Gaul (Buisson 1993; Le Bohec 1991) and Spain (Curchin 1997: 9). The study of funerary architecture, sculpture and epigraphy, in particular from Italy represents an exception to the generalisation made above and has become a central source for Roman society. The analysis of human remains is also not discussed here; its significance has been emphasised elsewhere although the number of cemetery publications to integrate discussion of skeletal data with other archaeological information remains small (Reece 1982; this volume). The emphasis of discussion in this paper lies primarily on current approaches to the burial practices of the northern provinces, especially of the early Roman period, although it is impossible to do equal justice to different national traditions of the study of Roman burial practice and it is hoped that generalisations will be forgiven.[1] The study of burials from Roman Britain should certainly not be considered as typical for the northern provinces: the greater priority given to burial evidence elsewhere is well demonstrated by the large number of cemetery related projects within the 'Romanisation project' sponsored by the Deutsche Forschungsgemeinschaft (Haffner and von Schnurbein 1996). Nevertheless despite these unavoidable restrictions of focus, the discussion considers some widely held assumptions in the study of burial in the Roman world.

Over the last two decades several studies have recognised the potential of burial evidence as a source for provincial Roman society and brought a diversity of perspectives to bear (e.g. Ferdière (ed.) 1993; Galliou 1989; Jones 1983; Philpott 1991; Reece (ed.) 1977; Struck (ed.) 1993; Fasold *et al.* (ed.) 1998). A growing database is also at the disposal of students of burial evidence. Figure 1.1 for example records the increase in the number of sites in Britain on which Roman period burials have been excavated since the early part of this century, an increase which matches that of other types of Roman period site (for which see Wilkes 1989: 247–9). However as others have pointed out (Jones 1993a; Reece 1982; Rife 1997), only a minority of analyses have critically considered the premises by which Roman society is reconstructed from burial evidence. In particular the 'post-processual' critique of the interpretation of mortuary practice has received little attention. This paper reviews current approaches to burial data in the light of general developments in two areas of debate, the archaeological study of mortuary ritual and debate on the nature of cultural change in the Roman world. The use of burial as evidence for cultural identity and social status is given particular attention. Drawing broadly on post-processual approaches, some methods are offered to develop and broaden analysis of Roman period burials, in particular through the study of burial evidence in tandem with that from other archaeological contexts.

Burial and cultural identity

If any one area of interest dominates the study of the burials of the Roman period (excluding the 'intellectualist' perspective), it is the relationship between burial and cultural identity. In the north-western provinces two examples of this approach are probably most familiar. Scholars have tried to differentiate between the burial practices of indigenous populations and those of incomers and to trace changes in local burial practices as manifestations of 'Romanisation'. In the study of the late Roman period the identification of settlers from beyond the boundaries of the empire through modes of burial furnishing has generated continuing discussion (Baldwin 1985; Clarke 1979; Cooke 1998; Halsall 1992; Hills 1979; James 1988), with study of skeletal evidence now making an important if so far limited contribution (Pilet 1995; Reece 1982; this volume). Given the comparative intensity of study of the late Roman period in this respect, attention is devoted here to the early Roman period.

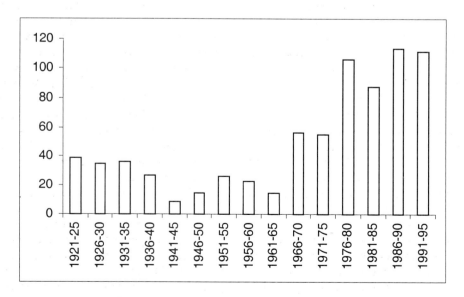

Fig. 1.1 *References to excavation of burials and cemeteries as recorded in archaeological summaries in JRS and Britannia (5 year blocks), 1920–1995.*

Distinctions between the burial practices of indigenous and intrusive groups in the early Roman period have been drawn on the basis of two criteria, grave goods and burial type. For example a suite of grave goods has been classed as 'Roman', in particular the presence of lamps, coins and unguent bottles (Philpott 1991: 218; Fasold 1993: 382–4; Fasold and Witteyer 1998). Metal dress accessories in burial assemblages have been used to attach ethnic affiliation to the occupants of graves, based on the regional costume types identified from relief sculpture and general distributions of dress accessories (Martin-Kilcher 1993a; Wild 1985). A criterion almost wholly ignored in Britain but given equal if not greater importance in study of the German provinces in particular and to a lesser extent in Gaul is the type of cremation burial. The manner of deposition of cremated bone, pyre debris and grave goods is the criterion for distinguishing between burial types, and the terminology adapted from that used for pre-Roman cremation burial types in central Europe: Bechert (1980) gives the most commonly accepted definitions although inconsistent usage persists, obstructing comparison between sites (Bridger 1996). Van Doorsaeler (1967) and Nierhaus (1959; 1969) offer cautious assessments of the cultural affiliations of different burial types.

Difficulties with this approach are partly practical. Discontinuous distributions can certainly be established within the burial record of the north-western provinces, but those based on as full a range of evidence as possible will be more convincing than those based on single features (see further below for archaeologically recoverable types of burial evidence). The presence of individual 'exotic' artefacts is of doubtful value in determining the origin of the deceased. Reece (1982) argued that to define an intrusive burial rite also requires a secure knowledge of the burial rite of the area in which it is supposed to have originated. However archaeological understanding of burial practices across the empire is highly variable. Particularly problematic is the lack of a 'base line' for identifying a Roman burial rite in the provinces. The monumental aspects (epigraphic, architectural, sculptural) of burial practice in central Italy of the late Republic and early empire have been intensively studied (see note 1), but grave assemblages much less so (Fasold 1993: 382–4; Fasold and Witteyer 1998). We should also beware of applying too rigid a definition of 'Roman' burial to compare to the provinces but remain alert to variability in what might be defined as a 'Roman' burial practice, perhaps the most obvious being the second century change to inhumation. In Britain the identification of intrusive burial traditions is frustrated by the lack of modern excavation of cemeteries used by non-indigenous populations, especially those of the military (Jones 1984b; Society for the Promotion of Roman Studies 1985: 5). The identification of indigenous burial traditions is also often not straightforward; for example not only in many parts of Britain, but also in other areas incorporated within the empire, are archaeologically visible burial practices largely

unknown in the pre-Roman Iron Age (e.g. Collis 1977; Pion and Guichard 1993; Whimster 1981).

On the other hand the vastly increased volume of burial data from some areas has made scholars increasingly wary of earlier generalisations. Local variation within the different categories of cremation burial is increasingly appreciated (e.g. Bridger 1996; van Doorsaeler and Rogge 1985; Vermeulen 1992: 233) while broad types previously sometimes considered particular to the north-western provinces are now known to occur at least occasionally in Italy (e.g. Groeneveld 1998: 394–5) and Asia Minor (F. Vermeulen pers. comm.). The extent of the area over which potential parallels might be sought is also intimidating. The structure of empire permitted movement and interaction on an unprecedented scale between a daunting diversity of groups. The consequent difficulty of assigning origin to a particular practice is well illustrated by Struck's (1993b) identification of four possible areas in the empire from which the *bustum* burial type in Britain might have been derived.

R. Jones (1987; 1991; 1993b) has argued that a multi-layered formulation resolves these complexities; different burial rituals can be associated with cultural rules shared by communities at local, regional and empire-wide levels. The identification of the high degree of local difference has led several scholars to a bolder conclusion, that the persistence of local practices indicates a relatively slow 'Romanisation' of burial practice, and indeed that only the spread of inhumation from the late second century marks its completion (van Doorsaeler 1967: 67; Morris 1992: 68; Struck 1995: 147; Wightman 1985: 188).

The relationship of these localised burial practices to the local / regional groups, the existence of which we know for example from literary and epigraphic evidence, needs careful evaluation. It has been demonstrated from many ethnographic examples that the identities ascribed in funerary ritual do not directly reflect those defining them in life; 'the pattern of death reinforces a societal ideal which is only part of what exists in practice and about which there is concern' (Hodder 1982a: 143). While Hodder's emphasis on the link between a strong group identity in burial and 'stress' has been disputed (Morris 1992: 28), the basic point remains in force: the patterning we identify in burial is unlikely to have a direct relationship with local communities. Care is required in identifying the transition of burial practice from a non-discursive component of *habitus* to a conscious and explicit ethnic signifier (S. Jones 1997).

S. Jones reminds us that the categories we use to label burial practice, in this case for example Roman or Germanic, or pertaining to a tribe or *civitas*, are not static or given – the perceptions of the colonial power and the response of the societies incorporated within empires can transform identities. The exact relationship of Roman political geography to pre-Roman formations, especially in the northern provinces, is in most cases unclear although we can offer general models (e.g. Haselgrove 1984). We cannot for example plot all of the formations which the literary sources reveal to us, often around the period of conquest, onto post-conquest political geography (e.g. Raepsaet-Charlier 1995). The relevance therefore of the Roman administrative map for grouping burial evidence should be tested rather than assumed.

As the recent study of 'Romanisation' also demands (see above), we need to explore how and why burial practice became 'Romanised'. The most successful consideration of burial evidence in this regard is of provincial manifestations of the monumental aspects of Roman funerary culture. Different regional and local chronologies of epigraphic commemoration have been established within the general manifestation of the 'epigraphic habit' (MacMullen 1982), for example in Hope's (1994) comparison of corpora of inscriptions from Mainz, Aquileia and Nîmes. A recurring theme is the selective adoption or assimilation into existing local repertoires of certain Roman monumental forms or motifs, for example in the eastern empire (Cormack 1997; Schmidt-Colinet 1997), Africa (Ferchiou 1995), Spain (von Hesberg 1993) and Gaul (Hatt 1986; Freigang 1997). Tumuli, the most popular monumental form in Britain, Gallia Belgica and Noricum / Pannonia, have been interpreted during this century in sharply opposed terms, as a revival of native forms or the imitation of late Republican examples from Rome (Becker 1993). Wigg (1993) and Morris (1992: 51) have convincingly argued that their popularity drew on their resonance in both indigenous and Roman traditions. The creation of innovative forms in a funerary context is also demonstrated in the assemblages of a small group of burials from northern Gaul and Britain in the first century BC and first half of the first century AD. The amphorae, imported ceramics, and metal vessels are argued to demonstrate elite connections to Roman power, access to Roman goods and the adoption of certain forms of 'symposium' culture, combined with local signifiers of status such as weapons and hearth furniture (Ferdière and Villard 1993; Haselgrove 1987; Metzler *et al*. 1991; Woolf 1998: 247). While these burials have been central to our understanding of the late Iron Age, the substantial burial assemblages of the later first and second centuries AD of the north-western provinces await exploitation as evidence for social processes.

The relationship of burial to social status

Monuments bearing inscriptions and sculpture can only ever have been raised by a small minority of the empire's inhabitants, but have dominated some syntheses of burial practice (e.g. Hatt 1986; Toynbee 1971). The systematic identification in burial evidence of ranking within provincial Roman society as a whole was the concern of R. Jones' (1983; 1984a; 1984c) survey of first to third century cemeteries in the western provinces. Within different local burial traditions, he defined groups of burials through multivariate analysis of burial assemblages

which he associated with social status. The study is the most extensive application of a processual approach to Roman period burial evidence (Binford 1972; Chapman *et al*. 1981).

Like many 'processual' analyses of burial practice (J. Brown 1981), Jones concentrated on the social status dimension of identity. The principal conclusion that provincial Roman society was stratified is unsurprising, but even if this particular approach has not been repeated on other samples it has helped to engender a more rigorous quantitative approach to the analysis of cemeteries (e.g. Bridger 1996; Millett 1993; Struck 1993c; van Lith and Randsborg 1985).

Criticisms of Jones' approach are possible within a 'processual' framework. Jones' analysis was based primarily on the container for the body and the grave goods. These assemblages are usually the most reliably recorded aspect of burials, but need not have been those on which most energy was expended. Thorough excavation and documentation of cemeteries have made it increasingly clear that other parts of the burial ceremony may be archaeologically visible, especially those connected with cremation. On well preserved sites, comprising an individual or small number of burials, different deposits can be related to a convincing sequence of ritual. The cremation and burial sites of the emperor Galerius and his mother provide a spectacular demonstration (Srejovic and Vasic 1994) but there are also several examples from LPRIA and early Roman north-western Europe (Jessup 1954; Metzler *et al*. 1991; Roosens 1976). In larger cemeteries used over a long period of time it is not so easy to distinguish features related to individual ceremonies but it still possible to reconstruct the sequence of ritual in more general terms (e.g. Haffner 1989; Fitzpatrick 1997). The recovery of this information has shown that conclusions based on grave goods alone need not be reliable. At Wederath for example one might have inferred a declining investment in burial from the lower numbers of ceramics in second century graves, but large contemporary deposits of burnt ceramics have been recorded from the *Aschengruben* (Haffner 1989: 114). Detailed analysis of the cremated human bone also has great potential for reconstruction both of the cremation process itself and other pre-burial aspects of funerary ritual (e.g. McKinley, in Fitzpatrick 1997: 55–73). It is less easy to apply this approach to inhumation burials although exceptional preservation conditions may permit fuller reconstruction of funerary rituals (e.g. Audollent 1922; Radolescu *et al*. 1973).

Jones' analysis was based on large and well-recorded groups of cemeteries usually associated with individual settlements. The cemeteries of a single settlement are unlikely to encapsulate all the variation in the status-determined burial practice of a particular society. A regional approach is necessary even if this compromises data quality (J. Brown 1981; 1995). It also remains to be demonstrated that the burial forms, within which Jones analysed variation, were the same for all social groups in his study areas. Given that the burial practices of many areas later incorporated into the Roman empire are invisible in the pre-Roman Iron Age, a significant proportion of the Roman period population of some provinces may well not have received formal burial or an archaeologically visible burial mode. The occurrence of bones and bone fragments on settlement sites (e.g. Hessing 1993) supports such a hypothesis.

The assumption on which Jones' and other processual studies were based, that variation in funerary rite directly reflects the deceased's status cannot stand unchallenged. Ethnographic and historical examples show that the status inferred from investment in funerary rituals need not reflect that attributed in life (Hodder 1982a: 146; 1982b; Ucko 1969). This position has been most trenchantly set out by analysts drawing on structural Marxism, for whom funerary ritual manifests an ideologically conditioned view of the world, either by universalising, naturalising or disguising social relations (e.g. Parker Pearson 1982; Shanks and Tilley 1982). The political theatre of the aristocratic Roman republican period funeral, dividing elite and commoners, provides an example of the universalisation of difference (Morris 1991). In the funerary sphere also certain groups can express themselves with a freedom not permitted, for instance, in other public spaces or in other ceremonies. The funerary culture of freedmen, over-represented in the epigraphic record at Rome, provides an example of this (Taylor 1961; Dyson 1992: 149–52). Funerary monuments bearing sculpture and / or inscriptions in Roman Britain were little employed by the *civitas* elites, nor where more common in the military areas by the highest status groups (Biró 1975; Hope 1997). Rather, according to Hope, it was 'outsiders' who made more extensive use of the medium, for example the unofficial wives of Roman soldiers:

> 'To these immigrants, who dwelt on the margins of acceptance, the funerary memorial created a sense of permanency and legitimacy not always achieved in life.' (Hope 1997: 258)

The context of burial

The difficulties of direct readings of burial evidence have been outlined above. The major contribution of the 'post-processual' critique has been to demonstrate that the treatment of the dead does not directly reflect the identity of the living, whether it be their ethnic affiliation or social status. Society is presented in an idealised form, a model constructed by and presented to participants in the ritual (Morris 1992: 5–15). We can only use burial as a source for Roman societies if we understand this transformation and establish the place of the dead in the culture under consideration. Many of the Roman provinces are poor in relevant literary evidence. We must therefore examine the archaeological approaches offered in the study of death and burial in prehistory that may be usefully applied in the Roman period.

The identification of a unified post-processual perspective for the study of burial is not possible, but a common emphasis of recent work is that to establish the significance of the dead in a particular context involves comparison across the conventionally separated elements of the archaeological record, settlements, cemeteries and sacred sites. Parker Pearson (1993) has distilled some of the methods offered in a threefold approach. Briefly summarised, this compares the location of the dead relative to other features in the landscape, the structure of cemetery and settlement by age, gender, status or other variable, and the deposition of artefact types across cemetery, votive and settlement deposits. It seeks to establish the significance of the dead in the life of the living, is their presence for example apparent in day to day movement in the landscape or are they only met with on specific occasions? As absolute notions of proximity between dead and living are difficult to establish, a diachronic approach is essential in order to determine the relative proximity of settlement and cemetery over time. Do the same variables, such as gender or status organise cemeteries and settlements, or do discrepancies suggest for example that the presentation of the dead masks inequalities among the living? Is the realm of the dead a focus for the expenditure of energy in the form of monuments or the deposition of prestige goods, and thus a realm of overt consumption, or is it insignificant compared for example to votive or settlement architecture or deposits? How do cycles of display and restraint in burial practice compare to those in other spheres (cf. Cannon 1989)?

The building blocks of such analysis are not easily established in their own right, for example the gendered organisation of settlement layout, and form major research topics in their own right. Many data sets, including that exploited by Parker Pearson, are dominated either by cemeteries, settlements or monuments (e.g. Bradley 1984). This is not simply inconvenient – the emergence of a visible burial tradition in the late Iron Age and Roman period in some parts of Britain and elsewhere is of probable historical significance in itself (Hill 1995). Different items will also be differentially visible across the archaeological record. For example precious metals may be widely circulating outside the burial / votive sphere but because of recycling may be virtually unrepresented in settlement deposits.

This type of analysis has been taxed with reducing funerary and other rituals to the cynical manipulation of power relations (Barrett 1991). The extent to which dominant ideologies are heeded outside dominant groups can be questioned (McGuire and Paynter 1991). Indeed the contested identity of the dead by different participants in funerary rituals becomes clear in ethnographic accounts (e.g. Huntington and Metcalf 1992). The concentration on power relations has also been insufficiently sensitive to individual emotional responses to the event of death (Meskell 1994; Tarlow 1999; Treherne 1996). Literary evidence however allowed all of the latter to explore such responses for at least some of their contexts of study, and in the absence of such evidence empathetic interpretations may project culture-specific responses to death onto the burial practices of the past. While there are dangers of reductionism to a cynical view of burial practice, nevertheless the perspective set out above offers fresh archaeological approaches to Roman period burial evidence.

Putting Roman burial in context

The following approaches are therefore suggested to explore the relationships between the living and the dead through archaeological evidence, first during the mortuary rituals themselves and second in the interrelationship of dead and living in the landscape.

1. Funerary rituals

For the sake of convenience general comparisons between different archaeological data sets, for example from settlements, cemeteries and votive sites, and comparisons between the structure of these different data sets, are treated separately in the following discussion.

It is sometimes assumed that certain artefact types represent the deposit of prestige goods (see above) but the relationship of burial deposits to those associated with other contexts, for example in public or private buildings, in temples or in votive deposits has rarely been systematically compared (see van Lith and Randsborg 1985 for an exception). Examples of considerable 'energy investment' in burial can be identified, such as gold jewellery (Rottloff 1995), but is it possible to recognise wider trends? If burial practice is argued to reflect cultural identity, how do the spatial distributions of types of grave good compare with the distribution of the same artefacts outside a burial context? The study of the 'Durotrigian' burial rite of the first centuries BC and AD from this perspective has yet to be repeated in other contexts (Blackmore *et al.* 1979).

Comparison of the ceramic assemblages from different contexts should be particularly fruitful, given the existence of large samples of ceramics from many cemetery and settlement contexts. Some differences have been outlined – for example storage and preparation vessels are relatively rare in tombs in Britain, and a small number of ceramics distinguished by their poor quality, miniature size or by traces of deliberate damage are particular to graves (Philpott 1991: 36; Tuffreau-Libre 1992: 113–23). However although individual studies have shown differences within the tableware category between burial and settlement (e.g. Millett 1993: 279), the subject deserves wider study. Given the relatively rapid change in availability of certain items and the likely changes in their prestige connotations (Bradley 1988), as close a chronological and spatial control as possible should be maintained over the deposits compared.

In drawing any comparisons we must be sensitive to all the archaeologically recoverable forms of burial practice, the pre-burial rituals, grave goods and monuments, although in practice for much of the northern provinces, monuments, the burial container and grave goods remain the most frequent elements of assemblages sufficiently well recorded to allow statistical analysis.

Diachronic comparison between contexts is also essential. If we can identify cycles of mortuary display analogous to those noted by Cannon (1989), how do these compare to depositional practice or monument building in other contexts? For example the average number of grave goods in some burial samples during the early Roman period in Britain seems to have declined in the post-conquest period (Millett 1995: 123–4; Struck 1995). It has also been widely proposed that the 'Romanisation' of burial practice is slow in comparison to other spheres, such as public architecture (see above). These propositions can further assessed by examination of trends in all types of burial evidence, not only grave goods, and by explicit comparison between trends in burial evidence and other archaeological contexts.

How does the structure of burial evidence compare to that visible in other data sets? If we can identify, like Jones, a quite marked hierarchy within or between sets of burials based on combinations of grave goods, how does this compare with the differentiation that students of settlement evidence have established (e.g. Hingley 1989; Smith 1997)? Does change in both sets of data take place at the same rate over time?

The construction of age and gender identities through burial also merits greater attention. In contrast to the study of Roman funerary art (Matheson, in Kleiner and Matheson 1996: 182–95) the relationship of archaeological evidence of burial practice to gender has attracted relatively limited interest. The most fruitful area of study has been reconstruction of female costume, especially of the early Roman period in the Rhine and Danube provinces, based on dress accessories in burial assemblages as well as sculpture (e.g. Wild 1985; Martin-Kilcher 1993a). Care is needed to eliminate unsupported assumptions of gender-specific grave goods (Allason Jones 1995). Studies of individual cemeteries are increasingly rigorous (e.g. Bridger 1996) but analysis of change over time in gender-specific burial treatment based on several categories of artefacts is rare; Foster's study (1993) represents a recent exception. The 'missing' women from many cemeteries from late Roman Britain are notorious but how does this inform our understanding of gender relations?

The most familiar age based difference is the burial of infants on settlements rather than in cemeteries, but even in this apparently well understood phenomenon recent studies have shown that further patterning can be extracted (Scott 1990, Struck 1993a). The lavish burial treatment of some very young individuals is particularly striking (e.g. Taylor 1993; Ruprechtsberger 1996) but there has been little general analysis of the relationship between burial treatment and age.

The increasing number of cemeteries with full publication of both human remains and artefact assemblages should allow this field of study to expand. Study should be made of broad changes in the treatment of age and gender in burial over time, to compare with changes identified in funerary epigraphy, for example (e.g. Shaw 1984; 1991) and with gender-related use of settlement space.

2. Burial in the landscape

Burials and other dimensions of the archaeological record can be compared as analytical categories but together they formed part of the same past landscape and their relationship in that landscape deserves study. On the general view passage through its encircling cemeteries marked arrival at and departure from the Roman town. Von Hesberg and Zanker (1987) have shown that behind this familiar picture lie subtle but important shifts in the relationship of the dead to these road frontages. Their analysis is largely traced through a small number of mainly Italian cemeteries. The extent to which this relatively precise model applies elsewhere has not been extensively tested (Roth-Congès 1990), partly because few cemeteries enjoy the same preservation. Nevertheless recent large-scale investigation shows that considerable stretches of *Gräberstrassen* associated with towns and military sites survive even beneath dense modern occupation in the north-western provinces. Individual examples show some differences. In the stretches excavated at Mainz-Weisenau (Witteyer and Fasold 1995) and Haltern (Berke 1990) for example, monuments are relatively closely packed close to the roadside. However south-east of St Albans (Frere 1990: 328–30) and south-west of Tongeren (Vanvinckenroye 1984) occasional monuments occur on the road frontage within spreads of burial which do not otherwise favour immediate roadside location. The sample of excavations on this scale is too small yet to allow meaningful generalisations, but the plotting of older scattered discoveries of monuments can yield useful results in this regard (e.g. Jones 1984b; Spiegel 1994). Further assessment of the relationship of cemeteries to the suburban landscape is also desirable (Esmonde Cleary 1987; Purcell 1987).

For a fuller appreciation of the location of burial display, analysis must transcend the confines of the urban cemeteries. Jones (1983: 81) suggested that early Romano-British elites favoured the countryside over the town for funerary display. Wightman (1985: 163–68) demonstrated that the preference for raising funerary monuments in town or country varied between neighbouring *civitates* in Gallia Belgica. Fiches (1993) has argued that more dynamic groups in the landscape around Nîmes could be identified from the more rapid adoption of funerary innovation both in the pre-Roman and Roman period. Many other areas have sufficient evidence to allow similar analysis, exploring the location of changing modes of burial display from the pre-Roman period onwards, combining monumental and artefactual evidence.

As around towns however rural burials must also be closely located in their context to characterise their impact on the living. A variety of relationships between funerary monuments or enclosures and their immediate settlement context have been documented. They may be located centrally within villa complexes (e.g. Lafon and Adam 1993), by their entrances (e.g. Bayard 1993), outside the settlement area but overlooking it (e.g. Williams and Zeepvat 1994) or be relatively secluded and inaccessible (e.g. Martin-Kilcher 1993b). The example of Bancroft (Bucks) not only demonstrates the highly obvious and visible locations in which such monuments might be placed, but also suggests the possible links between the 'life-cycle' of burial monuments and the histories of the settlements with which they are associated (Williams and Zeepvat 1994). Monuments like Bancroft of the 'temple-mausoleum' form may accommodate ancestral cults, perhaps like the *heroa* of the eastern provinces (e.g. Castella 1993: 242), although explicit designation as such is rare (Hatt 1986: 69–70).

Martin-Kilcher (1993b) has argued that large groups of burials, characterised by modest assemblages and lack of monuments, assumed to be those of the lower status element of the villa population, are usually buried in less conspicuous locations, but the sample is very small. In excavation of rural sites in Britain small clusters of graves or individual burials are frequently found in or close to non-grave features, such as ditches and pits (Philpott 1991: 232). Philpott and Reece (1993) have argued that these are the dead of low status groups, burying where expediency dictated and not maintaining a permanent cemetery, in the absence of a tenurial attachment to land. On the basis of a sample from Hampshire in southern Britain, this has been disputed (Pearce 1999). Such burials did not appear to have been made at random but recurring preferences in location could be identified and the burials were treated with as much 'respect', indicated by grave container and furniture, as contemporary burials at local urban sites.

Other landscape locations have been noted as potentially influential on the setting of rural burials. Proximity to roads is commonly assumed to determine monument location, forming the rural counterparts of urban *Gräberstrassen* (Grenier 1934: 213–22; Dunning and Jessup 1936). This however is not a wholly adequate generalisation (Wigg 1993: 379). There is some literary evidence for the placing of tombs on estate boundaries (Meffre 1993), attaching rights to land through ancestral presence, but such boundaries are notoriously difficult to identify archaeologically. Prehistoric sites seem to have been only rarely favoured in Britain as locations for Roman period burial (Williams 1998) but were more popular elsewhere (Dark 1993; Galliou 1989: 28, 31).

The example of Bancroft illustrates the positioning of monuments with regard to both their immediate and wider context. The temple mausoleum on the hill overlooking the settlement area was also visible from Watling Street 2.5 km to the south-east. The broader study of the location of cemeteries within Roman period landscapes offers exciting opportunities for GIS based analysis which have been more fully exploited by students of prehistoric landscapes.

In summary, a variety of observations have been made on the relationship between rural burial and other features of the rural landscape. The next step is to examine, where possible exploiting new technologies, the strength of these propositions, in conjunction with the acquisition of good regional data sets, spread over several centuries of burials or cemeteries and settlements excavated in conjunction. With exceptions (e.g. Gaitzsch 1993) such data sets remain rare and their acquisition should be a priority of rural settlement archaeology.

Conclusion

In the earlier part of this paper some practical and theoretical problems were identified in two of the most common approaches to burial evidence from the Roman world, the attribution of cultural identity and status to deceased individuals. We lack adequate archaeological evidence for some commonly cited burial 'types', for example 'Roman' burials from central Italy in the first century BC and the earliest centuries AD. More attention must also be paid to the fullest possible recovery of archaeological evidence for burial ceremonies, in order to establish both regional patterns in mortuary practice or degrees of 'energy investment' in burial more securely. The direct reading of ethnicity and status from burial is challenged by the many studies which demonstrate that burial is a transformation rather than a direct reflection of identity. This transformation depends on culturally specific attitudes towards death and the dead. While literary evidence to help establish such attitudes is available for some areas of the Roman world, in many provinces, especially those of north-western Europe, there is little or none. Some archaeological methods for establishing the significance of the dead to the living in particular contexts can however be offered, based on a broadly post-processual approach, although this offers no 'cookbook'. The essence of such an approach is not to examine burial evidence in isolation. Rather it is most fruitfully interpreted when examined within the context provided by other forms of archaeological evidence.

In the latter part of the paper some possible approaches to Roman period burial evidence were outlined, based on this perspective. These approaches were proposed both to strengthen interpretation in current areas of debate and to broaden the concerns addressed through burial evidence. They are by no means intended to suggest definitive areas of study. Many useful propositions have already been offered to explain patterning in Roman burial practice. These need application to larger samples and to be set within a broader context to give them greater force, as well as further examination of the assumptions that lie behind them.

It is clear that the Roman period offer one of the best opportunities to examine burial practice from a contextual perspective. The wealth of archaeological material pertaining to burial, as well as literary evidence, albeit unevenly distributed, and the abundance of data from other contexts, from settlements and votive sites, is almost unparalleled before the medieval period. The potential for contextual analysis should not be missed.

Acknowledgements

The earliest form of this paper was sent out to potential contributors in order to outline the issues which the colloquium was intended to address. It has been extensively rewritten to take account of the responses of colloquium participants and of recent literature. Thanks are owed to Manuela Struck and Martin Millett for their comments on an earlier version and to Ralph Häussler for his on a later draft.

Note

1. General bibliographic sources for death and burial in the Roman world can be found in Morris' (1992) bibliographic essay and in Rife's (1997) review of the re-issue of Toynbee's 'Death and Burial in the Roman World'. Collections of papers edited by Hinard (1987; 1995) discuss literary and epigraphic evidence largely from Rome and Italy. Recent literature on funerary architecture, sculpture and epigraphy is massive and the following references are simply offered as some general guides (von Hesberg 1989; 1992; von Hesberg and Zanker (eds) 1987; Kleiner 1988; Morris 1992: 156–73; Rife 1997; Woolf 1996; Koortbojian 1996). Morris (1992: 70–102) gives a general flavour of recent work in the Greco-Roman world. The volumes edited by Ferdière (1993), Struck (1993) and Fasold *et al.* (1998) as well as Bridger's (1996) monograph on the cemetery at Tönisvorst-Vorst include very extensive bibliographies on recent cemetery excavations from the north-western provinces in particular and from Italy. The publication of the cremation burials from Stettfeld (Wahl and Kokabi 1988) and Westhampnett (McKinley in Fitzpatrick 1997: 55–72) and of inhumations from Poundbury (Farwell and Molleson 1993) and St Martin de Fontenay (Pilet 1995) illustrate the potential variety of approaches based on the study of cremated and inhumed human remains from particular cemeteries. Comparison of differences in diet inferred from isotope ratios with differences in burial treatment also bridges the gap between study of the human remains and study of artefactual and structural evidence from cemeteries (Richards *et al.* 1998).

Bibliography

Addyman, P. and Black, V., eds, 1984. *Archaeological Papers from York Presented to M.W. Barley.* York: York Archaeological Trust

Allason-Jones, L. 1995. 'Sexing' small finds. In Rush 1995, 22–32

Alcock, S. ed., 1997. *The Early Roman Empire in the East.* Oxford: Oxbow

Aßkamp, R. and Berke, S., eds, 1991. *Die römische Okkupation nördlich der Alpen zur Zeit des Augustus: Kolloquium Bergkamen 1989.* Munster: Aschendorff

Audollent, A. 1922. Les tombes gallo-romaines à inhumation des Martres-de-Veyre (Puy-de-Dôme). *Mémoires présentés par divers savants à l'académie des inscriptions et belles-lettres, XIII,* Paris: Imprimerie Nationale

Baker, P. *et al.*, eds, 1999. *Proceedings of the Eighth Annual Theoretical Roman Archaeology Conference Leicester 1998,* Oxford: Oxbow

Baldwin, R. 1985. Intrusive groups in the Late Roman cemetery at Lankhills, Winchester – a reassessment of the evidence. *OJA,* 4: 93–105

Barrett, J.C. 1991. Towards an archaeology of ritual. In Garwood *et al.* 1991, 30–41

Barrett, J.C. 1997. Theorising Roman archaeology. In Meadows *et al.* 1997, 1–7

Bayard, D. 1993. Sépultures et *villae* en Picardie au Haut-Empire: quelques données récentes. In Ferdière 1993, 69–80

Bechert, T. 1980. Zur Terminologie provinzialrömischer Brandgräber. *Archäologisches Korrespondenzblatt,* 10: 253–58

Beck, L.A., ed., 1995. *Regional Approaches to Mortuary Analysis.* London: Plenum Press

Becker, M. 1993. Einführung von neuen Begräbnissitten: neue Bevölkerungsströmung oder eine autochthone, romanisierte, Bevölkerung. In Struck 1993, 361–70

Berke, S. 1991. Das Gräberfeld von Haltern. In Aßkamp and Berke 1991, 149–58

Binford, L.R. 1972. *Mortuary practices: their study and potential.* In Binford 1972, 208–43

Binford, L.R., ed., 1972. *An Archaeological Perspective.* New York: Academic Press

Biró, M. 1975. The inscriptions of Roman Britain. *Acta Archaeologica Academiae Scientiarum Hungariae,* 27: 13–58

Blackmore, C., Braithwaite, M. and Hodder, I. 1979. Social and cultural patterning in the late Iron Age in southern England. In Burnham and Kingsbury 1979, 93–111

Blagg, T.F.C., Jones, R.F.J. and Keay, S.J., eds, 1984. *Papers in Iberian Archaeology.* BAR International Series, 193, Oxford: BAR

Blagg, T.F.C. and King, A.C., eds, 1984. *Military and Civilian in Roman Britain.* BAR British Series, 136, Oxford: BAR

Blagg, T. and Millett, M., eds, 1990. *The Early Roman Empire in the West.* Oxford: Oxbow.

Bradley, R. 1984. *The Social Foundations of Prehistoric Britain.* London: Longman

Bradley, R. 1988. Status, wealth, and the chronological ordering of cemeteries. *PPS,* 54: 327–29

Brandt, R. and Slofstra, J., eds, 1983. *Roman and Native in the Low Countries.* BAR International Series, 184, Oxford: BAR

Bridger, C. 1996. *Die römerzeitliche Gräberfeld 'An hinkes Weißhof', Tönisvorst-Vorst, Kreis Viersen.* Köln: Rheinland Verlag

Brown, J. 1981. The search for rank in prehistoric burials. In Chapman *et al.* 1981, 25–37

Brown, J. 1995. On mortuary analysis – with specific reference to the Saxe-Binford research programme. In Beck 1995, 3–26

Buisson, A. 1993. Le monde des morts en Gaule rurale à l'époque romaine: l'apport des textes littéraires et épigraphique. In Ferdière 1993, 23–28

Burnham, B.C. and Kingsbury, J., eds, 1979. *Space, Hierarchy and Society.* BAR International Series, 59, Oxford: BAR

Cannon, A. 1989. The historical dimension in mortuary expressions of status and sentiment. *Current Anthropology,* 30: 437–58

Castella, D. 1993. Un sanctuaire augustéen autour d'une sépulture à incinération à Avenches, Canton de Vaud (Suisse). In Struck 1993, 229–45

Chapman, R., Randsborg, K. and Kinnes I., eds, 1981. *The Archaeology of Death.* Cambridge: Cambridge University Press

Clarke, G. 1979. *Pre-Roman and Roman Winchester, Part 2: The Roman Cemetery at Lankhills.* Oxford: Oxford University Press

Cliquet, D. *et al.*, eds, 1993. *Les Celtes en Normandie. Les rites funéraires en Gaule (IIIème – Ier siècle avant J.-C.).* Rennes: Revue Archéologique de l'Ouest

Collis, J. 1977. Pre-Roman burial rites in north-western Europe. In Reece 1977, 1–12

Cooke, N.H. 1998. *The definition and interpretation of late Roman burial rites in the western empire.* Unpublished Ph.D. thesis, University of London

Cormack, S. 1997. Funerary monuments and mortuary practices in Roman Asia Minor. In Alcock 1997, 137–56

Curchin, L.A. 1997. Funerary customs in central Spain: the transition from pre-Roman to Roman practice. *Hispania Antigua,* 21: 7–34

Czysz, W. ed., 1995. *Provinzialrömische Forschungen: Festschrift für Günther Ulbert zum 65. Geburtstag.* Espelkamp: Verlag Marie Leidorf

Dark, K.R. 1993. Roman-period activity at prehistoric ritual monuments in Britain and in the Armorican peninsula. In Scott 1993, 133–47

van Doorsaeler, A. 1967. *Les nécropoles d'époque romaine en Gaule Septentrionale.* Dissertationes Archaeologicae Gandenses 10, Bruges: De Tempel

van Doorsaeler, A. and Rogge, M. 1985. Continuité d'un rite funéraire spécifique dans la vallée de l'Escaut de l'Âge du Fer au Haut Moyen Âge. *Les Études Classiques,* 53.1: 153–70

Drenth, E., Hessing, W.A.M. and Knol, E., eds, 1993. *Het tweede leven van onze doden.* Amersfoort: ROB

Dunning, G.C. and Jessup, R.F. 1936. Roman barrows. *Antiquity,* 10: 37–53

Dyson, S. 1992. *Community and Society in Roman Italy.* Baltimore/ London: Johns Hopkins University Press

Elsner, J., ed., 1996. *Art and Text in Roman Culture.* Cambridge: Cambridge University Press

Esmonde Cleary, S. 1987. *Extra-Mural Areas of Romano-British Towns.* BAR British Series, 169, Oxford: BAR

Farwell, D. and Molleson, T. 1993. *Excavations at Poundbury, Dorchester, Dorset, 1966–1980. Volume 2: the cemeteries.* Dorchester: Dorset Natural History and Archaeological Society

Fasold, P. 1993. Romanisierung und Grabbrauch: Überlegungen zum frührömischen Totenkult in Rätien. In Struck 1993, 381–97

Fasold, P. *et al.*, eds, 1998. *Bestattungssitte und kulturelle Identität. Grabanlagen und Grabbeigaben der frühen römischen Kaiserzeit in Italien und den Nordwest-Provinzen.* Cologne: Rheinland-Verlag

Fasold, P. and Witteyer, M. 1998. 'Römisches' in den Gräbern Mittel- und Norditaliens. In Fasold *et al.* 1998, 181–90

Ferchiou, N. 1995. Architecture funéraire de Tunisie à l'époque romaine. In Trousset 1995, 111–37

Ferdière, A., ed., 1993. *Monde des morts, monde des vivants en Gaule rurale.* Tours: FERACF.

Ferdière, A. and Villard, A. 1993. *La tombe augustéenne de Fléré-la-Rivière (Indre) et les sépultures aristocratiques de la cité des Bituriges en Berry au début de l'époque gallo-romaine.* Mémoires du musée d'Argentomagus, Saint-Marcel: Musee d'Argentomagus

Fiches, J.-L. 1993. Les élites nîmoises et les campagnes au Haut-Empire: caractérisation, place et signification de leurs sépultures. In Ferdière 1993, 333–39

Fitzpatrick, A.P. 1997a. *Archaeological excavations on the route of the A27 Westhampnett bypass, West Sussex, 1992. Vol. 2. The late Iron Age, Romano-British, and Anglo-Saxon cemeteries.* Salisbury: Trust for Wessex Archaeology

Forcey, C., Hawthorne, J., and Witcher, R., eds, 1998. *Proceedings of the Seventh Annual Theoretical Roman Archaeology Conference.* Oxford: Oxbow

Foster, J. 1993. The identification of male and female graves using grave goods. In Struck 1993, 207–213

Freeman, P. 1993. Romanisation and Roman material culture. *JRA*, 6: 438–45

Freigang, Y. 1997. Die Grabmäler der gallo-römischen Kultur im Moselland. Studien zur Selbstdarstellung einer Gesellschaft. *JRGZM*, 44.1: 278–440

Frere, S.S. 1990. Roman Britain in 1989: Sites Explored. *Britannia*, 21: 303–64

Gaitzsch, W. 1993. Brand- und Körpergräber in römischen Landsiedlungen der Jülicher Lößborde. In Struck 1993, 17–41

Galliou, P. 1989. *Les tombes romaines d'Armorique: essai de sociologie et d'économie de la mort.* Dossiers d'Archéologie Français, Paris: Editions de la Maison des Sciences de l'homme

Garwood, P., Jennings, D., Skeates, R. and Toms, J., eds, 1991. *Sacred and Profane.* Oxford: Oxford University Committee for Archaeology

Grenier, A. 1934. *Manuel d'archéologie gallo-romaine, tome 2(1); L'archéologie du sol: les routes.* Paris: Picard

Groeneveld, S. 1998. Zur Beigaben- und Bestattungssitte vorcoloniazeitlicher Gräber im Bereich der Colonia Ulpia Traiana im 1. Jh. n. Chr.. In Fasold *et al.* 1998, 383–98

Haffner, A. 1989. Das Gräberfeld von Wederath-Belginum vom 4. Jahrhundert vor bis zum 4. Jahrhundert bach Christi Geburt. In Haffner 1989, 37–130

Haffner, A. ed., 1989. *Gräber – Spiegel des Lebens.* Mainz: von Zabern

Haffner, A. and von Schnurbein, S. 1996. Dem Kulturwandel unter Roms Einfluß auf der Spur. *Archäologie in Deutschland*, 1996.2: 6–9

Halsall, G. 1992. The origins of the *Reihengräberzivilisation*: forty years on. In Drinkwater and Elton 1992, 196–207

Haselgrove, C.C. 1984. 'Romanization' before the conquest: Gaulish precedents and British consequences. In Blagg and King 1984, 5–65

Haselgrove, C. 1987. Culture process on the periphery: Belgic Gaul and Rome during the late Republic and early Empire. In Rowlands *et al.* 1987, 104–24

Hatt, J.-J. 1986. *La tombe gallo-romaine* (2nd ed.). Paris: Picard

von Hesberg, H. 1989. Neuere Literatur zur römischen Grabbauten. *JRA*, 2: 207–14

von Hesberg, H. 1992. *Römische Grabbauten.* Darmstadt: Wissenschaftliche Buchgesellschaft

von Hesberg, H. 1993. Römische Grabbauten in den hispanischen Provinzen. In Trillmich *et al.* 1993, 159–83

von Hesberg, H. and Zanker, P. 1987. Einleitung. In von Hesberg and Zanker 1987, 9–20

von Hesberg, H. and Zanker, P., eds, 1987. *Römische Gräberstrassen – Selbstdarstellung, Status, Standard.* Munich: Bayerische Akademie der Wissenschaften

Hessing, W.A.M. 1993. Ondeugende Bataven en verwaalde Friezinnen?: Enkele gedachten over de onverbrande menselijke resten uit de ijzertijd en de Romeinse tijd in West- en Noord-Nederland. In Drenth *et al.* 1993, 17–40

Hill, J.D. 1995. *Ritual and Rubbish in the Iron Age of Wessex. A Study in the Formation of a Specific Archaeological Record.* BAR British Series, 242, Oxford: Tempus Reparatum

Hills, C.M. 1979. The archaeology of Anglo-Saxon England in the pagan period. *Anglo-Saxon England*, 8, 297–330

Hinard, F. ed., 1987. *La mort, les morts et l'au-delà dans le monde romain.* Caen: Université de Caen

Hinard, F. ed., 1995. *La mort au quotidien dans le monde romain.* Paris: De Boccard

Hingley, R. 1989. *Rural Settlement in Roman Britain.* London: Seaby

Hingley, R. 1997. Resistance and domination: social change in Roman Britain. In Mattingly 1997, 81–102

Hodder, I. 1982a. *The Present Past.* Cambridge: Cambridge University Press

Hodder, I. 1982b. *Symbols in Action.* Cambridge: Cambridge University Press

Hodder, I. ed., 1982. *Symbolic and Structural Archaeology.* Cambridge: Cambridge University Press

Hope, V. 1994. *Reflexions of Status: a contextual study of the tombstones of Mainz, Aquileia and Nîmes.* Unpublished Ph.D. thesis, University of Reading

Hope, V.M. 1997. Words and pictures: the interpretation of Romano-British tombstones. *Britannia*, 28: 245–58

Huntington, R. and Metcalf, P. 1992. *Celebrations of Death: the Anthropology of Mortuary Ritual* (2nd edition). Cambridge: Cambridge University Press

James, E. 1988. *The Franks.* Oxford: Blackwell

Jessup, R.F.J. 1954. Excavation of a Roman barrow at Holborough, Snodland. *Archaeologia Cantiana*, 68: 1–61

Jones, R.F.J. 1983. *Cemeteries and Burial Practice in the Western Provinces of the Roman Empire.* unpublished Ph.D. thesis, London

Jones, R.F.J. 1984a. The cemeteries of Roman York. In Addyman and Black 1984, 34–42

Jones, R.F.J. 1984b. Death and distinction. In Blagg and King 1984, 219–26

Jones, R.F.J. 1984c. The Roman cemeteries of Ampurias reconsidered. In Blagg *et al.* 1984, 237–65

Jones, R.F.J. 1987. Burial customs of Rome and the provinces. In Wacher 1987, 812–38

Jones, R.F.J. 1991. Cultural change in Roman Britain. In Jones 1991, 115–20

Jones, R.F.J. ed., 1991. *Britain in the Roman Period. Recent Trends.* Sheffield: J.R. Collis Publications

Jones, R.F.J. 1993a. Backwards and forwards in Roman burial. *JRA*, 6: 427–33

Jones, R.F.J. 1993b. Rules for the living and the dead: funerary practices and social organisation. In Struck 1993, 247–55

Jones, S. 1997. *The Archaeology of Ethnicity: Constructing Identities in the Past and Present.* London: Routledge

Kampen, N. 1981. *Image and Status: Roman Working Women in Ostia.* Berlin: Gebr. Mann

Kertzer, D.I. and Saller, R.P., eds, 1991. *The Family in Italy from Antiquity to the Present.* New Haven: Yale University Press

Kleiner, D. 1988. Roman funerary art and architecture: observations on the significance of recent studies. *JRA*, 1: 115–119

Kleiner, D. and Matheson, S. B. 1996. *I Claudia. Women in Roman Art.* Austin: University of Texas Press

Koortbojian, M. 1996. *In commemorationem mortuorum*: text and image along the 'Streets of Tombs'. in Elsner 1996, 210–34

Lafon, X. and Adam, A.-M. 1993. Des morts chez les vivants? Tombes et habitat dans la France du nord-est. In Ferdière 1993, 113–20

Le Bohec, Y. ed., 1991. *Le Testament du Lingon: Actes de la Journée d'Étude du 16 mai 1990.* Paris: De Boccard van Lith, S. and Randsborg, K. 1985. Roman glass in the West: a social study. *BROB*, 35: 413–532

McGuire, R.H. and Paynter, R. 1991. The archaeology of Inequality: material culture, domination and resistance. In McGuire and Paynter 1991, 1–27

McGuire, R.H. and Paynter, R., eds, 1991. *The Archaeology of Inequality*. Oxford: Blackwell

MacMullen, R. 1982. The epigraphic habit in the Roman empire. *American Journal of Philology*, 103: 233–45

Martin-Kilcher, S. 1993a. Römische Grabfunde als Quelle zur Trachtgeschichte im zirkumalpinen Raum. In Struck 1993, 181–204

Martin-Kilcher, S. 1993b. Situation des cimetières et tombes rurales en Germania Superior et dans les régions voisines. In Ferdière 1993, 153–64

Mattingly, D.J. 1997. *Dialogues in Roman Imperialism: Power, Discourse and Discrepant Experience in the Roman Empire*. JRA Supplementary Series, 27, Portsmouth, R.I.: JRA

Meadows, K., Lemke, C. and Heron, J., eds, 1997. *TRAC 96. Proceedings of the Sixth Annual Theoretical Roman Archaeology Conference*. Oxford: Oxbow

Meffre, J-C. 1993. Lieux sépulcraux et occupation du sol en milieu rural dans la cité antique de Vaison sous le Haut-Empire. In Ferdière 1993, 371–87

Meskell. L. 1994. Dying young: the experience of death at Deir-el-Medina. *Archaeological Review from Cambridge*, 13.2: 35–46

Metzler, J., Waringo, R., Bis, R. and Metzler-Zens, N. 1991. *Clemency et les tombes de l'aristocratie en Gaule Belgique*. Luxembourg: Musée National d'Histoire et d'Art

Metzler, J., Millett, M., Roymans, N. and Slofstra, J., eds, 1995. *Integration in the Early Roman West. The Role of Culture and Ideology*. Luxembourg: Musée National d'Histoire et d'Art

Millett, M. 1990. *The Romanization of Britain*. Cambridge: Cambridge University Press.

Millett, M. 1993. A cemetery in transition: King Harry Lane reconsidered. In Struck 1993, 255–83

Millett, M. 1995. *Roman Britain*. London: Batsford/English Heritage

Morris, I. 1987. *Burial and Ancient Society: the rise of the Greek city-state*. Cambridge: Cambridge University Press

Morris, I. 1991. The Archaeology of Ancestors: the Saxe-Goldstein hypothesis revisited. *Cambridge Archaeological Journal*, 1.2, 147–69

Morris, I. 1992. *Death Ritual and Social Structure in Classical Antiquity*. Cambridge: Cambridge University Press

Nierhaus, R. 1959. *Das römische Brand-und Körpergräberfeld 'Auf der Steig' in Stuttgart – Bad Cannstatt*. Stuttgart: Silverburg

Nierhaus, R. 1969. Römerzeitliche Bestattungssitten im nördlichen Gallien: autochthones und mittelmeerländisches. *Helinium*, 9: 245–62

Parker Pearson, M. 1982. Mortuary practices, society and ideology: an ethnoarchaeological study. In Hodder 1982, 99–113

Parker Pearson, M. 1993. The powerful dead: archaeological relationships between the living and the dead. *Cambridge Archaeological Journal*, 3:2: 203–29

Pearce, J. 1999. The dispersed dead: preliminary observations on burial and settlement space in rural Roman Britain. In P. Baker *et al*. 1999, 151–62

Philpott, R. 1991. *Burial Practices in Roman Britain. A survey of grave treatment and furnishing A.D. 43–410*. BAR British Series, 219, Oxford: BAR

Philpott, R. and Reece, R. 1993. Sépultures rurales en Bretagne romaine. In Ferdière 1993, 417–23

Pilet, C. 1995. *La Nécropole de Saint Martin de Fontenay*. Gallia Supplément No. 54, Paris: CNRS

Pion, P. and Guichard, V. 1993. Tombes et nécropoles en France et au Luxembourg entre le IIIème siècle et le Ier siècle avant J.-C. Essai d'inventaire. In Cliquet *et al*. 1993, 175–200

Purcell, N. 1987. Tomb and suburb. In von Hesberg and Zanker 1987, 25–42

Radolescu, A., Coman, E. and Stavru, C. 1973. Un sarcofago di età romana scoperto nella necropoli tumulare di Callatis (Mangalia). *Pontica*, 6: 247–65

Raepsaet-Charlier, M. 1995. Cité et municipe chez les Tongres, les Bataves et les Canninéfates. *Ktéma*, 21: 251–72

Reece, R., ed., 1977. *Burial in the Roman World*. CBA Research Report, 22, London: CBA

Reece, R. 1982. Bones, bodies and dis-ease. *OJA*, 1: 347–58

Rife, J.L. 1997. Review Article on J. M. C. Toynbee, Death and Burial in the Roman World (1996 reprint). *Bryn Mawr Classical Review*, 8: 583–94

Richards, M. P. *et al*. 1998. Stable isotope analysis reveals variations at the Poundbury Camp cemetery site. *JAS*, 25: 1247–52

Roosens, H. 1976. Bestattungsritual und Grabinhalt einiger Tumuli im Limburger Haspengouw. *Helinium*, 16: 139–56

Roth-Congès, A. 1990. Les voies romaines bordées de tombes. *JRA*, 3: 337–51

Rottloff, A. 1995. Der Grabfund von der Blauen Klappe in Augsburg. Bemerkungen zu römischen Frauengräbern des 2. und 3. Jahrhunderts n. Chr. mit Goldschmuck. In Czysz 1995, 371–86

Rowlands, M., Larsen, M. and Kristiansen, K., eds, 1987. *Centre and Periphery in the Ancient World*. Cambridge: Cambridge University Press

Roymans, N. 1996. The sword or the plough. Regional dynamics in the Romanisation of Belgic Gaul and the Rhineland area. In Roymans 1996, 9–126

Roymans, N. ed., 1996. *From the Sword to the Plough. Three Studies on the Earliest Romanisation of Northern Gaul*. Amsterdam: Amsterdam University Press

Ruprechtsberger, E.M. 1996. *Ein spätantikes Säuglingsgrab mit reichen Beigaben aus Lentia / Linz*. Linz: Stadtmuseum Linz

Rush, P. ed., 1995. *Theoretical Roman Archaeology: Second Conference Proceedings*. Aldershot: Avebury

Schmidt-Colinet, A. 1997. Aspects of 'Romanization': the tomb architecture at Palmyra and its decoration. In Alcock 1997, 157–77

Scott, E. 1990. A critical review of the interpretation of infant burials, with a particular reference to Roman Britain. *Journal of Theoretical Archaeology*, 1: 30–46

Scott, E. ed., 1993. *Theoretical Roman Archaeology: First Conference Proceedings*. Aldershot: Avebury

Shanks, M. and Tilley C. 1982. Ideology, symbolic power and ritual communication: a re-.interpretation of Neolithic mortuary practices. In Hodder 1982, 129–54

Shaw, B. 1984. Latin funerary epigraphy and family life in the Later Roman Empire. *Historia*, 33: 457–97

Shaw, B. 1991. The cultural meaning of death: age and gender in the Roman family. In Kertzer and Saller 1991, 66–90

Smith, J.T. 1997. *Roman Villas: a Study in Social Structure*. London: Routledge

Society for the Promotion of Roman Studies 1985. *Priorities for the Preservation and Excavation of Romano-British Sites*. London: Roman Society

Spiegel, E.M. 1994. Die römische Westnekropole an der Aachener Strasse in Köln. Ansätze zu einer Strukturanalyse. *KJVF*, 27: 595–609

Srejovic, D. and Vasic, C. 1994. 'Emperor Galerius' buildings in Romuliana (Gamzigrad, eastern Serbia). *Antiquité Tardive*, 2: 123–41

Struck, M., ed., 1993. *Römerzeitliche Gräber als Quellen zu*

Religion, Bevölkerungsstruktur und Sozialgeschichte, Mainz: Johannes Gutenberg Institut für Vor- und Frühgeschichte

Struck, M. 1993a. Kinderbestattungen in romano-Britischen Siedlungen – der Archäologische Befund. In Struck 1993, 313–19

Struck, M. 1993b. Busta in Britannien und ihre Verbindungen zum Kontinent. In Struck 1993, 81–94

Struck, M. 1993c. Les rites funéraires ruraux en Rhétie du nord-est aux deuxième et troisième siècles après J.-C. In Ferdière 1993, 425–32

Struck, M. 1995. Integration and continuity in funerary ideology. In Metzler *et al.* 1995, 139–47

Tarlow, S. 1999. *Bereavement and Commemoration. An Archaeology of Mortality.* Oxford: Blackwell

Taylor, A.F. 1993. A Roman lead coffin with pipeclay figurines from Arrington, Cambridgeshire. *Britannia*, 24: 191–227

Taylor, L.R. 1961. Freedmen and freeborn in imperial Rome. *American Journal of Philology*, 82: 113–32

Terrenato, N. 1998. The Romanisation of Italy; global acculturation or cultural bricolage. In Forcey *et al.* 1998, 20–27

Todd, M. ed., 1989. *Research on Roman Britain: 1960–1989.* London: Roman Society

Toynbee, J. 1971. *Death and Burial in the Roman World.* Ithaca, New York: Cornell University Press

Treherne, P. 1995. The warrior's beauty: the masculine body and self identity in Bronze Age Europe. *Journal of European Archaeology*, 3.1: 105–44

Trillmich, W. *et al.*, eds, 1993. *Hispania Antiqua: Denkmäler der Römerzeit.* Mainz: von Zabern

Trousset, P. ed., 1995. *L'Afrique du Nord antique et médiévale: monuments funéraires, institutions autochtones.* Paris: C.T.H.S

Tuffreau-Libre, M. 1992. *La céramique en Gaule romaine.* Paris: Editions Errance

Ucko, P.J. 1969. Ethnography and the archaeological interpretation of funerary remains. *World Archaeology*, 1: 262–80

Vanvinckenroye W. 1984. *De Romeinse Zuidwest-Begraafplaats van Tongeren (Opgravingen 1972–81).* Tongeren: Provinciaal Gallo-Romeins Museum

Vermeulen, F. 1992. *Tussen Leie en Schelde.* Archeologische Inventaris Vlaanderen. Buitengewone Reeks 1. Ghent

Wacher, J.S. ed., 1987. *The Roman World.* London: Routledge

Wahl, J. and Kokabi, M. 1988. *Das römische Gräberfeld von Stettfeld. I: osteologische Untersuchung der Knochenreste aus dem Gräberfeld.* Stuttgart: Konrad Theiss

Webster, J. 1996. Roman imperialism and the post-imperial age. In Webster and Cooper 1996, 1–18

Webster, J. and Cooper, N.J. eds, 1996. *Roman Imperialism: Post-colonial Perspectives.* Leicester: School of Archaeological Science

Wigg, A. 1993. Barrows in north-eastern Gallia Belgica: cultural and social aspect. In Struck 1993, 371–80

Whimster, R. 1981 *Burial Practice in Iron Age Britain.* Oxford: British Archaeological Reports

Wightman, E. 1984. *Gallia Belgica.* London: Batsford

Wild, J.P. 1985. The clothing of Britannia, Gallia Belgica and Germania Inferior. *ANRW* II. 12.3, 362–422

Wilkes, J.J. 1989. A prospect of Roman Britain. In Todd 1989, 245–50

Williams, H. 1998. The ancient monument in Romano-British ritual practices. In Forcey *et al.* 1998, 71–86

Williams, R.J. and Zeepvat, R.J. 1994. *Bancroft: a Late Bronze Age / Iron Age Settlement, Roman Villa and Temple/Mausoleum.* Aylesbury: Buckinghamshire Archaeological Society

Witteyer, M. and Fasold, P. 1995. *Des Lichtes Beraubt. Totenehrung in der römischen Gräberstraße von Mainz-Weisenau.* Wiesbaden: Landesamt für Rheinland-Pfalz

Woolf, G. 1996. Monumental writing and the expansion of Roman society in the early empire. *JRS*, 86: 22–39

Woolf, G. 1998. *Becoming Roman: the Origins of Provincial Civilization in Gaul.* Cambridge: Cambridge University Press

The Reconstruction of Mortuary Rituals

The papers grouped in this section all discuss the reconstruction of funerary rituals based on archaeological evidence and the implications of such reconstructions. Fitzpatrick combines a polemic with a series of case studies from recently excavated late Iron Age cemeteries in France, Luxembourg and England. He is concerned for the importance of recognising ritual, including the ceremonies preceding burial, burial itself and subsequent activities at burial sites, an opportunity which these recent excavations afford. He draws attention to the different working of common elements in the ceremonies which took place at these sites, arguing that we should study Iron Age and Roman societies in their own right rather than as instances of broader patterns like Romanization. Polfer and McKinley focus on the evidence for cremation rituals in Roman cemeteries. Drawing on a broad range of material Polfer considers the archaeology of *ustrina* and their place in funerary practice. His study of artefact assemblages associated with pyre and burial deposits from the cemetery of Septfontaines-Dëckt (Luxembourg) demonstrates the use of different objects at different stages of funerary ceremonial. McKinley's fundamental review raises important questions about the role of cremated bone within graves and challenges previous archaeological identifications of features related to burial rituals. Finally, two papers by Kreuz and Tuffreau-Libre examine different aspects of grave assemblages, respectively botanical remains and ceramics. Recent attention to botanical remains is shedding much new light on the cremation process and on the items with which the dead were furnished on the pyre, as Kreuz's examples from Germany and Switzerland indicate. Tuffreau-Libre advocates the detailed analysis of assemblages of ceramics, rather than of single vessel types, based on statistically meaningful numbers of graves, for a better founded study of cemetery chronologies and change in burial practice.

That careful excavation can reveal different stages in funerary and subsequent ceremonies is also demonstrated by papers in later sections, especially in association with individual burials or monuments. This is well illustrated in Schucany and Abegg-Wigg's examination of rural burial monuments, and particularly in Niblett's discussion of the Folly Lane complex at Verulamium, where a very full range of archaeological evidence is brought to bear. Topál and Jovanovic's analyses of the cultural affinities of different cremation burial types depend on the close recording of burial features, although both show that the processes which account for the archaeological observations are not always fully understood, and will benefit from further work of the type advocated by McKinley, especially with regard to the cremated human bone. Spanu's paper shows that careful extrapolation from architectural evidence can also sometimes reveal evidence for funerary rituals, even where tombs have been robbed and no artefactual or skeletal evidence survives.

Several papers demonstrate the value of comparison between cemetery and settlement deposits. Tuffreau-Libre cautions against dependence on burial assemblages for constructing general ceramic typologies and chronologies, given the discrepancies which can now be shown between cemetery and settlement deposits. Using examples from northern Gaul she produces significant evidence for local choices of ceramics used and deposited in different contexts. Fitzpatrick also draws attention not only to differences in variation in types of pottery but also in a broader range of artefacts deposited on settlement, cemetery and votive sites. His approach seeks to show that funerary rituals transformed the symbolism of everyday life. Both of their studies, as well as Schucany's comparison of assemblages from different contexts on the villa at Biberist-Spitalhof, draw their strength from comparison between deposits closely associated in space and time. Other contributors, including Martin-Kilcher and de Santis, also exploit archaeological and literary evidence for the significance of artefacts to the living to explore their meaning when placed with the dead.

2. Ritual, sequence, and structure in Late Iron Age Mortuary practices in North-West Europe

A. P. Fitzpatrick

Introduction

In the 1970s and 1980s anglophone prehistorians attempted a grand theory for the study of mortuary practices (Härke 1989). Summarised simply it was that 'grave goods speak for the dead'. Such assumptions drew on the idea that the social categories to which individuals belonged in life are displayed in mortuary rituals in ways which can be recovered archaeologically. Some of the most sophisticated and influential expositions of this thesis are set out in works by Binford, Brown, Saxe and Tainter.

Yet such a view, largely formulated in the analysis of inhumation burials and their associated grave goods, contrived to separate the social from the material. The world of material goods was conceived as secondary to, and a passive reflection of, the social. The social world was itself was determined by the 'economic'. It is such a view which was propounded by O'Shea who when writing of 'funerary remains as archaeological evidence' (1984, 32–49), identified the linkage between the two (the social and the material) as the major difficulty to be overcome, and as one which could be achieved through the development of a middle range theory.

The ultimate goal appeared to be the linking of general principles to particular cases, and the description of particular cases in terms of the general. In the tension between region and empire such an uneasy dichotomy also haunts much work on 'romanisation'. Much of the debate about the potential contribution of burial practices to the study of 'romanisation' can, as with debates about 'romanisation' generally (e.g. Millett 1990), be constituted in terms of elites and emulation, with material culture interpreted in terms of prestigious goods. The aims of such analyses may not be the construction of a grand theory of 'romanisation', which as Woolf (1993) points out is not without its difficulties, but the methods available to assess it, many of which derive from the 'New Archaeology', are essentially normative. As these methods allow comparison between burials and cemeteries, they may seem to offer a particularly sensitive index of 'romanisation' (*cf.* Struck 1995), particularly where the quality of the data are limited.

Yet this immediately points to another tension, that between the variability in religion and ritual which is accepted by most students of 'romanisation', and the normative methods often employed to study mortuary practices. Although most archaeologists would agree that beliefs are, at best, a difficult area of study, there seems (to me) to be little point in attempting to study mortuary practices without being willing to at least try and interpret the rituals which were guided by those beliefs. The present paper, which is largely concerned with cremation burial, attempts therefore to make two points. Firstly that something of the ritual process can be recovered archaeologically and secondly, that if the Later Iron Age is viewed simply as part of a process of 'romanisation', then the study of both the Iron Age and the Roman periods are diminished.

The dead hand of 'romanisation'

The King Harry Lane, St Albans, cemetery

Some of the limitations of what is essentially a normative approach in which the ritual process is afforded comparatively little attention may be illustrated by reference to Millett's (1993) carefully worked analysis of the King Harry Lane cemetery at St Albans, Hertfordshire, in southeast England. This well-known cemetery lies on the northern boundary of the Prae Wood component of the *oppidum* of *Verlamion*. For the purposes of this paper, attention is directed towards the Iron Age phase(s) of the cemetery, although some of the points made are also appropriate to the Romano-British phases.

In the excavation report Stead and Rigby (1989) suggested that the cemetery was founded in *c.* AD 1, but there is some uncertainty as to the absolute chronology of the phases, particularly with regard to whether some (Phases 2–3) are pre- or post-Conquest in date (Stead and Rigby 1989, 84, 98, 204–10, fig. 47; Mackreth 1994; Haselgrove and Millett 1997, 291–2). For present purposes, however, the phasing presented in the excavation report is followed and *contra* Pearce (1997, 176) the Iron Age phase (Phase 1) is treated separately from the

Romano-British ones. Some 73 burials were attributed to Phase 1, with many more potentially being either pre- or post-conquest.

The cemetery was set out around a series of small rectangular, ditched, enclosures (Fig. 10.5 in Niblett, this volume). At the centre of the enclosures there was a frequently a 'central burial' which was comparatively well furnished with grave goods. Most of the burials are cremation burials, but there were also a number (17) of generally undated inhumation burials, at least some of which might be dated to Phase 1.

The excavators regarded cremation burials with four or more pots as 'rich'. These burials were interpreted as 'founder burials' within an enclosure and they, and unenclosed groups of burials, were regarded as the burials of 'family groups'. In reviewing the excavation report, while welcoming it as a work of international significance, criticism was directed at the restricted interpretation of the mortuary rites (Fitzpatrick 1991). Although some difficulties are caused by the size of the sample, it is difficult to accept the interpretation of the cemetery as representing 'ordinary family groups'.

Considerable emphasis was placed on imported Roman goods in the excavation report by Stead and Rigby, but they were ascribed the same analytical value as indigenous goods in determining whether a grave was 'rich'. On closer examination, only 42% of the 'founder burials' in Phase 1 are both relatively early, and also well-furnished. As Millett has shown (1993), less than half of the burials attributed to Phase 1 also lie within these enclosures, so from the outset there is rather more variability than the concept of 'a family group' buried in an enclosure might suggest.

However, Millett also proposed that;

> *If we follow the suggestion ... that the grave goods were deposited by people attending the burial, then it becomes possible to think of them as representing not the wealth the dead person controlled in life as conventionally assumed, but instead the size of their social network* (Millett 1993, 275).

He suggested that the decline in the number of objects placed in each grave over time (both pots and other objects) indicates a decline in the scale of social networks of those buried. The cause of this is suggested to have been 'settlement nucleation [which] was disrupting kinship networks and those who settled in the developing towns were increasingly socially disembedded' (Millett 1993, 276).

Although Millett suggested that this attempts to explore 'social networks rather than wealth hierarchies' (1993, 277; repeated in Haselgrove and Millett 1997, 292), in analytical and methodological terms, it does little more than alter the equation of 'pots = wealth of deceased' to the slightly larger one of 'pots = mourners of deceased = social status of deceased.' In part Millett is able to pursue this avenue by considering questions of lineage and clan

as being subsidiary to the size of the ('larger') 'grave assemblages'. Consideration of 'gender' is restricted to biological sex and the efficacy of pyre technology in destroying this evidence. In doing this Millett appears to take lineage and patrilineal descent as unproblematic, and as something which will be corroborated by the materials buried with the deceased.

Millett attempted to relate the evidence from his careful analysis of the cemetery to that from contemporary Romano-British settlements. However, while numerical analyses of grave goods may allow comparison between burials at different sites or cemeteries, in isolation, they may fail to allow for the variability within sequences of mortuary rituals, leading to what has been termed a 'death in a material world' (Fitzpatrick 1991, 325–7). It is precisely the combination of the different stages of the mortuary ritual prior to burial and the variability within them, that may contain some of the most important archaeological information. This point may be amplified by examining the way in which pyre goods are treated in Millett's analysis.

That analysis effectively concentrated on objects offered as grave goods. As the unburnt animal bone was lost prior to reporting, this category could not be included in the analyses but the only offerings that Millett appears to have considered as burnt grave goods [i.e. pyre goods], are those objects which are heavily melted or otherwise deformed by fire. Pyre goods in the form of the offering of animals and birds appear not to have been considered. While acknowledging their potential importance, Millett concluded 'that none of the [burnt] objects shows any obvious pattern of distribution according to the age, sex or spatial groups of the dead.' (Millett 1993, 265). In effect, the analysis concentrated on one stage of the mortuary rituals only.

However, the cremated remains of pig and/or chicken were included in 87 of the 445 (c. 20%) cremation burials of Late Iron Age and Romano-British date. Artefacts offered as pyre goods were identified in only 6% of all of the cremation burials but cremated animal and/or bird remains were also found in 50% (14/28) of these graves. As Niblett has shown (this volume), the distribution of graves containing pyre goods displays a strong association with the so-called 'focal burials', many of which are dated to Phase 1. Eight out of 10 of the 'focal burials' contained burnt artefactual pyre goods, while one of the remaining two graves had been disturbed (perhaps in antiquity).

In view of the small numbers of graves being considered, this association must be regarded as significant. It strongly suggests that as well as the statuses enacted in the burial rites by, for example, the act of enclosure, the size (square) and shape of grave, and the number of grave goods, status was also distinguished during the cremation.

These data prompt the question whether any of the objects, regarded as unburnt grave goods may actually have been pyre goods. A very high proportion of the artefacts other than pottery were found in direct association with the cremated remains. In 25% of the graves from both the Late Iron Age and Romano-British phases in which the location of the brooches which can certainly or probably be determined, the brooches were found *amongst* the bones of the unurned burials. *Prima facie* it might be thought that there is a strong case for regarding these objects as pyre goods. Although the case is not as strong, a similar argument may also be advanced for the brooches found with the cremated bones in urned burials (68%). Brooches not directly associated with cremated bone represent only 7% of the graves where their location can certainly or probably be determined.

It is often assumed that objects placed on the funeral pyre will be characterised by signs of burning or melting but this is not so. The location of the object on the pyre and whether it remains in that position as the pyre collapses as it burns will effect whether an object is physically altered by heat (Northover and Montague 1997, 90). How many of the other types of objects from burials at King Harry Lane might also have been pyre goods? Although there are a number of unidentified objects, most of the non-ceramic finds from the cemetery are certainly or possibly associated with costumes or toiletry, and the deceased may have been placed on the pyre dressed or adorned with them.

The point which may be emphasised here is not whether the suggestions made above are correct or not, but that an approach in which the cremation itself is seen as one part of a ritual process in which it may be of equal, if not greater, significance than burial, offers possibilities for different and perhaps rather more interesting analyses.

Some of the most important and interesting recent work on Roman burials come from work on the cremated materials. In part this derives from the improved and more frequent application of scientific analyses which make it possible to approach the questions of selection and significance of materials chosen for the pyre (Kreuz 1994/ 95; this volume) or for sealing graves (Niblett, this volume) and have, for example, allowed the identification of breads and pastries at Wederath-Belginum, Germany (Cordie-Hackenberg *et al.* 1992). Yet not all of these developments have been contingent on scientific analyses. At Septfontaines-Dëckt, Luxembourg, Polfer (1996, 108–18; this volume) was able to determine from the surface condition of much of the pottery whether it had been affected by heat and so presumably placed on the pyre. The pottery placed on the pyre was dominated by forms associated with eating, and samian comprised *c.* 40% of these vessels. Yet the pots which had been placed as pyre goods and which were then subsequently placed as grave goods were dominated by forms associated with drinking, with the proportion of samian dropping to 4%. The selection of vessels chosen as grave goods proper (if indeed this is what they are, rather than pyre goods which were simply unaffected by the pyre) is different again. Similar complexity is apparent in the *Aschengruben* at Wederath-Belginum (Abegg 1989; Wigg 1993).

In the light of such work the 'reading-off' of grave goods as an index of the social persona of the deceased, whether as possessions or of mourners appears, at the very least, very questionable.

Late Iron Age mortuary practices
'Romanisation before the Conquest'

As applied to the Later Iron Age of north-west Europe, analyses of mortuary data using quantitative methods have also been sophisticated. Most have been devoted to assessing the significance of the occurrence of Roman imports in burials, particularly in 'elite' burials, although the presence of a single amphora in a burial has often been considered sufficient to define a grave as being an 'elite' one (e.g. Metzler-Zens *et al.* 1991, 112–36). In the most cogent and influential of these analyses Haselgrove, by quantifying the Number of Artefact Types (NAT) in 'Aylesford' type cremation burials in south-eastern England, was able to demonstrate clearly for the first time the recurrent association of imported goods with a large number of other objects (Haselgrove 1982).

Such analyses have been the dominant interpretative method used in the study of burials of Late Iron Age date. However, there is the possibility that in pursuing such analyses the Late Iron Age is viewed as little more than the predecessor of the Roman occupations, denied of its own internal logic and histories (Fitzpatrick 1989, 42–4; 1993, 233–5, 241), so much so that the question of 'romanisation' before the Conquest can be seen as the most important subject in the study of Late Iron Age mortuary practices (e.g. Pearce 1997, 174). It is difficult to reconcile this approach with the diversity of the evidence from Later Iron Age Europe, which includes abundant evidence for different stages in the mortuary rituals.

The richness of these data may be demonstrated by examining three Late Iron Age mortuary sites; Clemency, Acy-Romance, and Westhampnett (Fig. 2.1). At all three sites the burial rite is cremation burial, there is some evidence for associated pyre sites, and there are other structures which may have been associated with the mortuary rituals. All three excavations have been published recently (Metzler *et al.* 1991, Lambot *et al.* 1994; Fitzpatrick 1997) and include analyses of the cremated bones (human and animal), and all date wholly, or in part, to the first half of the first century B.C.; a time when considerable 'romanisation' before the conquest(s) has been claimed.

In reviewing this evidence, two points are taken as being axiomatic. Firstly, that while the focus of archaeological studies of mortuary practices *has* to be on the individuals who were buried or their remains otherwise disposed of, the study is as much about the living as the dead. Secondly, that a better understanding of mortuary practices is dependent on analysing them in the context of information from other types of archaeological

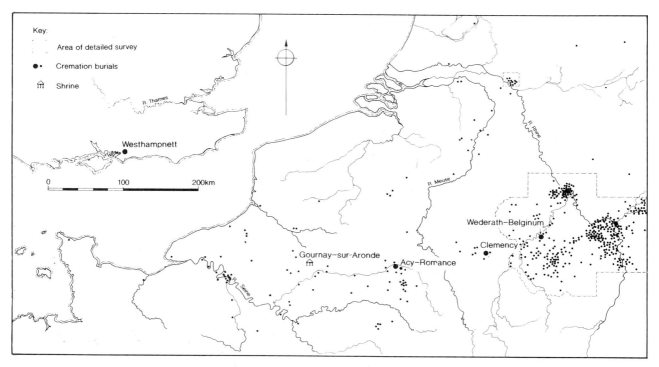

Fig. 2.1 *Distribution of Later Iron Age cremation burials in north-west Europe (after Fitzpatrick 1997, fig. 116).*

contexts, such as settlements and shrines. A third point is the definition of what is meant by ritual. Definitions of this abound, but that offered by one of the most perceptive and incisive scholars of the subject, Victor Turner, in *The Drums of Affliction* is followed here;

> By ritual I mean prescribed formal behaviour for occasions not given over to technological routine, having reference to beliefs in mystical beings or powers (Turner 1967, 19).

Perhaps the most important element of this definition in the present context is its incorporation of beliefs in mystical beings or powers, who play important parts in many mortuary rituals (Metcalf and Huntington 1992).

Clemency

At Clemency, in Luxembourg, *c.* eight kilometres from the *oppidum* of the Titelberg, a single very well-furnished burial of a 40–50 year old man was found (Metzler *et al.* 1991). The grave was sited on the side of a low hill, not far below the summit. The man had died around 80 BC (during La Tène D2a) and he was buried in a wooden vault or chamber which was probably covered by a low, circular, tumulus which itself lay within a square enclosure ditch (Fig. 2.2, A–C). The tumulus has been destroyed by cultivation. In the excavation report Nicole Metzler-Zens distinguished three main stages of offerings (*dépôts*) in the mortuary rituals. It is likely that the first of those stages was preceded by the construction of the elaborate

timber burial vault. As with many well-furnished 'elite' burials in north-western Europe the grave was square, and broadly aligned on the cardinal points.

The first stage of the offerings as defined by Metzler-Zens, was the cremation of the man with, or wearing, a bear-skin. His costume may have been pinned by a brooch. Remains of what appears to be the pyre were found (Fig. 2.2, D) and a deposit, or 'pavement', of 20–30 partly burnt Dressel 1 A/B wine amphorae found nearby probably derived from it (Fig. 2.2, E). The 'pavement' overlay a square, five-post structure, which it is suspected was associated with mortuary rituals, perhaps for displaying the corpse before his cremation.

The second stage of offerings was the unurned burial of the cremated remains, the sacrifice and butchering of four or more boars, and the offering of a series of grave goods. These included a wide range of pots (over 30), a gridiron, a copper alloy bowl, a Campanian ware lamp and *c.* 10 Dressel 1 wine amphorae which had not been placed next to the funeral pyre (Fig. 2.3). It is suggested by the excavators that six pots, and part of a *tuyère* from a metalworking furnace were placed on the roof of the wooden vault before the tumulus was raised over it.

The third stage of offerings is represented by 29 small pits found on the south-east of the tumulus (Fig. 2.2, I). All of these contained pyre debris and deposits of cremated animal bone, with a few containing fragments of molten metal objects. In one instance a piece of cremated human bone was found but it is uncertain if this derives from a burial which had subsequently been

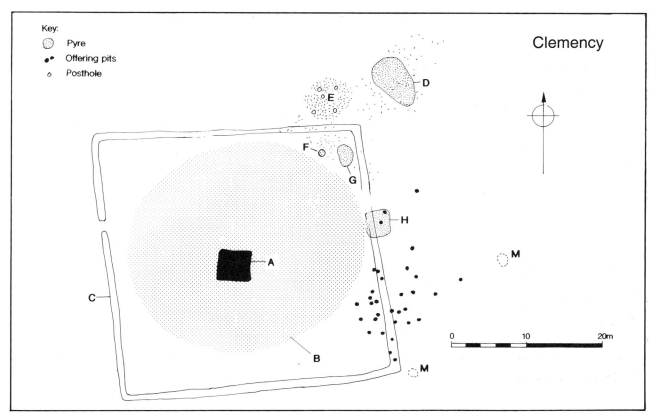

Fig. 2.2 *Clemency: plan of burial and associated features. A: burial vault, B: suggested extent of tumulus, C: enclosure ditch, D: 'principle' pyre, E: 'amphorae pavement' and five-post structure, F: pit, G: pyre? H: 'secondary' pyre, I, offering pits, M: modern fires? (after Metzler* et al. *1991, fig. 27).*

Fig. 2.3 *Clemency: reconstruction of the burial vault viewed from the west by Foni le Brun (from Metzler* et al. *1991, fig. 109).*

disturbed. A pyre site (Fig. 2.2, H) containing comparable animal bones and molten metal objects was found. As the pyre site overlies the partly filled ditch, and some of the pits cut the ditch (Fig. 2.2, I), but all respect the suggested area of the tumulus, it is clear that these offerings were made after the burial. It is possible that other fires (Fig. 2.2, M) which were suggested as perhaps being modern in date, could be ancient.

At a later date, perhaps 30–40 years later, the grave appears to have been robbed and many of the grave goods destroyed (and weapons allegedly robbed). The excavators do not associate this robbing with the third stage of offerings, the sacrifice, cremation and burial of animals and the destruction of metal objects. However, as iron working slags were found in the fill of the ditches, and the *tuyère* was suggested to have been placed on the roof of the timber vault, it is possible that they are contemporary and may represent a further stage of rituals involving the deliberate destruction of part of the tomb.

These archaeologically identifiable rituals may be glossed as follows;

Clemency: mortuary rituals
- display of the corpse
- building of vault
- cremation
- destruction of pyre goods ('pavement' of amphorae)
- sacrifice of animals (boars)
- burial
- raising of the tumulus
- sacrifice and cremation of animals
- robbing?/destruction of tomb

For understandable reasons, not least the prodigious quantity of Italian wine consumed or destroyed in the mortuary rituals (Fig. 2.3), the main emphasis of the excavator's interpretation is the proximity of the burial to the *oppidum* at the Titelberg and the links with the well-furnished and slightly later burials at Goeblingen Nospelt. No detailed comparison is made with 'non-elite' burials or the evidence from settlements (although comparatively little of the contemporary occupation at the Titelberg has yet been examined, *cf.* Metzler 1995, 102–10), although this may be anticipated with the publication of the contemporary cemetery recently excavated at Lamadelaine which lies below the western gate of the Titelberg (see now Metzler-Zens *et al.* 1999).

The kernel of the preferred interpretation is Roman trade as a stimulus to urbanism, with the large grave vaults and, in particular the wine amphorae, indicating a local elite whose wealth is based on the ownership of land and the exploitation of ores and who emulated the funerary rites of the Mediterranean elite, such as the symposium, with which the amphorae are suggested to be associated. The emphasis is very much on continuity between the Late Iron Age and Roman periods.

Acy-Romance

While there is only a single burial at Clemency, at Acy-Romance in the French Ardennes, two cemeteries, 'La Croizette' and 'La Noue Mauroy I', have so far been published (Lambot *et al.* 1994). The two cemeteries lie within a kilometre of each other, either side of the contemporary settlement of 'La Warde' (Lambot and Méniel 1992). Two other unexcavated cemeteries are also known close to 'La Warde', at 'La Noue de Barue' and another at 'La Noue Mauroy II'. Both of the excavated cemeteries are small, enclosed, and were more or less completely excavated. As well as the settlement, a contemporary sanctuary is also known *c.* three kilometres away at Nanteuil-sur-Aisne (Lambot 1989).

The 'La Croizette' cemetery was sited on a limestone ridge overlooking the settlement of 'La Warde' about 300 metres away. Most, but not all, of the 21 cremation burials lay within a long, narrow, rectangular ditched enclosure, *c.* 80 metres long by 21 metres wide (Fig. 2.4). In the centre of the enclosure was a large, 9m square, twelve-post structure with a central pit which contained cremated bone. A single posthole to the north may be associated. Thirteen of the burials lay immediately to the south of the structure, with the others dispersed within the enclosure, but one (120) lay outside it. A single pyre site, cut by a later burial, (112) was identified. Two of the burials (110 and 113) are suggested to have been made next to trees.

Some of the burials date to the mid-La Tène, from slightly before the middle of the second century BC, but over half are dated by the excavators to La Tène D1, *c.* 120/110–70/60. The 21 graves contained the remains of at least 28 individuals, with five graves containing the remains of more than one individual. Both sexes appear to represented in approximately equal numbers and most age groups were represented. However, infants and children were found most frequently in multiple burials accompanied by an adult. Cremated human bones were found in the pit in the centre of the structure, which the excavators are reluctant to see as a grave, drawing parallels instead with the chthonic pit at the temple site of Gournay-sur-Aronde in Picardy.

It seems probable that the enclosure and the post-built structure which is similar to a shrine or temple (Fig. 2.5) were built at the same time. They share the same alignment and probably represent one of the first phases of the mortuary rituals enacted on the site.

Only one possible pyre site was discovered, overlying a burial (112). This observation demonstrates that there must have been more than one pyre site. Although pyre sites could have been destroyed by cultivation, as no trace of cremated material was found in the extensively excavated enclosure ditch, it seems likely that the pyres were sited elsewhere.

The observed or demonstrable sequence of the mortuary rituals is that sacrificed animals or parts of them, usually pigs, and numerous pots were placed on the pyre alongside the deceased. The dead were cremated either

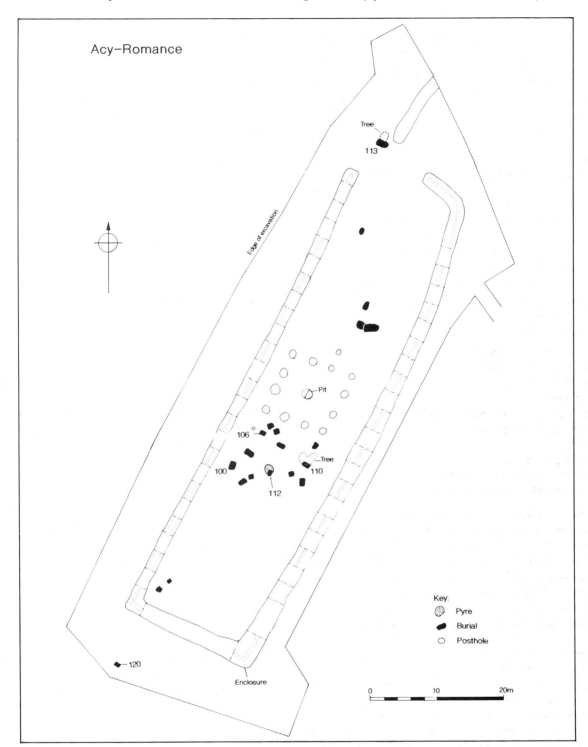

Acy-Romance

Tree
113

Edge of excavation

Pit

106

100   Tree
110

112

120

Enclosure

Key:
⊛ Pyre
◆ Burial
○ Posthole

0   10   20m

Fig. 2.4 *Acy-Romance 'La Croizette': plan of enclosure (after Lambot et al. 1994, fig. 10).*

wearing, or adorned by, costumes which are represented amongst the pyre goods by brooches, belt chains, belt hooks, glass bracelets or anklets. It is likely that the keys and knives found were also suspended from a belt, perhaps like a *châtelaine*.

The graves were often square or rectangular, and at least some were timber lined. Others may have had bases made of planks. The burials were both urned and unurned. Only a part of the cremated bones was chosen for burial but there appears to have been little attempt to remove quite large pyre goods from the cremated bones, for example the knife and belt chain from grave 100. Grave goods include joints of meat from animals and birds, often the same joints but from different animals as those

Fig. 2.5 *Acy-Romance 'La Croizette': hypothetical reconstruction of cemetery by Bernard Lambot (from Lambot* et al. *194, fig. 77).*

sacrificed for the cremation, and numerous pots which were often stacked in small piles (Fig. 2.6). Most, but not all, of these pots had been subjected to intense heat, presumably the funeral pyre. There is a suspicion that grave goods were placed more frequently around the north, south and western sides of the graves, with the eastern side either empty or occupied by grave goods of organic materials. The rectangular burials appear to be better slightly furnished with grave goods than the square ones.

The sequence of these archaeologically identifiable rituals may be glossed as;

Acy-Romance: mortuary rituals
  – creation of enclosure
  – sacrifice of animals
  – placing of pyre goods
  – cremation
  – sacrifice of further animals
  – burial

The burials span approximately one hundred years and, on this basis, the 28 burials might represent those of a small community, perhaps either a farm, or a small section of the population of the settlement at 'La Warde', a settlement which shows clear spatial organisation with

what may be a series of individual farms each with their own clearly defined spatial patterning, all ranged round a central open space. The other contemporary cemeteries could be for other families or clans resident in 'La Warde'.

As the excavators note, human bone, presumably excarnated, is found on the settlement at 'La Warde' and also at the sanctuary of Nanteuil-sur-Aisne, but there is no detailed attempt to compare the assemblages from these different types of sites. Where comparisons between finds from settlement and funerary contexts have been made (Lambot and Friboulet 1996), they have been primarily for chronological reasons. As the work at Acy-Romance is part of a detailed study of a micro-region the excavators are able to place it in a landscape setting, and in particular to draw together previously scattered evidence to show, at a regional scale, the range of burials, including several 'elite' ones, contemporary with the suggested *oppidum* at Chateau-Porcien (Lambot 1993; 1996). However, even though it is clear that the Roman imports which are found at the Acy-Romance settlement were not selected for burial in the cemeteries (Lambot *et al.* 1994, 147; Lambot 1996), the main thrust of the interpretation is again to see the burials as an indicator of social status.

Westhampnett

In contrast to the cemetery at 'La Croizette', the religious site at Westhampnett in West Sussex, England, seems to have been used by a wider community. At this site, which lies on a low, but locally prominent hill, at least two and probably four shrines, numerous pyre sites and related features, and 161 graves were excavated (Fig. 2.7). An early Romano-British cremation burial cemetery, a small Anglo-Saxon inhumation burial cemetery, and a Bronze Age ring ditch were also excavated. The graves and all features thought to be related with cremation were subject to whole-earth recovery allowing the recovery of evidence which would have been missed in manual excavation. Westhampnett is one of the largest late Iron Age cemeteries in western Europe yet published where the human bones are reported on (Fitzpatrick 1997).

The Late Iron Age site appears to have been used for only approximately 40 years, perhaps between 90–50 BC (La Tène D1b–D2b). On this basis it may be suggested that the cemetery was used by a community of around 90 people, but at present no types of settlements which could have housed a population of this size are known to have been occupied in the region. It seems probable then that this site was used as a burial ground by several communities. One exactly contemporary settlement has been excavated 1.5 kilometres to the south (at Copse Farm, Oving), and a number of other broadly contemporary farms are known. The Westhampnett site was called a religious site in the excavation report as it is not known with certainty what role the shrines played in the mortuary rituals, or when they were used. The purpose(s) of the short rows or alignments of timber posts is also unknown.

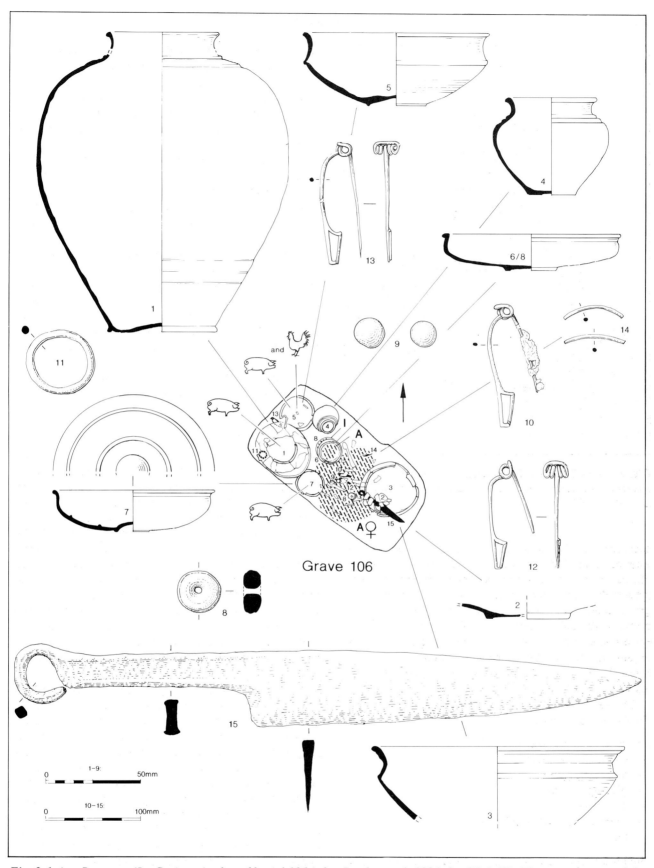

Fig. 2.6 *Acy-Romance 'La Croizette': plan of burial 106 (after Lambot* et al. *1994, fig. 25 & 27). The grave contained the burials of at least one female aged 25–30 and an immature infant aged between 1–3. Most of the cremated bone was placed in the centre of the grave and in pots 6/8 but some was also found in pots 1 and 5. Pyre goods included the right half of a pig's head, two brooches (nos 10 and 12) and perhaps the two ceramic rattles (9) and the spindle whorl (8), while a number of the pots had been placed on or near to the pyre. Grave goods may include knife 15 and brooch 13, both placed away from the cremated bone and the uncremated remains of a chicken in pot 5 and further joints of pork in pot 1.*

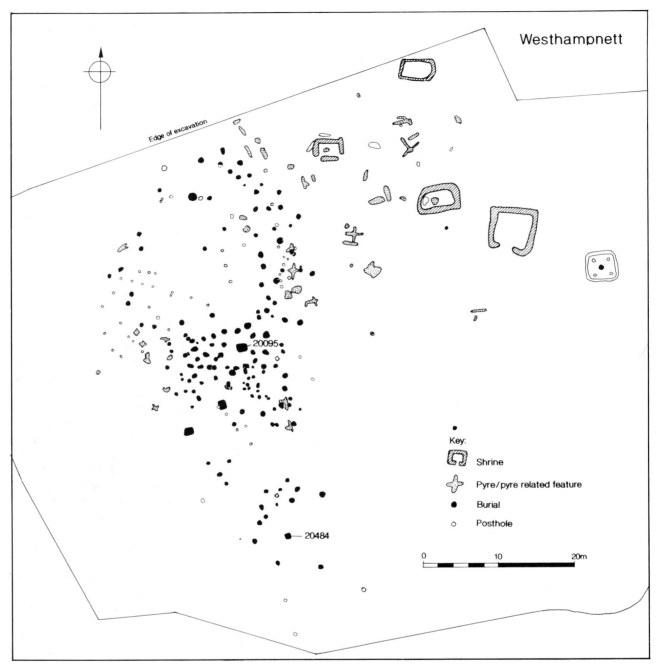

Fig. 2.7 *Westhampnett: plan of Iron Age features (source: author).*

It is, however, considered likely that the shrines were referred to throughout the mortuary rituals and so they are considered first here.

At least some of the shrines are readily paralleled in settlements, allowing them to be distinguished from funerary monuments. The small, square, shrines contrast with the large round houses of the British Iron Age. Most Iron Age shrines have been found on settlements and on these sites the entrances of the shrines face east; at Westhampnett they face south.

The pyre sites are indicated by a variety of linear features which are suggested to represent underground flues to draw up oxygen to assist the pyre to burn. If, as seems likely, the flues were along the long axis of the pyre, then many of the dead were cremated facing north or south. The pyres were usually made using oak from managed woodland and also re-used timbers from buildings or other objects. The dead were cremated wearing, or adorned by, a costume. Portions of sacrificed animals were also placed on the pyre. Pots were also placed in, or near to, the pyre.

The deposits within the flues of the pyres were often

mixed, which is quite different from the sequences which experimental cremations would lead us to expect (McKinley 1997, 65–6, pl. 17, fig. 46). This suggests that the pyres were deliberately disturbed after their final firing. A number of the pyres had pots, which had been on or near to the pyre, smashed on them as a final 'closing' signature after their final firing.

Although it is probable that all the cremated bones were collected from the pyre, only a small quantity, sometimes very small indeed, was chosen for burial which was usually unurned. Children appear to be under-represented, otherwise the ages and sexes of the deceased suggest what is commonly understood to be a 'normal' population. The most frequent grave goods were pots but at least some burials also had wooden vessels, probably bowls, placed in them. Preserved in the corrosion products of metal fittings or repairs on these wooden vessels is evidence for textiles and hides, and possibly straw, having been placed in the graves. The acidic soil left no trace of any unburnt sacrifices of animal meat. The graves must have been clearly marked as very few of them inter-cut.

It might be thought that in such a comparatively large and short lived cemetery such as Westhampnett, there would be clear evidence for social stratification, but in fact there was comparatively little obvious evidence for this. As assessed by the Number of Artefact Types (NAT), women appear to have been provided with fewer grave goods by their mourners than men, and younger people had fewer grave goods placed with them than adults.

A number of square graves do appear to echo elite well-furnished graves, perhaps appearing as 'focal' burials. They generally contained more grave goods (Fig. 2.8), but this was not statistically significant. Even so it is seems unlikely to be coincidental that the one grave in which a tiny fragment of gold was found (Grave 20095) was one of these.

If the object of the analyses was solely to isolate the material correlates of particular social types or social complexity, or to infer archaeologically something of the *social persona* of the deceased, this might seem disappointing. Yet because nearly all, if not all, of the plan of the religious site at Westhampnett was recorded, it was possible to explore other avenues. During analysis, a small group of broadly contemporary sites in the region was selected for comparison. They comprised the temple at Hayling Island, two small farms (Copse Farm, Oving, and North Bersted), and the slightly earlier hillfort of the Trundle. Some simple comparisons allowed some important insights into the character of the religious site at Westhampnett and the clearly prescribed nature of the materials used at it. Three examples of these comparisons may suffice to illustrate the point;

– unburnt human remains were present at these other sites, showing that the excarnation of corpses, with some parts of the dead being eventually being brought to a settlement, appears to have continued to be practised. Excarnation was probably the dominant burial rite before the adoption of cremation burial, so in the Late Iron Age cremation burial was not necessarily adopted by all communities

– most of the animals sacrificed for the funeral pyre at the religious site were pig and sheep. Although between them these species comprised 40–50% of the faunal assemblages on the settlements, the dominant species there was cow. However, at the Hayling Island temple, only pig and sheep were sacrificed

– although the forms of the pots offered as grave goods by the mourners at Westhampnett could be paralleled on settlements, the fabrics they were made in revealed clear choices. At the settlements pottery in grog-tempered fabrics comprises *c*. 3% of the assemblage. In the graves it is 40%, and many of the pots are highly decorated. This suggests that the pottery was specially chosen, if not made especially, for the grave. The choice may have been determined by the fact that this sort of fabric can be highly burnished to a dark, almost black, colour.

The recording of the almost complete plan of the religious site also allowed some suggestions to be made on the ways in which space had been structured, and how the architecture of the shrines and pyres guided the movements and pathways of the mourners.

The burials were made around a large circular area, with the pyre sites lying beyond them. Some of the rows of posts lay within the circular space, but others were outside it. What appears to be a second, smaller, circular setting of graves lay to the south of this main group. The shrines lay to the north-east of the main group, and the one grave which was marked by a mortuary structure lay to the east.

Using some of the cosmological referents embodied in the domestic architecture of the period and their use of space, it was suggested that the circular setting was an analogue of the Iron Age round house, and that the disposition of the graves to the south-east echoes and alters the usual orientation of the entrances to round-houses by turning it to the right. A similar movement is apparent in the rotation of the entrances of the shrines by 90°. The single grave marked by a funerary structure lies on the modern equinoxes. It appears that older people were buried preferentially close to the circular setting, although analyses using a Geographic Information System (GIS) (Loader 1996) show that this distribution is not significant statistically.

All four of these points, i) the continuing excarnation of some of the dead, ii) the selection of certain animals for sacrifice, iii) the particular decoration of pots, and iv) the cosmological referents of the sacred space and architecture by defining differences from the everyday also serve to refer the analysis back to it. By their nature everyday routines structure action, time and space, and sanctified by tradition, they constitute the *locales* in which the recursive face-to-face of everyday life, Bourdieu's,

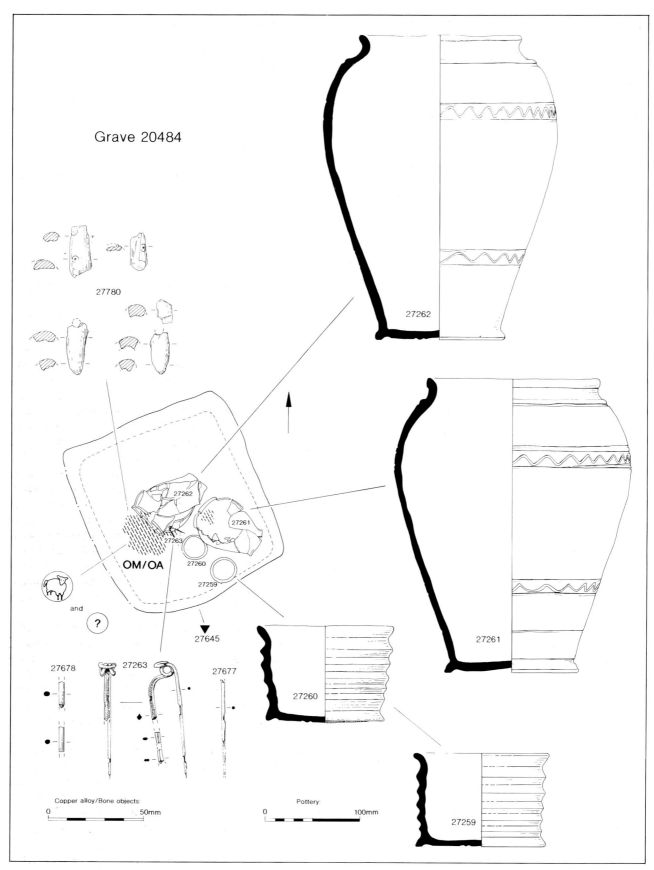

Fig. 2.8 *Westhampnett: plan of grave 20484 (after Fitzpatrick 1997, fig. 95). The grave contained the remains of an older-mature/older adult (26+ years) whose sex could not be determined. Pyre goods included all or parts of a lamb and another, unidentified, animal, two antler toggles which were probably costume fasteners, three brooches and further fragments of copper alloy, perhaps from another object. The two matching pairs of pots were placed as grave goods.*

habitus, is played out (Bourdieu 1977). It is precisely the links between these different fields – the everyday and death – which help to give ritual its significance.

At Westhampnett this sense of community was suggested to be close to Turner's formulation of *liminality* and *communitas*, developed out of the liminal phase of van Gennep's rites of passage. Van Gennep argued that all rites of passage or transition have a tripartite structure marked by three phases: separation, liminality, and reincorporation, but in funeral ceremonies the transitional phase is so distinct that it requires separate consideration. Turner's *communitas* is suggested to be a model emerging which;

> *recognisably in the liminal period, is of society as an unstructured or rudimentary structured and relatively undifferentiated comitatus, community, or even communion of equal individuals who submit to the general authority of the ritual elders* (Turner 1969, 96).

This levelling, when people are released from social structure into *communitas*, is one characteristic of the structure, rituals and also the symbolism of the Late Iron Age religious site at Westhampnett. A possible sequence for Iron Age mortuary ritual and some possible archaeological correlates were proposed.

Westhampnett: mortuary rituals

SEPARATION: BIOLOGICAL DEATH

Mourning >

– Dress/ adorn the dead in costume appropriate to age, sex and statuses
– Carry body to religious site
– ?Dead laid out on platform in symbolic house of ancestors in cemetery
– Gather pyre materials from settlement (culture) and woods (nature)
– Construct pyre, incorporating pots within it?
– Sacrifice animals, reserve portions for deceased and place on pyre
– ?Scatter grain on pyre

TRANSITION

– Light pyre
– Cremation
– Leave pyre to cool overnight
– Collect all of the cremated human bone, reserving a portion from all parts of the body, and tokens of the costume fittings and animal bone
– Turn over and mix the pyre site
– Smash burnt pots on pyre
– ?Curation of selected cremated remains (tokens) in shrines
– Dispersal of cremated remains

– Excavate grave outside symbolic house of ancestors
– Re-wrap *selected* cremated bones (incorporating pyre goods) in cloth or place in bag?
– Burial
– Place grave goods, pots, wooden vessels
– ??Place reserved portions of sacrificed animals
– ?Cover burial with straw
– Close grave
– Erect grave marker

INCORPORATION: DEAD PERSON ADMITTED TO ANCESTORS

< Formal mourning ceases

Conclusion

Many of these elements are common to Clemency, Acy-Romance 'La Croizette', and Westhampnett. At all three of these Iron Age sites there is a constant distinction between cremation and burial, when the actor becomes acted upon, but this was reformulated in different ways. It is perhaps shown most clearly by the sacrifice of animals and birds, and the offering of reserved portions of them to the pyre or the grave. Pots may or may not be burnt before inclusion in the grave, and sometimes, as at Westhampnett, where they were pyre goods, they were smashed. However, the deceased's costume was not separated from the cremated bones chosen for burial.

The location of the sites is consistent. Sited on hills they are above and away from settlements, but also visible from them. Their architecture, whether as mortuary structure and then tumulus at Clemency, or the shrines and timber posts at both Acy-Romance and Westhampnett, served to inscribe a new sort of religious space in the landscape. At Clemency and Acy-Romance this was emphasised by the an act of enclosure (Figs 2.2, 2.4). As the excavators of both sites note, this recalls the rituals enacted at Gaulish sanctuaries such as Gournay-sur-Aronde.

The destruction of people, animals and worldly goods in these places suggests that this was to enable their transferral to the gods not as material goods, but as metaphysical essences. These sacred spaces are also microcosms of the everyday lives of the community where the mourners re-negotiated their emotions and relations with the living and the dead, the dead, and their gods. It is arguable that this local, everyday, setting is a particularly appropriate context for the study of burial practice.

These suggestions about ritual, sequence, and structure derive essentially from contextual analyses, not the normatism of the 'New Archaeology', and from recent projects where the reporting of so-called 'environmental' data is standard. In comparison the concept of 'romanisation' as it is widely portrayed and how it is deployed in the analyses of the Clemency and Acy-Romance projects, with its emphasis on ideology, elites and emulation, and on material culture and prestigious goods, seems poorly equipped both to forge links between these diverse and complex series of localised beliefs and rites evident in

Late Iron Age mortuary practices. The case for 'romanisation' before the Conquest appears to have been overstated (Fitzpatrick 1993, 241–2; Haselgrove 1996, 168–75). Instead one of the challenges for the study of provincial Roman burial practices is to incorporate this diversity or heterogeneity of Late Iron Age mortuary rituals within the concept of 'romanisation' which can, whether by accident or by design, become a concept of homogeneity.

Acknowledgements

I am grateful to Rosalind Niblett for allowing me to read her paper in advance of publication and to Colin Haselgrove for his comments on a draft of this paper. The illustrations were prepared by S.E. James, and Figures 2.3 and 2.5 are reproduced by kind permission of Jeannot Metzler and Bernard Lambot respectively.

Bibliography

Abegg, A. 1989. Die Aschengrube 82/28. In *Gräber – Spiegel des Lebens. Zum Totenbrauchtum der Kelten und Römer am Beispiel des Treverer-Gräberfeldes Wederath-Belginum* (ed. A. Haffner). Trier: Rheinisches Landesmuseum Trier, 395–400.

Bourdieu, P. 1977. *Outline of a Theory of Practice.* Cambridge: Cambridge University Press.

Cordie-Hackenberg, R., Gerdes, C. and Wigg, A. 1992. Nahrungsreste aus römischen Gräbern und Aschengruben des Trierer Landes. *Archäologisches Korrespondenzblatt* 22: 109–17.

Fitzpatrick, A.P. 1989. The uses of Roman imperialism by the Celtic Barbarians in the later Republic. In *Barbarians and Romans in North-West Europe from the Later Republic to Late Antiquity* (eds J.C. Barrett, A.P. Fitzpatrick and L. Macinnes). Oxford: British Archaeological Reports International Series 471, 27–54.

Fitzpatrick, A.P. 1991. Death in a material world: the Late Iron Age and Romano-British cemetery at King Harry Lane, St Albans, Hertfordshire. *Britannia* 22: 323–7.

Fitzpatrick, A.P. 1993. Ethnicity and exchange: Germans, Celts and Romans in the Late Iron Age. In *Trade and Exchange in Prehistoric Europe* (eds C. Scarre and F. Healy). Oxford: Oxbow Monograph 33, 233–44.

Fitzpatrick, A.P. 1997. *Archaeological Excavations on the Route of the A27 Westhampnett Bypass, West Sussex. Volume 2: the Late Iron Age, Romano-British, and Anglo-Saxon cemeteries.* Salisbury: Wessex Archaeology Report 12.

Härke, H. 1989. Die Anglo-Amerikanische Diskussion zur Gräberanalyse. *Archäologisches Korrespondenzblatt* 19: 185–94.

Haselgrove, C.C. 1982. Wealth, prestige and power: the dynamics of political centralisation in south-east England. In *Ranking, Resource and Exchange: aspects of the archaeology of early European society* (eds C. Renfrew and S.J. Shennan). Cambridge: Cambridge University Press, 79–88.

Haselgrove, C.C. 1996. Roman impact on rural settlement and society in southern Picardy. In *From the Sword to the Plough. Three studies on the earliest romanisation of northern Gaul.* Amsterdam: Amsterdam Archaeological Studies 1, 127–87.

Haselgrove, C. and Millett, M. 1997. *Verlamion* reconsidered. In *Reconstructing Iron Age Societies: new approaches to the British Iron Age* (eds A. Gwilt and C. Haselgrove). Oxford: Oxbow Monograph 71, 282–96.

Kreuz, A. 1994/1995. Funktionale und konzeptionelle archäobotanischen Daten aus römerzeitlichen Brandbestattungen. *Berichte der Kommission für Archäologische Landesforschung in Hessen* 3: 1994/1995, 93–7.

Lambot, B. 1989. Le sanctuaire gaulois et gallo-romain de Nanteuil-sur-Aisne, lieu-dit 'Népellier' (Ardennes). *Bulletin de la Société Archéologique Champenoise* 4: 33–44.

Lambot, B. 1993. Habitats, nécropoles et organisation du territoire a La Tène finale en Champagne septentrionale. In *Monde des Morts, Monde des Vivants en Gaule rurale. Actes du colloque ARCHEA/AGER (Orleans 7–9 fevrier 1992)* (ed. A. Ferdière). Tours: 6e supplément à la Revue Archéologique du Centre de la France, 121–51.

Lambot, B. 1996. Les Rèmes à la veille de la romanisation. Le Porcien au Ier siècle avant J.-C. In *De la ferme indigène à la villa romaine. Actes du deuxième colloque de l'association AGER tenu à Amiens (Somme) du 23 au 25 septembre 1993* (eds D. Bayard and J.L. Collart). Amiens: Revue Archéologique de Picardie no. special 11, 13–38.

Lambot, B. and Friboulet, M. 1996. Essai de chronologie du site de La Tène finale d'Acy-Romance (Ardennes). *Revue Archéologique de Picardie* 3–4, 1996, 123–51.

Lambot, B. and Méniel, P. 1992. *Le site protohistorique d'Acy-Romance (Ardennes) I. L'habitat gaulois 1988–1990.* Reims: Mémoires de la Société Archéologique Champenoise 7/ Dossiers de Protohistoire 4.

Lambot, B., Friboulet, M. and Méniel, P. 1994. *Le site protohistorique d'Acy-Romance (Ardennes) II. Les nécropoles dans leur contexte régionale (Thugny-Trugny et tombes aristocratiques), 1986–1988–1989.* Reims: Mémoires de la Société Archéologique Champenoise 8/ Dossiers de Protohistoire 5.

Loader, E. 1996. *Spatial Analysis of the Late Iron Age Cremation Cemetery at Westhampnett, West Sussex.* Southampton: University of Southampton. Unpublished MSc. Dissertation.

McKinley, J.I. 1997. The cremated human bone from burial and cremation related contexts. In A.P. Fitzpatrick, *Archaeological Excavations on the Route of the A27 Westhampnett Bypass, West Sussex. Volume 2: the Late Iron Age, Romano-British, and Anglo-Saxon cemeteries.* Salisbury: Wessex Archaeology Report 12, 55–73.

Mackreth, D. 1994. Late La Tène brooch, 49–50. In R. Thorpe and J. Sharman with P. Clay. An Iron Age and Romano-British enclosure system at Normanton le Heath, Leicestershire. *Transactions of the Leicestershire Archaeological and Historical Society* 68: 1–63.

Metcalf, P. and Huntington, R. 1992. *Celebrations of Death: the anthropology of mortuary ritual.* (second edition) Cambridge: Cambridge University Press.

Metzler, J. 1995. *Das treverische Oppidum auf dem Titelberg (G.-H. Luxemburg). Zur Kontinuität zwischen der spätkeltischen und der frührömischen Zeit in Nord-Gallien.* Luxembourg: Dossiers d'Archéologie du Musée National d'Histoire et d'Art 3.

Metzler, J., Waringo, R., Bis, R. and Metzler-Zens, N. 1991. *Clemency et les tombes de l'aristocratie en Gaule Belgique.* Luxembourg: Dossiers d'Archéologie du Musée National d'Histoire et d'Art. 1.

Metzler-Zens, N., Metzler-Zens, J., Méniel, P., Bis, R., Gaeng, C. and Villemeur, I., 1999. *Lamadelaine: une nécropole de l'oppidum du Titelberg.* Luxembourg: Dossiers d'Archéologie du Musée National d'Histoire et d'Art 6.

Millett, M. 1990. Romanization: historical issues and archaeological interpretation. In *The Early Roman Empire in the West* (eds T. Blagg and M. Millett). Oxford: Oxbow Monograph 6, 35–41

Millett, M. 1993. A cemetery in an age of transition: King Harry Lane reconsidered. In *Römerzeitliche Gräber als Quellen zu*

Religion, Bevölkerungsstruktur und Sozialgeschichte (ed. M. Struck). Mainz: Archäologische Schriften Instituts für Vor- und Frühgeschichte der Johannes Gutenberg Universität Mainz 3, 255–82.

Northover, J.P. and Montague, R. 1997. Heat-altered metal. In A.P. Fitzpatrick, *Archaeological Excavations on the Route of the A27 Westhampnett Bypass, West Sussex. Volume 2: the Late Iron Age, Romano-British, and Anglo-Saxon cemeteries.* Salisbury: Wessex Archaeology Report 12, 90–1.

O'Shea, J. 1984. *Mortuary Archaeology: an archaeological investigation.* London: Academic Press.

Pearce, J. 1997. Death and time: the structure of late Iron Age mortuary ritual. In *Reconstructing Iron Age Societies: new approaches to the British Iron Age* (eds A. Gwilt and C. Haselgrove). Oxford: Oxbow Monograph 71, 174–80.

Polfer, M. 1996. *Das gallorömische Brandgräberfeld und der dazugehörige Verbrennungsplatz von Septfontaines-Dëckt, (Luxemburg).* Luxembourg: Dossiers d'Archéologie du Musée National d'Histoire et d'Art 5.

Stead, I.M. and Rigby, V. 1989. *Verulamium. The King Harry Lane site.* London: English Heritage Archaeological Report 12.

Struck, M. 1995. Integration and continuity in funerary ideology. In *Integration in the Early Roman West. The role of culture and ideology* (eds J. Metzler, M. Millett, N. Roymans and J. Slofstra). Luxembourg: Dossiers d'Archéologie du Musée National d'Histoire et d'Art 4, 139–50.

Turner, V.W. 1967. *The Forest of Symbols: aspects of Ndembu ritual.* Ithaca: Cornell University Press.

Wigg, A. 1993. Zu Funktion und Deutung der 'Aschengruben'. In *Römerzeitliche Gräber als Quellen zu Religion, Bevölkerungsstruktur und Sozialgeschichte* (ed. M. Struck). Mainz: Archäologische Schriften Instituts für Vor- und Frühgeschichte der Johannes Gutenberg Universität Mainz 3, 111–15.

Woolf, G.D. 1993. European social development and Roman imperialism. In *Frontières d'empire. Nature et signification des frontières romaines* (eds P. Brun, S. van der Leeuw and C.R. Whittaker), Nemours, Mémoires du Musée de Préhistoire d'Ile-de-France 5, 13–20.

3. Reconstructing funerary rituals: the evidence of *ustrina* and related archaeological structures

Michel Polfer

Definitions

In the scientific literature, even in contemporary excavation reports, a considerable lack of terminological precision as far as the different categories of archaeological structures occurring in provincial Roman funerary contexts are concerned must be acknowledged. The explanation for this terminological 'flou artistique' is not difficult to find: whereas Roman literary and epigraphic sources (Buisson 1993) provide us with rich evidence for the Latin terminology (Fellmann 1993) for individual graves, funerary monuments and cemeteries (e.g. *cenotaphium, monumentum, titulus, ossuarium*) we have at our disposal no Latin words for structures related to the cremation of the dead, except for the terms *bustum* (Struck 1993b and Bel/Tranoy 1993), the literary expressions *rogus* and *pyra* and the more common *ustrinum*. *Busta* and *ustrina* are defined by Festus (*De significatu verborum* (ed. W. M. Lindsay, Leipzig, 1913), p. 29, s.v. *bustum*) (Witteyer (1993) discusses their archaeological identification).

> << *bustum proprie dicitur locus, in quo mortuus est combustus et sepultus (...); ubi vero combustus quis tantummodo, alibus vero est sepultus, is locus ab urendo ustrina vocatur*>>

Archaeologists therefore have to devise their own terminology for all other structures which we are likely to encounter in funerary contexts, resulting in a considerable amount of terminological variation. Before we try to provide an overview of the present state of our knowledge on these structures, it might therefore seem not only useful but even necessary to start with a few definitions. As far as the northern provinces of the Roman empire are concerned, the current state of research suggests that we can distinguish between at least five categories of archaeological structures in funerary contexts other than graves and funerary monuments:

- *ustrina*, i.e. cremation areas, either individual or collective
- postholes encountered either beneath or in the immediate surroundings of *ustrina*. Ethnographic evidence (Wahl and Wahl 1983) suggests that most of these posts served to stabilise individual pyres.
- single pyre debris pits which were filled with the remains of an individual cremation after those pyre goods that were to be transferred into the grave had been sorted out. There is no established term in English for this type of structure, for which the expressions *Aschengruben* and *fosses à cendres* are commonly used in German and French respectively.
- larger pits which were filled with the material collected while cleaning an cremation area. Depending on the number of cremations per year and the frequency of cleaning sessions, these structures may contain more or less chronologically coherent material left over by a large number of cremations.
- small pits which contain materials deposited as offerings in the context of the funerary ritual, either during or after the actual burial. As this category of structures is not directly related to the cremation of the deceased, it will not be taken into account in the present paper.

The present state of knowledge

If after these few introductory remarks we turn to the present state of information on *ustrina* and related structures, we must immediately recognise that, although a large number of them have been recognised and excavated since the 19th century and despite the fact that they are quite often referred to in excavation reports (see Van Doorselaer 1967: 34ff for a list of references concerning northern Gaul) our knowledge remains very limited and fragmentary. Probably because they contain heavily burned archaeological materials, which are difficult to analyse and not suited to museological purposes, they have until now not been granted any sustained attention in provincial Roman funerary archaeology. Even in recent excavation reports a regrettable lack of interest in these categories of archaeological structures may be observed. For example, in a recent report on the cemetery of Kohlberg at Héraples (Moselle-France), only a few lines are devoted to the 26 pyre debris pits which were discovered in direct relationship to cremations of the first century AD (Hoffmann 1995: 15).

1. Ustrina

Our documentation, as fragmentary as it may be, nevertheless allows us to distinguish between two major types of structures used for the cremation of the deceased:

– permanent *ustrina* built in durable materials
– non-permanent areas used for a single or several cremations

Ustrina of the first type are in most cases though not exclusively to be found on urban cemeteries, where the large number of cremations per year made permanent structures if not necessary then at least useful, as they allowed a more efficient and faster cremation.

The known examples of this type are constructed in tiles or in dry stone walling and are quadrangular or circular (often doubled and concentric) in plan (Fig. 3.1). Such permanent *ustrina* are known from Britain, for example from Colchester and Verulamium (Black 1986), from Austria (Holter 1970: 35ff; Rieß 1974: 155; Ruprechtsberger 1983: 23) and from Gaul (Brun 1985:

13; Bel 1987: 36; Bailleu/Carbezuelo 1989). The best preserved example of a permanent *ustrinum* however comes from the Rhineland, more precisely from Rheinzabern (Ludovici 1908: 201). Recent discoveries of permanent *ustrina* in the context of rural cemeteries (Fourteau-Badarji et al. 1993: 268; Faye 1993: 90) however show that this type of cremation structure was not restricted to urban cemeteries.

The fact that permanent *ustrina* were not absolutely necessary even in large cemeteries is best illustrated by the cemetery of the small town of Wederath-Belginum (Haffner 1989): more than 2500 graves and a considerable number of cremation areas have been excavated, but none of the latter was a permanent structure. It seems clear that on smaller rural cemeteries, where only a limited number of cremations per year had to be accomplished (e.g. one cremation every 10 months in the rural cemetery of Courroux (Switzerland) (Martin-Kilcher 1976); one every 11 months in that of Septfontaines (Luxembourg) (Polfer 1996: 20)), the construction of such permanent *ustrina* was the exception rather than the rule. In most cemeteries in the provinces non-permanent cremation areas were thus sufficient. Established on the ground itself, they consist of simple depressions of shallow depth, filled with the remains of pyre debris. They present no evidence for internal features and no clear external boundary.

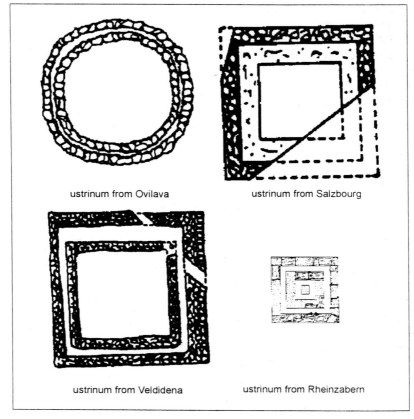

ustrinum from Ovilava

ustrinum from Salzbourg

ustrinum from Veldidena

ustrinum from Rheinzabern

Fig. 3.1 *Examples of permanent ustrina*

In the present state of research, we are able to distinguish two different subtypes of such non-permanent cremation structures:

-   small areas (2–3m², sometimes even less), used only for one or for a very limited number of cremations. Examples of this type are quite common and appear on rural as well as on small town and urban cemeteries (for examples in a rural context see Noël 1968: 18; Thill 1970: 375ff; Schindler 1973: 61; Metzler 1976; Ludwig 1988: 61; for examples in a small town/urban context see Vanvinckenroye 1967: 129; Witteyer 1993; Faber 1998: 167–175).
-   cremation areas which are much larger, often exceeding 100 m². These areas, which were in for use up to 150 years, were formed in the course of time by the overlapping of a considerable number of individual pyres. Until now only two examples of this second type are known: Vatteville-la-Rue (France-Seine Maritime) (Lequoy 1986: 56 and 64) and Septfontaines (Luxembourg; Fig. 3.2) (Polfer 1996).

2. Single pyre debris pits

Although they must have been a very common structure on every burial site in the northern provinces of the Roman empire, well documented single pyre debris pits (Wigg 1993) remain even less frequent than *ustrina*. Most of the known examples have been discovered under or in the direct surroundings of tumuli (e.g. Roosens/Lux 1973: 17–20 and 36–38; Leva/Plumier 1985: 169–196; Abegg 1989: 171–278; Wigg 1993: 114; Polfer 1996: 22). Their shape as well as their dimensions vary considerably. The pits contain more or less cremated and fragmented archaeological materials of different types, ashes and charcoal but no or very few cremated human bones.

The fact that only a small number of structures of this category has been discovered on rural (Thill 1970: 373–375; Roth-Rubi/Sennhauser 1987: 51; Barthélemy/Depierre 1990: 67ff.; Faye 1993: 89–92; Polfer 1996: 22–25; Liéger 1997: 14) or urban (Vanvinckenroye 1967: 84–86 and fig. 47) cemeteries may find its explanation in different factors:

-   many may have been destroyed without notice being taken of them, either before or during excavation
-   many may have been interpreted as graves (in particular in older excavation reports there are frequent references to so-called 'graves' without any records of cremated bones having been discovered)
-   many seem to have been situated outside the area of the actual graves, beside or around the cremation areas, which have also not been discovered in most cases

3. Other structures filled with pyre debris

As far as the reconstruction of funerary rituals is concerned, single pyre debris pits, containing the remains of an individual cremation, have to be clearly separated from other categories of archaeological structures, close to them in shape and in content, but the product of a completely different process in funerary rituals. One of these categories is constituted by pits which were filled with cremation debris during or after the more or less regular cleaning of a cremation area.

In practice however, this differentiation between all these categories is very often difficult to establish. Until now, only a few exceptionally large features from Destelbergen (Belgium) (De Laet 1962: 77; De Laet/Thoen/Van Doorselaer 1970: 3–30), Velzeke (Belgium) (Van Doorselaer/Rogge, 1985: 159–165), Nuits-Saint-Georges (France), (Planson 1982: 36s. and 164) and York (Great Britain) (Black 1986: 210), filled with a very rich and chronologically heterogeneous material may be identified with a high degree of probability as belonging to the later category. When discovered, these structures were interpreted respectively as *ustrina* (Nuits-Saint-Georges) or as mass-graves related either to epidemic diseases or war (Destelbergen, Velzeke). But a more precise analysis of their contents clearly shows that their filling took place over a long period of time, with material originating from a large number of cremations. It seems therefore likely, that these pits were filled in the course of time during the occasional cleaning of cremation areas with the material that had been left behind after several individual cremations.

One of the aims of future research in provincial Roman burial practice must therefore be to pay a greater degree of attention to all these categories of archaeological structures directly linked to the cremation process, thus allowing the development of criteria to permit their clear identification and distinction from one another.

The analytical potential of structures related to the cremation process for future research in provincial Roman burial practice

In order to justify this last remark, it might be useful to add a few general remarks concerning the analytical potential of structures such as *ustrina* and pyre debris pits.

Until recently, research into provincial Roman burial practice has almost exclusively shown interest in the graves themselves and the objects they contain, thus neglecting all other categories of archaeological structures which may be observed on cemeteries. But archaeologists involved in the study of burial sites are nowadays becoming increasingly aware that funerary practice is a *process*. It must therefore be accepted that if we want to improve our understanding of the funerary process and the ritual concepts behind it and if we are to reconstruct provincial Roman burial practice and to put it in its social and religious context, a first and essential condition will be to take account of all the different stages and aspects of the funerary process itself.

In pursuing this aim, structures such as *ustrina* and single pyre debris pits represent an invaluable source of information, because they offer us the only possibility of apprehending – at different levels of analysis – stages and aspects of the funerary ritual that may not be approached through the graves and the grave-goods themselves. This is especially true of two important stages of the funerary process: the cremation itself and the selection of those pyre goods which are to be transferred to the grave.

If we try to go further than these general remarks, the potential for future research of the structures which have been briefly presented in this paper may be situated on two different analytical levels. First, these structures present very often conditions of preservation of the archaeological material different from those encountered in the graves. Thus, if excavated with the same methodological meticulousness as the graves themselves, these structures can be a source of archaeological materials which are not found in the grave itself. The results obtained by A. Abegg-Wigg and her colleagues (Abegg 1989: 397; Abegg/Cordie-Hackenberg 1990) on some of the single pyre debris pits from the cemetery of Wederath (Germany) show the great potential for future research in this domain into animal (Lepetz 1993) and plant remains (Marinval 1993) as well as for other types of material

such as wooden containers. Second, these structures and the material they contain offer an invaluable possibility of contrasting the grave-goods with an archaeological material not only contemporary to them but also originating from the same social milieu and deposited in an identical *ideological* context. Seen from this point of view, their analysis deserves the same attention as that of the graves themselves.

So far, only one such comparative study (Polfer 1996) has been carried out. The main results of this case-study may however illustrate the great potential of this new kind of approach.

The case-study of Septfontaines (Luxembourg)

The *ustrinum* of Septfontaines (Figs. 3.2, 3.3) , covering about 160 m², belongs to a rural burial site in use from the Claudian period to the first decades of the third century AD. Altogether 181 cremations and one inhumation were discovered. The cremation area itself consisted of an ovoid depression of 15.75 m in length and 11.25 m in width. The maximum depth of the structure was 0.53 m. The analysis of the material showed that the structure was formed progressively by the overlapping of a large number of individual pyres between the Flavian period and the first decades of the third century AD. Around the

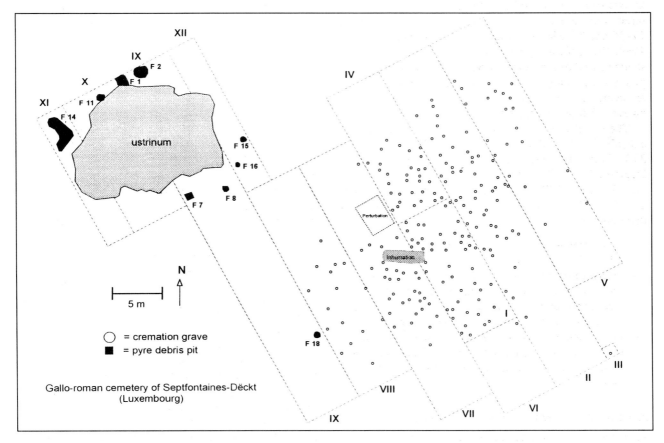

Fig. 3.2 *Gallo-Roman cemetery of Septfontaines-Dëckt (Luxembourg)*

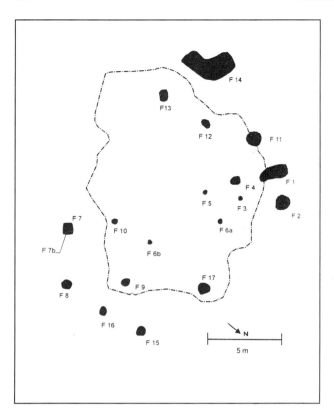

Fig. 3.3 Ustrinum *from Septfontaines-Dëckt. The shaded features are post-holes and single pyre debris pits, the outlined area indicates the spread of pyre debris*

cremation area and beneath it were discovered eleven single pyre debris pits.

Most of the material discovered in the *ustrinum* consisted of pottery sherds. A detailed analysis distinguished a minimum of 504 different vessels. In the graves 305 unburned ceramic vessels and 413 vessels used as pyre goods could be identified. The total minimum number of 1221 ceramic vessels thus obtained offered a sufficient base for comparative statistical analysis. This analysis was conducted from two different perspectives: the qualitative (fabric) and the functional (form) properties of the ceramics involved in the different steps of the funerary process.

The Qualitative Analysis

For this purpose, the ceramic vessels were sorted into six categories: samian, Gallo-Belgic ware, burnished ware, smoothed ware, granular ware and ceramics of which the fabric could no longer be determined (All percentages and numbers indicated refer to the minimum number of vessels of each category).

The results of the comparative analysis (Fig. 3.4) were significant for two of these categories: First of all the percentage of smoothed ware in the graves is twice that in the material from the cremation area. Secondly the samian, which represents only 2.5% of the vessels from the graves, accounts for 37.6% of the vessels and is by far the most common fabric in the material from the *ustrinum*. Of the 504 vessels from the cremation area, 198 are samian!

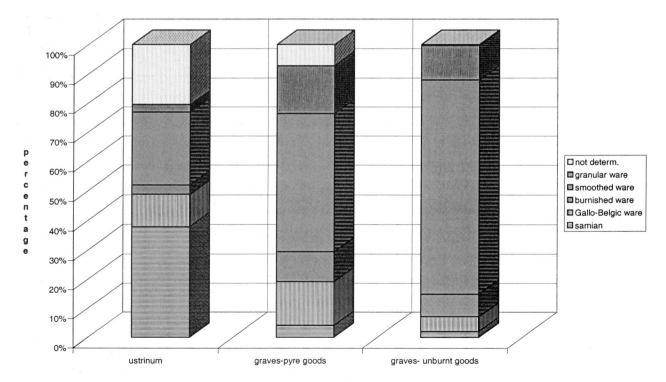

Fig. 3.4 A comparison of vessel fabrics from different contexts from Septfontaines-Dëckt

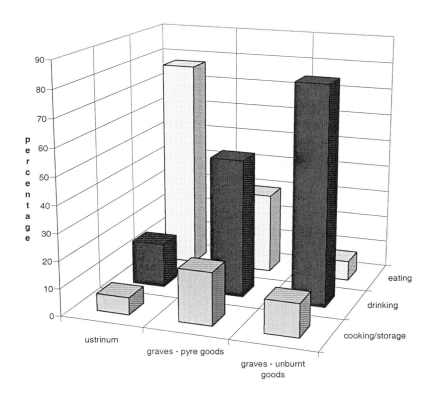

Fig. 3.5 *A comparison of vessel forms from different contexts from Septfontaines-Dëckt*

The qualitative analysis thus reveals a first fundamental difference in the use of ceramic fabrics: in Septfontaines samian was clearly used almost exclusively during the cremation process, only very rarely as a grave good. This first result has important consequences. For if we ask what the reasons for such a specialised use of some ceramic fabrics during the funerary process might be, a look at the ceramic forms (Fig. 3.5) represented in the material from the *ustrinum* gives a first clue: all vessels in samian ware belong to types linked to the service of solid food. The privileged use of samian ware during the cremation process might thus find a functional explanation.

To assess whether the specialised use of samian might be linked to fundamental functional differences between the ceramics involved in the cremation and those involved in the burial, a functional analysis was carried out: beakers and jars were considered to relate to the serving of liquids, plates and platters as well as the large relief-decorated bowls and small cups in samian ware to the serving of solid food, mortaria, pots and large bowls in granular ware to the preparation/storage of food.

The Functional Analysis

The results are very clear (Fig. 3.5). Whereas vessels linked to the service of liquids constitute 76% of the unburned grave goods, they represent only 17% of the vessels from the *ustrinum*. A large majority of the later

(78%) are linked to the service of solid food. The comparative functional analysis thus reveals two different steps in the funerary process!

A comparison between the material from the *ustrinum* and the burned ceramic vessels from the graves is also quite revealing. If the selection of the pyre offerings that were transferred into the graves had been made randomly, we should expect the burned vessels from the graves to reflect the results obtained for the vessels from the *ustrinum* as far as their function is concerned, i.e. to be mainly be linked to the service of solid food. But this clearly is not the case. On the contrary: like the unburned grave goods, the burned vessels from the graves are mainly linked to the service of liquids. This shows that the selection of pyre goods to be placed in the grave was far from random and clearly made on functional criteria.

In other words: the case-study of Septfontaines suggests that a major traditional assumption made in provincial Roman funerary archaeology, namely that the grave goods may be considered as representative for the whole material involved in the funerary process, is correct neither from a qualitative nor from a quantitative nor from a functional perspective.

Conclusions: methodological issues

The results obtained in the case-study of Septfontaines allow us to end the present paper with a few general conclusions. They concern methodological results that might be drawn – at two different levels – from this type of analysis.

- First of all, if we are to advance in our understanding of Roman burial practice, it will in the future be indispensable to take account of all the information available. Only this kind of approach will allow us to gain a more precise view of all the different steps of the funerary process, a necessary condition for the study of the psychological, social and religious concepts underlying it.

- Secondly, results such as those of the comparative analysis on the material of Septfontaines clearly show the dangers of interpretations and conclusions based only on the grave goods. Future research must be aware that the objects discovered in the graves represent only a sample of all the materials involved in the funerary process and that there is no *a priori* guarantee that the grave sample is representative, neither in a quantitative, nor in a qualitative, nor in a functional perspective. As long as our knowledge of other steps of the funerary process, preceding or following the actual burial, remains very limited, inter-regional comparisons based only on the grave-goods themselves will be difficult to justify. The same is true for arguments *a silentio* (i.e. based on the absence of certain categories of objects or of certain fabrics in the graves) and the conclusions based on them concerning the social or economic status of the deceased.

Bibliography

Abegg A. 1989. Der römische Grabhügel von Siesbach, Kreis Birkenfeld. *Trierer Zeitschrift* 52: 171–278.

Abegg A. and Cordie-Hackenberg R. 1990. Die keltischen Brandgräber und römischen Aschengruben mit Brot- und Gebäckresten von Wederath-Belginum. *Trierer Zeitschrift* 53: 225–240.

Bailleu M. and Carbezuelo U. 1989. La nécropole de Bruère-Allichamps (Cher) (IVe–XVIIe s.). In: *Cahiers d'Archéologie et d'Histoire du Berry* 98, 23–36.

Barthèlemy A. and Depierre G. 1990. *La nécropole gallo-romaine des Cordiers à Macon*. Macon.

Bel V. 1987. La nécropole gallo-romaine de Saint-Paul-Trois-Châteaux (Drôme). In *Nécropoles à incinération du Haut-Empire. Table ronde de Lyon 30 et 31 mai 1986*. Lyon: Rapports Arch. Préliminaires de la Région Rhône-Alpes 4, 35–42.

Bel V. and Tranoy L. 1993. Note sur les busta dans le Sud-Est de la Gaule. In Struck 1993, pp. 95–110.

Black E.W. 1986. Romano-British burial customs and religious beliefs in south-east England. *Arch. Journal* 143: 201–239.

Brun J.-P. 1985. La nécropole de Saint-Lambert. In *Les nécropoles gallo-romaines de Fréjus. Trois années d'action du service archéologique municipal*. Fréjus, pp. 13–19.

Buisson A. 1993. Le monde des morts en Gaule rurale à l'époque romaine: l'apport des textes littéraires et épigraphiques. In Ferdière 1993, pp. 23–28.

De Laet S.J. 1962. Het gallo-romeinse grafveld van Destelbergen.

Kultureel Jahrboek van de provincie Oost-Vlaanderen 23, vol. 2: 23–78.

De Laet S.J., Thoen S.J. and Van Doorselaer A. 1970. La tombe collective de la nécropole gallo-romaine de Destelbergen-lez-Gand (Flandre orientale). *Helinium* 10: 3–30.

Faber A. 1998. *Das römische Gräberfeld auf der Keckwiese in Kempten. II. Gräber der mittleren Kaiserzeit und Infra-strukturen des Gräberfeldes sowie Siedlungsbefunde im Ostteil der Keckwiese*. Kallmünz/Opf: Cambodunumforschungen VI.

Faye O.A. 1993. Une nécropole rurale du Haut-Empire à Gravelotte (Moselle). In Ferdière 1993, pp. 89–92.

Fellmann R. 1993. Texte zum Grabrecht und Grabbrauch. In Struck 1993, pp. 11–15.

Ferdière A. (ed.) 1993. *Monde des morts, Monde des vivants en Gaule rurale. Actes du colloque ARCHEA / AGER (Orléans 7 – 9 février 1992)*. Tours.

Fourteau-Badarji A.-M. et al. 1993. La nécropole gallo-romaine des Vernes à Faverdines (Cher). In Ferdière 1993, pp. 265–271.

Haffner A. 1989. Das Gräberfeld von Wederath-Belginum vom 4. Jahrhundert vor bis zum 4. Jahrhundert nach Christi Geburt. In *Gräber, Spiegel des Lebens. Zum Totenbrauchtum der Kelten und Römer am Beispiel des Treverer-Gräberfeldes von Wederath-Belginum (ed. A. Haffner)*. Mainz, pp. 37–129.

Hoffmann R. 1995. *La nécropole du Kohlberg au Héraples (Moselle)*. Metz: Sources et Documents, série Histoire Régionale Antique, Nr. 1.

Holter K. 1970. Beobachtungen über römerzeitliche Funde auf dem Gelände des ehemaligen Friedhofs in Wels (Baustelle Gerngross-Markthalle), 1970/71. *Jahrbuch des Musealvereins Wels* 17: 24–42.

Lepetz S. 1993. Les restes animaux dans les sépultures gallo-romaines. In Ferdière 1993, pp. 37–44.

Lequoy M.-C. 1987. La nécropole gallo-romaine de Vatteville-La-Rue (Forêt de Bretonnes-Les Landes -Seine Maritime). In *Nécropoles à incinération du Haut-Empire. Table ronde de Lyon 30 et 31 mai 1986*. Lyon: Rapports Arch. Préliminaires de la Région Rhône-Alpes 4, pp. 55–68.

Leva Ch. and Plumier J. 1985. Tombe gallo-romaine de Sombreffe (fouilles de 1959 et 1962). *Ann. Soc. Arch. Namur* 64: 169–196.

Liéger A. 1997. La nécropole gallo-romaine de Cutry (Meurthe-et-Moselle). Nancy: Etudes Lorraines d'Archéologie Nationale 3.

Ludovici W. 1908. *Urnengräber römischer Töpfer aus Rhein-zabern und III. Folge dort aufgefundener Stempelnamen und Stempelbilder bei meinen Ausgrabungen 1905–1908*. Rhein-zabern.

Ludwig R. 1988. Das frührömische Brandgräberfeld von Schank-weiler, Kreis Bittburg-Prüm. *Trierer Zeitschrift* 51: 51–366.

Marinval Ph. 1993. Etude carpologique d'offrandes alimentaires végétales dans les sépultures gallo-romaines: réflexions préliminaires. In Ferdière 1993, pp. 45–65.

Martin-Kilcher St. 1976. *Das römische Gräberfeld von Courroux im Berner Jura*. Derendingen, Solothurn: Basler Beiträge zur Ur- u. Frühgeschichte, Vol. 2.

Metzler J. 1976. Ein Gräberfeld des 3. und 4. Jahrhunderts in Dreiborn. *Hémecht* 28: 55–64.

Noël J. 1968. La nécropole romaine du Hunenknepchen à Sampont (commune de Hachy). *Arch. Belg.* 106.

Planson M. 1982. *La nécropole gallo-romaine des Bolards, Nuits-Saint-Georges*. Paris.

Polfer M. 1996. *Das gallorömische Brandgräberfeld und der dazugehörige Verbrennungsplatz von Septfontaines-Dèckt (Luxemburg)*. Luxembourg: Dossiers d'Archéologie du Musée National d'Histoire et d'Art V.

Rieß W. 1974. Die Ustrina des westlichen römischen Gräberfeldes von Ovilava. *Oberösterreichische Heimatblätter* 28: 154–156.

Roosens H. and Lux G.V. 1973. Grafveld met gallo-romeinse tumulus te Berlingen. *Arch. Belg.* 147.

Roth-Rubi K. and Sennhauser H. R. 1987. *Römische Straße und Gräber, Verenamünster Zurzach. Ausgrabungen und Bauuntersuchung 1*. Zürich.

Ruprechtsberger E.M. 1983. *Zum römerzeitlichen Gräberfeld von Lentia-Linz*. Linz: Linzer Arch. Forschungen, Sonderheft 5.

Schindler R. 1973. Das ummauerte Familiengrab der gallo-römischen Wüstung in Landscheid. *Trierer Zeitschrift* 36: 57–76.

Struck M. (ed.) 1993. *Römerzeitliche Gräber als Quellen zu Religion, Bevölkerungsstruktur und Sozialgeschichte*. Mainz: Archäologische Schriften des Instituts für Ur- und Frühgeschichte der Johannes Gutenberg-Universität Mainz, Vol. 3.

Struck M. 1993b. Busta in Britannien und ihre Verbindung zum Kontinent. Allgemeine Überlegungen zur Herleitung der Bestattungssitte. In Struck 1993, pp. 81–94.

Thill G. 1970. Ummauerter römischer Friedhof bei Lellig (1. Jahrhundert n. Chr.). *Hémecht* 22: 371–379.

Van Doorselaer A. 1967. *Les nécropoles gallo-romaines en Gaule septentrionale*. Brugge: Diss. Arch. Gandenses.

Van Doorselaer A. and Rogge M. 1985. Continuité d'un rite funéraire spécifique dans la vallée de l'Escaut de l'âge du fer au haut moyen âge. *Les Etudes Classiques* LIII: 153–170.

Vanvinckenroye W. 1967. *Gallo-romeinse grafvondsten uit Tongeren*. Tongres.

Wahl S. and Wahl J. 1983. Zur Technik der Leichenverbrennung. I. Verbrennungsplätze aus ethnologischen Quellen. *Archäologisches Korrespondenzblatt* 13: 513–520.

Wigg A. 1993. Zur Funktion und Deutung der *Aschengruben*. In Struck 1993, pp. 111–115.

Witteyer M. 1993. Die Ustrinen und Busta von Mainz-Weisenau. In Struck 1993, pp. 69–80.

4. Phoenix rising; aspects of cremation in Roman Britain

Jacqueline I. McKinley

Introduction

Cremation, as a mode of disposal of the dead, clearly represents a mortuary rite different, in at least some of its attendant beliefs, from those associated with the burial of an unburnt corpse. Whilst there would appear to be similarities between the two mortuary rites with respect to the rituals surrounding the act of *burial*, there are many indications that within the one rite the cremation itself was of primary significance. The two events, of cremation and subsequent burial, should not, though they frequently are, be considered or referred to as synonymous.

Most archaeologists tend to refer to cremation burials as 'cremations', which they are not. *The cremation* comprised the burning pyre with the corpse, or corpses, and any attendant artefacts and/or other offerings placed upon it. The common, though perhaps understandable 'short-hand' use of imprecise and potentially misleading terminology implicitly discards many hours of activity; preparation of the pyre and the corpse, the cremation, the collection and burial of the cremated remains and the subsequent clearing-up processes. All of these activities, to some degree, may potentially be deduced from the analysis of the archaeological remains.

As in all osteological analyses, the study of cremated bone serves to provide demographic and pathological data. An additional aim, however, should be to gain insights into aspects of pyre technology, and the rituals and rites attendant upon the funerary practice. To achieve these latter objectives, an understanding of the process of cremation is imperative if erroneous interpretations based on assumptions about what occurs are to be avoided. What is also clear is that any methodology must include detailed reference to the form and condition of the context from which the cremated remains were recovered. That is to say, the osteological analysis cannot be divorced from the excavation data and general archaeological analysis.

It is the intention of this paper to focus on three specific types of cremation-related deposits, and by using examples drawn from a number of Romano-British rural and urban cemeteries, to illustrate the potential for the recovery of data of a form which may increase our understanding of the whole mortuary practice of cremation, not just the burial.

Pyre Sites

The earliest identifiable stage of the cremation rite evident in the archaeological record is represented by the pyre site. Convincing evidence for these features in the Roman period in Britain is relatively scarce and predominantly includes sites with negative (i.e. below-ground) pyre-related features. Jessup (1959: 19) noted that pyre sites were recorded at several of the Romano-British walled cemeteries included in his survey. Unfortunately, some of the features were not described in the early antiquarian accounts, and the descriptions of others were either too subjective or inconclusive for interpretation of the features as pyre sites (see **Redeposited Pyre Debris**). Black (1986: 210–211) documented two cemeteries which had 'enclosed crematoria', Colchester and St Stephen's in St Albans. In the former, two tiled structures had evidence of burning in confined areas. At St Stephen's, Davey (1935) recorded three structures which contained 'vast quantities of wood and bone ash'; the structures comprised brick-lined pits and no cremated bone was recovered from the fills (Davey, *pers. comm.*). If these structures did comprise cremators it would be interesting to know how they functioned. Of the 15 sites listed by Philpott (1991: 48–49, figure 5) and Struck (1993: 92–3) where the excavators had recorded features interpreted as *busta*, i.e. pyre sites which also functioned as the place of burial, *c.* 67% had under-pyre pits (*Grubenbusta* – ibid.) and 27% were flat sites covered by a mound (*Flächenbusta* – ibid.), the remaining 6% were not classified.

By way of explanation for the apparent dearth of pyre sites in Roman Britain, Philpott has suggested that 'the great majority of cremations were carried out on pyres away from the final burial site' (1991: 8). This statement was made with specific reference to the 'south east of England' but no comment was made as to the probable situation in the rest of the country. Over the last decade or so much evidence has been collected to demonstrate that graves were frequently dug close to the pyre sites in much of Roman Britain. Contrary to Philpott's comment that 'pyre sweepings were not usually incorporated in the grave fill', pyre debris (see below) has frequently been recovered from cremation graves; for example from the Baldock – Area 15 cemetery 78% of the unurned burials and 16.5% of the urned burials had pyre debris in the grave fills (McKinley 1991), as did 50.5% of the burials from the St Stephen's cemetery in St Albans (Niblett *pers. comm.*, McKinley 1992) and 23% of the urned burials from the East London Cemeteries (McKinley 2000). The low number of known Romano-British pyre sites is probably related to more practical, or rather, technical reasons common to all periods in which the rite was used.

There may have been slight variations in form but all pyres would require fuel and needed to perform the same function; to provide a stable, body-sized support for the corpse and any pyre goods, to allow circulation of oxygen to facilitate combustion, and to accommodate enough fuel to give sufficient time and temperature for cremation to complete (McKinley 1994: 72–81). How much of the corpse needed to be burnt to comprise 'complete' cremation probably varied culturally (temporally and geographically), and there is certainly evidence from Roman Britain to suggest that full oxidation of the *bone* may not always have been considered necessary. For example, charred bone was recovered from several graves in the cemetery at Derby Racecourse (Philpott 1991: 48), whilst the remains of two partially cremated corpses (4110 and 4848) were excavated from the Baldock-Area 15 cemetery (McKinley 1991). In burial 4110 the leg (below the knee) and foot bones and the bones of the hands and forearm were fully cremated, the distal femurs (thigh bones) and humeri (upper arm bones), and parts of the skull were charred; the proximal femur and humeri and the axial skeleton were unburnt. This pattern of burning demonstrates that the bones with little soft tissue coverage had burnt, having been relatively quickly exposed to the fire, whilst there had been insufficient time for the soft tissues around those bones with a dense coverage to burn off and expose the bone to the effects of the fire. A large minority of black, blue and grey bone fragments are fairly frequently noted in Romano-British cremation burials (McKinley 2000), colour being a macroscopic indicator of the level of oxidation (Shipman *et al.* 1984, McKinley 1994: 75 and 77, Holden *et al.* 1995).

Anthropological (Dubois and Beauchamp 1943, Hiatt 1969, Wahl and Wahl 1983, *Stern* magazine 1975), historic (Schama 1987: plate 5) and archaeological (Holck 1986: figure 2) sources all indicate the use of a similar pyre structure over a wide temporal and geographical range, with slight variations only in detail. The majority of pyres appear to have been constructed directly on the ground surface. Minor variations include under-pyre scoops or pits to aid draught and posts at the corners presumably to help stabilise the structure. Deeper under-pyre pits (*Grubenbusta* – Struck 1993) appear confined

to the Roman period (certainly in Britain); the inferred technique in this instance being to let the pyre burn down into the pit then bury the remains *in situ*, i.e. the feature represented both pyre site and grave. This type appears to be that defined by Festus: '*Bustum propriae dicetur locus in quo mortuus est combustus et sepultus*' (*De significatu verborum*, W. M. Lindsay ed. 1913, 29, s.v. *bustum*; 'The place was properly said to be a tomb where the dead person had been cremated and buried...').

During cremation the pyre collapses gradually, down on to itself, there being little spread beyond the original limits, and the image left on the underlying surface presents a close plan of the structure. Throughout the process, the corpse remains in the same position relative to the pyre structure, i.e. above the wood. In the final stages, the cremated bone and charred soft tissues lie in correct anatomical position on the bed of wood ash. The shallow depth to which the effects of the pyre penetrate the ground have been demonstrated in experiment (*pers. obs.*) and is also illustrated by the 2–5cm thickness of burning noted by Topál (1981) in many of the *busta* excavated at Matrica.

This background evidence suggests that a basic archaeological requirement for a 'pyre site' would be evidence of *in situ* burning of a pyre-sized area, though the definition of 'pyre-sized' may be subject to numerous variables dependent, for example, on the size of the individual, the position of the body, the number of pyre goods included and availability of fuel. However, a pyre constructed on a flat ground surface obviously leaves ephemeral traces of its existence, easily eradicated by soil movement, plough damage or other disturbance. This 'fragility' is, to a large extent, probably responsible for the paucity of evidence for pyre sites in the archaeological record. It may be significant to note that, in Britain, known pyre sites have most frequently been observed below Bronze Age barrows, e.g. the ten from Wessex listed by Grinsell (1941) and, more recently, the several found at Linga Fold in Orkney by Downes (1995a, 1995b and in prep.); the sites being subject to preferential preservation in consequence of the protection offered by the mound.

The presence of a 'negative' pyre-related feature may indicate the location of a pyre site even where truncation has occurred. For example, several under-pyre draught-pits were recorded at the Iron Age cemetery of West-hampnett in West Sussex (Fitzpatrick 1997: figure 6). These features took a variety of forms including linear, 'T' or 'L' shaped and cruciform; all were relatively shallow, *c.* 0.10–0.20m, and around 1.50–2m in length.

There is growing evidence to suggest that pyre sites were often cleared of debris immediately or shortly after use (see **Redeposited Pyre Debris**), so there may be little or no fuel ash or other burnt material (including cremated bone not collected for burial) to support the identification of a possible pyre site. However, in some instances, e.g. in some of the Iron Age under-pyre draught-pits at Westhampnett (*ibid.*), matrices of fuel ash (including length of charred wood), fragments of burnt clay and often, though not always, cremated bone, were recovered. It is essential, however, to consider the relative distribution of the various archaeological components within such matrices to gain a proper understanding of the nature of the deposits and the formation processes involved. It should not be automatically assumed that large quantities of wood ash indicate a pyre site; there are other alternatives (see **Redeposited Pyre Debris**).

In view of the way in which a pyre collapses, an unmanipulated, *in situ* pyre site should demonstrate an ordered deposition of components. With the body placed in the upper part of the pyre, as most sources suggest it was and continues to be, the vast majority of the cremated bone should be on or close to the surface, above most of the fuel ash. In *Grubenbusta*, the relatively deep (>0.35m) under-pyre pits should contain large quantities of fuel ash within the lower levels since, unlike on flat pyre sites, the finer-fraction fuel ash would not blow away. This latter observation would also have an effect on the form of *Flächenbusta*, though the quantity of the finer-fraction wood ash recovered from these features would depend on the wind strength during and immediately after cremation and on how rapidly after cremation the mound was raised. Large fragments of charred logs would tend to remain in the *Grubenbusta*, as in the under-pyre draught-pits at Westhampnett (Fitzpatrick 1997), since in such relatively deep pits the oxygen supply needed to complete combustion would be curtailed.

A *bustum* burial, of either type, which had not suffered truncation, disturbance or some other form of manipulation, should contain the complete skeletal remains of the cremated individual, even if, as appears to have been the case in a few instances, some of the bone had been collected and placed in an urn before burial. The minimum weight of bone expected from an a (modern) adult cremation is *c.* 1000g (an elderly, gracile, female; McKinley 1993), though an average weight of *c.* 1600–2000g would be more common. Where there had been no separate collection of bone for inclusion in an urn, one would expect the cremated bone, to a large extent, to be lying above the fuel ash or at least in the upper levels of the fill, still roughly in anatomical order.

An experimental bustum cremation recently conducted by the writer (Birdoswald, Northumbria 1999; funded by *Time Team* for their seventh series), using an under-pyre pit of 1.0 × 0.7m, 0.5m deep and eight tiers of logs in the pyre construction, resulted in a variable depth of fuel ash within the pit from a maximum of *c.* 0.30m at the corners to a minimum of 0.10m in the centre. The sides and base of the pit – cut through a mid-brown natural of clayey silt – were burnt a salmon-pink, as was a margin of 0.08–0.60m around the top marking the outermost limits of the pyre structure represented by the base logs. The bone (sheep) was recovered from above or within the upper levels of the fuel ash.

Of those features from Romano-British sites denoted as *busta*, specifically *Grubenbusta* (Philpott 1991: 48–49, Struck 1993), the interpretation as pyre sites appears valid, there being clear evidence for *in situ* burning around the rim of many of the pits and they contain large quantities of charcoal. However their interpretation as *in situ* burials is not so conclusive. In the 10 such possible features from St Stephen's cemetery in St Albans examined by the writer (McKinley 1992) and one from the East London Cemeteries (McKinley 2000), the cremated bone was mixed throughout the fill with the fuel ash and only relatively small quantities were recovered, 98–410g from the former and 838g from the latter (which was disturbed). Although the latter may represent a disturbed *Grubenbustum,* the former do not. The same pattern of small amounts of bone mixed with the fuel ash also appears to be the case in many other examples of this type of feature recorded in Britain. Four of the supposed *Grubenbusta* from Petty Knowes, High Rochester (Charlton and Mitcheson 1984) contained no cremated bone at all (2, 6, 8 and 9) whilst the others appear to have contained very small quantities. Grave 1 contained 'minute fragments of heavily incinerated bone', grave 3 'small fragments of well-cremated bone', grave 4 'fragments of incinerated bone' and, although grave 5 contained 'much bone' the osteologist could not identify any of the fragments. Unfortunately no bone weights were recorded and the excavators' comments are rather subjective, but there was clearly nothing like the >1000g which would be expected within such a feature. At Minning Low (Philpott 1991: 40) the presence of 'grave goods' and 'much charred wood' was interpreted as a 'cremation *in situ*'. Records from 1846 and 1862 of masses of burnt material on the old ground surface surrounded by stones at Harley Hill (Marsden 1986: 46) led to similar interpretations. Various other sites appear to have qualified as *busta* on the basis of such criteria. The one description which appears convincing is that from Beckfoot (Philpott 1991: 48) where the 'discovery of a pyre with the bier *in situ* and calcined bones laying over the mass of charcoal suggest *in situ* cremation'... but again, there is no record of the quantity of bone recovered.

In general, the interpretation of these features in Britain seems to have ignored the quantity of cremated bone, sometimes appearing to assume (erroneously) that the small quantity of bone recovered was indicative of a highly efficient cremation. The position of the various archaeological components within the fill, including the cremated bone, has also received scant attention. Consideration of such factors are, however, imperative to the interpretation and further understanding of the formation processes associated with these features. What many of them actually appear to represent are pyre sites with some *in situ* debris, but from which most of the cremated bone was removed, presumably for burial or distribution elsewhere? (see below **Burial – Memorial?**).

Redeposited Pyre Debris

One form of cremation-related context which has not yet achieved full recognition, nor been exploited to its full potential, is redeposited pyre debris. Pyre debris is the material remaining at the end of cremation, including fragments of cremated human bone and pyre goods not collected to form part of the formal 'burial' within the grave. The predominant component of pyre debris is fuel ash, generally wood ash (including charcoal pieces) in Romano-British contexts, though coal was also recovered from Trentholme Drive, York (Wenham, 1968: 21). It may also include, depending on the associated soil type, burnt flint, burnt stone, burnt clay and fuel ash slag (a general hearth slag which forms in association with soils with a high silica content). The salient point is the mixed nature of the archaeological components. Even in graves which have pyre debris within the fills, the bone *collected for burial* tends not to be mixed with the other debris, but is generally observed in a concentration (possibly originally held in some form of organic container), usually, though not exclusively, towards or at the base of the grave. This is the case not only within the Romano-British period but also for the other phases in which the rite was practised.

All archaeological cremation burials, with the possible exception of some combined pyre site and grave features (*busta*, see above), are essentially token; rarely, if ever, were the entire cremated remains of an individual collected for burial. There is a very wide variation in the quantity of bone recovered from cremation burials; e.g. from >4000 of all periods examined by the writer, a range of 57–3000g of bone was recovered from undisturbed adult burials. On average, 40–60% of the expected bone weight was recovered (see above, McKinley 1993). Consequently, the recovery of large quantities of cremated bone from non-grave contexts is only to be expected. The fragments of cremated bone and pyre goods within redeposited pyre debris form an important and often substantial component of the cremated remains, in some instances representing larger quantities than were buried in the grave. For example, in the Migration period cemetery of Liebenau, where many of the graves were cut through the corresponding pyre site, Cosack (1983) observed that the vast majority of pyre goods were left on the pyre site rather than included in the grave. Recent work by Polfer (1993, this volume) has indicated a distinction between the type of goods *selected* from the pyre site for inclusion in the burial and those left amongst the pyre debris.

Redeposited pyre debris has been recovered from a variety of context types in the British Isles of all periods including; the backfills of cremation graves, over cremation graves, within pre-existent features, un-contained spreads, and in apparently deliberately excavated features (McKinley 1997a). It is usually found in the vicinity of a burial or within the confines of a cemetery, and its presence indicates the proximity of a pyre site, including those cases where all traces of the latter may have been eradicated.

1. in grave fills

Varying quantities of pyre debris have frequently been recovered from the backfills of Romano-British graves. An additional example to those illustrated above from Baldock, St Stephen's and East London (see **Pyre Sites**) would be all the grave fills from Low Borrowbridge (17 urned and 21 unurned; McKinley 1996a: 120). Ten of the 53 urned burials from Trentholme Drive, York (Wenham 1968: 27–28) had pyre debris, including fragments of pyre goods, in the backfills of the graves. The base and sides of the grave at Knobs Crook, Dorset were lined with charcoal (Fowler 1964). The presence of pyre debris in grave fills was also not uncommon elsewhere within the Roman period; for example Struck (1995a) records that 'remnants of the pyre' were frequently included in cremation graves from Raetia. It may be of significance that in the Baldock-Area 15 cemetery, a much greater percentage of the unurned (78%) as compared with the urned burials (16.5%) contained pyre debris (McKinley 1991).

2. in pre-existent features

The redeposition of pyre debris in pre-existent features has been observed in British cremation cemeteries of the Bronze Age (e.g. the barrow ditch at Twyford Down, McKinley 1997a: 138; McKinley in press), Iron Age (e.g. redundant under-pyre draught pits at Westhampnett, McKinley 1997b: 57 and 71) and Romano-British period. In one area of the East London Romano-British cemeteries, several redundant quarry pits were filled with redeposited pyre debris (Barber and Bowsher *pers. comm.*, McKinley 2000). There was a considerable range in the size of these deposits, from those representing the debris of a single cremation (128.3g bone), to the largest context which contained a total of 26,039.5g of cremated bone, representing the remains of a minimum of 19 individuals (McKinley 2000). Only about one-third of the latter context had survived as a result of medieval disturbance. Although only one possible pyre site was discovered within the East London cemeteries (see above), these dumps of pyre debris clearly demonstrate the close proximity of the pyre sites, which were located within specific areas of the cemetery (*ustrina* – the place in which cremation took place) and obviously cleared after cremation, presumably to facilitate re-use. A level of organisation is indicated, suggesting these cemeteries were run by professionals, rather than the cremation being conducted by the deceased's relatives/social circle as appears to have been the case in pre-Roman or smaller, rural cemeteries. Toynbee (1996: 45–46) discusses the range of professional personnel who may have been involved in various parts of Roman funeral arrangements, and it would seem likely that at least some semblance of that organisation reached the towns of Roman Britain.

3. in spreads

Spreads of redeposited pyre debris have been recorded from several Romano-British cremation cemeteries. There are also instances where redeposited pyre debris has been erroneously interpreted as the actual pyre site. For example, at Langley (Jessup 1959: 27) ...'a prominent layer two inches thick containing charcoal, ashes, burnt bones'...was recorded which ...'was thought to mark the site of the funeral pyres'. Whilst doubtless in the general vicinity, the absence of any indication of *in situ* burning or associated structure is indicative that the material was not *in situ*. It is worth noting here that both charcoal and cremated bone qualify as ashes; the Oxford English Dictionary gives the definition of 'ash' as the 'residue, chiefly earthy or mineral, left after combustion of any substance'. Unfortunately, the term 'ashes' is used somewhat indiscriminately to refer specifically to cremated bone or charcoal and to some unspecified type of ash. This makes interpretation of some excavation records rather difficult and inconclusive if one is trying to distinguish between burials with/without pyre debris and cremation-related deposits of any other sort.

One of the most substantial deposits of this type was excavated at Trentholme Drive, York (Wenham 1968: 21–26), spread over a radius of *c.* 10m to a maximum depth of *c.* 0.39m. The debris is described as comprising charred wood, fragments of cremated human and animal bone, coal and coal ash together with fragments of pyre goods. Unfortunately, there is no note of the quantity of cremated bone or charred wood, and there is no indication of the possible number of cremations from which the debris may have derived (the cremated bone from this context does not appear to have been subject to any osteological analysis).

Twenty-seven separate spreads of pyre debris were located around the northern edge of the Baldock Area 15 cemetery (Burleigh, *pers. comm.*), indicating the probable location of the pyre sites, though none were actually found (?plough damage). Each spread represented remains from a single cremation, with the weight of cremated bone recovered ranging from <1g to a maximum of 572.2g (McKinley 1991).

4. deliberately excavated features

Formal buried deposits of pyre debris have been identified from several Bronze Age cremation cemeteries in Britain (McKinley 1997a: 139). Similar features may also have existed in some Romano-British cemeteries. Jessup (1959: 7) records that at Holborough '...remains from the pyre were swept up and buried with scant attention in four different places'. The 'four places' comprised the grave and three 'ritual pits', the latter of which contained fragments of cremated human and animal bone, and pyre

goods, though there is no mention of any fuel ash. Such deliberate separation of pyre goods for burial in separate pits in this way hardly seems indicative of 'scant attention' but rather to signify great attention to ritual detail.

In the East London cemeteries, some pits containing redeposited pyre debris held as little as 6.2g of cremated bone, i.e. a maximum of 0.6% of the expected weight of bone from an adult cremation (McKinley 1993). The excavators recalled (Barber and Bowsher *pers. comm.*) that these very small quantities of bone were mixed in with the other debris. Although there was insufficient detail of the distribution of the archaeological components within the pits to be conclusive in interpretation, these features may represent deliberately redeposited pyre debris.

Burial or Memorial?

Why was all the bone remaining after cremation not collected for burial in the grave? It would not have been particularly difficult to recover, although perhaps time consuming (see **Pyre Sites** for position of cremated bone above wood ash). Clearly, the inclusion of all the cremated bone in the burial was not considered a pre-requisite; a 'random' selection of bone fragments from each skeletal area are generally found, and with one or two very rare exceptions (e.g. Wells 1981, Skeleton Green) there is no indication for deliberate selection of certain bones for burial.

Why was there such a large variation in the amount of bone placed in the graves, and what happened to the rest of it? The evidence presented above shows that much of the bone remaining at the end of cremation was simply left with the other pyre debris and 'discarded'. Furthermore, recent evidence from a Bronze Age site in Orkney suggests that cremated bone *collected* from the pyre site (i.e. not just left with the pyre debris) may not all have been included in the formal burial within the grave. Pyre debris was spread over the capstone of cist grave 5 at Linga Fold (Downes 1995a: 399, 1995b and in prep.), which had been cut through the cleared pyre site. That the bone from the pyre debris was from the same adult male as the bone in the grave was proven by joins between fragments (McKinley 1996b). However, it was clear that even combined the bone from the two contexts did not comprise what would have been the entire cremated remains: some had been removed, presumably for some other purpose. Was it used in some other ceremonial activity, was it scattered, or were fragments distributed amongst attendants at the funeral? There is evidence for the latter practice amongst Aboriginal Australians in the 19th century (Hiatt 1969).

Having established that the vast majority, if not all, cremation burials are essentially 'token', what is the threshold at which the quantity of bone becomes so small as to render the classification of a feature as a 'grave' – along with those containing a more 'representative' quantity of bone – unsuitable, and change the probable function of the feature to that of a 'memorial' or 'cenotaph'?

Grave-like features, some of which contained 'grave goods' (as distinct from pyre goods) and varying quantities of pyre debris, and from which either very small quantities (often >10g) or no cremated bone was recovered, have been identified within some late Iron Age and Romano-British cemeteries. Some of these features may have represented formal deposits of pyre debris but in others, particularly those which had 'grave goods', what little bone they did contain was noted to be present in 'a concentration' (though how concentrated <10g of bone can be may be open to debate).

Six features within the late Iron Age cemetery at Westhampnett, West Sussex were denoted as possible 'memorials' by the writer (McKinley 1997b: 71–72), all contained <30g of cremated bone, most <10g. Thirteen other features referred to as 'grave cuts' by the excavators contained no bone at all. The well-furnished 'Welwyn'-type 'burial' from Baldock -The Tene (Stead and Rigby 1986: 53) contained only 10.5g of cremated bone, mostly comprising bear phalanges; the report gives no indication of the identification of human bone. There was some slight disturbance to the feature prior to excavation, but it would be rather odd if the bronze, wood, cremated and unburnt animal bones were to have survived whilst all the cremated human bone was lost. At Hertford Heath, another 'Welwyn'-type 'burial', the grave, also disturbed prior to excavation, contained only 7.5g of cremated bone (Hüssen 1983: 45). At King Harry Lane (Stirland 1989) 29 burials were noted as comprising only small bone fragments of <25g in weight. Features devoid of human bone have also been found in Iron Age cemeteries in France and are referred to as 'cenotaphes' by Flouest (1993: 204).

Similar features have been noted within several Romano-British cemeteries. Philpott (1991: 19–20) notes the find of a group of 'grave goods' near the Roman fort at Camelon, Stirlingshire which 'probably represents a cremation burial... although no cremated bone was recovered'. At St Stephen's cemetery, St Albans, two undisturbed 'burials' with grave goods (145 and 261) had little (0.4g) or no bone respectively (McKinley 1992), and only 14 of the 'burials' from Low Borrowbridge held >50g of bone (McKinley 1996a: 119–121).

That such features were related to the ritual deposition of the dead is not in question, but their role in that ritual needs to be considered more carefully rather than simply assuming they qualify as 'burials' in the same way as any other. Since graves are often classified depending on the quantity and quality of their associated artefacts it seems somewhat absurd that the extreme paucity or even absence of human remains should not be considered of more consequence.

What was the role of human remains in the various features that are referred to as 'burials'? Cremation is a process of transformation of the physical remains of the deceased, and beliefs frequently link it with the freeing of

the spirit from its earthly bonds. If this were so, the physical remains may have been viewed as 'empty' once devoid of the spirit. Alternatively, a direct link, in the form of the physical remains of the individual being remembered, may not have been seen as a necessary inclusion within a memorial or offering to the dead. Whatever the interpretation, the implication is that there was more than one type of ritual deposit, perhaps viewed as one *of* and one *to* the dead.

Toynbee (1996: 54) notes the use of cenotaphs 'if a person's body was not available for burial' or 'for some person whose remains were buried elsewhere'. Wheeler (1985) suggested that some of the roadside tombs from Derby may have been 'memorials for people whose remains were lost or interred elsewhere'. Wenham (1968: 25) presents Herodian's account of the cremation of the Emperor Septimius Severus in York in A.D. 211. Although the Emperor was cremated in Britain, and the remains of his pyre site and even debris from the pyre may remain somewhere in York, the burial took place elsewhere: 'Afterwards the bones were put in a porphyry urn and carried to Rome and placed in the tomb of the Antonines'. Is it possible that a similar practice may have been afforded to lesser mortals, perhaps to those soldiers serving away from home and unfortunate enough to die whilst away? This may explain the paucity of bone in burials, including those interpreted as *busta* (see **Pyre Sites**), within some of the northern frontier Forts, particularly since the *busta* are seen as 'foreign' imports (Struck 1995a, 1995b) and the 'immigrants' to Britain chiefly comprised soldiers (Struck 1993).

Bibliography

Alcock, J.P. 1980. Classical religious beliefs and burial practice in Roman Britain. *Arch. J.* 137: 50–85

Black, E.W. 1986. Romano-British burial customs and religious beliefs in south-east England. *Arch. J.* 143: 201–239

Charlton, B. and Mitcheson, M. 1984. The Roman cemetery at Petty Knowes, Rochester, Northumberland. *Archaeologia Aeliana* 5 (12): 1–31

Cosack, E. 1983. *Das sachsische Gräberfeld bei Liebenau.* Teil. 1. Berlin: Gebr. Mann

Davey, N. 1935. The Romano-British cemetery at St Stephen's, near Verulamium. *Trans. St Albans and Hertfordshire Architectural and Archaeological Society* 4: 243–275.

Downes, J. 1995a. Linga Fold. *Current Archaeology* 142: 396–399

Downes, J. 1995b. Linga Fold, Sandwick, Orkney; Excavation of a Bronze age barrow cemetery 1994. GUARD 59.2 Glasgow University.

Downes, J. in prep. The excavation of a Bronze Age barrow cemetery at Linga Fold, Lyling, Orkney.

Dubois, J.A. and Beauchamp, H.R. 1943. *Hindu manners, customs and ceremonies.* Oxford: Clarendon

Fitzpatrick, A.P. 1997. *Westhampnett, West Sussex, Volume 2: The Iron Age, Romano-British and Anglo-Saxon Cemeteries excavated in 1992.* Wessex Archaeology Reports 12, Salisbury: Trust for Wessex Archaeology.

Flouest, J.-L., 1993. L'organisation interne des tombes à incinération du IIème au Ier siècle av. J.-C. Essai de description méthodique.

In Cliquet, D., Remy-Watte, Guichard, V. and Vaginay, M. (eds.) *Les Celtes en Normandie. Les Rites Funéraires en Gaule (IIIème au Ier siècle avant J.-C.). Actes du 14ème colloque de l'Association Française pour l'Etude de l'Age du Fer, Evreux – mai 1990*. Revue Archéologique de l'Ouest Supplément 6. Rennes, pp. 201–9

Fowler, P. J. 1964. A Roman barrow at Knob's Crook, Woodlands, Dorset and a reconsideration of the evidence for Roman barrows in Wessex. *Antiquaries Journal* 45: 22–53

Grinsell, L.V. 1941. The Bronze Age round barrows of Wessex. *PPS* 7(3): 73–113

Hiatt, B. 1969. Cremation in Aboriginal Australia. *Mankind* 7(2): 104–115

Holck, P. 1986. *Cremated bones: A medical-anthropological study of an archaeological material on cremation burials*. Anthropologiske skrifter 1, Oslo: Anatomisk Institutt – University of Oslo.

Holden, J.L., Phakey, P.P. and Clement, J.G. 1995. Scanning electron microscope observations of incinerated human femoral bone: a case study. *Forensic Science International* 74: 17–28

Hüssen, C.M. 1983. *A Rich Late La Tène Burial at Hertford Heath, Hertfordshire*. British Museum Occ. Papers 44, London: British Museum.

Jessup, R.F. 1959. Barrows and walled cemeteries in Roman Britain. *J. British Archaeological Association* 22: 1–32.

Marsden. B.M. 1986. *The Burial Mounds of Derbyshire*. (Revised edition) Bradford/Ilkley.

McKinley, J.I. 1991. Cremated Bone from the Area 15 cemetery, Baldock, Hertfordshire. Unpublished report for Letchworth Museum.

McKinley, J.I. 1992. Cremation and inhumation burials from St Stephen's cemetery, St Albans. Unpublished report for R. Niblett, Verulanium Museum.

McKinley, J.I. 1993. Bone fragment size and weights of bone from modern British cremations and its implications for the interpretation of archaeological cremations. *International J. Osteoarchaeology* 3: 283–287

McKinley, J.I. 1994. *The Anglo-Saxon cemetery at Spong Hill, North Elmham Part VIII: The Cremations*. East Anglian Archaeology 69, Gressenhall: Norfolk Archaeological Unit.

McKinley 1996a. The cremated human bone. In Lambert, J. (ed.) *Transect through time: the archaeological landscape of the Shell north-western ethylene pipeline*. Lancaster: Lancaster University Archaeological Institute, pp. 118–121

McKinley, J.I. 1996b. Linga Fold, Sandwick, Orkney: Human Bone, pyre technology and ritual Unpublished report for GUARD.

McKinley, J.I. 1997a. Bronze Age 'Barrows' and Funerary Rites and Rituals of Cremation. *PPS* 63: 129–145

McKinley, J.I. 1997b. The cremated human bone from burials and cremation-related contexts. In Fitzpatrick, A.P. pp. 55–72, 244–252

McKinley, J.I. in press. Human Bone and Funerary Deposits. In Walker, K.E. and Farwell, D.E. *M3 Bar End to Compton: Archaeological Investigations on Twyford Down*. Hampshire Field Club Monograph, 9, pp. 85–117.

McKinley, J.I. 2000. Chapters 3 'Funerary Practice' and 7 'Cremated Bone', in Barber B. and Bowsher, D. *The Eastern Cemetery of Roman London: Excavations 1983–1990*. MOLAS Mono. 4, pp. 60–81, 360–65.

Philpott, R. 1991. Burial Practices in Roman Britain. *BAR* (British Series) 219.

Polfer, M. 1993. La nécropole gallo-romaine de Septfontaines-Dëckt (Grand-Duché de Luxembourg) et son *ustrinum* central: analyse comparative du matériel archéologique. In Ferdière, A. (ed.) *Monde des morts, monde des vivants en Gaule rurale Actes des colloque AGER/ARCHEA*, Tours: FERACF, pp. 173–176

Schama, S. 1987. *The Embarrassment of Riches* London: Fontana

Shipman, P., Forster, G. and Schoeninger, M. 1984. Burnt bones and teeth, an experimental study of colour, morphology, crystal structure and shrinkage. *J.Arch.Sci.* 11: 307–325.

Stead, I.M. and Rigby, V. 1986. *Baldock: The excavation of a Roman and Pre-Roman settlement, 1968–72*. Britannia Monograph Series 7, London: Society for the Promotion of Roman Studies.

Stern magazine 1975. Berlin

Stirland, A. 1989. The cremations from the Iron Age cemetery. In Stead, I.M. and Rigby, V. *Verulamium: the King Harry Lane site*. English Heritage Arch. Report 12, London: English Heritage, pp. 240–49

Struck, M. 1993. *Busta* in Britannien und ihre Verbindungen zum Kontinent. Allgemeine Überlegungen zur Herleitung der Bestattungssittte. In Struck, M. (ed.) *Römerzeitliche Gräber als Quellen zu Religion Bevölkerungsstruktur und Sozialgeschichte*. Archäologische Schriften des Instituts für Vor-und Frühgeschichte der Johannes Gutenberg-Universität Mainz. Band 3, pp.81–93

Struck, M. 1995a. Analysis of social and cultural diversity on rural burial sites in North-Eastern Raetia. In Rush, P. (ed.) *Theoretical Roman Archaeology: second conference proceedings*. Aldershot: Avebury , pp. 70–80

Struck, M. 1995b. Integration and continuity in funerary ideology. In Metzler, J., Millett, M., Roymans, N. and Slofstra, J. (eds.) *Integration in the early Roman west*. Dossiers d'Archéologie du Musée National d'Histoire et d'Art 4, Luxembourg: Musée National, pp. 139–150

Topál, J. 1981. *The Southern Cemetery of Matrica* (Szazhalombatta-Dunafured) Fontes Archaeologicae Hungaricae, Budapest: Akademiai Kiado.

Toynbee, J.M.C. 1996. *Death and Burial in the Roman World*. Baltimore / London: Johns Hopkins University Press.

Wahl, J and Wahl, S. 1983 Zur Technik der Leichenverbrennung: I. Verbrennungsplätze aus ethnologischen Quellen. *Archäologisches Korrespondenzblatt* 13: 513–520

Wells, C. 1981. Report on three series of Romano-British cremations and four inhumations from Skeleton Green. In Partridge, C. *Skeleton Green: a late Iron Age and Romano-British site*. Britannia Monograph series 2, London: Society for the Promotion of Roman Studies, pp. 283–303.

Wenham, L.P. 1968. *The Romano-British cemetery at Trentholme Drive. York*. London: HMSO.

Wheeler, H. 1985. The Racecourse cemetery. In Dool, J. Wheeler, H. *et al*. Roman Derby: Excavations 1968–1983. *Derbyshire Archaeological J.* 105: 222–80.

5. Functional and conceptual archaeobotanical data from Roman cremations

Angela Kreuz

The centuries immediately before and after the birth of Christ seem to have been a time of substantial cultural and ecological change. To get a complete picture of the nature of the interaction between native customs and those introduced by the Roman empire not only data from civil and military settlements but also from cemeteries can be considered. As part of the research programme 'Kelten, Germanen, Römer im Mittelgebirgsraum zwischen Luxemburg und Thüringen. Archäologische und naturwissenschaftliche Forschungen zum Kulturwandel unter der Einwirkung Roms in den Jahrhunderten um Christi Geburt' (known as the 'Romanisierungsprojekt', of which this is publication 28), supported by the Deutsche Forschungsgemeinschaft (DFG), investigations of botanical macroremains from Roman cemeteries are being conducted to analyse the degree of change.

It is very likely that the individual persons buried in graves belonged to a local population. Their ethnic affiliation, i.e. whether Celtic or Germanic, is however unknown and is therefore the subject of archaeological research. For this reason archaeobotanical investigations can only provide a general contribution to the question of change in burial rites.

Theoretical and methodological aspects must first of all be considered. How did plant remains arrive in graves and how can we interpret the plant assemblages found? In this context it is important to differentiate between *bustum* graves (Fig. 5.1), where the cremation has taken place *in situ* in or above a grave pit, and other burial forms, ritual pits etc., where for example ashes and other remnants are collected from burnt-down pyres and later deposited in the ground in pits or in wooden and other containers. In the first case there is a possibility of recovering almost all the plant material charred during cremation, as long as the *bustum* remained undisturbed later. In the second case an anthropogenic selection of the material has very probably taken place.

Another important differentiation is that between primary and secondary grave goods (for example Struck 1993a): outside water-logged sites only charred plant remains and in rare cases mineralised material can be expected. Therefore all the secondary botanical grave goods which did not come into contact with the fire could not be charred and therefore have left no trace. That is why we always recover only part of the botanical material involved in the burial rite and – worse – an unknown fraction of the original. The degree of what might be missing was shown for example by the finds of water-logged wicker-baskets filled with whole fruits at the site of Les Martres-de-Veyre (Audollent 1922, cited in Marinval 1993: 48).

Apart from the charcoal, the plant remains from graves could have been deposited for example as a sacrifice to the gods, as remains of the funerary feast, or as food for the deceased (belief in an immortal soul). In most cases this cannot be reconstructed. In this article these different things are generally called grave goods.

To answer the question of whether botanical macroremains from graves can give a clue to culturally induced changes of rites we can use Härke's and others' differentiation between 'functional' and 'conceptual' data (Fig. 5.2;

Fig. 5.1 *During the burning of the pyre the vegetation and, if ripe, seeds and fruits from the surrounding area can char from the heat of the fire. In the case of a* bustum *the plant remains fall into the grave pit together with the other remains of the pyre (from Kreuz 1995a: 112, fig. 3, after Bechert 1980).*

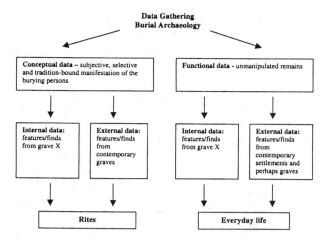

Fig. 5.2 *Structural differentiation of data from graves and related features (after Härke 1993; explanation in the text).*

Härke 1993 with further references). 'Conceptual' data are those which correspond with the subjective and probably tradition-bound actions of the persons carrying out the burial. 'Functional' data however are un-manipulated remains and therefore can represent everyday life. It is not possible to apply the conceptual data directly to the context of everyday life as they reflect the specific ideas of the participants in the rite. These ideas are only a part of daily reality, and it is very difficult to understand their meaning. The differentiation of the botanical data according to their inherent characteristics, their origin and their purpose is theoretically very important, but difficult to achieve in practice.

In Central Europe the investigation of plant remains from burial sites is very much in its infancy. At present there are about 46 (published) sites investigated archaeo-botanically, most of them situated to the west of the river Rhine (for references for 43 sites see Kreuz 1995a and b, in addition: Gale 1997: 77, 83 and 253; Jacomet and Bavaud 1992; König 1995; Petrucci-Bavaud 1996: 253ff.; Wigg 1993: 102 and 159). Further archaeobotanical research into ritual deposits has been done in England, for example by W. Carruthers, P. Murphy and V. Straker but is not yet fully published. Several hundred samples from two further burial sites (Wölfersheim-Wohnbach 'Am Kieselberg', Niedermörlen 'Am Grabstein') from the Wetterau landscape north of Frankfurt (Hesse) are being currently investigated by the author in the context of the 'Romanisierungsprojekt' (see also Rupp and Lindenthal 1995).

To make the botanical evidence from the 46 sites more easily comprehensible the species found have been arranged into groups of plant remains (Table 5.1). The cereals include wheat species (*Triticum* spec.), barley (*Hordeum* spec.), rye (*Secale cereale*), millets (*Panicum miliaceum, Seataria italica*) and oats (*Avena* cf. *sativa*). The recovery of stalks as well as grains might indicate

that cereals were sometimes deposited as bunches. The second group, the remains of pastries and bread, are in most cases very difficult to differentiate from the remains of fruit flesh. The pulses include lentils (*Lens culinaris*), peas (*Pisum sativum*), Celtic bean (*Vicia faba*) and bitter vetch (*Vicia ervilia*) and the oil-plants gold-of-pleasure (*Camelina sativa*), poppy (*Papaver somniferum*) and flax or linseed (*Linum usitatissimum*). Wild fruits and nuts include raspberry (*Rubus idaeus*), hazel (*Corylus avellana*), sloe (*Prunus spinosa*) and others. Fruits and nuts cultivated in the garden comprise vines (*Vitis vinifera*), walnut (*Juglans regia*) and plum (*Prunus insitita* ssp. *insitita*). Imported plants includes olive (*Olea europaea*) and stone-pine (*Pinus pinea*). There is also the group of spices, magical and medicinal plants, for example vervain (*Verbena officinalis*) or coriander (*Coriandrum sativum*), weeds, ruderals and meadow species like corn-cockle (*Agrostemma githago*), rocket (*Sisymbrium* spec.), dandelion (*Taraxacum* cf. *officinale*) or grasses (for example *Phleum pratense*). Wood and charcoal have also been identified. Finally there are other organic remains, such as fragments of textiles, possibly from the corpse's clothes or the wrappings of grave goods.

Most of these groups could represent conceptual data, as they were probably added to the cremation intentionally. There are however two groups for which this is rather unlikely, the weeds and the ruderal plants. The weed seeds could have arrived in the burial with the crop plants, so it is interesting to compare the weed species with those from adjacent settlements.

More interesting for the reconstruction of the burial rite itself are the ruderals and meadow plants. Ruderal plants grow on nitrogen- and nutrient-rich soils, such as those found at the edges of settlements, on rubbish dumps, beside paths or roads and so on. During the burning of the pyre the vegetation in the surrounding area can be disturbed and even charred by the heat of the fire. Thus plant remains – like seeds and fruits – from the vegetation

Table 5.1 *Groups of charred plant remains from 46 Roman burial sites (references in the text). The frequency is the percentage of the 46 sites where a certain species-group has been found.*

Groups of plant remains	Frequency (%)	Number of sites (n = 46)
cereals	47.8	22
pastries and bread (/fruit)	13	6
pulses	37	17
oil-plants	6.5	3
wild fruits and nuts	41.3	19
cultivated fruits and nuts	**50**	**23**
imported plants	**45.7**	**21**
spices, magic and medicinal plants	8.7	4
weeds	21.7	10
ruderals/meadow species	21.7	10
wood/charcoal	100	46
other (textiles etc.)	6.5	3

on the cremation site can char. They might fall into the grave pit together with the other pyre remains, in the case of a *bustum* (Fig. 5.1), or they can be collected later with the other pyre remnants and placed in a pit. That is why the finds of such plant species tell us something about the vegetation at the place where the cremation took place. Roman cremation sites seem not always to have been as clean and well cared-for as modern cemeteries.

Furthermore the months during the year when the fruits and seeds, for example, of ruderal, meadow and wild species found in graves and adjacent features ripen can be of interest. Sometimes this hints at which season a body was cremated, for example at Okarben 'Nordweg' (Hesse) (Kreuz 1995a: 117) or Augusta Raurica (Switzerland) (Petrucci-Bavaud 1996: 255). The finds of weeds, ruderals and meadow plants are examples of functional data, un-manipulated remains which can therefore more directly represent – along with the burial rite – everyday life. Another example of such data could be the physical anthropological data.

The groups of cereals, pulses and wild-growing fruits and nuts belong to the regular deliberately deposited grave goods in Roman burials (conceptual data). They have been found in more than 40% of investigated Roman sites (Table 5.1). Oil plants are rather rare – only 6.5% of the 46 sites – which might be due to their lesser chances of preservation. The cereals, pulses, oil plants and wild fruits and nuts are groups of remains which also occur in archaeological features on Celtic and Germanic settlements (Kreuz 1995c; 1999; van Zeist *et al.* 1991). Therefore they are no indicator for a change in burial customs due to Roman influence but rather represent a continuity of rites.

In more than 50% of the cemeteries or graves investigated archaeobotanically (Table 5.1) we have evidence for garden plants, such as peach (*Prunus persica*), garlic (*Allium sativum*) or chestnut (*Castanea sativa*) and/or evidence for imported plants such as date (*Phoenix dactylifera*), olive (*Olea europaea*) or stone-pine (*Pinus pinea*). As these two groups of plant species – the garden plants and the imported plants – have not so far been found on settlement sites north of the Alps before the Roman conquest (for references see above), they do not belong to a pre-Roman tradition, and therefore can be interpreted as indicators of a discontinuity in dietary customs and burial rites. The same holds true for imported animals as grave goods, indicated by zoological finds, for example of pheasant (Kunter 1996: 238).

It is striking however, that exotic species are quite frequent but do not appear in every grave investigated archaeobotanically. For example at the two sites investigated in the Wetterau landscape contemporary graves both with and without exotic plant species exist alongside each other (Kreuz, unpublished data). What could be the reason for the lack of such 'Roman' species be? Of course it is problematic to use negative evidence as a basis for interpretation: if certain plant species are lacking, this might be due for example to the status of the deceased, the season of the year, the location of the settlement, preservation conditions or sample size, and need not be the expression of the non-Romanized dietary customs of the deceased or the bereaved.

However, as such garden plants often have fruits with large stones, nutshells or pips they have an above-average chance of being seen during excavation in the field and especially in the laboratory. If they were primary goods their chance of getting charred were likewise very good, as stones or pips are often lignified. For both reasons therefore they have a relatively good chance of being detected, and it is not very probable that their lack is always due to methodological reasons.

Furthermore no connection can so far be detected between the presence or absence of such botanical finds and either region, the date of burial or the amount of archaeological finds in the graves concerned (Kreuz 1995a and b; Petrucci-Bavaud 1996: e.g. fig. 35). As mentioned already graves without exotic plant remains co-exist with graves containing such species at the same graveyard in the same period.

Doubtless there need not be a direct relationship between the botanical grave goods and the economic situation of the deceased individual, as the bereaved community can have reasons to select or to refuse. At the other extreme the community can also demonstrate a wealth which does not correspond with the real prosperity of the person buried during their lifetime. However, we have no evidence that the existence or absence of such exotic species relates to the wealth of the deceased person. On the contrary we know of rich grave monuments, for example at Augst (Jacomet 1986) or the tumulus of Büchel (Piening 1986), where botanical samples revealed large amounts of usual crop plant species and no Roman imports. This cannot be explained by the season of burial, as many of the exotic species like date (*Phoenix dactylifera*), fig (*Ficus carica*), chestnut (*Castanea sativa*), garlic (*Allium sativum*) and others were available in dried form the whole year round. For all these reasons it cannot be excluded that imported and garden plant species given as grave goods represent 'Romanised' dietary customs of the bereaved community or the deceased person.

The wood species used for the cremation might also give clues to the rites (conceptual data). Most of the charcoal found in graves and related features is likely to derive from firewood for the pyre. However sometimes we find the remains of wooden objects. As an example some preliminary results of charcoal identification from two cemeteries are presented (Table 5.2 and Fig. 5.3). The identification of the charcoal was carried out by N. Boenke with the financial support of the Deutsche Forschungsgemeinschaft. 9,399 pieces of charcoal from 58 samples from 24 features/graves were analysed. The two sites concerned, Wölfersheim-Wohnbach 'Am Kieselberg' and Niedermörlen 'Am Grabstein', are dated to the mid second century AD (V. Rupp/J. Lindenthal

	Augst	Reinach	Bern	Biberist	Avenches	Wederath	Siesbach	Vorst	Wölfersheim	Niedermörlen	A27
Fagus sylvatica, beech	dom.	+	dom.	+	dom.	dom.	+	dom.	dom.	+	
Quercus spec., oak	+				+		+	frequ.	+	dom.	dom.
Acer spec., maple					+				+	+	+
Alnus cf. *glutinosa*, alder								+	+		
Betula pend. /pubesc., birch								+	+	+	+
Buxus sempervirens, box									+		
Carpinus betulus, hornbeam								+	+	+	
Corylus avellana, hazel								+			+
Fraxinus excelsior, ash								+			+
Pomoideae									+		+
Populus spec., poplar					+				+		
Prunus spec.	+										+
Rosa spec., rose											+
Salix spec., willow								+			
Salix /Populus	+										
Abies alba, fir	+				+				+		
Picea abies, spruce					+						
Pinus cf. *sylvestris*, pine								+	+		
other						+					

Table 5.2 *Wood species identified as charcoal from Roman burial sites (references in the text;* dom. *dominant,* frequ. *frequent,* + *present).*

pers. comm.; see also Rupp and Lindenthal 1995) and both are situated in a loess landscape (the Wetterau, Hesse). The distance between them is not more than a few kilometres.

Figure 5.3 shows the percentages of the weight of charcoal species per grave at the two sites. It makes no sense to use the percentages of the number of charcoal-pieces, as their number might be the result of recovery method (for example breakage during wet sieving). The most frequent wood species are beech (*Fagus sylvatica*; horizontal dashes), and oak (*Quercus spec.*; black with white dots). The other species – maple (*Acer* cf. *campestre*), alder (*Alnus glutinosa*), birch (*Betula pendula/pubescens*), box (*Buxus sempervirens*), hornbeam (*Carpinus betulus*), Pomoideae, fir (*Abies alba*) and pine (*Pinus* cf. *sylvestris*)- appear in small quantities only. As *Abies* (and *Buxus*?) probably did not grow naturally in Hesse at the time, it is likely that they belonged to wooden objects and not to the firewood.

It is striking that oak is the dominant species in most graves at Niedermörlen, but only in less than half of the graves at Wölfersheim. There beech seems to be the favourite firewood for cremation. There are two further sites in Hessen where the charcoal has been investigated by the author, and there oak was also dominant (Kreuz 1995a). Unfortunately in these latter cases the botanical material was not representative for the graves or features as a whole. For comparison we can take external data from four contemporary settlement sites, where oak is the dominant contemporary firewood-species (unpubl. data). It cannot be excluded that the use of beech as firewood is

something exceptional for the Wetterau landscape at that time.

There are only a few other sites where the charcoal in cremations has been investigated and where there is data for comparison. In Switzerland relevant sites are Augst, Reinach Brüel and Bern-Engehalbinsel (references in Haeffelé 1996: 260), Avenches (Castella and Flutsch 1989: 276) and Biberist (Schucany 1995: 145), in Germany Wederath-Belginum (Haffner pers. comm.), Siesbach (Wigg 1993: 102) and Tönisvorst-Vorst (Tegtmeier 1996), in England the A27 Westhampnett Bypass (Gale 1997: 77 and 253). At most of these sites beech is the dominant wood species (Table 5.2).

Certainly oak *or* beech were the most suitable wood species as fire-wood for cremations. In general the choice of a certain species might have been influenced by the availability of the wood in the surrounding woodland or the access to such woodland, technical aspects (for example ease of chopping), heat potential of the wood (for the characteristics of fire wood species see for example Ebert 1981, Gayer 1954, Kreuz 1988).

As for conceptual aspects, the symbolic meaning of the firewood and other plant species within the rites can be considered. Trees have been described as the residence of gods and wreathes made from their leaves to honour people for gallantry (in the field) or success in competition (for example Pliny the Elder, cited in Lenz 1859: 155ff., 189, 191, 399; Martin-Kilcher this volume). Tacitus wrote of the Germans that the bodies of famous men were burned with particular kinds of wood (*Germania* 27). In addition it is possible that particular tree or shrub species rep-

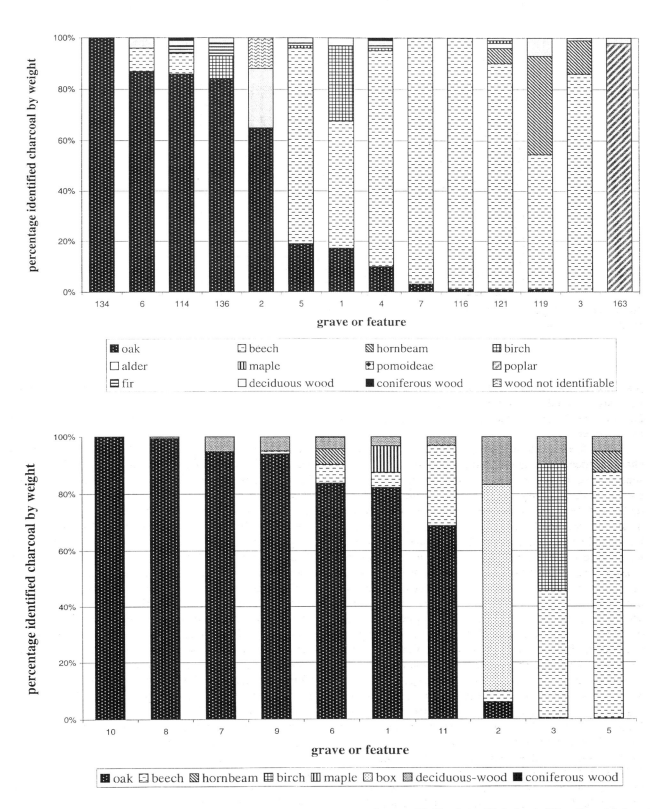

Fig. 5.3 *Percentages of the weight of charcoal species per grave at the sites Wölfersheim-Wohnbach 'Kieselberg' (above) and Niedermörlen 'Am Grabstein' (below). Explanations in the text.*

resented special characteristics, such as strength, longevity or tenacity. As different practices of burial co-existed in the same cemeteries in the Roman period (for example Bechert 1980, Fasold 1992, Haffner 1989, Struck 1993b), differentiated religious beliefs can be expected which might be expressed in the use of certain wood species and the deposition of certain plant species as primary goods on the pyre.

From the written sources it is known that for example poppy (*Papaver somniferum*) was the bringer of sleep and death, the flowers of the Celtic bean (*Vicia faba*) were a symbol of death and their seeds were eaten during the funerary feast (Körber-Grohne 1988: 127 and 401; Pliny the Elder, in Lenz 1859: 184). Furthermore, it cannot be ruled out that dates, *Phoenix dactylifera*, for example, were a symbol of reincarnation, like the holy bird of the same name. The evergreen stone-pine, *Pinus pinea*, was probably also a symbol of immortality. Pine cones are often shown on gravestones and monuments (Wigg this volume). At this point we quickly pass from interpretation to pure speculation, so we must await additional botanical and other results before offering further interpretation.

In future more attention needs to be paid to intra-site spatial variation of plant remains in different kinds of features. A more solid data base must be obtained by routinely sieving the entire contents of graves and other ritual features excavated, with a sieve of at least a 1mm mesh (0.5mm is better). For an interpretation of the primary botanical grave goods it seems necessary to sieve the entire contents of the graves and other ritual features. To assess the presence or absence of plant remains, at the very least all plant remains *preserved* should have the same chance of being recovered from the samples.

The investigation of botanical remains from burial sites is therefore very much at an early stage. For this reason this paper had to pose more questions concerning the interpretation of botanical finds than provide answers. However it is hoped that the potential contribution of archaeobotanical investigations to the reconstruction of burial rites in the Roman period has been well demonstrated.

Acknowledgements

I would like to thank D. Wigg, Frankfurt/M., for improving the English.

Bibliography

Audollent, A. 1922. Les tombes gallo-romaines à inhumation des Martres-de-Veyre. *Mémoires présentés par divers savants à l'Academie des Inscriptions et Belles lettres*, 13: 275–328.

Bechert, T. 1980. Zur Terminologie römischer Brandbestattungen. *Arch. Korrbl.* 10: 253–258.

Castella, D., Flutsch, L. 1989. La nécropole romaine d'Avenches VD-En Chaplix. Premiers résultats. *Jahrb. Schweiz. Ges. Ur- u. Frühgesch.* 72: 272–280.

Ebert, H.-P. 1981. *Mit Holz richtig heizen in Ofen, Herd und Kamin*. Ravensburg.

Fasold, P. 1992. *Römischer Grabbrauch in Süddeutschland*. Schriften des Limesmuseums Aalen 46.

Gale, R. 1997. Charcoal. In *Archaeological excavations on the route of the A27 Westhampnett Bypass, West Sussex, 1992* (ed. A.P. Fitzpatrick). Wessex Archaeology Report No. 12: 77ff. and 253.

Gayer, S. 1954. *Die Holzarten und ihre Verwendung in der Technik*. Leipzig.

Haeffelé, C. 1996. Die römischen Gräber an der Rheinstraße 46 des Nordwestgräberfeldes von Augusta Raurica. *Jahresberichte aus Augst und Kaiseraugst* 17: 217–310.

Haffner, A. 1989. *Gräber – Spiegel des Lebens. Zum Totenbrauchtum der Kelten und Römer am Beispiel des Treverer-Gräberfeldes Wederath-Belginum*. Trier.

Härke, H. 1993. Intentionale und funktionale Daten. Ein Beitrag zur Theorie und Methodik der Gräberarchäologie. *Arch. Korrbl.* 23: 141–146.

Jacomet, S. (unter Mitarbeit von M. Dick) 1986. Verkohlte Pflanzenreste aus einem römischen Grabmonument beim Augster Osttor (1966). *Jahresber. Augst u. Kaiseraugst* 6: 7–53.

Jacomet, S. and Bavaud, M. 1992. Verkohlte Pflanzenreste aus dem Bereich des Grabmonumentes ('Rundbau') beim Osttor von Augusta Raurica: Ergebnisse der Nachgrabungen von 1991. *Jahresberichte aus Augst und Kaiseraugst* 13: 103–111.

König, M. 1995. Botanische Grabinhalte und ihre Aussagemöglichkeiten. In *Des Lichtes beraubt. Totenehrung in der römischen Gräberstraße von Mainz-Weisenau* (eds. M. Witteyer and P. Fasold). Ausstellungskatalog Museum für Vor- und Frühgeschichte Frankfurt.

Körber-Grohne, U. 1988. *Nutzpflanzen in Deutschland*. Stuttgart.

Kreuz, A. 1988. Holzkohle-Funde der ältestbandkeramischen Siedlung Friedberg-Bruchenbrücken: Anzeiger für Brennholz-Auswahl und lebende Hecken? In *Der prähistorische Mensch und seine Umwelt* (Festschrift Körber-Grohne, ed. H. Küster). Forsch. u. Ber. zur Vor- u. Frühgesch. Baden-Württemberg 31: 139–153.

Kreuz, A. 1995a. Pflanzenreste aus römischen Brandgräbern und ihre kulturhistorische, agrar- und vegetationsgeschichtliche Bedeutung. In Archäologische und naturwissenschaftliche Untersuchungen an zwei römischen Brandgräbern der Wetterau (P. Blänkle, A. Kreuz, V. Rupp). *Germania* 73, 1. Halbb.: 110–123.

Kreuz, A. 1995b. Funktionale und konzeptionelle archäobotanische Daten aus römerzeitlichen Brandbestattungen. *Berichte der Kommission für Archäologische Landesforschung in Hessen* 3 (1994/1995): 93–97.

Kreuz, A. 1995c. Landwirtschaft und ihre ökologischen Grundlagen in den Jahrhunderten um Christi Geburt: zum Stand der naturwissenschaftlichen Untersuchungen in Hessen. *Berichte der Kommission für Archäologische Landesforschung in Hessen* 3 (1994/1995): 59–91.

Kreuz, A. 1999. How to become a Roman farmer: a preliminary report of the environmental evidence for the Romanisation project. In *Roman Germany: Studies in cultural interaction*. (eds. J. Creighton, R.J.A. Wilson). Journal of Roman Archaeology, Supplementary series, 32: 71–98.

Kunter, M. 1996. Anthropologische Untersuchung des Leichenbrandes aus dem Gräberfeld von Roßdorf. In *Römerzeitliche Gräber aus Südhessen. Untersuchungen zu Brandbestattungen* (R.H. Schmidt). Materialen zur Vor- und Frühgeschichte von Hessen 17 (Wiesbaden 1996), 222–240

Lenz, H.O. 1859. *Botanik der alten Griechen und Römer*. Reprint 1966, Vaduz.

Marinval, P. 1993. Étude carpologique d'offrandes alimentaires végétales dans les sépultures gallo-romaines: réflexions préliminaires. *Monde des morts, monde des vivants en Gaule rurale* (A. Ferdière). Orléans: 45–65.

Petrucci-Bavaud, M. 1996. Pflanzliche Speisebeigaben in den Brandgräbern. In *Die römischen Gräber an der Rheinstraße 46 des Nordwestgräberfeldes von Augusta Raurica* (C. Haeffelé). Jahresberichte aus Augst und Kaiseraugst 17: 253–259.

Piening, U. 1986. Verkohlte pflanzliche Beigaben aus einem frührömischen Grabhügel bei Büchel, Kreis Cochem-Zell. *Trierer Zeitschr.* 49: 257–271.

Rupp, V. and Lindenthal, J. 1995. Römische Tumuli rechts des Rheins. *Arch. Deutschland* 1995/4: 45–46.

Schucany, C. 1995. Eine Grabanlage im römischen Gutshof von Biberist-Spitalhof. *Archäologie der Schweiz* 18/4: 142–154.

Struck, M. 1993a. Busta in Britannien und ihre Verbindung zum Kontinent. Allgemeine Überlegungen zur Herleitung der Bestattungssitte. In *Römerzeitliche Gräber als Quellen zu Religion, Bevölkerungsstruktur und Sozialgeschichte* (ed. M. Struck). Mainz : 81–94.

Struck, M. (ed.) 1993b. *Römerzeitliche Gräber als Quellen zu Religion, Bevölkerungsstruktur und Sozialgeschichte.* Mainz .

Tegtmeier, U. 1996 Holzkohleuntersuchungen aus Brandbestattungen in Vorst. In *Das römerzeitliche Gräberfeld 'An Hinkes Weißhof' in Tönisvorst-Vorst, Kr. Viersen* (Clive. J. Bridger). Rheinische Ausgrabungen 40: 179–189 (Köln).

Van Zeist, W., Wasylikowa, K., Behre, K.-E. 1991. *Progress in Old World Palaeoethnobotany. A retrospective view on the occasion of 20 years of the International Workgroup for Palaeoethnobotany.* Rotterdam u. Brookfield.

Wigg, A. 1993. *Grabhügel des 2. und 3. Jahrhunderts n. Chr. an Mittelrhein, Mosel und Saar.* Trierer Zeitschrift Beiheft 16. Trier.

6. Pottery assemblages in Gallo-Roman cemeteries

Marie Tuffreau-Libre

Cemeteries have always been an important source of information for pottery specialists. The graves resemble closed assemblages, relatively easy to date and provide intact material, which is thus relatively easy to classify. As the last resting-place of the dead, they have been viewed as a mirror of daily life, with the grave vessels reflecting those in use at the point of death. From such discoveries, numerous general chronological typologies have been constructed.

It was not until pottery from settlements and workshops began to be studied systematically that an alternative picture of Gallo-Roman pottery gradually emerged. Once the regional repertoires were better known and better dated, it was clear that burial material posed a number of problems. There seemed to be a complete chronological disparity between the dates derived from funerary contexts and those coming from settlements, and there was a need to re-consider ceramic assemblages from burials in a different way, taking into account their specific nature.

In addition, the long life-span of numerous pottery forms has demonstrated that it is difficult to assign a precise date to an isolated item, and that the only dateable ceramic groups are those which have been systematically quantified. It is also clearly apparent that in funerary contexts a date cannot be derived from an individual grave good, a coin, a pot or a glass-vessel, as has often been the case, but that one must take into account the associations of objects, and also weigh up the presence and absence of certain types, in order to refine the chronology.

I will therefore try to re-define the characteristics of pottery assemblages in burials, to identify more precisely what information they provide and their limitations. These aspects are now mostly well-known but it seems appropriate to restate them, in view of some recent publications of funerary assemblages, which have repeated past mistakes which are better avoided. I shall conclude with an example drawn from a study of the material from the cemetery at Baralle (Pas-de-Calais, France).

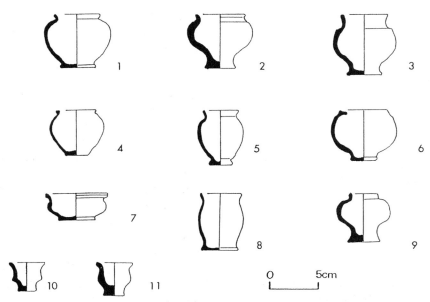

Fig. 6.1 Miniature pots from Gallo-Roman cemeteries: 1–8: La Forêt de Compiègne, 9–11: Soissons.

The characteristics of grave evidence and the limitations of its interpretation

I am not going to deal with the treatment of the pottery in its funerary context (for example ritual breakage) nor its layout, but only its typological characteristics. Two aspects characterise the pottery from burial assemblages, independently of the period and the region studied during the Gallo-Roman era.

1. The specific nature of pottery in burial contexts

Certain forms were preferred: for example, vessels for holding liquids, such as flasks and jugs, are over-represented in comparison with settlement finds. At Baralle (Pas-de-Calais, France) for instance, 23% of the assemblage comprised flasks and jugs, but only 9% on a contemporary settlement (Tuffreau-Libre 1989; 1992). In

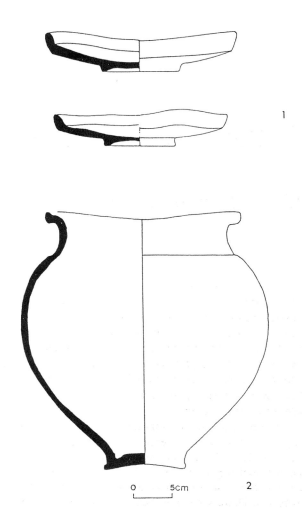

Fig. 6.3 Vessels with potting faults found in the cemetery of Baralle, Pas-de-Calais (1) and in the cemetery of L'Image in Saint-Marcel (Indre) (2)

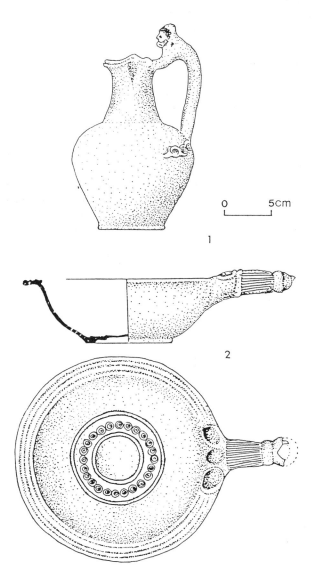

Fig. 6.2 Sets of vessels, oinochoe-type jug and patera found in the cemetery of Vimy (Augustan-Claudian).

late Roman cemeteries in general, the same forms account for between 20 and 43% of vessels, as opposed to 6% in urban settlements (Tuffreau-Libre and Jacques 1992; Tuffreau-Libre 1992). Beakers and flat platters are similarly over-represented. In contrast culinary vessels, such as mortaria, casseroles, and traditional bowls, are rarer.

A quantitative study of the pottery of the Limousin undertaken by Guy Lintz (1994), shows the proportionate differences between types of pottery from cemeteries and settlements; the study also noted that pots in burial assemblages were consistently smaller in size than those from settlements.

In tandem with the vessel forms, certain sorts of fabric are more common, mainly because they represent table-ware, conventionally known as fine wares. *Terra nigra*, *terra rubra*, mica-dusted and red-slipped wares constituted 58% of vessels at Baralle, 73% at Vimy (Monchy 1977), 41% at Noyelles-Godault (Bastien and Demolon 1975). This is much more than the 21 to 39% found in contemporary settlements.

Certain forms present in funerary contexts occur only rarely or are totally absent from settlements. For example there are miniature pots (Fig. 6.1), sets of vessels such as oenochoe-type jugs, *paterae* (Fig. 6.2), and small cups for offerings, the same that those found in sanctuaries (Tuffreau-Libre 1994).

It is clear, in fact, although not a new idea, that some grave goods had been bought for the occasion at stalls sited near the cemeteries, which must have sold sub-standard pieces of work, a probability suggested by the large number of vessels which have potting or firing faults (Fig. 6.3). Many examples indicate the existence of workshops near cemeteries: Blicquy, Harfleur (Evrard 1994), and rue Saint-Jacques in Paris (Robin, 1993; Tuffreau-Libre 1995).

2. The conservative nature of funerary assemblages

Some of the objects were deposited in the grave after prolonged use, attested by their worn state and frequent repairs. This characteristic suggests two interpretations which are not mutually exclusive: these were objects which belonged to the deceased and his or her family, and therefore had a sentimental value, or alternatively, worn objects may have been placed in the grave for reasons of economy, to avoid using new vessels.

Certain types of material appearing in cemeteries were already markedly old-fashioned. Vessels in *terra sigillata* form a good example. This fabric only seems to appear late in northern cemeteries. In the cemeteries at Noyelles-Godault, Vimy and Baralle, it was only placed in graves belonging to the last quarter of the first century, although it occurs from the end of the Augustan period in adjacent Atrebatic settlements at Arras, Remy and Hamblain-les-Pres (Tuffreau-Libre and Jacques 1985; Tuffreau-Libre 1989).

Here again, two explanations are possible: one cultural, a refusal to place in the graves objects which were not traditional, or which did not originate in that region. The other explanation is an economic one; *sigillata* was only placed in graves when it had become a less rare or less expensive commodity, or after a long period of use.

What, therefore, emerges from all these observations is the very disparate nature of ceramic funerary assemblages; this inevitably restricts their use for typologically-based chronologies. Cemetery pottery is thus far from representative of pottery in daily use. To be sure, it allows one to draw up typologies, but they are typologies of ceramic grave-goods, even if a large part of the material was capable of serving two functions. All these factors explain the apparent lack of sychroneity each time settlement material has been compared with cemetery material. The late Roman pottery of Northern Gaul is a good example. Whereas settlement excavations have provided precise chronological reference points, they have revealed chronological discrepancies of fifty years or even

more with the dates provided by cemeteries. The comparisons between the dating of the pottery from the urban settlement of Arras (Tuffreau-Libre and Jacques 1992) and the dating of the assemblages of the cemetery of Oudenburg (Mertens and Van Impe 1971) for example make this clear.

Indeed, the moment we enter the field of ritual, we cannot treat this material as if it were everyday tableware. Pottery found in settlements poses other problems, such as residuality, which I will not rehearse here; it does not necessarily provide a better picture of reality, it just gives us another picture. In any case it is clearly not possible to establish typologically-based chronologies from burial sites, and in particular, to use them to date settlement sites.

The cemetery of Baralle (Pas-de-Calais, France)

We must, in fact, ignore records which are too slight for productive studies of assemblages. There are few recent publications of cemeteries, and the countless cemetery assemblages which fill the stores of museums are no longer any use for this sort of study. We have many small groups of a few graves, either because they relate to very small communities, or because the excavation was necessarily partial. Finally, many graves contain only one or two pottery vessels.

For these reasons, I have chosen the Gallo-Roman cemetery of Baralle (Pas-de-Calais, northern France), as an example of a study in relationships and quantification (Hosdez and Jacques 1989; Tuffreau-Libre 1989). This has the advantage of having been completely excavated, and produced 100 graves. The quantification of the material and its association will facilitate the establishment of an internal chronology for the cemetery, and will also produce very interesting data for the study of ritual and the progressive Romanisation of material.

The number of pots

A quantified study of all the pottery from the cemetery shows, first of all, a very neat sequence in the number of grave vessels; 15 graves contained more than seven pots and alone accounted for 45% of the ceramic grave goods; 39 graves each had between three and six vessels; 38 had less than three pots each. As a general rule, this breakdown is related to the type of grave and its date. The square graves are mainly the oldest and richest, but nevertheless some exceptions exist. Several square graves have few goods, whereas certain oval graves have many (Fig. 6.4). They fit into the overall picture of aristocratic graves in North Gaul and two features may be noted: first of all, the presence of a number of objects probably reflects the social status of the deceased. Second, the number of objects decreases gradually in the course of the first century, in tandem with the Romanisation of the material.

From the fine wares and their associations, a number

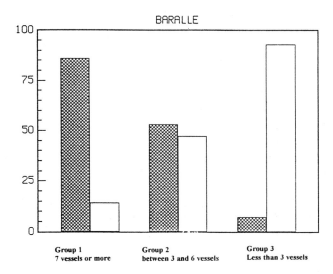

Fig. 6.4 *Breakdown of the pottery by numbers of pots into three groups. 1. 7 vessels or more 2. 3–6 vessels, 3. Less than 3 vessels. The shaded columns represent square graves and the open columns represent oval graves.*

of points emerge. The square graves contain 63% of the *terra nigra*; but 91% of the *sigillata* is in the oval graves. *Terra rubra* vessels are never associated with *sigillata*; the latter on the other hand occurs in association with all other fine wares (Fig. 6.5).

The study of the distribution patterns of the various types of objects provides additional information (Fig. 6.6). Thus high-shouldered jars are often associated with globular flasks decorated with facet burnishing. These graves all generally contain items of *terra rubra*, or numerous *terra nigra* vessels. Associations of this type should date the first series of graves to the Claudian period. A good example of such an assemblage is Grave J27 (Figs 6.7, 6.8).

A second series of graves exhibit different assemblages. The fine wares are represented by *terra nigra*, mica-coated ware, and red-slipped vessels, but the *terra rubra* has disappeared. In association with the newer forms, one can see old-fashioned types of vessel, such as the globular decorated flasks. By contrast, *sigillata* is still absent, an absence that also applies to the new forms

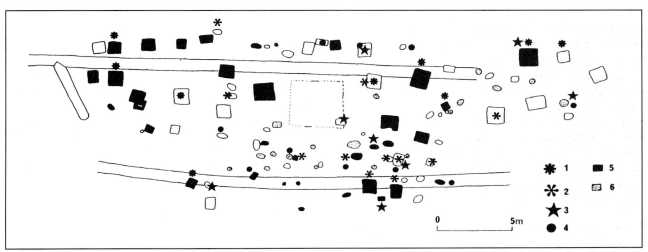

Fig. 6.5 *Distribution of fine wares 1. Chunky cog-like stars = terra rubra, 2. fine stars = mica-dusted wares, 3. pointed stars = red-slipped ware, 4. circles = sigillata, 5. solid black = mostly terra nigra, 6. light shading = absence of terra nigra.*

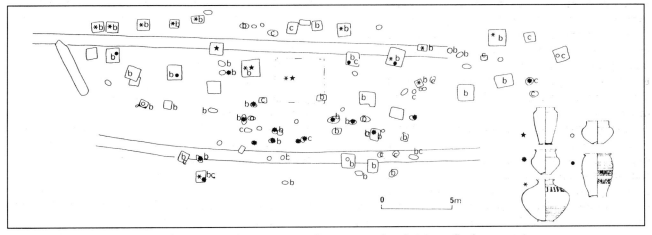

Fig. 6.6 *Distribution of pottery according to type. b = bottle or flasks, c = a jug.*

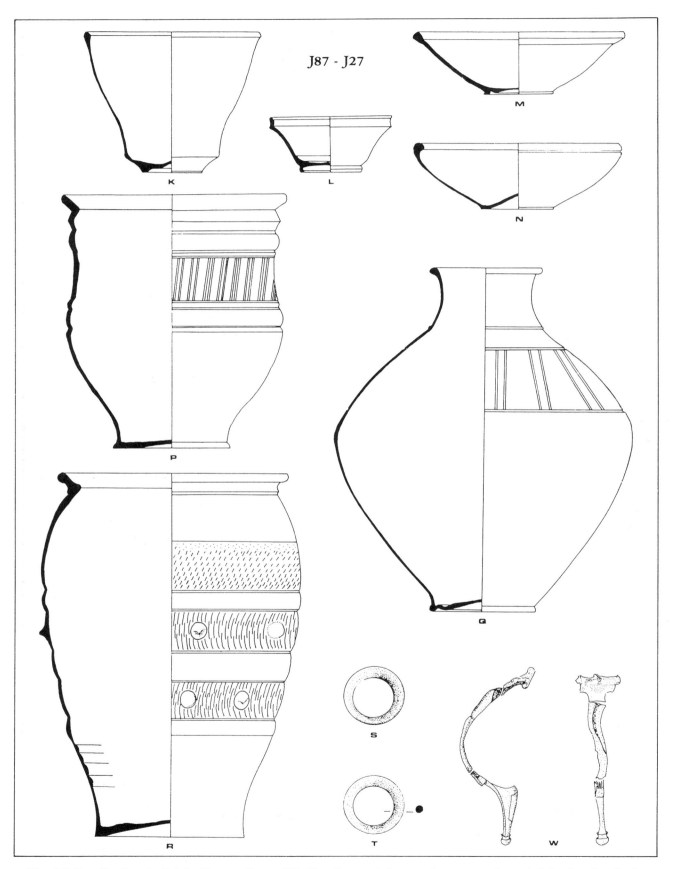

Fig. 6.7 *Baralle, Pas-de-Calais, France, Grave J27, Claudian period,* terra nigra, terra rubra, *girth beaker, butt beaker.*

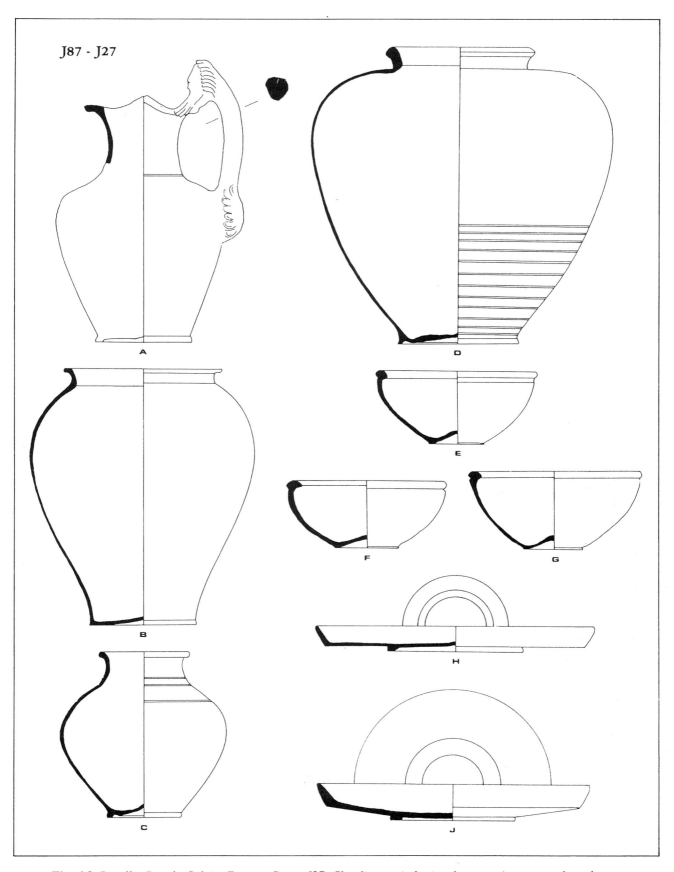

Fig. 6.8 *Baralle, Pas-de-Calais, France, Grave J27, Claudian period, oinochoe-type jug,* terra rubra *platters.*

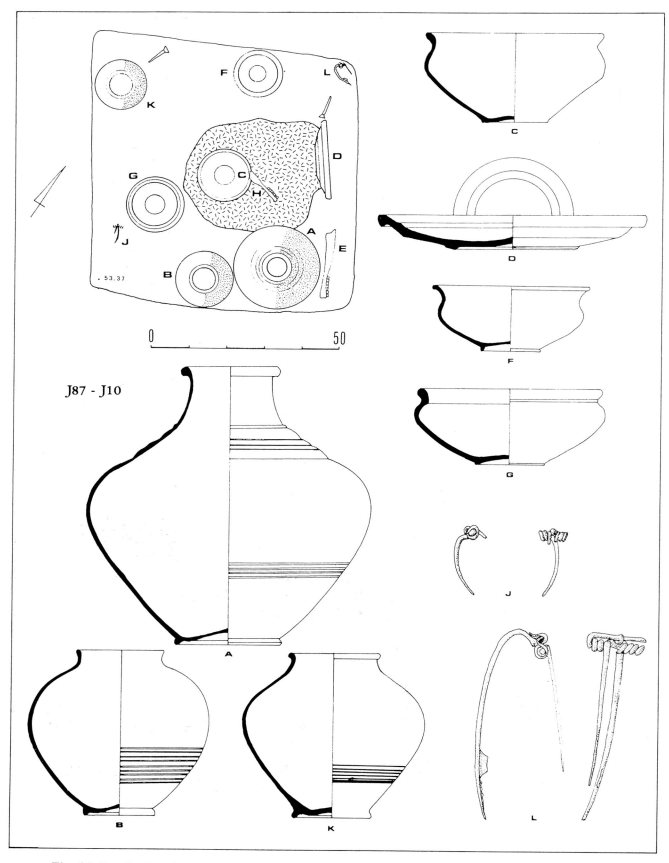

Fig. 6.9 Baralle, Pas-de-Calais, France, Grave J10, Claudian to about AD 70, flask, terra nigra, mica dust.

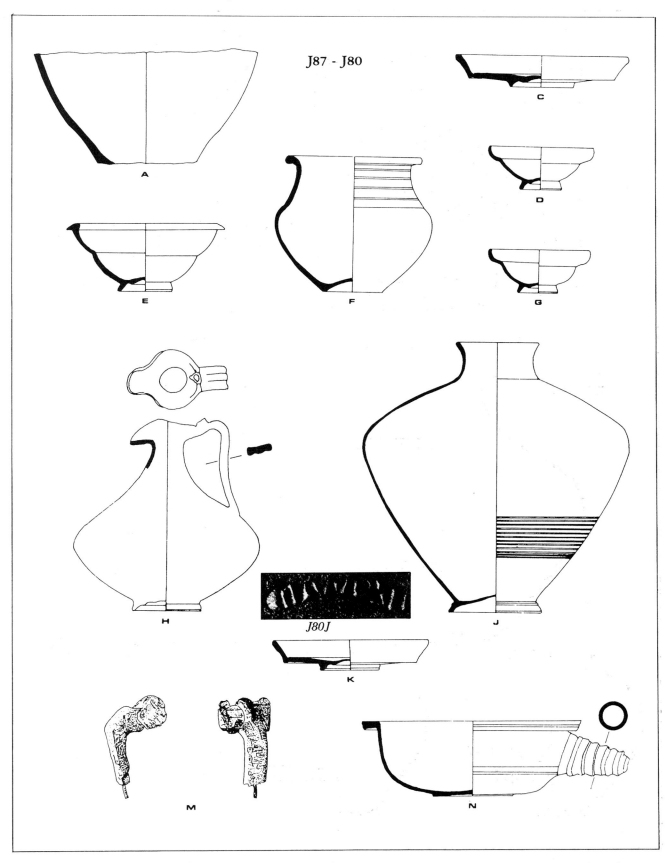

Fig. 6.10 *Baralle, Pas-de-Calais, France, Grave J80, 70–90 AD, 'vase tronconique' imitations, terra sigillata, Bourlon bowl.*

such as the 'vase tronconique' (already current on other types of site in the vicinity). These assemblages characterise the period from Claudius to about AD 70. An example is grave J10 (Fig. 6.9).

The third group of burials relates to the last phase of square graves and the appearance of oval graves, a period of transition when new pottery types appear: platters with splayed walls and a 'Pompeian' red-type slip, 'vases tronconiques', tall or globular vessels with a carinated girth, moulded vessels, a carinated bowl in a white fabric of local manufacture from Bourlon. Jugs replace flasks; *sigillata* appears in association with fine wares, such as mica-coated or red-slipped vessels, or *terra nigra*. This phase spans the period about 70–90 AD: for example, Grave J80 (Fig. 6.10).

The last series consists of quite poor grave groups which contain new ceramic types, such as the 'vases tronconiques', but from which the other fine wares have disappeared with the exception of *terra nigra*, which persists in certain graves. This phase should span the period 90–110 AD. An example is grave J 01.

To sum up, the dates are thus derived, not from the status of a single vessel, nor from certain pots in the graves whose dating is well-known elsewhere. All pots are taken into account and it is their groupings which determine the suggested dating. It demonstrates the interest of assemblages *per se*, and the need to utilise them and not just isolated objects. No dating derived from an isolated vessel, however typical, can be any more than a pointer to a very wide date-span. To be sure, this method requires graves sufficiently rich, and burial assemblages sufficiently significant for the results to be convincing and reliable.

This, then, demonstrates the possibilities of constructing a finer internal chronology for one particular cemetery, but it is impossible to use the assemblages from this burial site to date other assemblages, except for an adjacent burial context or for a site sufficiently close. Finally, it is clear that the study of pottery from burial sites has much to offer for ritual, social and economic studies, but great care must be taken over its chronological interpretation.

Acknowledgements

I want again to express here my warm thanks to Vivien Swan who translated this paper, and agreed to present it in Durham in 1997 when I could not be present.

Bibliography

Bastien J.M. and Demolon P. 1975. Villa et cimetière du Ier siècle après J.C. à Noyelles-Godault (Pas-de-Calais). *Septentrion*, 5.

Evrard, M.N. 1994. Un atelier de potiers à Harfleur (76)(Ier-milieu IIIème siècle), in *La céramique du Haut-Empire en Gaule Belgique et dans les régions voisines: faciès régionaux et courants commerciaux*, Tuffreau-Libre M., Jacques A. dir., Nord-Ouest Archéologie, 6, 195–203.

Hosdez, C. and Jacques, A. 1989. *La nécropole à incinérations de Baralle (Pas-de-Calais)*, Nord-Ouest Archéologie, 2.

Lintz, G. 1994. Quelques aspects de la céramique du Bas-Empire en Limousin, in *La céramique du Bas-Empire en Gaule Belgique et dans les régions voisines*, Tuffreau-Libre M., Jacques dir., Revue du Nord, 6, 201–212.

Mertens, J. et van Impe, L. 1971. Het laat gallo-romeins grafveld van Oudenburg, *Archaeologia Belgica*, 135.

Monchy, E. 1977. *Sépultures du Ier siècle ap.J.C. à Vimy*, 71 p.

Robin, S. 1993. Un atelier de potiers du Haut-Empire à Paris: l'atelier de la rue Saint-Jacques, *Trésors de terre*, 1993, 51–55.

Tuffreau-Libre, M. 1989. La céramique gallo-romaine de Baralle, *Nord-Ouest Archéologie*, 2, 205–222.

Tuffreau-Libre, M. 1992. *La céramique en Gaule romaine*, Editions Errance, 74 p

Tuffreau-Libre, M. 1994. La céramique dans les sanctuaires gallo-romains, *Actes du Colloque d'Argentomagus*, Editions Errance, 128–137.

Tuffreau-Libre, M. 1995. Céramiques communes gallo-romaines, *catalogue du Musée Carnavalet, Paris musées*, 160 p.

Tuffreau-Libre, M. and Jacques, A. 1985. La céramique gallo-romaine du Ier siècle dans le Sud de l'Atrébatie, *Gallia*, 43.1, 127–145.

Tuffreau-Libre, M. and Jacques, A. 1992. La céramique gallo-romaine du Bas-Empire à Arras (Nemetacum) (Pas-de-Calais), *Gallia*, 49, 99–127.

Burial and social status

The papers in this section approach different aspects of social status. Whilst recognising the difficulties in addressing this issue they exhibit a variety of aspects of the subject through both general surveys and case studies.

The first three papers explore the archaeological evidence for the mortuary practices of three different groups. Martin-Kilcher investigates the burial rites for those young women who died before marriage. She takes what appears to be a cross-cultural type, the 'bad death', and explores one of its specific manifestations in a Roman context, setting the burial evidence against other types of data. The burials of young individuals are often argued to be evidence for ascribed rather than achieved status: her discussion shows the situation to be more complicated. The combination of evidence of different types allows a much more nuanced analysis of these data and their culturally specific meanings. By contrast, Dexheimer examines the use of funerary portraits in northern Italy. She demonstrates how these were used by a group of relatively low social status – freed slaves – as an alternative mode of public display to those denied them by virtue of their social positions, borrowing portrait types from monuments in public spaces within towns which they were not themselves allowed to erect. Struck considers the general problem of how we might identify high status burials through cemetery evidence. With particular reference to Roman Britain, she reviews a series of studies which use both artefacts and site characteristics. Her conclusions provide new ideas about social status within the province and point towards both regional and chronological variations.

The study of high status burials is also reflected in the case studies presented by Niblett, Schucany and Abegg-Wigg. Niblett's study draws together evidence from around the Romano-British town of Verulamium, with particular emphasis on the burial at Folly Lane, exploring changing forms of status display in the early Roman period through the burial rite, the use of pyre goods as well as grave goods, and enclosures for burials. The latter two examine important recently excavated funerary monuments, within the compound / enclosure of a Swiss villa and within a Roman cemetery probably also related to a villa in the Saarland. Schucany situates the burial ceremony, construction of the monument and its remodelling in relation to the history of its villa setting. Through study of the Wadern-Oberlöstern cemetery, especially its monumental aspect, Abegg-Wigg discusses the creation of a new mode of high status burial display in a Roman province, which draws its power from both indigenous and 'Roman' burial traditions. A more holistic approach to society is taken by Murail and Girard who explore the social structure of a rural cemetery at Chantambre in Gaul throughout its history. Through a combination of bioanthropological and artefactual analyses their work demonstrates pattern of long term social and population stability which contrasts with the standard model for social and population change in this area.

The relationship of burial to social status is a recurrent theme among other papers in the volume. Most common is the identification of status difference from the degree of care taken in placing the body in the grave, the choice of burial container, or the number or value of grave goods (e.g. Riedel, Jovanovic, Topál); Quensel-von-Kalben is the only contributor to explore social differentiation in burial practice through more sophisticated multivariate analyses. The papers in the preceding section demonstrate that numbers of grave goods, for example, are unlikely to have been the only forms of burial display. Kreuz's observation that burials conspicuous by their large artefactual assemblages or monuments are no more likely than less well furnished burials to contain exotic plant remains, illustrates the potential of this form of evidence to modify interpretations based on grave goods alone.

In the later Roman period del Moro reminds us of changing media for the expression of social difference in burial; location within the cemetery, especially in cemeteries connected to churches becomes increasingly significant, while the analysis of grave goods demonstrates little difference between graves, although Martorelli's survey of dress evidence reminds us of a form of display of which the evidence has often been lost. De Santis also suggests that the scarcity of glass contributed to its relatively high value and prestigious associations as a burial marker.

7. *Mors immatura* in the Roman world – a mirror of society and tradition

Stefanie Martin-Kilcher

Death as the end of life is an elementary fact. Archaeology and other disciplines such as anthropology and psychology, have found similar patterns of behaviour concerning the end of life and dealing spiritually with death. Up till the present day we assume that a person's life has to pass through certain stations in order to end 'richly fulfilled', as we read in obituaries, grieved by the family and society. However, concepts of a 'fulfilled life' are manifold and differ according to society, religion and period. On a basic level, there are three stations in life, which in 1909 the folklorist Albert van Gennep defined in the 'rites de passage': birth, marriage and death (van Gennep 1909). Marriage also means reproduction, which is legalised and desired by society in order to maintain itself; death is only expected in old age.

Premature or unusual death therefore does not correspond to the acknowledged order of things. That this was no different in Roman times is demonstrated by textual references to *mors immatura* (Ter Vrugt-Lenz 1960), or to those who had died *ante suum diem*, i.e. before their predestined day or before the fulfilment of their predestined purpose in life according to the acknowledged order of things.

Four groups belong to this category of prematurely deceased individuals:

1) Infants who died before, during or shortly after birth.
2) Children and juveniles and, in many cultures, unmarried or childless adults.
3) Women who died in childbirth. They always have a special status, although their death relates them to individuals of the first and particularly of the fourth group.
4) People who died in special or horrible circumstances – the 'bad death'. These can be soldiers fallen in battle, victims of accidents, strangers who died far from home, murder victims, suicides, executed criminals or people who died of certain diseases.

Different sources inform us about the response towards *mors immatura* in the Roman period. Most of the written sources concern the Mediterranean region (Ter Vrugt-Lenz 1960); they express the deep feelings caused by premature death in a family and in society in general. They also provide help in the interpretation of archaeological data. However, the most plentiful sources for the treatment of *mors immatura* are the burials themselves. Together with physical anthropology (Schwidetzky 1965) and other scientific analysis – for example the analysis of animal bones and of plant or food remnants (Petrucci-Bavaud / Jacomet 1997) – archaeological interpretation continues to find new perspectives.

Thanks to the large number of burials, chronological and regional patterns of burial practice can be recognised. As in many cultures and periods, so too in the Roman world prematurely deceased individuals were dealt with in a different way to the rest of the population. In the archaeological record this is registered through the grave itself: the treatment and position of the body, the furnishing of the grave, sometimes also the position of the grave inside or outside the cemetery. This relates to the moment of interment in the mortuary ritual.

However, the structure of a grave expresses only part of the burial rite – although it is very important. In Roman times most graves were marked above ground and often it is this part of the grave which indicated the status of the deceased, not only supplementing the below ground treatment but even being the exclusive status indicator. This is attested by numerous tomb inscriptions and funerary monuments, even if associated burials have only been preserved in exceptional cases.

Archaeological terminology defines a class of 'extraordinary burials' which differ from the norm ('Sonderbestattungen'; for a detailed discussion cf. Pauli 1975). Although the term 'extraordinary burial' has to be specially defined for each region and period, it is possible to recognise a number of patterns sometimes with a wide distribution, which mirror the treatment of *mors immatura*. An essential precondition for this is that there was a consistent rite of grave furnishing. As so often the case we mainly have information on the middle and upper classes of society.

Rituals conducted before the interment hardly ever

show in the archaeological record (However increasing attention is being paid to other rituals; see for example papers in the first section of this volume). However, as this applies for all ages and both sexes, it can be neglected in our discussion.

Prematurely deceased unmarried individuals

This paper will deal with the second group of prematurely deceased, the *immaturi et innupti* of the written sources (Tertullian, *de Anima* 56ff.). A number of graves, in particular those of richly furnished girls and very young women, dating from the 1st to the 4th or early 5th centuries AD in the western *Imperium Romanum* will be the focus of our attention (for contrasting evidence concerning boys and young men cf. below).

Girls with pupae and crepundia

The burial of Crepereia Tryphaena from Rome will be used here as an example; she died aged 14–17 years and was buried in a marble sarcophagus in the area of the *horti Domitiae* (Fig. 7.1) (Bedini 1995: 64–75; Crepereia Tryphaena 1983). She lived in the second quarter of the 2nd century AD. According to the report of the discovery in 1889, she was crowned with a wreath of box leaves and blossoms and was adorned with gold jewellery: earrings, a necklace and finger rings. On the chest there was a splendid brooch, 4.5 cm in length, with hooks on the rear side. The head was slightly turned to the left, towards an ivory doll. At the side of the deceased were placed a spindle and distaff as well as a tiny casket with a miniature mirror and combs.

The grave-goods of Crepereia Tryphaena are not unique, as illustrated by a whole group of girls and very young women (Table 7.1) who as far as is known died, with one exception, aged between 5 and 20 years. These

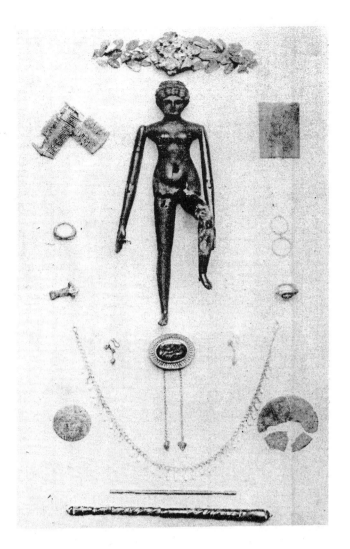

Fig. 7.1 Rome. Grave goods of Crepereia Tryphaena. After Crepereia Tryphaena 1983: 31.

Date	Findspot	Context		Age (years)	Burial type	Sarcophagus	Diadem/wreath	Jewellery (gold)	Spindle/distaff	Writing set	Mirror	Cistella	Amulet	Miniature implements	Doll (ivory)	Notes
0–50	Near Rome	(villa?)	'Girls grave'		?		●	●	●	●	●	●	●	●		
0–50	Puglia	(villa)	Young girl		I		●	●			●		●	●		Tile grave
(2. c.)	Brescello		Iulia Graphide	15	C									●		Altar
150	Rome, Prati Castello	villa	Crepereia Tryphaena	14/17	I	▢	●	●	●		●	●	●	●	●	
150/180	Rome, Via Cassia	(villa)		8	I	▢		●			●	●	●	●		
150/180	Vetralla	(villa)		ca. 20	I	▢		●	●		●	●	●			
180/200	Rome, Vallerano	villa		16/18	I	▢		●	●		●		●			
200	Tivoli	(villa)	Cossinia (Vestal)	66	I	▢						●			●	Altar
280	Bonn	(villa?)		9	I	▢	●			●	●		●			
300	Trento			12	I	▢	●				●		●	●	●	
300?	Lyon, Trion		Claudia Victoria	10	I	▢									●	Bronze & bone pins
4./5. c.	Tarragona (Grave 152)			5	I	▢									●	
4./5. c.	Yverdon			14	I										●●	

Table 7.1 Graves with ivory dolls and/or crepundia *and miniatures. For references cf. list 1.*

burials have a wide geographical and chronological distribution. Table 7.1 includes information on the site, the date and the character of settlement to which the grave belonged (i.e. whether from an urban cemetery or a villa). As tomb inscriptions were more common in the more literate south than in the north, we know the names of the deceased in four cases: Crepereia Tryphaena in Rome, Cossinia in Tivoli, Iulia Graphide in Brescello on the river Po and Claudia Victoria in Lyons. Apart from the grave from Brescello, probably a cremation, where the contents are very likely to be incomplete, they are all inhumations, mostly in sarcophagi. The grave inventories of the girls from Tarragona and Yverdon mirror the decrease in furnishing during the 4th century; apart from the dolls they contained neither jewellery nor any other grave-goods. However, the lower part of the grave from Yverdon was disturbed, so a vessel with food or drink, for example, may originally have been present; jewellery, on the other hand, should have been preserved (cf. Fig. 7.9).

Three categories of grave-goods are listed in Table 7.1:

A) *Gold jewellery and elements of costume* – golden personal ornaments and a sarcophagus testify to the fact that the deceased came from wealthy families. There are earrings, necklaces, bracelets and finger rings, in most cases combined with precious stones and pearls (for coloured figures cf. Bedini 1995). The burials of Crepereia Tryphaena in Rome and of the young woman in Rome-Vallerano also produced brooches and a *fibula* (Fig. 7.2). In several grave inventories fine gold threads and little gold spirals indicate textiles interwoven with gold. For three older graves a diadem or wreath is also reported. The wreath and certain elements of jewellery will be mentioned below.

B) *Personal implements* – These comprise spindles and distaffs as well as mirrors and, less often, writing equipment. The writing equipment in some of the graves shows that these young girls learnt to read and write (education of girls in schools is occasionally depicted on sarcophagi, cf. Amedick 1991).

The spinning of wool belonged to everyday female tasks. The large number of women of every age with a spindle and distaff as grave-goods and the depiction of spinning equipment on many funerary monuments underline the importance of this activity. Pirling (1976) explains the practice of providing a spindle and distaff for a deceased woman with reference to the cult of the Parcae. A connotation of the spinning Parcae and the thread of life is indeed possible in particular cases. However, the spindle and distaff, used so frequently in daily life, were characteristic female attributes and grave-goods over a huge area and a vast chronological range, and can therefore be regarded as symbols of womanhood in general. For that reason I cannot agree with the oft-repeated interpretation of distaffs, especially those of amber, jet and glass, as non-functional, purely symbolic and specially manufactured for the burial. This impression results from uneven conditions of preservation and therefore unequal knowledge of the objects themselves: badly fragmented and consequently mostly unpublished from settlements, and completely preserved and consequently published from graves (Martin-Kilcher 1998: 211).

The mirror, an indispensable toilet utensil, is at the same time an important attribute of Venus, the goddess of love and beauty. In antiquity the spindle, distaff and mirror symbolised the female world (Fig. 7.3).

C) *Dolls and miniature equipment* – Finally, we must discuss the furniture which distinguishes these individuals

Fig. 7.2 *Rome, Vallerano. The three brooches of the rich girl's grave (grave 2). Gold and semiprecious stone. After Bedini 1995b: 15–17.*

Fig. 7.3 Pisa. Tomb inscription of P. Ferrarius Hermes, his wives Caecinia Digna and Numeria Maximilla, and his son P. Ferrarius Proculus. Symbols of the female world are spindle and distaff as well as the toilet articles represented, comb, mirror, unguentarium. *After Zimmer 1982: No. 90.*

from the mass of prematurely deceased girls and young women: dolls and miniature implements. Both groups of objects can occur in graves together.

The dolls, ranging in height from *c*.15 to *c*.25 cm and made of the precious material ivory, were dressed, and sometimes adorned with gold jewellery made to scale, although clothes were not preserved. The dolls always represent adult women (Fig. 7.1). In the two early graves there is no doll (at least not of non-perishable material; in a Claudian grave inventory, probably of a girl, from Carmona in southern Spain a 3 cm long miniature bone comb was discovered, which could point to the presence of a doll made of perishable material [Fernandez-Chicarro y de Dios 1978]). In view of the absence of ivory dolls in the two early graves from Italy (probably both containing inhumations), it is indeed possible that dolls of this precious material were then unusual or simply were not provided in the graves until the second century.

Outside Italy for several reasons burials with ivory dolls are known from the later 3rd and 4th century. In the north-western provinces cremation which limits a complete understanding of the grave furnishings, was the usual rite from the 1st to the 3rd century, whereas in the Mediterranean region inhumation already became the predominant rite in the 2nd century. After AD 300 grave furnishing declined in Italy while it continued in Gaul and the north-western provinces for at least another 100 years, especially for girls and women (Martin 1991: 293 – 299).

A variety of miniature objects and amulets, many of valuable rock-crystal and amber, are found in almost all these grave inventories until the time around AD 300 (Fig. 7.4). Some are medallions and pierced amulets which

Fig. 7.4 'Girl's grave' from Rome. Some crepundia *of amber and rock crystal. Photos Antikensammlung, Staatliche Museen zu Berlin, Preussischer Kulturbesitz, I. Geske.*

could be worn, some are unpierced of most varied shapes, and there are also miniatures of crockery and tools which could be held in the hands. The whole group can be described with the Roman term *crepundia*. The word *crepundia* derives from the verb *crepare*, to rattle or to make a noise, which indicates that rattling was once important for their effect and function. According to descriptions and colloquial usage of that time, miniatures of different kinds with a form or made of a material thought to be apotropaic, were called *crepundia*.

L. Pauli has subdivided objects normally called 'amulets' from prehistoric graves north of the Alps into five groups (Pauli 1975: 116 – 135), which may include the classic *crepundia*:

1. noise producing ('Geräusch verursachend')
2. meaningful shape ('Äussere, sinnfällige Form')
3. exterior qualities ('Äussere Beschaffenheit')
4. remarkable objects and curiosa ('Auffälligkeiten und Curiosa')
5. material valued for its special properties ('Stoffwert')

Whereas some shapes and materials were widely distributed and used over a long chronological span, others were particular to periods and areas. Furthermore, their material value corresponded to the social milieu and ideological tendency of their owners. Apart from the shape and material, in Roman times an inscription or pictorial representation were thought to have a powerful effect.

From the classical texts we know that *crepundia* were either pierced or unpierced and either worn on strings, chains or rings or kept in small caskets, the so-called *cistellae*. A lively impression can be gained from a scene in the *Rudens* of Plautus, v. 1140 ff., in which a girl describes her golden *crepundia* contained in a *cistella*, which included miniature tools. In Herculaneum an older child (a girl?) fled from the eruption of Vesuvius, wanting to save her most precious possessions; these comprised an agate bowl and a number of *crepundia* and amulets, for example of amber, rock-crystal and lead/tin in a *cistella* (De Carolis 1993/94: 175–176). *Cistellae* were also found in several of the girls' graves under discussion here (Table 7.1). These tiny boxes should not be confused with the jewellery and toilet caskets from many other female burials (Martin-Kilcher 1976: 8 -88) – for example from Rome (the so-called Tomb of a Girl: Vierneisel 1978: 184), Vallerano (Bedini 1995: 39) and Vetralla (Bordenache Battaglia 1983: 76 Nr. 40).

Dolls and miniatures as grave-goods and the 'non-attained wedding'

The interpretation of the third category of grave-goods (C) varies from an explanation as simple toys for the after-life of the children (Degani 1951/52; Rossi 1993: 156) to a symbolic explanation in connection with the dolls (Manson 1978). However, G. Lafaye (DAC s.v. *matrimonium*) and M. Manson (1978: 864) have drawn

attention to texts describing how girls dedicated their amulets and toys (including dolls) to the gods before their wedding.

According to Roman law girls were marriageable at the age of 12 years (Hopkins 1965; Treggiari 1991). Of the individuals which interest us here, a five year-old girl from Tarragona is the youngest (4th century AD). However according to the other cases where precise information is available, the girls had died aged between 12 and almost 20 years; thus they were – like the 'fanciulla' from Puglia – of marriageable age. The only exception is Cossinia from Tivoli who had died at the age of 6 × 11 years, as the short tomb inscription puts it poetically, and was therefore an aged woman, considering life expectations in the ancient world. Nevertheless, a precious doll was placed to the right of her head and a small casket, a *cistella*, in her right hand; the *cistella* was found to contain textile remains. Cossinia had been a priestess of Vesta, and they never married.

The grave of this woman, dated to the Severan period after the hair-style of the doll, lay under a stepped pedestal, alongside the inscribed grave altar which also stood on a pedestal (Fig. 7.5). G. Mancini (1930) reckons that the priestess was buried under the pedestal – which must have supported a statue of the priestess of Vesta. However, G. Bordenache Battaglia (1983: 124–38) has doubted the link between the inscription and the grave, as one side of the grave's pedestal overlies the lowest steps of that of the altar. She therefore supposes that this was a later interment and, because of the complete set of teeth mentioned by Mancini, she believes that it was the grave of an unidentified young woman. However there was no grave beneath the altar, and Mancini emphasises the identical construction of both pedestals. Moreover, the orientation of the burial (in a coffin *c*.1.80 m in length) was exactly the same as the altar. Finally, if it were the grave of a girl of the Severan period, we would expect it to be furnished with more jewellery, comparable with Rome-Vallerano. Unfortunately an anthropological analysis is not available. From the published photograph B. Kaufmann (Anthropologisches Forschungsinstitut Aesch), identifies an adult woman of gracile build. According to Kaufmann, the complete set of teeth is not relevant for a more precise determination of age. Further statements are of course not possible without examination of the skeleton. However, in my opinion, the context does not contradict the connection between the grave and the inscribed altar.

Like the dolls, amulets and *crepundia* were already in the possession of the girls during their lifetime; but these objects were not toys either. We know about toys in the ancient world (*Les Dossiers d'Archéologie* Nr. 168, 1992). But miniature objects were not only for children's use and play: representation of real things in miniature form also had a magical meaning. In numerous sanctuaries and burials miniatures of different material were dedicated

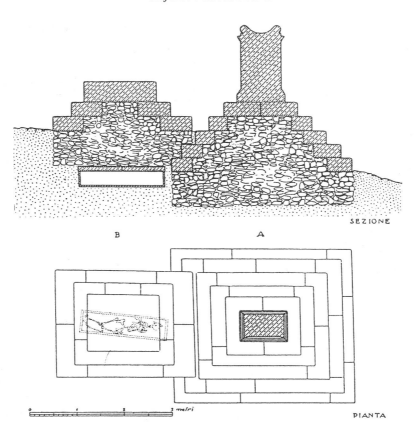

Fig. 7.5 Tivoli. Funerary monument of the Vesta priestess Cossinia. After Mancini 1930: Fig. 9.

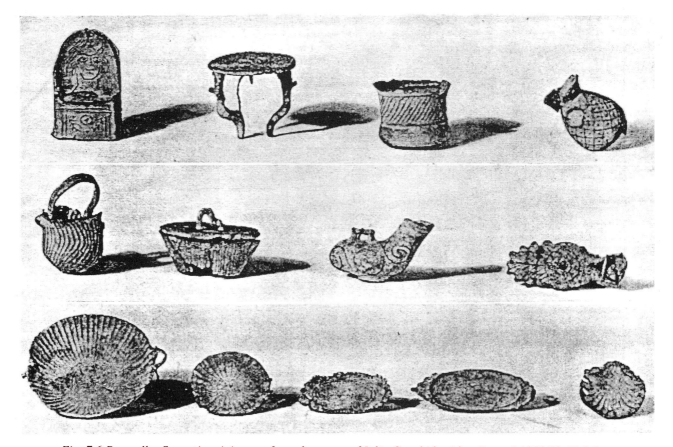

Fig. 7.6 Brescello. Some tin miniatures from the grave of Iulia Graphide. After Degani 1951/52: Taf. 1.

and deposited either singly or in groups. This will not be discussed here; examples from the Roman period are the many miniature votives of tin, lead and pottery.

In the lavishly furnished graves of our girls the miniatures and *crepundia* are mainly made of valuable ivory, amber and rock-crystal. But we find *crepundia* in other materials too. The tin crockery and implements from a grave in Brescello which hitherto have been interpreted as doll's accessories (Fig. 7.6) belong to this context. Most of them are probably casts from tin (cf the analysis of the pieces from the unfortunately disturbed context from the 'quartier Vénéjean' at Montbrun (Dép. Drôme): *Bulletin de la Société des Antiquaires de France* 1903: 269). The 15 year old Iulia Graphide was buried in the funerary enclosure ('Grabgarten') of her *patronus* and foster parents, with her own carefully carved grave altar. She is very unlikely to have played with the 2–4 cm long figures which apparently were mass produced and of low quality; rather these miniatures were votives which she would have dedicated to the gods before her wedding as symbols of a completed childhood. A group of similar miniature figures has, for example, been found in a pit next to the main temple of the sanctuary of Terracina, where among others Venus was venerated (e.g. Barbera 1991 with further examples from Pesaro – a grave or sanctuary?) and possibly from the grave at Montbrun, Dép. Drôme (see above).

Apotropaic and magic power in classical theory were not only attributed to amber and rock-crystal (Pliny, *N.H.* XXXVII, 9 ff.), but also to lead and tin, as these metals melt fast and can easily be moulded (Pliny, *N.H.* XXXIV, 48 ff.). These magic powers are still sometimes consulted by pouring molten lead and tin at New Year's Eve.

However, true toys were dedicated to the gods as well, as for instance a recently discovered ivory doll of outstanding quality from Segobriga in Spain demonstrates. The doll came to light on the edge of the *forum* where the excavators postulate a temple of Venus (Almagro Gorbea/ Sesé 1996). We can also assume that the small silver table service from the so-called 'Tomb of a Girl' near Rome (Zahn 1950/51) was a proper toy and would have been dedicated to the gods before the wedding, if the girl had lived long enough.

If we not only consider single elements of grave furnishing, but take a comprehensive look at the burial, in my opinion we can recognise further indications of the 'non-attained marriage' in the archaeological context of several of these graves. The grave of Crepereia Tryphaena in Rome is especially informative: her sarcophagus was placed directly next to the sarcophagus of L. Crepereius Euhodus who, judging from his name, was probably her father or brother. If Crepereia Tryphaena had been married, we would expect her to be buried in the mausoleum or funerary enclosure of her husband's family. The *cognomina* Euhodus and Tryphaena point to their status as freedmen (Crepereia Tryphaena 1983: 31). They were not a married couple of freedmen of the same *patronus* L. Crepereius,

Fig. 7.7 Rome. Sarcophagus of Crepereia Tryphaena: the deceased lying on the bed is mourned by her parents. After Crepereia Tryphaena 1983: 34.

because the relief decoration on the Tryphaena sarcophagus shows the grieving parents on the death-bed of their daughter (Fig. 7.7). They lost their daughter in the prime of her youth and provided her doll and miniature implements and *crepundia* in the grave, the items which she would have dedicated to the gods before her wedding. One of the golden rings of Tryphaena is engraved with the name Filetus and could have been a gift from her fiancé.

According to the miniatures, Iulia Graphide also belonged to the *immaturae et innuptae*, although at her age she could have been married (15 years, 2 months, 11 days). Her foster parents erected her grave altar in their funerary enclosure (Degani 1951/52: 16). Cossinia, the priestess of Vesta from Tivoli who came from an old equestrian family, was certainly unmarried (Mancini 1930). Although she had died at the age of 66 years, she was accompanied by a doll and a *cistella*. Priestesses of Vesta could of course not marry and had to be celibate. The doll and the tiny box are therefore symbols of her virginity and unmarried status.

The age and the grave-goods of the other girls suggest that they too were treated in this special way as they had died unmarried, some of them possibly shortly before their wedding. One might even suggest that Crepereia Tryphaena was buried in her wedding costume. Like a bride she was wearing a wreath of blossoms: Treggiari (1991: 163) describes the most important elements of the bridal outfit: the *tunica recta* with a *cingulum*, a wreath of blossoms and the *flammeum*, a red veil (Lucan, *De bello civili* 355 ff. describes a bride of the republican upper class: she wears a *corona*, the *flammeum* covers her face, her dress is belted and she is adorned with necklace and upper arm rings). The large oval brooch in the grave of Crepereia Tryphaena could have belonged to the *flammeum* or to a bridal girdle. However, the box leaves (*buxus semper virens*) of the wreath were sacred to the underworld gods (Crepereia Tryphaena 1983: 38 – not myrtle, as stated in

Bedini 1995: 71). Haberey (1938) also records a box posy in a late Roman grave near Mayen.

Golden diadems or *coronae*, possibly produced specially for the grave and representing probably bridal jewellery, were discovered in both graves of the early principate from Rome and Puglia (Table 7.1). Diadems or *Scheitelschmuck* in a few rich late Roman girls' graves are also interpreted as bridal jewellery (Martin 1991). Wreaths of unperishable materials, especially gold, were never widely used on corpses in the Roman west – in contrast to the east.

From this point of view, the mirrors, spindles and distaffs in the graves of these prematurely deceased girls gain an additional meaning. As symbols of womanhood (cf. Fig. 7.3) the mirror had a special meaning during the adornment of the bride, and spindle and distaff were carried at the traditional Roman bridal procession (DAC s.v. *matrimonium*).

The treatment of premature death – a mirror of society and tradition

The precious nature of the objects and the use, in some cases, of marble sarcophagi and the funerary monuments all indicate the wealthy social background of these girls. According to the inscriptions we know that Cossinia was of noble birth. Iulia Graphide from Brescello, on the other hand, was the adopted daughter of a wealthy freedman; she was equipped with tin miniatures, which were chosen for the special properties of the material rather than its value. Crepereia Tryphaena may have belonged to the class of freedmen (see above). However to judge from the location of the burial in the *Horti Domitiae*, the imperial gardens in which a short time earlier Hadrian had built his mausoleum, the family must have had direct connections with the imperial court.

The location of burial is a further means to express

Fig. 7.8 Rome, Vallerano. The proprietorial funerary enclosures with the burial of an immatura *(grave 2, circled) and the spatial organisation of the cemetery which results from the social status of the deceased. The funerary enclosures are reconstructed from walls and aerial photographs of the excavation. After Bedini 1995b: Fig. 1; Bedini et al. 1995a: Fig. 35.*

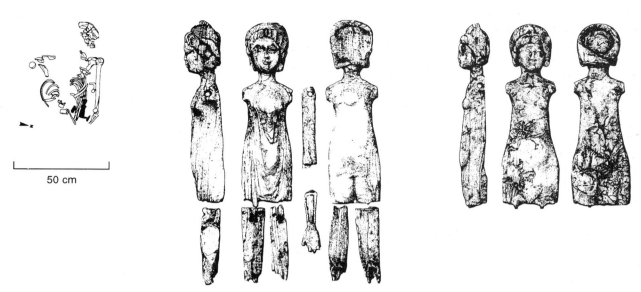

50 cm

Fig. 7.9 *Yverdon-les-Bains (VD). Late-Roman girl's grave with two ivory dolls (scale 1:2). After Rossi 1993: Fig. 6.7.*

high status or wealth; this is confirmed by the other graves (cf. Table 7.1). Apart from the latest burials they were placed in private funerary enclosures outside the urban cemeteries. These private funerary monuments too were generally situated in topographically prominent places, well visible for posterity. We often notice that wealthy families chose a burial place close to a country-seat or *villa suburbana*. The proprietorial funerary enclosures can dominate the cemeteries of the staff and servants by acting as their foci or can be completely separated from them (Ferdière (ed.) 1993: *passim*).

In this context the site of Vallerano, a few kilometres south of Rome, is an interesting example: along a Roman road large parts of a cemetery have been excavated, belonging to a *villa suburbana* which unfortunately has been destroyed. Along the access road to the villa there were two funerary enclosures, adjoined by the simple graves, probably of the servants (Fig. 7.8). The large central enclosure contained five exceptionally large and elaborate tombs, without doubt originally covered by altars and monuments. In grave 2, the only one with a sarcophagus, one of the lavishly furnished young girls considered here was interred (Table 7.1). The other graves of the cemetery were, according to contemporary custom at Rome, accompanied by only a few grave-goods: single lamps, coins, rarely a ceramic vessel. The cemetery was used from the middle of the 2nd into the 4th century, always respecting the proprietorial funerary enclosure.

The girl from Tarragona was buried in the 4th century in a Christian *memoria* close to a martyrial church. She came, therefore, from a rich Christian family. This is probably also the case for the girl from Yverdon who died at roughly the same time, although no buildings in connection with this grave are known (Fig. 7.9). However, the grave from Yverdon was situated in a prominent position, directly on the road from *Castrum Eburodunense* to *Aventicum*.

Moreover, the *immaturae et innuptae* include a further group of girls with special grave-goods: *crotala*, clackers and a tambourine. In this connection a poem by a Hellenistic author, cited in the *Anthologia Palatina*, has been neglected. It describes how Timareta, daughter of Timaretos, dedicates her tambourine, her ball and her dolls, including their clothes, to Artemis before her wedding (Manson 1978: note 5). Such musical instruments have been found in Roman graves dated from the 2nd to the early 5th century AD, and they again testify to a close relationship between grave-goods, votive offerings and the symbolic end of childhood before the wedding ceremony. The jewellery and the rest of the grave inventory demonstrate that these prematurely deceased individuals came from wealthy families (Martin 1991: 51–57; Pirling 1993; Rottloff 1995: 381–383). Due to the decline in grave furnishing noted above, the latest examples again concentrate in the area north of the Alps. It is interesting that the two combinations – dolls and *crepundia* on the one hand, musical instruments on the other hand – have not so far occurred together.

The wide geographical and chronological distribution of the girls' graves with rich (bridal) jewellery as well as dolls, *crepundia* or musical instruments, indicates the wide spread and consistency of the fundamental ideas which had their roots in Graeco-Roman traditions. In late Roman times there was a wealthy class in the provinces which had connections and property across the whole Empire (Painter 1988). The mobility and life-style of this social group and its milieu, and their treatment of the *mors immatura*, of which the archaeological traces have been preserved by the persistence of furnishing graves, explain the late Roman examples in the provinces.

In a Christian environment the doll would, of course, not be dedicated to the gods. The form of the tradition was maintained, but interpreted in a Christian way: the doll becomes the symbol of virginity, a virtue very much propagated by the church-fathers (Cooper 1996: esp. 45–67), and the girl becomes, as it were, a bride of Christ. The fact that in the catacombs bone dolls were pressed into the gypsum covers of the *loculi* even of small children – for instance on the *loculus* of the 15 month old girl Hermofilis in the catacomb of Novatian (Degen 1997: 35 Abb. 12) – also speaks for this *interpretatio Christiana*, whereas dolls and also symbols of the *mundus muliebris*, such as the mirror, spindle and distaff were not customary as grave-goods for girls before the age of five to seven in a pagan *Roman* environment (cf. Table 7.1).

Was it usual to represent the 'non-attained wedding'?

The pain experienced at the death of unmarried girls, some of whom had died just before the wedding which at that time, along with bearing children, was the most important social aim of a woman, is expressed by Juvenal (*Sat.* XV, 138 ff.): *naturae imperio gemimus cum funus adultae virginis occurrit.*

It must therefore be asked whether the custom of furnishing the graves of girls and young women in a particular way as *immaturae et innuptae* is also recognised in other classes and parts of Roman society. We often find that those burials in Rome and in the provinces which were more richly furnished with jewellery and other grave-goods than normal for the contemporary regional rite,

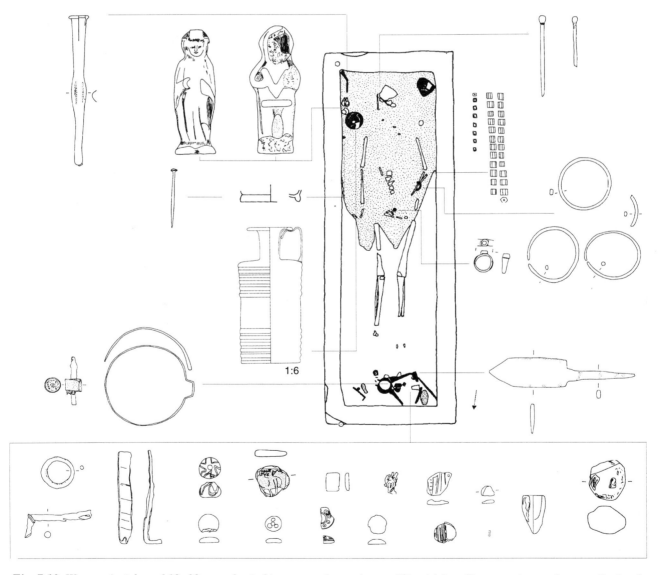

Fig. 7.10 *Worms. A girl aged 12–13 years buried in a sarcophagus (grave 58), with jewellery, amulets and* crepundia *(scale 1:4) in a casket at her feet. Mid 4th century. After Grünewald 1990: 212–217.*

and from which we know the age of the deceased, belong to girls or very young women (Pauli 1975: 181–191; Martin 1991: 293–299; Rottloff 1995: 381–382). However, if we seek elsewhere the furnishings which characterise our group of girls, we find that dolls of less valuable material are only known from a few graves (e.g. Marcelli 1989, grave 59), even if we consider the fact that wooden and textile dolls or *crepundia* of organic material rarely survive in the ground (cf. textile dolls from late antique Egypt: Bailey ed. 1996). Furthermore, the numerous amulets known from children's and women's burials of the Roman period do not share many formal characteristics with the *crepundia* under discussion here. Indeed, the basic idea of protection during life can be expressed in completely different ways. Nevertheless, it is worth consideration whether above-average jewellery combined with amulet-like objects in girls' burials may hint at the 'non-attained wedding' (cf. Fig. 7.10).

Dangerous dead and the immaturae et innuptae

In his study of mainly prehistoric amulets, L. Pauli (1975: 181) emphasised that the prematurely deceased could be regarded as dangerous, and he believes the amulets could be interpreted as protection of the bereaved *from* the dead. Such dangerous dead ('gefährliche Tote') can be identified in the Roman burial rite, but more by a special body position and an isolated situation in a cemetery than by the furnishings. It is highly improbable that amulets and *crepundia* found in the graves of Roman girls served as protection *from* the dead.

Another kind of mors immatura: death in childbirth

Distinct from the group of young girls is another specific group of female burials which could contain amulets: women who died in childbirth or with their baby. We refer to this kind of *mors immatura*, even though it does not belong to the group studied here, and which may therefore be possible to be distinguished archaeologically. It is, for example, certainly relevant that in the extremely rich grave of a 20 year old woman with a new-born baby or foetus in Bessines near Niort (dép. Deux-Sèvres) objects of the *pupa* and *crepundia* categories were not present (Mitard 1977). But in the archaeological context often only an exceptional or unusual grave inventory can be recorded, as more precise anthropological age determinations are missing or made difficult by the cremation process. As for cremation burials, further information is lost to the process of selecting the bones and the grave-goods after the cremation and to the very different rite of furnishing the grave with secondary (unburnt) grave-goods.

Finally two points shall be mentioned which, by providing a contrast, show the funerary customs of the prematurely deceased Roman girls in an even stronger light, firstly Roman boys and secondly girls beyond the Germanic *limes*.

Prematurely deceased Roman and Germanic boys

Roman boys from the middle and upper classes were taught in schools from the age of seven years onwards and, if in a position to, finished off at the age of 18 with a higher education from a *rhetor*, lasting three years. At 15 years they entered the world of men (Marquardt 1975: 127).

In contrast to girls, boys cannot or can hardly ever be recognised in Roman graves. Even in provinces north of

Fig. 7.11 *Chieti. Grave stele of the boy Alexander, c. AD 100 (?):* Alexander Maraidi Sex(ti) s(ervus) quot par parenti dequs facer(et) filius mors imatura ademit ut faceret mater filio Alexandro. *After Sanzi Di Mino / Nista 1993, no 38.*

the Alps, which are more generously provided with grave-goods, child burials (i.e. anthropologically determined *infans* II, 6/7 – 14 years) only very occasionally include tools used by men, such as an axe. Such grave-goods seem to belong to the world of adults. The case is different with the funerary monuments above ground and the grave reliefs in which – according to the classical hierarchy of gender – boys are mentioned and depicted more frequently than girls (Fig. 7.11).

Boys distinguished by above-average or rich grave-furnishings can be found neither in Rome nor in the Gallo-Roman world but they do however, occur in *Germania magna*. Three examples of 'Elbe-Germanic' (elbgermanische) cemeteries with representative numbers of burials dating to the 1st to 3rd century AD (Aubstadt: Völling 1995; Dessau: Laser 1965; Zauschwitz: Meyer 1969) will be used here to demonstrate that there are graves of small children with weapons, i.e. armed boys (Fig. 7.12); the quality of the grave furnishings can be outstanding, even compared with contemporary adult burials. Individuals with a higher social position were equipped with a lance and axe, other boys were only provided with an axe. This custom can be traced back to

the early Imperial period in Aubstadt, and then continued for example in Zauschwitz (3rd century AD) until the early medieval period (Ottinger 1974; Martin 1991: 307). The boys from Aubstadt and Zauschwitz were given weapons of children's size, which indicated their special production; a small boy in Zauschwitz was cremated with a male belt of normal size including a purse with fire-steel, awl, knife and comb.

Aubstadt Grab 1

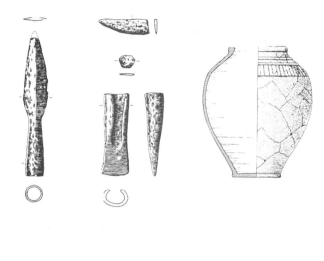

Zauschwitz Grab 14

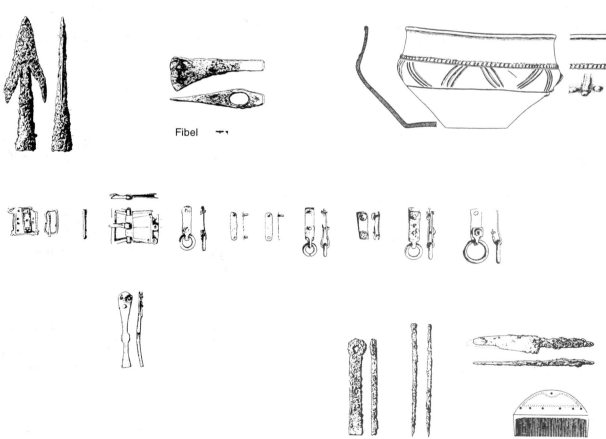

Fibel

Fig. 7.12 *Aubstadt (A) and Zauschwitz (B). Germanic boy's graves of the 1st and 3rd century AD. Scale 1:4 (urns 1:6). After Völling 1995; Meyer 1969.*

Certainly nobody will suggest that Germanic boys aged between 1 and 6 years walked around armed with weapons and wearing male belts, and despite their specially made weapons they were no warriors. Instead it mirrors the familial and social structure within Germanic society: the prematurely deceased son and heir is buried according to his warrior rank, possibly because of the belief that he would need these status symbols in the other world. These communities were dependants of armed leaders, whose image had an important impact on the representation of the social hierarchy.

The representation of Roman boys in a funerary context differs completely from these examples in *Germania*, although the social rank on both sides was determined by birth, and both societies were patriarchal. But in the Roman Empire social rank was defined by the state and the Emperor. Therefore the armed warrior was no longer the ideal, but instead, over most of the period, the career of a man as an official was crucial, in which military service only represented one stage. Moreover, representations and inscriptions could be used to show which career would have been expected for the deceased boy (cf. Walser 1979: No. 45). Exceptional grave furnishings were not necessary.

An atypical 'Elbe-Germanic' girl's grave from Gundelsheim

Unlike the Roman Empire, in the 'Elbe-Germanic' region boys but not girls were buried in an exceptional way, apart from a few cases, for example the grave of a girl

from Lalendorf (Gebühr 1976: Fig. 33). The three Germanic cemeteries noted above demonstrate that from the first to the third century AD there are indeed girls' burials furnished with female equipment earlier than in the Roman provinces (Fig. 7.13), but without any outstanding objects. This makes the grave of a three-year-old girl from Gundelsheim (Kreis Heilbronn) especially interesting (Roeren 1959) (Fig. 7.14).

Gundelsheim, north of Bad Wimpfen on the river Neckar, was, until AD 260, part of the province *Germania superior* east of the Rhine. The elaborate tomb was situated close to a Roman villa and probably belonged to one of the early Germanic settlements beyond the limes (Katalog Alamannen 1997: 121–141). The burial dates to the later 3rd century. Apart from brooches and beads of the 'Elbe-Germanic' costume, a shell-shaped rock-crystal pendant is striking and is doubtless a Roman product. A bronze basin and a glass beaker also come from the provinces, as does a miniature *patera* with ram's head terminal. The rock-crystal shell and the miniature bronze vessel lead us into the ideological world of the funerals of Roman girls considered here and are foreign in the Germanic environment. The adoption not only of Roman goods, for example bronze basins and glass vessels, but also of the custom of furnishing a girl at her death in an exceptional way, for example with miniatures, indicates the reception of Roman traditions in Gundelsheim. Note, however, that in the Roman world, the rite did not apply to very young girls up to the fourth century AD.

Contacts with *Germania Magna* are particularly clear

Zauschwitz Grab 56

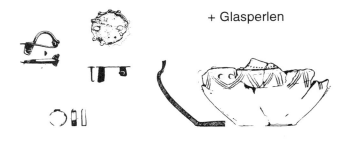

+ Glasperlen

Zauschwitz Grab 34

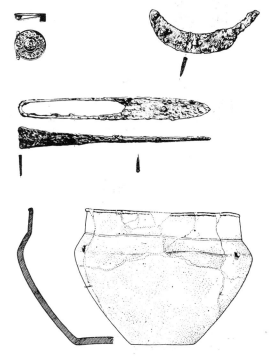

***Fig. 7.13** Zauschwitz. Germanic girl's graves of the 2nd and 3rd century AD. Scale 1:4 (urns 1:6). After Meyer 1969.*

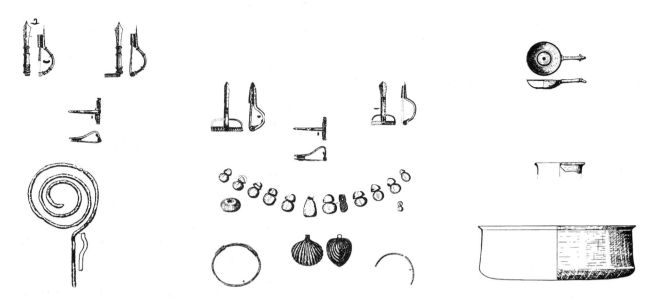

Fig. 7.14 *Gundelsheim. Rich 'Elbe-Germanic' girl's grave. Late 3rd century AD. Scale 1:4 (vessels 1:6). After Roeren 1959: Taf. 45.*

in the late 3rd century during the so called Gallic Empire (260–274). They resulted in the beginning of a Romanisation of the Germanic upper class on different levels, which can be most clearly seen in the Hassleben-Leuna group (Dusek 1992: 135–151). It is uncertain how the community of Gundelsheim was influenced by Roman culture. Family connections are possible, the mother of the girl might even have originated in the provinces. However, coming from a leading Germanic family, the girl had to be buried in Germanic costume.

Perspectives

The burial practices concerning prematurely deceased young girls and boys mirror different social structures and religious traditions. The girls studied here, from a wealthy and / or high status Roman social class with Graeco-Roman traditions, with their uniform grave furnishings, offer a reliable foundation for interpretation: they evoke the 'non-attained wedding' and female virtues. On the other hand, in the western provinces, girls with adornment and different amulets and even miniatures (*crepundia?*) are already known in the pre-Roman period (e.g. Alzey Grab 10: Stümpel 1991: 80 – 83) and continue until late Roman times (Fig. 7.10). Do they express the same concept of the unattained wedding? In Germania Magna, however, we see clear differences to the Roman western provinces. But which status do the girls have in the 'Elbe-Germanic region'? For the future it would be worthwhile to discuss burial rites for children and young people in a wider context, and contrast the archaeological results with comparative religion, folklore and anthropology.

List 1

In Table 7.1 elements of the following graves are listed: North of Rome, 'girl's grave': Zahn 1950/51; Vierneisel 1978: 184–195 (type of burial unknown, most probably inhumation). – Puglia: Arezzo, il Museo Archeologico Nazionale G. C. Mecenate. Florence 1987: 116. – Brescello: Degani 1951 / 52. – Rome, Prati de Castello: Crepereia Tryphaena 1983; Bedini 1995: 64–75. – Rome, Via Cassia: Bordenache Battaglia 1983: 49–78; Bedini 1995: 89–109. – Rome, Vallerano: Bedini et al. 1995; Bedini 1995: 31–57. – Tivoli: Mancini 1930; Bedini 1995: 84–87. – Bonn: Haberey 1961. – Trento: Endrizzi 1990: 25–33 (tomba A). – Emona: Petru 1972: 172 plate 115, 2. – Lyon: Allmer/Dissard 1890: no. 291. – Tarragona: Serra Vilaro 1944: 203–204; Balil 1962: 82; Almagro Gorbea/Sesé 1996: 176. – Yverdon: Rossi 1993.

Acknowledgements

This paper is part of my inaugural lecture entitled 'Mors immatura: Archäologische Aussagen zum Umgang mit dem vorzeitigen Tod in römischer Zeit' held in June 1995 in Bern. I wish to thank Manuela Struck, Birmingham, for the translation into English and A. Schaub, Bern, for some additional help, and E. Schmid, Institut für Ur- und Frühgeschichte und Archäologie der Römischen Provinzen, Bern, for the graphic design and lay-out of the figures. For archaeological information I am grateful to H. Chew, Musée des Antiquités Nationales, St-Germain-en-Laye, M. Martin, München/Basel, D. Castella and L. Steiner, Gollion.

Notes

1. For the written sources cf. DAC, s.v. *crepundia*; for other colloquial terms (*monumenta, signa*) cf. Manson 1978: 869 note 25. – The *bulla* is a specific amulet which was worn around the neck.

2. Admittedly the bronze sheet interpreted by Rottloff 1995 (Abb. 4, 6) as part of a *crotala* is very large (10 cm diameter) and is quite thin and may belong instead to a piece of furniture.

3. After the closure of this manuscript Degen (1997) has published a series of good illustrations of *pupae*, based on Manson (1978).

Bibliography

Allmer, A. and Dissard, P. 1890. Inscriptions antiques au Musée de Lyon 3. Lyon

Almagro Gorbea, M. and Sesé, G. 1996. La muneca de marfil de Segobriga. *Madrider Mitteilungen*, 37: 170–180

Amedick, R. 1991. *Die Sarkophage mit den Darstellungen aus dem Menschenleben. Teil 4: Vita privata* . Berlin

Balil, A. 1962. Munecas antiguas en España. *Archivo Español de Arqueologia*, 35: 70–85

Baratte, F. (ed.) 1988. *Argenterie Romaine et Byzantine. Actes table ronde Paris 1983*. Paris

Barbera, M. 1991. I crepundia di Terracina: Analisi e interpretazione di un dono. *Bolletino di Archeologia*, 10: 11–33

Bedini, A. 1995. *Mistero di una fanciulla*. Catalogue Rome

Bedini, A., Testa, C. and Catalano P. Roma 1995. Un sepolcreto di epoca imperiale a Vallerano. *Archeologia Laziale*, 12: 319–331

Bordenache Battaglia, G. 1983. *Corredi funerari di età imperiale e barbarica nel Museo nazionale romano*. Catalogue Rome

Cooper, K. 1996. *The Virgin and the Bride. Idealized Womanhood in Late Antiquity*. Cambridge, London.

Crepereia Tryphaena 1983. Catalogue Rome

DAC. Daremberg, Ch. and Saglio, E. *Dictionnaire des Antiquités Grecques et Romaines*. Paris

De Carolis, E. 1993/94. Lo scavo dei fornici 7 ed 8 sulla marina di Ercolano. *Rivista Studi Pompeiani*, 6: 168–186

Degani, M. 1951/52. I giocattoli di Giulia Grafide fanciulla Brescellese. *Bulletino comunale Roma*, 74: 15–19

Degen, R. 1997. Römische Puppen aus Octodurus/Martigny VS. *Helvetia Archaeologica*, 28: 15–38

Dusek, S. 1992. *Römische Handwerker im germanischen Thüringen*. Stuttgart

Endrizzi, L. 1990. *'Ai Paradisi'. Una necropoli romana a Trento*. Catalogue Trento

Fasold, P., Fischer, Th., v. Hesberg, H. and Witteyer, M. (ed.). *Bestattungssitte und kulturelle Identität. Grabanlage und Grabbeigaben der frühen römischen Kaiserzeit in Italien und den Nordwest-Provinzen*. Koll. Xanten 1995. Köln

Ferdière, A. (ed.) 1993. *Monde des morts, monde des vivants en Gaule rurale*. Actes colloque ARCHEA/AGER Orléans 1992. *Suppl. Revue Archéologique Centre*, 6

Fernandez-Chicarro y de Dios, C. 1978. Reciente decubrimiento de una tumba romana, del siglo I de la Era, en la zona del anfiteatro de Carmona. *Boletin de Bellas Artes*, 6: 139–161.

Gebühr, M. 1976. *Der Trachtschmuck der älteren römischen Kaiserzeit*. Göttingen

van Gennep, A. 1909. *Les rites de passage*.

Grünewald, M. 1990. *Der römische Nordfriedhof in Worms*. Worms

Haberey, W. 1938. Ein Buchssträusschen in einem spätrömischen Grab bei Mayen. *Rheinische Vorzeit in Wort und Bild*, 1:46–48

Haberey, W. 1961. Ein Mädchengrab römischer Zeit aus der Josefstrasse in Bonn. *Bonner Jahrbücher*, 161: 319–332

Haevernick, Th.E. and von Saldern, A. (ed.) 1976. *Festschrift Waldemar Haberey*. Mainz 1976

Hopkins, K. 1965. The Age of Roman Girls at Marriage. *Population Studies*, 18: 309–327

Katalog Alamannen 1997. *Die Alamannen*. Katalog Landesmuseum. Stuttgart

Lafaye, G. 1887. Pupa. In: DAC I.2: 768–769

Laser, R. 1965: *Die Brandgräber der spätrömischen Kaiserzeit im nördlichen Mitteldeutschland*. Forschungen zur Vor- u. Frühgeschichte 7

Mancini, G. 1930. Tivoli – Scoperta della tomba della Vergine Vestale tiburtina Cossinia. *Notizie degli Scavi*, 6: 353–369

Manson, M. 1978. Histoire d'un mythe: les poupées de Maria, femme d'Honorius. *Mélanges Ecole Française Rome* 90, 1978: 863–869

Marcelli, M. 1989. Su alcune tombe tardo-antiche di Roma: Nota preliminare. *Archeologia Medievale* 16, 1989, 525–540

Marquardt, J. 1975. *Das Privatleben der Römer*. Reprint Darmstadt

Martin, M. 1991. *Das spätrömisch-frühmittelalterliche Gräberfeld von Kaiseraugst (Kt. Aargau)*. Derendingen

Martin-Kilcher, S. 1976. *Das römische Gräberfeld von Courroux*. Derendingen, Solothurn

Martin-Kilcher, S. 1998. Gräber der späten Republik und der frühen Kaiserzeit am Lago Maggiore: Tradition und Romanisierung. In: Fasold, P., Fischer, Th., v. Hesberg, H. and Witteyer, M. (ed.): 191–252

Meyer, E. 1969. *Das germanische Gräberfeld von Zauschwitz, Kr. Borna*. Arbeits- u. Forschungsberichte sächsische Bodendenkmalpflege Beih. 6

Mitard, P-H. 1977. Une riche sépulture gallo-romaine découverte près de Niort (Deux-Sèvres). *Gallia*, 35: 201–227

Ottinger, I. 1974. Waffenbeigabe in Knabengräbern. *Festschrift Joachim Werner*. München: 387–410

Painter, K. 1988. Roman Silver Hoards: Ownership and Status. In: Baratte, F. (ed.): 97–112

Pauli, L. 1975. *Keltischer Volksglaube*. Münchner Beiträge zur Vor- und Frühgeschichte No. 28. Munich

Petru, S. 1972. *Emonske Nekropole*. Ljubljana

Petrucci-Bavaud, M. and Jacomet, S. 1997. Zur Interpretation von Nahrungsbeigaben in römerzeitlichen Brandgräbern. *Ethnographisch-Archäologische Zeitschrift* 38: 567–593

Pirling, R. 1976. Klothos Kunkel. In: Haevernick and von Saldern (ed.) 1976: 101–109

Roeren, R. 1959. Ein frühalamannischer Grabfund von Gundelsheim (Kr. Heilbronn). *Fundberichte Schwaben NF*, 15: 83–93

Rossi, F. 1993. Deux poupées en ivoire d'époque romaine à Yverdon-les-Bains VD. *Archäologie der Schweiz*, 16: 152–157

Rottloff, A. 1995. Der Grabfund von der Blauen Kappe in Augsburg. Bemerkungen zu römischen Frauengräbern des 2. und 3. Jahrhunderts mit Goldschmuck. In: *Provinzialrömische Forschungen. Festschrift G. Ulbert*. Espelkamp: 371–386

Sanzi Di Mino M.R. and Nista, L. 1993. *Gentes et Principes*. Catalogue Chieti

Schwidetzky, I. 1965. Sonderbestattungen und ihre paläodemographische Bedeutung. *Homo*, 16: 230–247

Serra Vilaro, J. 1944. Sepulcros y ataudes de la necropolis de San Fructuoso. *Ampurias*, 6: 179–208

Stümpel, B. 1991. *Beiträge zur Latènezeit im Mainzer Becken und Umgebung*. Mainzer Zeitschrift Beih.1, 1991

Ter Vrugt-Lenz, J. 1960. *Mors immatura*. Groningen

Treggiari, S. 1991. *Roman Marriage*. Oxford

Vierneisel, K. (ed.) 1978. *Römisches im Antikenmuseum*. Katalog Berlin

Völling, Th. 1995. *Frühgermanische Gräber von Aubstadt im Grabfeldgau (Unterfranken)*. Materialhefte Bayerische Vorgeschichte 67. Kallmünz

Walser, G. 1979. *Römische Inschriften in der Schweiz I*. Bern

Zimmer, G. 1982. *Römische Berufsdarstellungen*. Berlin

8. Portrait figures on funerary altars of Roman *liberti* in Northern Italy: Romanization or the assimilation of attributes characterising higher social strata?

Dagmar Dexheimer

Funerary altars with relief ornament are found in northern Italy from the early 1st centurty AD, while lavish decoration, figures and mythological scenes do not appear before the second quarter of the 1st century. By this time, northern Italy had been an integral part of the Roman Empire for well over a century. The confrontation with Roman life-style, customs and art over at least two generations made its mark on the fashioning of graves. There was an adjustment to metropolitan Roman burial rites in northern Italy. In both areas people of all social strata preferred burial along the principal roads leading in and out of towns. Burial places were styled modestly or impressively, mostly according to financial circum- stances. However, northern Italian funerary altars developed regional variations of placing and design which differ from those of the *urbs*. In Rome altars were erected, sometimes in numbers, in closed burial chambers which have a distinctly private character (Boschung 1987: 37). In northern Italy however altars were set up exclusively in the open air, in the centre or at the rear of a burial area enclosed by walls or by waist-high stone balustrades, and were visible from a distance. Thus, they were intended to address the public directly. Northern Italian monuments also differ from those of urban Rome in the choice of decorative forms and by the use of often large motifs visible from some distance. Urban Roman monuments in contrast generally display rather small neat decoration, meant to be viewed at close quarters.

As differences in types of grave and grave decoration between northern Italy and Rome persisted during the imperial period, northern Italian burial practices cannot be explained only as the result of a developing Romaniza- tion on the part of the local population. They must rather be viewed as a local artistic and subjective preference. Nevertheless to bring the question of Romanisation into clear focus, it must be considered whether from the heterogeneous mass of donors of altars a group can be isolated for which a direct confrontation with Roman *mores* and customs is not obvious. Such a group is undoubtedly that of slaves and *liberti*. They constantly faced the same choice, whether to continue their own native traditions, or to assimilate to the habits of their social environment – in this case to Roman life-styles and burial practices. The status of freedmen and slaves differs not only legally but also by their common subordinate social position from other donors of altars.

Of 247 altars which have been analysed within the framework of this study, only two were erected on behalf of slaves and only one for a slave by another slave (Gabelmann 1977: 218 fig. 17). Many more, 41, were built by *liberti* who are securely identifiable by way of their pseudofiliation. Together with those persons who, according to their *cognomina*, must also be assigned freedman status, they constitute more than half of all owners or donors of funerary altars in Northern Italy. The decision of slaves and *liberti* to choose a funerary altar as a monument already hints at an assimilation to Roman burial practices and in fact amounts to settling the question of Romanization in Northern Italy during the 1st and the early 2nd century AD. With the attainment of Roman citizenship, with emancipation, or with constant cultural confrontation, known Roman forms of expression in funerary art are adopted and publicly demonstrated.

When we scrutinise the funerary altars of *liberti* in greater detail, however, we find that the result of the confrontation with Roman funerary art reveals different degrees of intensity, finding its culmination within a small but significant group. Altars bearing relief decoration are divided equally between *liberti* and *ingenui*. This examina- tion makes clear the degree to which the will to adopt Roman models can also be seen in the decoration of the altar. The sides of such altars display portrait figures. These representations doubtless depict those persons with a direct connection to the monument, either as the deceased or as donors. On seven of the nine altars with portrait figures both sides are still well preserved (see appendix for list and references). Each of them reveals one female and one male figure, with the exception of the altar of Albius Vitalis, on which the female figure has no portrait quality. Previously these figures were regarded as representations of the deceased, but who were they really? A thorough examination, together with a consideration of

Fig. 8.1a Funerary altar of Quintus Cerrinius Cordus, left side, portrait of Iulia Donacine?

Fig. 8.1b Funerary altar of Quintus Cerrinius Cordus, right side, portrait of Quintus Cerrinius Corinthus?

the inscriptions leads to an alternative result of interest to the question posed above, i.e. whether the freedmen of northern Italy recorded on the funerary altars were deeply Romanised or merely adjusted to the practices of higher social strata.

In the case of the altar of Arrius Macer (1) the identity of the female figure is easily determined. The inscription mentions one Arria Trophime as the donor, arranging the construction of the altar during her lifetime. As she is the only female person mentioned in the inscription, the figure probably depicts Arria herself.

The inscription on the altar of Cerrinius Cordus (2) mentions only one female person who is therefore represented by the female figure, the donor's wife. Brusin (1929: 237) calls the male figure Cerrinius Cordus, i.e. the patron, whose name appears first in the inscription and in the dative form. Brusin takes it for granted that the naming of individuals in the dative case *per se* implies that they are dead. Thus he concludes that the two portraits on the sides of the altar represent the patron and the donor's wife. We must keep in mind, however, that the naming of an individual in the dative case is not proof

that they are dead. The inscription on the altar of Sextus Caesernius (3), for example, mentions five other persons – in addition to the patron – whose names are given in the dative case. Three of them are characterised as still living by a 'V' after their names. Evidence for the death of a named person can be obtained from information about the life-span of the individual in question, a comprehensive *cursus honorum* or the cause of death; for example the funerary altar of Lucius Atilius Saturninus in Aquileia records his murder by thieves (Dessau 1962: 8570). Attributes like *pientissimus* or *carissimus* generally characterise already deceased persons. *Dis Manibus* however, can also be used in an anticipatory sense, thus referring to all persons mentioned in the inscription, i.e. also to those still alive at the time of the erection of the altar. Therefore a certain degree of caution is required before making such generalisations and inscriptions have to be scrutinised in the light of this particular problem. In the case of the altar of Cerrinius, the patron may well be deceased, but we cannot necessarily assume the same for Iulia the donor's wife. Her picture is presented on the left side. On the opposite side her husband, Quintus Cerrinius

Fig. 8.2a *Funerary altar of Sextus Caesernius Libanus, left side, portrait of Caesernia Prima?*

Fig. 8.2b *Funerary altar of Sextus Caesernius Libanus, right side, portrait of Sextus Caesernius Cedrus?*

Corinthus, is depicted. This interpretation seems certainly more plausible than the combination 'patron and donor's wife'.

The inscription on the altar of Sextus Caesernius Libanus (3) admittedly names no less than four female persons, but the arrangement and combination of the names do not lend themselves to any other conclusion than that the portrait figures are identical with the two donors, Sextus Caesernius Cedrus and Caesernia Prima, both still living at the time of construction. The patron's (Sextus Caesernius Libanus) death was the occasion for the building of the monument.

On the altar of Tiberius Claudius Germanus (4), erected under the common auspices of Tiberius Claudius Germanus, his wife Julia Procne, and his son Tiberius Claudius Proculus, the donors' portraits probably figure as well. The situation, however, is not absolutely unequivocal, as parts of the inscription are missing and other individuals are mentioned to whom the images could

possibly refer. But we may assume on analogy with the aforementioned examples that reference is made to donors still living at the time of construction.

The circumstances of the erection of the altars of Maia Severa (5) and Albius Vitalis (6) must remain unclear. The slight remnants of the former's inscription do not furnish sufficient information concerning the donors, but merely name two of the individuals to whom the altar was dedicated. The relationship between these two persons cannot be ascertained. The latter altar permits both kinds of interpretation, i.e. that the portrait is of a friend who is the donor of the altar, or of the deceased.

There is no doubt as to the identity of the individuals depicted on the altar of Tiberius Claudius Astylus (7). Astylus himself is recognisable as *ingenuus* by his filiation; this cannot be taken for granted however for his father and wife. The inscription pertains to the donor and his wife. As the male figure on the side is endowed with a *dolabra*, we may take it for an image of the still-living

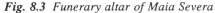

Fig. 8.3 *Funerary altar of Maia Severa*

Fig. 8.4 *Funerary altar of Albius Vitalis, right side*

donor, Tiberius Claudius Astylus, who claims to hold the office of *dolabrarius*. The female figure must be his wife, Julia Dionysia.

On the altar of Onesimus (8), too, the donor has had himself depicted, together with his already deceased wife, Illyria Severilla. The same holds true for the case of Caius Trosius Azbestus (9), whose image and that of his wife we find on the sides of his altar. He, and probably his wife too, were still living when the altar was raised; their son's death provided the occasion for the foundation.

Thus in seven out of nine cases the portrait figures on the altar sides are securely identifiable with donors who were still living at the time the altars were built. By representing male figures in togas and women in Roman dress, the donors made use of a formal idiom which clearly and unequivocally alluded to free-born Roman citizens. Employing this statuary type as a model for the reliefs is a clue to the significance of the image (see below). This aspect, the allusion to the free-born Roman, must above

all be viewed in the light of the reputation and social status of the people in question, as the dedicators were *liberti*, and thus individuals with a low social standing. The expression 'of lower social status' does not exclusively refer to their financial situation but to their position on the social pyramid constructed by Alföldy (1975: 131). In this sense *ingenui*, *liberti* and slaves constitute the lower classes. There may be gradual differences of ranking not always dependent on juridical status.

It is all the more astonishing therefore that in most cases, the donors unashamedly specify their status. They explicitly declare that they themselves are still among the living and, frequently, that they have commissioned the altar for some person of higher standing in the social hierarchy who had already gained acceptance within society. Thus Arria (1) declares herself to be a freedwoman of Arrius Macer. By mentioning her patron in the first place in the inscription and by also alluding to his military career and his decurionate in Aquileia, she hopes that his reputation is associated with her own. Thereby the ultimate motive for the donation seems not to be the death of her patron, but that of her son, Caius Varius Arrianus. The founders of Cerrinius' altar (2) too could bask in the glory of their patron's military career, which is presented at the very beginning of the inscription. Things are different with the donor of the altar of Sextus Caesernius (3). Here too the patron is represented in the first place, but he is not characterised as an outstanding member of society, but as someone to whom Sextus Caesernius Cedrus owes his freedom. The founder seizes the opportunity to name his own office. Onesimus (8) proceeds along the same lines, he calls himself *servus vilicus vectigalis*, an office which was evidently particularly prestigious. Caius Trosius Azbestus (9) did not hold any office; he and his wife were both freedmen of one Caius. Claudius Astylus (7) dedicates the altar to himself and to his wife. His father is honoured by detailed mention, even though he is not the 'dedicatee' of the altar in the proper sense of the word. Astylus himself also mentions his office of *dolabrarius*. It is not quite clear if this office is endowed with a lower social standing but the over-explicit reference to his father's military rank makes this likely.

Of all people the *liberti* chose a motif for the decoration of their grave for which the models are to be found among the statues of the public domain. The particular significance of these portrait figures can only be fully acknowledged when we focus our attention on these models. A statue on a pedestal with an inscription, set up in a public place generally recognised as such, was meant above all to publicise and preserve the achievements and the appearance of the honoured persons (Lahusen 1983: 135). The precursors of the honorific statues are those of Greek funerary decoration, the *schemata* of which can be traced back to Greek honorific statuary of the 4th century BC (Zanker 1992: 344). Zanker views the statement of achievement as already implied in Hellenistic statues. He regards the *liberti* of the late republican period as recipients or fresh creators of this manifestation in combination with Roman portraiture. Maia Severa's altar bears testimony to the concrete influence of Greek funerary decoration on the images on the sides of altars. The motif of a woman sitting on a throne does not appear, it is true, in Greek grave reliefs, but the similarity to Greek domestic or farewell scenes cannot be overlooked. It is a prerequisite for the honouring that the person in question belongs to a higher *ordo* endowed with *honos*; he must, therefore, already be socially accepted, although there are exceptions (Alföldy 1984: 61. 67; Lahusen 1983: 122; Rollin 1979: 26). Membership of a higher *ordo* is primarily based on free status. But it also depends on the pecuniary situation of the dedicatee, as well as on his willingness to accept public offices and to exert power and influence. The latter two aspects, however, can only be realised when there is a general acceptance within the social environment. Both requirements are interdependent. Thus the statue is the symbolic embodiment of those values which are closely associated with exemplary citizenship, i.e. free birth, membership of an elevated social stratum and possibly also political activity within the framework of a municipal community. Boschung (1987: 53) however interprets the wearing of the toga by those not authorised to as simply a sign of distinction.

Freed status precluded membership or advancement to a privileged *ordo* and therefore also the public erection of statues. This does not hold true to the same degree for veterans or the sons of freedmen, yet honorary statues and foundations were exceptional for this social class also (Ausbüttel 1982: 37). *Liberti* could hold public office only within the framework of a sevirate. To obtain honorary statues in public places was at best a posthumous honour (Alföldy 1984: 61). Notwithstanding this, the *liberti* wished to demonstrate their own exemplary citizenship and to present themselves as full members of society. Thus they adopted this form of funerary decoration, the demonstrative intent of which corresponds to that of a statue.

This demonstration of assimilation to higher social strata is reinforced by the fact the donors of the altar were still alive at the time of construction. The primary purpose of erecting a funerary altar does not therefore consist of the wish to preserve the memory of a deceased person and to extol him by artistic representation, but to underpin the aspirations of the donor to a higher social standing. By commissioning an altar on which he is depicted in the desired form, the donor combines the memorial function of the altar – which attains its real meaning only after the donor's death – with the representational function of a monument. Such a monument however could only be erected within the private realm, encompassing in juridical terms the area of the burial place. The juridical basis is decisive for the attribution of the grave to the private domain. The right to a grave is already constituted by the choice of the type of grave: individual grave, family grave, or hereditary grave. The donor, i.e. founder, as an individual, creates a right which is binding for others (private autonomy). By defining the purpose of the area as a burial site, it is withdrawn from normal jurisdiction and as *locus religiosus* is attributed to the *ius sepulchri* or to penal law

The strong rules of urban representational art were obviously not binding here. Considering the location of the sites on the principal roads to or from the towns which all travellers had to use, the portrait figures on the funerary altars almost amount to public honouring. Thus they constitute the most explicit evidence for the freedmen's aspirations to social acceptance. These aspirations in turn, led to the absorption of Roman representational forms in funerary art, but they are equally an indication of an intensifying Romanization process.

It is quite remarkable in this context that not one single Roman citizen certainly belonging to a higher *ordo* made use of this decorative form. Numisius Castor's altar is not an exception to the rule, as it is not absolutely certain that the donors were free-born Romans; the absence of filiation could also be an indication of freedman status. In addition, we lack information about offices and titles. On both sides we find one bearded *togatus*. In spite of a high artistic standard it is not clear whether the portraits are those of two different persons. However as the name of Marcus Numisius Castor appears on the right side below the presentation, the identification is unequivocal. Thus the representation on the on the opposite side must be that of Quintus Velucius Verus, who fulfilled his friend's testament. Identification of both *togati* with the deceased Marcus Numisius Castor would not be inconceivable, but quite uncommon. The remaining certainly free-born dedicators generally preferred motifs and ornaments with a more direct funerary symbolism. In the area of municipal Rome portrait figures on funerary altars are wholly absent. By choosing portrait figures as decoration, the *liberti* expressed their aspirations to be accepted as genuine Roman citizens on the one hand while on the other they differentiated themselves from other altar donors in a very conspicuous manner. This differentiation is possibly therefore also meant to be programmatic, pointing to an increased self-consciousness of this group. In the course of the 2nd century the differences in the choice of grave decorations between *ingenui* and *liberti* diminish visibly. This phenomenon can initially be explained by the art-historical development of the monumental form, a development which, so far as numbers and splendour are concerned, was already past its prime by the end of the 1st century. The increased acceptance of freedmen in society, manifesting itself officially in *the Constitutio Antoniniana* in the early 3rd century, must also have contributed to this process.

Appendix

Monuments

(All dimensions in centimetres (H=height, W=width, D=depth))

1. **Funerary altar of Lucius Arrius Macer**; Provenance: Aquileia, near S. Giovanni; Current location: Aquileia, Museo Archeologico; Inv.-Nr. 16; Material: Limestone; Dimensions: H. 189; W. 133; D. 91; L(ucio) Arrio / Macro / veterano milit(avit) ann(os) XXXVI / in aere inciso ab / Divo Vespasiano / decurioni Aquileiae / Arria L(uci) / l(iberta) Trophime / patrono v(iva) f(ecit) / sibiq(ue) et suis / C(aio) Vario Arriano annor(um) XV / ab amico deceptus. (Scrinari 1972: 130 Nr. 371 Abb. 371)

2. **Funerary altar of Quintus Cerrinius Cordus** (Figs. 8.1a and b); Provenance: St. Egidio near Aquileia. Current location: Aquileia, Museo Archeologico. Inv.-Nr. 1062; Material: Limestone; Dimensions: H. 120; W. 89; D. 63; Q(uinto) Cerrinio C(ai) f(ilio) / Cam(ilia tribu) Cordo / mil(iti) leg(ionis) VIII Aug(ustae) / patrono / Q(uintus) Cerrinius Q(uinti) l(ibertus) Corinthus / v(ivus) f(ecit) / Iuliae Sex(ti) l(ibertae) Donacini / contubernali / Base: l(ibertis) libertabusque. (Goette 1989: 118 Nr. 82)

3. **Funerary altar of Sextus Caesernius Libanus** (Figs 8.2a and b); Provenance: Aquileia, Via Petrada; Current location: Aquileia, Museo Archeologico; Inv.-Nr. 981; Material: Limestone; Dimensions: H. 120; W. 101; D. 77; Sex(to) Caesernio / Libano patron(o) / Sex(tus) Caesernius Cedrus / IIIIII vir et / Caesernia Sex(ti) l(iberta) Prima v(ivi) f(ecerunt) / Caeserniae Iridi f(iliae) / Caeserniae Iucundae v(ivae) / L(ucio) Plancio Antae amico v(ivo) / S(exto) Caesernio Diodoto conlib(erto) v(ivo) / Caeserniae Venustae lib(ertae) v(ivae) / l(ibertis) l(ibertabusque) suis. Base: L(ocum) m(onumenti) in (fronte). (Goette 1989: 126 Nr. 264)

4. **Funerary altar of Tiberius Claudius Germanus**; Provenance: Casa Bianca near Aquileia; Current location: Aquileia, Museo Archeologico; Inv.-Nr. 379/877; Material: Limestone; Dimensions: H. 150; W. 113; D. 96; Ti(berius) Claudius / Germanus / et Iulia Q(uinti) liberta / Proc(i)ne v(ivi) f(ecerunt) / Ti(berio) Claudio / Ti(beri) f(ilio) Proculo / ann(orum) XXVII / Iuli(ae) matr(i) et / M(arco) [—]vio Adiutori VI vir(o). (Scrinari 1972: 129 Nr. 367 Abb. 367)

5. **Funerary altar of Maia Severa** (Fig. 8.3); Provenance: Aquileia, S. Egidio; Current location: Aquileia, Museo Archeologico. Inv.-Nr. 1184; Material: Limestone; Dimensions: H. 132; W. 85; D. 73; Q(uinto) Albio Q(uinti) l(iberto) / Aucto / IIIIII vir(o) et / M[ai]a [S]everae / ann(orum) XXII / Ma[ia] v(iva) f(ecit). (Scrinari 1972: 129 Nr. 368 Abb. 368).

6. **Funerary altar of Albius Vitalis** (Fig. 8.4); Provenance: Aquileia, near Via Gemina; Current location: Aquileia, Museo Archeologico; Inv.-Nr. 440; Material: Limestone; Dimensions: H. 158; W. 83; D. 58; Memoriae / Albi Vitalis / IIIIII viri / C(aius) Vennonius / primus amicus. (Pochmarski Nagele 1992: 146)

7. **Funerary altar of Tiberius Claudius Astylus**; Provenance: Between Beligna and Belvedere, in the south of Aquileia Current location: Vienna, Kunsthistorisches Museum/ Antikensammlung; Inv.-Nr. III 1116; Material: Limestone; Dimensions: H. 105; W. 77; D. 48; Ti(berius) Claudius / Ti(beri) Claudi / Epaphroditian(i) / vet(erani) leg(ionis) VIII Cl(audiae) p(iae) f(idelis) / fil(ius) Astylus / dolabrar(ius) coll(egii) fabr(um) / vivos fecit sibi et / Iuliae Dionysiadi / coniugi / bene de se mer(enti). (Zaccaria 1987: 129)

8. **Funerary altar of Onesimus**; Provenance: Unknown; Current location: Udine; Museo Civico; Inv.-Nr. 163; Material: Limestone; Dimensions: H. 119; W. 77; D. 45; D(is) M(anibus) / Onesimus / ser(vus) vil(icus) / vectigal(is) / Illyr(ae) Severillae / uxori / pientissime / ann(os) XXV / et sibi vivus / fec(it). (unpublished)

9. **Funerary altar of Caius Trosius Azbestus**; Provenance: Belvedere bei Aquileia; Current location: Collaredo di Montalbano; Inv.-Nr. n. v.; Material: Limestone; Dimensions: H. 65; W. 55; D. 43; C(aius) Trosius (Caiae) l(ibertus) / Azbestus / Trosiae C(aiae) l(ibertae) / Nymphini coniugi / Flacco fil(io) ann(orum) XXII / l(ocus) m(onumenti) i(n) fr(onte) p(edes) XVI in agr(o) p(edes) XXXII. (CIL V 1419).

10. **Funerary altar of Marcus Numisius Castor**, Provenance: S. Lazzaro, near Modena; Current location: Modena, Museo Civico, Lapidario; Material: Marble; Dimensions: H. 159; W. 105; D. 97; M(arcus) Numisius / Castor sibi et / Q(uinto) Velucio Vero / contubernali / t(estamento) p(oni) i(ussit); (Rebecchi 1988: 383 Abb. 308)

Acknowledgements

For discussion of the law relating to Roman cemeteries I am obliged to Irmgard Wroblewski, Bonn.

Notes

1. 'Deceased' is defined here as 'no longer alive at the time of the building of the altar'. Brusin (1929: 65) offers the generalisation that all figures on the altars included in his guide are those of 'deceased persons', explicitly Cerrinius Cordus (1929: 237). According to Forlati Tamaro (1933–1934: 36) this applies to Maia Severa and according to Scrinari (1972: 128-129) to both Cerrinius Cordus and Maia Severa. Mansuelli (1958: 95) is of a different opinion on Cerrinius Cordus.

2. For the attribution of graves to sacral law or to penal law, in the course of intensified secularisation during the imperial period compare: RAC 1983: Grab 378; Robinson 1975: 175; Düll 1951: 161; Bürgin-Kreis 1986: 25.; Cicero *de leg.* 2, 18, 46; 2, 22, 57; 2, 26, 64 25.

Bibliography

Alföldy. G. 1975. *Römische Sozialgeschichte.* Wiesbaden: Steiner

Alföldy. G. 1984. *Römische Statuen in Venetia und Histria. Epigraphische Quellen.* Abhandlungen der Heidelberger Akademie der Wissenschaften, 3 Heidelberg: Winter

Ausbüttel. F.M. 1982. *Untersuchungen zu den Vereinen im Westen des römischen Reiches.* Kallmünz: Lassleben

Boschung. D. 1987. *Antike Grabaltäre aus den Nekropolen Roms.* Bern: Stämpfli

Brusin. G. 1929. *Aquileia.* Udine: Edizione de 'La Panarie'

Bürgin-Kreis. H. 1968. In *Provincialia. Festschrift für Laur-Belart*: pp. 25–41

Dessau. H. 1962. *Inscriptiones Latinae Selectae* [3].

Düll. R. 1951, Studien zum römischen Sepulkralrecht. In *2. Atti Congr. intern. Verona*, 3: 161–177.

Forlati Tamaro. B. 1933–1934. Sculture Aquileiesi. *Aquileia Nostra*, 4 – 5: 18–46

Gabelmann. H. 1977. Zur Tektonik oberitalischer Sarkophage, Altäre und Stelen. *Bonner Jahrbücher*, 177: 199–244

Gabelmann. H. 1987. Römische Grabbauten der Nordprovinzen im 2. u. 3. Jh. In *Römische Gräberstraßen* (eds. P. Zanker and H. v. Hesberg): pp. 291–308.

Goette. H. R. 1989. *Studien zu römischen Togadarstellungen.* Mainz: Zabern

Lahusen. G. 1983. *Untersuchungen zur Ehrenstatue in Rom.* Rome: Bretschneider

Mansuelli. G.A. 1958. Il ritratto Romano nell Italia settentrionale. *Römische Mitteilungen*, 65: 68–99

Pochmarski Nagele. M. 1992. *Die dionysischen Reliefs in Noricum und ihre Vorbilder.* Vienna: VWGÖ

Rebecchi. F. 1988. *Modena dalle origini all'anno mille I.* Modena: Panini

Robinson. O. 1975. The Roman law on burials and burial grounds. *Irish Jurist*, 10: 1975–186.

Rollin. J.P. 1979. *Untersuchungen zu Rechtsfragen römischer Bildnisse.* Bonn: Habelt

Scrinari. V.S.M. 1972. *Museo Archeologico di Aquileia. Catalogo delle Sculture Romane.* Rome. Istituto Poligrafico dello Stato

Zaccaria. C. 1987. Aspetti della produzione epigrafica funeraria Aquileiese tra la fine della Repubblica e gli inizi del Principato. *Antichità Altoadratiche*, 29: 129–144

Zanker. P. 1992. Bürgerliche Selbsdarstellung am Grab in römischer Kaiserreich. In *Die römische Stadt im 2. Jh. n. Chr.* (eds. H.J. Schalles, H. v. Hesberg und P. Zanker). Xantener Berichte No. 2: pp. 339–58

9. High status burials in Roman Britain (first – third century AD) – potential interpretation

Manuela Struck

Introduction

In anthropology as in sociology it has often been observed that treatment at death is closely related not only to ideology but also to social position in life. Superior burials are therefore generally linked with the élite of a society – an expression which will be used here for the politically and socially leading group. However, we must be aware that this treatment does not necessarily mirror status in life directly, but can represent an ideal – as V.M. Hope has demonstrated for Roman tombstones in Britain (Hope 1997: 257; for the modern period e.g. Nielsen 1997). Furthermore, status in life can also be influenced by status in death, which includes the circumstances surrounding death, for example heroic or premature death (Peebles 1971: 69; Martin-Kilcher this volume). This article will concentrate on the following three questions, to what extent is status in life reflected in the burial rite, do high status burials show patterns in distribution, chronology and burial rite, and do the results of burial analysis contribute to our understanding of the social structure of Roman Britain?

Ethnographic research has drawn attention to many ways of expressing status after death, and for the Roman period literature provides us with additional information (e.g. Toynbee 1982). There are several stages when status can be demonstrated after death:

1. The funeral process
2. The construction of a monumental form of funerary architecture
3. The treatment of the body
4. The provision of the dead with valuable objects and/or status symbols
5. The location of the grave

If display of status and wealth is forbidden 'much nonmaterial symbolism and lavish nonpermanent display (feasting, elaborate hearses, flowers, the presence of significant persons, etc.)' will be applied (Wason 1994: 69); this is difficult for us to recognise. The degree of display can be related to the so-called energy-expenditure theory which, according to J. Tainter (1977: 332), entitles a deceased of higher rank to a larger amount of corporate involvement in the act of interment, and to greater disruption of normal community activities for the mortuary ritual. Again, factors other than rank might influence the relative energy expended on death ritual, e.g. popularity, or a large family, which is also a form of status but not in a structural (political or economic) sense (cf. Metcalf/Huntington 1992: 150). An elaborate burial may also be conducted simply because of the deceased's connection to a high-status person. Finally the energy is not necessarily expended for grave digging, monument erection etc., and might therefore not leave any archaeological traces (Wason 1994: 78).

Recognising high status in the archaeological evidence

Returning to the first question and thus to the archaeological evidence, the first means suggested to express high status is hardest to identify archaeologically. Cases like the Holborough Knob barrow (Kent; Jessup 1955), St Albans-Folly Lane (Herts., Niblett 1992) and Colchester-Stanway (Essex, Crummy 1993), with remains of a complicated mortuary ceremony, are very rare, not only in Britain but also in other western provinces (cf. e.g. Nuber 1972; Schucany this volume). Customs like offering farewell presents to the dead during the funeral are known from ancient literature (Marquardt 1886: 381–382) and sometimes it is possible to show this with the archaeological evidence (cf. Struck 1996: 82–83). In this context it has been suggested that the quantity of grave-goods – being farewell presents – reflects the social network of the deceased (Millett 1993: 266 ff. esp. 275–277), which would enable us to evaluate his or her status. The success of this approach depends very much on the tradition of grave furnishing, and has so far only been applied to one site; in order to expand it to a wider range of data, for example from a whole province, many small scale studies are needed (for an example of contrasting traditions of grave furnishing in adjacent cemeteries, cf. Jones 1993: 250–251). Finally, there are reasons to

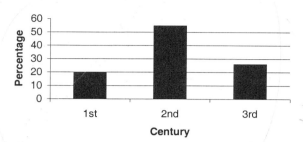

Fig. 9.1 *Chronology of burials. The percentages are calculated as a proportion of the total of datable graves in Roman Britain from the first to the third century.*

suppose that the *bustum* cremation type is connected with an above-average funeral as it requires its own *ustrinum*, meaning more space and effort, and it is often met together with barrows and/or elaborate grave inventories.

The second way to refer to the high status of a dead person is easier to estimate, although here we are faced with the problem of above-ground preservation. Roman Britain does not belong to the provinces and regions of the Roman Empire with a strong tradition of monumental tomb architecture. In total only *c*.2% of the burials in Roman Britain are connected with a funerary monument, which comprise remains of *mausolea*, monuments in stone, masonry tombs, wooden shrines on top of graves, single grave enclosures and barrows. The modest nature of Romano-British burial customs may, to a certain extent, be explained by reference to the weak visible burial evidence from Britain in the late pre-Roman Iron Age, where only five regional groups of burial traditions could be identified, most of the country not providing archaeological evidence for a distinct rite (cf. Whimster 1981). This seems to continue well into the Roman period. Thus about 10,000 known graves dating from the first to the third century contrast with an estimated population in Roman Britain of almost 4 million people (cf. Millett 1995: 45), and those 20% of graves which can be dated show a marked increase in burial numbers between the first and the second centuries AD (Fig. 9.1). It is therefore possible that formal burial, in itself, already indicated a certain status (M. Millett and J. Pearce pers. comm.). However, a precise judgement of this is entirely beyond our understanding.

Concerning the third means of demonstrating status, it has been suggested that careless arrangement of the dead in the grave meant a lack of respect, and certain cases of prone or crouched positions might indicate the deceased's status as a social outcast (Philpott 1991: 71–76. – for the continent see for example van Doorselaer 1967: 129; Mondanel 1989: 39; Friedhoff 1991: 55–56; Fasold 1992: 22). However, the term 'careful' is culturally specific and might not have been the same then as for us today (Millett pers. comm.). Furthermore, special body positions and treatment for high ranking individuals have not yet been

identified with certainty for our period, although there are cases when cremation in a sitting position seems possible (cf. Jessup 1955: 16).

The fourth point depends very much on the burial rite. For instance, to what extent did it comprise primary and secondary grave-goods (cf. e.g. Polfer this volume)? The burial rite varies in pre-Roman Britain and becomes increasingly heterogeneous in Roman times, with influences adopted from different parts of the Empire. Even before the late Roman period burials with grave-goods are far outnumbered by unaccompanied burials (Fig. 9.2). The fewest burials with grave-goods come from the *civitas* of the Dobunni (9.1%), most from the *civitas* of the Regni (44.1%). With the exception of the Corieltauvi, the Trinovantes and the Cantiaci the percentage of accompanied graves stays in most regions under 20%. This makes comparison very difficult.

Furthermore lavish grave inventories or valuable objects are not necessarily statements of high status: they might simply result from wealth. So-called rich grave inventories will therefore not be accepted as evidence for high status if there are no other reasons to consider them. This applies to a group of cremations with large pottery assemblages from East Hampshire (Millett 1987) and a group of cremations in wooden and stone cists on the Sussex Coastal Plain which is also characterised by large grave inventories, mostly of pottery, but also jewellery and toilet items (Philpott 1991: 218–219). However, some burials from Alton not only have large pottery assemblages but also show signs of a complicated funeral process, which would justify their inclusion according to our criteria. As Alton is among the few sites excavated under modern conditions, it gives us an idea of how much evidence for rituals we are missing from the majority of the less well observed burial grounds. The East Hampshire group will therefore be

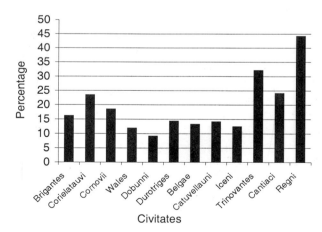

Fig. 9.2 *Distribution of burials with secondary grave-goods in Roman Britain (first–third century). Boundaries of* civitates *after Jones and Mattingly 1990: 154. Regions with less than 100 burials are not included (Scotland, and Atrebates, Dumnonii)*

considered in the final part of the article, but cannot be included in the statistical results. Another problem when accepting large grave assemblages as a criterion for élite burials is where to draw the line between élite and non-élite (cf. Haselgrove 1982: 82–83).

Expensive imported articles were connected with the late pre-Roman Iron Age élite in Britain. As soon as they were more easily available, in our region by the Neronian period, they lost their exclusive character and therewith their value as status symbols (Trow 1990: 108; Millett 1990: 58). In graves of the Roman period in Britain, extraordinarily expensive imports and antiques were absent. There might have been different reasons for the provision of the dead with other old items, e.g. sentimental, ritual or economic (cf. Mariën 1974: 9–19; Fasold 1987/88: 190; Struck 1996: 115–116; Going 1993: 49).

It is less difficult to interpret true status symbols, assuming that we can recognise them. The late pre-Roman Iron Age élite in Britain apparently projected their image as warriors, hunters and social drinkers (Millett 1990: 35–38). When occurring in pre-Roman graves, therefore, weapons and valuable banqueting vessels – mostly of metal – can be interpreted not only as an expression of wealth but of status as well (Philpott 1991: 123–124).

Mirrors might have fulfilled the same function in women's graves of the late pre-Roman Iron Age (Millett 1990: 38; Garbsch 1965: 10–11), but their meaning in post-conquest burials is difficult to estimate. Already in the early Roman period mirrors became a mass article (Haffner 1989: 111), which applies to Britain to a lesser extent. According to R. A. Philpott (1991: 277–278; 355) there are only 50 burials with mirrors of which two date to the fourth century, the rest being undated or belonging to the first three centuries. Mirrors were apparently still a luxury item but there is no indication for their function as a status symbol. Apart from their distribution, concentrated in the south-east of the province (Philpott 1991: 419 fig. 12; 461 fig. 29), mirror burials do not share any characteristics with the high status burials from the southeast (see below nos. 1 and 2): they occur in a Romanized environment, most frequently in urban cemeteries (0.6%), followed by cemeteries of secondary centres (0.5%) and military settlements (0.3%), least frequently (0.1%) at villa sites, as defined by Millett (1990: 91–92). The composition of the grave ensembles shows more links to a Romanized burial practice than to the native tradition in the south-east. Status symbols or elaborate grave architecture are missing. The grave-goods consist mainly of jewellery, toilet articles and objects of personal property; small dining services were occasionally provided. In general these assemblages indicate the wealth of the deceased with costly ossuaria, caskets and glass. The proportion of mirror burials is roughly the same over the first three centuries: 1.9% of the dated graves per century in the first, 1.8% in the second and 1.7% in the third century AD. Apart from the possible pre-Roman Iron Age custom there is no reason why mirrors in post-conquest graves should be regarded as status symbols and not simply as toilet items.

The character of status symbols of high ranking immigrants from other parts of the Roman Empire is less easy to define. There is a small number of possible insignia of power other than weapons and costly banqueting vessels. Firstly the *tumuli* of Holborough Knob (Kent, see above) and Bartlow Hill no. 4 (Essex, VCH Essex III 1963: 41–42) contained metal folding chairs which could be interpreted as *sellae curules* or *sellae castrenses*. These insignia of high ranking officials were sent as a reward to loyal allies (Wanscher 1980: 121 ff.). Even if the dead in the graves with *sellae* did not hold the original rank connected with this piece of furniture (cf. Nuber 1972: 171–172), the chairs were still a clear representation of high status. This is supported by the fact that the two British burials with folding chairs show other characteristics of élite burial as well. Secondly two inhumations without extraordinary grave constructions were each accompanied by two sceptres: one from Brough-on-Humber (Humberside, Corder 1938) and one from London (RCHM England 1928: 163–164).

Finally, certain favoured locations for élite burials have been encountered: an isolated prominent position (Jones 1987: 819–820) like the enclosure and burial mound from St Albans-Folly Lane (Herts.; Hunn 1994: 27 fig. 13) or the Holborough Knob *tumulus* (Jessup 1955: 2); close to an important road (including cemeteries along major roads, Cleary 1987: 174; also cf. Martin-Kilcher 1998: 219); and as a central grave for a group of burials or a whole cemetery, for example the King Harry Lane cemetery with the 'richest' graves in the centres of the enclosures (Millett 1993: 257 fig. 2 top) or Ampurias (Jones 1984: 249). However, spatial distinctions are only recognised by archaeologists if they correlate with other variables, such as special grave construction and/or inventory; otherwise they are difficult to detect (Wason 1994: 102).

The burial data in Roman Britain

Continuing with the second question, concerning patterns in distribution, chronology and burial rite, we have to turn to the burial data in Roman Britain. The analysis led to the recognition of several customs for high status burial which not only differ in their external appearance, but also in their geographical distribution, chronology, burial rite and grave furnishing. Although the distinguishing features are quite clear, it must be borne in mind that each custom has its exceptions, and that they overlap. The customs form two groups: the first comprising those rites continuing or developing late pre-Roman Iron Age traditions (nos. 1–5), the second probably representing customs imported to Britain in the Roman period (nos. 6–9). Within the first group, customs 1 and 2 bear clear signs of a superficial adoption and acceptance of Roman ways of life, whereas customs 3 to 5 seem to have resisted external influences more successfully.

1. The most frequent high status burial type in Roman Britain is formed by the large barrows with a diameter of more than 7 m, mainly in the south-east of the province (Jessup 1959: 10–11; Toynbee 1982: 179 ff. esp. 181–183) (Fig. 9.3). 1. It is a widely accepted opinion that they continue an élite burial custom from the late pre-Roman Iron Age, with or without stimulation from Gallia Belgica or Italy (Toynbee 1982: 180; von Hesberg 1992: 102–111; Wigg 1998). They show signs of wealth such as internal grave constructions, valuable containers and costly grave goods, and quite frequently contain status symbols. Almost always they appear as single monuments or in small groups with a preference for villa sites (2.6%), only 0.08 % are associated with other settlement types. 2. There are first century examples, but both the number and the proportion clearly increase from the first to the second century (Fig. 9.4).

2. 34 burials – mostly cremations – with valuable banqueting vessels continue another late pre-Roman Iron Age custom (Philpott 1991: 123). In most graves these vessels comprise a bronze jug and *patera*. In their distribution (Fig. 9.5), association with villas (cf. Philpott 1991: 124), grave furnishing and display of wealth and Romanized way of life (e.g. large table services, writing implements, bathing and gaming equipment, lamps, *unguentaria*, coins) they are very similar to the large barrows in the south-east. The proportion of graves during the first two centuries hardly decreases and only drops markedly in the third century (Fig. 9.6).

3. 13 wooden shrines of rectangular or circular plan, often with four-post-structures, also have pre-Roman predecessors (Black 1986: 205–210). Their distribution is restricted to south England and south Wales (Fig. 9.7). Whereas they occur mainly in urban cemeteries, there is only one example from a military site (Caerleon). There are no examples later than the second century (Fig. 9.8). The origin, chronology and distribution of the post constructions all make it probable that the examples dating to the Roman period are not only a cheaper version of the stone *mausolea* but could also represent a native alternative to them.

4. Late pre-Roman Iron Age examples such as Colchester-Stanway (Crummy 1993: 492; Cleary 1997: 433–434) and St Albans (Stead/Rigby 1989: 80 ff.; Niblett 1992) show that the at least 16 single grave enclosures in Britain follow a native tradition (cf. Bridger 1996: 246; Fitzpatrick 1997: 236). Most enclosures are small with sides between 2.70m and 8m. Grave furnishing is very modest, most examples lacking luxurious grave-goods, although there are a few lavishly furnished graves, mainly in large enclosures. A chronological development cannot be recognised. The distribution concentrates in the south and south-west of England (Fig. 9.7). Among the different types of settlements with which they were discovered,

native rural sites are represented. Apart from one weapon grave, the enclosures are therefore the only high status burial type associated with native rural settlements other than villas (Fig. 9.10). It is exceedingly difficult to judge to what extent these enclosures indicate burials of high ranking individuals. Their burial tradition is certainly distinct from that of the large barrows in the south-east, so it is tempting to interpret the single enclosures in the south and south-west as élite burials of yet another group of the native population in the province.

5. Three lavishly furnished south English barrows and a secondary burial in a grave enclosure from Colchester-Stanway (Essex, see above) contained weapons. However, there are 12 weapon graves in Britain without an elaborate grave construction; these are mainly inhumations without expensive containers and grave-goods. Weapon graves seem to continue two Iron Age traditions: one group consists of true warrior graves with swords, shields and/or other armour, certainly belonging to warriors (cf. Whimster 1981: 129 ff.). The Roman examples date exclusively to the first century AD and show a distribution matching that of the Iron Age (Fig. 9.5; cf. Whimster 1981: 132 Fig. 50). Other grave inventories contain weapons which could just as well be used for hunting, being a privileged pastime of the Iron Age élite (cf. Millett 1990: 36). Weapon graves date to the first and early second century AD (Fig. 9.6). As far as could be determined, they were discovered in urban (4), military (3) and rural native (1) cemeteries. Most burials contained only one item of weaponry, perhaps as a *pars pro toto*. This and the early chronology of the burials need not surprise us, considering that the native élite was disarmed when the province was founded (cf. Millett 1990: 58–59).

6. Apart from the so-called temple *mausolea*, the different architectural forms of the other stone built tombs originate in the Mediterranean world (Toynbee 1982: 164–172; von Hesberg 1992: 55 ff. – for the origin of the temple *mausoleum* cf. Meates 1979: 130–132; Black 1986: 205 ff.). In Britain there are remains of more than 42 *mausolea* and other stone monuments as well as 32 masonry tombs from the first three centuries AD. They have a wide distribution (Fig. 9.7) and are most frequent at military sites and urban cemeteries (Fig. 9.10), occurring therefore more often in large cemeteries than as isolated monuments. The proportion of *mausolea* and related monuments more than doubles between the first and second century (Fig. 9.8). Although masonry tombs are already attested for the late Iron Age in Britain (Whimster 1981: 154–155), in general they seem to date later than the *mausolea*. These monuments were built either by immigrants or by people who wanted to demonstrate that they took part in the Roman way of life.

7. According to M. Biró there are only 25 tombstones of higher ranking soldiers (centurion and superior officers)

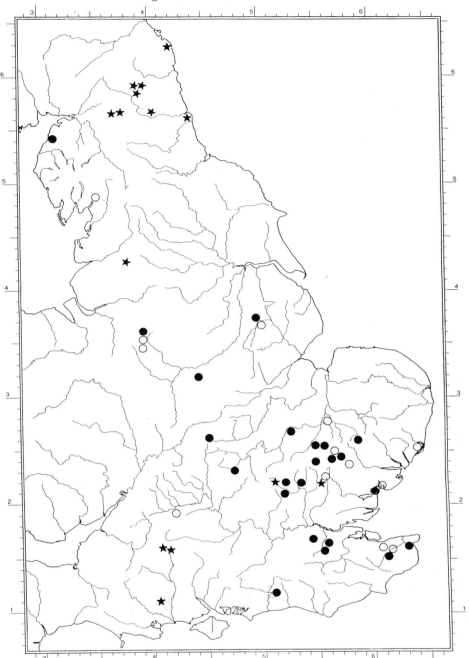

Fig. 9.3 *Distribution of barrows. Star: small barrow, diameter less than 7 m. – dot: large barrow, diameter greater than 7 m. – circle: barrow with undetermined dimensions.*

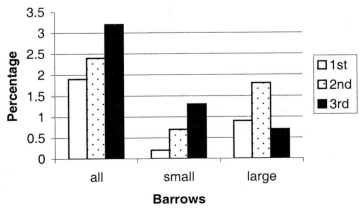

Fig. 9.4 *Chronology of the barrows.*

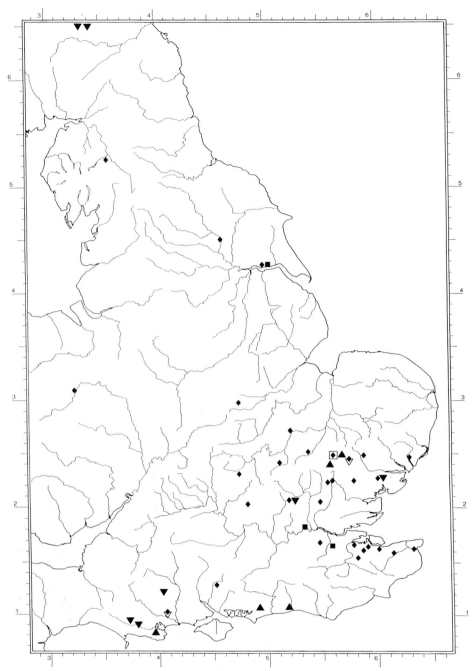

Fig. 9.5 *Distribution of graves with status symbols. Rhombus: valuable banqueting vessel(s). – triangle: weapon(s).*

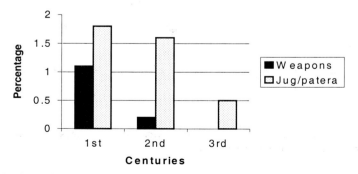

Fig. 9.6 *Chronology of weapon graves and graves with valuable banqueting vessels.*

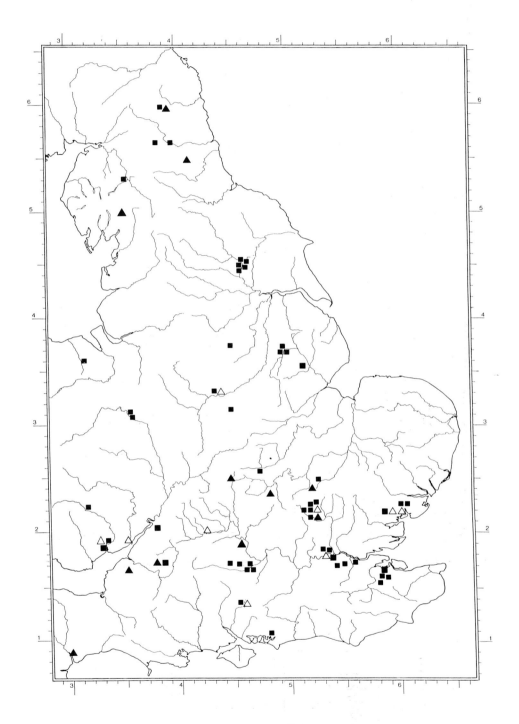

Fig. 9.7 *Distribution of funerary monuments other than barrows. Square: stone* mausoleum *or similar monument. – triangle (full): enclosure. – triangle (open): wooden post construction.*

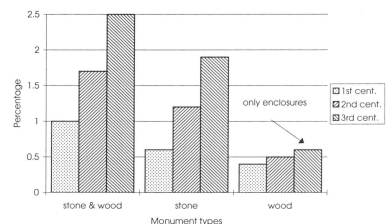

Fig. 9.8 *Chronology of funerary monuments other than barrows (types 3, 4 and 6).*

and five funerary inscriptions from the urban upper class (*decurio, sevir*) (Biró 1975: 46). As the majority of them were found separated from the original grave the burial rite cannot be described. They appear at military settlements and a few larger towns with villas being omitted from the distribution (Biró 1975: 42–47). Their popularity seems to have declined after the second century (Millett 1995: 124). In general, having a tomb inscription was an not a custom adopted by the native aristocracy (Hope 1997: 249).

8. At least 44 small barrows were found mainly in the north of the province (Fig. 9.3). Less than half of them are excavated with Rochester-Petty Knowes (Northumberland) being the best investigated cemetery (Charlton/ Mitcheson 1984). Conclusions concerning chronology and burial rite therefore derive mainly from this site. The northern examples do not date before the second century (Fig. 9.4) and form part of larger military and urban cemeteries. Their subterranean grave construction, containers and grave furnishings are very modest, but the *bustum* or cremation on a individual pyre (cf. McKinley this volume) is a burial type of more than average frequency. Although in size, construction effort and location the small burial mounds are far behind the impressive examples in the south-east, the *busta* indicate not only an elaborate funeral process, but also suggest a different cultural background for the deceased; the latter is further confirmed by the completely different fashion in which these graves are furnished (Struck 1993 b: 83). A continuity of the small *tumuli* from the pre-Roman Arras Culture in East Yorkshire of the fourth to the first century BC into the Roman period seems very unlikely (cf. Whimster 1981: 75 ff.), considering the chronological gap, the geographical distance and the different burial mode. A link to the Danubian area seems more likely, as there is a comparable burial custom with small mounds covering *busta* (Struck 1993 b: 88–89 with note 39) and a connection between the Danubian and the north British barrows could be suggested by the epigraphic evidence

for the *cohors I Dalmatorum* or *Dacorum* at High Rochester in the second century AD (cf. Charlton/ Mitcheson 1984: 19).

9. Of the roughly 25 certain *busta* only seven do not have an above-ground construction (cf. Struck 1993 b: 92). These graves are of modest appearance, and the same is true for the objects found in them. They are widely distributed in the province with a nearly exclusive association with cities and military sites. It is therefore tempting to interpret the scarcity or absence of grave furnishing as an expression of a Romanized burial practice.

Summary

All together almost 3% of all graves in Britain dating from the first to the third century AD show characteristics of élite burials, according to the criteria selected. The East Hampshire group demonstrates how easily this proportion can be increased if excavation is conducted under modern standards. Within the province the proportions of these burials vary remarkably (Fig. 9.9). A higher degree of status representation is found on the one hand in the north and north-west of Britain and in Wales, and on the other hand in the Trinovantian, Catuvellaunian and Cantiacian *civitates* of the south-east. The high proportion of élite burials in north England (8.3%) and Wales can certainly be explained by the smaller quantity of burials there (M. Millett pers. comm.). However, in the north high status is mainly detected in a military environment and the proportion of the élite was probably in reality even larger than the burial data suggest. This is indicated by the contrast between the numerous high ranking military personages documented in votive inscriptions and the small number of their tombstones. The only plausible explanation is that these high ranking soldiers left the province as soon as they had served their time (Biró 1975: 47). In the north, outside the zones of intensive military presence, the proportion of élite burials

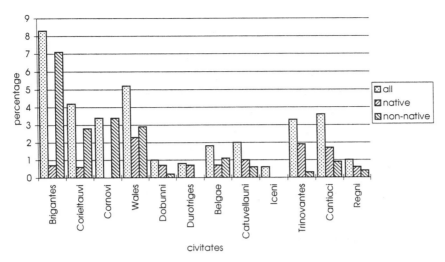

Fig. 9.9 *Distribution of élite burials in Roman Britain. Native: types 1–5, non-native: types 6–9. Boundaries of civitates after Jones and Mattingly 1990: 154. Regions with less than 100 burials are not included (Scotland, and Atrebates, Dumnonii)*

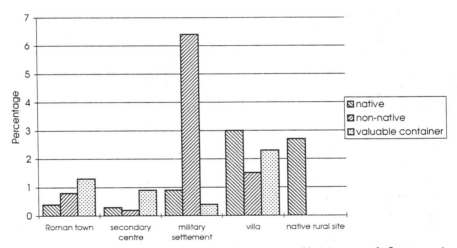

Fig. 9.10 *Associations of élite burials with different settlement types. Native: types 1–5, non-native: types 6–9.*

can be compared with Wales and the south-east. Whereas in northern Britain status is mainly demonstrated by small *tumuli*, *mausolea* and similar stone built monuments as well as *busta*, in the south-east this role is taken by large barrows and grave inventories with status symbols such as costly banqueting vessels. In Wales there is a mixture of *mausolea* and similar stone built monuments, wooden shrines and burials with status symbols. The noticeably fewer examples from the west comprise a large proportion of wooden structures and single grave enclosures.

Regarding the social environment in which status is expressed at death, it seems to be disproportionately frequent among villa dwellers (6.9%) and the army (7.6%) (Fig. 9.10). Cities follow with only 2.5%. Secondary centres very rarely have élite burials (0.5%). This pattern is also confirmed by the occurrence of the East Hampshire élite burials at non-urban cemeteries (Millett 1987: 63). The kind of status representation also differs: at villa sites large barrows, graves with valuable banqueting vessels

and large pottery assemblages dominate, *mausolea* and similar stone built monuments are less frequent; in the cemeteries of auxiliary forts and legionary fortresses small barrows, tombstones, *mausolea* and similar stone built monuments as well as *busta* fulfil the task. At the urban sites the whole variety is met with *mausolea* and wooden shrines in first place.

Several scholars have assumed that the native(?) élite lived outside the towns on their estates, as 'rich' graves are more likely to be found around villas than in the urban cemeteries (Jones 1983: 81; Cleary 1992: 31; 38). It was demonstrated above that the traditional forms of high status burial, such as large barrows and status symbols, have in most cases rich containers and furnishings. In addition to this, burials with valuable containers such as decorated stone and lead coffins, glass urns, lead ossuaria, wooden caskets and cists made from a single block of stone – as an indication for material wealth independent of the grave furnishing practice – are preferentially

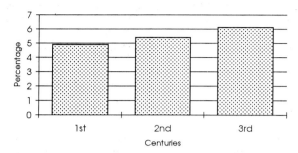

Fig. 9.11 *Chronology of élite burials. The percentages are calculated as a proportion of the total of datable graves per century.*

associated with villas (2.3%), to a lesser extent with towns (1.3%) and secondary centres (0.9%), and hardly ever with military sites (0.4%) (Fig. 9.10).

Surprisingly, the need for status demonstration in funerary display does not seem to have declined over the first three centuries AD (Fig. 9.11). However, as expected, forms which we regard as connected with non-Roman traditions (nos. 1, 2, 3 and 5 see above) became less frequent as time progressed.

The number of graves with analysed skeletal material is too small to allow general conclusions, for example when asking whether élite burial was gender specific, or whether certain forms were reserved for, or preferred by, men or women. The present state of research only makes clear that neither gender was excluded from status representation, and small barrows and *mausolea* were even erected for children (infans I and II). This could be a typical case for demonstrating status of a non-structural kind as certainly the children did not achieve their rank by themselves, but only by their association with a high ranking individual or family. Alternatively, their status at death could differ from their status in life, as in many cultures prematurely deceased individuals received special treatment (cf. Struck 1993c: 317 note 31; Berger 1993: 324–325; Martin-Kilcher this volume).

Conclusions

To what extent do these results add to our understanding of the social structure of Roman Britain? A few ideas will be presented here.

The proportion of *c*.3% is a realistic figure for the size of the élite in Roman Britain. Compared with an estimate for Rome and Italy, this is roughly what we have to expect (6 million inhabitants, 20,000 members of the senatorial and equestrian *ordo*; N. McKeown pers. comm.). However, a comparison between the extreme north-western province and the homeland reveals certain problems.

The clear distinction between the north (and west) and the south-east of the province shown by other phenomena and developments (Jones/Mattingly 1990: 43 ff.; Millett

1990: 9 ff.), is confirmed by the élite burials. In the north a social structure different from the south-east is indicated by settlement patterns (Jones/Mattingly 1990: 61), archaeobotanical analysis (van der Veen 1991: spec. 449) and the ancient written sources (cf. Salway 1980: 13). The Brigantes are described as a loosely organised tribal confederation. With an unstable social structure like this, a strong need for status demonstration is to be expected (cf. e.g. Reinert 1993: 356): but neither in the pre-Roman nor in the Roman period are there sufficient numbers of native élite burials. High status is demonstrated mainly in a Romanized or non-native way. The rare evidence for possible native forms of élite burial did not survive the Roman occupation for long. As mentioned above, formal burial in itself could indicate status, or the local aristocracy must have had other ways than burial practice to represent their status. So power was either held by non-natives or there was no pride in demonstrating status in a traditional way. The fact that self-administration by the local élite had not succeeded in northern Britain is suggested by other sources (cf. Millett 1990: 99).

In the south-east, status at death is demonstrated in traditional ways, especially by the large barrows, assemblages with status symbols and large pottery inventories from the early East Hampshire group. These types are predominantly associated with private estates and continue for the whole Roman period. Although a certain degree of prosperity can be detected in the graves of urban cemeteries, this does not correlate with status representation. At the villas, by contrast, the two are associated. This seems to reinforce the epigraphic evidence, which indicates that the native élite in Roman Britain competed less in towns than in other provinces (cf. Millett 1990: 82; Cleary 1992: 38), and the fact that houses of obviously rich people, who probably held political power, are difficult to identify in the towns before the middle of the second century (Walthew 1975). The demonstration of high status on one's own property implies seclusion from the masses, and the exclusivity of this kind of burial may have reinforced the demonstration of status, as a normal funeral would have taken place on the common cemetery of the settlement. That it was a demonstration is clear by the highly visible locations of the monuments. It might also reflect the growing distance between an aristocracy increasingly integrated in an imperial élite and the rest of the population (Cleary 1998: 51). The choice of a barrow as a funerary monument should not necessarily be understood as an anti-Roman statement, as the *tumulus* was a well acknowledged architectural form in Rome (cf. von Hesberg 1992: 94–107). On the other hand, it was the type of funerary monument familiar to the indigenous population. This means that in contrast to a Latin inscription, it was understandable, and that the villa inhabitants may have presented themselves with pride as natives (as on the funerary monuments in the Moselle valley).

The variety of high status burial types is greatest in the

south-east which could mirror an influx of different people associated with the economic upswing. Hardly any demonstration of status is found at secondary centres. Burials can, however, be moderately wealthy. This is not surprising, as according to the building types and small finds from these settlements, the main tasks of small towns and roadside settlements were economic and artisanal: administrative functions played only a minor role (cf. Millett 1990: 145; Cleary 1992: 38).

Acknowledgements

I am most grateful to M. Millett and J. Pearce for reading my article and commenting upon various questions. I also want to thank A. Fitzpatrick, S. Martin-Kilcher and V. Swan for their constructive contributions in the discussion.

Notes

1. Full details and literature will be provided in M. Struck, *Romano-British burial practices from the 1st to the 3rd century AD*. BAR British Series (in preparation).
2. All percentages used here and in connection with settlements in the following text refer to the overall burial numbers per settlement type.

Bibliography

Berger, L. 1993. Säuglings- und Kinderbestattungen in römischen Siedlungen der Schweiz ein Vorbericht. In Struck 1993 a: 319–328.

Biró, M. 1975. The inscriptions of Roman Britain. *Acta Archaeologica Academiae Scientiarum Hungaricae*, 27: 13–58.

Black, E. W. 1986. Romano-British burial customs and religious beliefs in south-east England. *Archaeological Journal*, 143: 201–239.

Bridger, C. 1996. *Das römerzeitliche Gräberfeld 'An Hinkes Weißhof' Tönisvorst-Vorst, Kreis Viersen*. Cologne: Landschaftsverband Rheinland: Rheinische Ausgrabungen 40.

Charlton, B. and Mitcheson, M. 1984. The Roman cemetery at Petty Knowes, High Rochester, Northumberland. *Archaeologia Aeliana* 5th Series, 12: 1–31.

Cleary, A.S.E. 1987. *Extra-mural areas of Romano-British towns*. Oxford: BAR British Series 169.

Cleary, A.S.E. 1992. Town and country in Roman Britain? In *Death in towns. Urban responses to the dying and the dead, 100–1600* (ed. S. Bassett). Leicester: Leicester University Press, pp. 28–42.

Cleary, A.S.E. 1997. Roman Britain in 1996. *Britannia*, 28: 414–453.

Cleary, A.S.E. 1998. The origins of towns in Roman Britain: the contribution of Romans and Britons. In A.R. Colmenero (ed.), *Los orígines de la ciudad en el Noroeste Hispánico. Actas del Congreso Internacional Lugo 15–18 de Mayo 1996*. Lugo: Servicio de Publicaciones Disputación Provincial San Marcos: 35–54.

Corder, P. 1938. A Roman-British interment, with bucket and sceptres, from Brough, East Yorkshire. *Antiquaries Journal*, 18: 68–74.

Crummy, P. 1993. Aristocratic graves at Colchester. *Current Archaeology*, 132: 492–497.

van Doorselaer, A. 1967. *Les nécropoles d'époque romaine en Gaule septentrionale*. Bruges: Dissertationes Archaeologicae Gandenses 10.

Fasold, P. 1987/88. Eine römische Grabgruppe auf dem Fuchsberg bei Günzenhausen, Gem. Eching, Lkr. Freising. *Bericht der Bayerischen Bodendenkmalpflege*, 28/29: 181–215.

Fasold, P. 1992. *Römischer Grabbrauch in Süddeutschland*. Stuttgart: Gesellschaft für Vor- und Frühgeschichte in Württemberg und Hohenzollern e. V.: Schriften des Limesmuseums Aalen 46.

P. Fasold *et al* (eds.) 1998. *Bestattungssitte und kulturelle Identität. Grabanlagen und Grabbeigaben der frühen römischen Kaiserzeit in Italien und den Nordwest-Provinzen*. Xantener Berichte 7. Cologne: Rheinland Verlag.

Fitzpatrick, A.P. 1997. *Archaeological excavations on the route of the A27 Westhampnett Bypass, West Sussex, 1992. Volume 2: the late Iron Age, Romano-British, and Anglo-Saxon cemeteries*. Wessex Archaeological Report 12.

Friedhoff, U. 1991. *Der römische Friedhof an der Jakobstraße zu Köln*. Mainz: Philip von Zabern: Kölner Forschungen 3

Garbsch, J. 1965. *Die norisch-pannonische Frauentracht im 1. und 2. Jahrhundert*. Munich: Münchner Beiträge zur Vor- und Frühgeschichte 11.

Going, C. 1993. Pottery vessels. In N. Crummy, P. Crummy and C. Crossan, *Excavations of Roman and later cemeteries, churches and monastic sites in Colchester, 1971–88*. Colchester: Colchester Archaeological Trust Ltd.: Colchester Archaeological Report 9, 47–49.

Haffner, A. 1989. *Gräber – Spiegel des Lebens. Totenbrauchtum der Kelten und Römer*. Mainz: Philip von Zabern: Schriftenreihe des Rheinischen Landesmuseums Trier 2.

Haselgrove, C.C. 1982. Wealth, prestige and power: the dynamics of late Iron Age political centralisation in south-east England. In C. Renfrew and S.J. Shennan (eds.), *Ranking, resource and exchange: aspects of the archaeology of early European society*. Cambridge University Press: 79–88.

von Hesberg, H. 1992. *Römische Grabbauten*. Darmstadt: Wissenschaftliche Buchgesellschaft

Hope, V.M. 1997. Words and pictures: the interpretation of Romano-British tombstones. *Britannia*, 28: 245–258.

Hunn, J.R. 1994. *Reconstruction and measurement of landscape change. A study of six parishes in the St Albans area*. Oxford: Tempus Reparatum. BAR British Series 236.

Jessup, R.F. 1955. Excavations of a Roman barrow at Holborough, Snodland. *Archaeologia Cantiana*, 68: 1–61.

Jessup, R.F. 1959. Barrows and walled cemeteries in Roman Britain. *Journal of the British Archaeological Association*, 22: 1–32.

Jones, B. and Mattingly, D. 1990. *Atlas of Roman Britain*. Oxford: Basil Blackwell.

Jones, R.F.J. 1983. *Cemeteries and burial practice in the western provinces of the Roman Empire*. Unpublished PhD Thesis, University of London.

Jones, R.F.J. 1984. The Roman cemeteries of Ampurias reconsidered. In *Papers in Iberian archaeology* (eds. T.F.C. Blagg, R.F.J. Jones and S.J. Keay). Oxford: BAR International Series 193, pp. 237–265.

Jones, R. 1987. Burial customs of Rome and the provinces. In *The Roman World* II (ed. J. Wacher). London: Routledge, 812–844.

Jones, R. 1993. Rules for the living and the dead: funerary practices and social organisation. In Struck 1993a: 247–254.

Kimes, T., Haselgrove, C. and Hodder, I. 1982. A method for the identification of the location of regional cultural boundaries. *Journal of Anthropological Archaeology* 1: 113–131.

Mariën, M.E. 1974. Objects de bronze comme 'antiquités'. *Bulletin des Musées Royaux à Bruxelles* Series 6, 46: 9–19.

Marquardt, J. 1886. *Das Privatleben der Römer* (Second edition). Leipzig.

Martin-Kilcher, S. 1998. Gräber der späten Republik und der frühen Kaiserzeit am Lago Maggiore: Tradition und Romanisierung. In Fasold *et al*: 19–252.

Meates, G.W. 1979. *The Roman villa at Lullingstone, Kent I: the site*. Ashford: Kent Archaeological Society.

Metcalf, P. and Huntington R. 1992. *Celebrations of death: the anthropology of mortuary ritual* (Second edition). Cambridge: Cambridge University Press.

Millett, M. 1987. An early Roman burial tradition in Central Southern England. *Oxford Journal of Archaeology*, 6: 63 – 68.

Millett, M. 1990. *The Romanization of Britain. An essay in archaeological interpretation*. Cambridge: Cambridge University Press.

Millett, M. 1993. A cemetery in an age of transition: King Harry Lane reconsidered. In Struck 1993 a: 255–282.

Millett, M. 1995. *Roman Britain*. London: Batsford, English Heritage.

Mondanel, C. and D. 1989. *Sépultures et nécropoles gallo-romaines en Auvergne*. Revue Archéologique Sites, Paris: Hors-Serie 34.

Niblett, R. 1992. A Catuvellaunian chieftain's burial. *Antiquity*, 66: 917–929.

Nielsen, K.H. 1997. From society to burial and from burial to society? In Jensen, C.K. and Nielsen, K.H. (eds.), *Burial and society. The chronological and social analysis of archaeological burial data*. Aarhus University Press: 103–110.

Nuber, H.U. 1972. Ein römischer Grabfund aus Ludwigshafen-Maudach. *Mitteilungen des Historischen Vereins der Pfalz*, 70: 111–137.

Peebles, C.S. 1971. Moundville and surrounding sites: some structural considerations of mortuary practices II. In *Approaches to the social dimensions of mortuary practices* (ed. J.A. Brown). Memoirs of the Society for American Archaeology 25, pp. 68–91.

Philpott, R. 1991. *Burial practices in Roman Britain. A survey of grave treatment and furnishing A.D. 43–410*. Oxford: Tempus Reparatum: BAR British Series 219.

RCHM England 1928. *An inventory of the Historical Monuments in London III. Roman London*. London: Royal Commission on Historical Monuments (England).

Reinert, F. 1993. Frühkaiserzeitliche 'Fürstengräber' im westlichen Treverergebiet. In Struck 1993 a: 345–360.

Rivet, A.L.F. 1958. *Town and country in Roman Britain*. London: Hutchinson

Salway, P. 1980. The *vici*: urbanisation in the north. In *Rome and the Brigantes* (ed. K. Branigan). Sheffield University Press: 8–17.

Stead, I.M./Rigby V. 1989. *Verulamium: The King Harry Lane site*. London: English Heritage.

Struck, M. 1993 a. *Römerzeitliche Gräber als Quellen zur Religion, Bevölkerungsstruktur und Sozialgeschichte*. Mainz: Archäologische Schriften des Instituts für Vor- und Frühgeschichte der Johannes Gutenberg-Universität Mainz 3.

Struck, M. 1993 b. *Busta* in Britannien und ihre Verbindungen zum Kontinent. Allgemeine Überlegungen zur Herleitung der Bestattungssitte. In Struck 1993 a, pp. 81–94.

Struck, M. 1993 c. Kinderbestattungen in romano-britischen Siedlungen – der archäologische Befund. In Struck 1993 a, pp. 313–318.

Struck, M. 1996. *Römische Grabfunde und Siedlungen im Isartal bei Ergolding, Landkreis Landshut*, Kallmünz/Opf.: Michael Lassleben: Materialhefte zur Bayerischen Vorgeschichte A 71.

Tainter, J. 1977. Modelling change in prehistoric social systems. In *For theory building in archaeology* (ed. L.R. Binford). New York Academic Press, pp. 327–352.

Toynbee, J.M.C. 1982. *Death and burial in the Roman world*. London: Thames and Hudson

Trow, S.D. 1990. By the northern shores of Ocean. Some observations on acculturation process at the edge of the Roman world. In *The early Roman Empire in the West* (eds. T. Blagg and M. Millett). Oxford: Oxbow, pp. 103–118.

van der Veen, M. 1991. Native communities in the frontier zone – uniformity or diversity? In *Roman frontier studies 1989* (eds. V.A. Maxfield and M.J. Dobson). Exeter: University Press, 446–450.

VCH Essex III 1963. *The Victoria County History of the Counties of England. A History of Essex* III. London: University of London/OUP London.

Walthew, C.V. 1975. The town house and the villa house in Roman Britain. *Britannia* 6: 189–205.

Wanscher, O. 1980. *Sella Curulis, the folding stool- an ancient symbol of dignity*. Copenhagen: Rosenkilde and Bagger.

Wason, P.K. 1994. *The archaeology of rank*. Cambridge: Cambridge University Press

Whimster, R. 1981. *Burial practice in Iron Age Britain. A discussion and gazetteer of the evidence c.700 B.C.–A.D. 43*. Oxford: BAR British Series 90.

Wigg, A. 1998. Römerzeitliche Grabhügel im Trierer Land: Assimilation einer autochthonen Bestattungssitte an eine mittelitalische Grabdenkmalform. In Fasold *et al*: 295–305.

10. Funerary rites in Verulamium during the early Roman period

Rosalind Niblett

There are nearly 1200 recorded burials from Verulamium spanning the period from the first to the early fifth centuries AD. They have been found in two main areas. First, second and early third century burials concentrate south and south-west of the Roman town, in a wide arc from the west end of King Harry Lane (Stead and Rigby 1989) to St Stephen's Hill (Davey 1935; Frere 1987: 329; Frere 1990: 338); later burials are mainly found on the north and north-east of the town, near the junction of the modern Redbourn road with Batchwood Drive (Frere 1983: 287–8) and east through Kingsbury to the area around the modern lake in Verulamium Park (Wheeler and Wheeler 1936: 135–8). In addition a smaller area of burials is known south of the Chester Gate (Wheeler and Wheeler 1936: 134–35), while in the 1980s Martin and Birthe Biddle found part of a late and early post Roman cemetery on the south side of St Albans Abbey *(pers. comm.* Martin Biddle) (Fig. 10.1).

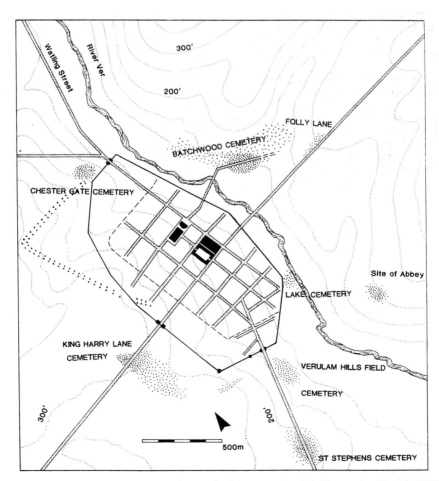

Fig. 10.1 *Verulamium Cemeteries, 1st–early 5th centuries AD.* Drawn by David Williams.

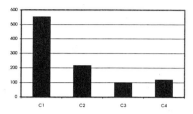

Fig. 10.2 *Total number of recorded burials per century at Verulamium*

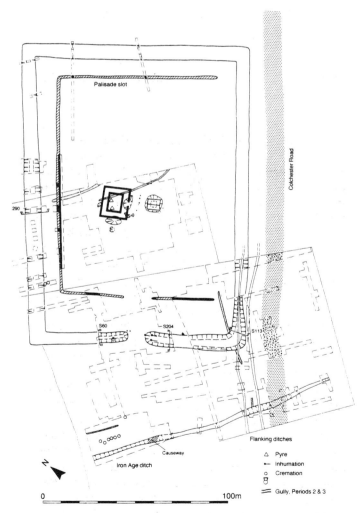

Fig. 10.3 *The Folly Lane Ceremonial Enclosure.* Drawn by David Williams

As a result there is considerable amount of data available, much of it of comparatively good quality and covering the whole of the Roman period, although as figure 10.2 indicates, there is a disproportionate number from the first century, a distortion resulting from the growth of modern development (and hence excavation) on the south of the Roman town.

During the first half of the first century AD a number of burial customs are apparent in the Verulamium district. Since Ian Stead's excavation of the King Harry Lane cemetery in 1966–8 the best known of these customs is the practice of cremation burial, usually in an urn, and in groups or clusters, within or adjacent to, rectilinear ditched enclosures (Stead and Rigby 1989). At least 8 of these enclosures were excavated at King Harry Lane, and 2 further examples have been recognised more recently south-west of Stead's site (Niblett and Thompson, forthcoming). There are also examples in the St Stephen's and Verulam Hills cemeteries (Anthony 1968: 10–21). From the point of view of material goods these burials are not particularly well equipped – certainly they are nowhere near as rich as the Harpenden burial 8 km. to the north (Page 1914: 153), or the Welwyn Garden City burial 13 km. to the north-east (Stead 1967).

Nevertheless at the time of the conquest the burial rituals practised at Verulamium could be highly complex – it was not simply a matter of cremation followed by the burial of ashes with greater or lesser quantities of grave offerings, depending on the wealth of the individual or the generosity of his family and friends. In 1992 the picture of first century burial customs locally was transformed by the discovery of a high status burial at Folly Lane, on the north side of the Ver valley, 700m north-east of the Roman town. The site lay within the area of the pre-Roman oppidum, in a prominent position overlooking the centre of Verulamium. During the early part of the first century AD it had been occupied, but by the Claudian period the site had been cleared and a rectilinear enclosure laid out, covering just over 2 hectares and surrounded by a 3m deep ditch with a single entrance on the south-west side. Central to the enclosure was a low mound consisting of the upcast from a large shaft that had been dug on its eastern side (Fig. 10.3). The shaft was 8m square and 3m deep and on its base were the remains of a rectangular timber chamber, measuring 3 × 4m. The vertical sides of the shaft were reveted by an elaborate double revetment and in the south-west corner there were indications of an entrance ramp (Fig. 10.4).

The shaft structures had all been deliberately destroyed, after which the shaft had been filled with a massive deposit of turf and humus, brought from a variety of locations, including a stockyard and meadow, marsh and heathland (Wiltshire 1999: 365).

Immediately adjacent to the shaft, on its north-east side, was a much smaller pit which contained a single adult cremation accompanied by cremated animal remains (cattle, pig, sheep and hare or cat), large quantities of

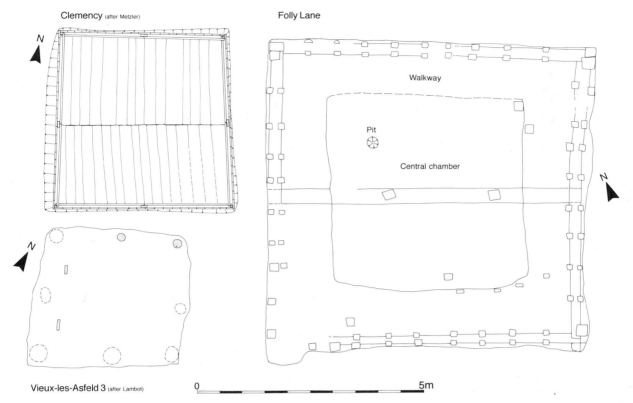

Fig. 10.4 *The Folly Lane Mortuary Shaft, and shafts from Clemency (after Metzler) and Asfeld (after Lambot)* Drawn by David Williams.

pyre debris and the remnants of a collection of exceptionally rich pyre offerings including remains of a cart or chariot, horse gear, fragments from an ivory mounted chair or couch, iron mail, and over 4 kilograms of solidified molten silver.

The pyre debris had been put in the burial pit while it was still hot, as it had singed the edges of the surrounding turf. Nevertheless the degree of scorching did not suggest that the cremation had taken place in the pit. Instead, the site of the pyre almost certainly lay in the centre of the enclosure, on the top of the mound of upcast material from the shaft. Here several areas of heavy burning survived, embedded in which were fragments of solidified molten silver and bronze.

Although the Folly Lane shaft shared some characteristics with timber burial shafts on the Continent, for instance at Clemency (Metzler *et al.* 1991), which also had a double wall, it was not a burial pit. Apart from a few crumbs of cremated bone, care had been taken to deposit the cremated remains outside the shaft, in an adjacent, but quite separate burial pit. The function of the shaft can only be speculated on but the most likely explanation is that it was used as a mortuary chamber in which to house the dead before the final funeral rites took place. Philip Crummy has suggested a similar use for the smaller but more or less contemporary timber lined pits, that he has excavated within ditched enclosures at

Stanway, outside Colchester (Crummy 1992; 1997: 23–8). Although it is impossible to determine how long the deceased was kept in the pit, the Folly Lane structures were exceptionally stoutly built, and could easily have stood for 20 years or more. Evidence from cremation burials in Luxembourg and Champagne suggests that in some cases the human bone was already dry and brittle by the time it was cremated, suggesting a protracted period of exposure prior to the funeral (Lambot *et al.* 1994: 135–141). Unfortunately the bone from Folly Lane was too heavily comminuted to tell whether it was too was dry at the time of cremation, and it is not known how long the deceased had been kept in the shaft before the final funeral. Equally, the shaft could already have been used for earlier funerals before it was finally demolished at the time of the final funeral on the site.

The rites performed in the shaft, apart from simply exposing or storing the corpse, are also largely a matter of guesswork. They may well have included processions or dances around the central chamber in the base of the shaft. The shaft floor, between the chamber and the revetment showed signs of trampling, reminiscent of the evidence for processing or dancing at Clemency. On the floor of the Folly Lane shaft were sherds from at least 41 vessels, most of them from amphorae and tableware, all of which suggest feasting; while the date of the pottery shows that however long the body may or may not have

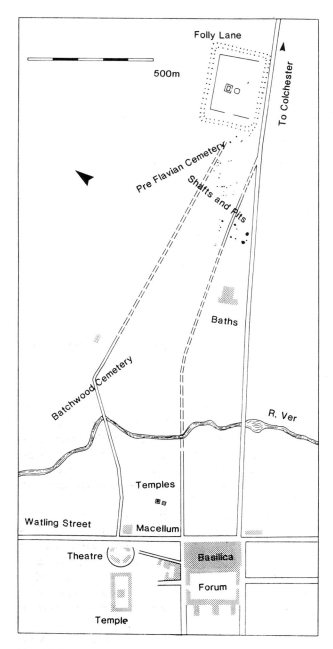

Fig. 10.5 *The Folly Lane site in the early 3rd century AD in relation to the Verulamium temples and theatre. Drawn by David Williams*

from the pyre debris and scattered in the shaft as it was being backfilled. A few handfuls of un-burnt sherds from the same pots were also thrown into the shaft at intervals. Apart from this token amount however, no attempt was made to sort the remaining cremated bone, animal and human, which was simply placed in the burial pit; mixed with smouldering pyre debris. Nevertheless, although the fill of the entire burial deposit was removed to the laboratory and sieved, it contained less than 25% of the total bone for an adult cremation.

It is equally apparent that not all the pyre offerings were placed in the burial pit. Even allowing for the fact that the silver and bronze were often melted beyond recognition, there were insufficient fragments of the fire dog, chariot or furniture for anything more than token portions of these objects. Of the 41 ceramic vessels represented in the shaft, sherds from only 4 (2 amphorae and 2 platters) were found in the burial pit.[1]

All this suggests that at Verulamium it was the pre-funeral rituals, and above all the actual cremation itself that was the most important aspect – what happened to the cremated remains afterwards was of less importance. It is interesting that the pyre occupied the centre of the enclosure, while the funerary shaft was to one side, with the burial pit tucked into to one edge of it. Furthermore, it was the site of the pyre that was subsequently commemorated, first by a standing post, resting on a deposit of pyre debris, and subsequently by a Romano-Celtic temple. By the second century the temple had become the focus of an extensive religious site, incorporating a large suite of baths and numerous apparent ritual shafts, with a direct road link to the Verulamium theatre and its associated temple (Fig. 10.5).

Clearly the funerary ceremonies at Folly Lane involved a period of exposure, or 'lying in state' in a sunken mortuary chamber. The rites culminated with the cremation during which everything connected with the preliminary ceremonies was destroyed. A token amount of the debris and pyre offerings were then buried close by (what happened to the remainder is still a mystery), while a few unburnt sherds from the funerary feast were scattered in the back filling of the mortuary shaft. All this was in marked contrast to the rite characterised by the wealthy 'Welwyn' graves, where what was presumably the equipment for the funeral feast was placed in the grave largely intact, together with the cremated remains of the deceased. The rich satellite burials in the Stanway enclosures and the wealthier burials at King Harry Lane are probably examples of the same rites.

Occasionally small quantities of pyre debris were included in the 'Welwyn' graves, as at Hertford Heath (Hüssen 1983) and Welwyn Garden City (Stead 1967). There is a certain amount of evidence to suggest that the deposition of a token amount of debris from pyre offerings was a mark of relatively high status burials within a particular group of people. Just over 8% of the pre-Flavian cremations from King Harry Lane and St Stephen's

resided in the shaft, this final meal took place in about AD 55.

It appears that the material on the floor of the shaft had been used during rites that took place before the pyre was lit. This material was not itself burnt, suggesting that before the actual cremation took place, the pottery and other objects were broken up and that only a very small proportion were left on the floor of the shaft, either deliberately or accidentally. Once the cremation had taken place, a small quantity of the cremated bone and a few fragments of burnt pottery and metalwork were collected

Fig. 10.6 *The King Harry Lane cemetery, showing graves with pyre offerings. (After Stead and Rigby). Drawn by David Williams*

contained deposits of solidified molten metal and occasionally burnt pottery and glass- all presumably remnants of pyre offerings. Furthermore, as figure 10.6 demonstrates, these cremations tend to occupy central positions within enclosures, or clusters of burials. Of the 24 graves from King Harry Lane producing this material, half were in central positions within enclosures or were close to clusters of burials, and every enclosure had one or more 'pyre offering' burials in central positions. It has to be admitted that in many cases the quantity of molten metal was very small, but the metalwork found in the Folly Lane burial pit only represented a tiny proportion of what must originally have existed;- so the modest amounts from the King Harry Lane and St Stephen's burials may nevertheless represent a collection of pyre offerings that originally was perfectly respectable. It should be emphasised that it was *only* in the graves shown on figure 10.6 that any 'pyre offerings' were found; thus however small the quantity of pyre material, its presence alone suggests that the burials containing it reflect a rite that was confined to a section of society. This section tended to be accompanied on the pyre by high quality objects, and to have been buried in central positions in the burial enclosures, which in turn suggests that the individuals buried here occupied a 'special' place in society. We can only speculate as to the relative social position of someone buried in a rich 'satellite' grave to that of someone in an apparently poorer 'pyre offering' grave at the centre of an enclosure. It is tempting to see the size of the enclosure, and the number of burials within it as a measure of their status. Folly Lane is the largest enclosure with the fewest number of burials (1 cremation and 3 inhumations) giving an average of

4,670 sq. m. per burial while at King Harry Lane the smallest fully excavated enclosures (Millett's enclosures B and E) (Millett 1993) have 44 and 26 burials respectively giving averages of approximately 3.8 and 5.4 sq. m. per burial. The Verulam Hill enclosure, which appears to be intermediate in size, produced 29 burials giving an average of 117 sq. m. per burial.[2]

Cremation was not the only method of disposal of the dead that was current at Verulamium at the time of the conquest. There are also a significant number of inhumations associated with mid first century cemetery enclosures. Verulamium has produced 32 inhumations dating from the pre-Flavian period, and of these 28 are within, or aligned upon, the ditches of cremation enclosures.

The inhumations were normally without grave goods, and those in ditches had simply been placed on the floor of the ditch, with no sign of a grave cut. Unlike late Roman inhumations at Verulamium, none of the first century examples were in coffins. The marked contrast between the inhumations and the cremation burials within the enclosure has usually been seen as an indication of differences in social class with the inhumations being those of poorer retainers of the individuals buried within the enclosures. This may well be the case. On the other hand, a possibility that cannot be discounted entirely is that, prior to cremation, the dead were sometimes exposed on the banks or in the ditches surrounding cremation cemeteries. The surviving inhumations may simply be bones that were never 'retrieved' for cremation, possibly, in the case of Verulamium, because the family or group to which the individuals had belonged, were dispersed as a result of the Roman conquest or the Boudiccan revolt.

Developments of Funerary Rites in the Roman Period

The practice of enclosing areas of the cemetery or entire cemeteries within rectilinear ditches seems to have died out by the early second century. Nor have any other mortuary shafts like Folly Lane been found in the area. In 1985 however, Adrian Havercroft excavated a curious structure in a ditched enclosure in St Stephen's cemetery(*pers. comm.* A.B. Havercroft). It was supported on cill beams, and in many ways resembled a mortuary chamber at Acy-Romance (Lambot *et al.* 1994: fig. 45). Neither structure contained any burials, but both were close to small clusters of cremations, those at Acy Romance dated from the second quarter of the first century BC, those from St Stephen's from the late first and early second centuries AD. For both these structures, a use as a

mortuary chamber connected with rites similar to those suggested for the Folly Lane/ Stanway pits, seems eminently possible (Fig. 10.7).

Another possible mortuary chamber was excavated in the 1980s by David Neal, at Wood Lane End, 4 km. west of Verulamium (Neal 1984). Here a substantial temple/ mausoleum and associated bath block were built, probably early in the Hadrianic period, and enclosed in a walled precinct. The Wood Lane End *cella* included a rectangular sunken pit or chamber, 4.5 × 2.5m. and just over a metre deep. The pit's purpose is unknown, but it is possible that it fulfilled a similar function to that of the Folly Lane shaft, as a place where the dead person was exposed, before being finally cremated. The ashes may either have been buried elsewhere or stored in the tower-like super-structure of the temple.

In the course of the second century a large number of apparently ritual pits were dug within and peripheral to cremation cemeteries. A total of 41 are known from Verulamium, 15 of which contained stray human bones,

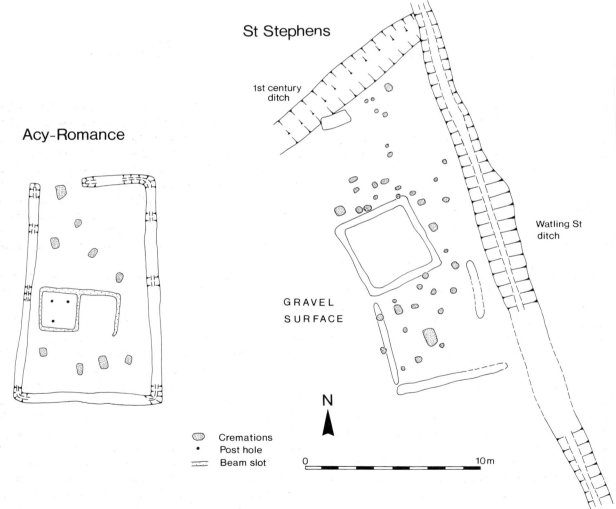

Fig. 10.7 *The possible mortuary structure at St Stephens, and the structure at Acy-Romance (after Lambot). Drawn by David Williams*

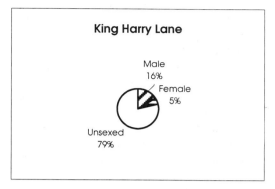

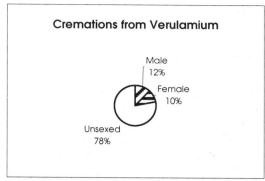

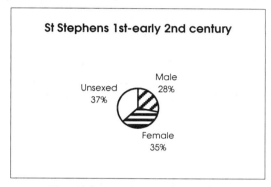

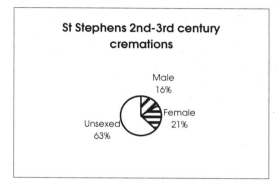

Fig. 10.8 *Sexed cremation burials of the first and second centuries AD at Verulamium*

including one skull that had been carefully defleshed (Mays and Steele 1996). It seems possible that these 'stray' bones result from a continuation of exposure rites in the Roman period, with pits as places where the dead were placed temporarily.

Neither the practice of placing pyre debris in selected graves nor the custom of throwing unburnt sherds into the pit fill was universal. In the King Harry Lane and St Stephens cemeteries, pyre debris has been recorded in approximately 8% of burials, and unburnt sherds in the filling of approximately 15% of the burial pits. Only at Folly Lane were both customs practised together. No pyre offerings have been recorded in burials after the early second century, and indeed the custom may already have been in decline at the time of the conquest. The custom of throwing unburnt fragments of pottery into the filling of the grave however persisted throughout the Roman period, and has been recorded in late Roman graves south of St Albans Abbey (Martin Biddle *pers. comm.*).

There is growing evidence that cemeteries were already being deliberately and carefully positioned in the pre-conquest period and that traditions concerning the location of burials persisted into the early Roman period. The pre-Flavian cemetery that grew up on the south-west side of the Folly Lane enclosure, as well as the King Harry Lane and Verulam Hill cemeteries are all approximately 800m. from the ditched enclosure underlying the Verulamium Forum (Frere 1983: 193). Furthermore, if, as has been

argued elsewhere, the earliest north/south axial road in Verulamium was on the west side of the Forum (Niblett 1999: 412), the early nuclei of all three cemeteries lay on the left hand side of routes out of the centre of Verulamium. This preference for the left continued into the Roman period. There are indications that in its earliest phase Watling street ran roughly on the line of King Harry Lane (Niblett and Thompson, forthcoming); this means that the early cemetery enclosures at St Stephen's lay on its left hand side as it left the town. The second-third century inhumation cemetery south of the Chester Gate also lay 800m from the Forum on the left hand side of Watling street and the road leading out to Wood Lane End as they left Verulamium.

Many questions remain to be answered. In the King Harry Lane cemetery, which appears to have gone out of use by the Flavian period, if not before, two thirds of the sexed burials were those of men. Sexing of cremated remains is beset with difficulties, and these figures have to be treated with great caution, although with 7 male and 1 female, the inhumation burials from Verulam Hills field show a similar bias. There seems to have been a change in the later first century however. The St Stephen's cemetery contains over 400 graves dating from the Claudian to the early Antonine periods, although most fall within the bracket *c.*90–200. The cemetery has not been published, and indeed little post-excavation work has been carried out on it but the human remains have been examined by J. McKinley who has produced an interim report.[3] Of the sexed cremation burials from St Stephen's, two thirds were female (Fig. 10.8). Why should this be? In both King Harry Lane and St Stephen's, burials of men, women and children were found right across the cemeteries, with no sign of special grouping in particular areas. Is this dearth of men in late first and early second century burials at Verulamium the result of local youths being encouraged to serve in the Roman army, or do these discrepancies simply underline the difficulties in sexing cremated remains? If it were possible to sex the large numbers of unsexed burials in both cemeteries the ratios could well be changed dramatically.

Other questions concern the relationship between people who were buried with pyre goods, and those with burial goods. In c.AD 85, the ashes of an elderly individual were buried on the outskirts of the King Harry Lane cemetery, together with a complete samian dinner service, strigils, gaming counters, a bronze bowl and a folding chair (Niblett and Reeves 1991). At first sight this burial provides a vivid example of the 'Romanisation' of the local elite, especially when compared to the rites practised a generation earlier, at Folly Lane. On the other hand, no pyre material was included in the burial, and it could equally well be seen as a continuation of the traditions that separated the section of society who went to the grave accompanied by all the furniture of the funerary feast (as at Welwyn Garden City) from those where everything connected with the pre-funerary rituals was carefully destroyed.

Notes

1. In the course of the excavation all the area within the funerary enclosure that was threatened by re-development was excavated down to natural subsoil, and no further deposits of pyre debris were found. Subsequently a geophysical survey was carried out over the remaining area: when the housing development was completed, topsoil over the northern (unexcavated) portion of the enclosure was removed and a careful watching brief was maintained. No further pyre deposits were found. There had been a certain amount of small scale gravel and sand extraction over much of the enclosure during the 18th and 19th centuries however, and it is possible that further deposits of pyre debris were removed without record.

2. These figures have to be treated with extreme caution. It is by no means certain that all the burials within the enclosures were found; the King Harry Lane site was very eroded and shallow burials may have been lost, while the size of the Verulam Hill enclosure can only be estimated.

3. I am grateful to J McKinley for permission to quote from her report.

Bibliography

Anthony, I.L. 1968. Excavations in Verulam Hills Field, St Albans, 1963–4. *Hertfordshire Archaeology*, 1.9–50.

Crummy, P. 1992. Aristocratic Graves at Colchester. *Current Archaeology*, 132, 492–7

Crummy, P. 1997. *City of Victory.* Colchester Archaeological Trust. Bath.

Davey, N. 1935. The Romano-British cemetery at St Stephens, near Verulamium. *Trans. St Albans and Hertfordshire Architectural and Archaeological Society*, 4, 243–75

Frere, S.S. 1983. *Verulamium Excavations Vol.II.* Rep.Res.Comm of Society of Antiquaries of London. 28. Oxford.

Frere, S.S. 1987. Roman Britain in 1986. *Britannia*, 18, 301–59

Frere, S.S. 1990. Roman Britain in 1989. *Britannia*, 21, 304–64

Hüssen, C.M. 1983. *A Rich La Tène Burial at Hertford Heath, Hertfordshire.* British Museum Occasional Paper 12.

Lambot, B., Friboulet, M. and Méniel, P. 1994. *Le site protohistorique d'Acy-Romance (Ardennes) II: Les nécropoles dans leur contexte régional.* Mémoires de la Société Archéologique Champenoise, 8. Reims.

Mays, J. and Steele, J. 1996. A mutilated human skull from Roman St Albans. *Antiquity*, 70, 155–60

Metzler, J., Waringo, R., Bis, R., and Metzler-Zens, N. 1991. *Clemency et les tombes de l'aristocratie en Grande Belgique*, Dossiers d'Archéologie du Musee National d'histoire et d'art. I. Luxembourg.

Millett, M. 1993. A cemetery in transition: King Harry Lane reconsidered. In Struck, M. (ed.) *Römerzeitliche Gräber als Quellen zur Religion, Bevölkerungsstruktur und Sozialgeschichte*, Mainz: Johannes Gutenberg Institut für Vor- und Frühgeschichte, pp. 255–82

Neal, D. 1984. A Sanctuary at Wood Lane End, Hemel Hempstead. *Britannia*, 15, 193–215

Niblett, R. and Reeves, P. 1991. A wealthy early Roman cremation from Verulamium. *Antiquaries Journal*, 70, pt. II, 441–446

Niblett, R. 1992. A Catuvellaunian chieftain's burial from St Albans. *Antiquity*, 66, 917–929.

Niblett, R. 1999. *The Excavation of a Ceremonial Site at Folly Lane, Verulamium.* Britannia Monograph 14.

Niblett, R and Thompson, I., forthcoming, *St Albans – From Prehistory to Dissolution.* English Heritage Monograph

Page, W. 1914. *The Victoria County History: Hertfordshire. Vol.IV*

Stead, I.M. and Rigby, V. 1989. *Verulamium, the King Harry Lane Site.* English Heritage Archaeological Report no. 12. London.

Stead, I.M. 1967. A La Tène III burial at Welwyn Garden City. *Archaeologia*, 101, 1–62

Wheeler, R.E.M. and Wheeler, T.V. 1936. *Verulamium, a Belgic and Two Roman Cities.* Rep.Res.Comm Society of Antiquaries of London, 11. Oxford.

Wiltshire, P. 1999. The Palynographic Analysis of the Filling in the Funerary Shaft. In Niblett, R., *The Excavation of a Ceremonial Site at Folly Lane, Verulamium*, Britannia Monograph 14, 347–65

11. Biology and burial practices from the end of the 1st century AD. to the beginning of the 5th century AD: the rural cemetery of Chantambre (Essonne, France)

Pascal Murail and Louis Girard

Introduction

The Chantambre cemetery is situated in the department of Essonne, France, in the large forest of Fontainebleau (co-ordonnées Lambert: x = 605,125, y = 72,01; average height above sea level: 72 m). The cemetery site, in sandy soil, was surrounded by large sandstone boulders and demarcated to the north by a Roman road (Fig. 11.1).

The complete excavation of the site was carried out by Louis Girard between 1976 and 1992. From the study of the human remains and archaeological data, we have defined the biology and the burial practices of this population (Murail 1996) and this paper will deal with the most important results.

The excavation has yielded 495 graves (Fig. 11.1): 35

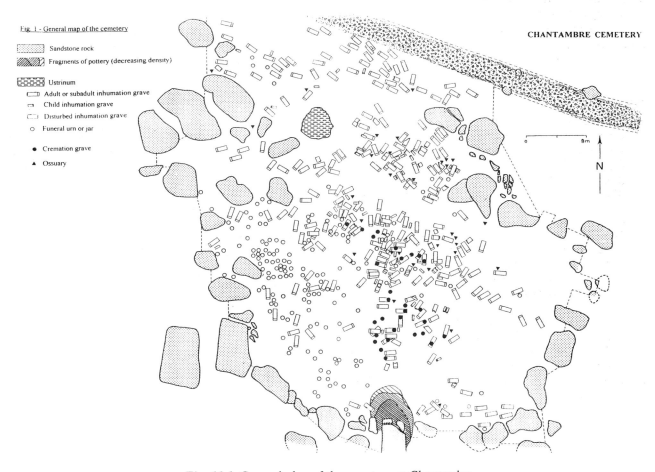

Fig. 1 - General map of the cemetery

Sandstone rock

Fragments of pottery (decreasing density)

Ustrinum

Adult or subadult inhumation grave

Child inhumation grave

Disturbed inhumation grave

Funeral urn or jar

Cremation grave

Ossuary

CHANTAMBRE CEMETERY

N

Fig. 11.1 General plan of the cemetery at Chantambre

cremation graves, 31 ossuaries, 155 inhumation burials in ceramic containers and 274 inhumation graves (247 individual and 27 multiple graves). A significant concentration of pottery fragments in the south of the cemetery and an *ustrinum* were also recovered. Monuments or inscriptions, typical in the Gallo-Roman period of a strongly Romanized population, are lacking (Molleson 1989; Ferdière 1993a). Nor is there any trace of a settlement close to the cemetery. An aerial photograph has revealed some traces of settlement, possibly farms, located four kilometres away. These characteristics and the lack of rich gravegoods suggest that the cemetery is that of a poorly Romanized rural population.

Chronology

The chronological development of the cemetery has been determined from ceramics, radiocarbon dating and the organisation of the cemetery. The site was in continuous use from the end of the 1st century AD to the beginning of the 5th century. It was possible to determine five areas

differentiated by date (Fig. 11.2). The earliest graves were situated to the south (areas I and II), and the cemetery expanded over time from area III to area V (Fig. 11.3). It is important to note that use of the cemetery was continuous and that there was no interruption between the Early and the Late Empire as observed in many other cemeteries (Martin-Kilcher 1993; Fourteau-Bardaji *et al.* 1993; Van Ossel 1993; Troadec 1993).

Burial typology and practices

The cremation graves took the form of pits with burned human and animal bones associated with many gravegoods. They date only to the earliest phase during the 2nd century. No evidence of containers was found. Individuals were not selected for cremation according to age since all age groups are represented. The greater frequency and richness of associated gravegoods differentiate cremation from inhumation burials (Fig. 11.4). Some of the cremation burials cut inhumation burials but others were disturbed by inhumation burials, proof of the co-existence of the two rites in the 2nd century.

The ossuaries were defined by the discovery of disarticulated bones which belonged to one or several individuals. It has been proven that these bones came from the intercutting of inhumation graves. In this case, disturbed bones were removed and reburied in shallow pits. Respect for disturbed bones is also indicated by the reburial of gravegoods with the bones.

It is therefore a question of mortuary behaviour linked to the phenomenon of 'réduction', a term applied in the study of mediaeval cemeteries in France to the deliberate re-opening of a grave with a view to its re-use (Bonvalot 1988; Crubézy and Raynaud 1988). Here however the disturbance of the burial seems to have been random. It differed therefore in that it was not deliberate but nevertheless showed respect for the disturbed bones. Here therefore we prefer the term of 'secondary reburial', recently described by Courtaud (1995), i.e. that bones are removed from the burial pit or original burial container, as opposed to 'primary reburial', the replacement of bones in their original funerary context. The intensity of the reworking varies across the site. Sector V, the latest, is least affected. This lack of disturbance is in agreement with the observations that inhumations in this sector are more widely spaced and that grave orientation is more homogenous. The difference between the overall frequency of burial in sectors III–V and sector V is significant and therefore represents a development in the management of cemetery space for placing inhumation burials.

Intercutting of burials, the displacement and redeposition of bones have already been noted in other Gallo-Roman cemeteries (Grange *et al.* 1960; Viet 1982). The intercutting might suggest that the location of burial place was soon forgotten and that there was limited management of the cemetery (Theureau 1983). Alternatively, it might

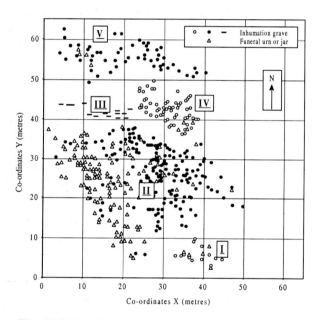

Fig. 11.2 *Dated sectors in the cemetery of Chantambre*

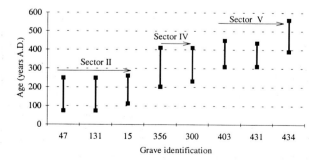

Fig. 11.3 *Radio-carbon dates for a samples of burials from Chantambre (95% confidence interval)*

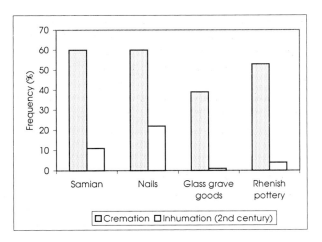

Fig. 11.4 Differences in grave goods between cremation and inhumation burials

indicate a concern to place individuals together after death. The latter hypothesis cannot be dismissed out of hand. It would obviously require a grave marker above ground level. Such structures were not recovered in excavation but an organic grave marker is possible. In general rural Gallo-Roman cemeteries are characterised by a lack of destruction of earlier tombs, in contrast to urban cemeteries with limited space. At Chantambre, intercutting occurs even when space is still available. The significant decrease in the frequency of intercutting in the final phase of the cemetery perhaps indicates a change in grave markers. The fact that the disturbed burials were of individuals buried directly in the earth without a coffin leads us to prefer the hypothesis of chance intercutting of burials.

A total of 155 ceramic burials (jars 82% and urns 18%) were excavated. The vast majority of human remains from these containers belonged to neonatal individuals, i.e. slightly premature stillborn babies or children deceased in the first week after birth. Some other remains were of children deceased between two and four years of age. The jars were cut in half longitudinally, creating two half vessels. The body was laid into one and sometimes covered by the other. A cover made of perishable material for other burials cannot however be ruled out. The bodies of young children were introduced into urns through their mouths. No special adjustment was therefore required. Such containers, also observed on other sites, have been called 'vases funéraires' (Ancien 1980).

Most of the other inhumation burials were in a wooden coffin or without a coffin. Only in one case was a burial lined with stone. The graves were mostly of individuals but there were also a few cases of multiple interments. A large majority of individuals had been laid out in supine position and all possible arm positions were observed. In some cases (10%), the skeleton was in a strange position, with the arms displaced as if the body had been carelessly thrown into the grave. This hypothesis is also supported by the regular absence of gravegoods in these graves.

Gravegoods were recovered from some but not all inhumation burials and where found were of modest quality but relatively abundant. The ceramic coarsewares were mostly represented by flagons and beakers. As with coarsewares, the frequency of terra sigillata declined from sector I to V. No difference between age groups was noted. Glass grave goods were represented by cups, a flask, a stemmed vessel and a bath flask. They were only associated with the burials of adults and sub-adults. The four adult graves with glass vessels were of young women. Faunal deposits comprised chicken, cock and pig, the typical species of Gallo-Roman cemeteries (Lepetz 1993), and were only associated with adult inhumations. The frequency of ornaments was low and was similar across all sectors. They were placed with 5% of adult and child burials and were absent from those of adolescents. Worn shoes were identified from the 'ghosts' of soles in the form of several rows of hobnails (four or five) with the feet. In some cases shoes were deposited away from the feet: such deposits were rarely associated with worn footwear. 16% of adult inhumations contained a deposit of nails, placed at the head or the feet, by the hands or in ceramic vessels. Their presence probably possessed a magical symbolism (van Doorsaeler 1967). The deposition of a charcoal layer at the bottom of inhumation burials is a phenomenon observed many times in contemporary cemeteries (van Doorsaeler 1967: 132).

Burial practices linked to age and gender

The statistical analysis of the various archaeological data has made it possible to determine burial practices linked to age and gender (Fig. 11.5). These links are statistically significant at the 0.05 level. The burial type, the depth of the grave and the associated gravegoods isolated three

Links to age at death	Neonates	Children (under 15 years)	Adults and subadults (over 15 years)
Grave type	urn or jar	in wooden coffin or in soil	in wooden coffin or in soil
Depth	low depth (average = 1.17 m)	moderate depth (average = 1.40 m)	greater depth (average = 1.56 m)
Associated deposit	none	frequent deposits of nails and ashes	frequent deposits of shoes

Links to sex	– Inhumation in wooden coffin more frequent for women than men – Glass gravegoods deposits specific to young women

Fig. 11.5 Burial practices linked to gender and age (0.05 statistical significance level)

age groups: neonates, children aged under 15 years and individuals aged over 15. It is however difficult to draw a parallel between these three age groups and a social distinction in the corresponding living population. Gender distinctions include the more frequent burial of female than male inhumation burials in wooden coffins and the presence of glass gravegoods only with young women aged between 15 and 25 years.

Evolution of the burial practices

Grave orientation is not homogeneous. The earliest phases (I and II) were characterised by random orientation without distinction linked to age or gender. In the early Roman period, burials in some cemeteries have a homogenous orientation, most often north-south (e.g. Viet 1982; Troadec 1993). Some homogenisation is observed in phase IV at Chantambre and in the latest phase (V) 90% of the graves were excavated east-west. This apparent break is a typical observation and is often interpreted as the widespread adaptation by Gallo-Roman populations of certain funerary practices particular to the end of the late Roman period and the beginning of the early mediaeval period. Thus in the Verdier cemetery at Lunel-Viel (Hérault) a change in burial orientation from north-south to east-west occurs halfway through the fourth cemetery (Raynaud 1987).

Figure 11.6 shows a significant decrease in the frequency of several categories of grave goods, worn footwear, coarsewares, samian, ashes, nails and footwear. However many other aspects of burial practice remain unchanged, such as the burial types or the specific burial practices for neonates.

Burial practices at Chantambre in a Gallo-Roman context

The Chantambre cemetery presents some typical characteristics of Gallo-Roman cemeteries. The objects

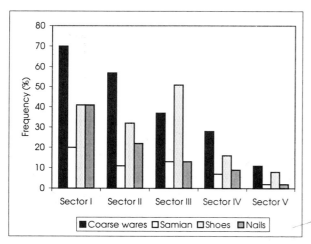

Fig. 11.6 *The frequency of different types of grave good over time (inhumation burials)*

recovered correspond to the concept of the tomb as a temporary residence (van Doorsaeler 1967: 125), where everyday objects are present (ceramics, animal offerings). Elements related to religious belief have also been recovered, notably the frequently present 'magic nails' placed at the bottom of the grave of which the function would be to prevent the return of 'evil spirits' (van Doorsaeler 1967: 122). The presence of an important concentration of ceramic sherds is reminiscent of the ritual breakage often referred to in Gallo-Roman cemeteries. The deliberate breakage is attested from the Iron Age onwards (van Doorsaeler 1967: 203). Its presence at Chantambre illustrates the longevity of certain mortuary practices.

Rites of cremation and inhumation coexisted during the earliest phase (2nd century AD). It is now accepted that rites of cremation and inhumation coexisted in the Gallo-Roman world, with a progressive predominance of inhumation during the 2nd and the 3rd centuries (Bel *et al.* 1991; Van Ossel 1991). The case of Chantambre illustrates this theory, save for the predominance of the inhumation rite at the end of the first century and the early disappearance of the cremation rite. The general spread of inhumation does not therefore seem to be linked to Christianization. The cremation graves also have richer and more frequent gravegoods than inhumation graves. Without indulging in over-speculative interpretation, the presence of glass, terra sigillata and 'Rhenish wares' in clearly higher proportions than in inhumation graves clearly signifies a social difference, the cause of which might be attributed to different social status or to different funerary ideologies.

The specific nature (in burial practice and location) of mortuary ritual related to the dead of the peri-natal age group is commonly observed in Gallo-Roman cemeteries (Planson 1982; Bel *et al.* 1991; Duday *et al.* 1995). The major difference lay generally in the inhumation of the latter while older children and adults were cremated. However the modes of inhumation varied, including tiled inhumations, beneath *imbrices* (Planson 1982; Barthelèmy and Depierre 1990), in jars cut in half (Despriée 1971; Petit 1976; Pladys 1985), in urns (Hugoniot *et al.* 1975; Gouiric and Pradeau-Moisson 1977; Ancien 1980) or amphorae (Raynaud 1987) or even outside the cemetery (Hugoniot *et al.* 1975; Duday *et al.* 1995). At Chantambre the specific nature of mortuary practices related to neonates lay in the container type, the depth of inhumation and in spatial grouping. There was no contrast between inhumation and cremation. This particular burial treatment endured throughout the entire period of use of the site into the later empire. The particular nature of funerary rituals for neonates and their absence from many cemeteries has given birth to the idea of 'baby cemeteries' in the Gallo-Roman world (Joly 1951). Chantambre therefore provides, by the number of its urned (infant) burials and by their location, a reference point for our understanding of the funerary rituals of neonates in rural Gaul. Rather than a baby cemetery, Chantambre was characterised by the reservation of one area to this age group within the burial space used by the whole population.

The decrease in the occurrence of grave goods in the course of the development of the cemetery has already been observed elsewhere (Van Doorselaer 1967: 139; Philpott and Reece 1993). The example of Chantambre perfectly illustrates the progressive adoption of new funerary practices, with a progressive decrease in grave furniture between sectors II, IV and V. This phase of the cemetery lacking grave goods, which can be dated from the 4th to the beginning of the 5th centuries, is of a period which is particularly poorly represented in cemeteries. This is in some sense a response to the problem posed by Ferdière (1993b: 438), who has noted a common reticence in attributing burials without grave goods to the later Roman period. The early to late Roman transition, to which numerous upheavals in the rural world are attributed (Ferdière 1988; Van Ossel 1993), manifests itself at Chantambre not only by the change in certain funerary practices but also by the continued use of the same cemetery and of certain practices such as the urned inhumation of very young children.

Results of the biological study

The following presents information derived from the biological study of this population. Firstly, the sex-ratio is balanced and all age groups are present in the proportion to be expected for a population with a pre-industrial mortality rate (Fig. 11.7). It means that all the members of the community could have been buried on this site. Indeed, unlike many Gallo-Roman or medieval sites in France, no selection according to age is observed. The size of the human group which used this cemetery can be estimated to lie between 50 and 80 people, which could have corresponded to approximately ten families.

The large sample of Chantambre also allows us to describe the morphology of this rural population. The skull vault is mesocranic, the cranial capacity is strong and the face is orthognathous. Many skulls show a posterior development of the occipital bone known as the occipital bun (Fig. 11.8). This trait is typical of this period and is not linked to sex. In European populations it disappears during the early middle ages. Sexual dimorphism is very marked at Chantambre in terms of stature, the average stature of males being approximately 172 cm and that of females 160 cm.

Non-metrical traits of the skeletons were also studied in order to determine some linkage between individual characteristics and location within the cemetery, but this was not successful. It can be interpreted either as indicating random organisation or a strong degree of homogeneity among this population. Indeed anthropological data have identified elements which point to a strong homogeneity in the population and its strong stability over time. For example many analyses of cranial and post-cranial metrical data have shown that it is impossible to identify differences between the parts of the cemetery used at different periods. This homogeneity is also supported by the occurrence of a very rare pathology, osteochondroma, an isolated benign tumour which is a faulty ossification of the growth plate between the diaphysis and the epiphysis. At Chantambre, 5% of the males have an osteochondroma on the femur (Fig. 11.9). The aetiology of this pathology is related to exostosis multiplex which is a genetic trait. The frequency observed in Chantambre is similar to that in one very closed contemporary native Canadian population in Manitoba (Black *et al.* 1993). Osteochondroma occurs in each area and therefore each period of the cemetery. It seems thus that the rural population which used this funeral site remained stable over time and was very closed. This indication gives credence to arguments based on archaeological data for a progressive evolution of burial practices within the same population.

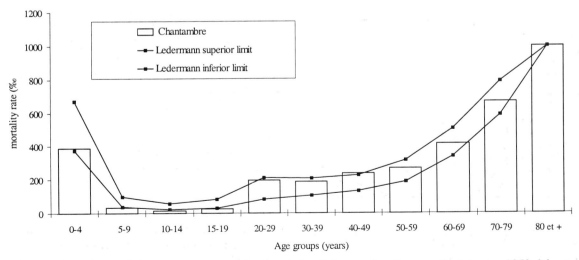

Fig. 11.7 *Chantambre age distribution compared to a pre-industrial mortality diagram (Ledermann 1969, life expectancy at birth of 30 years; further details in Murail 1996)*

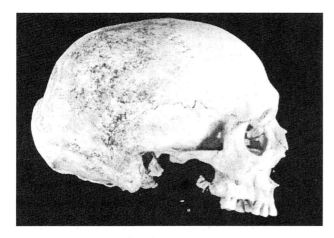

Fig. 11.8 Right lateral view of the calvarium of a male individual from Chantambre showing the occipital bun, a very frequently observed trait in this population. It corresponds to a posterior development of the occipital bone which defines a notch in the parieto-occipital region (Ducros 1967).

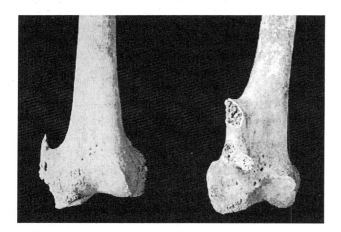

Fig. 11.9 Two examples of osteochondroma localised at the medial and distal part of left femurs

The Chantambre population also presents the classic pathologies observed in past skeletal populations which need not be detailed here. We must however note that 62% of the individuals present some enamel defects on their permanent dentition. These occurred at Chantambre between two and four years old, a common pattern that is sometimes associated with nutritional stress after weaning.

There is also one exceptional medical treatment. A male aged over 30 years at death and belonging to the earliest phase of the cemetery (2nd century) has a dental implant where the right second upper premolar would have been. This implant is made of iron and the retro-alveolar X-ray showed that the alveolar wall and the pseudo-root fit perfectly together. The implant is thus very well integrated into the jawbone. According to available data the necessary period for osseo-integration

is a minimum of three to six months. We do not know the reasons for its insertion. Anthropological and archae-ological data do not distinguish the man from other burials within the group. However this discovery is a remarkable piece of evidence for the knowledge of medicine and anatomy in this rural community of the 2nd century AD (more details in Crubézy *et al.* 1998).

Conclusion

Chantambre appears to have been a highly organised cemetery with burial practices linked to age and sex. The differences between cremation and inhumation, or between burials deposited in wooden coffins and those not may have signified difference in social status or reflected the economic condition of individuals. The description of the funerary practices observed at Chantambre introduces new areas for discussion and supports van Ossel's proposition for a great diversity in the management of death in Roman Gaul, a diversity which can perhaps be explained by the persistence of some practices inherited from the Iron Age (Galliou 1993).

Scholars have often argued that in France the transition between the Early and the Late Empire was strongly affected by migrations from the east that produced many changes in the indigenous population, particularly with reference to burial practice and the choice of burial site (Ferdière 1988 ; Van Ossel 1993). The case of Chant-ambre does not support this idea in this rural population, as archaeological and anthropological data provide evidence of a strong homogeneity in the population and a large scale stability over time. Likewise, no indirect evidence (for example particular grave furniture or an increase in the diversity of practice) was observed which might signify the invasions of the 3rd or 4th centuries. As Chantambre is the only cemetery in this region both to have been completely excavated and to cover both the early and late Roman periods, are these characteristics particular to this cemetery, or is it a representative sample? Only the excavation and study of similar sites will make it possible to reply to this question and to discuss its interpretation in historical terms.

Finally this example of a cemetery study also stresses that a successful global understanding (biology and palaeoethnology) of a past population needs constant interaction between both the archaeological and the anthropological analyses, as well as exhaustive excavation and a well-defined chronology. Without such pre-conditions, the Chantambre osteo-archaeological sample might well have led us to incorrect interpretations.

Bibliography

Ancien, A.M. 1980. Inhumations d'enfants en urne dans le quartier gallo-romain du château d'Albâtre à Soissons (Aisne). *Revue Archéologique de l'Oise*, 19:1 0–12.
Barthelèmy, A. and Depierre, G. 1990. *La nécropole gallo-romaine des Cordiers à Macon*. Macon.

Bel, V., Tranoy, L., Béraud, I. and Gébara, C. 1991. Les nécropoles à incinérations et à inhumations en Gaule Méridionale. In *Incinérations et inhumations dans l'Occident Romain aux trois premiers siècles de notre ère*, Actes du Colloque International de Toulouse-Montréjeau, Octobre 1987, pp. 9–40.

Black, B., Dooley, J., Pyper, A. and Reed, M. 1993. Multiple hereditary exostoses. An epidemiologic study of an isolated community in Manitoba. *Clinical Orthopaedics and Related Research*, 307: 212–217.

Bonvalot, N. 1988. Le problème des inhumations successives dans les nécropoles du Haut Moyen Age. In *La mort à travers l'archéologie Franc-comtoise*, pp. 83–86.

Courtaud, P. 1995. Les ensembles sépulcraux. *Dossiers d'Archéologie*, 208: 34–43.

Crubézy, E., Murail, P., Girard, L. and Bernadou J.P. 1998. False teeth of the Roman World. *Nature*, 391: 29.

Crubézy, E. and Raynaud, C. 1988. Le passage de la sépulture individuelle à la sépulture collective du IIIe siècle au XIIe siècle dans le sud-ouest de la France. In *Anthropologie et histoire ou anthropologie historique?*, Actes des Troisièmes Journées Anthropologiques de Valbonne, CNRS Ed., 195–208.

Despriée, J. 1971. Quatre sépultures d'enfants à Averdon (Loir-et-Cher). *Revue Archéologique du Centre,* 39–40: 229–237.

Ducros, A. 1967. Le chignon occipital : mesure sur le squelette. *L'Anthropologie* (Paris), 71 (1–2): 75–96.

Duday, H., Laubenheimer, F. and Tillier, A.m. 1995. *Sallèles d'Aude: nouveau-nés et nourrissons gallo-romains.* Centre de Recherches d'Histoire Ancienne, volume 144, série Amphores 3.

Ferdière, A. 1993a. Sépultures dans le monde gallo-romain: le cas de la Beauce. In *Monde des morts et monde des vivants en Gaule rurale*, Actes du colloque d'Orléans, 6ème supplément à la Revue Archéologique du Centre de la France, pp. 209–239.

Ferdière, A. 1993b. Conclusion du colloque. In *Monde des morts et monde des vivants en Gaule rurale*, Actes du colloque d'Orléans, 6ème supplément à la Revue Archéologique du Centre de la France, pp. 433–447.

Ferdière, A. 1988. *Les campagnes en Gaule Romaine. Tome I: les Hommes et l'environnement en Gaule rurale.* Errance

Fourteau-Bardaji, A.M., Marinval, P., Ruas, M.P. and Marguerie, D. 1993. La nécropole gallo-romaine des Vernes à Faverdines. In *Monde des morts et monde des vivants en Gaule rurale*, Actes du colloque d'Orléans, 6ème supplément à la Revue Archéologique du Centre de la France, pp. 265–271.

Galliou, P. 1993. Monde des morts et monde des vivants dans les campagnes de l'Armorique Romaine. In *Monde des morts et monde des vivants en Gaule rurale*, Actes du colloque d'Orléans, 6ème supplément à la Revue Archéologique du Centre de la France, pp. 241–246.

Gouiric, N. and Pradeau-Moisson, F. 1977. *Fouille de sauvetage d'une nécropole gallo-romaine*, Catalogue d'exposition, Dourdan.

Grange, A., Parriat, H. and Perraud, R. 1960. La nécropole gallo-romaine et barbare de Briord (Ain). *La Physiophile*, 52:17–46.

Hugoniot, E., Thévenon, R. and Vannier, B. 1975. Les sépultures gallo-romaines tardives de Bruères-Allichamps (Cher). *Revue Archéologique du Centre*, numéro spécial: 85–92.

Joly, J. 1951. Un cimetière gallo-romain de bébés à Alise-Sainte-Reine (Côte d'Or). *Revue Archéologique de l'Est*, 2: 119–120.

Ledermann, S. 1969. *Nouvelles tables types de mortalité.* INED, Travaux et documents n°53, Presses Universitaires de France, Paris.

Lepetz, S. 1993. Les restes animaux dans les sépultures gallo-romaines. In *Monde des morts et monde des vivants en Gaule rurale*, Actes du colloque d'Orléans, 6ème supplément à la Revue Archéologique du Centre de la France, pp. 37–43.

Lequoy, M.C. 1992. Inhumations et incinérations dans deux nécropoles de la basse vallée de la Seine: Rouen et Vatteville-La-Rue. In *Incinérations et inhumations dans l'Occident Romain aux trois premiers siècles de notre ère*, Actes du Colloque International de Toulouse-Montréjeau, Octobre 1987, pp. 231–233.

Martin-Kilcher, S. 1993. Situation des cimetières et tombes rurales en Germanie supérieure et dans les régions voisines. In *Monde des morts et monde des vivants en Gaule rurale*, Actes du colloque d'Orléans, 6ème supplément à la Revue Archéologique du Centre de la France, pp. 153–164.

Molleson, T. 1989. Social implications of mortality patterns from juveniles from Poundbury Camp, Romano-british cemetery. *Anthropologische Anzeiger*, 47 (1): 27–38.

Murail, P. 1996. *Biologie et pratiques funéraires des populations d'époque historique: une démarche méthodologique appliquée à la nécropole gallo-romaine de Chantambre (Essonne, France).* Thèse de l'Université de Bordeaux I, unpublished.

Petit, M. 1976. *Nécropoles gallo-romaines de Lutèce.* Thèse de l'Université Paris IV, unpublished.

Philpott, R.A. and Reece, R. 1993. Sépultures rurales en Bretagne romaine. In *Monde des morts et monde des vivants en Gaule rurale*, Actes du colloque d'Orléans, 6ème supplément à la Revue Archéologique du Centre de la France, pp. 417–423.

Pladys, C. 1985. La nécropole gallo-romaine de Clos-Fontaine. *Bulletin du Groupement Archéologique de Seine et Marne*, 26: 21–25.

Planson, E. *et al.* 1982. *La nécropole gallo-romaine des Bolards, Nuits-Saint-Georges.* CNRS Ed.

Raynaud, C. 1987. Typologie des sépultures et problèmes de datation :nécropoles languedociennes de l'Antiquité Tardive et du Haut Moyen Age. *Revue Trimestrielle de la Fédération Archéologique de l'Héraut*, 4: 121–132.

Theureau, C. 1983. *Le cimetière médiéval de Saint-Pierre-le-Puellier, à Tours*, Diplôme de l'Ecole Pratique des Hautes Etudes, Laboratoire d'Anthropologie Biologique.

Troadec, J. 1993. Le complexe funéraire de Lazenay, Bourges (Cher). In *Monde des morts et monde des vivants en Gaule rurale*, Actes du colloque d'Orléans, 6ème supplément à la Revue Archéologique du Centre de la France, pp. 313–318.

Van Doorselaer, A. 1967. Les nécropoles d'époque romaine en Gaule septentrionale. *Dissertationes Archaeologicae Gandenses*, X, Bruges.

Van Ossel, P. 1993. L'occupation des campagnes dans le nord de la Gaule durant l'Antiquité tardive: l'apport des cimetières. In *Monde des morts et monde des vivants en Gaule rurale*, Actes du colloque d'Orléans, 6ème supplément à la Revue Archéologique du Centre de la France, pp. 185–196.

Van Ossel, P. 1991. Incinération et inhumation dans le nord de la Gaule Belgique durant le Haut-Empire. In *Incinérations et inhumations dans l'Occident Romain aux trois premiers siècles de notre ère*, Actes du Colloque International de Toulouse-Montréjeau, Octobre 1987, pp. 209–218.

Viet, J. 1982. La nécropole du Bas Empire d'Ouchamps (Loir-et-Cher), étude d'une population. *Revue Archéologique SITES*, Hors Série n°16.

12. A Roman cemetery in the eastern *Civitas Treverorum*. Preliminary report on the excavations in Wadern-Oberlöstern in Northwestern Saarland (Germany)

Angelika Abegg-Wigg

Few cemeteries, parts of cemeteries, or groups of graves from the *Civitas Treverorum* have been published upon which a general assessment of Roman funerary customs there can be based, and detailed overall studies are almost non-existent (Massart 1989; Stein 1989: 117 f.; Cüppers 1993). There is insufficient background information to identify regional peculiarities, yet the burial practices in this area, which includes parts of the present-day states of France, Belgium, Luxembourg and Germany, were remarkably varied.

This paper will look at one particular cemetery in order to consider how a group of graves in a rural landscape can illuminate individual expressions, traditions within the community, and the conflict between indigenous and intrusive funerary rites. What information can the data collected provide about changes in burial customs which might be the result of Italic or Roman influence? Above all, what role did funerary architecture play in the 'Romanisation' of the rural population?

It is important to view Roman funerary rites at several

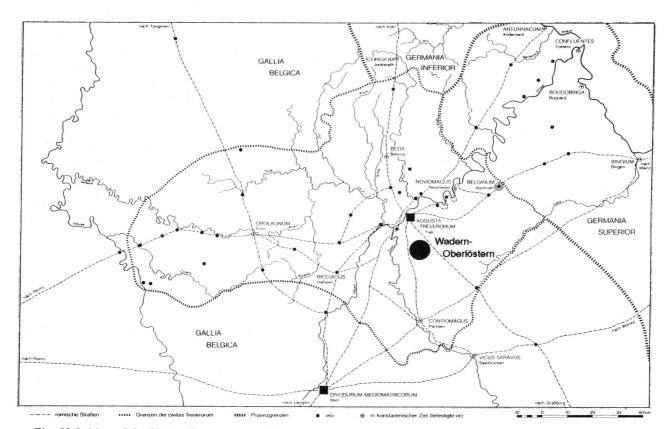

Fig. 12.1 *Map of the* Civitas Treverorum *with the cemetery of Wadern-Oberlöstern (after Haffner 1989: 24 Abb. 9)*

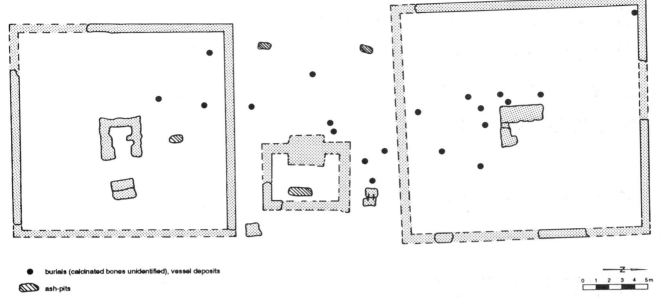

● burials (calcinated bones unidentified), vessel deposits

▨ ash-pits

N
0 1 2 3 4 5m

Fig. 12.2 *Plan of the cemetery of Wadern-Oberlöstern*

levels, at the regional or local, as well as at the supra-regional or provincial (Jones 1991). The regional evidence can say something about the rules prevalent within a local individual society. The widespread similarity of the arrangement of graves demonstrates that, on the whole, there were cultural rules and conventions governing the treatment of the dead. Burial customs are not just an expression of the beliefs of one person or a group of persons, for example a family, but are also dependent on broader social factors (Schlette 1991). On the other hand a comparison of the rites which can be identified in various regions will always show that there was significant variation.

Alongside such local manifestations phenomena can also be identified which remain the same throughout several regions. As far as locally restricted phenomena are concerned, it is often difficult in individual cases to tell whether they are the result of Italic or Roman influence, as local factors can also produce results which, on the surface, appear to be expressions of 'Romanisation'. Only when tendencies are repeated at a supra-regional or provincial level are we perhaps justified in talking of genuine acculturation or even 'Romanisation' (Jones 1993).

Oberlöstern, part of the town of Wadern in Saarland, lies in the east of the *Civitas Treverorum* (Fig. 12.1). The State Archaeological Service (Staatliches Konservatoramt des Saarlandes) excavated there from 1991 to 1996, on the eastern slope of a long ridge to the west of the village dividing the Löster and Wadrill valleys. A Roman cemetery was uncovered over an area of some 2000m². (Reinhard 1992a; Reinhard 1992b; Schönwald 1992). It was related to a Roman settlement, probably a *villa*

rustica, some 400m away. The site for the cemetery was carefully chosen, on a prominent spur which was visible from far and wide. Some 200m further down the slope the stream of the Lohbach will have provided the settlement with water. A road seems to have run close by, perhaps providing access to the settlement.

So far two tumuli with rectangular retaining walls, and a rectangular enclosure between them have been discovered, together with an ash cist and a funerary altar. There are also a number of burials in simple earth graves, as well as various scatters of ash, deposits of vessels, and ash-pits which are associated with the cremation ceremonies (Fig. 12.2). As it has not yet been fully explored, it is not possible to provide a definitive assessment of the entire complex. Rather individual aspects will be presented, which can throw light on the questions discussed above.

The rectangular walled enclosure which lies between the two tumuli (Fig. 12.2) measures 6 by 4.90m, and only the foundation had survived. All that remained of the wall were a few fragments of blocks in the southeast corner and in the foundations on the north side. In the west a 2.1m long section of the foundation was wider, and supported a stone monument which has been completely robbed out.

Within the eastern part of the enclosure, only slightly off the central axis, and in alignment with the wall and the monument, was an oblong-shaped pit measuring 1.8 by 0.7m. Apart from fragments of some 50 to 60 vessels, including a large amount of samian ware, the pit mainly contained pyre remains, such as glass and metal objects. The few calcined bones, which have not yet been analysed, lay mainly in the southwest sector. Charred pieces of wood provide a date of AD 137 (dendrochronological analysis by Dipl.-Forstwirtin M. Neyses, Rheinisches Landesmuseum Trier), and the charred plant remains provide a typical spectrum of cereals and pulses of the Roman period (see Kreuz this volume); mainly spelt and peas, together with a little barley, emmer, lentils and beans (archaeobotanical analysis by Dr H. Kroll, University of Kiel). The position of the pit suggests that it was associated with the enclosure wall, and so probably dates the enclosure to the middle of the second century AD.

Various stone architectural fragments, together with the carved remains of human figures and of an inscription lay nearby, at a distance of no more than 6m. Some of this will have belonged to the funerary monument built on the foundation in the west wall. Not all of the material has been studied, but very probably it was part of a tower-tomb with scale roof, such as are typical of the Moselle region. The fragments include sections of cornice, floral decorative elements, and parts of the scale roof. Elements of arms, hands, legs and feet confirm that there was a field with figured decoration.

Two identical sandstone heads were found to the northeast. The faces are framed by hair with stylised long curls drawn up together above the forehead, a hair style typical of ancient theatre masks. With a height of 0.5m they compare well in size with other stone masks from Gaul and Germany, which were used as frontal or corner acroteria on ostentatious funerary monuments. This element of funerary architecture had probably spread north from Gallia Narbonensis, where many particularly fine large examples are known (Hallier et. al. 1990: 186–194; Peters 1992).

In front of the southeast corner of the enclosure was a large ash cist of green, very porous sandstone. Only fragments of the lid are preserved, and it was inscribed with the letters DM, the usual abbreviation in funerary inscriptions of the second century AD for *Dis Manibus*. The size of the cist, and various individual elements set it apart from the simpler types which we know from other rural cemeteries in the *Civitas Treverorum*.

A feature to the north was probably a funerary altar measuring 1.15 × 0.85m. All that was left of the main structure were two stone blocks which had been joined by a bracket and were still in situ. Funerary altars have their origins in Italy, although they drew on elements from the Greek world.

The enclosure of funerary precincts and monuments with stone walls was a common feature in the Roman Empire (Decker 1976/77; von Hesberg 1992: 57 f.). Structures of this kind are known in Italy from the late second century BC, and they are a characteristic element of cemeteries in the late Republic. In North Italy there are direct prototypes for the plan found at Oberlöstern, which in turn drew on funerary monuments from Rome, Central Italy, as well as the Hellenistic East (Mansuelli 1963: 32–43).

A good parallel for the layout of the complex at Oberlöstern is provided by a funerary enclosure from Boretto by Brescello ('Monument of the Concordii') (Fig. 12.3), which is dated to the third quarter of the first century AD (Aurigemma 1931; Pflug 1989: 178–179). A rectangular wall measuring 10.8 × 9.2m enclosed several cremation burials, and a 2 × 1.28m foundation was built into the front. This was surmounted by a monumental rectangular stele 4.19m high, with architectural and figured decoration.

In Gaul graves enclosed with ditch systems are already found in the La Tène period (Metzler et. al. 1991; Becker 1995; Bridger 1996: 245–249), and continue into the second/third centuries AD. From the first century AD we also find stone enclosures. For example in the mainly military cemetery at Mainz-Weisenau there are simple stone enclosure walls, as well as those with tombstones incorporated into the front (Fig. 12.3) (Witteyer/Fasold 1995: 20–21). This *Gräberstrasse*, which follows Italic models, was in use from the Tiberian period until the fourth century.

Both temporal and religious motives have been suggested for the construction of these funerary enclosures. They have been interpreted as a boundary between the sacred and profane, between this world and the next, or as a cult place for the worship of ancestors. Others have emphasised the desire to demarcate a family plot, or else to demonstrate the social prestige of the deceased through the construction of a monumental complex (Mackensen 1978: 132–133; Becker 1995: 75).

Walled funerary enclosures are known in large numbers from rural cemeteries in the *Civitas Treverorum*, and vary in size from 11 to 83 m². They are mainly dated to the second and third centuries, and can be divided into two groups; those with simple surrounding walls (Schindler 1973: 64–68), and those with a foundation for a funerary monument incorporated into them, as at Oberlöstern. An example of the latter type was found in 1970/1971 in Luxembourg, on the Roman road from Trier to Altrier at Lellig-Wasserbillig ('Weiler', Friedhof D) (Fig. 12.3.; Thill 1971: 496–497; Thill 1972: 368–369), and is very similar to Oberlöstern. Measuring 8.2 by 6.35m, it was only a little larger, and enclosed three burials of the second century. The surrounding wall is interrupted by a platform measuring 2.4′ 1.55m, which was probably the base for an altar or a tombstone. Facing the road, on the opposite side to the platform and outside the wall, was another foundation, either for an ash cist or a funerary altar.

In the north of Gallia Belgica there are also tumuli with a square enclosure wall incorporating a foundation for an altar (Wigg 1993a: 34 f.). At Lösnich the sides of the wall are 15m long, and a foundation for a funerary altar is built into both the north and west walls. At Siesbach a circular retaining wall was surrounded by an additional square wall 24.5m square, with an altar foundation on the north side.

The two tumuli at Oberlöstern are also surrounded by a rectangular wall (Fig. 12.2). Tumulus 1, to the south of

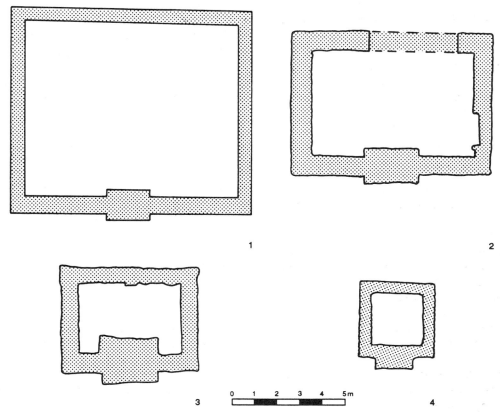

Fig. 12.3 *Comparative sizes of walled funerary enclosures. 1. Boretto, 2. Lellig-Wasserbillig, 3. Wadern-Oberlöstern, 4. Mainz-Weisenau*

the small funerary enclosure, had been badly eroded, and was only recognisable as a mound 0.6m high and 29m from north to south. After the mound had been removed, an enclosure wall measuring 16m square externally came to light. The original mound must have had a diameter of 14m (the internal dimension of the enclosure wall), and been at least 2.7m high. The visible remains of the northern tumulus 2 had a diameter of 34m, and it was preserved to a height of 0.8m. Its original size must have been some 16.5m, and the rectangular enclosure wall was 18.5m square.

Simple rectangular enclosure walls for tumuli, which were not structurally necessary, are rare in the northwest provinces (Fig. 12.4). The two tumuli at Oberlöstern, enclosing areas of 256 m² for tumulus 1, and 342 m² for tumulus 2, are the largest known examples of this kind. As was already seen above some tumuli with a circular surrounding wall were enclosed additionally within a square wall (Wigg 1993b: 376). The largest example is the monumental tumulus at Nennig, with an area of 9403 m².

A stone foundation was found in the centre of both tumuli, and probably indicates the presence of a burial chamber. The base of the rectangular chamber beneath tumulus 1 was set below the ancient ground level, and constructed of stone blocks laid in a U-shape 3m long.

The entrance was in the east. It was probably roofed with sandstone blocks which were found to the east of the entrance. The chamber had already been robbed, and the 5m wide shaft dug into the hill is visible in the profile. No human remains or finds which might help date the construction of the chamber were present. Beneath tumulus 2 there was also a stone structure, but because nothing had survived other than the foundation, it cannot be certain that it was indeed a burial chamber. However, the presence of a burial mound discounts the possibility that we have here the base for some other sort of funerary monument, such as is known from Wavre, which stood within a 13m square enclosure (Bridel 1976).

Tumuli with a burial chamber of the late first to the third centuries are rare in Gallia Belgica (Wigg 1993a: 48–55; Wigg 1993b: 378; Wigg 1993c). Because they are frequently so badly preserved it is hard to date them or produce a typology. For example it is often not possible to determine the exact position of the chamber beneath the mound, and technical details of the structure can be unclear. Nevertheless west of the Rhine it is possible to divide the Roman tumuli with burial chamber – which is normally built of sandstone – into two groups. The chambers at Oberlöstern are of type 1. These are rectangular structures, which can be up to 6m long, and had no external access once the mound had been constructed

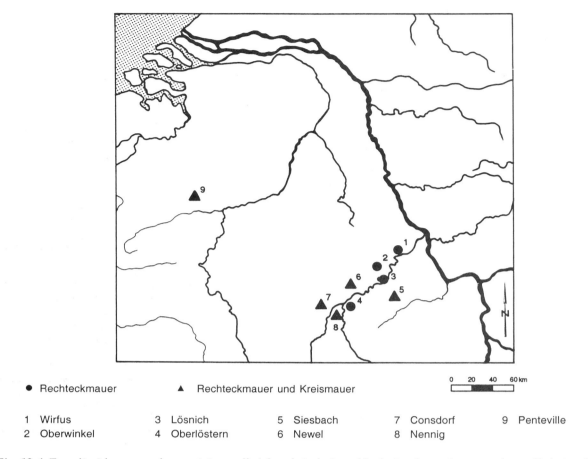

● Rechteckmauer   ▲ Rechteckmauer und Kreismauer

1	Wirfus	3	Lösnich	5	Siesbach	7	Consdorf	9	Penteville
2	Oberwinkel	4	Oberlöstern	6	Newel	8	Nennig		

Fig. 12.4 *Tumuli with rectangular retaining walls (closed circles), and both circular and rectangular walls (triangle) in the eastern* Civitas Treverorum *and adjacent areas*

over them. As far as can be determined they range from 6 to 28 m². in size. Type 2 chambers are characterised by a corridor leading from the edge of the mound to a circular or rectangular chamber.

The cemetery at Oberlöstern almost certainly belonged to a nearby *villa rustica*. The ostentatious architecture is typical of the graveyards of the rich landowners, especially in the second century. They are often sited above the main house, and are visible from far and wide (Martin-Kilcher 1993). Oberlöstern fulfils two of the most important requirements for such a monument: suitable sandstone was available at a distance of some 1.5 km. to the north and labour was to hand. The monuments surely reflect the social status of those buried beneath them. But at the same time a group identity was expressed through the use of particular architectural forms, and it is significant that two virtually identical monuments stood next to each other. Perhaps this uniformity was meant to demonstrate that the deceased had a similar standing, or that they were related. Was a bond to be visible even after death, or was the intention to achieve similar status? The linear arrangement of the various monuments are in some ways similar to an Italic *Gräberstrasse*.

What relevance does the architecture of the cemetery

above ground have then for the problems discussed at the beginning of this paper? Funerary complexes with similar arrangements can be found not just locally or regionally, but also across the provinces. We have seen an almost exact parallel example of an enclosed funerary precinct from nearby Luxembourg, and Oberlöstern fits well into the known pattern of monumental funerary architecture from rural cemeteries of the second century AD in the Roman Empire.

Although the practice of enclosing a burial precinct with a ditch was already common locally in the late Iron Age, the form chosen here for the enclosure, incorporating a foundation for a funerary monument, has its origins in Italo-Roman models. The immediate prototype need not have come direct from Italy itself, but like the stone masks may have been transmitted from provinces where the process of 'Romanisation' was already advanced. This led to a mixture of older native elements and external influences.

This synthesis of tradition and the new is further embodied in the two tumuli from Oberlöstern. Burial mounds were widespread in northern Gallia Belgica in the pre-Roman Iron Age, but there does not seem to have been an uninterrupted continuity of the tradition into the

Roman period. They only appear again from the mid-first century AD, often with very ornate architecture, and fit in well with other Roman funerary monuments in the region.

Thus the architecture and planning of the cemetery at Oberlöstern are in many ways an outward expression of an assimilation of Italo-Roman burial rites. Some individual elements can be traced back to indigenous traditions, but this should not be interpreted as a sign of resistance to new funerary customs, or of a conscious adherence to old practices. Rather, the mixture of different elements led to a new form of expression, in which we can also see the desire to conform to certain standards which is so typical of the rich landowning classes in the provinces. This is one of the main characteristics of Italo-Roman burial customs. The result is not a one-sided phenomenon, but rather a dialogue between Italo-Roman and indigenous elements (Hitchner 1995). In other words the assimilation of Italo-Roman funerary architecture did not lead to mere imitation, but became characteristic of the so-called Gallo-Roman (provincial) culture, which involved both native Celtic and Roman aspects (Freeman 1993; von Hesberg 1995). We can indeed see an external expression of 'Romanisation'. But whether the population actually identified itself with this is another matter.

Bibliography

Aurigemma, S. 1931. Il monumento dei Concordii presso Boretto. *Rivista del R. Istituto d'Archeologia e Storia dell'Arte*, 3: 268–298

Becker, S. 1995. Die Grabgärten der Latènezeit in Mittel- und Westeuropa. *Archäologische Informationen*, 18/1: 75–78

Bridel, Ph. 1976. Le mausolée de Wavre. Etude des fragments architecturaux du Musée archéologique de Neuchatel. *Jahrbuch der Schweizerischen Gesellschaft für Ur- und Frühgeschichte*, 59: 193–201

Bridger, C. 1996. *Das römerzeitliche Gräberfeld "An Hinkes Weißhof", Tönisvorst-Vorst, Kreis Viersen*. Köln/Bonn: Rheinische Ausgrabungen 40

Cüppers, H. 1993. Sépultures et cimetières ruraux en pays trévire. In *Monde des morts, monde des vivants en Gaule rurale* (ed. A. Ferdière). Tours: Revue Archéologique du Centre de la France Supplément 6, pp. 81–88

Decker, K.-V. 1976/77. Steinerne Grabeinfassungen (Grabgärten) vom oberen Laubenheimer Weg. *Mainzer Zeitschrift*, 71/72: 228–230

Freeman, P.W.M. 1993. Romanisation and Roman material culture. *Journal of Roman Archaeology*, 6: 438–445

Haffner, A. et. al. 1989. *Gräber – Spiegel des Lebens. Zum Totenbrauchtum der Kelten und Römer am Beispiel des Treverer-Gräberfeldes Wederath-Belginum*. Trier: Schriftenreihe des Rheinischen Landesmuseums Trier 2

Hallier, G. et. al. 1990. Le mausolée de Cucuron (Vaucluse). *Gallia*, 47: 145–202

von Hesberg, H. 1992. *Römische Grabbauten*. Darmstadt: Wissenschaftliche Buchgesellschaft

von Hesberg, H. (ed.) 1995. *Was ist eigentlich Provinz? Zur Beschreibung eines Bewußtseins*. Köln: Schriften des Archäologischen Instituts der Universität zu Köln

Hitchner, R.B. 1995. The culture of death and the invention of culture in Roman Africa. *Journal of Roman Archaeology*, 8: 493–498

Jones, R.F J. 1991. Cultural Change in Roman Britain. In *Roman Britain: Recent Trends* (ed. R.F.J. Jones). Sheffield: Recent Trend Series Volume 5, pp. 115–120

Jones, R. 1993. Backwards and forwards in Roman burial. *Journal of Roman Archaeology*, 6: 427–432

Mackensen, M. 1978. *Das römische Gräberfeld auf der Keckwiese in Kempten*. Kallmünz: Materialhefte zur bayerischen Vorgeschichte A 34

Mansuelli, G.A. 1963. Les monuments commémoratifs romains de la vallée du Po. *Monuments et Mémoires E. Piot*, 53: 19–93

Martin-Kilcher, St. 1993. Situation des cimetières et tombes rurales en Germania superior et dans le régions voisines. In *Monde des morts, monde des vivants en Gaule rurale* (ed. A. Ferdière). Tours: Revue Archéologique du Centre de la France Supplément 6, pp. 153–164

Massart, C. 1989. Les rites funéraires dans la province de Luxembourg à l'époque gallo-romaine. In *Les vivants et leurs morts. Art croyances et rites funéraires dans l'Ardenne d'autrefois*. Bastogne: Musée en Piconrue, pp. 35–56

Metzler, J. et. al. 1991. *Clemency et les tombes de l'aristocratie en Gaule Belgique*. Luxembourg: Dossiers d'Archéologie du Musée National d'Histoire et d'Art 1

Peters, R. 1992. Masken von römischen Grabmälern. In *Colonia Ulpia Traiana. Grabung, Forschung, Präsentation. 7. Arbeitsbericht*. Köln: Rheinland-Verlag, pp. 60–65

Pflug, H. 1989. *Römische Porträtstelen in Oberitalien. Untersuchungen zur Chronologie, Typologie und Ikonographie*. Mainz: Verlag Philipp von Zabern

Reinhard, W. 1992a. Monumentale Grabhügel der Römerzeit aus Wadern-Oberlöstern. In *Der Kreis Merzig-Wadern und die Mosel zwischen Nennig und Metz* (eds. J. Lichardus and A. Miron). Stuttgart: Führer zu archäologischen Denkmälern in Deutschland 24, pp. 160–163

Reinhard, W. 1992b. Monumentale Grabhügel der Römerzeit von Oberlöstern, Stadt Wadern, Kr. Merzig-Wadern. *Archäologie in Deutschland*, 1992/1:56

Schindler, R. 1973. Das ummauerte Familiengrab der gallorömischen Wüstung in Landscheid. *Trierer Zeitschrift*, 36: 57–76

Schlette, F. 1991. Geistig-religiöse und soziologische Erkenntnisse aus dem ur- und frühgeschichtlichen Bestattungswesen. In *Bestattungswesen und Totenkult in ur- und frühgeschichtlicher Zeit* (eds. F. Horst and H. Keiling). Berlin: Akademie-Verlag, pp. 9–21

Schönwald, J. 1992. Neueste Ergebnisse bei der Grabung römischer Grabhügel in Oberlöstern. *Archäologie in Deutschland*, 1992/4: 54

Stein, F. 1989. Die Bevölkerung des Saar-Mosel-Raumes am Übergang von der Antike zum Mittelalter. Überlegungen zum Kontinuitätsproblem aus archäologischer Sicht. *Archaeologia Mosellana*, 1:89–195

Thill, G. 1971. Neue Ausgrabungsergebnisse in 'Weiler' zwischen Wasserbillig und Lellig. *Hémecht*, 23: 489–506

Thill, G. 1972. Nachtrag zum Grabungsbericht über den Gräberbezirk 'Weiler' (Wasserbillig-Lellig). *Hémecht*, 24: 367–372

Wigg, A. 1993a. *Grabhügel des 2. und 3. Jahrhunderts n. Chr. an Mittelrhein, Mosel und Saar*. Trier: Trierer Zeitschrift Beiheft 16

Wigg, A. 1993b. Barrows in Northeastern Gallia Belgica: cultural and social aspects. In *Römerzeitliche Gräber als Quellen zu Religion, Bevölkerungsstruktur und Sozialgeschichte* (ed. M. Struck). Mainz: Archäologische Schriften des Instituts für Vor- und Frühgeschichte der Johannes Gutenberg-Universität Mainz 3, pp. 371–379

Wigg, A. 1993c. Zu römerzeitlichen Grabhügeln mit gemauerter Grabkammer in Großbritannien. *Germania*, 71: 532–538

Witteyer, M./Fasold, P. 1995. *Des Lichtes beraubt. Totenehrung in der römischen Gräberstraße von Mainz-Weisenau*. Wiesbaden: Wiesbadener Graphische Betriebe

13. An elite funerary enclosure in the centre of the villa of Biberist-Spitalhof (Switzerland) – a case study

C. Schucany

The study presented here shows how a well preserved archaeological feature which was excavated and fully documented allows the detailed reconstruction of burial rites and the customs concerning the deposition of grave goods.

Context

The villa of Biberist-Spitalhof lies in the valley of the river Aare, 1.5 km south-west of the *vicus* of Salodurum (Solothurn), on a flat terrace on the southern side of the valley, 25 m above the river. The situation, near a navigable river, the main road from Aventicum (Avenches) to Augusta Raurica (Augst) and a presumed road from Salodurum to the *vicus* of Berne-Engehalbinsel (Fig. 13.1), was perfect for the distribution of the products of the villa. Prior to the construction of a highway, the archaeological service of the canton of Solothurn (Kantonsarchäologie) excavated about 40% of the villa's area in 1982/83 and 1986–1989 (Schucany 1986; Archäologie des Kantons Solothurn 1987; 1989; 1991). The occupation of the villa can be divided into three periods: I. a probably rather small farm dated to the final third of the 1st century; II. a *c.*5 ha large villa, dated to the late 1st/early 2nd to mid-3rd century; III. a small farm, dated to the late 3rd century and perhaps later.

In the northern part of the large inner courtyard of the

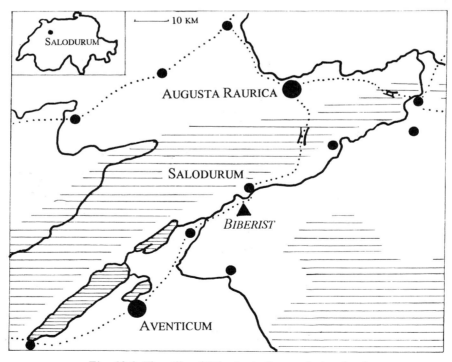

Fig. 13.1 *The villa of Biberist in Roman Switzerland.*

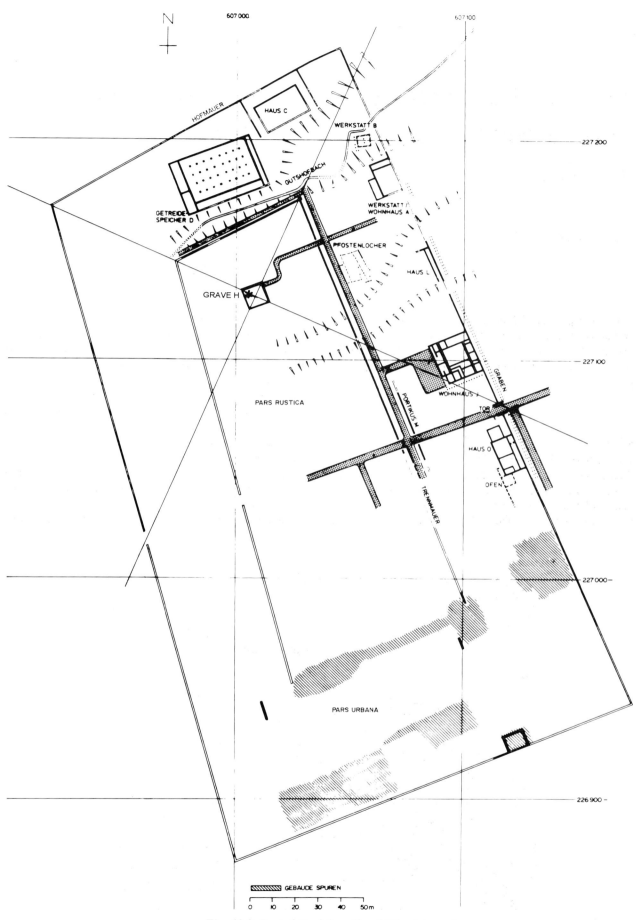

Fig. 13.2 *Period II of the villa of Biberist.*

Fig. 13.3 Funerary enclosure (Photograph looking east)

villa's 2nd period (Fig. 13.2), we discovered a funerary enclosure (Fig. 13.3) with a *bustum*, dated to the 3rd quarter of the 2nd century (Schucany 1995; 1996a). Opposite the *pars urbana*, at a distance of 170 m, it lay probably on the central axis of the whole complex, as its situation on the diagonal axis through the corner of the yard wall and through the principal door indicates. The walls of the enclosure comprised an area of c.9 × 9m. The entrance was presumably near the north-eastern corner, from which a path led to a gateway in the eastern wall of the inner courtyard, passing a tree at the north-eastern corner of the grave garden.

The funerary enclosure had two phases (Fig. 13.4): the northern and the eastern wall were enlarged in a 2nd phase. The elements of the first phase are:
– the *bustum*: an almost 1 m deep pit (1.30 × 1.30m), lying on the east-west central axis, with a charcoal layer at the bottom (Fig. 13.5), filled with burnt material rich in finds, the remains of the pyre goods;
– the urn: a stone block (0.88 × 0.63 × 0.60m), set into the soil on the central axis of the cremation-pit and close to the diagonal axis of the north western quarter of the enclosure (Fig. 13.4), with a hollow of 15 litres filled and covered with the burnt debris. Two stone fragments may be part of the lid which was later broken.

The burnt layer contained 3 kg of highly fragmented burnt human bones. The proportion by level shows that the burnt bones lay mostly in the lower part of the pit where the deceased fell when the pyre had collapsed; more or less all of the burnt bones therefore seem to be preserved. The anthropologist (Bruno Kaufmann, Aesch CH) identified a 50–year old man with very good teeth and without osteological indicators of stress, together with a neonate. Glass beads from a necklace and a cosmetic tablet may indicate also the presence of a female individual (Schucany 1995: fig. 13). The pyre-goods, which had been placed by the sides of the pyre, in the main represented a complete set of household vessels (46 kg of potsherds, 16 kg of amphora sherds, 2 kg of molten glass, 0.5 kg bronze, 1.5 kg iron, 0.3 kg lead, 1 kg of animal bones).

The *spolium*, over 2 m long and semicircular in section, lying askew in the cremation-pit (Fig. 13.5) can be interpreted as a grave-stone. Its top was covered by the burnt layer and it penetrated some 0.05m into the base of the pit at a point approximately 0.2m from the centre of the pit which lay on the central axis of phase 1, but exactly on the central axis of phase 2 (Fig. 13.4). This change explains this otherwise obscure 2nd phase of the monument. By widening the two walls of the north-eastern corner, the interior of the enclosure became smaller so that the new east-west central axis passed exactly through the grave-stone. This explanation is supported by the location of two offering pits: one lay on this axis in the centre of the enclosure, the other outside but lying on an east-west axis through the centre of the southern half of the enclosure. In the first pit was an unburnt lustre-ware dish, in the second some charred fruits and nuts. Unburnt fragments of square glass bottles were found in the uppermost level in front of the cremation-pit and the grave-stone. After the cremation, perhaps some time later, a cattle-skull was buried in a small pit outside the funerary enclosure.

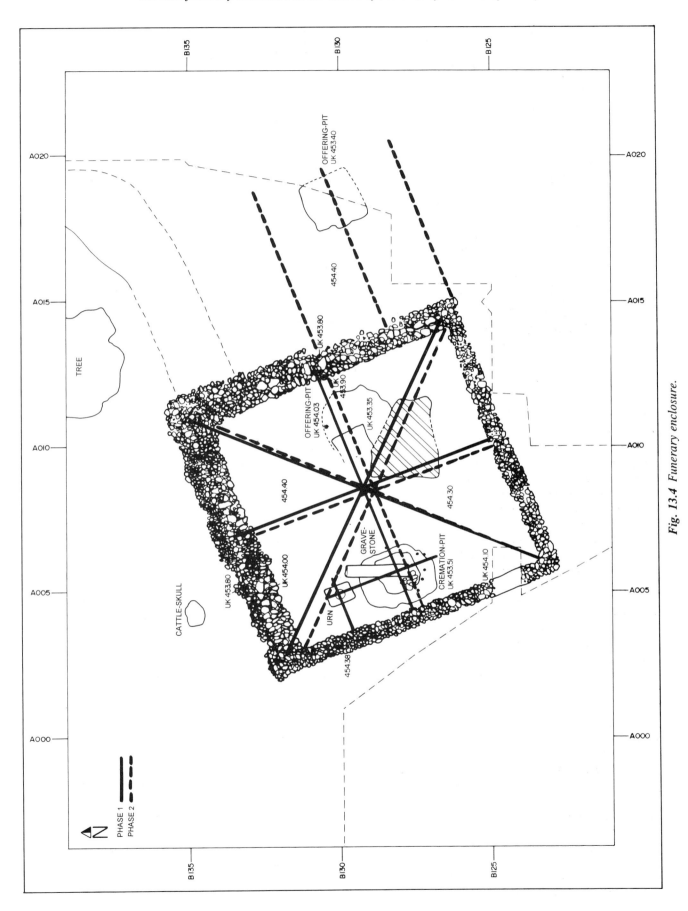

Fig. 13.4 Funerary enclosure.

Fig. 13.5 *The stratigraphy of the cremation-pit (Photograph looking west).*

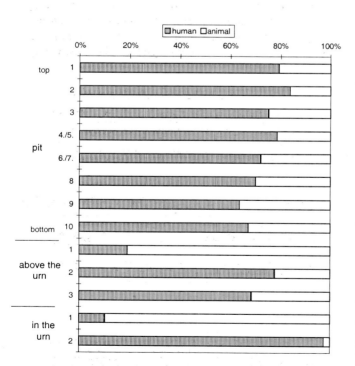

Fig. 13.6 *Proportion of human and animal bones by level.*

Ritual

We might reconstruct the burial ritual as follows, after members of the villa owner's family, perhaps the whole family, died at the same time or shortly one after the other. The dependants conveyed the deceased in a cortège from their home in the *pars urbana*, outside along the eastern wall of the inner courtyard, through a gateway to the funerary enclosure and through the entrance in its north-eastern corner to the pyre built of beech-wood. They set the deceased on top of the pyre. The skull bones, found mostly but not exclusively in the northern part of the cremation-pit, and lower leg bones, found only in the southern part, indicate that the heads of the deceased pointed to the north and their feet to the south. On top of the pyre, next to the deceased, the dependants put personal effects and also some glass vessels, samian and lustre-ware dishes. They placed a complete set of household vessels (a minimum of 333), by the sides of the pyre, the amphorae probably to the south, the dolium, the cooking vessel and the mortaria at the base, the latter to the east. The quantities of the vessels indicate an intentionally assembled set (Schucany 1995: tab. 1; see below). The palaeo-botanical study (conducted by Marianne Petrucci-Bavaud, Basel CH) shows that some vessels must have contained food-offerings including lentils, grain, and fruit. There were the remains of twelve animals, including one chicken, one lamb/kid, two sheep / goats, five to seven pigs, one cow and one frog. Some of them seem to have been cooked (B. Kaufmann).

The proportion of bone is lower in the deepest but one

level of the *bustum* than in the other levels (Fig. 13.6), and in this level, the proportion of bones of human origin is also lower. The dependants seem to have taken the bones from this level to put into the urn which was then sealed with a lid. The remnants of the pyre and the pyre-goods were broken into small pieces. They were deposited well mixed into the pit and accumulated on top of it. In setting up the stone grave marker, contrary to their intention they missed the centre of the cremation-pit which lay on the central axis of the first phase of the funerary enclosure. Deep irritation over this mistake caused the dependants to adjust its position (phase 2): by widening the two walls of the north-eastern corner the interior of the enclosure became smaller so that the stone grave marker lay exactly on the new east-west central axis. The two offering pits cut subsequent to the burial respect this second axis. Both may have contained food-offerings. The unburnt fragments of square glass bottles, found in front of the cremation-pit, might suggest drink-offerings. The cattle-skull, later buried outside the funerary enclosure could represent an apotropaic sign which may have originally been placed above the entrance or on one of the walls (Deschler-Erb 1999).

The grave seems to have been desecrated at a later date. The lid of the urn was obviously broken and the grave-stone was pushed over, consequently forming a depression in the soil beneath. It was covered so that no surface marker pointed to the grave any longer. Perhaps the burial of the cattle-skull outside the grave garden must be interpreted in the same way. An important lack of human bone in the uppermost level of the urn (Fig. 13.6) might suggest that the physical remains of the deceased had been partially removed. The reason for this could be a change of ownership, as extensive re-building in the whole area of the villa at the end of the 2nd or the beginning of the 3rd century indicates.

Further Reflections

The deceased were not the founders of the villa, nor the constructors of the villa's 2nd period. The grave garden was not a family monument with a long tradition. There were no tombs of ancestors nor of descendants; rather the monument was constructed especially for these particular individuals. The desecration of the grave, and the fact that the dependants may have taken some physical remains of the deceased when they left, might nevertheless be an argument for a kind of ancestor worship. It seems possible that they wanted the presence of their ancestors in their new home. The grave points to the east, to the sunrise, but so does the whole villa and thus the houses of the living. Separated from the *pars urbana* by some distance and from the *pars rustica* by a wall, the grave was isolated from the living but by respecting the alignment of the villa the deceased were nevertheless connected with the living. There were no other graves, so that the deceased were also isolated from the dead. Opposite the *pars*

urbana (Fig. 13.2), the grave seems to constitute an alternative second centre for the villa; but it was a private one because it was not visible from the exterior.

The artefacts with the deceased can be considered as equipment for a new life; according to classical sources no meal took place before or during the burning of the pyre (*RE* III: 358), so that the burnt finds must be the remnants of the goods presented to the deceased on the pyre. This rite seems to go back to Celtic traditions (Caesar Bell. Gall. VI 19). The equipment was not a normal household assemblage (Fig. 13.7): compared to the ceramic assemblage from one of the villa workshops of the same phase, there are too few cooking vessels, more storage vessels and more eating related vessels (plates: e.g. Drag. 18/31). Differences exist also in the eating-related vessels between the grave and workshop assemblage. There are more sauce-dishes (e.g. Drag. 27, Drag. 35), and more flat dishes (e.g. Drag. 36) than deep bowls (e.g. Drag. 37) so that we may conclude that it resembles rather a Mediterranean dining set (Schucany 1993; Schucany 1996b: 209–216). The same can be said about the drinking-vessels: there are many more serving-vessels, specially flagons, and fewer beakers. Compared to the workshop, the grave's vessels are much more in the Roman tradition (Fig. 13.8).

In conclusion, this rite is still Celtic in structure – the grave goods represent an outfit for a new life – but the pottery forms recall the Roman tradition. This confirms Nathan Wachtel's (1974) acculturation theory, according to which the values of the dominating civilisation are integrated into the traditional system of the dominated one and often act as new status symbols. Thus the newly

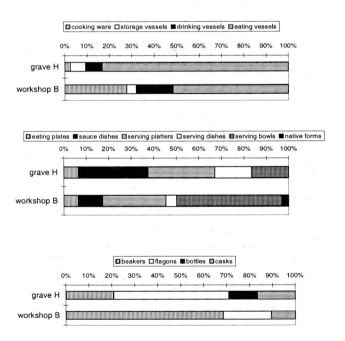

Fig. 13.7 *Comparison of ceramic assemblages between grave and villa workshop.*

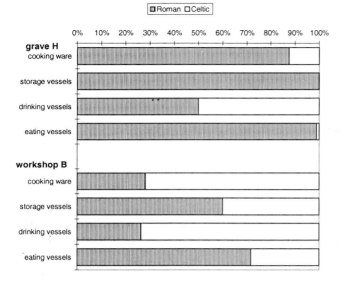

Fig. 13.8 *Comparison of ceramic traditions between grave and villa workshop:*

formed amalgamated culture remains bound to its traditional structure, its form however is assimilated to the dominant culture. The burial of Biberist-Spitalhof indicates that during the Roman period death rituals in our area structurally still followed Celtic representations, where grave goods are assembled according to the needs of the deceased in their new life – a rite aimed towards the future. Mediterranean ideas, accommodated to the memory of the deceased and depicting how they had lived – a rite reflecting the past – do not seem to have been integrated

Acknowledgements

Thanks to Clive Bridger, Xanten, to Carlotta Caviola-Schucany, Liestal, and to Herman Fetz, Luzern, for their assistance with my English.

Bibliography

Archäologie des Kantons Solothurn 5, 1987: 158–159; 6, 1989: 131–136; 7, 1991: 112–115.

Deschler-Erb, S. 1999. Rinderschädelkult in der römischen Villa von Biberist. *Archäologie der Schweiz 23: 100–103.*

Schucany, C. 1986. Der römische Gutshof von Biberist-Spitalhof. Ein Vorbericht. *Jahrbuch der Schweizerischen Gesellschaft für Ur- und Frühgeschichte* 69: 199–220.

Schucany, C. 1993. Tradition indigène – tradition méditerranéenne: un essai appliqué à la céramique des Ier et IIe siècles d'Aquae Helveticae (Baden, Suisse). *Société Française d'Etude de la Céramique en Antique Gaule. Actes du congrès de Versailles:* 249–266.

Schucany, C. 1995. Eine Grabanlage im römischen Gutshof von Biberist-Spitalhof. *Archäologie der Schweiz* 18: 142–154.

Schucany, C. 1996a. Le jardin funéraire de la villa romaine de Biberist. *L'Archéologue/Archéologie nouvelle* 25: 35–38.

Schucany, C. 1996b. Aquae Helveticae. Zum Romanisierungs-prozess am Beispiel des römischen Baden. *Antiqua* 27. Basel.

Wachtel, N. 1974. L'acculturation. In *Faire de l'histoire. I Nouveaux problèmes*, J. Le Goff and P. Nora (eds.). Paris: 174–202.

The Dead in the Landscape

The four papers in this section examine burials within different landscape contexts. Esmonde Cleary explores principles behind the placing of the dead in Roman Britain from two perspectives, to what degree settlement type influences burial location, and the locations in which certain types of burial practice take place. Placing the dead on boundary locations could resolve the paradox of providing for proper burial, of keeping the dead within the memory of the living, yet at the same time distancing the living from their potentially malign influence. His survey draws attention to some previously neglected burial types and locations, in particular the occurrence of individual body parts or skeletal fragments on settlement contexts.

Other papers in this section consider the placing of burial in the different contexts identified by Esmonde Cleary. Tranoy focuses on the question of suburban cemetery location at Lyons. Here it is possible to see contrasts between the highly visible location of monumental tombs of Italian inspiration and the more general array of burials. It is again evident that there was no simple pattern of cemetery growth and distribution around the town and that burial could take place in very close proximity to inhabited areas and to 'craft production.' Spanu provides a synthesis of aspects of the burial evidence from Asia Minor. Despite the relatively poor quality of the data he is able to offer important insights into the location of grave tombs, especially the most monumental types, which demonstrates significant differences from those familiar in the western provinces; a topographically prominent location appears to have been more important than proximity to roads or immediate accessibility to passers-by. Vermeulen and Bourgeois focus on a detailed case study of part of Gallia Belgica to explore the issue of the reuse of past monuments in burial location. In exploring this aspect of the evidence they review a range of interpretative possibilities and demonstrate how different sites illustrate a complex and heterogeneous pattern of landscape use into the Roman period. Their paper demonstrates the value, for both the study of burial and landscape, of including burial evidence in survey programmes.

The relation of burials to their landscape is investigated at a variety of scales in papers in other sections. Taking a provincial or supra-provincial perspective, Struck, in particular, and Martin-Kilcher make the case that elites buried their dead in small rural cemeteries rather than large urban graveyards. The difference in the preferred settings for funerary altars between the towns of central and northern Italy, noted by Dexheimer, have implications for the relationship of these monuments with their immediate surroundings and with those passing by. Niblett offers some intriguing possibilities to explain cemetery location around the Romano-British town of Verulamium. One of the most striking changes in urban life in late Antiquity is the movement of the dead *intra muros*. Meneghini and Santangeli Valenzani's paper demonstrates how close attention to the urban context of these burials, even where information is relatively poor, shows subtle but important patterning. At the local level in a rural context Schucany examines the spatial relationships between a burial monument and the villa compound within which it was set, while Abegg-Wigg alludes to the importance of visibility in the wider surroundings. Botanical evidence allows Kreuz an interesting alternative perspective on the environs of tombs and cemeteries. Fitzpatrick briefly compares the orientation of cemeteries with contemporary settlements, an approach finding favour in study of the Iron Age, but yet to have the same impact on that of the Roman period, although Schucany's case study illustrates the potential for further examination.

14. Putting the dead in their place: burial location in Roman Britain

Simon Esmonde Cleary

Introduction

'Gone but not forgotten': the dead may have been transformed beyond recall, yet individually and collectively they remain a vital part of the world of the living. Death may deprive society of a full and active participant, but (s)he may still be able to intervene in the world of the living for good or ill and their influence may therefore need to be entreated or propitiated. The dead may form an extension of the society of the living, indeed they may have a society (often idealised) of their own over against that of the living (as in classic Christian theology). This paper is a preliminary attempt to look both at the surprisingly wide range of places in which the dead were disposed of in Roman Britain, but also to use this information to suggest some lines of enquiry about how the dead were viewed by the living.

Anthropologists and archaeologists are much obsessed with death. They have used funerary ritual and burial evidence to try to reconstruct past societies' beliefs about death and the hereafter, an eschatological approach; or they have used it to try to reconstruct past societies' structures especially along the axes of age, gender and status, a sociological approach. The approach here may be termed cosmological, inferring the place and powers of the dead in the conceptual landscape of the living from the placing of the dead in the physical landscape. This paper thus relates to current concerns in archaeology with landscape, with spatial patterning and with how these both respond to and create ideological structures.

There is a huge anthropological and archaeological literature on the practices and symbolisms in the transformations undergone by the dead, on their post-mortem treatment and on how they are eventually deposited in their 'long home' (cf. Metcalf and Huntington 1992; Morris I. 1992 both with refs.). But there is surprisingly little on the processes and symbolism of the choices made about where to place the dead. Archaeologists have become increasingly concerned with this, particularly in examining the placing of burials vis-à-vis earlier burials and other monuments, generally in a discourse about the conscious creation of relations with 'ancestors' (real,

appropriated or mythical) and thus the legitimation of the present by recourse to the past (cf. Barrett 1994; Bradley 1993; Carr 1995). Parker Pearson (1993) has drawn attention to the 'Powerful Dead', and how their ability to intervene in the affairs of the living needs to be controlled or mitigated by conscious choices about the relation of their remains to the domains of the living.

This paper will therefore take it as axiomatic that the placing of the dead was generally purposive rather than random, though of course rationales differed in time and space and according to cultural context rather than being fixed. It will proceed by looking at the remaining physical evidence for burial locations before drawing any general conclusions about the place of the dead in the physical landscape, thus enabling consideration of more theoretical implications of the empirical data.

One final general comment or *caveat* should be entered. The archaeologically-visible dead of Roman Britain are unbalanced in space, probably time, and by type of site. They are much more common in the South and East than in the North and West (cf. Philpott 1991, 217–28). They are more common in the later than the earlier Roman period. Even in the South and East they cluster at towns and are less common in the countryside (e.g. Taylor 1993, fig. 6), a reversal of the actual population distribution. It is quite possible that the majority of the population of Roman Britain was over time disposed of by means which leave little or no archaeological trace, and that the little that remains of such means may be difficult to detect and interpret. This also means that this paper will be almost exclusively be concerned with the South and East, but perhaps more importantly it also means that we must look out for traces of otherwise non-visible rites and their influence on those that are visible. Moreover, as will be seen, this can be difficult, since the presence of so many formal cremation and inhumation burials has led to a general perception that this was the normative style for the disposal of the dead in Roman Britain. This has in turn been emphasised by the natural archaeological preference for the study of positive over negative or absent evidence, giving a premium to the study of cemeteries. Thus, as will be seen, other 'non-normative' occurrences of human bodies or body-parts have often been played down, leaving them poorly represented in the archaeological literature, and thus poorly understood.

N.B. In a publication such as this it is not practical to give a full list of sites/burials; examples of the types of burial and sites with good instances are given. A full literature search will be necessary before detailed treatments of individual burial-types can be undertaken – an essential next step.

Burial by site-type

A convenient way of breaking down the vast number of known Romano-British burials into manageable categories is by looking at them according to the type of site from which they come. This does have the advantage of contextualising burial and not isolating it from other human activity. It is acknowledged that it does have the weakness of responding to modern categories, which can be inappropriate for the period we are studying, though sometimes these modern categories do correspond with

observable differences in the evidence. Instances both of good and poor 'fit' will be noted as appropriate; the use of these categories is more of an heuristic device than a prescriptive formulation.

Major Towns

The large cemeteries attached to the these towns are the most intensively studied class of Romano-British burial, and at some towns a combination of modern excavation with antiquarian records permits a general outline of the location and development of burial to be drawn. A good example of this is Winchester (Kjølbye-Biddle 1993) (Fig. 14.1). Initially, in the first and second centuries, the principal cemetery seems to have been the extensive cremation cemetery outside the north gate, between the Cirencester and Silchester roads. Other cremation burials are known outside the west, south and east gates, along the major roads (cf. Kjølbye-Biddle 1993, fig. 2). As at many towns, the third century is poorly represented, making even more obscure the chronology and processes of the shift from cremation to inhumation. In the fourth century, there were extensive, 'managed' inhumation cemeteries of a type familiar at most large towns. At

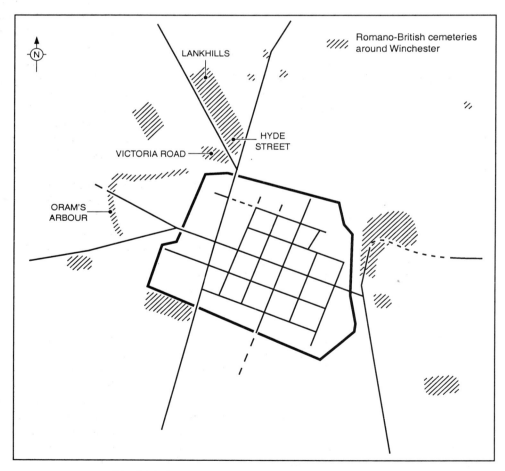

Fig. 14.1 Romano-British cemeteries around Winchester

Winchester the principal cemetery still seems to have been outside the north gate, though in different areas to the earlier cremation cemetery. The best-known part of this cemetery is that in the grounds of Lankhills School (Clarke G. 1979), where a cemetery was laid out *de novo* at the beginning of the fourth century in a plot bounded to the west by the Cirencester road and to the east by a substantial boundary ditch (eventually colonised then spread beyond in the latter part of the century). Other, smaller areas of the cemetery have been excavated more recently around Victoria Road (Kjølbye-Biddle 1993, 216; Richards 1999, Ch.4). Another large fourth-century cemetery lay north-east of the east gate (cf. Morris M. 1986), with smaller groups outside the south gate. Also in the fourth century, the largely-infilled Iron Age defensive ditch at Oram's Arbour to the west of the Roman defences became a burial zone. In general, therefore, burial at a major town such as Winchester took place in extensive, bounded, ordered cemeteries. There is little evidence for more random extra-mural burial and equally little for intra-mural burial, save some skeletons of infants. This pattern seems to hold good for the other large towns of the province, and it is possible to suggest that this class of site had a fairly uniform burial pattern, one which as we shall see sets it somewhat apart from other classes of settlement.

Small Towns

Burial at these sites is both like and unlike that at major towns. It is clear that at several of these towns, especially in the fourth century, there were extensive, ordered cemeteries to the pattern of those we have just seen at the major towns (cf. Esmonde Cleary 1992, 33). The exceptional site at Baldock (Herts.) (Burleigh 1993; 1995) has a suite of earlier cemeteries, Dorchester-on-Thames (Oxon.) a range of fourth-century and later cemeteries (Cook and Rowley 1985, 26–8). Other small towns with published cemeteries include Great Dunmow (Essex) (Wickenden 1988, 12–23) and Kelvedon (Essex) (Rodwell 1988, 26–52). But it is equally clear that there was also a range of other burial sites and types. Again, to take a single town as an example, we may turn to Ilchester in Somerset (Leach 1982; 1994) (Fig. 14.2). In the fourth century there was a large, 'managed' cemetery across the Ivel from the north gate in the Northover area, with large numbers of inhumations, some distinguished by more elaborate rites such as the presence of lead coffin-linings (Leach 1994, 91–102). But excavations to the south of the defences at Little Spittle and Townsend Close (Leach 1982, 61–91, 92–106) have identified a very different context. During the fourth century inhumation burials were inserted into the backlands of plots fronting onto Fosse Way, which had occupied buildings along the road frontage. The burials were generally located around the edges and beside or occasionally in the boundary ditches. These are suggested to be burials of the family inhabiting the property. A somewhat similar situation can be seen at the site of Shepton Mallet, north-east along Fosse Way from Ilchester (Leach forthcoming). There in the fourth century were small burial groups away from Fosse Way, within ditched enclosures, usually also containing buildings. These 'backland' burials clearly blur the expected distinction in the Roman period between the domains of the living and the dead, so visible at the major towns. They also place more emphasis on the relationship between particular groups of living and dead, rather than removing the latter into the wider anonymity of a large cemetery.

This pattern of 'backland' burial, once recognised, can be seen at a number of other small towns. Sometimes, as at Ilchester and Shepton Mallet, it is reasonably orderly both in the placing of the graves and of the bodies within them. But there are other sites where the disposal is less regular. There are single burials, or a number of burials, apparently placed randomly rather than in relation to each other or to other features such as ditches or structures. Sometimes these burials can be removed from 'normative' treatment. For instance, a recent excavation in a 'backland' area at Godmanchester (Cambs.) revealed a number of apparently random inhumations, of which one was the decapitated corpse of a juvenile placed in a disused pottery kiln and the kiln dome collapsed on the body. Scott (1991) has noted some other instances of juveniles associated with heat-using installations such as kilns, ovens and corn-driers. Other 'backland' burials have been noted at sites such as Alcester (Warws.) (Mahany ed. 1994, 144–47), Asthall (Oxon.) (Booth 1997, 64–73), Springhead (Kent) (cf. Burnham and Wacher 1990, 192–98) and Towcester (Northants.) (Brown, Woodfield and Mynard 1983, 65–8). In some ways it is distinctive of small towns, since it does not occur at the major towns. It is also difficult to parallel precisely at villas and other rural settlements, though there is some overlap between the smallest and most informal groups of burials at small towns and some of the burials at rural sites (see below p. 131). This may be an instance where modern site categorisation risks obscuring a widespread phenomenon of single graves or small groupings at a range of site-types.

Forts and Vici

The study of burial at military sites can hardly even be described as being in its infancy. Few burials have been excavated and fewer cemeteries targeted for excavation. A little is known of the locations of the cemeteries of the legionary fortresses at Caerleon (including the Great Bulmore cemetery) (Evans and Maynard 1997; Vyner 1978), Chester (Mason 1987) and the heavily-compromised cemeteries of York (RCHM (E) 1962, 67–110; Wenham 1968). A small number of fort cemeteries such as the one at High Rochester (Charlton and Mitcheson 1984) or the twenty-nine fourth-century infant burials from within the fort at Malton (Corder 1930) have been excavated and published, but they generally remain *terra incognita*. It is to be hoped that this situation will change, since they may have important information on burial rites derived from the homelands of the garrisons, on assimilation to British practices, and the relationships between the garrisons and the inhabitants of the *vici*. This is as true for the forts of the Saxon Shore as it is for the forts in the North.

Villas

Excavated villa cemeteries and burial sites are rare in Britain, in contrast to neighbouring areas of the western provinces (cf. Ferdière ed. 1993; Struck ed. 1993). It is possible that this reflects a real lack of such cemeteries, but it may also be an artefact of archaeologists' concentration on the main domestic buildings. A small number of monumental structures associated with villas

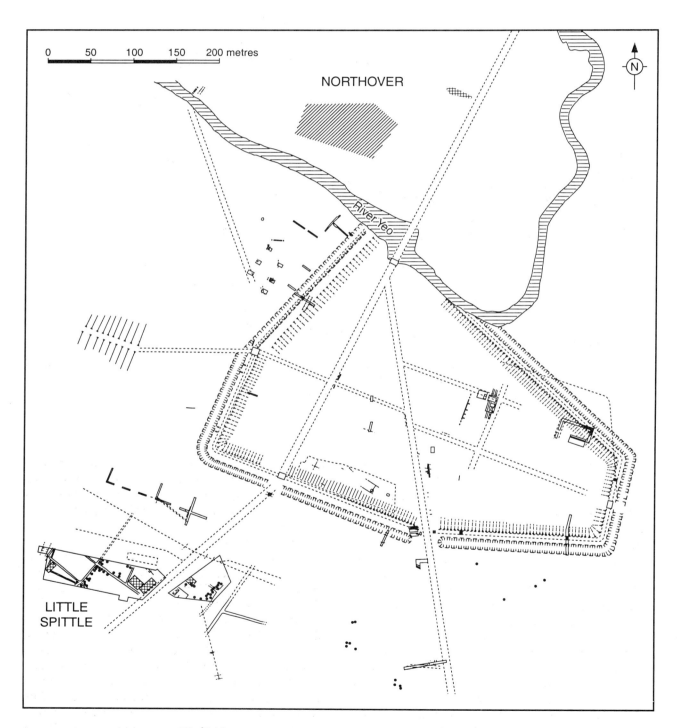

Fig. 14.2 *Late Roman cemeteries and settlement at Ilchester*

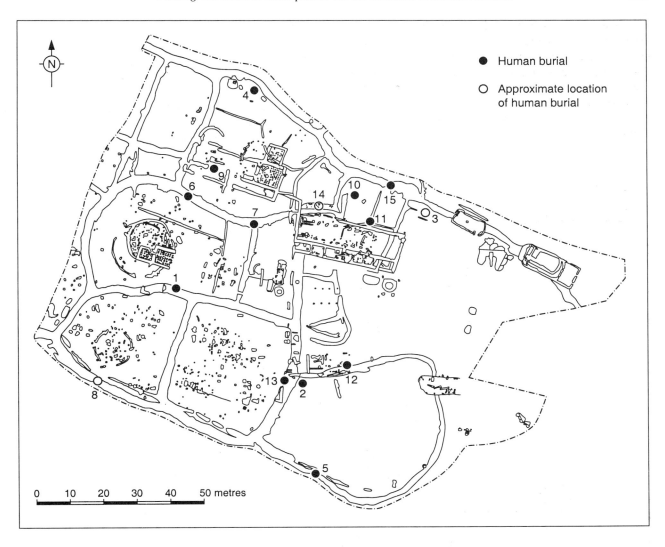

Fig. 14.3 *The distribution of burials at Dalton Parlours, West Yorkshire*

is known, including mausolea at sites such as Bancroft (Bucks.) with a later small cemetery (Williams R.J. and Zeepvat 1994, 88–102) and Lullingstone (Kent) (Meates 1979, 122–32) (cf. below p. 134), or barrows such as Bartlow Hills (Essex) (Gage 1836), Borough Hill (Northants.) (Brown 1977) or Holborough (Kent) (Jessup 1954). There were also walled cemeteries, notably in Kent (Jessup 1959). Other monuments such as the mausoleum at Harpenden (Herts.) (Rook, Walker and Denston 1984) and the probable mausoleum at Wood Lane End (Herts.) (Neal 1983) may have been associated with villas. The mausolea in particular are placed in locations such as hill-tops or false crests which are very visible, particularly from the principal residence. A similar situation obtains with the cemetery (with late Iron Age antecedents) which lies on a hill to the north-east of the villa of Bledlow-cum-Saunderton (Bucks.) (Collard and Parkhouse 1993). The villa at Barton Court Farm (Oxon.) (Miles ed. 1984,

15–16) had an infant cemetery in the south-eastern corner of the main enclosure. A large number of infant burials are also famously known from the northern part of the courtyard of the villa at Hambleden (Bucks.) (Cocks 1921, 150; Scott 1990; 1991).

Other villas have yielded isolated burials from spots either in or around buildings or further away, sometimes in boundary ditches. Good examples of these include Dalton Parlours (W. Yorks.) (Manchester and Bush in Wrathmell and Nicholson 1990, 171–4) (Fig. 14.3), Rudston (E.Yorks.) (Stead, 1980, 146–8), Stanton Low (Bucks.) (Woodfield and Johnson 1989) and Winterton (Lincs.) (Stead 1976, 290–300). Given the small numbers over what can be long periods of time, it is clear that only a small proportion of any likely population of inhabitants was buried in this manner. Furthermore, many of the burials at the sites mentioned were isolated, or were adjacent to other activity areas, suggesting that disposal of the dead could be integrated with other land-uses and activities rather than set apart in a separate domain. This is similar to the practice to be seen at other types of rural settlement (cf. below), so again modern categorisations should not be allowed to obscure a recurring pattern.

Other Rural Settlements

This category covers a large number of sites which vary widely in location, form and period. It is also a category about whose burials little is known and where a major literature search needs to be undertaken. The few remarks appended here are more to draw attention to the deficiencies in our knowledge and the need to remedy them, than to say anything comprehensive or particularly coherent. Occasionally groups of burials associated with

such sites can be identified. The most often quoted is that at Lynch Farm (Cambs.) (Jones 1975), where a small group of mainly adult inhumations was placed in the south-west corner of a ditched field, with another, smaller group of inhumations in the south-eastern corner of the next field to the west. Another instance is at Owslebury (Hants.) (Collis 1977, cf. Pearce 1999), where principally earlier Roman burials lay in small enclosures, and there were a number of infant burials in enclosure ditches. Ashville (Oxon.) (Parrington 1978) exhibits a similar pattern for the later period.

Groups of burials and scattered burials can be demonstrated at a number of individual sites of differing morphology and probably social structure and status. The 'village' at Catsgore (Soms.) (Leech 1982, 147–8; Ellis 1984, 6–7) has a number of burials, principally of infants

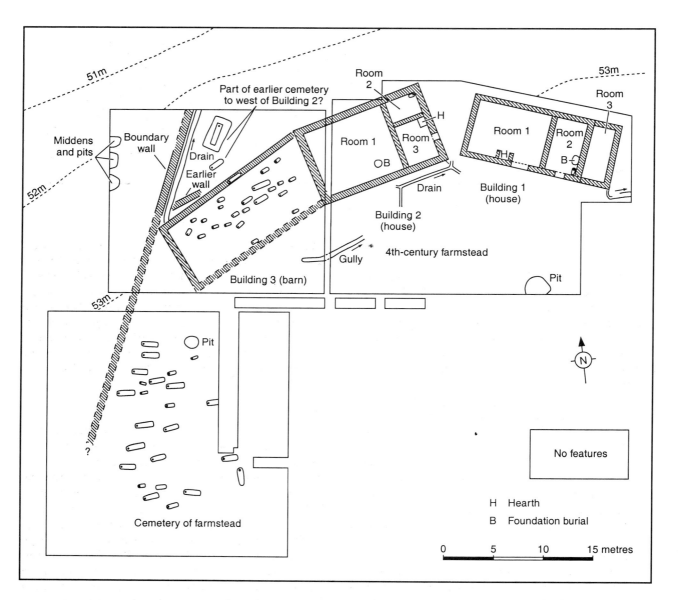

Fig. 14.4 *Cemeteries and burials at Bradley Hill, Somerset*

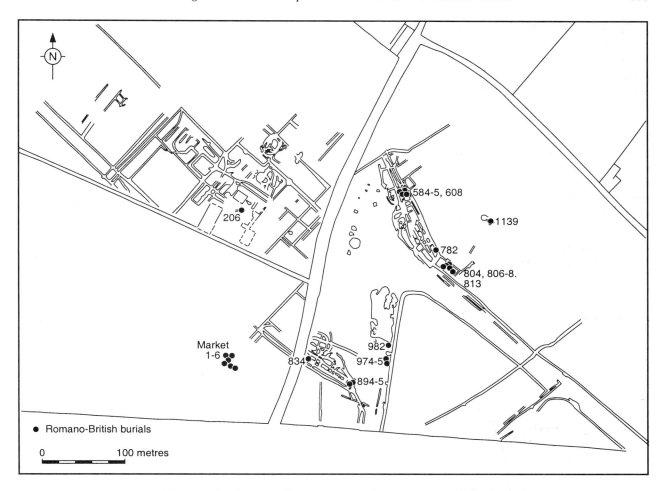

Fig. 14.5 The distribution of burials at Roughground Farm, Gloucestershire

and many associated either with buildings or in ditch fills. At another Somerset site, Bradley Hill (Leech 1981) a cemetery to the south of the farmstead buildings consisted of fifteen adults and ten children (Fig. 14.4). Within one of the structures, Building 3, was a cemetery of twenty-one infants, with two adult and one infant burials possibly pre-dating the structure. Building 1, Room 2 contained a 'foundation' deposit and an infant burial. The floor of Building 2, Room 2 sealed a triple infant burial. Building 3 contained a re-burial within its north wall, and two adult and one child burials possibly pre-dating the construction, and forming part of an earlier cemetery to the north. In the interior of the building was a cemetery of twenty-one infant burials. The postulated 'estate centre' at Kingscote (Glos.) (Timby ed., 1998, 275–6) yielded three adults, seven infants and a child, and the site at Syreford Mill, Wycomb (Timby ed. 1998, 315–18, 331–2, Fig. 130) a small cemetery of at least four adults, four children and two infants. Another Gloucestershire site, Roughground Farm, Lechlade (Allen, Darvill, Green and Jones 1993, esp. 95–101) yielded seventeen inhumations (one from the centre of the villa courtyard, five from a ditched enclosure, the other mainly in groups alongside or in enclosure ditches – one decapitated, two prone) and three

infants (Fig. 14.5). This is a small and entirely random sample of sites, but it does show that a range of burial types was possible, from small, formal cemeteries through small groups and isolated burials. As noted above with the villas, human remains were not necessarily disposed of in discrete areas, but were one of a range of activities carried on at the site. Infants clearly were an important component of the burial repertoire in, under and in the immediate vicinity of buildings (cf. below p. 135).

Temples

In the Classical world a strict separation between temples or shrines and the dead was observed. The reason for this was the ritual pollution attendant upon the physical remains of the dead (cf. Harries 1992), which would defile any sanctuary. The account of whited sepulchres in Matthew 23.27 shows this attitude to 'dead men's bones and all uncleanness'. In Britain this separation between cult and the dead seems generally to have been observed, though it needs to be nuanced (cf. Forcey 1998). Rarely, if ever, does a temple act as the focus for a cemetery or have a cemetery directly associated with it. The case of Lancing Down (Bedwin 1981) may be a partial exception, but the precise spatial and chronological relationships between burials and temple remain uncertain. The temple at Cosgrove contained an adult inhumation and two human skulls set in the *cella* wall (Quinnell 1991). There are also temples, such as Springhead IV (Penn 1961, 121–2, fig. 4; 1968), which overlie infant burials, but this may be part of the wider question of infant burials and 'foundation burials' considered below (p. 136). Forcey (1997) has also pointed to the association between temples and 'ritual' shafts or pits, some of which contain human and/or animal remains. Clearly in some cases there is such an association, though again precise chronological and spatial relations need to be borne in mind: for instance, are the shafts within or outside the *temenos*; are shafts and temples contemporaneous? Shafts and wells are considered further below (p. 134). So there are circumstances where human remains do intrude into sanctuary space, but the exceptions should not prove too far the rule of separation between the temples, *temene* and the dead.

In the south-east Midlands there appears to have been a regional tradition of appropriating the form of the Romano-Celtic temple for mausolea or other funerary purposes, such as the mausolea at Bancroft, Harpenden, Welwyn and probably Wood Lane End (not forgetting the instance in Kent at Lullingstone [Meates 1979, 122–32]). There is also the exceptional case of the temple later constructed to one side of the Folly Lane, St Albans high-status burial (Niblett 1999). This last may be some sort of *heroon*. These temple-mausolea are set in prominent positions in the local topography (hill-tops or other sky-line settings); the building itself would make the spot the more prominent. But the appropriation of a widespread cultic architectural form may have been purposely to impart some notion of 'divinity' to the individuals or family interred within, thus further strengthening their dominance over the landscape within which their mausoleum was set and augmenting the legitimacy within the 'natural order of things' of living descendants. The subsequent demolition of the Bancroft temple-mausoleum with its replacement by a shrine and the replacement of the Wood Lane End building may witness to substantial change in the ownership of the landscape. At Verulamium, did Alban replace the Folly Lane burial as corpse-in-residence?

Prehistoric Monuments

The association of Roman-period burials with prehistoric monuments has recently been the subject of a preliminary review by Williams (1998a; cf. Williams H. 1997; 1998b for more extended considerations of the significance of this practice for the Anglo-Saxon period), and it would be otiose to duplicate his valuable work here. It is clear that such monuments were occasionally re-used, though there is considerable regional and chronological variation. The class of monument most commonly used was the barrow, particularly the early Bronze Age round barrow, perhaps because their original function was known or because they

resembled the barrows constructed within the Roman period in south-eastern Britain and northern Gaul. Sometimes the Roman-period burial was inserted into the mound, but they could also be inserted into the tail of the mound, the berm or the ring-ditch. Sometimes the barrow itself was respected, but acted as a focus for the development of a cemetery (cf. Mucking). In such cases it is clear that current discussion by prehistorians on the symbolism of such actions in relating the present to the past (real, imagined or mythic) and the rôle of the past in constructing and legitimating the present are entirely apposite for the Roman period (cf. Bradley 1993; Williams 1997). It should be remembered, though, that it is not a universal practice for Roman Britain, and evidence such as the way in which Ackling Dyke Roman road strides across the Oakley Down (Dorset) barrow cemetery on an exaggerated *agger* (cf. Crawford and Keiller 1928) shows that other attitudes to the past were possible (cf. Petts 1998).

Wet Places, Wells, Shafts, Pits

It is becoming increasingly clear that there was a lively tradition of depositing human remains in such places. The best-known instance of the wet-place deposition of a human is Lindow Man (Stead, Bourke and Brothwell 1986), whose ^{14}C dates stubbornly refuse to allow prehistorians to claim him as undoubtedly theirs in point of chronology, though in point of practice there are clear similarities. Other possible Roman-period instances of 'bog burial' are catalogued by Turner and Briggs (in Stead, Bourke and Brothwell 1986, 148–50). Another well-known incidence of human remains from a wet-place context is the skulls from the Walbrook, London (Bradley and Gordon 1988; Merrifield 1995), to which can now be added other instances of human skulls from roadside ditches in the city (Cotton 1996).

A growing number of wells has yielded evidence for the deposition of complete human skeletons or parts of skeletons, along with a range of other animal and inanimate material. Some of the earlier occurrences of such material, such as that in the wells at Brislington (Soms.) and North Wraxall (Wilts.) have been 'explained away' by recourse to episodes such as the *barbarica conspiratio* of A.D.367 (e.g. Branigan 1976, 136–7), which probably says more about unwillingness to countenance 'non-normative' burials than about the real reasons behind their deposition. Wells containing human remains are now known from a range of sites, including major and small towns, villas, farmsteads and temples. Generally, the back-fill of the well exhibits 'structured' deposition, usually of a restricted range of materials: human remains; animal remains; building material and architectural fragments; coins; complete pots, metal vessels. The range and number of human remains is considerable. Sometimes it is only body-parts, with a preference for skulls. Sometimes there is a single human skeleton. But in some cases there are multiple human bodies, up to twenty-three adults and three children in the well at Oakridge (Hants.) (Oliver 1992). Wells with such deposits also occur at temple sites, for example Pagan's Hill (Boon 1989; Rahtz and Watts 1989) (cf. above p. 133). It should be noted that wells (i.e. shafts designed for abstracting water) appear to be over-whelmingly a Roman-period phenomenon, and those with human deposits often fourth-century A.D., making arguments for a linear continuity from 'Celtic' practice difficult to sustain.

The distinction between wells and shafts can be nebulous (though the presence of lining/steyning may favour the former), and the latter are again often involved in a 'Celtic'/Iron Age construct. The best-known shafts with human remains from Roman Britain are those in the annexe to the fort at Newstead (Borders) (Curle 1911; Clarke S. 1997). Again 'explanations' of the presence of these remains in terms of exceptional factors (here the practices of the Roman army, especially non-British auxiliaries) have been proposed. Other shafts of the Roman period are known from sites such as Greenhithe (Kent) (Gatrill 1880) and Hardham (Sussex) (Dawkins 1864).

The sites at Dragonby (Lincs.) (Harman in May 1996, 139–41) and Hambleden (Bucks.) (Cocks 1921, 150) have yielded human remains from the fill of pits, a location also for animal remains deposited in a way which suggests they are not food remains. These, however, do not resemble the well-known Iron Age 'storage pits' with structured deposits found at hill-forts and other sites in southern Britain. It remains to be determined whether this latter tradition had already ceased before the end of the Iron Age, or was discontinued after the Roman invasion.

Murders and Sacrifice?

There are two sites at least from Roman Britain where the location and character of the burials strongly suggest violent death and subsequent concealment. One is the two skeletons buried in unusual postures and with two swords in a pit at Canterbury (Bennett, Frere and Stow 1982, 43–6); the other is the two skeletons from under the floor of a building in the *vicus* of Housesteads, the evocatively-named 'Murder House' (Birley, Charlton and Hedley 1933, 87–8).

Lindow Man (Stead, Bourke and Brothwell 1986) is generally accepted as the subject of ritual killing, with at least three different elements to his death. It is also worth noting the possibility raised at the Lankhills fourth-century cemetery that some burials were deliberately placed as satellites of other, 'special' graves (Clarke G. 1979, 372–5), possibly even as the result of deliberate sacrifice since there were possible instances of coercion. Perhaps the most striking examples of this were the decapitated skeleton inserted into the upper fill of the cenotaph Grave 400 (cf. below p. 138) and of the 'intrusive' Grave 443. Indeed, the whole practice of decapitation, common in the fourth century but known as early as the second (Philpott 1991, 77–89; Wheeler H. 1985), might be viewed as having

sacrificial connotations, whether or not the individuals concerned were alive or dead at the commencement of the operation (they would certainly be dead by its end), since the body has been purposely mutilated. One might wonder also how it was that the desired number of dead infants for the sorts of foundation deposits noted above came to be available in sufficient numbers, even in a society with high infant mortality. Isserlin (1997) has suggested that some of the body parts found on habitation sites might be explained by sacrifice. This phenomenon is referred to below, where alternative explanations are advanced. Nevertheless, the possibility of sacrifice should not be ruled out without further debate, however transgressive it would be of known Roman prohibitions.

This brief overview has, it is hoped, demonstrated that there was a range of possible places in and at which to dispose of human remains, of which conventional cemeteries was only one, albeit an important one. Possible meanings for these locations will be considered below. But simply categorising by site-type can obscure other significant features of deposition, of which two will now be considered.

Children

It is widely recognised that juveniles in general but particularly infants (less than six months old at death) are grossly under-represented in the burial record from Roman Britain, given what must have been the mortality pattern of this population. This under-representation is particularly noticeable in formal cemeteries, and though it has been posited that the children may have been put in a reserved area of the cemetery no such 'kiddies corners' have actually yet been found. A number of separate burial-grounds have been noted above, at the fort at Malton (E. Yorks.), the villas at Barton Court Farm (Oxon.) and Hambleden (Bucks.) and the settlement at Bradley Hill (Soms.), this latter within a still-standing building. The Roman-period burials at Owslebury (Hants.) show a predominance of infants (Collis 1977). Nonetheless, infant burials are most commonly to be found associated with buildings (cf. Struck 1993).

It is noted by Kjølbye-Biddle (1993, 212) that infants are virtually the only humans buried within the walls of Roman Winchester: twenty-six infant burials were found in the Greyhound Yard, Dorchester (Dorset) excavations (Woodward, Davies and Graham 1993, 314–5), and ten in Wheeler's Verulamium excavations (Wheeler R. and Wheeler T. 1936, 138–9; cf. Frere 1983, 46, 238). Clearly, infants were not comprehended within the usual separation of the living and the dead and this may well be because, as Ucko (1969) notes, there is extensive anthropological evidence that infants lacked a definite social *persona* which would entitle them to/enjoin on them normative burial practices including exclusion from the domain of the living. This attitude is also clear in Roman com-mentators, for Italy at least (cf. Watts 1989).

The association with buildings as at Bradley Hill is maintained in what is probably the most widespread locus for the placing of infant burials, in association with the construction of buildings (cf. Mays 1993). Examples of this have again been noted above, for instance at Bradley Hill and Catsgore in Somerset, and Springhead Temple IV in Kent. Both Philpott (1991, 97–102) and Scott (1991) list other example of this practice. It may also provide an alternative context for discussion of infant remains from forts such as Housesteads instead of (or in addition to) the discussion of whether soldiers' families were housed in the fort in the later Roman period. The interpretation of these infant burials is debated. A 'minimalist' stance would be that as infants lacked an independent *persona*, they could simply be 'tidied away'. This sort of attitude is visible in the Roman prescriptions to bury infants under the eaves of houses (cf. Watts 1989, 372), though even this begs the question of why there? But the widespread phenomenon of infant burials under buildings does seem more purposive, justifying the term 'foundation burial'. The association with buildings may signify that because infants had no developed *persona*, they did not bring with them the possibility of ritual pollution in the way that an older person might, as well as not meriting separate disposal. This liminal status between not-being and being may also have meant that the usual proscriptions did not yet apply. New-born infants as a symbol of accomplished fertility might also have been appropriate talismans for the construction, interior or surroundings of a building; perhaps birth and death following each other so closely epitomised the cycles of fertility and fatality.

Body-parts

Also associated with buildings is the small but growing repertoire of human body parts from habitation sites. These can be an extreme example of the unwillingness of excavators to consider 'non-normative' disposal, since the only notice of the presence of such material may be tucked away in the specialist bone reports. We have already (p. 134) noted the human skulls from the Walbrook and elsewhere in London. Skulls from the decapitated burials at Walkington Wold barrow (E. Yorks.) (Bartlett and Mackey 1972) were inserted into the mound of the Bronze Age barrow (? an execution site, possibly post-Roman). Isserlin (1997) has noted a number of sites where this phenomenon may be observed, and a casual trawl of site reports can easily add to it from a range of site-types (e.g. Woodward, Davies and Graham 1992, 315 [Dorchester, Dorset]; May 1996, 140 [Dragonby]; Kjølbye-Biddle 1993, 211–2 [Winchester]). Isserlin (1997) raises the possibility of human sacrifice. This has been alluded to above (p. 135), but for these scattered pieces of bone it is a more difficult hypothesis to sustain. It is, of course, possible that the presence of these bones is fortuitous, the result of disturbance of earlier burials by later activity. But is does also raise the notion that we should be alive

to the possibility of post-mortem manipulation of the dead, in a way very familiar to prehistorians. At the beginning of this paper it was noted that we should be on the look-out for evidence for the archaeologically-invisible disposal rites of the majority of the population; this may be such an instance.

Discussion

In what ways may we set about trying to analyse and interpret the wide range of contexts for the disposal of human remains in Roman Britain? Universalising answers are always dangerous, particularly here where the preceding discussion has made it clear that there are very substantial differences in time and space in the means of disposal of the dead (and that is just the archaeologically-visible rites). Nevertheless, a number of recurrent patterns in the evidence suggest that there are some broad avenues of approach.

The Dead in the Landscape

As stated at the beginning of this paper, one approach is to use the placing of the dead in the physical landscape to draw conclusions about their place in the conceptual landscape. In general, it is clear that the dead were not 'out of sight, out of mind'. Recurrently they are sited where the living would have been aware of them. A number of different patternings may be noted.

At the major towns the dead occupied an important place in the overall urban morphology. The date of the earliest urban cemeteries suggests that these areas were set apart for the dead from the beginning (cf. Esmonde Cleary 1992, 31). The laying-out of a civitas-capital involved the imposition of a hefty piece of Roman-style cosmology onto the landscape. We know that the ceremonies for the *deductio* of a *colonia* involved formal definition of binary opposites such as inside:outside, well-omened:ill-omened; we may imagine that something similar may have taken place at the civitas-capitals, with formalisation of the relations between the domains of the living and of the dead. A consequence is that the dead were the first of a town's citizens to be encountered on entering the town, and the last to be left behind on quitting it. Few Romano-British towns had anything like a monumentalised 'street of tombs' in the Italian or even Rhineland style, but nevertheless such monuments as there were, the presence of grave-mounds and the formal setting-aside of bounded cemeteries would alert the passer-by. Thus a town was ringed by its ancestors and over time this would help make its presence seem natural and age-old, softening the rawness of its original creation. It is interesting to note that this link with the past was not static. In the summary of the development of the cemeteries of Winchester (p. 128) it was noted how the late Roman cemeteries are on new, different sites, a phenomenon observable at many major towns. At a number of towns the late cemeteries are inhumation cemeteries, displaced from the cremation cemeteries, which may be telling us something about the much-debated shift from cremation to inhumation and how it was negotiated and rationalised by individual communities and larger regions (cf. Morris I. 1992, Ch.2). It is also one of the changes which ought to be factored into future discussions of the changes from early to late Roman urbanism in Britain. The towns of Roman Britain did not, of course, survive long enough to see the dead become protectors and guardians of the town with the Christianisation of urban topography (cf. Harries 1992), though the idea may have resonances for the earlier period especially at sites such as Folly Lane, Verulamium (Niblett 1999). One other feature of these cemeteries at major towns is their size and relative lack of differentiation in the visible parts of the burial. Given the lack of monuments and tombstones, most of the burials must have seemed uniform in their mounded anonymity (the more so in the late period when civil Roman Britain had lost whatever tenuous grasp it had ever had on the 'epigraphic habit'). Clearly families would have known where individual graves or groups of graves lay, witness the probable family group defined by the ditched enclosure F.6 at Lankhills, or the presence of offerings on grave-mounds in the boundary ditch F.12 at the same site (Clarke G. 1979, 97–99, 100–5), also the mausolea at cemeteries such as Butt Road, Colchester (Crummy, Crummy and Crossan 1993) or Poundbury, Dorchester (Farwell and Molleson 1993), but the overall impression of sameness would have remained. Burial in a large cemetery at a major town or the ones at some small towns would to an extent have meant assimilation into the generality of the town's past inhabitants rather than retaining sharply-defined individual or family identity. This too would have increased with time as families died out and cemeteries shifted.

By contrast, at many small towns and at most rural sites, the dead seem to retain much of their individual or family identity. The 'backland' cemeteries at small towns, the cemeteries that there are at villas and other rural sites and the monumentalised burials such as mausolea all attest differing strategies for retaining the memory of the deceased. The mausolea are clearly designed to be visible. Many villa and other cemeteries are placed near, and visible from, the habitation. Barrows may be a similar case, perhaps trying to create a 'landscape of ancestors'. The placing of the Borough Hill (Northants.) Romano-British barrows within a hillfort not only gave them a prominent physical position but also a significant relationship to an important earlier monument. Other burials were placed near tracks and other routes, maintaining them in the eye and mental map of the inhabitants and passers-by. The 'backland' burials at the small towns are not on public display in the same way, but they do form part of the day-to-day experience of the living, including presumably relicts and descendants. The placing of more scattered and individual burials does seem to betoken a different attitude to the significance of the dead, with them integrated into other land-uses. To us this may look a more casual attitude, but this of course is writing our perceptions on the past. At present there is perhaps too much of an understandable tendency to load a series of discrete events, including burial, in an area onto one palimpsest plan for publication. More chronological discrimination may separate out the funerary phases from other activities. The treatment of infants has been outlined above (p. 135) and shows that this group had an important and distinctive relationship with settlements and buildings, perhaps out of proportion to their importance in life.

Boundaries and Boundedness

The deposition of the dead within bounded enclosures and in association with boundary features is an important recurring feature of burial practice in Roman Britain. Cemeteries and smaller groups of burials at major towns, small towns, villas and rural settlements are generally to be found within enclosures, usually ditched, occasionally walled, and ranging in date from the first to the fourth centuries. Clearly boundedness was a major issue. It is possible to argue that this was simply a function of property and rights over space. For urban cemeteries where there may have been pressure on space and fragmented ownership patterns, this may up to a point be plausible. But the reinforcement of cemetery boundaries themselves by burial, and other evidence for delimiting funerary space discussed below suggest that this simple argument should not be pursued too far. It is even less convincing for rural sites, where space was not at a premium. At one level these bounded areas may be analogous to the Christian concept of 'consecrated ground', that land was not just physically but also ritually set apart and made suitable for burial. Roman law recognised a similar legal and ritual separateness through the performance of the necessary rituals (cf. Toynbee 1971, 50–1). In addition, there is, of course, extensive anthropological and folk-lore evidence for the belief in the powers of the dead to intervene in the affairs of the living. In some beliefs this can be because the dead can rise in some form, more usually it is that the souls or spirits of the dead in some sense live on, to a greater or lesser extent tied to the remains of the body. These dead can then 'walk' to inflict harm, more rarely to benefit, the living; in this way are the dead Powerful. Therefore the need to be able to prevent or control the ability of the dead to leave the place of burial is evident. A physical boundary such as a ditch would be the archaeological evidence for a ritual boundary, fortified by the rites appropriate for constraining the dead. Conversely, the dead can themselves be subject to malign influence of spirits and other maleficent agencies: the Powerful Dead can be the Vulnerable Dead. The apparent lack of such boundedness in many of the more scattered and isolated burials at villas and other rural sites is another index of the somewhat deviant nature of this means of disposal, though some of them are near boundaries such as ditches. Also, there are boundaries which may have left little or no trace in the archaeological record, such as fences or hedges.

Another commonly-recurring pattern is the presence of burials beside and especially in boundary ditches. This can be seen at major cemeteries such as Lankhills, Winchester where the original boundary ditch F.12 was later colonised by burial, before (and perhaps making possible?) the expansion of the cemetery beyond that boundary (Clarke G. 1979, fig. 105). Within the Lankhills cemetery, the F.6 complex has a number of burials inserted into the corners and sides of the enclosure. It also had a grave in its entranceway, closing off the gap, perhaps sealing the monument after the last burial. At Winchester the fourth-century colonisation of the Iron Age defensive ditch at Oram's Arbour has also been noted (p. 129). A similar pattern can be observed at other major fourth-century urban cemeteries such as Butt Road Colchester (Crummy, Crummy and Crossan 1993) and Poundbury, Dorchester (Farwell and Molleson 1993). The 'backland' burials at Ilchester (Fig. 14. 2) are placed alongside the boundary ditches and sometimes in them. At Harpenden, the enclosure ditch of the mausoleum contained formal burials, whereas the berm between the ditch and the mausoleum was kept clear of them. At villas such as Dalton Parlours (Fig. 14. 3) and rural sites such as Roughground Farm (Fig. 14. 5) there is a recurrent association between boundary ditches and burials.

The functional/rational explanation of such positioning would be that the ditches were ground which was of little use for other purposes, but suitable for the placing of the dead. Another use for ditches was the disposal of refuse such as waste bone. In this case, the burial of the dead would be the higher rubbish disposal. But the way in which the dead were disposed of, even in ditches, was not the same as the dumping of waste. The close physical association and alignment with ditches suggests something more purposive and symbolic. In the physical world ditches are boundaries, in the conceptual world they are liminal positions. The intermediate and indeterminate conceptual position of boundaries makes them features ripe for definition and confirmation by the presence of a range of possible ritual deposits (cf. Bradley 1990). In the Roman period burials seem to be a favoured type of deposit in this context, though other types of offering have also been found. Conversely, the ambiguous status of a boundary may be what made it attractive for the deposition of a type of deposit (i.e. human burial) whose presence in areas of more defined activities might be disruptive, and not just by its physical presence. The association of burial with boundary might also help bound the possible influence of the dead.

Burial and Patterns of Ritual Deposition

Lankhills Grave 400 (Clarke G. 1979, 82–3, fig.66) is a fascinating assemblage. On the floor of the grave lay a coffin, but there had been no skeleton: a cenotaph. Where the right hand would have been was a group of five coins. Immediately above the 'head' end of the coffin was the complete and articulated skeleton of a dog. In the fill of the grave were some human leg-bones (no earlier burial was disturbed by Grave 400) and the dismembered remains of a dog near the 'foot' end. Cut into the grave fill was a later burial, Grave 427, which contained a decapitated skeleton and in the fill of which were three human skull fragments. These graves were surrounded by the gulley F.40. Though the form of the deposit (a grave) and its location (a formal cemetery) bring it within the category 'funerary', there are features of it such as the complete human and animal skeletons, the parts of human and animal skeletons and the coins which relate it to other types of ritual deposition.

In considering the deposition of human remains in wet places, wells and shafts (p.134) it was noted that human remains occur with other categories of material such as animal remains, whole pots, coins, metal vessels (cf. Poulton and Scott 1993) and architectural material. All of these, apart from architectural material, also occur as grave-goods. Metalwares and coins also occur in hoards, plausibly seen as ritual manifestations as well as/rather than the concealment of valuables or the product of monetary instability. Coins and other objects also recur in votive material at temples, both on 'dry land' and in major wet-place temple contexts such as the Sacred Spring at Bath (Cunliffe 1988) and Coventina's Well (Northumberland) (Allason-Jones and McKay 1985). Animals form a regular part of burial practice in well and shaft fills. (Such deposits form a plausible late Roman context for the 'ritual' pits and their contents dug through the latest Roman deposits at Silchester, Insula IX [Fulford and Clarke 1999]). All of these have in common deposition in a place which penetrates into the earth, or at which something issues from the earth: grave, pit, shaft, spring, well. This again is a liminal context, and this seems to be important in wet-place sites (cf. Bradley 1990). But the penetrations created by humans may also have chthonic significance by their disturbance of the established categories and boundaries and by bringing light and air into the dark and closed. Proper ritual to propitiate chthonic deities or to re-establish equilibrium may have been necessary. There are also the sexual connotations of these penetrations, particularly if the components of the natural world were gendered.

The presence of animal remains in funerary contexts is perhaps more common than is often realised, and not just as 'grave-goods' (cf. Sidell and Rielly 1998). Animal remains can on rare occasions apparently be focal in the development of human cemeteries, for instance the burial of a horse and two dogs at the start of the burial sequence in the eastern cemetery of London (Barber, Bowsher and Whittaker 1990, esp. 9–10). In an adjacent part of the same cemetery, at West Tenter Street, the upper fill of a gravel quarry filled in to make way for the cemetery contained the complete skeleton of a horse (Whytehead 1986, 31–2). There was also a deep shaft which did not penetrate the water-table and whose backfill contained 'some rubble as well as domestic refuse' (Whytehead 1986, 65). Two of the burials contained deliberately deposited domestic fowl, a practice also observed at Lankhills and the Bath Gate, Cirencester cemetery (Whytehead 1986, 64–5 and refs.). The dogs in Lankhills Grave 400 have already been noted, as has the occurrence of dogs in other contexts such as wells. Horses are also recorded (albeit in antiquarian records) from the main *colonia* cemetery at York (RCHM[E] 1962, 79). The human burials from the Dalton Parlours villas have already been noted (p. 131), but both Iron Age and Romano-British pits from this site produced animal bones, including Iron Age dog burials (Berg in Wrathmell and Nicholson 1990, 174–89). At Barton Court Farm (Miles ed. 1984, 15–16) three of the burials in the infant cemetery had animal skulls placed with them (two dogs and a sheep). Scott (1991, 117–18) notes other occurrences of animal skulls, particularly again with infants including those associated with buildings. Many animal species were and are invested by humans with properties and qualities such as power, speed, loyalty, cunning, which may be an approach to interpreting their presence. Alternatively, animals can be seen as companions or attributes of particular deities and thus associate a site with that deity and his or her qualities, or place the site under their protection.

Clearly, therefore, we must be wary of decontextualising the deposition of human bone by separating it from other classes of ritual deposition. Even in large cemetery sites, apparently dedicated to the ordered disposal of human bodies, there are overlaps with other contexts of ritual deposition. In the case of features such as wells and shafts the overlap is clearer, both in the context of the place of deposition and in the context of the other classes of material deposited along with the human. It also reinforces the point made in connection with boundaries that human burials and bones are powerful and efficacious beyond simply cemetery contexts. It also means that the objects found in graves should not be considered simply as grave-goods, but as one context of deposition of materials which can also occur in other ritual contexts. Equally, it must also raise serious questions over simply functional interpretations of animal bone (for instance, in terms of diet and agricultural economy), particularly animal bone from ritual contexts, shaft, wells, or the burials of (near-)complete animal skeletons where there is no evidence of butchery for hides, tendons, meat etc. Consideration of the reasons for the presence of not only the human remains but also the other material from such contexts, and also of the contexts themselves should in due course offer ideas as to the reasons for the deposition of human remains in particular places.

Origins and Influences

As has been seen, there is a wide range of locations for burial and of variations in the treatment of human remains in Roman Britain. An obvious question is when and where these practices developed, allied with the extent to which there is chronological variation and development alongside those by region, site-type and age (cf. Black 1986). One strand in such a discussion has traditionally been to seek for the influence of 'Roman' burial practices on Britain (cf. Alcock 1980). Some features of Romano-British funerary ritual do seem to have Mediterranean origins, though explaining them directly in terms of the evidence from Rome and Italy (especially the literary evidence) is problematic and currently unfashionable. First we may examine some of the major traits in Romano-British burial practice which seem to have been influenced from outside the island. The use of archaeologically-visible rites of disposal is far more widespread than in the preceding Iron Age, and it is noticeable that it is most prevalent at towns, probably forts and to an extent villas. These are the types of site most open to and reflective of innovation from outside Britain; more 'Romanised' if one must express it that way. The general change from cremation to inhumation from the late second century is also an instance where Britain forms part of a much wider whole. Philpott (1991) has demonstrated how a range of burial practices are either imported from outside Britain or reflect the influence on British burial practice of rites from other areas of the western empire. This of course begs the question of whether there ever was a distinctively 'Roman' burial rite, rather than a range of possibilities both in metropolitan Italy and more widely in Gaul. Nonetheless, it is clear that it is impossible to see the development of funerary practice in Britain in isolation from influence from across the Channel. We need a more developed notion of burial locations and rites and of other sites for ritual deposition in Gaul, especially in Belgica.

Another approach, currently more fashionable, is to trace the development of practices in the Roman period out of the later Iron Age. This is an entirely reasonable approach, particularly for the earlier Roman period, though one must beware of privileging what was happening in the late Iron Age at the risk of denying invention and innovation to the Romano-British. The situation becomes more complicated when attempts are made to attach to such practices the ethnic label 'Celtic'. It is clear that many features of Roman-period burial have analogues in the later Iron Age. The burial of children and of animals such as horses and dogs can be detected in the Iron Age. The deposition of human and other remains in shafts and, possibly, wells is present, though there has been perhaps too much of a tendency to try to date them to the Iron Age, and they have suffered particularly from interpretation in terms of 'Celtic' ritual (Webster 1997; cf. Wait 1985 Ch.3). Pit-burial is also a well-known Iron Age rite, though as noted above (p.134) it may not have survived into the Roman period. Clearly there was deposition of valuables in wet places, above all the lower Thames, in the Iron Age, though how much deposition of human remains there was remains debatable. One form of such deposition was that of skulls. All of these practices are represented in the Roman period. There is a natural tendency to regard the Roman as a development out of the pre-Roman, an approach given a premium by recent interest in 'Romanisation' and in the rescuing of indigenous contribution from the obscurity into which it is cast by imperialist discourses. There is, though, a consideration which may counsel caution and the possibility of more complex development. Many of the practices and instances discussed in the body of this paper are best-attested in the fourth century. Many of the burials in ditches, many of the child burials, some of the animal burials date to the later Roman period. In a way this is not surprising, since they reflect the numerical predominance of fourth-century inhumation, and inhumation is probably more visible to the archaeologist. One of the rites, deposition in wells, which seems to have clear Iron Age antecedents in shaft deposition, is a similar problem. Most of the dated instances of human remains and other material in wells date to the fourth century rather than the first and second. Indeed, as noted above, this practice forms part of a complex pattern of late Roman ritual deposition. The purpose of this argument is not to deny the influence on pre-Roman on Roman rites. It is to urge caution and complexity rather than over-confidence and an over-linear approach. It is to urge more detailed study than has been possible here of development and change through time of individual rites and practices. It is also to draw attention to the fact that the fullest range of practices is visible in the fourth century, some three hundred years after the Conquest and allowing ample time for the development of new ideas and ideologies on death and the dead. Future enquiry might consider whether these later Roman burial rites and sites influenced developments in the post-Roman period, or is part of the archaeological distinction between Roman and post-Roman that the societies of the latter period chose to found their burial-grounds anew?

Envoi

In sum, it is clear that the archaeological evidence for the ways in which the dead were placed in the physical landscape of Roman Britain shows that the dead were a real part of the conceptual landscape of living Romano-Britons. Equally clearly, the dead had some sort of afterlife, which could affect the living. Even after the rituals of the passing of life, of the funeral and of the burial the dead remained potentially formidable. The places in which they were deposited, the ways in which they were deposited and the materials with which they were deposited all attest to the need of the living to provide for the proper treatment of the dead. They attest also to the need to ensure that the influence of the dead was at least confined and did not act to the detriment of the living, or was at best turned to the advantage of the living, especially descendants. They also show that the dead were part of a wider spectrum of materials and contexts of deposition, all of which attest to

'burial' as an important facet of Romano-British ritual practice. Others of the dead, perhaps the majority, remain, of course, invisible to us.

Acknowledgements

I am very grateful to the editors for their initial invitation to take part in the conference, and for their subsequent forbearance during the writing of the text. My research student, Tina Simpson, kindly discussed her work on well fills of the Roman period. Sally Crawford and Roger White commented on a draft, to its considerable improvement, as did the anonymous referee.

Bibliography

Alcock J.P. 1980. Classical Religious Beliefs and Burial Practice in Roman Britain, *Archaeological Journal* 137: 50–85

Allason-Jones L. and McKay B. 1985. *Coventina's Well*, Chesters: Trustees of the Clayton Collection

Allen T.G., Darvill T.C., Green L.S. and Jones M.U. 1993. *Excavations at Roughground Farm, Lechlade, Gloucestershire: a prehistoric and Roman landscape*, Thames Valley Landscapes: the Cotswold Water Park, Volume 1, Oxford: Oxford University Committee for Archaeology

Baker P., Forcey C., Jundi S. and Witcher R. (eds.) 1999. *TRAC 98: Proceedings of the Eighth Annual Theoretical Roman Archaeology Conference Leicester 1998*, Oxford: Oxbow Books

Barber B., Bowsher D. and Whittaker K. 1990. Recent Excavations of a Cemetery of *Londinium, Britannia* 21: 1–12

Barrett J. 1994. *Fragments of Antiquity*, Oxford: Blackwell

Bartlett J.E. and Mackey R.W. 1972. Excavations on Walkington Wold 1967–1969, *East Riding Archaeologist* 1.2: 1–93

Bassett S.R. (ed). 1992. *Death in Towns; urban approaches to the dying and the dead, 100–1600*, Leicester: Leicester University Press

Bedwin O. 1981. Excavations at Lancing Down, West Sussex, *Sussex Archaeological Collections* 119: 37–56

Bennett J., Frere S.S. and Stow S. 1982. *Excavations at Canterbury Castle*, The Archaeology of Canterbury Vol.I, Maidstone: Kent Archaeological Society

Bird J., Hassall M. and Sheldon H. (eds.) 1996. *Interpreting Roman London: papers in memory of Hugh Chapman*, Oxford: Oxbow Monograph 58

Birley E., Charlton J. and Hedley P. 1933. Excavations at Housesteads in 1932, *Archaeologia Aeliana 4th Series* 10: 82–96

Black E.W. 1986. Romano-British Burial Customs and Religious Beliefs in South-East England, *Archaeological Journal* 143: 201–39

Boon G.C. (ed.) 1978. *Monographs and Collections I: Roman Sites*, Cardiff: Cambrian Archaeological Association

Boon, G.C. 1989. A Roman sculpture rehabilitated: the Pagans Hill dog, *Britannia* 20: 201–17

Booth P.M. 1997. *Asthall, Oxfordshire: Excavations in a Roman 'Small Town'*, Thames Valley Landscapes Monograph No. 9, Oxford: Oxford Archaeological Unit

Bradley R. 1990. *The Passage of Arms*, Cambridge: Cambridge University Press

Bradley R. 1993. *Altering the Earth*, Edinburgh: Society of Antiquaries of Scotland Monograph No.8

Bradley R. and Gordon K. 1988. Human skulls from the Thames, their dating and significance, *Antiquity* 62: 503–9

Branigan K. 1976. *The Roman West Country*, Newton Abbot: David and Charles

Brown A.E. 1977. The Roman Barrow Cemetery on Borough Hill, Daventry, *Northamptonshire Archaeology* 12: 185–90

Brown A.E., Woodfield C. and Mynard D.C. 1983. Excavations at Towcester, Northamptonshire: The Alchester Road Suburb, *Northamptonshire Archaeology* 18: 43–140

Brown A.E. (ed.) 1995. *Roman Small Towns in Eastern England and Beyond*, Oxford: Oxbow Monograph 52

Burleigh G. 1993. Some aspects of burial types in the cemeteries of the Romano-British settlement at Baldock, Hertfordshire, England, in Struck (ed.) 41–9

Burleigh G. 1995. The plan of Romano-British Baldock, Hertfordshire, in Brown (ed.) 177–82

Burnham B. and Wacher J.S. 1990 *The 'Small Towns' of Roman Britain*, London: Batsford

Carr C. 1995. Mortuary practices: their social, philosophical-religious, circumstantial and physical determinants, *Journal of Archaeological Method and Theory* 2 (2): 105–200

Charlton, B. and Mitcheson, M. 1984. The Roman cemetery at Petty Knowes, Northumberland, *Archaeologia Aeliana 5th series*, 12: 1–33

Clarke G. 1979. *The Roman Cemetery at Lankhills*, Oxford: Winchester Studies 3.II

Clarke S. 1997. Abandonment, Rubbish Disposal and 'Special Deposits' at Newstead, in Meadows, Lemke and Heron (eds.) 73–81

Cocks A.H. 1921. A Romano-British Homestead in the Hambleden Valley, Bucks, *Archaeologia* 71: 141–98

Collard M. and Parkhouse J. 1993. A Belgic/Romano-British Cemetery at Bledlow-cum-Saunderton, *Records of Buckinghamshire 35: 66–75*

Collis J. 1977. Owslebury (Hants.) and the problem of burials on rural settlements, in Reece (ed.) 26–34

Cook J. and Rowley T. (eds.) 1985. *Dorchester through the ages*, Oxford: Oxford University Department for External Studies

Corder P. 1930. *The Defences of the Roman Fort at Malton*, Leeds: Roman Malton and District Report No.2

Cotton J. 1996. A miniature chalk head from the Thames at Battersea and the 'cult of the head' in Roman London, in Bird, Hassall and Sheldon (eds.) 85–96

Crawford O.G.S and Keiller A. 1928. *Wessex from the Air*, Oxford

Crummy N., Crummy P. and Crossan C. 1993. *Excavations of Roman and later cemeteries, churches and monastic sites in Colchester, 1971–88*, Colchester: Colchester Archaeological Report 9

Cunliffe B.W. 1988. *The Temple of Sulis Minerva at Bath: Volume 2 The Finds from the Sacred Spring*, Oxford: Oxford University Committee for Archaeology Monograph 16

Curle J. 1911. *A Roman Frontier Post and its People: the fort of Newstead in the parish of Melrose*, Glasgow: James Maclehose and Sons

Dawkins W.B. 1864. On a Romano-British cemetery and a Roman camp at Hardham in West Sussex, *Sussex Archaeological Collections* 16: 52–64

Ellis P. 1984. *Catsgore 1979. Further Excavation of The Romano-British Village*, Gloucester: Western Archaeological Trust Excavation Monograph No.7

Esmonde Cleary A.S. 1992. Town and Country in Roman Britain?, in Bassett (ed.) 28–42

Evans E.M and Maynard D.J. 1997. Caerleon Lodge Hill cemetery: the Abbeyfield site 1992, *Britannia* 28: 169–243

Farwell D.E and Molleson T.I. 1993. *Excavations at Poundbury 1966–80 Volume II: The Cemeteries*, Dorchester: Dorset Natural History and Archaeological Society Monograph Series No.11

Ferdière A. (ed.) 1993. *Monde des Morts, Monde des Vivants en Gaule Rurale*, Tours: FERACF

Forcey C. 1998. Whatever Happened to the Heroes? Ancestral cults and the enigma of Romano-Celtic temples, in Forcey, Hawthorne and Witcher (eds.) 87–98

Forcey C., Hawthorne J. and Witcher R. 1998. *TRAC 97 Proceedings of the Seventh Annual Theoretical Roman Archaeology Conference Nottingham 1997*, Oxford: Oxbow Books

Frere S.S. 1983. *Verulamium Excavations Volume II*, London: Thames and Hudson

Fulford M. and Clarke A. 1999. Silchester and the end of Roman towns, *Current Archaeology* 161: 176–80

Gage J. 1836. A letter from JOHN GAGE, Esq. F.R.S., Director, to HUDSON GURNEY, Esq. F.R.S., Vice-President, communicating the recent discovery of Roman sepulchral relics in one of the greater Barrows at Bartlow, in the parish of Ashdon, in Essex, *Archaeologia* 26, 300–17

Garwood P., Jennings D., Skeates R. and Toms J. (eds.) 1991. *Sacred and Profane: Proceedings of a Conference on Archaeology, Ritual and Religion Oxford, 1989*, Oxford: Oxford University Committee for Archaeology

Gatrill J.M. 1880. Notes on a discovery at Greenhithe, *Archaeological Journal* 37: 193–95

Gwilt A. and Haselgrove C.C. 1997. *Reconstructing Iron Age Societies: new approaches to the British Iron Age*, Oxford: Oxbow Monograph 71

Harries J. 1992. Death and the dead in the late Roman West, in Bassett (ed.) 56–67

Isserlin R. 1997. Thinking the Unthinkable: Human Sacrifice in Roman Britain, in Meadows, Lemke and Heron (eds.) 91–100

Jessup R.F. 1954. Excavation of a Roman Barrow at Holborough, Snodland, *Archaeologia Cantiana* 68: 1–61

Jessup R.F. 1959. Barrows and Walled Cemeteries in Roman Britain, *Journal of the British Archaeological Association* 22: 1–32

Jones R.F.J. 1975. A Romano-British farmstead and its cemetery at Lynch Farm, near Peterborough, *Northamptonshire Archaeology* 10: 94–137

Kjølbye-Biddle B. 1993. Dispersal or concentration: the disposal of the Winchester dead over 2000 years, in Bassett (ed.) 210–47

Laurence R. and Berry J. (eds.) 1998. *Cultural Identity in the Roman Empire,* London: Routledge

Leach P. J.1982 *Ilchester Volume 1 Excavations 1974–5*, Bristol: Western Archaeological Trust Excavation Monograph No.3

Leach P.J. 1994. *Ilchester Volume 2 Archaeology, Excavations and Fieldwork to 1984*, Sheffield: Sheffield Excavation Reports 2

Leach P.J. forthcoming *Fosse Lane: Excavation of a Romano-British Roadside Settlement at Shepton Mallet, Somerset, 1990*, London: Britannia Monograph

Leech R. 1981. The Excavation of a Romano-British Farmstead and Cemetery on Bradley Hill, Somerton, Somerset, *Britannia* 12: 177–252

Leech R. 1982. *Excavations at Catsgore 1970–1973 A Romano-British Village* Bristol: Western Archaeological Trust Excavation Monograph No.2

Mahany C. (ed.) 1994. *Roman Alcester: Southern Extra-Mural Area 1964–1966 Excavations Part 1: Stratigraphy and Structures*, York: Council for British Archaeology Research Report 96

Mason D.J.P. 1987. Chester: the Canabae Legionis, *Britannia* 18: 143–68

May J. 1996. *Dragonby: Report on Excavations at an Iron Age and Romano-British Settlement in North Lincolnshire*, Oxford: Oxbow Monograph 61

Mays S. 1993. Infanticide in Roman Britain, *Antiquity* 67: 883–88

Meadows K., Lemke C. and Heron J. (eds.) 1997. *TRAC 96 Proceedings of the Sixth Annual Theoretical Roman Archaeology Conference Sheffield 1996* Oxford: Oxbow Books

Meates G.W. 1979. *The Lullingstone Roman Villa Volume I The Site*, Chichester: Phillimore and Kent Archaeological Society

Merrifield R. 1995. Roman metalwork from the Walbrook – rubbish, ritual or redundancy, *Transactions of the London and Middlesex Archaeological Society* 46: 27–44

Metcalf P. and Huntington R. 1992. *Celebrations of Death: the Anthropology of Mortuary Ritual* (second edition), Cambridge: Cambridge University Press

Miles D. (ed.) 1984. *Archaeology at Barton Court Farm, Abingdon, Oxon*, Oxford: London Archaeological Unit Report 3, Council for British Archaeology Research Report 50

Morris I. 1992. *Death Ritual and Social Structure in Classical Antiquity*, Cambridge: Cambridge University Press

Morris M.1986. A Lead-lined Coffin Burial from Winchester, *Britannia* 17: 343–46

Neal D.S. 1983. Unusual Buildings at Wood Lane End, Hemel Hempstead, Herts., *Britannia* 14: 73–86

Niblett R. 1999. *The Excavation of a Ceremonial Site at Folly Lane, Verulamium*, London: Britannia Monograph Series No.14

Oliver M. 1992. The Iron Age and Romano-British settlement at Oakridge, *Proceedings of the Hampshire Field Club and Archaeological Society* 48: 55–94

Parker Pearson M. 1993. The powerful dead: archaeological relationships between the living and the dead, *Cambridge Archaeological Journal* 3 (2): 203–29

Parrington M. 1978. *The excavation of an Iron Age settlement, Bronze Age ring ditches and Roman features at Ashville Trading Estate, Abingdon (Oxfordshire) 1974–76*, London: Oxfordshire Archaeological Unit Report 1, Council for British Archaeology Research Report 28

Pearce J. 1999. The Dispersed Dead: preliminary observations on burial and settlement space in rural Roman Britain, in Baker, Forcey, Jundi and Witcher (eds.), 151–62

Penn W.S. 1961. Springhead: Temples III and IV, *Archaeologia Cantiana* 74: 113–40

Penn W.S. 1968. Possible Evidence from Springhead for the Great Plague of A.D. 166, *Archaeologia Cantiana* 82: 263–71

Petts D. 1998. Landscape and cultural identity in Roman Britain, in Laurence and Berry (eds.) 79–94

Philpott R. 1991 *Burial Practices in Roman Britain: A survey of grave treatment and furnishing A.D. 43–410*, Oxford: Tempus Reparatum, British Archaeological Reports British Series 219

Poulton R. and Scott E, 1993. The Hoarding, Use and Deposition of Pewter in Roman Britain, in Scott (ed.): 115–32

Quinnell H. 1991. The Villa and Temple at Cosgrove, Northamptonshire, *Northamptonshire Archaeology* 23, 4–66

Rahtz, P. and Watts, L. 1989. Pagans Hill revisited, *Archaeological Journal* 146: 330–71

Reece R.M. (ed.) 1977. *Burial in the Roman World*, London: Council for British Archaeology Research Report 22

Royal Commission on the Historic Monuments of England 1962. *Eburacum Roman York*, London: Her Majesty's Stationery Office

Richards J. 1999. *Meet the Ancestors*, London: BBC Publications

Rodwell K.A. 1988. *The prehistoric and Roman settlement at Kelvedon, Essex*, London: Chelmsford Archaeological Trust Report 6, Council for British Archaeology Research Report 63

Rook T., Walker S. and Denston C.B. 1984. A Roman Mausoleum and Associated Marble Sarcophagus and Burials from Welwyn, Hertfordshire, *Britannia* 15: 143–62

Scott E. 1990. A critical review of the interpretation of infant burials in Roman Britain, with particular reference to villas, *Journal of Theoretical Archaeology* 1,

Scott E. 1991. Animal and Infant Burials in Romano-British Villas: A Revitalization Movement, in Garwood, Jennings, Skeates and Toms (eds.) 115–21

Scott E, (ed.) 1993. *Theoretical Roman Archaeology: first conference proceedings*, Aldershot: Avebury

Sidell J. and Rielly K. 1998. New evidence for the ritual use of animals in Roman London, in Watson (ed.) 95–99

Stead I.M. 1976. *Excavations at Winterton Roman Villa and other Roman sites in North Lincolnshire 1958–1967*, London: Her Majesty's Stationery Office

Stead I.M. 1980. *Rudston Roman Villa*, Leeds: Yorkshire Archaeological Society

Stead I.M., Bourke J.B. and Brothwell D. 1986. *Lindow Man: The Body in the Bog*, London: British Museum Publications

Struck M. 1993. Kinderbestattungen in romano-britischen Siedlungen – der archäologische Befund, in Struck (ed.) 313–18

Struck M. (ed.) 1993. *Römerzeitliche Gräber als Quellen zu Religion, Bevölkerungsstruktur und Sozialgeschichte*, Mainz: Johannes Gutenburg-Universität

Taylor A. 1993. A Roman Lead Coffin with Pipeclay Figurines from Arrington, Cambridgeshire, *Britannia* 24: 191–225

Timby J. (ed.) 1998. *Excavations at Kingscote and Wycomb, Gloucestershire: a Roman estate centre and small town in the Cotswolds with notes on related settlements*, Cirencester: Cotswold Archaeological Trust

Toynbee J. 1971. *Death and Burial in the Roman World*, London: Thames and Hudson

Ucko P. 1969. Ethnography and the archaeological interpretation of funerary remains, *World Archaeology* 1: 262–80

Vyner B. 1978. Excavations at Great Bulmore, near Caerleon, in Boon (ed.) 25–62

Wait G. 1985. *Ritual and Religion in Iron Age Britain*, Oxford: British Archaeological Reports British Series 149

Watson B. (ed.) 1998. *Roman London: Recent Archaeological Work*, Newport, RI: Journal of Roman Archaeology Supplementary Series No. 24

Watts D. 1989. Infant Burials and Romano-British Christianity, *Archaeological Journal* 146: 372–83

Webster J. 1997. Text expectations: the archaeology of 'Celtic' ritual wells and shafts, in Gwilt and Haselgrove (eds.) 134–44

Wenham L.P. 1968. *The Romano-British Cemetery at Trentholme Drive, York*, London: Her Majesty's Stationery Office

Wheeler H. 1985. The Racecourse Cemetery, *Derbyshire Archaeological Journal* 105: 222–80

Wheeler R.E.M. and Wheeler T.V. 1936. *Verulamium: A Belgic and Two Roman Cities*, London: Report of the Research Committee of the Society of Antiquaries of London No.11

Whytehead R. 1986. The Excavation of an Area within a Roman Cemetery at West Tenter Street, London E1, *Transactions of the London and Middlesex Archaeological Society* 37, 23–124

Wickenden N.P. 1988. *Excavations at Great Dunmow, Essex*, Chelmsford: Chelmsford Archaeological Trust Report No.7, East Anglian Archaeology Report No.41

Williams H.M.R. 1997. Ancient Landscapes and the Dead: The Reuse of Prehistoric and Roman Monuments as Early Anglo-Saxon Burial Sites, *Medieval Archaeology* 61, 1–32

Williams H.M.R. 1998a. The Ancient Monument in Romano-British Ritual Practices, in Forcey, Hawthorne and Witcher (eds.) 71–86

Williams H.M.R. 1998b. Monuments and the past in early Anglo-Saxon England, *World Archaeology* 30 (1): 90–108

Williams R.J. and Zeepvat R.J. 1994. *Bancroft: a late Bronze Age/Iron Age Settlement, Roman Villa and Temple-Mausoleum*, Aylesbury: Buckinghamshire Archaeological Society Monograph Series No.7

Woodfield C. and Johnson C. 1989. A Roman site at Stanton Low, on the Great Ouse, *Archaeological Journal* 146: 135–278

Woodward P.J., Davies S.M. and Graham A.H. 1993. *Excavations at the Old Methodist Chapel and Greyhound Yard, Dorchester, 1981–1984*, Dorchester: Dorset Natural History and Archaeological Society Monograph Series No. 12

Wrathmell S. and Nicholson A. 1990. *Dalton Parlours Iron Age Settlement and Roman Villa*, Wakefield: West Yorkshire Archaeology Service

15. Continuity of prehistoric burial sites in the Roman Landscape of Sandy Flanders

Frank Vermeulen and Jean Bourgeois

Long lived burial sites in the Romanised landscape

As John Pearce rightly remarks in his introductory text, meant to hand out themes for this symposium, burial practice not only is an important source for the study of religious belief. If properly treated much more can be learnt from it about research areas such as the social context of ancient societies and the human perception of former landscape surroundings. In this paper we will focus especially on these two areas, and in particular on the general position of tombs and cemeteries in the landscape over time, combined with aspects of regional topography and of the social environment. As problems concerning continuity are crucial, our story will deal almost as much with later prehistory as with the Roman world.

Central in our discussion is the question of which considerations played a role in the past in the choice of where to bury the dead and especially whether the presence of (much) older graves on the spot had any significance. In this context, it is essential to drop our modern, rather economic-utilitarian point of view, namely that the distribution and location of graves – as well as of settlements and holy places – in past landscapes were always the result of rational decisions. In accordance with Tilley's (1994) lead on this matter we stress the active role that the symbolic potential of the landscape plays in the relationship of man with his (prehistoric or Roman) environment. The landscape acquires this special cultural dimension through daily use. As a result of different events and activities, places in the landscape, in time, built their own history with related meanings and associations. These meanings, accumulated over a long time, thereupon play a crucial role when one has to decide which spot is suited for burial, the adoration of ancestors, for the living, etc.

Such historic-cultural meanings are then weighed against the physical and symbolic qualities of the landscape. A place which was or is in use as a cemetery will evoke other feelings than a ploughed field or a fancy rock formation, and because of that all these spots have a different potential in the spatial choreography. Tilley remarked with reason that the use and organisation of the landscape by man is not therefore a purely economic phenomenon, but a cultural manifestation, strongly linked with power and the balance of power. It looks as if the landscape is situated at the cross-roads of ecology and ideology.

The adaptation of tribal communities to a well structured Roman form of society, is certainly responsible for a much more rational-economic treatment of the landscape. One only has to think of systems of centuriation, introduced in many provinces to rationalise agriculture, and of their consequences for the location of settlements and cemeteries (Chouquer and Favory 1991). In the less deeply Romanised world of the north-western provinces such fundamental interventions were rather exceptional. From region to region different gradations in the Roman impact on the landscape exist here. But even regions which easily accepted Roman innovations and whose landscapes gradually show marked changes in occupation pattern – mostly due to political and economic reasons – kept much of their funeral habits unchanged. This confirms the persistent and conservative character of the burial tradition. As well as widespread practice of cremation and the ritual acts that accompany it, this is especially valid for the respect for the places of burial. Archaeological research in the north-western provinces confirms that during the Early Roman period graves and cemeteries were firm values in the rural landscape which could not simply be obliterated. This is particularly clear in the lack of disturbances to the cemeteries and by the fact that burial grounds were seldom given new functions (Ferdière 1993). Their position near the edge or completely outside the settlements was accepted by the whole community and no doubt enjoyed widespread recognition. Thanks to markers above ground – whose character often remains obscure to us – but especially because of their particular place in the collective memory, they fulfilled an important role in the cultural landscape of the period.

As these north-western provinces were populated with essentially indigenous communities, one would also expect the *pre-Roman* cemeteries to be treated with some respect. This was certainly the case when grave markers or other recognisable witnesses of the presence of a cemetery (enclosures, gates, monuments, ...) were maintained for some time or resisted surface erosion. As several regions have produced proof for this great respect for ancient burial grounds (Bayard 1993; Cüppers 1993; Galliou 1989; Hessing 1993; Lafon and Adam 1993; Lambot 1993; Roymans 1995 etc.) or the continued use or re-use of old cemeteries, one can of course try to explain the phenomenon.

Why are Roman graves – isolated or not – often found on older prehistoric cemeteries and is there more than a simple topographic relation? In other words is there a kind of real continuity of burial places, not resulting from the mere fact that the chosen grounds are the only ones within the landscape suitable for living and the deposition of the dead? Although we are very well aware that answers to these questions cannot be over simplistic, we distinguish at least five explanations relevant for the Early Roman rural landscape of the regions considered. We will discuss them briefly in random order, without trying to evaluate their relative importance.

1. In principle Roman law ensured that a cemetery was shielded against tomb robbers or desecrators (Cicero, *De Legibus*: II, 22, 55). The presence of a grave on private or public terrain changes the latter into a *locus religiosus* to be held in respect. Although there is some proof for deliberate desecration, it is generally agreed that this law, with a natural fear for the dead and communal respect, certainly protected most tombs. In northern *Gallia* this sacralisation of the cemetery and the related fear for the dead is also indirectly proven by the many coin hoards deposited on burial grounds in times of trouble (e.g. the 3rd century): it was hoped that fear of disturbing the soul of the deceased would ensure enough protection (Galliou 1989: 26).

We have no reason to believe that most traditional cemeteries of later prehistory, which were still in use lost their original role when the Romans incorporated the conquered territories in the new provincial framework and introduced a new judicial structure. Rather it seems likely that these prominent places, especially those with clear markers, retained their natural protection. Of course much depends on the specific character of the above-ground aspect (burial mounds, ditched enclosures, posts...), on the degree of respect for these places and on the stability of the local community. In this perspective it was only very natural to dig new graves in old cemeteries, at least if the landscape and its population were not too much disrupted.

2. Another explanation for the (re)use of older burial grounds is even more pragmatic. Thanks to a better knowledge of the road network we now know that in Roman times graves were often located near roads. Beside offering better accessibility, this also had the advantage that the places where the dead had to be honoured were easier to find. The recovery of an ancestral tomb, one or two generations after the funeral, was probably no sinecure, especially when isolated graves or very small rural cemeteries are involved and when the markers were very transitory. Each distinct element in the landscape, such as a road, but also a particular tree, a small hill or a rock would have been used as fixed point, and this no doubt was also true for (very) old burial grounds with, for example, remnants of grave mounds or ditched enclosures. In Brittany this phenomenon is very well known: many isolated Roman graves were discovered near megalithic monuments or monumental *stelae* of the La Tène period or just dug into older *tumuli* (Galliou 1989: 28). The conscious choice for old burial places is here therefore only made by the descendants (or the deceased) in order to locate the grave easily.

3. The judicial function of graves and especially of some burial monuments as markers of landed property in the Roman Empire cannot be disputed. Several texts of the *agrimensores* leave little room for doubt. A passage in *De sepulcris* (*Gromatici Veteres*: 271–272) clearly stresses the role played by the grave as an emblem to signal ownership (Meffre 1993). Siculus Flaccus (*Gromatici Veteres*: 134–165) reveals in his *De condicionibus agrorum* that graves were often dug near the limits of a domain and not seldom in uncultivated areas or on land unsuitable for agriculture. He does not mention whether ancient burial places were effectively used to demarcate an estate – which would in fact stimulate their reuse as cemeteries – but such an interpretation seems very acceptable.

Above ground elements of tombs are obviously indissoluble parts of land division and use in the Roman agrarian space. This signalling function was apparent for some very visible and very 'Roman' monuments, such as the Treveran funeral pillars (Cüppers 1993) or the Central-Belgian and Rhenish tumuli (Amand 1960; Wigg 1993). The erection of such monumental and often rich tombs could – as at the end of the La Tène period in the Alsace (Lafon and Adam 1993) – be explained as proof for new property divisions. This special form of burial display might also be a reaction and an effort by the local elites to counter immigrants in their pursuit of new land during restructuring of the countryside. If such is the case, a re-use of older cemeteries would certainly be a logical choice. As a result these old burial grounds also became structuring elements in the landscape, marking the limits of rural estates. Their continued use guaranteed the 'eternity' of landed property, for which they functioned as landscape beacons.

In communities who partially or totally owned the land and whose wealth arose from the inherited domain, descendants considered it worthwhile to invest on a long-term basis in a familial or communal cemetery, or to perpetuate existing graveyards. These kinds of groups are probably responsible for the well-organised larger cemeteries, with enclosures and several monuments, found in different regions of the north-western provinces (Philpott and Reece 1993). A well-studied example of these is Wederath-*Belginum* in the Moselle region (Cüppers 1993), where protohistoric grave monuments of the 4th century BC are the base for a continued use of the cemetery into the later Roman period (4th century AD). This cemetery serves as a model for a region with a very stable population and with a continuing pre-Roman tradition, where the occupants of scattered farms make use of one central funerary area. It is not clear whether regions with less stable population structures display the same form of continuity. Recently excavated sites from the Southern Netherlands, such as the well-organised Roman cemetery of Mierlo-Hout, which developed around ditched funerary monuments of the Early Iron Age (Roymans 1995), seem to demonstrate that also in this area protohistoric cemeteries remained beacons within the new judicial context. As in other regions it is absolutely necessary, however, to be able to link such burial places to related contemporary settlements. Only then can archaeology start with a plausible delimitation of ancient territorial units and evaluate the exact juridical function of large communal graveyards (Parker Pearson 1993).

4. In some cases the above ground witnesses of earlier cemeteries and cult places were obviously more than useful landmarks to the later Romanised inhabitants of the area. Their function was commonly known and to be respected. Especially in regions of the Empire where the long-term evolution of the population was less stable, people were confronted in their immediate environment with special places whose original, many centuries old, ritual meaning was lost. Such sacred and often funerary places and remains of old forgotten monuments, were no doubt sometimes linked to magic or dark forces. How else would we explain the hearths and depositions of Roman objects in or at the foot of many (at least two millennia older) monuments in Brittany? Some of these Roman 'intrusions' near megalithic monuments are funerary and often consist of one or two isolated graves. Therefore, one can presume that not solely pragmatic reasons – such as an easy location of the tomb (*cf. supra* 2) – prevailed, when the place for burial was chosen. Rather these practices, fairly well represented all over western and northern Gaul (Van Doorselaer 1967: 178–179), probably betray ritual intentions of magical protection. We think it is unlikely that such magical practices are part of a collective cult for all the deceased (Galliou 1993: 71). We rather interpret them as more isolated phenomena linked to respect and especially fear for the unknown. A direct relation between funerary practices of (much) older periods and those of the Roman period seems unlikely here.

5. Finally the prolonged and deliberate use of ancient cemeteries, on a communal base, can be explained by the cult of ancestors. In that case the burial location first of all has to be seen as a kind of sanctuary. Comparative historical research of religions (Eliade 1959) – especially in the Indo-European world where the ancestral cult has its roots (Hatt 1951) – demonstrated that in all religions the sacred discloses itself in particular places of the landscape. If a certain religious experience – such as a formal funeral – is shared with relations and associates, then the place of this event can become a locus of worship where special sacred forces are thought to be permanently present (Derks 1991; Derks 1996: 15). It grows into a frontier place in the landscape where the sacred and the profane meet (Leach 1976). The physical appearance of this liminal zone is often clearly marked, for instance with an enclosure or a burial mound. This fixes not only the border of both worlds, but also the area for future ritual activity and burial. If a cemetery has formal characteristics, such as a certain order in lay-out, the presence of boundaries and a lasting exclusive use for burial purposes, then this could point at communal descent and identity of the local group. Such cemeteries were the focus of ritual activities, in which communication with the ancestors stood central (Roymans 1995: 6). These activities were probably part of a collective cult for all the deceased of the community. The departed enter the 'club' of ancestors, guarantee tradition and take care of the continuity of the family: they are the fathers and mothers of the living (Galliou 1989: 71). It is believed that the role of such cemeteries in the ancestral cult was closely related to their status as territorial markers, which laid the symbolic claim of the community on the land (*cf. supra* 3). Such graveyards could thus become a core element in the mythical ordering of the landscape, as in many ancient societies, the ancestors and not the living were regarded as its owners (Roymans 1995: 7).

In Roman Italy ancestral cult was strongly formalised in official festivals, the so-called *Parentalia* (Ovid, *Fasti*: 2–533–70), while the worship of *lares* and *manes* permeated domestic life. From about 100 BC onwards, the funerary rituals increasingly show different forms and levels of public display, later reinforced by the imperial family cult, after the erection of the mausoleum of Augustus (Morris 1992; Toynbee 1971; Zanker 1988). Like processing with or privately displaying ancestral masks, many of these rituals tend to divide rather than unite the community (Morris 1991: 159). Like some of the legal texts, these activities confirm the link between death rituals and the linear transfer of property.

In the north-western provinces we recognise several reflections of these ancestral cult practices. Iconography and some textual information, as well as archaeology, bear witness to funerary family- or heroic cults. Some of the best known archaeological indications come from the sites of Avenches 'en Chaplix' (Castella 1993) and Newel (Cüppers and Neysens 1971), where we see associations of formal cemeteries with a *fanum*. Although such sites have been considered as founder burials, sometimes approximating in form to a *heroon* and relating to Greco-

Roman processes of dynastic succession (Pearce: this volume), we need not search for a direct influence or impulse from the South. In most cases indigenous traditions are responsible for lasting respect for the (important) tombs, which sometimes grow into larger communal cemeteries or retain a special place in the landscape. In both ways the community is constantly confronted with the image of society that these particular dead may have portrayed. A typical example is the association of special tombs with the entrances or boundaries of certain villas in Picardy (Bayard 1993). These tombs, probably those of the founders of the villa-complexes, long remained integral to their surroundings and assumed an important place in the local mythical landscape. As we see from research in northern Champagne (Lambot 1993), such a close relation between well-structured farms ('fermes indigènes') and groups of (aristocratic?) monumental graves can go back to the La Tène II-period.

It is clear from different regions, therefore, that expressions of ancestral cult in provincial Roman contexts have much deeper roots than the period of the earliest Romanisation. We have already considered the example of Wederath-Belginum and the Treveri (Cüppers 1993), where a continuity of almost eight centuries – starting from Iron Age round barrows – is observed. On the sandy soil of the southern Netherlands a comparable example of continuity exists (*cf. supra* 3). This region has a tradition of cemeteries with circular or rectangular grave enclosures in the Roman period, no doubt going back to the enclosed cemeteries of the Late Iron Age, also seen in other 'Celtic' areas, northern France, the Rhine and Moselle region and even eastern Yorkshire (Hessing 1993). From his study of these problems of cemetery continuity Roymans (1995) concludes that this region shows an important continuity of indigenous tribal ideologies and attitudes towards older burial grounds in the landscape – at least half of the now known rural Roman cemeteries lie on or near an older urnfield of the Late Bronze-Early Iron Age. None of the inventorized urnfields of the period considered (1100–450 BC) made way for Roman settlement or ploughing. These prehistoric cemeteries seem to be fully incorporated into the indigenous-Roman cultural landscape which, according to Roymans is to be explained by the persistence of ancestral cult and a positive appraisal of the landscape by the indigenous-Roman inhabitants, actively reworking or invoking ancient values.

Sandy Flanders as a test region

To test some of these theoretical statements we will focus on one particular region and put an archaeological research strategy into operation. To do this we will first briefly present this testing area, report the current state of fieldwork and sketch the outlines of what is known about later prehistoric and early Roman occupation and burial history. The chronological framework will be the Bronze

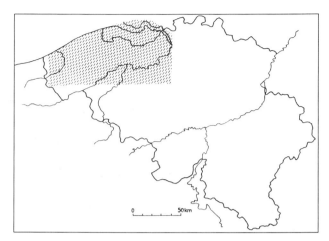

Fig. 15.1 *Location of the study area (within present day Belgium).*

and Iron Ages and the Early Roman period, i.e. between ca. 1800 BC and AD 200. Restricted space prevents us from exploring later Roman developments. This would involve study of the complex and still quite ill-understood Germanisation of north-west Gaulish society, in our region a process which sets in shortly after the raids of the Germanic *Chauci* around AD 170. The impact of this and other processes, such as Christianisation, on later Roman burial practices is a subject for future research.

The region of sandy Flanders is dominated by a large coversand plateau of some 4,000 km² located in north-western Belgium (Fig. 15.1). It stretches between the coastal plain and the clay-rich polder landscape to the west and north, the broad valley of the river Scheldt to the east and the central Belgian loam or loess area to the south. Along its eastern and southern fringes it incorporates areas (circa 1,000 km²) dominated by sandy loam soils, which we will not omit from this study as they are well integrated in the Pleistocene sand landscape (Fig. 15.2). Although the broad river plains of Lys, Durme and Scheldt, each fed by several streams and brooks, traverse this generally flat to slightly undulating landscape, the region is remarkably homogenous. The sandy soils, known for their relatively poor agricultural value, are the cohesive elements that structured and conditioned the cultural history of this area. In the protohistoric past, these landscape features always led to a system of mixed farming. The best arable land was especially concentrated on the slightly higher sandy ridges and on the more loamy soils, while the many badly drained soils and valleys attracted intensive animal husbandry. These general features of rural land use still dominate the study unit today, although the urbanisation of the modern countryside continues, especially near the major cities in the area, Ghent, Bruges, Courtrai and Sint-Niklaas.

Until the late fifties sandy Flanders was almost an archaeological *terra incognita*. After the more systematic but still occasional fieldwork of the sixties and seventies,

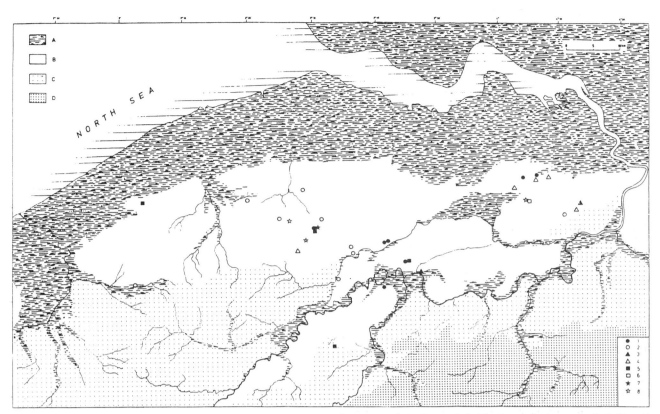

Fig. 15.2 *Dispersion of prehistoric burial sites in sandy Flanders west of the River Scheldt. Legend: **A.** coastal plain and polders, **B.** sand region, **C.** sandloam region, **D.** loam region. **1.** Bronze Age barrows related to Roman graves, **2.** Bronze Age barrows not related to Roman graves, **3.** Late Bronze/Early Iron Age urnfields related to Roman graves, **4.** Late Bronze/ Early Iron Age urnfields not related to Roman graves, **5.** Late Iron Age burials related to Roman graves, **6.** Late Iron Age burials not related to Roman graves, **7.** Iron Age cult-places related to Roman graves, **8.** Iron Age cult-places not related to Roman graves.*

a period of much more intensified and less subjective archaeological surveys began. The boom in discoveries during the past fifteen years or so is the result of several long term projects initiated by the archaeological department of Ghent University.

The first of these projects, initiated in 1979, is the *Archeologische Inventaris Vlaanderen* (De Mulder 1994a; Vermeulen 1983; Vermeulen 1986). It is principally based on active field survey, using the methods of the German 'Landesaufnahme', i.e. a combination of fieldwalking with the use of a range of other 'fast' prospection techniques – such as the investigation of vertical aerial photographs, old maps, written documents, and archaeological collections. In this attempt to inventorize the archaeological potential of rural Flanders as completely and accurately as possible, up till now some 80 municipalities are fully investigated. Of these some 40 lie partly or completely in our sandy region.

This kind of intensive field survey contrasts with earlier surveys because research is now directed towards testing the actual distribution of past settlement as objectively as possible and thereby revealing the limitations of current knowledge. For the first time one could – keeping in mind

several interpretative pitfalls – try to reconstruct a more 'total' image of earlier occupation of the landscape, closer to the real density of ancient habitation. On the sandy soils of Flanders, this work produced a much denser scatter of Roman period sites (e.g. some 60 new settlements), but the Bronze and Iron Ages – both clearly less visible on surface level – were still difficult to grasp. This phenomenon was further reinforced by the results of two intensive Roman period survey projects in specific micro-regions – around Oudenburg (Hollevoet 1992) and between Lys and Scheldt (Vermeulen 1992; Vermeulen 1995) – which also involved several excavations on selected or endangered sites.

A second project, developed by the Ghent team since the mid-eighties, involves a very thorough survey of the whole region considered using oblique aerial photography. It is the first time that this kind of remote sensing has been executed on a systematic basis in such a large area in Belgium and although the rural landscape consists of small parcels here and agricultural land use is extremely varied, the results so far are impressive (Ampe *et al.* 1996: 45–58; Bourgeois and Semey 1991). The aerial photographs, now more than 50,000, containing several thousands of sites and ancient landscape features, have extended the archaeological database of the region in an almost 'alarming' way. The Bronze Age especially has produced the most spectacular results, thanks to its characteristic morphology of circular ditches surrounding former burial mounds (Ampe *et al.* 1996: 58–84). The settlements of that era, as well as occupation remains of the Iron Age and the Roman period, were initially much less easy to trace from the air. An intensification of flights since the late eighties, combined with growing experience with the landscape, has, however, produced results for these periods too. Ancient roads, field-systems, cemeteries, enclosed cult-places and settlements, all obviously of pre-medieval date, are some of the main features now registered on a regular basis. Precisely the discovery and interpretation of such phenomena offer an important surplus value to systematic research into the periods concerned here. As total coverage of the region is pursued, we can state that this prospection technique is used here in a very objective way. It is also Important that this aerial survey has stimulated much excavation work, especially on sites endangered by destruction, but also on selected features, such as some of the enclosed protohistoric burial

places (Ampe *et al.* 1996; Bourgeois and Semey 1991). Although many of these excavations remain too small-scale for a more total image of past settlement history – a typical 'Belgian archaeology' problem linked with chronic lack of funding – this fieldwork has for the first time produced the minimum of results necessary for tackling the question of burial-continuity.

Bronze and Iron Age burial cultures

Our knowledge of Bronze and Iron Age burial cultures in the western part of Belgium is of rather recent date. Papers by De Laet (1954; 1961) on the Hilversum-phenomenon mentioned several Early and/or Middle Bronze Age burials in the southern part of Flanders. Studies by the University of Ghent in the '50s and '60s on the so-called Urnfield-culture (De Laet *et al.* 1958; Desittere 1968; Desittere 1974; Desittere 1976) revealed new cemeteries dating from the Late Bronze Age up to the Early Iron Age. Burials of later periods remained almost unknown. At the end of the 70s the situation changed radically, especially due to aerial photography carried out by Jacques Semey and Ghent University (Ampe *et al.* 1996a;

Table 15.1 *Excavated protohistoric burials sites in Sandy Flanders and their connection with Roman cemeteries (see also table 15.2).*

ID: see legend	Site	Date	large scale info.	Roman burial or cemetery	Roman settlement
1	Sint-Denijs-Westrem	E+MBA	-	+	+
1+5	Gent – Hoge Weg	E+MBA / LIA	+	+ (1 with square enclosure, LIA or ROM)	-
1	Evergem – Ralingen	E+MBA	-	+	-
1	Evergem – Molenhoek	E+MBA	-	+	-
2	Oostwinkel – Veld	E+MBA	-	-	-
2	Lovendegem – Brouwerijstraat	E+MBA	-	-	+ (Roman road)
2	Lovendegem – Vellare	E+MBA	-	-	-
1	Oedelem - Drie Koningen	E+MBA	-	-	-
1+5+7	Ursel – Rozestraat	E+MBA / LIA	+	+ (69, LIA + Early ROM)	-
1	Sint-Gillis-Waas Reepstraat	E+MBA	+	+	+ (road/ rural settlement)
1	Kemzeke – Verkeerswisselaar	E+MBA	+	+	+ (buildings)
2	Vosselare – Kouter	E+MBA	-	-	-
2	Sint-Niklaas Europark Zuid	E+MBA	+	-	+
2	Knesselare – Flabbaert	E+MBA	+	-	+ (road/ rural settlement)
2	Maldegem – Vliegplein	E+MBA	+	-	-
4	Aalter – Oostergem	LBA	+	-	-
3	Destelbergen – Eenbeekeinde	LBA	-	+	+ (buildings etc.)
4	Sint-Gillis-Waas Ripstraat	LBA	+	-	-
4	Sint-Gillis-Waas Loeverstraat	LBA	-	-	-
3	Temse – Veldmolenwijk	LBA	+	+	-
4	Temse – Velle	LBA	+	-	+ (pits)
4	Stekene	LBA	-	-	-
6+8	Kemzeke – Kwakkel	LIA	+	-	-
5	Huise – Lozerbos	LIA	+	+	+
8	Aalter – Woestyne	LIA	+	-	+ (road)
8	Knesselare	LIA	+	-	-

Vanmoerkerke, Semey and Bourgeois 1990). In less than 15 years almost 1,000 circular ditched structures – mostly remnants of Early and/or Middle Bronze Age burial mounds – were discovered. These discoveries completely changed our interpretation of human presence in the Bronze Age. From 1985 onwards, several (rescue) excavations yielded new data about the cemeteries and funeral practices of later periods and increased our knowledge of the settlement systems and patterns of all periods of the Bronze and Iron ages (Bourgeois 1989; Bourgeois and Verlaeckt in press; Verlaeckt (ed.) 1996). It is probably too early to think that our information about burial cultures is complete and comprehensive (De Mulder 1994b), but the time has come to make some basic statements.

The period of the last two millennia BC can be subdivided into three main phases: the (Early and) Middle Bronze Age, up to about 1100 BC, the Late Bronze Age and the Early Iron Age, from 1100 to 450 BC, and finally the Late Iron Age, from 450 BC to the Roman invasion. All three periods show clearly different burial practices and settlement patterns (Fig. 15.2 and Table 15.1).

The (Early and) Middle Bronze Age is characterised by a landscape of burial mounds. Most of these – with the exception of some mounds in the Flemish Ardennes area (De Laet 1982: 440–456) – were discovered by aerial prospection in sandy Flanders. In 1992–1994, the Research Council of the University of Ghent supported an inventory of this type of structure and during the late eighties and early nineties several excavations were carried out (Ampe *et al.* 1996b). Some 914 of these monuments have been detected and registered, but every year new circles appear. The geographical setting of the majority of these monuments is clearly connected with the Pleistocene sands, although some of them are discovered on loamy-sandy and even loamy soils, while a few barrows lie in the Polder area of Zeeuws-Vlaanderen (the Netherlands). We realise that this distribution pattern is (partly?) due to the prospection technique used, but some features, such as the large concentration of circles around the so-called 'cuesta' of Maldegem-Zomergem, are too obvious and cannot be underestimated. It is clear that the population generally chose to install and erect its monuments on sandy ridges, places where they were easily visible, although we may note a few exceptions, such as some barrows located on low-lying sandy soils near the confluence of the rivers Scheldt and Lys.

When one tries to group the Bronze Age barrows into cemeteries – a risky business, because of the technical limitations of the survey method – it seems that still 65% of all circles appear to be isolated. The other circles group in graveyards of two to five barrows (almost 80%); larger cemeteries can group more than ten barrows. They are organised in rows or clusters, according to soil-context and (probably) landscape features, although it still is a risky activity to define a 'necropolis'. If we accept this definition of cemeteries, the clustering of these in the

area east of Bruges, along a 25m-high cuesta, is remarkable. In this area, every one or two kilometres is marked by such a cluster of mounds.

Although our information is still rather scarce, it is probable that the Early and Middle Bronze Age occupation is especially situated on exhausted, podzolised sandy soils. Excavations clearly show that in many cases the barrows are built in areas where podzolisation had already been going on for a long time. Palynological studies (Bourgeois 1995) show that the landscapes around the barrows are in most cases characterised by heath, sometimes by poor grasslands.

At about 1100 BC the situation changes totally. In the western part of Belgium, some 20 cemeteries of the Late Bronze Age and the Early Iron Age are recorded (Bourgeois 1989; De Laet *et al.* 1986). Typical is their large number of urned graves, from 10/20 up to more than one hundred in some cases. All cemeteries seem to have been occupied for a long period, over several generations, so they need not be proof for the existence of large central settlements. Most of them continue to be used into the Early Iron Age (Ha C, sometimes Ha D). Information on possible funeral monuments is problematic. Almost all cemeteries were discovered in the 19th century or in the early '50s of this century during sand exploitation. In most cases there was no opportunity to excavate in normal conditions. However, at some cemeteries investigated more recently, such as Destelbergen, funeral monuments were indeed present. But the two excavated circular monuments here are smaller than in the previous period (no more than about 10 m diameter) and other types of monuments appear: Late Bronze Age oval ditched monuments of the 'langbed'-type (known also from aerial prospections) and square ditched monuments less than 10m wide, situated in the Early Iron Age part of this cemetery (*cf. infra*).

The location of these burial places is interesting: in most cases, they are situated close to the valley of the Scheldt or other rivers, the only real exception being the finds in Aalter, Velzeke and especially in the 'Land van Waas', west of Antwerp. As already mentioned, most of these urnfields were still in use during the Early Iron Age, but they do not continue into the Late Iron Age. Here again, it is possible to see a clear break in occupation patterns and burial practices.

Only three cemeteries of the Late Iron Age are well recorded. The first of 13 cremation burials was discovered in 1988 during the excavation of a rectangular enclosure in Kemzeke (Bourgeois 1991). They are very poor and probably related to a square funeral monument. The scarce artefacts date this cemetery to the Early La Tène-period. Another cremation cemetery of 69 graves, in Ursel, was discovered in the late '80s during excavation of a Bronze Age barrow and Late Iron Age rectangular enclosure (Bourgeois 1989). All are rather poor, but characterised by the deposition of some metal artefacts, mostly iron copies of Nauheim-fibulae. This cemetery was in use from the 1st century BC until at least the 1st century AD, when more typically Roman practices and objects appear (*cf. infra*). At that moment, another – typical Roman – cemetery was installed several hundreds of metres north-east of the first site. Very recently a third cemetery of the Late Iron Age was discovered in Knesselare (Vermeulen and Hageman 1997). Four simple cremation burials were surrounded by a rectangular ditched monument, with posts at each corner. The presence of other contemporary post-holes in the immediate vicinity, of two possible burials dug into the upper layers of the ditch and of an Early Roman (1st century AD) deposit near the monument, suggest some prolonged ritual activity connected with this small cemetery.

It is still too early to confirm the presence of other funeral monuments in the Late Iron Age landscape of sandy Flanders. The excavation of a Bronze Age barrow at Gent-Hogeweg (Vanmoerkerke 1985) produced a small rectangular grave enclosure between the inner and outer circular ditches, but the minute finds cannot help us decide whether a date in the Late Iron Age or the Roman period should be put forward. Several aerial photographs in the region suggest that many other rectangular funerary monuments existed, but excavations are awaited to date and interpret them.

Another typical phenomenon of this period is the appearance of large rectangular ditched enclosures, constructed neither as burial monuments nor dwellings (Bourgeois and Semey 1991). These large uninterrupted structures (of sides between 20 to 50 m) probably played a temporary religious role. This is suggested by their particular history – their ditches were filled only a few days after the construction – and by some special archaeological finds, such as pottery deposits (cf. Aalter). They could have fulfilled a regional role as cult-places of larger social units.

The pattern of Early Roman occupation

In the first two centuries of our era sandy Flanders could be characterised as a poorly Romanised rural region. Its situation too far from the Rhine *limes* and in the northern part of the only slightly urbanised *Civitas Menapiorum* is responsible for a very limited Roman military engagement in the area (Vermeulen 1996b). Since it had no role to play in the organisation of Augustan offensives and as the coastal defence line was only fully developed here after the *Chauci* raids, this area probably knew no large military settlements before the last third of the second century (Thoen and Vermeulen 1997).

However there are enough archaeological indications for an increase in population in most parts of the area from the beginning of our era onwards. This is especially obvious by the time of Claudius' reign, when archaeological visibility of the settlements increases substantially due to the spread of Roman imports and Gallo-Belgic goods. By the end of the first century the concentration of habitation in suitable landscapes, such as near the rivers (e.g. Lys and Scheldt), or near clays exploitable for pottery industries (e.g. the cuesta in the north-eastern 'Land van Waas'), are comparable to the dense occupation of the fertile soils of central Belgium and northern France. In some areas this distribution obviously shows some continuity with the pre-Roman situation, although concentrations of rural sites near central places (e.g. Courtrai, Kruishoutem) and later near military structures (e.g. Oudenburg, Bruges) and probably also roads, indicate some reorganisation under Roman rule. On the other hand it seems that there are also large areas with a much lower habitation density, especially those with land less suited to arable, which were probably used as woodland and for extensive pasture. Therefore the rather low site density of a maximum of one site per three km² calculated for the micro-region between Lys and Scheldt during the 2nd century (Vermeulen 1992: 234–237) can probably be extrapolated to most parts of sandy Flanders.

Another marked contrast with the fertile central Belgian loam area, bordering to the south, is the almost complete lack in Roman Sandy Flanders of well-organised small towns and of villas. The role of the small towns is partly taken over by several evenly spread river- or roadside habitation centres, such as Courtrai, Harelbeke, Waasmunster and Kruishoutem. These appear to be rather humble rural centres that also combine some commercial, semi-industrial and religious functions. From their beginnings in the mid-first century or earlier they develop into *foci* for the surrounding countryside, without however receiving the status and appearance of their well-known central-Belgian counterparts, known as *vici*, along the Boulogne-Köln axis (e.g. Liberchies, Braives). According to the low degree of Romanisation, observed from building-construction, pottery evidence and spatial organisation, these centres were essentially inhabited by a native population with strong rural ties. This is also visible in the cemeteries, where the rite of un-urned cremation burial, with deposition of the cremated remains and some burnt personal items in a simple pit, is predominant. Still we note that some burials of the partly excavated cemeteries of these centres show signs of a more pronounced Romanisation. The first century cemetery of Kortrijk-Molenstraat (Leva and Coene 1969), for instance, even displays a majority of urned cremations. In Waasmunster (Van Hove 1996) several elements, such as at least two stone monuments, a ditched enclosure and a *bustum* grave, seem to indicate southern influences, while in Oudenburg (Hollevoet 1993), where recently more than 500 cremation burials were excavated, two square ditched enclosures surround graves with remarkable Mediterranean imports.

Of specific relevance to us here is the situation in rural context outside these centres. As in the Kempen, another major sandy region situated east of ours (Slofstra 1991), fully developed Gallo-Roman villa-estates seem to remain absent. Only in the adjoining sandy loam areas, on the southern fringes of the sand plateau, is their presence really attested (Rogge, Thoen and Vermeulen 1990).

Instead the settlement pattern was completely dominated by small native-style settlements. Many of these started as isolated farms, but developed from Flavian times onwards into what can be called 'habitats rapprochés' (Meffre 1993: 379). These are loose, more or less dispersed groupings of three to seven farmhouses – 'rural hamlets' – established in crucial zones of the exploitable agrarian territory. Certain excavated sites, such as the riverside settlements of Eke, Sint-Martens-Latem and Sint-Denijs-Westrem (Vermeulen 1992), seem to indicate a very low level of hierarchy between the individual units. Not much differentiation in their receptivity of Roman innovations and modes can be deduced from their characteristic indigenous-Roman houses and other structures (such as enclosures, wells, silos), nor from the associated artefacts and graves (*cf. infra*). Some small-scale discoveries on sites as Nevele, Aalter, Belsele and Merendree, seem to demonstrate, however, that more Romanised larger units – perhaps of the kind of proto-villas recognised in the Kempen (Slofstra 1991) – might be part of this system in the course of the second century. This interesting hypothesis should, however, first be tested by excavations on a reasonable scale.

Anyhow, the grouping of loosely connected settlements in favoured rural zones seems typical for this landscape during the Principate. This implies that the agrarian space around and between these settlements had a well struc-tured morphology. The presence of infields, axes for circulation, water sources and ponds, enclosures and ditches used for drainage and land division, is obvious on aerial photographs and has been confirmed here and there by fieldwork. Of course burials and cemeteries are part of this immediate environment of the settlements. In the region studied and of the period considered nearly 50 rural cemeteries were identified (Fig. 15.3 and Table 15.2). Although all burials were found outside the inhabited space, they were often situated only some tens of metres from the nearest house compound, sometimes at a greater distance, but presumably never more than 350–400m away from the settlement area. Their location seems generally to depend more upon the choice of settlement location than upon environmental factors.

Small cemeteries of between 5 and 40 cremation graves seem to have been predominant. The minimum and maximum numbers of graves are difficult to grasp, as circumstances of discovery were seldom ideal and some burials were certainly lost or remain to be uncovered. These reasons may explain why in some instances very isolated burials were found, although large scale excavations in Sint-Denijs-Westrem (Vermeulen 1993) and on prehistoric cemeteries (*cf. infra*) have demonstrated that not all Roman burials were grouped. An isolated position further from the living area, near a trackway or other visible landscape marker, was clearly no exception. Larger

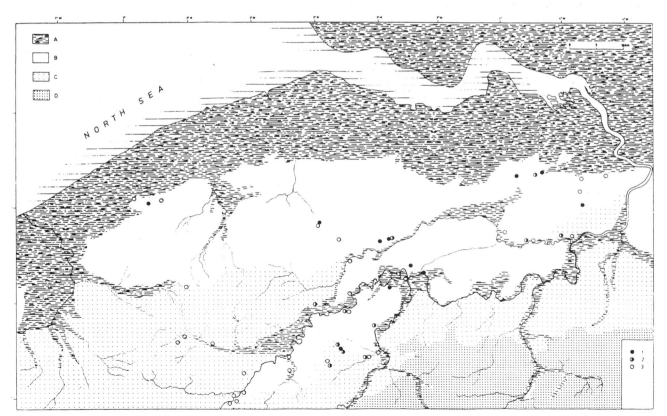

Fig. 15.3 *Dispersion of Roman cemeteries in sandy Flanders west of the River Scheldt. Legend: A. coastal plain and polders, B. sand region, C. sandloam region, D. loam region. 1. Roman cemetery with nearby prehistoric burials, 2. Roman cemetery with nearby prehistoric settlement, 3. Roman cemetery without apparent prehistoric traces.*

Table 15.2 Roman cemeteries with graves found in situ and their connection with Early (E), Middle (M) or Late (L) Bronze Age (BA) and Iron Age (IA) burials and settlements in Sandy Flanders.

ID	Site	Number of Roman graves	Protohistoric burials	Protohistoric settlement
1	Zomergem-Ro	1	-	-
2	Ursel-Rozestraat	3	circle E+MBA, monument EIA, cemetery LIA	-
3	Ursel-Konijntje	13	circles E+MBA	-
4	Merendree-Kasteel ter Wallen	1	-	-
5	Sint-Martens-Leerne Damstraat	15	-	-
6	Evergem-Molenhoek (Belzele)	1	-	IA
7	Evergem-Ralingen	2	circles E+MBA	IA
8	Zeveren-Blekerij	1	-	LIA
9	Gent-Pekelharing	1	-	-
10	Gent-Kathedraal	1	-	-
11	Destelbergen-Eenbeekeinde	ca. 200	urnfield LBA/EIA	-
12	Evergem-Spoorwegstraat	1	-	LIA
13	Melsele-Den Es	(?)	-	-
14	Nieuwkerken-Cauwerwijk	1 (?)	-	-
15	Vrasene-Schuilhoek	1	-	-
16	Waasmunster-Pontrave	ca. 400	-	-
17	Waasmunster-Eekhout	4	-	LIA
18	Temse-Veldmolenwijk	ca. 10	urnfield LBA/EIA	-
19	Elversele Lage Heirweg	17	-	-
20	Tielrode-Nieuw Gelaag	(?)	-	-
21	Lokeren-Kriktestraat	1	-	-
22	Kemzeke Verkeerswisselaar	2	circle E+MBA	IA
23	Sint-Gillis-Waas Reepstraat	8	circle E+MBA	E+LIA
24	Sint-Gillis-Waas 't Hol	1	-	LIA
25	Astene-Beekstraat	2	-	-
26	Astene-Steenweg	2	-	LIA
27	Eke-Molen	6	-	LBA/EIA
28	Asper-Jolleveld	8	-	-
29	Huise-'t Peerdeken	3	-	LIA
30	Huise-Lozerbos	1	graves LIA	LIA
31	Huise-Lozer Zuid	39	-	LIA
32	Huise-Bekestraat	5	-	-
33	Kruishoutem-Wijkhuis	1	-	E+LIA
34	Kruishoutem-Kerkakkers	ca. 20	-	-
35	Kruishoutem-Kapellekouter	6	-	LIA
36	Waregem-Ringlaan	min. 1	-	-
37	Sint-Denijs-Westrem Vliegveld	140	circle E+MBA	LBA, EIA, LIA
38	Sint-Eloois-Vijve	1	-	-
39	Kortrijk-Molenstraat	ca. 110	-	-
40	Hulste-Kuurnestraat	10	-	-
41	Emelgem	ca. 70	-	-
42	Roeselare-Haven	4	-	-
43	Roksem-Hoge Dijken	1	grave LIA	-
44	Oudenburg	ca. 500	-	-
45	Jabbeke-Klein Strand	1 (?)	-	-
46	Harelbeke-Zandberg	2	-	-
47	Kortrijk-Klackaertsbeek	1	-	-
48	Roeselare-Geldberg	1	-	-
49	Lichtervelde-Vrijgeweid	1	-	-
50	Gent-Hogeweg	1	E+MBA, LIA	EIA

groupings of more than 100 graves, the result of a common and prolonged use of the cemetery grounds by different families of one (big) hamlet, were also identified. In Sint-Denijs-Westrem (Vermeulen 1993) and on the semi-rural site of Destelbergen-Eenbeekeinde (Van Doorselaer and Thoen 1969) such cemeteries were located immediately outside the build up area (*cf. infra*).

Even more than on the burial grounds of the rural

centres described above, these smaller rural cemeteries are dominated by, or often consist exclusively of, an indigenous pre-Roman type of cremation burial (Van Doorselaer 1969, Van Doorselaer and Rogge 1985). This typical grave is un-urned and the cremated remains, together with remnants of the pyre, nails and some burnt personal items, are simply deposited in a rectangular pit. Interestingly this is often inhumation-sized. Intact grave goods, normally placed in a niche beside the pit, are rare (Vermeulen 1985). In most cases the grave objects are restricted to a few pieces of simple regional pottery and/ or one or two personal items such as brooches. Some burials, however, especially in the better off sandy loam zones, contain finer ceramic imports and glass (Vermeulen 1992: 231–232). The deposition of goods typical of a more Romanised rite, e.g. coins, lamps and *unguentaria*, is very exceptional. So is the discovery of a Flavian burial in Temse, containing a *gladius* and *umbo* (Thoen 1989: 112). Other external influences, such as the occurrence of particular grave monuments or other non-perishable grave markers, have not been observed. Only one or two examples are known of a small rectangular ditch, enclosing a simple grave (Ursel-Konijntje, Gent-Hogeweg?; *cf. supra*).

It seems clear that throughout the first two centuries most of these rural cemeteries are in perfect accordance with the development of the settlements. Both present the picture of a predominant indigenous population which was slow and restricted in assimilating Roman-style attitudes and displayed a certain continuity in life-style and ideology. While the rural settlements seldom revealed hard proof for an exact topographic continuity with the last phase of the La Tène period, it is now our task to investigate a possible stronger tie between the burial places of both periods. The weak continuity of habitation areas is easy to explain. First there is the demographic growth from the pacified and well organised Claudian era onwards, which demonstrably resulted in an important increase in new settlements (Vermeulen 1992: 164–165). Secondly we think that especially the first century (or pre-Flavian) settlement system and agrarian use of the land was still quite similar to the late Iron Age pattern of 'Wandersiedlungen'. This pattern, typical for less fertile sandy regions where more primitive agriculture cannot prevent the rapid exhaustion of the soil, implied a movement of settlement area every few generations. Although there is no final proof for such a pattern in the La Tène period in sandy Flanders, some indications point in that direction (De Laet 1982: 661, Vermeulen 1992: 150). If correct, it would help to explain why early Roman settlements are seldom located precisely on top of the remains of late La Tène habitations.

For the cemeteries things may have been different. The same demographic argument surely implies that new cemeteries were necessary and that the number of Roman burial places will be much higher than in the later Iron Age. However, the second (agricultural) argument seems less relevant. Indeed, the regular movement of a settlement to a new place need not necessarily have been very far, so that the same cemetery could have been in use for a longer time. And, of course, burial grounds – as demonstrated above – had a stronger ideological significance for the community, which can easily explain their more persistent use. We are thus encouraged to look into this matter further by comparing the locations of pre-Roman and Roman cemeteries in the region, in particular in relation to some well-documented sites.

Testing continuity in cemetery topography: three case-studies in sandy Flanders

Although large scale excavations are still exceptional in Flemish archaeology, a handful of recently excavated examples can be put forward to test problems of cemetery continuity. From our region of sandy Flanders we present three cases. They are very different and therefore, help us to demonstrate that there is much variation in the way ancient cemeteries were used in Roman times. All three lie in the province of East Flanders and were excavated by Ghent University.

1. Sint-Gillis-Waas

Since 1989 a site located at Sint-Gillis-Waas ('Reepstraat', 'Kluizenmolen') has been excavated almost uninterruptedly in close collaboration with the archaeological service of the 'Land van Waas' (Bourgeois 1991b; Van Doorselaer and Bourgeois 1996). The circumstances of this rescue excavation are far from ideal, but the excavated surface (today more than five hectares) is large enough to try out some of the questions put forward in this paper (Fig. 15.4).

The oldest occupation is attested by two round barrows of the Early/Middle Bronze Age. Only one of them was completely investigated. It was surrounded by a ditch of 20 m diameter, containing some fragments of Hilversum-pottery. Radiocarbon analyses suggest a date around 1735–1464 BC (1 sigma). Interestingly, the barrow was, at a later date, marked by a surrounding circle of widely spaced posts. During the Early Iron Age (6th century BC?), an area directly north and west of the grave mound was chosen for settlement. Several rectangular wooden houses and smaller buildings were erected within an orthogonal system of ditched compounds of 15 to 30m wide. It is remarkable that this settlement did not overlap the earlier burial mound, but was located near the edge of it. The precise character of the settlement – a small isolated farm or a more nucleated hamlet? – as well as its duration of occupation, are still unclear. A complete lack of 5th century Marne-pottery may be significant, but it is possible that 5th century contexts are to be found in the surroundings.

The site was again inhabited and used for burial purposes in full Roman period. A few metres from the barrow three Early Roman cremation graves were found, each in a more or less isolated position. Some hundred metres north-east of that same Bronze Age monument the excavators discovered parts of a Roman settlement (1st– 3rd century). Two or three well-structured compounds, surrounded by ditches and situated along an earthen road, have been cleared. Nearby this settlement another five Roman burials were found recently. This excavation

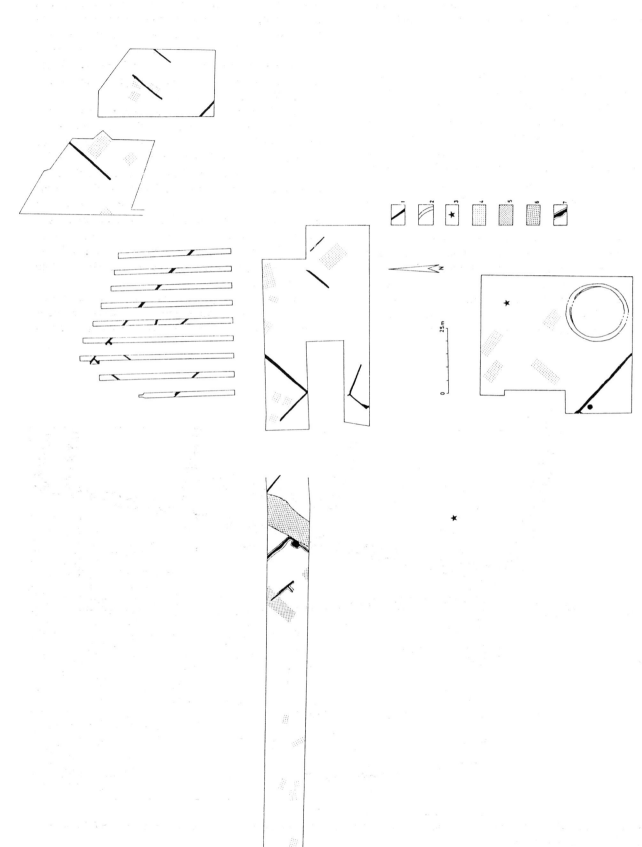

Fig. 15.4 *The site of Sint-Gillis-Waas/Kluizenmolen. Legend: 1. Protohistoric ditches, 2. Ditch enclosure of Bronze Age burial, 3. Roman burial, 4. Protohistoric buildings (Late Bronze/Early Iron Age), 5. Roman buildings, 6. Roman road, 7. Roman ditches. On-going excavations on this site have already led to the discovery of 4 new graves.*

therefore seems to prove that a monumental Bronze Age tomb played a certain role in the following millennia. It probably acted as a landmark for later communities and maybe it even attracted subsequent settlement and burial.

2. Ursel

The site of Ursel-Rozestraat was discovered in the mid-eighties thanks to aerial photography. Traces visible from the air were a circular structure and several rectangular monuments. Between 1986 and 1989 excavations were carried out in and around these features (Bourgeois *et al.* 1989). The circular structure was identified as a ditched enclosure around a barrow with a complex and long history. Different phases have to be distinguished, starting at the beginning of the Bronze Age until the coming of the Romans (Fig. 15.5):

– phase 1: the original monument comprised two concentric ditches (respective diameters: 7.5m and 17m), the inner circle being filled in when the barrow was constructed. The central grave was completely eroded, but remnants of a Hilversum-urn were found in the filling of the ditch. Several charcoal-datings suggest that this monument was erected near the

beginning of the second millennium, around 2109–1931 cal BC (1 sigma).

– phase 2: after steadily silting up, the outer ditch was re-dug, but, as a result of the dominant western winds the barrow mound had slightly moved, thus moving the new ditch a little towards the east. A few potsherds found in the fill of the ditch can be dated to the Early Iron Age. Radiocarbon dates suggest the period around 775–539 cal BC (1 sigma).

– phase 3 A: in the course of the Late Iron Age, when the outer ditch was completely filled, the mound was surrounded by a narrow square ditch, as if to close or isolate the prehistoric monument. The lay-out of this square ditch, precisely above the outer ditch of the barrow, proves that the mound was still visible at the time. This square is part of a larger complex of enclosures, which cannot be fully interpreted as it extends outside the excavated area. Because of a lack of datable artefacts, this monument can only be situated stratigraphically between the Early Iron Age and the Roman period.

– phase 3 B: also in the course of the Late Iron Age, a large rectangular monument (49′ 16m) was constructed north of the round barrow. Two other ditched

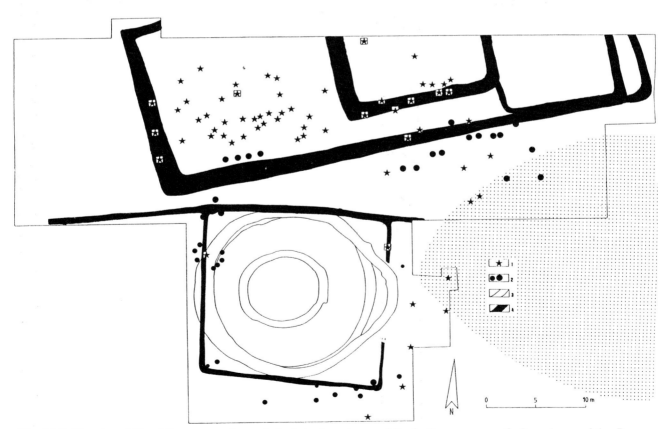

Fig. 15.5 *The site of Ursel-Rozestraat. Legend: 1. Late Iron Age and Early Roman grave, 2. Iron Age and /or Roman posthole, 3. Bronze Age ditch, 4. Iron Age ditch.*

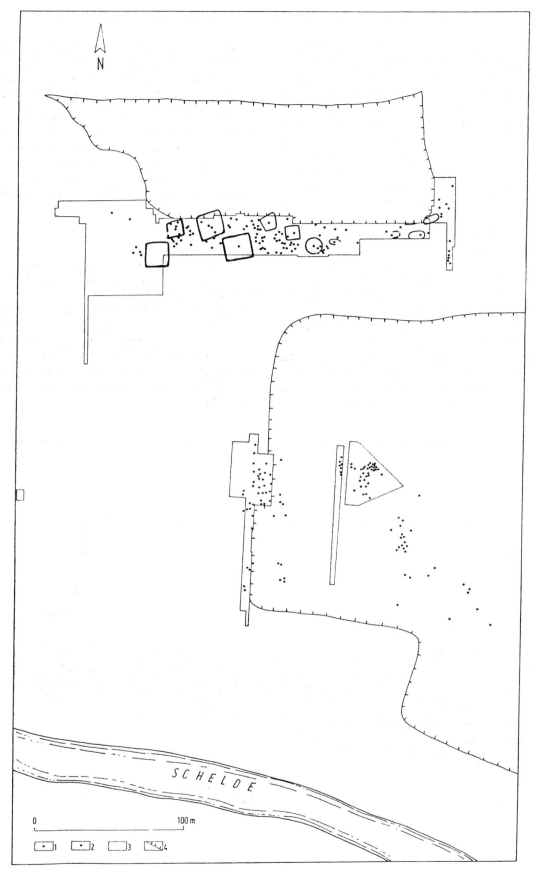

Fig. 15.6 *General location of the Roman period cemetery (near the Scheldt) and Hallstatt-urnfield at the site of Destelbergen-Eenbeekeinde. Legend: **1**. Late Bronze Age or Early Iron Age burial, **2**. Roman burial, **3**. Roman settlement area (see fig. 6), **4**. Modern sand extraction area.*

monuments with the same orientation are connected with it, but their full extent remains unknown. This large enclosure is characterised by four particular interconnected posts in its south-western corner, not to be seen as an entrance or bridge construction. The ditch had a very short life and its deliberate filling followed a specific scenario: first the yellow (natural) sand, which was then tamped and covered by the humic sand. Several elements indicate that this monument, like those in nearby Aalter and Kemzeke (Bourgeois 1991a ; Bourgeois and Semey 1991), is of 4th–3rd century BC date.

– phase 4: after its abandonment the rectangular monument was replaced by a cemetery, of which some 69 cremation graves were discovered (*cf. supra*). The burials are poor. Some contain iron copies of Nauheim-brooches and pottery of 1st century BC date, while the youngest are larger cremation graves with a niche containing wheel-turned pottery and Roman brooches, dated to the 1st century AD. A series of radiocarbon dates confirm this interesting chronology. The position of the burials is remarkable, around and not within the square monument, which probably means that the round barrow was deliberately avoided. It seems,

therefore, that the Bronze Age burial mound of Ursel-Rozestraat has a history of many centuries, possibly even two millennia. Its remains were still respected in the Late Iron Age and Early Roman period.

Finally the ancient cemetery was possibly abandoned in the course of the 1st century AD to install a new cemetery a few hundred metres to the north-east, from which the thirteen cremation burials excavated date principally to the later 1st and 2nd century AD (Bungeneers *et al.* 1987). They are more typically Roman in shape and content.

3. Destelbergen

The somewhat older excavations on the site of Destelbergen-Eenbeekeinde, near Ghent, also produced some interesting conclusions for this debate. Between 1960 and 1984 more than one hectare was systematically excavated here while rescue interventions during large scale sand extraction resulted in many related discoveries. It must however, be stressed that a large part of the site remains uninvestigated and that modern exploitation of the sandy soil certainly destroyed much data (Figs. 15.6 and 15.7).

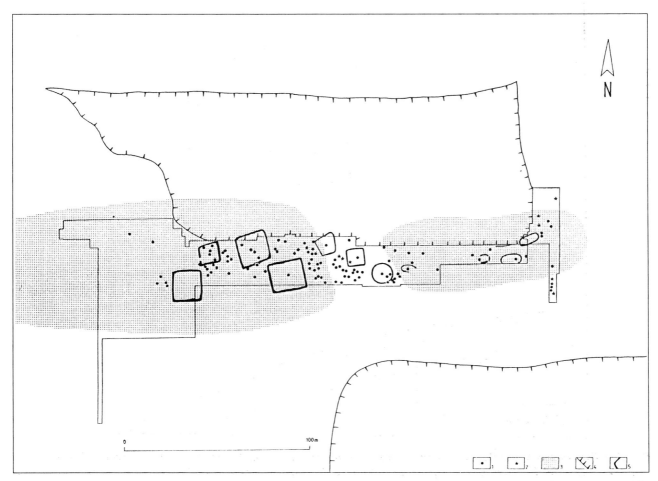

Fig. 15.7 *Details of fig. 6. Legend: 1.– 4. (see fig. 5), 5. Ditched burial enclosure of Late Bronze or Early Iron Age. The eastern extension of the settlement is still unknown.*

From the Late Bronze Age onwards an east-west oriented sandy ridge, parallel to the river Scheldt, functioned as a cemetery. Of this more or less planned urnfield some 105 graves were found. Not more than thirteen burials belong to the earliest phase (Ha B). One of these was surrounded by a small four-post construction and a circular ditch of 11m diameter. This monument no doubt also comprised a grave mound. The other Bronze age graves almost all lie east of the round barrow and several of these were the centre of an oval ditch of the so-called 'langbed'-type.

The cemetery developed further in the Early Iron Age (Ha C and D). Now only the western part of the ridge was used, thus giving the circular mound a central position. Six of these Iron Age graves were part of monuments with a square ditch (sides: between 8 and 19m). All the monuments are evenly spread over the available area.

After an interruption in the occupation of the site during the Late Iron Age, this well-situated zone was again intensively used during the Roman period. While the somewhat lower area nearer the river also contains traces of habitation, the core of a large native-Roman settlement was found on the same ridge as the prehistoric urnfield. Between the middle of the 1st century and the third quarter of the 3rd century – with a short interruption around the *Chauci*-raids of AD 172–174 – a settlement with mixed character (crafts and agriculture) developed here. The living areas were concentrated in two cores, lying directly on top of the former cemetery. Both cores, however, were separated by a small open area, probably containing a road system which linked them to the river Scheldt. This open area includes the zone of the Bronze Age round barrow, which was, therefore, spared by the Roman living quarters. A large Early Roman cemetery, whereof only some 130 graves were excavated in good conditions, extends from the settlement area towards the riverside. Several of its cremation graves lie near the edge of the inhabited zone, but although one burial is dug into the fill of the circular ditch, it seems that the barrow itself was again avoided.

At first sight Destelbergen appears as a typical example of non-continuity on the funerary level. An urnfield with planned monuments of Late Bronze/Early Iron Age date was built over by the Gallo-Romans and the existence, in both periods, of funerary functions, seems more related to the topographic conditions. It must be stressed however that the dominating monument of the prehistoric cemetery, the Bronze Age round barrow, was evidently spared in the process. This probably indicates that some aspect of the barrow was still visible and could even suggest that the ancient monument was a focus for later habitation activities and their related funeral functions.

Conclusions

A first analysis of the Roman use of prehistoric cemeteries in sandy Flanders, partly based on the information grouped on the distribution maps (Figs 15.2 and 15.3), presents a very heterogeneous situation. We can elucidate this picture by grouping the burial data in three major chronological phases whose funerary context is very different. The difference in funerary habits by period causes a differential integration of the older burial places in the later Roman landscape.

The round barrow-landscape of the Early and Middle Bronze Age no doubt had a permanent influence on the environment of later periods. The aerial photographs already show quite clearly that only a very small minority of the more than 1000 detected circular structures are disturbed by younger traces, most of which can be attributed to post-Roman times. This observation is further confirmed by archaeological excavations: none of the 16 excavated circles has been build upon, ploughed over or disturbed by other burials before the Middle Ages. Of these excavated structures only five remain (for the time being) without Roman connections. At nearly half of the studied circles (seven barrows), Roman graves were found in the immediate surroundings.

This numerical information, as well as the situations observed in Ursel (square ditch around the barrow and a link with the Roman cemetery) and Gent-Hogeweg (square Late Iron or Early Roman Age monument constructed precisely between the two concentric circles), proves beyond doubt that at least part of the Bronze Age monuments remained visible in the landscape for two millennia and more. It also indicates a certain respect for these past monumental burial places and it is likely that some of them even attracted later (Roman) funerary practices.

It can not be unequivocally explained precisely why such places were again much used for burial in the Roman period. The huge distance in time and especially the two major ruptures in the settlement history that divide the Middle Bronze Age and the Early Roman period (*cf. supra*), indicate that ancestral cult is a less likely explanation. The latter would indeed presuppose a direct link between both populations, for which there is no proof. Furthermore, not one round barrow could be related to possible traces of certain ritual activities of Roman date in its surroundings. If we must choose between the five options discussed above, then we propose to seek the possible explanation elsewhere. We think that certain elements in the native-Roman population of that time deliberately chose to bury their dead near such older monuments because they thought it would give the deceased some magic protection. They probably did this without even knowing that these obvious human creations of a distant past were also of a funeral nature. The burial continuity was, therefore, less deliberate than we might now think.

We should not exclude other, more pragmatic reasons. Such barrows, often whole groups of them, surely had the advantage of being very recognisable features in the landscape and, therefore, were very useful as topographic markers for Roman burial, surely helpful in finding the precise position of more or less isolated tombs, some time after the deposition of the dead. Neither can we exclude the possibility that they fulfilled a certain role in dividing and bordering the land and estates, a role that could have been confirmed by new burial in Roman context. Although this interesting hypothesis needs more proof, it remains remarkable that while no Late Bronze or Iron Age graves were dug near these barrows, such activities were indeed common in Roman times. Maybe the more total use of the landscape under Roman dominance is responsible for this and the search for dividing features between new property was quickly oriented towards these remarkable remnants of lost generations.

The situation is very different for the second main prehistoric period considered here, the Late Bronze-Early Iron Age, a time when whole urnfields were arranged for the dead. Because these large cemeteries were probably often completely devoid of surface monuments, they are still ill-documented today. Their aerial discovery is very difficult. The fragmentary and often older documentation available leaves only eight trustworthy burial sites of that period in the region. Only in two cases were Roman graves also found in the neighbourhood, while again two sites produced settlement traces of that later period. Nowhere is continuous utilisation of these urnfields into the Roman period detectable, as they all end somewhere in Ha C or Ha D and certainly before 450 BC. In Destelbergen we see that the only well excavated urnfield of the region was even superseded by a Roman settlement, thus at first sight demonstrating a complete break with the old funerary character of the place (*cf. supra*). Yet we noticed that something particular happened here: the most monumental and centrally placed (round) barrow was preserved by the Gallo-Romans, and even used by them as a pole of attraction for four of their own cremation graves. We have the impression that this monument, like those of Early and Middle Bronze Age date, was still a structure of some importance, to be respected by the community. The above ground markers of the other graves, however, were lost in the mists of time.

The Late Iron Age, with its often shallow and ill-structured graves, is even worse documented in the records. Only five cemeteries could be mapped. That four of them also contain Roman burials does indicate, however, that some continued use is likely. All four cemeteries have a late date (LT III) and, as convincingly demonstrated in Ursel (*cf. supra*), there seems to be no clear divide between the La Tène-burials and the Early Roman graves. This is in line with the information we have from some rural settlements of both periods, although many difficulties for precise dating in the transition period remain.

Furthermore it is interesting to remark that in the immediate surroundings of two out of the four known

open air sanctuaries of the Late Iron Age (Aalter, Kemzeke, Knesselare and Ursel), some Roman activity had taken place. As these monumental cult places functioned only for a very short time and as this type of continuity is only apparent on both sites which also had funerary functions in the Iron Age (Ursel and Knesselare), it can be assumed that not the religious but indeed the funerary aspect of these places was responsible for a prolonged use. In Ursel this continuity seems purely to be one of burial practice, while the monumental cemetery of Knesselare has probably attracted other ritual activities in later (Roman) times. Only the last case is presumably related to a kind of ancestor cult in the Early Roman period. Confirmation of this observation on other sites would be most welcome.

On Figure 2 we mapped all Early Roman cemeteries in sandy and sandy loam Flanders west of the Scheldt. That out of the 51 sites only 11 (22%) were found near older prehistoric burials need not be interpreted as proof for a radical breach in the funerary landscape. Many Roman graves and cemeteries were discovered in poor circumstances and large-scale excavations on them are scarce. In the 24 instances of more or less systematic excavation, only six provided no traces of older burials at all. Furthermore, the growth of the population during the *Pax Romana* must also account for an increase in cemeteries in the landscape.

We hope that our discussion of the evidence has shown that problems of burial continuity, in relation to topography and landscape, need a subtle approach. A lot of nuance is needed for several reasons. First the documentation of the finds should be excellent and much large-scale excavation work is needed. The latter in particular is not yet fulfilled in the region considered. Secondly part of the observed burial continuity must be explained by the special character of the regional landscape. Therefore, a regional approach is to be preferred and comparisons with other parts of the Empire are most delicate. Our generally flat region of dry and less fertile sandy soils no doubt restricted the choice for the early inhabitants to locate their settlements, cult places and cemeteries. This stimulated accidental forms of continuity in the best locations. Somewhat higher ridges and local dunes no doubt attracted settlers at all times, so that prolonged or renewed use of certain terrain for specific purposes was absolutely no exception. Still we were able to show that not all observed links between prehistoric and Roman burials are accidental; the deliberate continuity observed on many sites is not the result of our imagination. Finally some nuance is needed on the chronological level of research and regarding the typology of the graves – monumental or not. This implies that certainly not *one* explanation, and not always *the same* explanations, can be put forward to understand the renewed or prolonged use of ancient cemeteries in Roman times.

Notes

1. Compare with the European Christian Middle Ages, when such old pagan places were, willingly or not, attributed to all kinds of evil forces (Roymans 1995).
2. Situation at the end of 1995 (Ampe *et al.* 1996b). The years 1986, 1989 and 1990 yielded a huge number, with respective totals of 56, 53 and 101 monuments, but the summer of 1995 was probably the 'best of the century' with no less than 272 new barrows.
3. Soils (drainage, profile) for instance are important for visibility (Ampe *et al.* 1995).
4. The figures change every year, for new barrows can be found in the neighbourhood of earlier finds and thus form large graveyards.
5. The settlement at Kortrijk (*Cortoriacum*), also known from the *Tabula Peutingeriana*, probably had a more elaborate infrastructure than most central sites in sandy Flanders.

Bibliography

Amand, M. 1960. Roman Barrows in Belgium. In *Analecta Archaeologica. Festschrift Fritz Fremersdorf*. Köln: 69–81.

Ampe, C., Bourgeois, J., Crombé, PH., Fockedey, L., Langohr, R., Meganck, M., Semey, J., Van Strydonck, M and Verlaeckt, K. 1996. The circular view. Aerial Photography and the discovery of Bronze Age funerary monuments in East- and West-Flanders (Belgium), *Germania*, 74/1: 45–94.

Ampe, C., Bourgeois, J., Fockedey, L., Langohr, R., Meganck, M. and Semey, J. 1995. *Cirkels in het land. Een inventaris van cirkelvormige structuren in de provincies Oost- en West-Vlaanderen*. Ghent.(= *Archeologische Inventaris Vlaanderen, Buitengewone reeks* 4).

Bayard, D. 1993. Sépultures et villae en Picardie au Haut-Empire: quelques données récentes. In Ferdière A. (ed.) 1993: 69–80.

Bourgeois, I. 1995. Palynologisch onderzoek van grafheuvel-structuren uit de bronstijd in zandig Binnen-Vlaanderen, *Lunula. Archaeologia protohistorica*, III. Ghent: 9–11.

Bourgeois, J. 1989. De ontdekking van nieuwe gronstoffen en de eerst metaalbewerkers in Temse en in het Waasland. In Thoen H. (ed.) 1989 *Temse en de Schelde. Van IJstijd tot Romeinen*. Brussels: 44–68.

Bourgeois, J. 1991a. *Enclos et nécropoles du second âge du fer à Kemzeke (Stekene, Flandre orientale). Rapport provisoire des fouilles 1988*. Ghent, 1991 (= *Scholae Archaeologicae*, 12).

Bourgeois, J. 1991b. Nederzettingen uit de late bronstijd en de vroege ijzertijd in westelijk België: Sint-Denijs-Westrem en Sint-Gillis-Waas. In Fokkens, H. and Roymans, N. (eds.) 1991. *Nederzettingen uit de bronstijd en de vroege ijzertijd in de Lage Landen, Nederlandse Archeologische Rapporten*, 13. Amersfoort.

Bourgeois, J. and Semey J. 1991. Contribution de la photographie aérienne à l'étude de l'âge du fer en Flandre intérieure. In Thoen, H. *et al.* (eds.) 1991 *Studia Archaeologica. Liber Amicorum J.A. Nenquin*. Ghent: 89–100.

Bourgeois, J., Semey, J. and Vanmoerkerke, J. 1989. *Ursel. Rapport provisoire des fouilles 1986–1987. Tombelle de l'âge du bronze et monuments avec nécropole de l'âge du fer*. Ghent (= *Scholae Archaeologicae*, 11).

Bourgeois, J. and Verlaeckt, K., in press. Bronze Age and Early Iron Age occupation patterns in Western Belgium. In Assendorp J. (ed.) *Symposium zur bronzezeitlichen Besiedlung in Nordwesteuropa*. Hitzacker.

Bungeneers, J., Delcourt, A. and Rommelaere, J. 1987. *Excavations at Ursel (East Flanders) 1985–1986. Prehistoric occupation and Roman cemetery*. Ghent (= *Scholae Archaeologicae*, 7).

Castella, D. 1993. Un sanctuaire augustéen autour d'une sépulture à incinération à Avenches, Canton de Vaud (Suisse). In Struck, M. (ed.) 1993: 229–244.

Chouquer, G. and Favory, F. 1991. *Les paysages de l'Antiquité. Terres et cadastres de l'Occident romain (IVe s. avant J.-C. / IIIe s. après J.-C.)*. Paris.

Conso, D. *et al.* 1990. *Traduction de Siculus Flaccus, Les conditions de la terre*. Besançon.

Cuppers, H. 1993. Sépultures et cimetières ruraux en pays trévire. In Ferdière A. (ed.) 1993: 81–88.

Cuppers, H. and Neysens, A. 1971. Der römerzeitliche Gutshof bei Newel. *Trierer Zeitschrift*, 34: 143–225.

De Laet, S.J., 1954. De bronstijd en het begin van de ijzertijd in Vlaanderen in het licht van recente opgravingen, *Gentse Bijdgragen tot de Kunstgeschiedenis*, 15: 61–187.

De Laet, S.J. 1961. Quelques précisions nouvelles sur la civilisation de Hilversum en Belgique, *Helinium*, 1: 120–126.

De Laet, S.J. 1982. *La Belgique d'avant les Romains*. Wetteren

De Laet, S.J., Nenquin, J. and Spitaels, P. 1958. *Contributions à l'étude de la Civilisation des Champs d'Urnes en Flandre*, Brugge (= *Dissertationes Archaeologicae Gandenses*, IV).

De Laet, S.J., Thoen, H. and Bourgeois, J. 1986. *Les fouilles du Séminaire d'Archéologie de la Rijksuniversiteit te Gent à Destelbergen-Eenbeekeinde (1960–1984) et l'histoire la plus ancienne de la région de Gent. I. La période préhistorique*, Brugge (= *Dissertationes Archaeologicae Gandenses*, XXIII).

De Mulder, G. 1994a. *Het project A.I.V. Een bilan van 15 jaar systematische archeologische inventarisatie in Vlaanderen*. Universiteit Gent (brochure).

De Mulder, G. 1994b. Aspects of the funeral ritual in the Late bronze Age and the Early Iron Age in the western part of the Flemish region. *Helinium*, XXXIV/1: 94–133.

Derks, T. 1991. The perception of the Roman pantheon by a native elite: the example of votive inscriptions from Lower Germany. In Roymans, N. and Theuws, F. (eds.) 1991. *Images of the past. Studies on ancient societies in northwestern Europe*. Amsterdam: 235–265.

Derks, T. 1996. *Goden, tempels en rituele praktijken. De transformatie van religieuze ideeën en waarden in Romeins Gallië*. Amsterdam. 1996.

Desittere, M. 1968. *De Urnenveldenkultuur in het gebied tussen Neder- Rijn en Noordzee*. Brugge (= *Dissertationes Archaeologicae Gandenses*,XI).

Desittere, M. 1974. Quelques considérations sur l'âge du bronze final et le premier âge du fer en Belgique et dans le sud des Pays-Bas. *Helinium*, 14: 105–134.

Desittere, M. 1976. Autochtones et immigrants en Belgique et dans le sud des Pays-Bas au Bronze final. In De Laet, S.J. (ed) *Acculturation and continuity in Atlantic Europe*. Brugge: 77–94 (= *Dissertationes Archaeologicae Gandenses*, XVI).

Eliade, M. 1959. *The Sacred and the Profane. The Nature of Religion*. San Diego/New York.

Ferdière, A. (ed.) 1993. *Monde des morts, monde des vivants en Gaule rurale*. Actes du Colloque Archea/Ager (Orléans, 7–9 février 1992). Tours.

Ferdière, A. 1993. Conclusions. In Ferdière A. (ed.) 1993: 433–447.

Galliou, P. 1989. *Les tombes romaines d'Armorique. Essai de sociologie de la mort*. Documents d'Archéologie Française, 17. Paris

Gaillou, P. 1993. Monde des morts et monde des vivants dans les campagnes de l'Armorique romaine. In Ferdière, A. (ed.) 1993: 241–246.

Gromatici Veteres 1848 – Blume, F., Lachmann, K. and Rudorff, A. *Die Schriften der Römischer Feldmesser*, I. Berlin.

Hatt, J.J. 1951. *La tombe gallo-romaine: recherches sur les inscriptions et les monuments funéraires gallo-romains des trois premiers siècles de notre ère*. Paris.

Hessing, W. 1993. Nécropoles indigènes de la zone alluviale des Pays-Bas (50 av. J.-C. – 300 ap. J.-C.). In Ferdière A. (ed.) 1993: 105–112.

Hollevoet, Y. 1993. Ver(r)assingen in een verkaveling. Romeins grafveld te Oudenburg (prov. West-Vlaanderen. Interimverslag. *Archeologie in Vlaanderen* III-1993: 207–216.

Lafon, X. and Adam, A.-M. 1993. Des morts chez les vivants ? Tombes et habitat dans la France du Nord-Est. In Ferdière A. (ed.) 1993: 113–120.

Lambot, B. 1993. Habitats, nécropoles et organisation du territoire à La Tène finale en Champgne septentrionale. In Ferdière A. (ed.): 121–151.

Leach, E. 1976. *Culture and Communication. The logic by which symbols are conneted. An introduction to the use of structuralist analysis in social anthropology.* Cambridge.

Leva, CH. and Coene, G. 1969. Het Gallo-Romeins grafveld in de Molenstraat te Kortrijk. *Archaeologia Belgica* 114. Brussels.

Meffre, J.-C. 1993. Lieux sépulcraux et occupation du sol en milieu rural dans la cité antique de Vaison sous le Haut-Empire. In Ferdière A. (ed.) 1993: 371–387.

Morris, I. 1991. The Archaeology of Ancestors: the Saxe/Goldstein hypothesis revisited. *Cambridge Archaeological Journal*, I: 147–169.

Morris, I. 1992. *Death Ritual and Social Structure in Classical Antiquity.* Cambridge.

Parker Pearson, M. 1993. The Powerful Dead: Archaeological Relationships between the Living and the Dead. *Cambridge Archaeological Journal*, 3:2: 203–229.

Philpott, R. and Reece, R. 1993. Sépultures rurales en Bretagne Romaine. In Ferdière, A. (ed.) 1993: 417–423.

Rogge, M., Thoen, H. and Vermeulen, F. 1990. Oost-Vlaanderen in de Romeinse tijd, *VOBOV-info* 38–40: 59–63.

Roymans, N. 1995. The Cultural Biography of Urnfields and the long-term history of a mythical landscape. *Archaeological Dialogues*, vol. 2, nr.1: 2–24.

Slofstra, J. 1991. Changing settlement systems in the Meuse-Demer-Scheldt area during the Early Roman period. In Roymans, N. and Theuws, F. (eds.) 1991 *Images of the past. Studies on ancient societies in northwestern Europe.* Amsterdam: 131–199.

Struck, M. (ed) 1993. *Römerzeitliche Gräber als Quellen zu Religion, Bevölkerungsstruktur und Sozialgeschichte.* Archäologische Schriften des Instituts für Vor- und Frühgeschichte der Johannes Gutenbeg-Universität Mainz. Mainz

Thoen, H. (ed.) 1989. *Temse en de Schelde. Van IJstijd tot Romeinen.* Brussels.

Thoen, H. and Vermeulen, F. 1997. Etappen in der Germanisierung Flanderns in Mittel- und Spätrömischer Zeit. In Bridger, C., Gilles, K.-J., Luik, M.and Struck, M. (eds.) 1993, *Neue Untersuchungen zu spätrömischen Befestigungsanlagen in den Rhein- und Donauprovinzen*, British Archaeological Reports, International Series. Oxford.

Tilley, C. 1994. *A Phenomenology of Landscape. Places, Paths and Monuments.* Oxford/Providence.

Toynbee, J. 1971. *Death and Burial in the Roman World.* Ithaca/New York.

Van Doorselaer, A. 1967. *Les nécropoles d'époque romaine en Gaule septentrionale.* Dissertationes Archaeologicae Gandenses, 10. Brugge.

Van Doorselaer, A. 1969. Typische Gallo-Romeinse brandrestengraven in de Scheldevallei. *Helinium* 9: 118–137.

Van Doorselaer, A. and Bourgeois, J. 1996. Van boeren en adellijke heren. Sociale differentiatie in de Ijzertijd ca. 750 v.Chr.-Romeinen. In Van Roeyen, J.-P. (ed.) 1996. *Uit Vlaamse bodem. 10 archeologische verhalen.* Sint-Niklaas: 29–47.

Van Doorselaer, A. and Rogge, M. 1985. Continuité d'un rite funéraire spécifique dans la vallée de l'Escaut, de l'âge du fer au haut Moyen Age. *Les Études Classiques* LIII-1 (= Mélanges A. Wankenne): 153–170.

Van Doorselaer, A. and Thoen, H. 1969. Het Gallo-Romeinse grafveld van Destelbergen, Oudheidkundige Opgravingen en Vondsten in de Provincie Oost-Vlaanderen 5. In *Kultureel Jaarboek van de Provincie Oost-Vlaanderen* 23: 23–115.

Van Hove, R. 1996. Het Gallo-Romeins grafveld van de vicus Waasmunster-Pontrave. Stille getuige van de dodenzorg binnen een relatief welvarende handelsnederzetting ca. 70–275 n Chr. In *Uit Vlaamse bodem. 10 Archeologische verhalen.* Sint-Niklaas: 67–78.

Vanmoerkerke, J., 1985. Vierkante grafstructuur uit de IJzertijd aan de Hogeweg. *Stadsarcheologie*, jg. 9 – nr. 2 : 42–51.

Vanmoerkerke, J., Semey, J. and Bourgeois, J. 1990. Some Aspects and Results of Aerial Surveying and Archaeological Air Photography in East-Flanders. In Leva, C. (ed.) 1990, *Aerial Photography and Geophysical Prospection in Archaeology. Proceedings of the Second International Symposium, Brussels 8 – XI – 1986*, Brussels: 237–248.

Verlaeckt, K. (ed.), 1996. *Tussen heuvel en rivier. De bronstijd in Oost-Vlaanderen (ca. 2000–750 v.Chr.).* Dendermonde.

Vermeulen, F. 1983. *Sint-Martens-Latem.* Ghent.(=*Archaeologisch Inventaris Vlaanderen* I).

Vermeulen, F. 1985. *A Roman Cemetery at Sint-Martens-Leerne (Deinze, East Flanders)*, Ghent. (=*Scholae Archaeologicae 1*).

Vermeulen, F. 1986. La commune de Sint-Martens-Latem (Belgique). In *Documents d'Archéologie Française 3, La prospection archéologique. Paysage et peuplement.* Paris: 93–95.

Vermeulen, F. 1992. Tussen Leie en Schelde. Archeologische inventaris en studie van de Romeinse bewoning in het zuiden van de Vlaamse Zandstreek. *Archeologische Inventaris Vlaanderen. Buitengewone Reeks* 1. Ghent

Vermeulen, F. 1993. De Gallo-Romeinse nederzetting te Sint-Denijs-Westrem (gem. Gent, prov. Oost-Vlaanderen), *Archeologisch Jaarboek Gent 1992.* Ghent: 187–303.

Vermeulen, F. 1995. Sandy Flanders in the Roman Period: Towards a Regional Research Strategy. In Lodewijckx M. (ed.) 1995, *Archaeological and Historical Aspects of West-European Societies, Album Amicorum André Van Doorselaer*, Acta Archaeologica Lovaniensia Monographiae 8. Leuven: 135–143.

Vermeulen, F. 1996a. Moderate Acculturation in the Fringe Area of the Roman Empire: Some Archaeological Indications from the Civitas Menapiorum, *Bulletin van het Belgisch Historisch Instituut te Rome*, LXII: 5–41.

Vermeulen, F. 1996b. The Role of Local Centres in the Romanisation of Northern Belgica. In Metzler J. *et al.* (eds.) 1996, *Integration in the Early Roman West. The role of culture and ideology.* Luxembourg: 183–198.

Vermeulen, F. and Hageman, B., 1997. Een rituele omheining uit de late ijzertijd te Knesselare (O.-Vl.), *Lunula*, V: 29–33.

Wigg, A. 1993. Barrows in Northeastern Gallia Belgica: cultural and social aspects. In Struck M. (ed.) 1993: 371– 379.

Zanker, P. 1988. *The Power of Images in the Age of Augustus.* Ann Arbor.

16. The living and the dead: a struggle for space – approaches to landscape around Lyons

Laurence Tranoy

A number of studies carried out over the past fifteen years in Lyons have enabled researchers to explore the immediate surroundings of the ancient city. The consequent re-evaluation of our knowledge concerning the urban periphery of Lyons now makes it possible to address the notion of *suburbium* by bringing into question the role of the cemetery in the urban landscape.

In order to provide an impression of the landscape surrounding the colony, it is perhaps best to review briefly the current state of knowledge of the roads leading to and

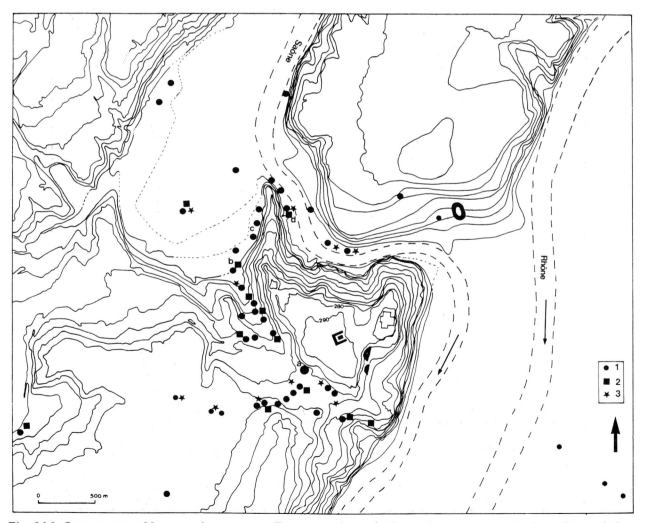

Fig. 16.1 *Contour map of Lyons and environs; a. Trion mausoleums b. Gorge-de-Loup c. quartier Saint-Pierre d. Quai-Arloing 1. grave 2. dwelling 3. craft areas*

from it. A distinction must be made between the tombs of prominent citizens, as illustrated by the great monuments of Trion, and the anonymous and more modest burial sites that have been discovered in recent years. It must be remembered that while Lyons possesses an extremely rich collection of funerary inscriptions, most of them have been severed from their context.

Urban limits, roads, and the first monumental tombs

The first topographical question to be raised concerns the urban limits of the *colonia* during the Early Roman Empire. It is currently acknowledged that the *colonia* at Lyons was founded in 43 BC and was simultaneously endowed with the privileged status of a Roman city (Goudineau 1986: 1989). It was long thought that this status implied the automatic erection of city walls (Février

1972), but the reality of the situation now appears to have been more complex (Gros and Torelli 1988: 255–256). In Lyons no archaeological remains have yet confirmed the presence of an enclosure erected during the Early Empire, and both epigraphic and literary sources are silent on the subject (Desbat 1987). Consequently, current knowledge does not allow us to trace a physical limit between the colony and the *suburbium*.

The tracing of the city's outline is dependent on topography and cemetery areas. The city spread over the Sarra plateau and along adjacent slopes to the north and south as the terrain allowed (Fig. 16.1). Beyond the urban limits, tombs are situated along roads that have been more accurately located thanks to recent archaeological field-work. Since the 19th century, the course of a road leading northward, the 'voie du Rhin', so named following Strabo (IV, 6, 11), has been known (Tranoy and Ayala 1994: 177–178). Several sections of roads belonging to the

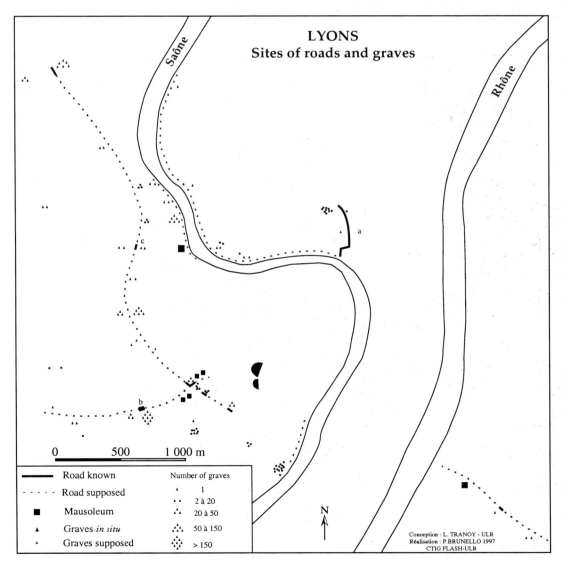

Fig. 16.2 *Sites of roads and graves*

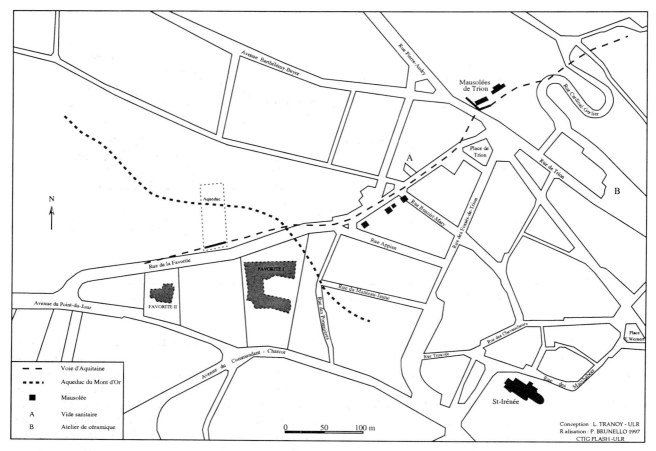

Fig. 16.3 *Map of the Trion district*

network established by Agrippa have recently been discovered. They have been linked to the so-called 'voie d'Aquitaine' heading west (Plassot 1995a: 114) and to the 'voie de l'Océan' leading north-west (Chastel *et al.* 1995; Frascone 1999) (Fig. 16.2).

Near the city's western exit, a group of tombs have been known since the 19th century, particularly after the unearthing of the Trion mausolea in 1885. As these monuments are well known, they will not be discussed in detail here (Allmer and Dissard 1890; Espérandieu 1910: 40; Kahler 1934: 170). A few additional details on the topographical and chronological context of these sites will suffice. The Trion mausolea, of which only the plinths remain, stood massively at the city's western exit on a slope. The natural relief accentuated the ostentatious aspect of these structures. Visible from afar, they adorned in monumental fashion the entrance to the city. The mausolea are entirely set within a monumental tradition of which the prototypes were erected in Italy at the end of the Republican period (Figs 16.3 and 16.4).

The severely eroded state of the mausolea discourages any detailed reconstruction. Within the typology of architectural tombs proposed by H. Gabelmann, the C. Calvius Turpio mausoleum (No. 1) features in the 'Mausoleumsgrundform' category, comprising monuments with a full plinth and open superstructure. The

Turpio mausoleum, and perhaps also that of the Salonii (No. 2) are to be more precisely placed within the 'colonnaded facade' group (the 'Saulenfronttypus') (Gabelmann 1977: 113–114; Roth-Congès 1987: 49).

The proposed dating based on analysis of epigraphy or decoration pertains solely to these two mausolea. The inscription preserved on the monument dedicated to Turpio, a freed slave and a *sevir*, situates the edifice within the Augustan period, around the first decade of the 1st century BC (Duthoy 1976; 1978). The monument of the Salonii might well be older. By combining F. S. Kleiner's analyses on workshops (1977) with A. Roth-Congès's studies on the mausoleum of the Julii at Glanum (1983: 130–131), we might date the Lyons monument to the triumviral period or the very beginning of the Augustan period. This hypothesis would require further development outside the scope of the present paper. We may bear in mind, however, that these proposed dates rely on the strong stylistic analogies that exist between the two mausoleums.

Following the hypothesis of an earlier dating, in accordance with A. Roth-Congès's proposed dating for Glanum, the monument of the Salonii would be contemporary with the *deductio* of the *colonia* and with the initial urbanisation of which few remnants are left. The oldest traces of the ancient city were discovered on the

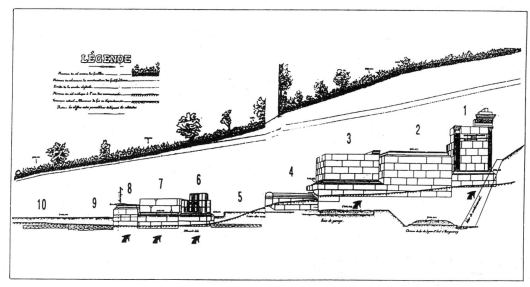

Fig. 16.4 *Trion mausoleums. Drawing by Chanel (Allmer et Dissard 1887). Arrows indicate preserved mausolea.*

Verbe-Incarné site. However the remains on this site that are traceable to around 40 BC are rare and extremely modest: the city appears to be in an embryonic state (Delaval 1994: 204; Desbat and Mandy 1991: 87). If a later date is attributed to the mausoleum of the Salonii (the first half of Augustus' reign), it as well as that of Turpio would be contemporary with the initial expansion of the city brought on by its status as provincial capital. The urban character (i.e. with street grid, insulae and monumental aspect) of the Verbe-Incarné site, like other sites in the Lyons area, only develops from 15–10 BC (Delaval 1994: 205; Tranoy, Ayala 1994: 176). However whether we privilege one hypothesis or the other, the fact remains that these Italic-inspired, self-honouring monuments were firmly implanted at *Lugdunum* right at the beginning of the colony's existence.

The development of burial spaces

The oldest Roman period tombs of Lyons are little documented. All along the 'voie de l'Aquitaine', cremation burials dating from the end of Augustus' reign at the earliest are approximately 320m from the Trion mausoleums. A cluster of 150 cremation burials dating from the end of the 1st century BC has been discovered 2.8 km from Trion, near the road to the north-west. The distance casts doubt on the connection of these tombs to the colony. During the course of the 1st century AD burial sites were concentrated around the city's periphery, but sites have also been located further away, sometimes at more than 1km, no doubt related to rural settlements. In the 2nd and 3rd centuries AD cemeteries were located around the entire urban periphery, as well as along the right bank of the Saône and the left bank of the Rhône (Fig. 16.1).

We already know that all sorts of activities and installations could often exist side by side with tombs in the great cities of the Roman Empire. In Lyons, despite the poverty of documentation, we can begin to trace the development of the suburbs. As observed elsewhere, in the immediate vicinity of the tombs were areas set aside for craftsmen and their workshops, in particular for pottery making and metal working. Older literary sources dating from the 19th century or earlier also signal the presence of mosaics or the remains of buildings in a zone also occupied by burials.

A number of examples aptly illustrate the diversity of the peri-urban landscape. No funerary monument has been unearthed on the 'voie d'Aquitaine' beyond the alignment of the Trion mausoleums and the rue de la Favorite, discovered in the 19th century. However, the sector nearest to the road has yet to be explored. The 'Favorite I' site is located at a distance of 320m south-west of the Trion mausoleums and at 40m from the Roman period road. Cremation took place in this area as early as the end of Augustus' reign (Fig. 16.3). Graves then accumulated in this area up to the 3rd century. In all 278 cremation and 143 inhumation burials have been brought to light. Cremation seems to have been the exclusive rite during the first half of the 1st century (period 1). Inhumation burial appears during the Flavian period (period 2); it must have been practised throughout the 2nd century (periods 3 and 4) but the grave goods and stratigraphy only allow us to recognise it at the end of the 2nd century and in the 3rd century (periods 4 and 5), a period at which a parallel decline although not abandonment of cremation can be noted (Fig. 16.5).

Busta play a particularly important role, accounting for 53% of all cremations. Among the 131 graves identified as of this type, 15 can be distinguished by their exceptional size, reaching 3.05m in length and 2.05m in width (Fig. 16.6). An extensive osteological study of the fills of these graves is lacking, but in terms of morphology

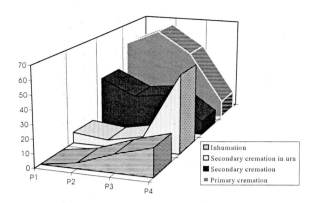

Fig. 16.5 *Proportion of tomb types by period*

and contents they resemble the pits defined as *ustrina* at Mainz-Weisenau (Witteyer 1993: 69–80).

Attempts to understand the spatial arrangement of the graves have met with numerous difficulties, in particular, the superimposition of burials, for which there may be different causes at different periods, the absence of traces of spatial organisation and the apparently random distribu-

tion of tombs. Nonetheless, locational and chronological analysis allows for the clarification of certain points:

1. The majority of intercuttings (54%) are due to inhumation burials cut into cremation burials or other inhumations. Half of these intercuttings affected cremation, half inhumation burials.
2. There are intercuttings linking cremation burials from different periods: 27% of these affected the cremated remains.
3. Intercuttings between contemporary burials are more surprising. They are fairly numerous (37 examples), and some date to the earliest use of the site.

Of intercuttings on the site as a whole, in all periods, 60% damaged deposits of cremated bone or skeletal remains. The degree of damage shows the discrepancy between the theoretical Roman legislation for the care of graves (de Visscher 1963: 49) and the actual management of an area occupied by modest graves which display little concern for ostentation.

Opposite the Favorite I site, on the other side of the road, no grave has been located. The contrast between a very densely occupied cemetery and a practically deserted piece of land is most probably due to the presence of an

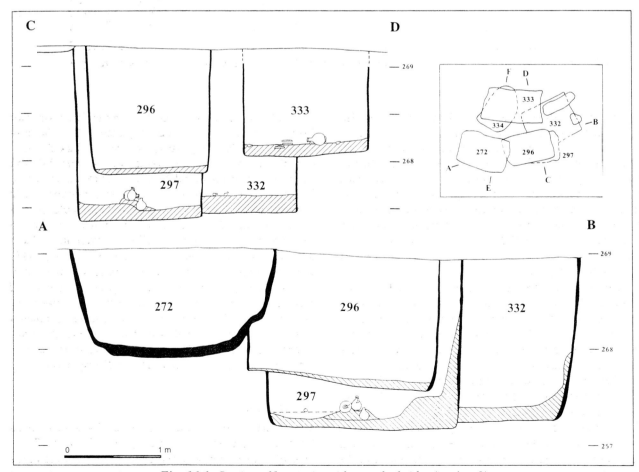

Fig. 16.6. *Section of large pits with scorched sides* (ustrina ?).

Fig. 16.7 *Plan of the Quai Arloing excavation (drawn by P. Gayte, and M-N. Baudrand. See Tranoy 1995)*

underground aqueduct. The path of the aqueduct may also explain the empty space on the north-eastern side of the Favorite site. One hundred metres to the west of Favorite I, the Favorite II site bears witness to the construction of a 1st century dwelling. The building seems to have been occupied while cremation and probably inhumation burials were made in the vicinity. The plan of the building is incomplete, but there are traces of metal working and of a hypocaust. The building was probably deserted at the end of the 1st century, and burials were made among its ruins from then on.

In the north-western part of the city, topography limited the installation of peri-urban sites on the slopes of a talweg (the Trion talweg). Evidence of occupation is known at the mouth of the valley or on the open land west of the Saône (plaine de Vaise, Fig. 16.1). In the talweg, traces of settlement show a variety of types of occupation, but the phenomenon is better illustrated at the mouth of the valley on the Gorge-de-Loup (Bellon 1995) and Quartier Saint Pierre sites (Chastel *et al.* 1995; Plassot 1995b). The latter includes a road bordered by graves and scattered cremation burials. 100m away were a fuller's workshop and a peristyle house of 630 square metres dated to the 1st century, thus contemporary with the cremations.

The Quai Arloing settlement area extended downward from the abrupt slope of the Sarra plateau, along the right bank of the Saône (Fig. 16.7). It comprised a collection of buildings in use from the 1st to 3rd centuries AD. The site also served for burial from the 1st to 4th centuries. To the south of this plot, highly fragmentary walls decorated with painted plaster probably belong to a building occupied during the 1st century AD. To the north lie the remains of an area identified as a warehouse dated to the middle or latter part of the 1st century. This warehouse underwent a series of changes to the initial layout (Tranoy 1995). Among the graves, a cluster of cremation burials dated to the end of the 1st century, but the expansion of the cemetery seems to have culminated in the 3rd century. On this plot burials and buildings clearly appear to co-exist; no spatial separation between the two types of utilisation could be distinguished.

Conclusion

This overview of the burial areas of *Lugdunum* sheds light on a number of important points. First, the Trion mausolea bear witness to the presence beyond the limits of the *Provincia* of patrons who from the very beginnings of the *colonia* commissioned specialists familiar with models inherited from an Italic repertory to construct extremely expensive, private and rare monuments.

Beyond the rows of monumental tombs, of which the alignment on the 'voie d'Aquitaine' recalls Italian models, developed clusters of anonymous and modest burials which over time were superimposed to the extent that all indications of spatial organisation were erased. Recent discoveries reveal a somewhat discontinuous cemetery fabric, comprising small groups of burials of varying concentration, developing in a seemingly disorganised and poorly managed way. The cemetery areas were spread across an urban halo in which craft activities, commerce and residence blended outside the normal regulation of urban space. Thus, on the margin of the city developed varied modes of occupation, spawned by a dynamic city that overran the initial framework of its foundation. The documents currently at our disposal beckon us to consider both the city and the *suburbium* from a new perspective.

Bibliography

Allmer, A. and Dissard, P. 1890. *Inscriptions antiques de Lyon*. Tome III, Lyons.

Bellon, C. 1995. L'occupation gallo-romaine de Gorge de Loup. In *Vaise, un quartier de Lyon antique*, DARA 11, Lyons: 169–174.

Chastel, J. *et al.* 1995. Le Quartier Saint-Pierre. In *Vaise, un quartier de Lyon antique*, DARA 11, Lyons: 39–70.

Delaval, E. 1994. Un îlot d'habitation romaine à Lyon, (Ier siècle av. J.-C. – IIIe siècle ap. J.-C.), Clos du Verbe Incarné, colline de Fourvière. In *Actes du premier Congrès Méditerranéen d'Ethnologie (Lisbonne), 4–8 novembre 1991*, Lisbon: 203–229.

Desbat, A. 1987. L'enceinte de Lyon au Haut-Empire. In *Les enceintes augustéennes dans l'Occident romain (France, Italie, Espagne, Afrique du Nord)*, Actes du Colloque international de Nîmes, IIIe Congrès Archéologique de Gaule Méridionale, 9–12 Octobre 1985, Ecole Antique de Nîmes, 18: 63–75.

Desbat, A. and Mandy, B. 1991. Le développement de Lyon à l'époque augustéenne: l'apport des fouilles récentes. In *Les villes augustéennes de Gaule*, Actes du Colloque international d'Autun, 6, 7 et 8 juin 1985, Autun: 79–97.

Duthoy, R. 1976. Recherches sur la répartition géographique et chronologique des termes de Sevir Augustalis, Augustalis,

Augustalis et Sevir dans l'Empire romain. In *Epigraphische Studien*, Cologne: 143–214.

Duthoy, R. 1978. Les Augustales. *Aufstieg und Niedergang der Römischen Welt*, II, 16–2, Berlin-New-York: 1255–1309.

Espérandieu, E. 1910. *Recueil Général des Bas-Reliefs, Statues et Bustes de la Gaule Romaine*. 3, Paris.

Février, P.-A. 1972. Enceinte et colonie (de Nîmes à Vérone, Toulouse et Tipasa). *Hommage à Fernand Benoît*, III: 277–286.

Frascone, D. 1999. *La voie de l'Océan et ses abords. Nécropoles et habitats gallo-romains à Lyon Vaise*. D.A.R.A., 18

Gabelmann, H. 1977. Römische Grabbauten in Italien und den Nordprovinzen, *Festschrift für F. Brommer*, Mainz: 101–117.

Goudineau, C. 1986. Note sur la fondation de Lyon. *Gallia*, 44: 171–173.

Goudineau, C. 1989. Les textes antiques sur la fondation et la topographie de Lugdunum. In *Aux origines de Lyon*, DARA, 2, Série lyonnaise n°1: 23–36.

Gros, P. and Torelli, M. 1988. *Storia dell'urbanistica. Il mondo romano*. Rome.

Kähler, H. 1934. Die rheinischen Pfeilergrabmäler. *Bonner Jahrbücber*, 139: 145–172.

Kleiner, F.S. 1977. Artists in the Roman world: an itinerant workshop in Augustean Gaul. *Mélanges de l'Ecole Française de Rome. Antiquités*, 89: 661–696.

Plassot, E. 1995a. Lyon, 5th arrondissement, 50 bis, rue de la Favorite. *Bilan scientifique 1994*, DRAC, Rhône-Alpes, Lyons: 114.

Plassot, E. 1995b. Le Quartier Saint-Pierre; la maison aux *Xenia*. In *Vaise, un quartier de Lyon antique*, DARA 11, Lyons: 71–129.

Roth-Congès, A. 1983. L'acanthe dans le décor architectonique protoaugustéen en Provence. *Revue Archéologique de Narbonnaise*, 16: 103–134.

Roth-Congès, A. 1987. Le mausolée de l'Île du Comte. In *Ugernum, Beaucaire et le Beaucairois à l'époque romaine*, II, Association pour la Recherche Archéologique en Languedoc Oriental, Cahier 16, Caveirac: 47–127.

Tranoy, L. and Ayala, G. 1994. Les pentes de la Croix-Rousse à Lyon dans l'Antiquité. État des connaissances. *Gallia*, 51: 171–189.

Tranoy, L. 1995. Le quai Arloing, artisanat et nécropole. In *Vaise, un quartier de Lyon antique*, D.A.R.A. 11, Lyons: 179–240.

Vischer de, F. 1963. *Les droits des tombeaux romains*. Milan.

Witteyer, M. 1993. Die Ustrinen und Busta von Mainz-Weisenau. In Struck, M., *Römerzeitliche Gräber als Quellen zu Religion, Bevölkerungsstruktur und Sozialgeschichte*, Archäologische Schriften des Instituts für Vor- und Frühgeschichte der Johannes Gutenberg-Universität Mainz, Band 3, Mainz: 69–80.

17. Burial in Asia Minor during the Imperial period, with a particular reference to Cilicia and Cappadocia

Marcello Spanu

Introduction

The intention of this paper is to present a synthetic account of burials in Asia Minor during the Imperial period. In general one should remember that Asia Minor included all the Anatolian provinces which, even if they correspond today to a single territorial entity (i.e. Turkey), were regions marked by deep cultural and social diversity, only partly mitigated by the Hellenizing phase which followed the conquests of Alexander the Great. Large migration from Italy (colonial settlements were rare in Asia and the presence of the army was mostly restricted to the *limes* strip along the Euphrates) did not follow Roman annexation of Anatolia, begun in 129 BC and ended by Vespasian, so numerous local traditions survived in these regions which were marginally affected by genuine 'Romanization'.

Contrary to what can be recorded for the Western provinces, in this area of the Empire – despite a very rich tradition of study of the artistic and the stylistic features and the symbolism of funerary representations – one must lament the almost total absence of extensive archaeological excavations of cemeteries, which is a lacuna only slightly offset by the state of preservation (sometimes excellent) of the funerary monuments, and by sporadic, restricted, rescue excavations, mostly unpublished or locally published and therefore difficult to find. Moreover a large number of funerary monuments remain totally unknown, particularly those of the peripheral areas, which are far from the renowned cities but are none the less significant.

This necessary introduction having been made, it nevertheless seems necessary to make some remarks on aspects of burial in these provinces, in view of the fact that a current summary (however generic) of the problems concerning the funerary culture of these regions during the Imperial period is missing. This situation is quite unusual (if not, in some ways, inexplicable): in the numerous papers in which funerary practices or rites of the *Roman world* are examined, Asiatic provinces are punctually given brief mentions or are very often left out (for example Reece 1977; Jones 1987; Amand 1987; Amand 1988; Millett 1990; Morris 1992; Struck 1993).

Given the guide lines of this meeting, such a contribution might not seem relevant: in fact it will concern mostly tombs and cemeteries which have not been archaeologically excavated and have in many cases been looted or found empty, a situation that does not allow any kind of quantification and statistical analysis. Therefore the following discussion will depend only upon the accidental survivals or – even better – upon the known survivals and so, paradoxically, evidence for funerary practices lacking not only proper excavation records but also even traces of the dead will be taken into consideration. Nevertheless, while aware of the lack of accurate information, it seems necessary to start to explore the Eastern provinces from these new perspectives even if this contribution will be able to offer mostly questions and hints on these subjects, rather than precise data which further studies must supply.

The tombs

If almost nothing can be said about the 'simple' burials (because of the lack of archaeological surveys), in contrast to the Western provinces, the Roman conquest of the Asiatic provinces did not apparently introduce any serious changes to funerary monuments. A well-rooted tradition of funerary architecture existed in these regions; therefore drastic changes due to the consequences of the Roman conquest, such as the emergence of new ruling elites, cannot be recorded. If radical innovations, in fact, do not seem to be perceived within the formal architectural aspects of tombs, gradual changes are visible, corresponding to the evolution of taste together with the slow reception of new architectural forms. This happens also with new building techniques (such as *opus caementicium*), the adoption of which reflects the more general revolution in the way of building begun in the Augustan period.

On the other hand, typically local features survive, above all rock-cut architecture. Rock-cut tombs in Anatolia belong to a tradition enduring over several millennia: in addition to the best known monuments boasting richly decorated façades with figural reliefs or with architectural

Fig. 17.1 *Karlik (Cappadocia). Rock-cut tomb*

forms, a large number of tombs situated in the Anatolian plateau are, in fact, plain and undecorated and having been looted or reused pose serious dating problems. However, we are certain of the existence of rock-cut tombs during the Imperial period thanks to figural or epigraphic evidence or to the topographical context: such persistence (which is scarcely recorded in Italy) seems to be peculiar of Central and Eastern Asia (particularly of Cappadocia) (Fig. 17.1), and located mostly in less urbanised areas.

From a formal point of view the tombs of Asia Minor of the Imperial period can be briefly divided according to these customary typologies:

– earth-cut pits (plain or containing chests, amphorae or urns) (isolated, within a precinct)
– buildings (house-shaped, temple-shaped, tower-shaped, exedrae)
– altars
– tumuli
– sarcophagi (on plinths, pillars or inside niche-shaped buildings), *chamosoria*
– hypogea
– rock-cut (sunk into the rock, chambers, niche-shaped) (with or without external decoration, with reliefs or architectural façades)

These definitions (or similar terms) substantially reflect the modern necessity of gathering the various types of monuments on architectural or compositional grounds, but it is well to remember how ancient names known from inscriptions (Kubinska 1968; Equini Schneider 1970) do not reveal any typological or qualitative difference, while the terms employed (which may vary from region to region) only indicate:

1) the tomb generically
2) the container for inhumation or cremation
3) functional parts of the funerary monument.

Setting aside in this context the elements of the architectural composition and of the decoration (or at least their historic-artistic and symbolic implications), let us concentrate on the most ignored data from monumental tombs, that is to say the 'structural' information (particularly of monument interiors), taking into consideration monumental tombs intended to receive several persons.

Among these we must include also a great number of containers that only seemingly can be defined as 'mono-somatic' such as open-air sarcophagi (or at the most, 'open' within niche-shaped monuments) lining the edges of 'streets of tombs' (Fig. 17.2). In addition to the several cases in which the inscriptions themselves mention permission to bury more than one person in the same tomb, we have the evidence offered by the surveys of the cemetery of Kalchedon (Asgari, Firatli 1978) and by rescue excavations at Kütahya (Türktüzün 1991: 225–227), in which the number of skeletons found inside sarcophagi is usually higher than that of the persons recorded in the inscriptions as entitled to be buried. Moreover in some regions it is possible to observe on this type of monument devices built into the sarcophagus to facilitate the removal of their lids (Alföldi-Rosenbaum 1980:29) (Fig. 17.3). Alternatively the absence of methods of closure by means of metal clamps, to fasten the lid to the chest, can also be noticed (Machatschek 1967: 22, 33; Koch, Sichtermann 1982: 20–21; Koch 1993a: 27). Such evidence shows how a single chest could be used for additional burials. This partially explains the dimensions of some containers which

Fig. 17.2 *Aphrodisias Museum. Sarcophagus with three portraits.*

Fig. 17.3 *Necropolis of Adrassos (Isauria): sarcophagus with devices for removal of the lid.*

sometimes are unusual for one single person, and which were intended to receive several persons (in most cases members of the same family). The choice of this type of monument could be partially explained as a means of lessening the expenses met with the purchase of the land and the construction of the tomb.

As for other types of funerary monument, several tombs in Asia Minor seem to be distinguished by receiving a number of burials higher than that which the actual space would let us suppose. In Asia Minor, in fact, tombs containing a large number of burials do not occur very frequently, while the prevailing plan both of built and rock-cut tombs consists of a square chamber (in front of which sometimes a courtyard or anteroom can be observed) with one side designated as the entrance and the other three with accommodation for burials (sarcophagi, funerary beds, *arcosolia*) (Fig. 17.4), according to the typical scheme of the οἶκος τρίκλινος, a formula epigraphically known (Kubinska 1968: 47; for the implicit relationships between 'house of the living' and 'house of the dead': Waelkens 1980; Waelkens 1982a). Given the great number of these tombs it seems probable that they had a 'familiar'

character (although some epigraphic evidence defines the tomb as a property of 'associative' type) but, assuming that the burial places were used only once, it would be desirable to know for which family members they were intended. Any assumption (e.g. father, mother, one child, the earliest three dead in the family) which does not admit more than the three burials leaves us perplexed and discontented. It seems at least plausible therefore to suppose that the tomb was used for subsequent burials.

Although the space was limited the evidence that these tombs were created in order to be used for several burials derives from many clues. In addition to the very few well known contexts of excavation which seem to confirm this assumption (Meriçboyu, Atasoy 1969; Atasoy 1974a; Tulay 1991: 28–30; Dedeoglu 1990) and to the figural decoration which is not easily thus explicable, we frequently find in these tombs both sarcophagi showing accommodation similar to that mentioned above for 'open-air' monuments (in Adrassos: Alföldi-Rosenbaum 1980: 23). There are also funerary beds of various types which do not seem either to provide definitive methods of closure, such as plain beds and above all *arcosolia*, the latter wide spread in built and above all in rock-cut tombs. The origin of the *arcosolium*-burial is still uncertain, but its presence in Asia Minor is certainly earlier than in Rome (where – despite large modifications – it was popular among Christian funerary monuments): the oldest dated example known to me in fact dates from the first half of the 1st century BC (in Kanytelleis in Cilicia: Machatschek 1967: 59).

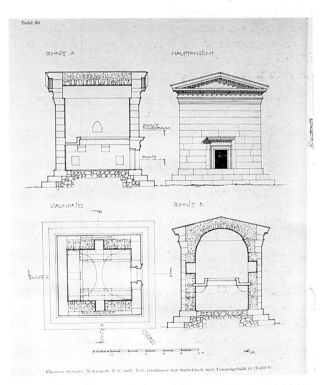

Fig. 17.4 *Necropolis of Elaiussa Sebaste (Cilicia): Monumental tomb (after Machatschek 1967)*

In rock-cut tombs the *arcosolium* consists of a surface scooped out inside an approximately semicircular niche: the presence of a cushion-shaped end in relief and the form of the niche itself prove that the dead person was not placed in a rigid container (whether of stone or wood) but simply laid on the funerary bed. We do not know how the lunette of the *arcosolium* was closed after the body had been laid, nor if it was actually closed, since we do not have archaeologically surveyed examples of perfectly preserved tombs. However, in the absence of any evidence (e.g. clamp holes, traces of masonry) for tombs which have already been looted, we cannot exclude that the lunette could remain open or that at most it was to be closed with easily removable material (wood? plaster?).

In built tombs the *arcosolium* was instead built in masonry, starting from the floor and ending with an horizontal surface of which the appearance suggests the possibility of a double burial, one inside the niche, the other above it. In these tombs the niche at least in most cases certainly could not house rigid chests. It remains totally uncertain whether it was closed, while the possibility of placing the deceased in closed containers (of masonry or other type) on the upper surface seems highly improbable (Machatschek 1967: 78–79; Alföldi-Rosenbaum 1971: 98–102).

A different type of burial occurring in tombs with a 'tricliniar' arrangement can be found in some cemeteries in Cilicia. Here the dead were laid in stone chests suspended on shelves lacking any room for the lid. Their internal dimensions do not allow the placing of rigid containers inside (Machatschek 1967: 76–78) (Fig. 17.4). In a structurally different but functionally similar way at Iasos in Caria, tombs show three 'perimetral' chests covered with stone slabs. The restricted area inside these (which is sometimes still partly occupied by the living rock, left unworked) has caused us to suppose that the dead were not laid down inside the chests but above the stone slabs (Tomasello 1991: 222).

Generally in all these tombs, whether built or carved out of the rock, with arcosolia or beds of any type, it seems very probable that the dead person, most likely wrapped in a shroud was simply and directly laid in the pre-arranged space but not in a rigid container, the use of which, besides, was hindered by the means of access to the tombs. This normally had reduced dimensions and – in the case of rock-cut tombs – could be placed some metres above ground level. Thus when there was a need to re-use the funerary bed, after a period of exposure the remains of the dead could therefore be removed, this involving a necessary 'secondary burial'.

Without a great quantity of available data, it is quite difficult to say how this practice was effected. At Iasos amphorae containing bones which were found close to built tombs but above all underneath internal floors have been recognised as belonging to 'secondary burials' (Levi 1961:552; Tomasello 1991: 218, 222). Sometimes bones

Fig. 17.5 *Perge Museum: Ostotheca with two portraits.*

could be gathered in an undercroft (for example bones belonging to several skeletons at Antiocheia ad Cragum: Rosenbaum 1967: 51) but we cannot exclude the possibility that in some cases the remains of the dead were simply moved aside, as seems to occur in at least one instance.

A widespread, if not the most extensive, practice provided 'secondary burial' in appropriate *ostothecai*, small stone or marble chests for a long time wrongly regarded as exclusively belonging to children's burials (Inan 1956: 69; Himmelmann 1970b: 17), which are preserved in several Turkish museums or in cemeteries but unfortunately always out of context (Fig. 17.5). Certainly, their function was that of receiving the remains of the dead person, which were by that time without flesh and soft tissues. They could therefore house several individuals, as a one-off example at Side has shown (Inan 1956: 69).

In conclusion, all this evidence suggests that a large number of the tombs of Asia Minor were used continually by the families that built them or at least by persons entitled to be buried there. The great number of epigraphic formulas recording curses or fines could therefore be explained as addressed not against occasional clandestine violators but against the possible occupation of the tomb by people unrelated to the family that owned it and who therefore might remove the original bodies. Among the consequences of this frequent and prolonged use of volumetrically restricted areas must be the tangible loss of grave furniture.

In the case of the 'multiple burial' sarcophagi, the superimposition of bodies in a restricted area could have caused the partial destruction of grave furniture and we cannot exclude the possibility that during the repeated re-openings some objects could have been removed in order to gain extra space or that furnishings could be robbed. As for burials in chamber-like tombs, we have found marked differences between the period of construction of the monument and the grave furniture, evidence that these tombs were used for a very long period of time, probably over several generations (Meriçboyu, Atasoy 1969; Atasoy, 1974a; Eskioglu 1989: 189–204).

Topographical context

In Asia Minor as well as in Italy tombs whether isolated or in groups are located outside the urban area, even if there are also cases of intramural burials which continue an ancient tradition of *ekistai* and dynasts' tombs in dominant positions, of which the Mausoleum of Halikarnassos is probably the most famous.

The presence of monumental tombs within the city has been well recorded for Ephesos, where some mausolea distributed in time between the late Republican age and the middle Empire flank the main street of the city. Similar evidence from the imperial period has been found at Aizanoi (Naumann, 1994), Assos (Clarke, Bacon, Koldewey 1902: 115–117), Miletos (Kleiner 1968: 124–134) and Priene (Wiegand, Schrader 1904: 278), obviously all tombs of well-deserving citizens.

Obviously most of the burials took place at the borders of the built-up areas: even in the absence of extensive systematically documented cases (in many cases the precise documentation of all the architectural evidence of individual cemeteries is also lacking), evidence confirms that the favourite place was along the main extra-urban street. However excluding some exceptions (above all those of Assos, Elaiussa Sebaste and Hierapolis of Phrygia), the overall effect generally is quite different from the most famous 'streets of tombs' in the Roman West. Sometimes in fact the type of funerary monuments gave a particular appearance to the cemetery, as in the case of rock-cut tombs. The configuration of the cemetery was conditioned by the orography and the landscape. Often the general development of the cemetery turned

out to be vertical rather than horizontal. Alternatively funerary monuments were built in isolation from others where specific conditions (rock-outcrops etc.) allowed. Rather than building immediately close to the road, what seemed to be most important was the striving, above all, for better visibility of the tomb, even if this might make it inaccessible, as can be observed – excluding the most ancient Lycian and Carian cemeteries – at Diokaisareia in Cilicia or at Sagalassos.

This desire can be recorded also for cemeteries where funerary monuments are built, as at Anemurion, Ariassos and Iasos. In these cases too there is an apparent lack of desire to give an organic appearance to the whole complex: the monuments climb up the hill away from the main roads, their distribution apparently related above all, to the desire to make the tomb somehow visible.

This characterises not only large urban cemeteries but also tombs in rural areas, as has been confirmed by recent surveys done in Cappadocia (Equini Schneider 1992–1993; Equini Schneider 1993), a scarcely urbanised area where villages were the predominant settlement type and the landscape was divided mostly into large estates. In spite of the lack of architectural evidence and the scarcity of surface material, small cemeteries or single rock-cut tombs are visible in this area which are sometimes notably constructed or richly decorated.

Rituals

The literary sources seem to agree that in the Greek world inhumation, *graecus mos* (Petr., *Satyricon* II, 2) prevailed and that its adoption in the Roman West caused the spread of the sarcophagus, still considered a foreign marvel in Rome at the end of the 1st century AD (Plin., *N.H.,* XXXVI, 131; *C.I.L.* XI, 1430).

Fig. 17.6 *Necropolis of Sagalassos (Pamphylia): Rock-cut tombs*

In 1960 in a well known paper on inhumation and cremation Audin wrote '*l'Asie Mineure constitua la citadelle de l'inhumation*' (Audin 1960:526; see also Nock 1932:326–327), but even if true as a rule, this view must be revised. It is not possible at the moment to quantify the presence of cremation in Asia but it is certain that it was widespread during the imperial period. The evidence is weak, but we have to bear in mind the structural diversity of funerary monuments and above all, the lesser possibility of preservation of cremation burials and containers. We cannot exclude the possibility that some of the above mentioned *ostothecai* could serve as containers for cremations.

For these reasons the few cases of partially surveyed cemeteries which have yielded examples of cremations are particularly significant, at Anemurion (Alföldi-Rosenbaum 1971: 94, 100), Ephesos (Pietsch, Trinkl 1994: 39–40), Eskisehir (Atasoy 1974: 258), Hierapolis of Phrygia (Verzone 1960–1961: 637), Iasos (Levi 1961–1962: 552), Pessinus and Sardis (Dedeoglu 1990; Dedeoglu, Malay 1991), as are instances where the tradition of the rock-cut monument occurs together with the rite of cremation, as at Sagalassos (Waelkens 1993: 47) (Fig. 17.6) or in Isauria (e.g. Swoboda, Keil, Knoll 1935: 89 no. 243). All these examples – although we must stress the absence of a large dossier of excavations – seem to suggest the cremation of the dead person in one place with the subsequent burial in another of ashes and bones in appropriate containers. The presence of cremation however cannot be regarded as evidence for 'Romanization' since such ritual occurs in Asia Minor also during the Hellenistic period, as the excavations at Mylasa (Akarca 1952), Myrina (Pottier, Reinach 1887: 57–75) and Sagalassos show (Waelkens, Hasendonckx, Owens, Arikan 1993: 338–341). These examples (of which the number is destined to increase) therefore seem substantially to revalue, at least partially, the words of Lucian (περί πένθου, 21), who, in total contrast to Petronius, defined cremation as a Greek custom.

Conclusions

The extremely fragmentary information available does not seem at the moment to allow final conclusions and not even to a guess at the number, of those who could afford monumental or, in any case, lasting tombs, although it would be a minority (the percentage we cannot say). Nevertheless, this synthesis shows how funerary practices in Asia Minor provide a panorama which is different from that usually understood, with several aspects that will have to be gradually confronted through new perspectives. In particular, the real presence of cremation (practised in whatever way) is to be verified, while everything concerning grave goods (their composition, nature and interpretation etc.) and therefore the rituals related to the dead person, either during the burial or afterwards, are yet to be studied. We are facing a series of questions which, at the moment, must be left unanswered, but the future answers will also have to take into consideration the religious and philosophical features of the Asiatic provinces which are historically more complex and for which there is a greater degree of literary evidence than those of the Western empire.

However, is it possible – from present knowledge – to find tangible clues of Romanization in the funerary practices of these provinces? In general, we can also wonder what 'Romanization' was and how deep it was in these provinces. The macroscopic effects of the Roman conquest of Europe are only partially found in Asia Minor: at a linguistic level Latin never took over from Greek, and the deep modifications of the landscape which occurred in Gaul, Spain and Britain with the foundations of cities or the organisation of the landscape were not necessary since they had already taken place there. As for the world of burial, apparently the answer seems to be no, since – as argued above – on the one hand formal traditional elements survive, on the other hand radical innovations do not seem to be recorded in the organisation of space within single tombs or cemeteries.

This negative picture should not mislead: rather than specific aspects an innovation can be observed in the vast extent of the phenomenon of the 'monumental tomb'. The richness and the luxury of urban cemeteries in Asia Minor seems to me the most remarkable factor from which to evaluate the major social changes which affected these regions during the imperial period. Monuments and ambitious buildings in this period are no longer dedicated to kings, high dignitaries or to a very restricted number of persons: rather the monumental or richly decorated tomb, made visible by whatever means, becomes more and more frequent. I interpret this as not only the emergence of a particular funerary ideology but also as clear evidence of a generalised and widespread level of wealth. In this context I think it is significant that in most cases we do not find monuments destined for an individual but – as we have seen before – to the burial of more than one person. The tombs do not seem therefore to show the emergence of single eminent persons, but they show the primacy of the most important families of the city.

As a confirmation of this, the funerary monuments of the rural areas have turned out to be particularly interesting, but they pose the problem of the rank of their owners, which is difficult to solve without epigraphic evidence. Considering their number I do not think it is possible to regard them as all belonging to affluent landowners, therefore a good number will have to be ascribed to members of the lower classes, determined at different levels to make their presence stand out in extra-urban areas through funerary monuments.

In conclusion we may assert that the deep difference between Hellenistic funerary monuments and Roman is mostly conceptual: no longer remarkable tombs for heroes or dynasts, but more and more frequent burials for families or groups, now marked by a 'bourgeois' spirit.

Notes

1. The accurately published contexts of non-monumental tombs of the imperial period are extremely few: amongst others, see the examples of Assos (Stupperich 1992: 4–6; Stupperich 1993: 6–12), Iasos (Berti 1990) and Pessinus (Devreker, Waelkens 1984: 51–74).

2. For rock-cut tombs of the imperial period, see Machatschek 1967: 49–61; Haspels 1971: 172–195; Thierry 1977; Alföldi-Rosenbaum 1980: 21–27; Wagner 1982: 138–141, 145–148; Thierry 1984: 659–666; Dardane-Longepierre 1985; Er 1991.

3. Cf. for example the stelai with a very stylised representation of a human figure carved on the façades of several rock-cut tombs in Cappadocia: in some cases we have found more than ten stelai belonging to tombs furnished with only three funerary beds.

4. Cf. the tumulus at Eskisehir (Atasoy 1974a: 260). The rarity of such evidence could be caused by the above mentioned absence of excavation surveys; see similar evidence of the Hellenistic period at Mylasa (Akarca 1952), Myrina (Pottier, Reinach 1887: 16–17), Dardanos (Duyuran 1960) or of the imperial period at Susa in Mesopotamia (Ghirsmann 1949: 198).

5. The cemetery surveyed in 1967–68 contained 25 inhumation burials (simple pit, pit coated with different materials, 'cist-shaped', sarcophagi) and 36 cremation burials (simple pit, pits coated with different materials). As stratigraphy was seriously disturbed, only 21 burials had evidence of date; in any case it was clear that both rites were contemporaneously practised throughout the period of the cemetery's use from the Hellenistic period to the 5th century AD (Devreker, Waelkens 1984: 51–74).

Bibliography

This selection has no claim to be complete: further bibliography is quoted in the titles given below (all published after 1900).

General Works

Audin, A. 1960. Inhumation et incinération. *Latomus*, 19: 312–322; 518–532.

Berciu, I. and Wolski, W. 1970. Un nouveau type de tombe mis au jour à Apulum et le problème des sarcophages à voute de l'Empire romaine. *Latomus*, 29: 919–965.

Hesberg von, H. and Zanker, P. (eds.) 1987. *Römische Gräberstrassen*. Munich: Verlag der Bayerischen Akademie der Wissenschaften.

Jones, R. 1987. Burial Customs of Rome and the Provinces. In Wacher J., *The Roman World*. London-New York: Routledge & Kegan Paul, pp. 812–831.

Koch, G. 1993a. *Sarkophage der römischen Kaiserzeit*. Darmstadt: Wissenschaftliche Buchgesellschaft.

Koch, G. (ed.), 1993b. *Grabeskunst der römischen Kaiserzeit*. Mainz am Rhein: Verlag Philipp von Zabern.

Koch, G. and Sichtermann, H. 1982. *Römische Sarkophage*. Munich: C.H. Beck'sche Verlagsbuchhandlung.

Millett, M. 1990. The Roman World – a world apart?. *Journal of Roman Archaeology*, 3: 213–216.

Morris, I. 1992. *Death-Ritual and Social Structure in Classical Antiquity*. Cambridge: Cambridge University Press.

Nock, A.D. 1932. Cremation and Burial in the Roman Empire. *Harvard Theological Review*, 25: 321–359.

Purcell, N. 1987. Tomb and Suburb. In *Römische Gräberstrassen* (eds. H. von Hesberg and P. Zanker) Munich: Verlag der Bayerischen Akademie der Wissenschaften, pp. 25–41.

Reece, R. (ed.) 1977. *Burial in the Roman World*. London: The Council for British Archaeology, Research Report, 22.

Struck, M. (ed.) 1993. *Römerzeitliche Gräber als Quellen zu Religion, Bevölkerungsstruktur und Sozialgeschichte*. Mainz: Institut für Vor- und Frühgeschichte der Johannes Gutenberg – Universität Mainz.

Toynbee, J.M.C. 1971. *Death and Burial in the Roman World*. London: Thames and Hudson.

Funerary Symbolism

Cumont, Fr. 1942. *Recherches sur le Symbolisme funéraire des Romains*. Paris: Libraire Orientaliste Paul Geuthner.

Nock, A.D. 1946. Sarcophagi and Symbolism. *American Journal of Archaelogy*, 50: 141–170.

Turcan, R. 1978. Les sarcophages romaines et le problème du symbolisme funeraire. In *Aufstieg und Niedergang der Römische Welt* II.16.2. Berlin-New York: Walter de Gruyter, pp. 1700–1735.

Tombs and funerary monuments in Asia Minor

Akarca, A. 1952. Mylasa'da Hellenistik bir mezar. A Hellenistic Tomb in Mylasa, *Belleten*, 16: 367–405.

Alföldi-Rosenbaum, E. 1971. *Anamur Nekropolü. The Necropolis of Anemurium* [Türk ve Tarih Kurumu Yayılarından, VI s., n. 12]. Ankara: Türk Tarih Kurumu Basımevi.

Alföldi-Rosenbaum E. 1980. *The Necropolis of Adrassus (Balabolu) in Rough Cilicia (Isauria)*. Vienna: Österreichische Akademie der Wissenschaften. Phil.-Hist. Klasse. Denkschriften, 146.

Amand, M. 1987. La réapparition de la sépulture sous tumulus dans l'empire romain. *L'antiquité classique*, 56: 163–182.

Amand, M. 1988. La réapparition de la sépulture sous tumulus dans l'empire romain. II. *L'antiquité classique*, 57: 176–203.

Anlağan, Ç. 1968. Akkuzulu Tümülüsü Kazısı, *Anadolu*, 12: 1–7.

Arkwright, W. 1911. Penalties in Lycian Epitaph of Hellenistic and Roman Times. *Journal of Hellenic Studies*, 31: 269–275.

Asgari, N. 1965. *Kleinasiatiche Ostotheken im Sarkophagform* [unpubl. Diss.]. Istanbul.

Asgari, N. 1977. Die Halbfabrikate kleinasiatischer Girlandensarkophage und ihre Herkunft. *Archäologischer Anzeiger*, 329–380.

Asgari, N. 1992. Prokonnesos-1990 çalışmaları. *IX Araştırma Sonuçları Toplantısı*: Ankara: 311–332.

Asgari, N. and Firatlı, N. 1978. Die Nekropole von Kalchedon. In *Studien zur Religion und Kultur Kleinasiens. Festschrift für Fr. K. Dörner*. Leiden: Études préliminaires aux religions orientales dans l'empire romaine, 66.1, pp. 1–92.

Atasoy, S. 1974a. The Kocakızlar Tumulus in Eskişehir, Turkey. *American Journal of Archaeology*, 78: 255–263.

Atasoy, S. 1974b. Aphrodisias Yöresindeki Tümülüsler. The Tumuli of the Environs of Aphrodisias. *Belleten*, 38: 351–360.

Atila, I.A. 1992. Olympos mezar odası kurtarma kazısı. *II. Müze Kurtarma Kazıları Semineri*. Ankara: 105–127.

Ayabakan, C. 1991. Maşattepe tümülüsü kurtarma kazısı. *I. Müze Kurtarma Kazıları Semineri*. Ankara: 49–62.

Başer, S.S. 1991. 1988–89 yılları Kibyra kurtarma kazıları. *I. Müze Kurtarma Kazıları Semineri*. Ankara: 235–260.

Bean, G.E. 1960. Notes and Inscriptions from Pisidia. Part II. *Anatolian Studies*, 10: 43–83.

Berges, D. 1993. Kleinasiatische Girlandesarkophage in Kleinasien. In *Grabeskunst der römischen Kaiserzeit* (G. Koch ed.), Mainz am Rhein: Verlag Philipp von Zabern, pp. 23–35.

Berti, F. 1990. Les Travaux à Iasos en 1988. *XI. Kazı Sonuçları Toplantısı*. Ankara: 229–243.

Borchhardt, J. (ed.) 1975. *Myra*. Berlin: Istanbuler Forschungen, 30.

Clarke, J.T., Bacon, Tr.H. and Koldewey, R. 1902. *Investigations at Assos*. London-Cambridge-Leipzig: The Hentzemann Press Boston.

Cormack, S. 1989. A Mausoleum at Ariassos. *Anatolian Studies*, 39: 31–40.

Dardane, S., Longepierre, D. 1985. Essai de typologie des monuments funéraires de *Sydima* (époque lycienne et romaine). *Ktema,* 10: 219–232.

Dedeoğlu, H. 1990. Roman Tomb. In *The Sardis Campaign of 1986* (C.H. Jr. Greenewalt, N.D. Cahill, H. Dedeoğlu; P. Hermannn eds.). *Bulletin of the American Schools of Oriental Research, Supplement* No. 26, pp. 161–164.

Dedeoğlu, H. and Malay, H. 1991. Some Inscribed Cinerary Chests and Vases from Sardis. In *Erol Atalay Memorial.* Izmir: Ege Üniversitesi Basımevi, pp. 113–120.

Devreker, J. 1989. Pessinus (Pessinonte) 1987. *X. Kazı Sonuçları Toplantısı.* Ankara: vol. II, 319–337.

Devreker, J.; Vermeulen, F. 1993. Pessinus (Pessinonte) 1991: Preliminary Report. *XIV. Kazı Sonuçları Toplantısı.* Ankara: vol. II, 261–271.

Devreker, J. and Waelkens, M. 1984. *Les Fouilles de la Rijksuniversiteit te Gent a Pessinonte. I. 1967–1973* [Dissertationes Archaeologicae Gandenses, XXII], Brugge: De Tempel.

Durugönül, S. 1989. *Die Felsreliefs im Rauhen Kilikien.* Oxford: BAR International Series, 511.

Duyuran, R. 1960. Découverte d'un tumulus près de l'ancienne Dardanos. *Anadolu*, 5: 9–12.

Equini Schneider, E. 1970. Note sulle iscrizioni funerarie di Hierapolis di Frigia. *Atti dell'Accademia nazionale dei Lincei. Classe di scienze morali, storiche e filologiche. Rendiconti,* S. VIII, XXV: 475–482.

Equini Schneider, E. 1972. *La necropoli di Hierapolis di Frigia.* Rome: Monumenti antichi pubblicati per cura della Accademia Nazionale dei Lincei, 48.

Equini Schneider, E. 1992–1993. Siti di età romana in Anatolia: indagini in Cappadocia 1993. *Scienze dell'Antichità,* 6–7: 387–407.

Equini Schneider, E. 1993. Classical Sites in Anatolia: 1993 Archaeological Survey in Cappadocia. *XI Araştırma Sonuçları Toplantısı.* Ankara:429–440.

Er, Y. 1991. Diversità e interazione culturale in Cilicia Trachea. I monumenti funerari. *Quaderni storici,* 76: 105–140.

Er Scarborough, Y. 1996. 1994 Isaura Yüzei Araştırması. *XIII Araştırma Sonuçları Toplantısı.* Ankara: 339–356.

Erdemgil, S. 1981. Kestel kazısı 1980 yılı çalişmaları. *III. Kazı Sonuçları Toplantısı.* Ankara: 63–66.

Eskioglu, M. 1989. Garipler Tümülüsü Ve Kayseri'deki tipi mezarlar. *Türk arkeoloji dergisi,* 28: 198–204

Evren, A.; Içten, C. 1993. Torbalı Pancar Tümülüsü kurtarma kazısı. *III. Müze Kurtarma Kazıları Semineri.* Ankara: 179–195

Fleischer, R. 1978. Eine späthellenistische Ostothek aus Pisidien. In *Classica et Provincialia. Festschrift E. Diez.* Graz: Akademische Druck- und Verlaganstalt, pp. 39–50.

Flacelière, R., Robert, R. and Robert, J. 1939. Bulletin épigraphique. *Revue des études grecques,* 52: 445–538.

Ghirsmann, R. 1949. Campagne de fouilles à Suse en 1948–1949. *Académie des inscriptions et belles-lettres. Comptes rendus des séances de l'année 1949,* pp. 196–199.

Gibson, E. 1981. The Rahm Koç Collection. Inscriptions. Part VIII, A Cinerary Chest from Sardis. *Zeitschrift für Papyrologie und Epigraphik,* 42: 215–216.

Haspels, C.H.E. 1971. *The Highlands of Phrygia.* Princeton: Princeton University Press.

Heberdey, R. and Wilhelm, W. 1900. Grabbauten von Termessos in Pisidien. *Jahreshefte des Österreichischen Archäologischen Institutes in Wien,* 3: 177–210.

Himmelmann, N. 1970a. Μία ὀστοθήκη ἀπο τὴν Κιλικία στή Λευκωσία. *Report of the Department of Antiquities, Cyprus,* pp. 146–148.

Himmelmann, N. 1970b. Der 'Sarkophag' aus Megiste. *Akademie der Wissenschaft und der Literatur in Mainz. Abhandlungen der Geistes- und Sozialwissenschaftlichen Klasse,* pp. 5–30.

Himmelmann, N. 1971. Sarcophage in Antakya und Bericht über eine Reise nach Kleinasien. *Archäologischer Anzeiger,* pp. 92–93.

Inan, J. 1956. Heykeltraşlık eserleri. Die Skulpturen. In *Side Agorası ve civarındaki binalar. Die Agora von Side und die benachbarten Bauten* (Mansel, A.M., Bean, G.E. and Inan, J. eds.) Ankara: Türk Tarih Kurumu Basımevi, pp. 49–77.

Işık, F. 1977. Zur Datierung des verschallenen Girlandensarkophags aus Alaşehir. *Archäologischer Anzeiger,* pp. 380–383.

Işık, F. 1984. Sarkophage aus Aphrodisias. *Marburger Winckelmann-Programm.* pp. 243–281.

Işık, F. 1993. Zur Kontinuitätsfrage der Kleinasiatischen Girlandesarkophage während des Hellenismus und der frühen Kaiserzeit. In *Grabeskunst der römischen Kaiserzeit* (G. Koch ed.), Mainz am Rhein: Verlag Philipp von Zabern, pp. 9–21.

Jobst, W. 1983. Embolosforschungen I. *Jahreshefte des Österreichischen Archäologischen Instituts in Wien, Beiblatt* 54: 149–152.

Keil, J. 1930. XV. Vorläufiger Bericht über die Ausgrabungen in Ephesos. *Jahreshefte des Österreichischen Archäologischen Instituts in Wien, Beiblatt,* 26: 5–66.

Keil, J. and von Premerstein A. 1914. *Bericht über eine dritte Reise in Lydien und den angrenzenden Gebieten Ioniens.* Vienna: Österreichische Akademie der Wissenschaften. Phil.-Hist. Klasse. Denkschriften, 57.1.

Kleiner, G. 1957. Hellenistische Sarkophage in Kleinasien. *Istanbuler Mitteilungen* 7: 1–10.

Kleiner, G. 1968. *Die Ruinen von Milet.* Berlin: Walter de Gruyter & Co.

Knibbe, D. and Langmann, G. (eds.). *Via Sacra Ephesiaca I.* Vienna: Berichte und Materialien herausgegeben von Österreichischen Archäologischen Institut, 3.

Knibbe, D. and Thür, H. (eds.). *Via Sacra Ephesiaca II.* Vienna: Berichte und Materialien herausgegeben von Österreichischen Archäologischen Institut, 3, pp. 19–48.

Kodan, H. and Günbattı, C. 1992. Tontar Roma Mezarı. *Türk arkeoloji dergisi,* 30: 83–103.

Kramer, J. 1983. Zu einigen Architekturteilen des Grabtempels westlich von Side. *Bonner Jahrbücher,* 183:145–166.

Kubinska, J. 1968. *Les monuments funéraires dans les inscriptions grecques de l'Asie mineure.* Warszawa: Panstwowe Wydawictwo Navkowe.

Lamprechts, P. 1969. Les fouilles de Pessinonte: la nécropole. *L'antiquité classique* 38: 121–146.

Levi, D. 1961–1962. Le due prime campagne di scavo a Iasos (1960–1961). *Annuario della Scuola archeologica di Atene e delle Missioni italiane in Oriente,* 23–24: 505–571.

Machatschek, A. 1967. *Die Nekropolen und Grabmäler im Gebiet von Elaiussa Sebaste und Korykos im Rauhen Kilikien.* Vienna: Österreichische Akademie der Wissenschaft. Phil.-Hist. Klasse. Denkschriften, 96.

Machatschek, A. 1974. Die Grabtempel von Dösene im Rauhen Kilikien. *Mansel'e Armağan. Melanges Mansel.* Ankara: Türk Tarih Kurumu Basımevi, vol. I, pp. 251–261.

Mansel, A.M. 1949. Perge nekropolünde yapılan Kazılar ve Araştırmalar. Excavations and Researches in the Necropolis of Perge. In *Pergede Kazılar ve Araştırmalar. Excavations and Researches at Perge* (Mansel, A.M.; Akarca, A. eds.). Ankara: Türk Tarih Kurumu Basımevi, pp. 1–34; 44–61.

Mansel, A.M. 1959. Die Grabbauten von Side. *Archäologischer Anzeiger,* 364–402.

Mansel, A.M. and Akarca, A. (eds.) 1949. *Pergede Kazılar ve Araştırmalar. Excavations and Researches at Perge* [Türk ve Tarih Kurumu Yayılarından, V s., n. 8]. Ankara: Türk Tarih Kurumu Basımevi.

Mansel, A.M., Bean, G.E. and Inan, J. 1956. *Side Agorası ve civarındaki binalar. Die Agora von Side und die benachbarten Bauten* [Türk Tarih Yayınlarından V S., No 11]. Ankara: Türk Tarih Kurumu Basımevi.

Mendel, G. 1912. *Catalogue des Sculptures grecques, romaines et byzantines. I.* Constantinople.

Mendel, G. 1914. *Catalogue des Sculptures grecques, romaines et byzantines. III.* Constantinople.

Meriçboyu, Y. and Atasoy, S. 1969. The Kanlıbag at Izmit. *Istanbul Arkeoloji Müzeleri*, 15–16: 67–95

Mitchell, St. 1992. Ariassos 1990. *IX Araştırma Sonuçları Toplantısı.* Ankara: 93–108.

Morey, Ch.R. 1921–1922. The Origin of the Asiatic Sarcophagi. *The Art Bulletin*, 4: 64–70.

Morey, Ch.R. 1923. The Chronology of the Asiatic Sarcophagi. *American Journal of Archaeology*, 27: 69–84

Morey, Ch.R. 1924. *The Sarcophagus of Claudia Antonia Sabina.* Princeton: Publications of the American Society for the Excavations of Sardis V.1.

Naumann, R. 1994. Römische Grabbau westlich des Zeus-Tempelareas in Aizanoi. *Istanbuler Mitteilungen* 44: 303–306.

Naour, Ch. 1976. Inscriptions et reliefs de Kibyratide et de Cabalide. *Zeitschrift für Papyrologie und Epigraphik*, 22:109–136.

Nollé, J. 1985. Grabepigramme und Reliefdarstellungen aus Kleinasien. *Zeitschrift für Papyrologie und Epigraphik*, 60: 117–135.

Özgen, E. and Özgen, I. 1988. *Antalya Museum.* Ankara.

Parrot, A. 1939. *Malédictions et violations de tombes.* Paris: Libraire Orientaliste Paul Geuthner.

Pietrogrande, A.L. 1935. Nuova serie asiatica di urne e di piccoli sarcofagi. *Bullettino del Museo dell'Impero romano* VI:17–37.

Pietsch, W. and Trinkl E. 1994. Der Grabungsbericht der Kampagnen 1992/93. In *Via Sacra Ephesiaca II* (D. Knibbe and H. Thür eds.). Vienna: Berichte und Materialien herausgegeben von Österreichischen Archäologischen Institut, 3, pp. 19–48.

Pinna Caboni, B. 1993. La necropoli romana di Alagün. *Annali della Scuola normale superiore di Pisa*, s. III, XXIII: 954–966.

Pottier, E. and Reinach S. 1887. *La nécropole de Myrina*, Paris: Ernest Thorin Éditeur.

Robert, R. and Robert, J. 1950. Bulletin épigraphique. *Revue des études grecques*, 43: 121–220.

Rodenwalt, G. 1933. Sarcophagi from Xanthos. *Journal of Hellenic Studies*, 53: 181–213.

Rodenwalt, G. 1948. Sarkophagprobleme. *Mitteilungen des Deutschen Archäologischen Instituts, Römische Abteilung*, 58: 1–26.

Rosenbaum, E. 1967. The Cemeteries. In *A Survey of Coastal Cities in Western Cilicia* (Rosenbaum, E., Huber, G. and Onurkan, S. eds.). Ankara: Türk Tarih Kurumu Basımevi, pp. 50–66.

Rosenbaum, E. , Huber, G. and Onurkan, S. 1967. *A Survey of Coastal Cities in Western Cilicia.* [Türk Tarih Yayınlarından V.S., No. 1, 8]. Ankara: Türk Tarih Kurumu Basımevi.

Strocka, V.M. 1996. Datierungskriterien Kleinasiatischer Girlandensarkophage. *Archäologischer Anzeiger*: 455–473.

Stupperich, R. 1992. Zweiter Vorbericht über die Grabung in der Westtor-Nekropole von Assos in Sommer 1990. In *Ausgrabungen in Assos 1990* (U. Serdaroğlu and R. Stupperich (eds.). Bonn: Asia Minor Studien, 5, pp. 1–31.

Stupperich, R. 1993. Dritter Vorbericht über die Grabung in der Westtor-Nekropole von Assos in Sommer 1991. In *Ausgrabungen in Assos 1991* (U. Serdaroğlu and R. Stupperich (eds.). Bonn: Asia Minor Studien, 10, pp. 1–35.

Swoboda, H., Keil, J. and Knoll, F. 1935. *Denkmäler aus Lykaonien, Pamphylien und Isaurien.* Brünn: Verlag Rudolf M. Rohrer.

Takaz, H. 1975. Amasya Külistepe Nekropol Kazısı ön Raporu. *Türk arkeoloji dergisi*, 22.1: 109–115.

Thierry, N. 1977. Un problème de continuité ou de rupture. La Cappadoce entre Rome, Byzance et les Arabes. *Académie des inscriptions et belles-lettres. Comptes rendus des séances de l'année 1977*, pp. 98–144.

Thierry, N. 1984. Découvertes à la Nécropole de Göreme (Cappadoce). *Académie des inscriptions et belles-lettres. Comptes rendus des séances de l'année 1984*, pp. 656–691.

Thür, H. 1990. Arsinoe IV, eine Schwester Kleopatras VII, Grabinhaberin des Oktogons von Ephesos? Eine Vorschlag. *Jahreshefte des Österreichischen Archäologischen Instituts in Wien, Hauptblatt*, 60: 43–56.

Tomasello, Fr. 1991. *L'acquedotto romano e la necropoli presso l'istmo* [Missione Archeologica Italiana di Iasos, II]. Roma: Giorgio Bretschneider Editore.

Torelli, M. 1988. Il monumento efesino di Memmio. *Scienze dell'Antichità*, 2: 403–426.

Tulay, A.S. 1991. Kabalar kurtarma kazısı 1989. *I. Müze Kurtarma kazıları Semineri.* Ankara: 25–39.

Türktüzün, M. 1991. Roma devri Nekropolü Kurtarma Kazısı. *Türk arkeoloji dergisi*, 29: 225–249.

Türktüzün, M. 1992. Çavdarhisar (Aizanoi) Roma devri nekropolü kurtarma kazısı. *II. Müze Kurtarma Kazıları Semineri.* Ankara: 81–94.

Türktüzün, M. 1993a. Zwei Säulensarkophage aus der Südwestnekropole in Aizanoi. *Archäologischer Anzeiger*, 517–526.

Türktüzün, M. 1993b. Çavdarhisar (Aizanoi) Roma nekropolü kurtarma kazısı. *III. Müze Kurtarma Kazıları Semineri.* Ankara: 151–166.

Ussishkin, D. 1977. Two Lead Coffins from Cilicia. *Israel Exploration Journal*, 27: 215–218.

Verzone, P. 1961–1962. Le campagne 1960 e 1961 a Hierapolis di Frigia. *Annuario della Scuola archeologica di Atene e delle Missioni italiane in Oriente*, 23–24: 633–647.

de Visscher, F. 1963. *Le droit des tombeaux romains.* Milan: Giuffré Editore.

Waelkens, M. 1980. Das Totenhaus in Kleinasien. *Antike Welt*, 11.4: 3–12.

Waelkens, M. 1982a. Hausähnliche Gräber in Anatolien vom 3. Jht. v.Chr. bis in die Römerzeit. In *Palast und Hütte* (eds. D. Papenfuss and V.M. Strocka). Mainz am Rhein: Verlag Philipp von Zabern, pp. 421–445.

Waelkens, M. 1982b. *Dokimeion. Die Werkstatte der Repräsentativen kleinasiatischen Sarkophage.* Berlin: Gebr. Mann Verlag.

Waelkens, M. 1986a. *Die Kleinasiatische Türsteine.* Mainz am Rhein: Verlag Philipp von Zabern.

Waelkens, M. 1986b. Marmi e sarcofagi frigi. *Annali della Scuola normale superiore di Pisa*, s. III, XVI: 661–678.

Waelkens, M., Hasendonckx, A., Owens, E. and Arikan, B. 1993. The Excavations at Sagalassos 1991. *XIV. Kazı Sonuçları Toplantısı*, Ankara. Vol. II, pp. 325–353.

Wagner, J. 1982. Neue Denkmäler aus Doliche. *Bonner Jahrbücher*, 182: 133–166

Wegner, M. 1974. Kunstgeschichtliche Beurteilung der Grabtempel von Olba/Diokaisareia. In *Mansel'e Armağan. Melanges Mansel*, Ankara: Türk Tarih Kurumu Basımevi, vol. I, pp. 575–583.

Wiegand, Th. and Schrader. H. 1904. *Priene.* Berlin:Georg Reimer.

Wiegartz, H. 1965. *Kleinasiatische Säulensarkophage.* Berlin: Gebr. Mann Verlag.

Wilberg, W., Theuer, M., Eichler, Fr. and Keil, J. 1953. *Die Bibliothek.* Vienna: Forschungen in Ephesos, V.1.

Wrede, H. 1990. Der Sarkophag eines Mädchens in Malibu und die frühen Klinensarkophage Roms, Athens und Kleinasiens. *OPA* 6: 15–46.

Wulf, U. 1993. Zwei Grabbauten in der Südwestnekropole von Aizanoi. *Archäologischer Anzeiger*, 527–541.

Burial and ethnicity

The papers in this section approach the complex and controversial issue of ethnic identity. In contrast to much contemporary British scholarship, which lays considerable emphasis on theoretical aspects of ethnic self-identification, these papers follow empirical approaches in Germanic and central European traditions.

The papers by Topál, Jovanovic and Fasold each examine the problem of ethnic identity in cemeteries in the Alpine and Danube provinces, while Riedel's focus lies on a single city, Cologne. They share an approach which attempts to identify aspects of grave layout, funerary tradition and artefact style with membership of particular ethnic groups, who according to archaeological, literary and epigraphic evidence peopled the areas in question prior and / or subsequent to Roman annexation, although confidence in the strength of these identifications varies among the contributors. Considerable emphasis is placed on the mixing of populations and all papers play down the role of Romanization in the patterns which emerge. At most, incorporation within the empire introduces further elements into what is already a complex mixture. Indeed a lack of obvious general change in burial ritual is noted by other contributors (Vermeulen and Bourgeois, Spanu). In the final section Meneghini and Santangeli Valenzani argue that in fifth-century Rome, groups of burials with and without grave goods reflect the maintenance of their identity by different groups arriving in the city, with the disappearance of these differences reflecting their integration into the general population. Such a model might be usefully applied to evidence from some of the cosmopolitan early Roman cities discussed in this section, such as Aquincum, Sirmium or Cologne.

Contributions in other sections are also of primary relevance to this question, from both a methodological and theoretical perspective. In order to identify different groups in their local burial traditions all of these papers are obliged to rely on characterisations of the burial practices of other areas which may be based on relatively scant information and which require substantial revision. Spanu assesses the generalisations made about burial practices in Asia Minor, in particular that inhumation remains a constant feature of burial practice there throughout the Roman period. His revisions, in particular the identification of a strong cremation tradition, are significant for our understanding of intrusive burial practices in the western provinces. Important also is his emphasis on the variability of burial types within Asia Minor. Differences in types of cremation burial have long been taken to signify difference in ethnic origin. Experimental reconstruction and detailed archaeological attention is now shedding further light on the complex cremation ceremonies of which some of these deposits are the residue, as papers by Polfer, McKinley and Kreuz show. Esmonde Cleary reminds us that the location of the dead can be as significant in terms of cultural identity as the form of burial. Only in Murail and Girard's paper is osteological evidence fully exploited. They demonstrate that the population buried at Chantambre remains the same, despite the changes in the material culture of death. Their approach depends on a long-standing local inhumation tradition. In many of the study areas the prevalence of cremation would not permit this type of skeletal analysis, although the case study from Cologne, as well as the recent excavations of the eastern cemetery of Roman London remind us that sometimes substantial samples of early Roman inhumation burials are available elsewhere for such approaches.

The uptake or rejection of imported material culture and of new types of burial rite by local populations, as discussed by Murail and Girard, is also the concern of several other papers elsewhere in the volume. Fitzpatrick stresses local appropriation and re-interpretation of exotic items and practices in the late Iron Age; in her study area, Tuffreau-Libre demonstrates that imported material, in the shape of terra sigillata, seems to have been rejected for burial for much of the first century AD despite its presence on settlement sites. Abegg-Wigg's paper shows that some aspects of burial practice, especially monuments, could carry meanings in both indigenous and Roman traditions. On the other hand Martin-Kilcher argues for the existence, at least at an elite level, of a common supra-regional ideology which endures over several centuries, manifested in the richly furnished graves of some young women.

However even where burial ritual appears little changed, Spanu's case study shows a need for sensitivity to which elements of the population employed it. In Asia Minor little change can be identified between the Hellenistic and Roman periods in burial ritual, funerary architecture or burial location. Nevertheless a monumental funerary vocabulary came to be exploited by a larger proportion of the population in the Roman period, especially in urban areas, than in the Hellenistic. In Vermeulen and Bourgeois's study region of Sandy Flanders, little change is visible between Iron Age and Roman period burial rites, but burials of the latter period are much more archaeologically visible. Might we propose that this increase also represents the adoption of an existing burial form by an increasing proportion of the population as well as population growth?

Finally it is worth noting that opportunities to study change in burial practice from the same cemetery or same area over 'transitional' periods, for example from the Iron Age to Roman period, or from the late Roman to early mediaeval, as well as through the course of the Roman period, remain all too rare. The sample of cemeteries around Verulamium and the possibility at Chantambre of detailed study of one cemetery over a long period of time remain somewhat exceptional.

18. Early Roman graves in Southern Bavaria – a review

Peter Fasold

The individualistic character of graves provides an excellent source for observing the formation of new political und social units. The question this paper seeks to answer is to what extent the study of burials can illuminate the early history of the provinces of Raetia and of northwest Noricum (see Dietz 1995 for the best recent summary of this area). Of particular interest is the ethnic composition of the provincial population and its effect upon the process of Romanisation which the native population experienced. Above all we must define what is 'native' and what is 'intrusive' or 'foreign' (Fasold 1993b: 382–289). For example we can look at jewellery and pottery which clearly come from outside, the distribution and origin of which can be clarified by other groups of finds, for example gravestones (e.g. Garbsch 1965: 119–128). Certain striking examples of funerary rites which were developed and practised elsewhere can also be informative. In contrast epigraphic evidence, including tombstones, is almost completely absent for Raetia in the first century AD. Thus we do not know which military units were stationed in the Voralpenraum in the first half of the first century (Dietz 1995: 58–59, 75; Schön 1986: 94–102). Yet epigraphic sources could, ideally (for example in the case of a building inscription and an excavated cemetery from the same fort), help to assign particular funerary rites to foreign, perhaps even exotic (auxiliary) troops. Furthermore, caution is still necessary when trying to localise the Celtic tribal groupings recorded for North Raetia (Dietz 1995: 33–34). Physical anthropology can also offer little help, for the few burials that have been recorded are mainly cremations and so provide insufficient material for such studies (Schröter 1993: 133–138). The lack of a greater amount of botanical remains also prevents analysis of the degree of change (Willerding 1978; see also Kreuz this volume).

From the Voralpenraum few cemeteries are known or have been published from the early imperial period, i.e. between the conquest in 15 BC and the establishment of the Danube Limes under Claudius. The *Gräberstraße* at Kempten-Cambodunum was established in the Augustan period. Most of the 435 burials recorded so far date to the

first century (Mackensen 1978; Faber 1992). Burials of the first half of the first century AD are known from the military station on the Lorenzberg near Epfach-Abodiacum (Müller-Karpe 1964). Little can be said about the few graves which were recovered from Augsburg-Augusta Vindelicum, mainly in the nineteenth century (Hübener 1958). The graves of the 'Heimstettener Gruppe' are concentrated in rural districts between the Iller and Inn and date to the period from Tiberius to Nero (Keller 1984).The earliest burials at Bregenz-Brigantium, in the Austrian Federal State of Vorarlberg, also date to the reign of Augustus (von Schwerzenbach 1909; von Schwerzenbach, Jakobs 1910).

Several cemeteries are known from northwest Noricum, which are included here for a number of good reasons. They began in the Claudian period and are Hörafing (Gerhardt, Maier 1964), Karlstein (von Chlingensperg 1896), Unteremmerting (Hochberger, Pittner 1962) and Salzburg-Maxglan (Hell 1934). It has not been possible to excavate systematically large areas of the cemeteries from the *municipium* of Salzburg-Iuvavum, as it has long been built over and plundered (Heger 1974: 94–97). Mention should also be made of the *Gräberstraße* at Seebruck-Bedaium, which started in the Vespasianic period (Fasold 1993a).

If we take a look at late La Tène funerary rites in southern Bavaria in order to establish a basis from which to look at further developments, then it is immediately apparent that burials of this period are quite simply absent. This phenomenon has long been the subject of heated debate (Christlein 1982; Fischer 1995; Gleirscher 1987a: 78–82; Krämer 1985: 34–38; Moosbauer 1997: 187–89; von Schnurbein 1985a: 32; von Schnurbein 1993; Schön 1984: 62–66, 85–93; Sommer 1988: 612–619; Sommer 1990; Struck 1996: 129–137). Sabine Rieckhoff has recently attributed the few graves of the so-called 'southeast Bavarian Group' to German immigrants from Central Germany, who then, according to her, soon left the area before about 60 BC (Rieckhoff 1995: 185–190). Archaeological features in the oppidum of Manching might indicate a radical change in funerary rites as early as the second century BC, which would certainly make the identification of 'normal' burials even more difficult (Lange 1983: 111–113; Hahn 1992: 229–232). However, native settlements from the last decades before the Roman occupation are also unknown. It is now generally accepted that the flourishing oppidum culture ended in southern Bavaria around 80/70 BC. Manching, the best-researched oppidum, was finally abandoned by a residual population about 40 BC (Gebhard 1991: 104; Rieckhoff 1995: 187). There are no other La Tène D2 remains between Iller and Inn, so that we must conclude that this area was more or less abandoned when Roman troops occupied it (Fischer 1995: 226; Rieckhoff 1995: 201; Sommer 1988: 614). The Bavarian Archeological Service is efficient, and would surely have found relevant evidence in an area which has produced ample information for other, earlier periods, and the reasons for this reduction in population must remain shrouded in darkness. Political factors might have played a role, or even a devastating plague (Rieckhoff 1995: 188). The remaining Celtic inhabitants will have been scattered in isolated farmsteads, which can only be discovered by chance. It is perhaps too optimistic to hope that environmental research might plug the gap. Positive evidence would be only too welcome, but has yet to be found (For a different viewpoint Küster 1986: 556–559; von Schnurbein 1993: 248). Significantly, it has been suggested that southwest Germany was also quite depopulated in the first century BC (Wieland 1996: 182).

The situation in Southeast Bavaria and the Salzburg area is different. Here too late La Tène graves are missing, but La Tène D2 settlements are known (e.g. Karlstein, Puch, Stöffling) (Irlinger 1991; Menke 1977; Moosleitner 1992: 398; Werner 1961). But it is still difficult to bridge the gap convincingly between the early Augustan decades and the earliest Roman finds of the Claudian period (Burmeister 1998: 18–20; Fasold 1993a: 71–73). Only the finds from a few villa sites would seem to indicate uninterrupted settlement (Christlein 1963: 52–55; Moosleitner 1985: 21).

What little we do know at present about the extensive area between Iller, Danube and Salzach in the Augustan to Claudian periods, and this in spite of the fact that it has been the subject of an archaeological survey, must be seen in the context of contemporary historical developments. The area to the north of the foothills of the Alps was most certainly not fully occupied militarily at the beginning of the first century AD (Mackensen 1978: 136–142; von Schnurbein 1985b: 22–23). Apparently a few military stations along the roads were enough to control and open up the land. We have almost no traces of civilian, urban foundations or of a rural population in the Augustan period. Only the western sector bordering Helvetian territory was developed at an early stage (Bregenz, Kempten, Auerberg). A linear frontier along the Danube was not completed until the reign of Claudius, thus concluding the work of Tiberius who had made Raetia a

province (Dietz 1995: 69–78; Mackensen 1987: 143–155). The province of Noricum was created at the same time (Alföldy 1974: 62, 78–81). Iuvavum received its civic charter, which must mean that the administrative boundary of the *municipium* and thus the border with the neighbouring province of Raetia along the Inn was also defined (Heger 1974: 19–20).

Similarly, there is little evidence for burial practices in the first half of the first century AD. What there is offers a very heterogeneous picture of the graves and their furniture. The Italic influence apparent in the *Gräberstraße* at Kempten provides a contrast to the inhumation burials of the 'Heimstettener Gruppe' and the tumuli in the Salzburg area (Fasold 1993a: 102–105; Keller 1984; Mackensen 1978; Urban 1984: 142–143). The grave furniture suggests that those buried came from Gaul, as well as the area populated by Germans and immigrants from the Mediterranean (Fasold 1993b: 392; Mackensen 1978: 181).

We should not neglect the Central Alps, that is the southern half of what was to become the province of Raetia, where the situation was somewhat different. It is here that we can locate the tribes who were the main target of the Alpine campaigns of 15 BC (Dietz 1995: 22–28). Much research has been done on their material culture recently, above all the metal dress items (Demetz 1992; Gleirscher 1987a; 1987b; 1992). The summer campaign of 15 BC 'pacified' the entire central Alpine region, which had until then been a regular source of disturbance in north Italy. At this time a specific cultural group had developed in North and South Tyrol, which, on the evidence of the characteristic fibulae with links to the eastern Po Valley, extended from the Etsch Valley across the main ridge of the Alps to the Upper Inn and the Salzach (Fig. 18.1). Funerary ensembles are, however, rare. Most of the archaeological material comes from settlements and votive deposits or cult sites (Gleirscher 1987a: 83).

If we compare the archaeological picture in Southern Bavaria with that from areas which were continuously occupied by the Celts, for example the region around Trier or even North Italy, then it is clear that we cannot really apply the term 'Romanisation' to the Voralpenraum. At best it must be redefined (Haffner 1989: 93–113; Tizzoni 1981). For this reason the evidence of graves should be decisive in answering the question as to how the Raetian-Norican provincial population originated.

The *Gräberstraße* in Kempten reveals that there must have been a number of Italic or at least highly Romanised persons from northern Italy or southern France at this central, urban site who had a decisive influence on the identity of the site. The Italic nature of the funerary architecture and grave furniture leaves no room for doubt here (Fasold 1993b: 392–395; Mackensen 1987: 179–180) (Fig. 18.2). East Gallic influences can also be identified. This element is perhaps Helvetian, and is even more apparent in Bregenz. Those areas of Gaul which

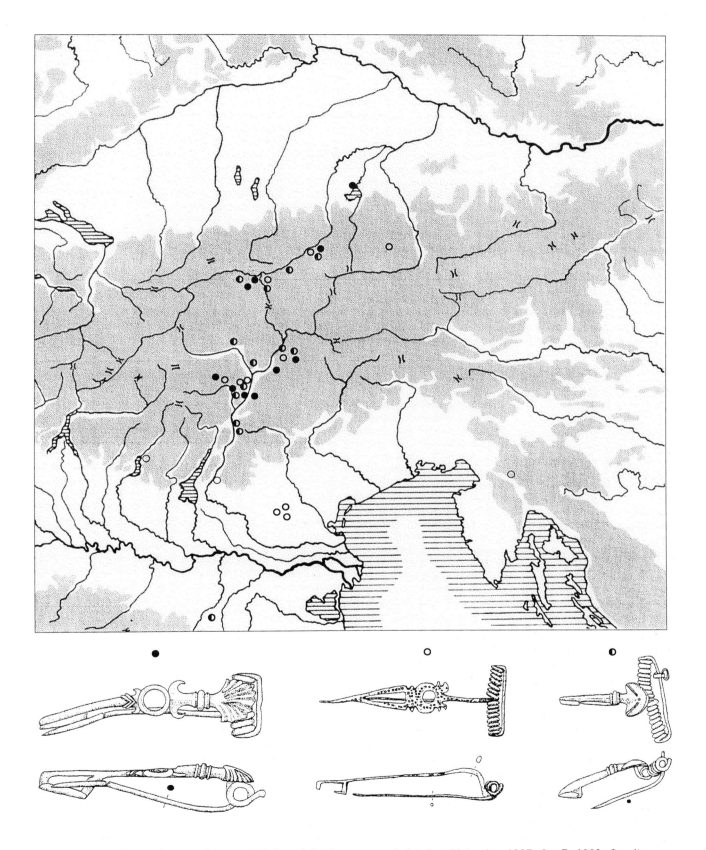

Fig. 18.1 *Distribution of Raetian fibulae of the first century BC (after Gleirscher 1987: fig. 7; 1992: fig. 4)*

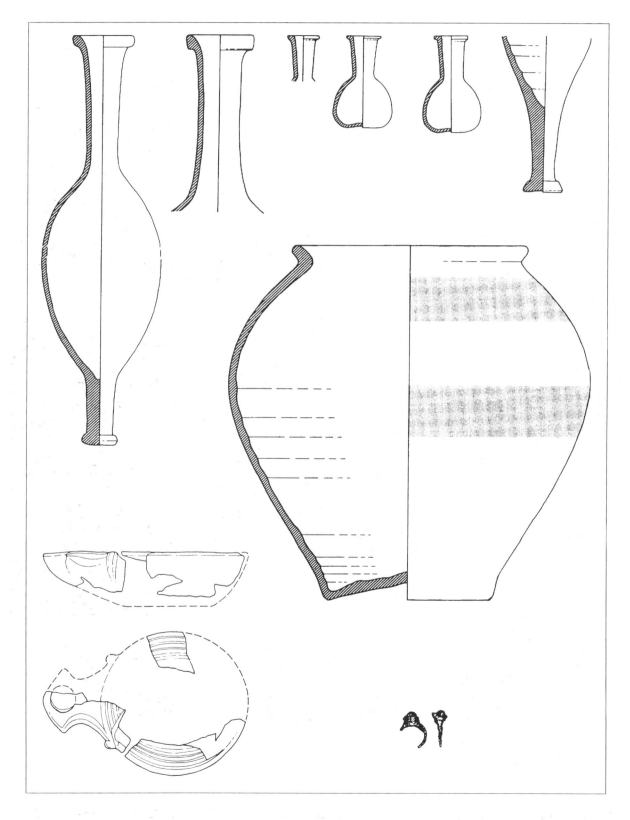

Fig. 18.2 *Furniture of grave 227, Kempten-Keckwiese (after Mackensen 1978: tab. 93) Scale 1:2*

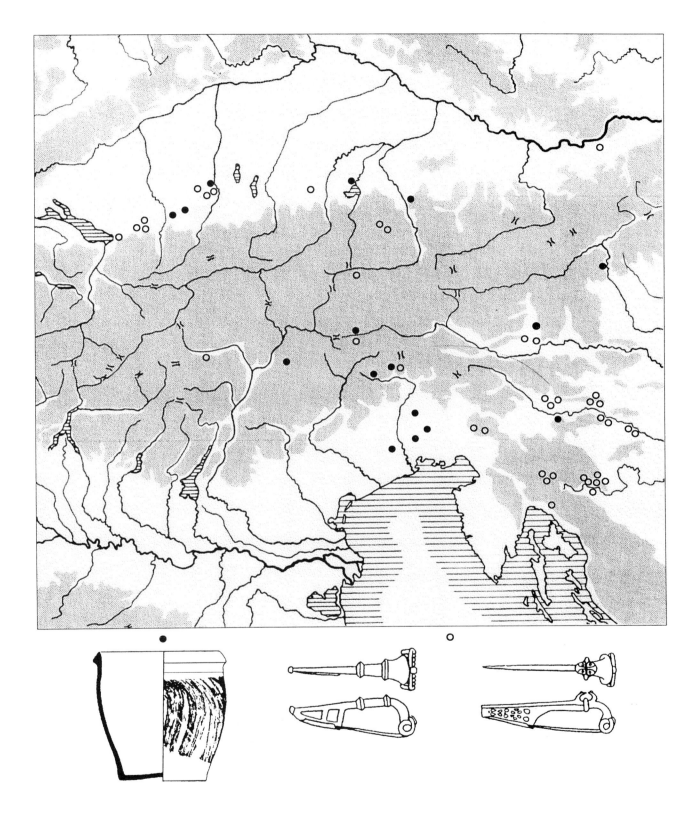

Fig. 18.3 *Draft for a distribution map of 'Auerberg ware' and Almgren fibulae 236 and 238 (after Buora 1984: fig. 1; Garbsch 1974: figs 6–9)*

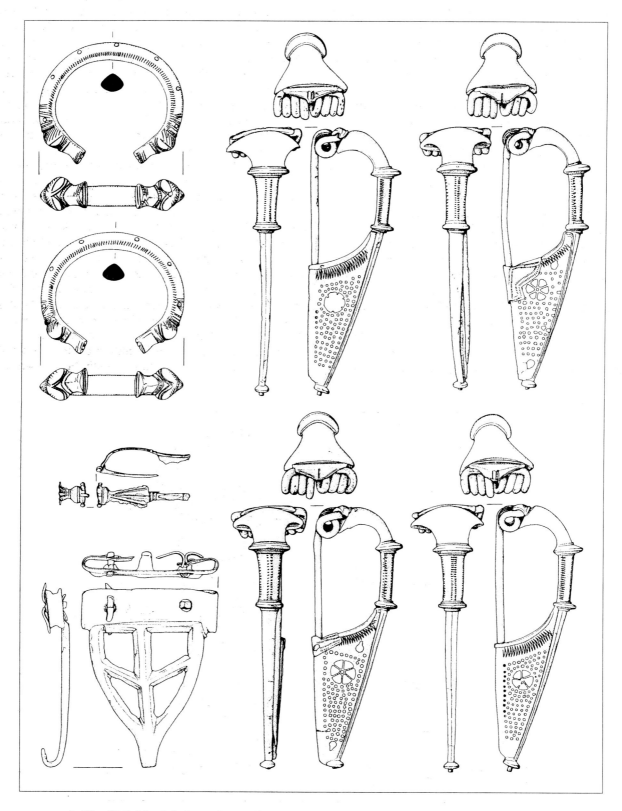

Fig. 18.4 *Metal fittings of grave 2, Heimstetten (after Keller 1984: tab. 5–6) Scale 1:2*

had already been subjected to Roman influence for several generations must have provided powerful impulses, which are reflected in characteristic finds (above all fibulae) rather than in funerary rites, which were already quite uniform by this time. Analysis of the pottery from the first generation of new settlements may also emphasise contacts with northern Italy / southern Gaul and with eastern Gaul / Switzerland. Other finds reveal a Germanic component in the population of early Raetia (Ulbert 1975: 430).

The early Roman material in Raetia has been the subject of various interpretations. It shows contacts with the Alpine region (Gleirscher 1987a: 78–82; Keller 1984: 50–53; Mackensen 1978: 49–51; Maier 1985: 249–251; Menke 1974). It is becoming increasingly clear that a type of pottery which is typical of early Raetia and is often referred to as 'Auerbergware' was in fact produced in the Augustan-Tiberian period in the central or eastern Alps (Buora 1984; Flügel, Schindler-Kaudelka 1995; Ulbert 1965: 87–91). From there it reached Raetia, where its influence is attested by local derivatives until the end of the first century (Fischer 1957: 13). In northwest Noricum it developed further into the 'norische Ware' and it is typical of burials from the Claudian period until the mid-third century (Fasold 1993a: 70–73). Alongside this typical pottery we find the Flügel- and Doppelknopf-fibulae, which have a similar distribution (Buora 1984: Fig. 1; Garbsch 1974: Abb. 6–9) (Fig. 18.3). The fibulae

and the 'Auerbergware' appear together in South Bavarian graves and indicate some kind of immigration from the (eastern) Alps. The burials from Tires and Aica to the east of Bozen form a link to the graves of the Caput Adriae, and if we include the 'kräftig-profilierten' fibulae which are typical of north Raetia and northwest Noricum, they are almost identical to burials north of the Alps (Rosada, Dal Ri 1985). These fibulae (Almgren 236, 238 and Almgren 67–69) are typical for the 'Heimstettener Gruppe' (Keller 1984: 36–37). This group of burials is of particular importance for any analysis of the history of early Roman Raetia, above all since the belt-hooks, arm and neck jewellery and metal amulets which are so characteristic of them also reveal connections with the Alpine region (Keller 1984: 32–36, 40–41) (Fig. 18.4). The dead were not normally cremated, and were often buried beneath tumuli. The inhumation burials from Ehrwald in Tyrol show identical rites and grave furniture (Franz 1955; Sydow 1984) (Fig. 18.5). R.A. Maier has mapped both these burials and Raetian sacrificial-places. Their distributions are so similar that he suggested that a Raetian-Alpine population was responsible for both the votive and funerary rites (Maier 1985: Abb. 1, 249–251; for a different viewpoint see Gleirscher 1987a: 78. 82) (Fig. 18.6). The archaeological evidence is quite clear. The contacts with the Alpenraum are too close for these characteristic groups of small finds to be the product of an indigenous Celtic population in south Bavaria, which,

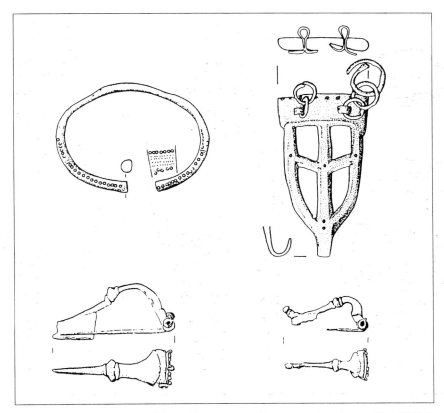

Fig. 18.5 *Grave furniture from Ehrwald in Tyrol (after Sydow 1984: fig. 674–679) Scale 1:2*

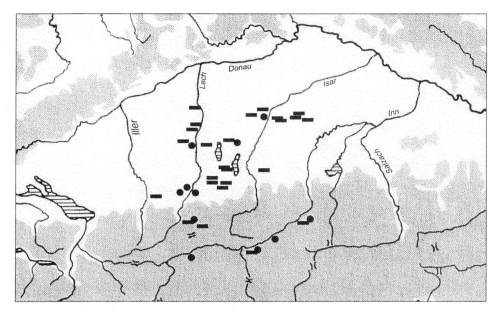

Fig. 18.6 *Graves (rectangles) and deposits (circles) of the 'Heimstettener Gruppe' (after Dietz 1995: fig. 70)*

as we have already seen, has left no recognisable traces either in the decades preceding or after the Roman conquest. It remains to be seen how this group, that is the 'Heimstettener Gruppe', which played such an important role in the settlement of north Raetia in the Tiberian-Neronian period, arrived in the area. Probably they are to be interpreted as the descendants of the Alpine-Raetian auxiliaries who were raised after the Alpine campaigns and who then settled in North Raetia once they had completed their military service. There they adopted elements of both east Gallic and Germanic dress from populations which had also migrated into the area (Keller 1984: 37, 51–53; for a different viewpoint see Faber 1995: 23).

The troops raised after the Alpine campaigns will mainly have come from the warlike tribes of the inner Alps. I believe that they can be identified in the archaeological record in Raetia as veterans, and are mentioned in detail in the historical sources. It was therefore quite correct that the Alpine Raetians rather than the Vindelici, who are archaeologically invisible, should have given their name to the province.

It is not possible to decide here to what extent a genuine 'Raetian' population is behind the 'Heimstettener Gruppe'. It is important to note that the Etsch Valley as far as the Bozen Basin was subject to north Italian/Roman influence in the first century BC (Demetz 1992: 640–642). For example we find there, along with other brooches which originated in North Italy, the fibula Almgren 65, which is thought to be the precursor of the 'Flügelfibel' (Demetz 1992: 635–637; Garbsch 1964: 49–50; Gleirscher 1987a: 75–76). This north Italian/Gallic influence, which is also apparent in the La Tène type forms of the 'Auerbergware', could indicate in addition

to Raetian elements the presence of Celtic components from northeast Italy and Istria which established themselves in the central and eastern Alps in the Caesarian / early Augustan period.

More work needs to be done on the role in the settlement of north Raetia of Alpine-Raetian and north Italian / Istrian groups of Gallic origin with different levels of Romanisation, a role which is becoming quite apparent. The same is true for the contacts between the Alps and the southern Alpenvorland at the end of the La Tène period, as the distribution of Tyrolean fibulae cannot be explained by trade (for a different viewpoint Gleirscher 1987a: 83).

The Raetian sacrificial-place from Forggensee includes Augustan material which would seem to suggest that Alpine groups were already spreading into the Voralpenraum before 15 BC. The votive site of Döttenbichl near Ettal does not have to be attributed to a residual Celtic-Vindelican population, but is rather to be seen in connection with Alpine-Raetian tribes (Fischer 1995: 226; Rieckhoff 1995: 201 note 282; Zanier 1994: 596).

The metal small finds indicate that the Norican population of south Bavaria, whose settlements (e.g. Karlstein, Stöffling) were still occupied in the Augustan period, also had contacts with the Alpenraum. However, it remains a riddle why their cemeteries do not start until the Claudian period, and are unknown here for the late La Tène period, too. At present it is hard to prove continuity of settlement and cult for the Alauni and Ambisontii, who can be localised here, above all because there was a wave of settlements founded in the Claudian period, although it is not clear to what extent they replaced existing native sites (Burmeister 1992: 193, 197–200; Heger 1974: 20; Irlinger 1991: 79; Menke 1977: 224–227). As in the neighbouring province of Raetia so here too funerary rites were varied in the pre-Flavian period. They included secondary burials in older tumuli (Maxglan), large stone mounds with internal structures (Hörafing), simple urn graves (Karlstein) and inhumation burials without grave goods (Seebruck). Only the characteristic accessories and the 'Norican' pottery reveal that a cultural unity is involved. But, as we have already seen, the finds do not necessarily indicate an indigenous population. It remains to be seen to what extent southeast Alpine influences are involved. Here the fibulae are relevant, as well as the furnishing with knives and the customs of placing comb-decorated graphite ceramic distaffs in graves, elements which are also common in the Gallic tombs of North Italy.

In other words the late Augustan – Claudian burials especially in the Raetian part of south Bavaria present a colourful picture. Above all the dress fittings indicate the presence of populations which had come from all directions to settle here. The various funerary rites also reveal various cultural traditions. Above all no particular indigenous element can be identified, and although the occurrence of secondary burials in older tumuli from the Tiberian period onwards is significant (Burmeister 1995: 226–227), it is no proof of continuity of population (Wieland 1996: 63–64). Celtic ceramic traditions are probably an indication of Gallic immigrants, for example from North Italy, rather than indigenous groups (for a different view Wieland 1993). It is now possible to identify a significant Alpine element in the provincial population, and this mixture of ethnic components prior to the foundation of the provinces of Raetia and Noricum is quite clear in the graves.

However, these characteristics then start to disappear. The heterogeneous nature of the burials becomes diluted and the graves more homogeneous. The best example of this process is the disappearance of the exotically furnished burials of the 'Heimstettener Gruppe' in the Neronian period. The 'Roman' elements of the central settlements will have acted as an influential model, and the sense of belonging to the Roman Empire will have spread increasingly, above all through the local ruling classes as a provincial society came into being, and will have found its expression in the adoption of fixed, Mediterranean fashions of honouring the dead (Fasold and Witteyer 1998: 181–83). We must also ask to what extent normative administrative measures encouraged the standardisation of burial practice. Perhaps the controls along the frontier between Raetia and Noricum put an end to the population fluctuations of the early period. The disappearance of Norican fibulae in Raetia at this time would seem to suggest this (Garbsch 1974: 178; Keller 1984: 37). Under the Flavians a provincial funerary culture developed in North Raetia which had its own characteristics, for example decorated samian bowls, mortaria and certain lamp and urn types, which start to become standard features in graves (Fasold 1993c; von Schnurbein 1982: 7–8). The metal dress fittings are now

almost entirely missing. Above all the 'Henkeldellenbecher' and other ceramic forms reveal Raetian-Alpine components in the provincial culture of the second century (Maier 1985: 247–249). The graves under discussion here show how the 'Romanisation' of North Raetia took the form of an assimilation of customs of various ethnic groups and was by no means an unqualified assumption of a dominant Romano-Italic culture by the subjected local population.

Acknowledgements

I wish to thank A. Faber, Frankfurt and M. Witteyer, Mainz, for useful remarks and D. Wigg, Frankfurt, for the translation.

Bibliography

Alföldy, G. 1974. *Noricum*. London.
Buora, M. 1984. Marchi di fabbrica su urne con orlo a mandorla dal medio Friuli. *Aquileia Nostra* 55, 6–32.
Burmeister, S. 1998. *Vicus und spätrömische Befestigung von Seebruck-Bedaium*. Kallmünz/Opf. Materialhefte zur Bayerischen Vorgeschichte 76.
Burmeister, S. 1995. Die römerzeitliche Besiedlung im Landkreis Starnberg. In W. Czysz et al. (eds.), *Provinzialrömische Forschungen. Festschrift Günter Ulbert*, Espelkamp, 217–236.
Von Chlingensperg auf Berg, M. 1896. *Die römischen Brandgräber bei Reichenhall*. Munich.
Christlein, R. 1963. Ein römisches Gebäude in Marzoll, Ldkr. Berchtesgaden. Vorbericht über die Grabungen 1959–1962. *Bayerische Vorgeschichtsblätter* 28, 30–57.
Christlein, R. 1982. Zu den jüngsten keltischen Funden Südbayerns. *Bayerische Vorgeschichtsblätter* 47, 275–292.
Demetz, S. 1992. Rom und die Räter. Ein Resümee aus archäologischer Sicht. In R. Metzger and P. Gleirscher (eds.) *Die Räter*, Bozen, 631–653.
Dietz, K. 1995. Okkupation und Frühzeit. In W. Czysz et al. (eds.), *Die Römer in Bayern*, Stuttgart, 18–99.
Faber, A. 1992. Früh- und mittelkaiserzeitliche Gräber von der Keckwiese in Cambodunum-Kempten. *Das archäologische Jahr in Bayern* 1991, 117–119.
Faber, A. 1995. Zur Bevölkerung von Cambodunum-Kempten im 1. Jahrhundert. Archäologische Quellen aus der Siedlung auf dem Lindenberg und dem Gräberfeld 'Auf der Keckwiese'. In W. Czysz et al. (eds.), *Provinzialrömische Forschungen. Festschrift Günter Ulbert*, Espelkamp, 13–23.
Fasold, P. 1993a. *Das römisch-norische Gräberfeld von Seebruck-Bedaium*. Kallmünz/Opf.: Materialhefte zur Bayerischen Vorgeschichte 64.
Fasold, P. 1993b. Romanisierung und Grabbrauch: Überlegungen zum frührömischen Totenkult in Rätien. In M. Struck (ed.), *Römerzeitliche Gräber als Quellen zu Religion, Bevölkerungsstruktur und Sozialgeschichte*, Mainz: Archäologische Schriften des Instituts für Vor- und Frühgeschichte der Johannes Gutenberg-Universität Mainz 3, 381–395.
Fasold, P. 1993c. Geschirr für das Jenseits: Gefäßkeramik als Beigabe in den Gräbern Nordraetiens. *Arbeitshefte des Bayerischen Landesamtes für Denkmalpflege* 58, 69–72.
Fasold, P. and Witteyer, M. 1998. 'Römisches' in den Gräbern Mittel- und Norditaliens. In *Römische Gräber des 1. Jahrhunderts n.Chr. in Italien und in den Nordwestprovinzen*, Köln: Xantener Berichte, 181–90.

Fischer, T. 1995. Kelten und Römer in Bayern. *Archäologische Informationen* 18/2, 225–229.

Fischer, U. 1957. *Cambodunumforschungen 1953–II. Keramik aus den Holzhäusern zwischen der 1. und 2. Querstraße.* Kallmünz/ Opf.: Materialhefte zur Bayerischen Vorgeschichte 10.

Flügel, C. and Schindler-Kaudelka, E. 1995. Auerbergtöpfe in Rätien, Noricum und der Regio Decima. *Aquileia Nostra* 66, 66–84.

Franz, L. 1955. Der Fund von Biberwier. In *Außerferner Buch,* Innsbruck: Schlernschriften 111, 74–75.

Garbsch, J. 1965. *Die norisch-pannonische Frauentracht im 1. und 2. Jahrhundert.* Munich: Münchner Beiträge zur Vor- und Frühgeschichte 11.

Garbsch, J. 1974. Ein Flügelfibelfragment vom Lorenzberg. Bemerkungen zu Fibeln der Frauentracht von Raetien und Juvavum. In G. Kossack and G. Ulbert (eds.), *Studien zur vor- und frühgeschichtlichen Archäologie. Festschrift Joachim Werner,* Munich: Münchner Beiträge zur Vor- und Frühgeschichte, Ergänzungsband I/1, 163–183.

Gebhard, R. 1991. *Die Fibeln aus dem Oppidum von Manching.* Stuttgart: Die Ausgrabungen in Manching 14, 104.

Gerhardt K. and Maier R.A. 1964. Norische Gräber bei Hörafing im Chiemgau. *Bayerische Vorgeschichtsblätter* 29, 119–177.

Gleirscher, P. 1987a. Tiroler Schüssel- und Palmettenfibeln. *Germania* 65, 67–88.

Gleirscher, P. 1987b. Die Kleinfunde von der hohen Birga bei Birgitz. *Berichte der Römisch-Germanischen Kommission* 68, 181–351.

Gleirscher, P. 1992. 'Tiroler' Cenisolafibeln? Eine neue Definition der Variante Vill. *Archäologisches Korrespondenzblatt* 22, 93–107.

Haffner, A. 1989. *Gräber – Spiegel des Lebens.* Ausstellungskatalog Trier, Mainz: Schriftenreihe des Rheinischen Landesmuseums Trier 2.

Hahn, E. 1992. Die menschlichen Skelettreste. In Maier *et al.* 1992, 214–234.

Heger, N. 1974. *Salzburg in römischer Zeit.* Salzburg.

Hell, M. 1934. Frühkaiserzeitliche Hügelgräber aus Maxglan bei Salzburg. *Mitteilungen der Anthropologischen Gesellschaft Wien* 64, 129–146.

Hochberger, K. and Pittner, M. 1962. Unteremmerting. Fundchronik für die Jahre 1961 und 1962. *Bayerische Vorgeschichtsblätter* 27, 251.

Hübener, W. 1958. Zum römischen und frühmittelalterlichen Augsburg. *Jahrbuch des Römisch-Germanischen Zentralmuseums Mainz* 5, 154–238.

Irlinger, W. 1991. Die keltische Siedlung in Stöffling. *Das archäologische Jahr in Bayern* 1990, 76–79.

Keller, E. 1984. *Die frühkaiserzeitlichen Körpergräber von Heimstetten bei München und die verwandten Funde aus Südbayern.* Munich: Münchner Beiträge zur Vor- und Frühgeschichte 37.

Krämer, W. 1985. *Die Grabfunde von Manching und die latènezeitlichen Flachgräber in Südbayern.* Stuttgart: Die Ausgrabungen in Manching 9.

Küster, H. 1986. Werden und Wandel der Kulturlandschaft im Alpenvorland. Pollenanalytische Aussagen zur Siedlungsgeschichte am Auerberg in Südbayern. *Germania* 64, 533–559.

Lange, G. 1983. *Die menschlichen Skelettreste aus dem Oppidum von Manching.* Wiesbaden: Die Ausgrabungen in Manching 7.

Mackensen, M. 1978. *Das Römische Gräberfeld auf der Keckwiese in Kempten I.* Kallmünz/Opf.: Materialhefte zur Bayerischen Vorgeschichte 34.

Maier, F. et al. 1992. *Ergebnisse der Ausgrabungen 1984–1987 in Manching.* Stuttgart: Die Ausgrabungen in Manching 15.

Maier, R.A. 1985. Ein römerzeitlicher Brandopferplatz bei Schwangau und andere Zeugnisse einheimischer Religion in der Provinz Rätien. In J. Bellot et al. (eds.), *Forschungen zur Provinzialrömischen Archäologie in Bayerisch-Schwaben,* Augsburg: Schwäbische Geschichtsquellen und Forschungen 14, 231–256.

Menke, M. 1974. 'Rätische' Siedlungen und Bestattungsplätze der frührömischen Kaiserzeit im Voralpenland. In G. Kossack and G. Ulbert (eds.), *Studien zur vor- und frühgeschichtlichen Archäologie. Festschrift Joachim Werner,* Munich: Münchner Beiträge zur Vor- und Frühgeschichte, Ergänzungsband l/I, 141–159.

Menke, M. 1977. Zur Struktur und Chronologie der spätkeltischen und frührömischen Siedlungen im Reichenhaller Becken. In *Symposium Bratislava, Bratislava: Ausklang der Latène-Zivilisation und Anfänge der germanischen Besiedlung im mittleren Donaugebiet,* 223–238.

Moosbauer, G. 1997. *Die ländliche Besiedlung im östlichen Rätien während der römischen Kaiserzeit.* Espelkamp: Passauer Universitätsschriften zur Archäologie 4.

Moosleitner, F. 1985. Latènezeitliche Siedlungsspuren in Loig. In E.-M. Feldinger et al. (eds.), *Die römische Villa Loig bei Salzburg. Ergebnisse der Grabungen 1979–81 sowie Forschungen zu den Mosaikfunden von 1815,* 17–22.

Moosleitner, F. 1992. Spätkeltische Siedlungsreste in Puch bei Hallein. In A. Lippert and K. Spindler (eds.), *Festschrift zum 50–jährigen Bestehen des Instituts für Vor-und Frühgeschichte der Leopold-Franzens-Universität Innsbruck,* Innsbruck: Universitätsforschungen zur Prähistorischen Archäologie 8, 385–400.

Müller-Karpe, H. 1964. Katalog des römischen Brandgräberfeldes in der Mühlau. In J. Werner (ed.), *Studien zu Abodiacum-Epfach 1,* Munich: Münchner Beiträge zur Vor- und Frühgeschichte 7, 28–52.

Rieckhoff, S. 1995. *Süddeutschland im Spannungsfeld von Kelten, Germanen und Römern.* Trier: Trierer Zeitschrift, Beiheft 19.

Rosada, G. and Dal Ri, L. (eds.) 1985. *Tires e Aica. Necropoli di epoca romana.* Verona.

Schön, F. 1986. *Der Beginn der römischen Herrschaft in Rätien.* Sigmaringen.

Schröter, P. 1993. Anthropologischer Bericht über kaiserzeitliche Körperbestattungen von Seebruck und Poing. In Fasold, P. 1993a, 121–144.

von Schnurbein, S. 1982. Die kulturgeschichtliche Stellung des nördlichen Rätien. *Berichte der Römisch-Germanischen Kommission* 63, 5–16.

von Schnurbein, S. 1985a. Die Funde von Augsburg-Oberhausen und die Besetzung des Alpenvorlandes durch die Römer. In W. Bellot et al. (eds.), *Forschungen zur provinzialrömischen Archäologie in Bayerisch-Schwaben,* Augsburg: Schwäbische Geschichtsquellen und Forschungen 14, 15–43.

von Schnurbein, S. 1985b. Die Besetzung des Alpenvorlandes durch die Römer. *Die Römer in Schwaben,* Arbeitsheft des Bayerischen Landesamtes für Denkmalpflege 27, 17–24.

von Schnurbein, S. 1993. Nachleben in römischer Zeit. in H. Dannheimer and R. Gebhard (eds.), *Das keltische Jahrtausend,* Mainz: Ausstellungkataloge der Prähistorischen Staatssammlung 23, 244–248.

von Schwerzenbach, K. 1909. Ein Gräberfeld von Brigantium. *Jahrbuch für Altertumskunde* 3, 98–110.

von Schwerzenbach, K. and Jakobs, J. 1910. Die römischen Begräbnisstätten von Brigantium. *Jahrbuch für Altertumskunde* 4, 33–63.

Sommer, C.S. 1988. Kastellvicus und Kastell. *Fundberichte aus Baden-Württemberg* 13, 457–707.

Sommer, C.S. 1990. Das römische Militär und sein Einfluß auf die Bevölkerung in Obergermanien und Rätien rechts des Rheins und nördlich der Alpen. *Akten des 14. Internationalen Limes-*

kongresses 1986 in Carnuntum, Wien: Der Limes in Österreich, Heft 36/1, 121–129.

Struck, M. 1996. *Römische Grabfunde und Siedlungen im Isartal bei Ergolding, Landkreis Landshut.* Kallmünz/Opf.: Materialhefte zur Bayerischen Vorgeschichte 71.

Sydow, W. 1984. Ehrwald. *Fundberichte aus Österreich* 23, 308–309.

Tizzoni, M. 1981. La cultura tardo La Tène in Lombardia. *Studi Archeologici* 1, 3–39.

Ulbert, G. 1965. *Der Lorenzberg bei Epfach. Die frührömische Militärstation (Epfach III).* Munich: Münchner Beiträge zur Vor- und Frühgeschichte 9.

Ulbert, G., 1975. *Der Auerberg in: Ausgrabungen in Deutschland, gefördert von der Deutschen Forschungsgemeinschaft 1950–1975, Teil 1.* Mainz: Römisch-Germanisches Zentralmuseum Mainz, Monographien 1,1, 409–433.

Urban, O. 1984. *Das Gräberfeld von Kapfenstein (Steiermark) und die römischen Hügelgräber in Österreich.* Munich: Münchner Beiträge zur Vor- und Frühgeschichte 35.

Werner, J. 1961. Bemerkungen zu norischem Trachtzubehör und zu Fernhandelsbeziehungen der Spätlatènezeit im Salzburger Land. *Mitteilungen der Gesellschaft für Salzburger Landeskunde* 101 (Festschrift M. Hell), 143–160.

Wieland, G. 1993. Spätkeltische Traditionen in Form und Verzierung römischer Grobkeramik. *Fundberichte aus Baden-Württemberg* 18, 61–70.

Wieland, G. 1996. *Die Spätlatènezeit in Württemberg.* Stuttgart: Forschungen und Berichte zur Vor- und Frühgeschichte in Baden-Württemberg 63.

Willerding, U. 1978. Die Pflanzenreste. In Mackensen 1978, 183–92

Zanier, W. 1994. Eine römische Katapultpfeilspitze der 19. Legion aus Oberammergau – Neues zum Alpenfeldzug des Drusus im Jahre 15 v.Chr. *Germania* 72, 587–596.

19. Early Roman graves in Cologne

Matthias Riedel

The subject of this paper, related to the theme of this conference, is a discussion of early Roman graves in Cologne. Specifically it will address the co-existence and inter-penetration of native and Roman burial customs that took place in Cologne. The evidence discussed comes from a section of a cemetery discovered in the north-western part of the city. The evaluation of the grave goods is still in progress and thus they will only be presented in outline here.

To begin a general view of the cemeteries of the provincial capital of Cologne is necessary (Fig. 19.1). Following the requirements of Roman law, the cemeteries lie outside the city along the major roads. The cemetery that interests us is rather extensive and lies outside the

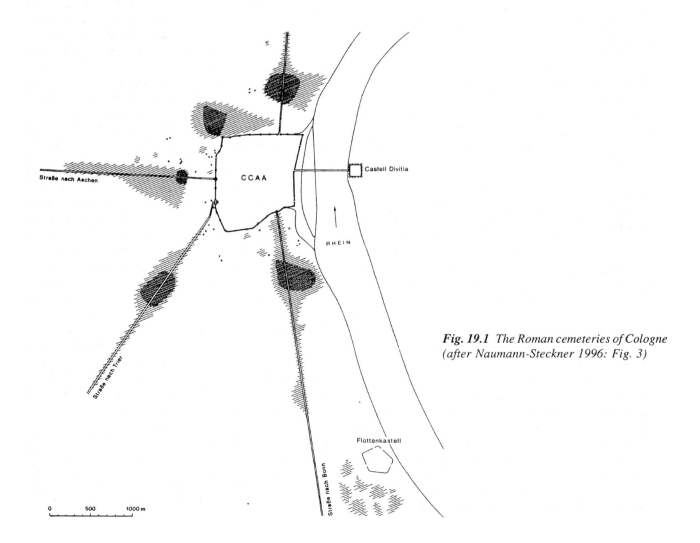

Fig. 19.1 *The Roman cemeteries of Cologne (after Naumann-Steckner 1996: Fig. 3)*

SPIESERGASSE

Fig. 19.2 *The main excavation area (1985/86 campaign) (P. Otten)*

north-west corner of the Roman city. Unlike others it did not lie near a main road: there is neither proof of a gate in this part of the city wall nor any sign of the systematic arrangement of graves in relation to such a road. An excavation in 1996 did find traces of a gravelled road but this was certainly a cemetery path rather than a main thoroughfare. From the Middle Ages into the twentieth century an incalculable number of Roman burials has been observed, excavated or plundered. Since the mid 1920s systematic excavation and observation of construction work by the appropriate government departments have brought to light more than 500 graves. Roughly two thirds of them are cremations, the rest inhumations. The use of the cemetery started at the beginning of the first century AD with isolated burials. The frequency of burial increased in the middle of the same century and concentrated subsequently around St Gereon into the post-Roman era. The whole cemetery was not in use from the early Roman period till the later post-Roman period: rather use of the cemetery shifted over time from south to north.

This impression was strengthened through an extensive excavation, conducted in 1985 and 1986 in a section of the cemetery, the publication of which is in preparation by the author (Fig. 19.2). This campaign alone unearthed another 734 graves within the cemetery, and in 1989 120 graves were found in an adjoining section to the east. In 1996 in a further adjoining area 160 graves were excavated, bringing the total to over 1500 graves.

The period into which the graves excavated in these three campaigns fall begins in the Tiberian period and ends in the early part of the second century AD. The occasional later graves, including a partially destroyed

burial in a stone coffin dated to the early fourth century, do not represent a general continued use of this area of the cemetery. The southern part of the cemetery was certainly no longer in general use by this time as it was levelled using rubble from the city in the third and fourth centuries. The intensive use of the cemetery did not begin before the founding of the *colonia* in 50 AD and the main emphasis of use was the second half of the first century AD.

Roughly three quarters of the graves from the two large campaigns of the 1980s were cremations, of which the majority were *Brandschüttungsgräber*, graves in which the calcined bones of the dead and the pyre debris including grave goods are deposited separately (Bechert 1980). Cremations were even more predominant among the burials excavated in the 1996 campaign, of which only 5% were inhumations. Contemporary cremation burials from this period are very closely packed. Typical grave goods from the main classes of material are the white single-handled Hofheim flagon with its smooth triangular rim (Fig. 19.3), bronze thistle brooches (Fig. 19.4), and the candlestick shaped unguent bottles Isings 82 B1. Cremation was almost the only known burial type in the Rhineland in the early and middle Roman period. This rite was that of both the pre-Roman indigenous population and that of the new Roman rulers. In this burial type therefore neither typically Roman nor typically native Ubian elements can be distinguished.

Thus approximately one quarter of the graves from these excavations are inhumations. This is a surprisingly high percentage for the first century AD, at least for the Rhineland. How many of these graves are those of the Ubian population is unknown. More plausible, but still lacking conclusive evidence, is the hypothesis that these

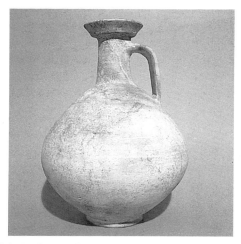

Fig. 19.3 *Hofheim 50 flagon from prone inhumation. Mid first century AD*

Fig. 19.4 *Two first century AD thistle brooches(1985/86 campaign)*

graves were those of an immigrant Gallic, for example Remic, population (van Doorsaeler 1967: 129).

The connection with the Remi is supported by the oldest and certainly best known of the tombstones in the cemetery, that of Bella (Galsterer and Galsterer 1975 no. 310). This tombstone, dated to the Tiberian period, shows the deceased in relief holding a child in her arms, suggesting that Bella died in childbirth. An inhumation burial with grave goods was excavated by the tombstone. Bella was the daughter of Vonucus, a member of the above mentioned tribe of the Remi, native to the region around Reims in northern Gaul. It seems likely that members of this and other Gallic tribes migrated into the Cologne region following the foundation of the oppidum Ubiorum and to an even greater degree on its elevation to the status of a colony in 50 AD. There initially at least they retained their burial form of inhumation. However there is no proof of this because many of the inhumations were either without grave goods or provided with only a very small number. It is however certain that this is a native, non-Roman burial type, accounting for a relatively high percentage of burials.

The inhumation burials like the cremations are often so tightly packed that they overlap and intercut one another. Despite this, grave goods show little chronological difference and indicate a similar date in the second half of the first century AD. Two supine inhumation burials, although in other respects out of the ordinary, demonstrate how closely burials were packed (Fig. 19.5). One burial with a tile at its feet set on its edge was overlain by another inhumation with a tile placed by the pelvis. The round hole in the skull of the lower burial showed no traces of healing on its rim which indicates a fatal projectile wound. Two similar wounds could be observed on the lower part of the left tibia. Such wounds were identified on at least seven skeletons, including on the skull of a child buried prone. Such injuries may indicate war-related incidents of which the victims were buried here.

In this context a number of further burials should be mentioned. In several cases the corpse had been thrown vertically head first into graves of which the sides were carelessly cut and steep, having been hurriedly dug (Fig. 19.6). The Norbertstraße excavation, in the same area of the cemetery, revealed two cases of the burial of the lower part of the skeleton, still articulated, in two obviously undisturbed grave pits. The dating of these and neighbouring graves to the later part of the first century AD suggests that they may be victims of the Batavian rebellion of 70 AD. In the course of this historically attested event fighting occurred in the area of Cologne (Tacitus, *Historiae* IV, 63–67). To apply the same interpretation to crouched burials, burials placed on their sides or others in unusual positions which occur here is too uncertain. Many of these burials might be those of socially marginal groups such as the poor, the diseased or criminals, as in a similar cemetery in Mainz (M. Witteyer pers. comm.).

Roughly two dozen inhumations were found face down in a prone position during this excavation campaign. Some of the damaged burials might also be attributed to this group. Among the few grave goods associated with such burials was a Hofheim 50 flagon of the type described above, dated to the second half of the first century AD. This burial position has been occasionally observed in the most varying regions of Europe from the Palaeolithic to the modern period and has been explained as having ritual significance. However this type of inhumation has been found not only in this area but over a large zone on the north-western border of the empire from Britain to upper Germany (C. Bridger pers. comm.). It is difficult to attribute it therefore to a particular ethnic origin although the ritual practice might have a common root.

A further unusual burial indicates the special character of this cemetery in the context of the first century AD. Among the cremation and inhumation burials was the skeleton of an approximately nine year old horse, the extremities of which have been disturbed by more recent activity. The horse was 1.25 to 1.3m high at the withers and may belong to an eastern European race (observations

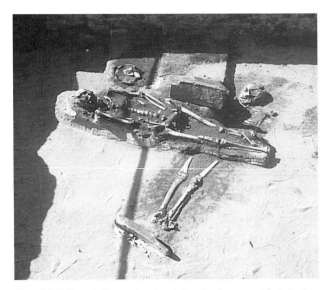

Fig. 19.5 Two inhumation burials, the lower with injuries. Second half of the first century AD

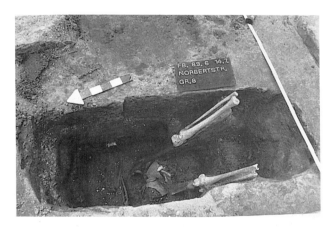

Fig. 19.6 *Inhumation of the second half of the first century AD (1989 campaign)*

comparison with the burials of men with horses at Krefeld-Gellep suggests itself (Pirling 1971). These were long argued to be connected to the revolt of the Batavi, although a later dating has been proposed (Bechert 1982: note 83). The difference between the first example described above and the others is the ritual killing of the horse.

There are five later horse burials of the mid- and late Roman period from the northern cemetery along the 'Neusser Straße' (Riedel 1990: 245). All these finds of horse burials might be attributed to a Germanic custom, especially because contemporary horse burials are frequent in Germania Libera, although it is not possible to identify which Germanic group. However these burials are not to be confused with the late Roman and migration period horse burials of central Europe, in which the horse is clearly the centre of the ritual and is buried alone (Müller-Wille 1971). The same ethnic background may lie behind the phenomenon, although it might also be linked to the presence of Thracian cavalry units (cf. Hessing 1993).

In conclusion it can be established that an above average number of individuals belonging to a non-Roman or non-Romanised element in Cologne's population was buried in this cemetery. The horse burials may suggest a Germanic affiliation, the inhumation burials a Gallic connection. There is much evidence that the burials are not those of the Ubian population, or if so they were those of the socially marginal.

Notes

1. Recent publications on the cemeteries of Roman Cologne include those of Friedhoff (1991), Päffgen (1993), von Boeselager (1993), Spiegel (1994), Neu (1995b) and Naumann-Steckner (1996).

of Mr H. Berke, Cologne). Its throat had been ritually cut; the neck is unnaturally bent back and one of the neck vertebrae shows cut marks. An iron knife found by the neck may support this interpretation. Although without datable finds other than the knife, on the basis of its immediate horizontal and vertical stratigraphic proximity to other graves on the southern edge of the cemetery the grave doubtless belongs to the main period of the cemetery's use in the second half of the first century AD. The spiral brooch of Hofheim Type I found in the disturbed area at the horse's extremities supports the date.

This grave belongs to a small group of horse burials of this period in Cologne. Two of these found in association with human burials in the same cemetery (Riedel 1990). Four other disturbed horse burials were discovered in other Roman cemeteries a few years ago (Neu 1995a: 268). The possibility of a related human burial cannot be discounted because of the degree of disturbance. A

Bibliography

Bechert, T. 1980a. Zur Terminologie provinzialrömischer Brandgräber. *Archäologisches Korrespondenzblatt*, 10, 253–58

Bechert, T. 1982. *Römisches Germanien zwischen Rhein und Maas*. Munich: Hirmer

von Boeselager, D. 1993. Die Beigabenkombination reicher Brandgräber in Köln. In M. Struck (ed.), *Römerzeitliche Gräber als Quellen zur Religion, Bevölkerungsstruktur und Sozialgeschichte*, 283–92. Mainz: Johannes Gutenberg Institut für Vor- und Frühgeschichte

van Doorsaeler, A. 1967. *Les nécropoles d'époque romaine en Gaule Septentrionale*. Dissertationes Archaeologicae Gandenses 10, Bruges: De Tempel

Friedhoff, U. 1991. *Der römische Friedhof an der Jakobstrasse zu Köln*. Kölner Forschungen 3. Mainz: Philipp von Zabern

Galsterer, B. and Galsterer, H. 1975. *Die römischen Steininschriften aus Köln*. Wissenschaftliche Kataloge des Römisch-Germanischen Museums Köln, Bd. 2, Cologne: Greven and Bechtold

Hessing, W.A.M. 1993. Horse burials in a cemetery of the middle Roman period at Kesteren, the Netherlands. In M. Struck (ed.), *Römerzeitliche Gräber als Quellen zur Religion, Bevölkerungs-*

struktur und Sozialgeschichte, 305–12. Mainz: Johannes
Gutenberg Institut für Vor- und Frühgeschichte
Naumann-Steckner, F. 1996. Death on the Rhine: changing burial
customs in Cologne, 3rd–7th century. In L.E. Webster and M.
Brown 1996. *The Tranformation of the Roman World AD 400–
900*, 143–57. London: British Museum Press
(see also Naumann-Steckner, F. 1997. *Tod am Rhein. Begräbnisse
im frühen Köln*. Exhibition catalogue. Cologne: Asmuth)
Müller-Wille, M. 1971. Pferdegrab und Pferdeopfer im frühen
Mittelalter. *BROB*, 20–21, 119–248
Neu, S. 1995a. Römische Gräber in Köln. In *Ein Land macht
Geschichte*, Ausstellungskataloge Köln, Mainz: von Zabern,
265–68

Neu, S. 1995b. Die Entdeckung des Achilles – in Köln. In *Ein
Land macht Geschichte*, Ausstellungskataloge Köln, Mainz:
von Zabern, 269–73
Päffgen, B. 1992. *Die Ausgrabungen in St. Severin zu Köln*. Kölner
Forschungen 5, 1–3. Mainz: Philipp von Zabern
Pirling, R. 1971. Ein Bestattungsplatz gefallener Römer in Krefeld-
Gellep. *Archäologisches Korrespondenzblatt*, 1, 45–46
Riedel, M. 1990. Eine Pferdebestattung im römischen Friedhof
um St. Gereon. *KJVF*, 23, 421–29
Spiegel, E.M. 1994. Die römische Westnekropole an der Aachener
Strasse in Köln. Ansätze zu einer Strukturanalyse. *KJVF*, 27,
595–609

20. The connection between funerary rites and ethnic groups in the cemeteries of north-eastern Pannonia

Judit Topál

In the last thirty years of research a certain ambivalence can be observed with regard to the ethnic composition of the population of the province of Pannonia. Pioneers in this sensitive theme of research cautiously began to explore the balance between indigenous and foreign elements in the population of the Middle Danube region. On the basis of newly discovered cemeteries and settlements, first at Intercisa, they tried to prove the existence of these different population components (Barkóczi *et al.* 1954; 1957). Their opponents were of the opinion that the information from the Roman Empire, especially of its latest period, was insufficient to recognize any distinction (Lányi 1972). Moreover, I. Bóna tried to prove (and not without effect) that all aspects of fourth-century material culture could have derived from a uniform, colourless and homogenous late Roman civilization (Vágó-Bóna 1976).

The present paper attempts to deal with some aspects of the ethnic components in this area. The starting point of this survey is a map of the Pannonian native peoples (Fig. 20.1) based upon the work of A. Mócsy (1974: 54 fig. 9). His most important authority was Pliny the Elder (*Nat. Hist.* III) who described the provinces and listed their inhabitants. His second source was the geographic work of Ptolemy (books II and III), a later listing of tribes arranged topographically.

The Celtic invasions reached the Carpathian region at the beginning of the fourth century BC. The gradual Celticization of this area took place during the following century. This was so complete, especially in the northern half of Pannonia, that pre-Celtic languages almost completely disappeared. In southern Pannonia, however, a thin Celtic upper class (*Scordisci*) was gradually absorbed by the conquered but numerically stronger native population namely the Pannonians who were related linguistically and culturally to the Illyrians, e.g. the *Breuci* and the *Andizetes* (named by Strabo). Nevertheless other tribes between the rivers Drava and Sava must have also been regarded as Pannonians (*Colapiani, Iasi, Oseriates, Amantini* and *Cornacates*). The western half of the Carpathian basin was dominated by the Celtic *Boii*. Like their Istrian kinsfolk, they inhumed their dead, although by the first century they commonly adopted cremation, probably under Roman influence.

After the Roman conquest of Pannonia the concentration of power among the Celts, such as the Boian network, probably dissolved, already having been weakened by the Dacians and Burebista's war. In this territory were to be found the *Boii, Arabiates, Azali, Eravisci*, who had invaded east Pannonia towards the end of the late La Tène period. All these tribes were of Celtic origin except the Illyrian *Azali* who were transferred from south Pannonia to the Danube at the time of Tiberius. (Mócsy 1974: 55). Among the recorded names of the *Asali* there is a small group (e.g. Aturo, Anbo, Ciliunus, Teitia) which point to contacts with Spain and Portugal. These names occur on tombstones decorated with so-called astral symbols, including sun disc, crescent and L-shaped motifs (*ianua coeli* = gates of heaven) (e.g. the tombstone of Sisiu at Ulcisia Castra: SzFM Lapidarium Inv.Nr. 77.29.1=RIU 923) which are frequent on tombstones in Salamanca (Schober 1923: 218; Cumont 1942: 203–251; Garcia y Bellido 1949; Mócsy 1974: 61, note 30) as well as generally in Pannonia (CIL 3372, 3687, 3690, 4372, 10571, etc., Nagy 1988: 93–111).

It is also generally known that in AD 50 Vannius, the king of the *Quadi,* was settled in Pannonia together with his followers while most of the tribe remained beyond the frontier. Some of the graves of this time and stray finds as well as those of settlements found between the Danube and the Lake Pelso (Balaton) show certain Dacian and Germanic characteristics (Mócsy 1974: note 13 with detailed literature).

On the basis of tombstones, the costumes and jewellery depicted on them, as well as epitaphs and, less frequently, burial rites and objects of personal equipment, it is possible to give a general outline of ethnic relations in the early Roman period. The habit of setting up tombstones was a Roman custom that had been rapidly adopted, though at the same time many traditional features of the native way of life and ideas survived. Celtic or Illyrian (Pannonian) names were not abandoned just because they appeared on Latin epitaphs. In the most fortunate circumstances the

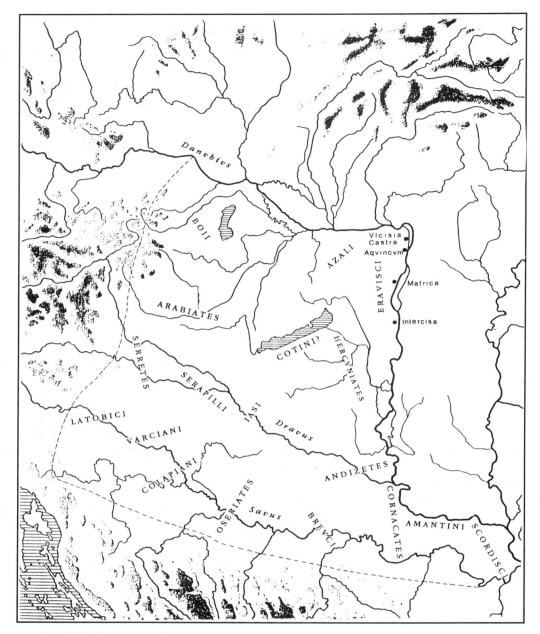

Fig. 20.1 *The native tribes of Pannonia (after A. Mócsy) and sites mentioned in the text.*

tombstones left *in situ* record the age, gender, social rank and time of the burial of the deceased. Even tombstones which have been moved from their original locations, sometimes several times before being reused or built into walls, contain valuable information through the names of those who erected them and those to whom they were raised. *Stelae* with Illyrian-Pannonian and Celtic (mainly Eraviscan) native names on them testify to the rapid, albeit slightly superficial, Romanization of the native population, for example the *stele* of Eburo Milionis f(ilius) (Aquincum Lapid. Inv. no. 63.10.20), that of Scorilo from the territory of Aquincum (Inv. no. 63.10.110, CIL 13379) or the Numio stone from Ulcisia Castra (Inv. no. 64.10.183, CIL 15173). However inscriptions will not be discussed here. Instead

I should like to discuss certain burial rites, objects and jewellery which were used in the burial tradition and can be related to a separate ethnic group or individuals. Two of the four main sites in question, Matrica and Aquincum, the capital of Pannonia Inferior, were excavated by the author herself, while at Ulcisia Castra (later Castra Constantia) and at Intercisa the author took part in exploring several graves. The conclusions, therefore, are based on personal examination of the evidence.

We start from the fact that cremation was a dominant burial rite in our region throughout the Empire. Both Pliny *(Nat. Hist. VII, 187)* and Cicero *(De leg. II, 22, 56)* named inhumation as the primitive rite at Rome and implied that this was later superseded by cremation. This is in keeping

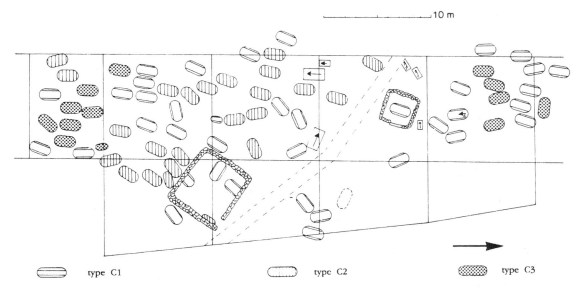

10 m

type C1   type C2   type C3

Fig. 20.2 *The distribution of grave types C1, C2 and C3 in a part of the Southern Cemetery of Matrica*

with the evidence of the Twelve Tables (III. 890–3) which assumed the existence of both rites. These rituals were, however, coloured by many local indigenous practices. Some of these can also be seen in the cremation graves at Matrica (Fig. 20.2.). A distribution of the main burial types in a part of the excavated area in the Southern Cemetery (Topál 1981: Suppl.1) shows three more or less exclusive groups. It seems, therefore, very likely that these grave-groups define separate ethnic groups. The grave-pits of type C1 were ritually purified by fire so that the sides and sometimes the bottom were burnt orange-red. After purification the pits were plastered with fine clay strikingly different from the earth in which they were dug. This type proved to be the most frequent form of burial at Matrica – half of the total number (Topál 1981: 75, notes 18–25) – and also in the Western cemetery of Aquincum (Topál 1993: 78).

Grave-pits of type C2 were also fired before the ashes were scattered into them, but they were not plaster-lined (Topál 1981: 76 ff, notes 26–32). The distinction between the burial types C1 and C2 cannot be distinguished from the finds alone as the furnishings of both types are fairly alike.

The small, oval pits of type C3 were neither burnt nor plaster-lined. The grave-goods discovered in these burials were evidently much more modest than those of the former types (Topál 1981: 77, notes 33–36). In the case of all three types of burials the corpses were cremated at a common firing place (*ustrinum publicum*) together with the bier (*lectus funebris*) and the funeral pyre (*rogus*). The cremation of the dead person on the very spot of burial the *rogus* had been erected **in** ('étage' pits: Topál 1981: note 40) or **above** the grave-pit, i.e. the *bustum* (type C4, Topál 1981: 77; 1993: 78, 80), is not discussed here. In all cases above the calcined bones were not selected from the

remains of the pyre but were simply scattered over the bottom of the grave without any container.

Grave-pits purified by ritual fire before the burial occur frequently in Noricum (Kloiber 1953: 19), Pannonia (Topál 1981: notes 21, 25–6; 1993: 78, 80), Dalmatia (Srejović 1962–63: 68), Upper Moesia (Srejović 1962–63: 69) and Dacia (Babeş 1970: 196). The custom of burial in ritually fired graves is attributed to the *Illyrii* in the Yugoslavian part of Pannonia, Moesia Superior, Dalmatia and Dacia (the so-called type Mala Kopasnica-Sase horizon, Babeş 1970: 198; Jovanović 1984: 152, map 19; Srejović 1962–3: 87; Jovanović this volume). For the same geographical reasons these groups may have lived at Matrica as well but to find such a large number in the territory of the *Eravisci* of certain Celtic origin seems to be interesting. Nevertheless several signs of survival of Illyrian traditions have already been noted, especially in the southern part of this region (Mócsy 1959: 61, note 314). On the basis of these data, the ritually fired graves may have been the autochthonous funeral tradition of the Illyrian-Pannonian populations in this region coloured by some south-western Celtic influence.

The fact that the grave-goods found in graves of type C3 were certainly poorer than those from the former grave-types suggests that this group may have belonged to peoples of lower social status. The low percentage of this type – ten percent at Matrica and only three percent in the Western Cemetery of Aquincum (Topál 1993: 78) – does not allow us to connect this group with any of the Celtic tribes (Babeş 1970: 203–4; van Doorselaer 1967: 91; Knez 1968: 236; Srejović 1962–3: 57). On that basis, this area would not have been rightly called *civitas Eraviscorum*. The presence of Illyrian-Pannonian (non-Celtic) elements in this area, together with the occurrence of names of Spanish origin and astral symbols on the tombstones of the *Azali* (CIL III

10571=RIU 942, MNM inv. nr. 104/1901) point to the possibility that Celtic culture in Pannonia was not solely derived from the Norican-Alpine civilization.

As a whole, the grave-goods found in the Matrica cremation burials are fairly similar to those of cemeteries along the *limes* (Aquincum: Topál 1993; Intercisa, furniture of almost 300 still unpublished graves). Some of them will however be discussed here as displaying certain non-Roman characteristics (Fig. 20.3). The two fragmentary Norican-Pannonian wing brooches of Garbsch type A238v deserve no particular explanation. One of them, however came to light together with a special kind of spiral brooch ('Distelfibel') which is generally accepted as an object of western Germanic influence (Behrens 1927: 55, fig. 8; Müller 1977: 65/15).

The brooch of Böhme form 19b occurs more frequently along the Upper German-Raetian *limes* (Böhme 1972: 18, 57–58, Fundliste 8, Taf. 33). The bronze brooch of Almgren form 101 was also favoured in *Germania Libera*

as well as along the *limes* (Kovrig 1937: type VIII, Taf. 41; Keller 1971: pp. 175–78; Böhme 1972: type 35c, 30–31, 64–65, Fundliste 30). On the basis of its provenance and distribution, the fork-shaped brooch (Böhme 1972: form 27c) has similar connections.

More detailed explanation should be rightly attached to our 'bow-tie' shaped brooch. We have not yet found parallels which can be compared to this open-work specimen of 'Maschenfibeln'. The other brooches of this kind, mostly from *tumulus*-graves, are made from iron or bronze plates decorated with geometric motifs (Fitz 1957: 146, note 88, Taf. 28,3 and 29,2–3), rosettes (Petres 1965: 98, fig. 26, 3–4), a human mask and figure (Topál 1981: 93, note 248, 250), or even a cicada (c.f. Felsőcikola and a recently found specimen in Lussonium). These brooches are often depicted on tombstones of this area, sometimes together with Norican-Pannonian brooches. They are however probably not an indigenous part of the costume of the *Eravisci*, being completely absent from their first-

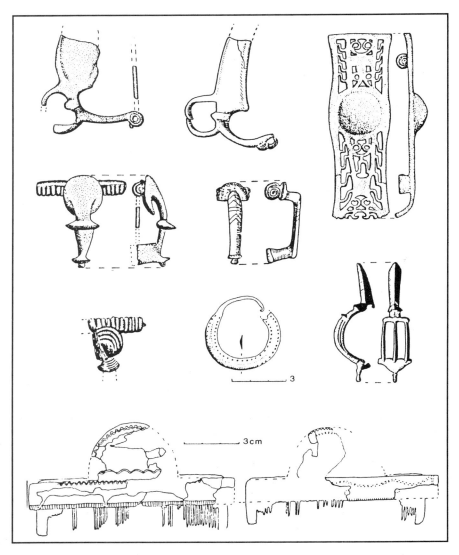

Fig. 20.3 *Artefacts of non – Roman character in the Southern Cemetery of Matrica.*

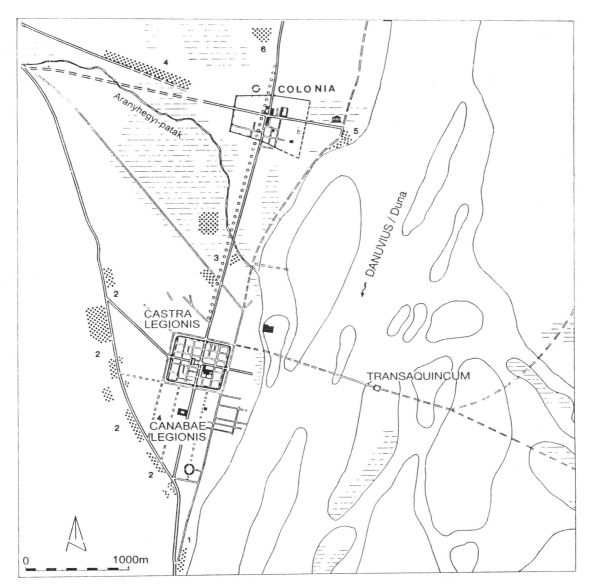

Fig. 20.4 *Roman cemeteries around the military and civil town of Aquincum. 1= Zsigmond tér (southern cemetery of the military town, C1-2 AD); 2= Kecske utca, Bécsi út (western cemetery of the military town, C1-4 AD); 3= Bogdáni út, Kaszásdűlő, Benedek E. utca (northern cemetery of the military town, C2-4 AD); 4= Aranyhegyi árok (western cemetery of the civil town, C1-2 AD); 5= Gázgyár (eastern cemetery of the civil town, C3-4 AD); 6= Csillaghegy (northern cemetery of the civil town, late C1 AD).*

century material. Neither do they occur among the genuine Pannonians in the south (Mócsy 1974: 63). Consequently in the southern part of the *territorium Eraviscorum* – an area roughly between Vetus Salina and Lussonium the costumes and burial practice *(tumuli)* are obviously affected by influences from the south-western Pannonian region between Celeia and Vindobona. This influence can be explained by the assumption that a west Pannonian ethnic group settled in East Pannonia towards the end of the first and beginning of the second century. The main cause of this migration may have been the *deductiones* for veterans, which robbed the native peoples of their homeland (Mócsy 1959: 62–64, 69). The inhumation grave

of a young girl in the Western Cemetery of Aquincum (graveyard I, Kecske u. grave 3, unpublished) provides additional information for this migration. A positively south-western Norican-Pannonian brooch of Garbsch type A238p on the left shoulder (the easternmost occurrence of this type so far) and a one-knobbed 'kräftig profilierte' brooch (Kovrig 1937: 52, 54; Patek 1942: IV/12) at the right shoulder reflect the power of tradition and fashion. More fragmentary, but also south-western, wing-brooches of Garbsch type A238v came to light in the cemetery of Ulcisia Castra (Maróti-Topál 1980: grave 118).

In Aquincum, south of the military town many burials were discovered in a narrow band on both sides of the *limes* road (No. 1) (Fig. 20.4). A few early tombstones raised over the graves of cavalrymen are associated with the first *ala* fort which preceded the legionary fortress, for example the *stele* of Cl. Severus of Vangionan origin (Aquincum Lapid. Inv.nr.63.10.98) and that of the Treveran Reginus (Inv.nr. 63.10.150).

Under Domitian Legio II Adiutrix was stationed here and the rapidly developing military town continued to use the southern cemetery (a famous *stele* of this period is that of Castricius from Como, Italy, Inv.nr. 64.10.2.) but use of the western cemetery (No. 2) along the Bécsi road soon began (one of the earliest tombstone is that of L. Varius Pudens from Parma, Inv.nr. 63.10.64) and lasted to the end of the fourth century. Significant differences are difficult to ascertain between the cremation graves of the native population and those similarly cremated burials of the first conquerors which were not marked by grave monuments. The grave furniture is fairly alike, mainly pottery vessels 'from the market', sometimes deliberately spoiled ones (see also Tuffreau-Libre, this volume). There is, however, one special type of flagon, one or two handled, similar to Gose type 389, which occurs in overwhelming quantity in graves, but so far never in settlement material from Aquincum. Exceptions to this lack of difference are the previously mentioned graves containing costume accessories revealing tribal affiliation and imported goods which had been personally brought by the settlers. In one of the graves from the western cemetery a handled beaker, an imitation of a silver vessel with a precious stone inlay (Fig. 20.5) was found (Topál 1993: 21, Plates 24–25 and 132). This has its closest parallel in Rome (Fig. 20.6; Comfort 1960: 273). In

Fig. 20.5 Imitation of a silver vessel with glass inlay from the Bécsi út cemetery , grave 29.

Fig. 20.6 Cup with glass inlay from Rome. Photo courtesy of the Archaeological Department of Heidelberg University.

Fig. 20.7 Reconstruction of an arca *found in the Bécsi út cemetery, grave 7.*

another grave we excavated a large wooden chest (*arca*) with heavy bronze fittings, which held a bronze bucket, bronze flagon, an amphora and cosmetic kit, and the cremated remains of a young woman. The rite of burial indicates a funerary rite of Italian origin (Topál 1993: 8–11, Pl. 3–6 and 118–120, Fig. 20.7). In more than one case we could observe that both cremation and inhumation occurred in one and the same grave-pit. We might imagine that in the case of the later burial (Nachbestattung), changes in funerary practice within one family took place fairly rapidly. Pliny observes (*Nat. Hist.* VII, 187) that many Roman families, especially the *gens Cornelia* retained inhumation, while others cremated, and Cicero writes (*De leg.* II, 22, 56) that Sulla was the first of the Cornelii to be cremated. Nevertheless, groups in the north-eastern area of Pannonia, especially women on the evidence of dress accessories in graves and tombstones, tried to protect traditional tribal customs for almost two centuries. Those tribes where inhumation was the ritual also continued to use it side by side with people practising cremation and vice versa.

In the absence of more convincing archaeological data we must be content with the hypothesis that the territory of the *Eravisci* – of which the Celtic origin has been repeatedly emphasised – must have been the region in which at least three ethnic groups merged: the auto-chthonous Illyrian-Pannonian population, which survived for centuries, the *Eravisci* transferred here in the late La Tène period and groups of south-western Celtic tribes (presumably *Boii* and *Taurisci*) who arrived as immigrants at the turn of the first century AD.

Bibliography

Almgren, O. 1923. *Studien über nordeuropäische Fibelformen der ersten nachtchristlichen Jahrhunderte mit Berücksichtigung der provinzialrömischen und südrussischen Funde.* Mannus-Bibliothek 32.

Ambros, A.K. 1966. *Fibuly juga-jevropejskoj casti SSSR.* Svod Arheologiceskih Istocnikov, Moscow.

Babeş, M. 1970. Zu den Bestattungsarten im nördlichen Flach-gräberfeld von Romula. Ein Beitrag zur Grabtypologie des römisches Daziens. *Dacia* 14, 167–208.

Barkóczi, L. and Soproni, S. 1981. *Die römischen Inschriften Ungarns* RIU, Band 3. Budapest.

Barkóczi, L., Alföldi, M. R., Radnóti, M., Sági, K. and Nemeskéri, J. 1954–1957. *Intercisa I–II,* Budapest

Behrens, G. 1927. Fibeldarstellungen auf römischen Grabsteine. *Mainzer Zeitschrift* 22, 52–55.

Böhme, A. 1972. Die Fibeln der Kastelle Saalburg und Zugmantel. *Saalburg Jahrbuch* 29.

CIL Corpus Inscriptionum Latinarum

Comfort, H. 1960. Roman Ceramic-and-Glass Vases at Heidelberg and New-York. *American Journ. Arch.* 64, 273.

Cumont, F. 1942. *Recherches sur le symbolisme funéraire des romains.* Paris.

Fitz J. 1957. Az eraviszkusz női viselet (Die Tracht der Eraviskerinnen). *Archaeologiai Értesítő* 84, 133–154.

Garbsch, J. 1965. *Die norisch-pannonische Frauentracht.* Munich.

Garcia y Bellido, A. 1949. *Esculturas romanas de Espana y Portugal* I–II. Madrid.

Gose, E. 1950. Gefäßtypen der römischen Keramik im Rheinland. Beiheft *Bonner Jahrbücher* 1.

Jovanović, A. 1984. *Rímske nekropole na teritoriji Jugoslavije. Forms of Burial in the Territory of Yugoslavia in the Time of the Roman Empire.* Belgrade.

Keller, E. 1971. *Die Spätrömischen Grabfunde in Südbayern,* Münchner Beiträge zur Vor- und Frühgeschichte, Munich: Beck.

Kloiber, A. 1957. *Die Gräberfelder von Lauriacum. Das Ziegelfeld.* Linz.

Knez, T. 1968. Oblike anticnih grobov na Dolenjskem (Antike Grabformen in Dolenjsko [Unterkrain]. *Arheoloski Vestnik* 19, 221–238.

Kovrig, I. 1937. *Die Haupttypen der kaiserzeitlichen Fibeln in Pannonien.* Dissertationes Pannonicae II,4. Budapest.

Lányi, V. 1972. Die spätantiken Gräberfelder von Pannonien. *Acta Archaeologica Hungarica* 24, 53–213.

T.Maróti É.- Topál J. 1980. Szentendre római kori temetője.(Das römerzeitliche Gräberfeld von Szentendre). *Studia Comitatensia* 9, 95–177.

Mócsy, A. 1959. *Die Bevölkerung von Pannonien bis zu den Markomannenkriegen.* Budapest.

Mócsy, A. 1974. *Pannonia and Upper Moesia. A History of the Middle Danube Provinces of the Roman Empire.* London and Boston.

Müller, G. 1977. *Novaesium VII. Die römischen Gräberfelder von Novaesium.* Limesforschungen 17. Berlin.

Nagy, M. 1988. Die nordpannonische Gruppe der mit sog. Astralsymbolen verzierten Grabsteine. *Communicationes Archaeologicae Hungariae,* 93–111.

Patek, E. 1942. *Verbreitung und Herkunft der römischen Fibeltypen von Pannonien.* Dissertationes Pannonicae II,19. Budapest.

Petres É. 1965. A mányi eraviszkusz temető. (Das eraviskische Gräberfeld von Mány). *Folia Archaeologica* 17, 87–100.

Reece, R. (ed.) 1977. *Burial in the Roman World.* Council for British Archaeology Research Report 22, London.

RIU see Barkóczi and Soproni

Salamon, Á. and Barkóczi, L. 1973. Archäologische Angaben zur spätrömischen Geschichte des pannonischen Limes – Gräberfelder von Intercisa I. *Mitteilungen des Archäologischen Instituts der Ungarischen Akademie der Wissenschaften* 4, 73–95.

Schober, A. 1923. *Die römischen Grabsteine von Noricum und Pannonien.* Vienna.

Srejović, D. 1962–63. Rímske nekropole ranog carstva u Jugoslaviji (Nécropoles romaines du haut empire en Yougoslavie). *Starinar* 13–14, 49–88.

Topál, J. 1981. *The Southern Cemetery of Matrica (Százhalombatta-Dunafüred).* Fontes Archaeologici Hungariae. Budapest.

Topál, J. 1993. *Roman Cemeteries of Aquincum, Pannonia. The Western Cemetery (Bécsi Road) I.* Budapest.

Toynbee, J.M.C. 1971. *Death and Burial in the Roman World.* London.

Vágó, E.B. – Bóna, I. 1976. *Die Gräberfelder von Intercisa I. Der spätrömische Südostfriedhof.* Budapest.

van Doorselaer, A. 1967. *Les nécropoles d'époque romaine en Gaule septentrionale.* Brugge.

21. Romanization and ethnic elements in burial practice in the southern part of Pannonia Inferior and Moesia Superior

Aleksandar Jovanović

Introduction

My aim here is to present the results of research related to burial practice during the Early Empire (first to third centuries) in the southern part of Pannonia Inferior and Moesia Superior. An attempt to determine the ethno-cultural identity of the creators of particular forms of burial procedure and graves will be emphasised.

Pannonia Inferior – southern part

Conclusions on basic aspects of burial practice in early Roman cemeteries have not been attainable due to a relatively inadequate exploration of the southern part of the province of Pannonia Inferior. Therefore, my suggestions are only preliminary.

The basic elements noted in the majority of graves derived directly from the La Tène tradition, hence they were ascribed to the indigenous Pannonian and Celtic population (Jovanović 1984: 49–51). Simple burial pits of circular, rectangular or irregular shape were recorded, containing the remnants of cremated individuals which were not separated from the remains of the pyre, or (less frequently), a ceramic urn. Grave goods consisted of the following items: ceramic vessels – often resembling the La Tène form; iron bindings from wooden boxes; occasional jewellery; coins; glass vessels, and lamps. Torques and fibulae prevailed among the jewellery. It is remarkable that anchor-like silver fibulae, which were elements of the local costume, were found in these graves (Marijanski-Manojlović 1987: 36; Popović and Borić-Brešković 1994: 20–22). Besides, these graves are directly related to pre-Roman burial forms in the region of study, reflected in the following basic funerary elements: cremation on the pyre (*ustrinum*); cremated human remains mixed with the pyre remnants; a similar proportion of graves containing an urn and those lacking it (circa 10:1) and the presence of weapons in grave inventories (Todorović 1974: 55–63). As for grave goods, the autochthonous elements are also represented by particular forms of jewellery, along with wooden boxes with metal binding. Similar continuity has also been recorded on the indigenous settlements of this part of Pannonia (Brukner 1995: 91–136). The occasional presence of lamps, coins and glass vessels in graves could be of secondary character, attributable to a greater degree to a social and economic diversification of the autochthonous population than to a process of Romanization. The chronology of graves covers a time span between the beginning of the first and the late fourth century AD. The same form of graves was recorded in urban cemeteries (Sirmium/Sremska Mitrovica,

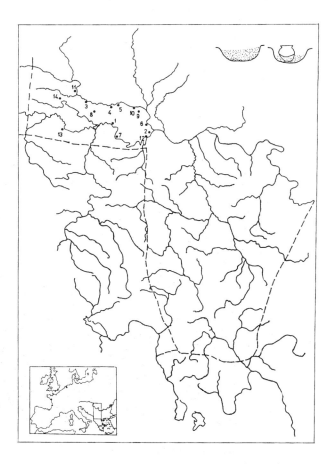

Fig. 21.1 *Simple cremation burials of the indigenous tradition (Pannonia Inferior)*

Taurunum/Zemun), fortifications (Cornacum/Sotin, Bononia/Banoštor, Burgenae/Novi Banovci), at *civitates peregrinae* (Gomolava), rural settlements (Beška) or villas (Tovarnik) (Fig. 21.1). It is remarkable that this form of grave persisted for a long time in the cemeteries of Sirmium. It has also been recorded in the fourth century (Ercegović-Pavlović 1980: 6–12), confirming that traditional, autochthonous forms of burial endured even in the most fully-developed urban backgrounds.

Graves of this type were recorded at a large number of cemeteries in Pannonia Superior and Pannonia Inferior, encompassed by the same ethno-cultural complex (Buócz 1961: 219–239; Demo 1982: 279; Fülep 1958: 371; Gregl 1984; Horvath 1972: 257; Szanto 1953: 53–62).

Concurrently with this form, another type of burial with similar traits has been recorded in the cemeteries of Sirmium and Beška. The similar elements are represented by cremated human bones mixed with the remains of pyres, absence of urns, reduced grave inventories and the similarity of grave goods. On the other hand, the burial form was different. Graves of the second group are slightly larger in size, mainly rectangular in shape, sometimes with stepped sides ('en étage') and with walls burned in an intense contact with fire. A question remains open whether the burning was a consequence of cremation at

the place of burial (*bustum*), or of lustration of the grave area and its purification by fire. In archaeological publications, such graves are labelled the Mala Kopašnica-Sase type after the eponymous sites (Garašanin 1968: 5–35). They have an extensive distribution in the north of the Balkan peninsula, notably in the provinces of Moesia Superior, Pannonia, East Dalmatia and Dacia, and their appearance is explained by translocation of miners from the regions of Moesia Superior and East Dalmatia (Babeš 1970: 167–206; Protase 1971: 141–160).

In view of their basic elements, these graves are not significantly different from the characteristic form occurring previously in Pannonia. A different shape of burial pit and burning of its walls could be of secondary character, if an assumption about ritual 'purification' of the grave area was accepted. However, if it was a consequence of cremation at the very spot of burial (*bustum*), then one may speak of a different sacral concept. The question may thus be put as to whether these graves were a manifestation of Romanization? It is difficult to reply in the affirmative to this question, notwithstanding the appearance of these graves in large urban centres where a more intensive Romanization could be observed. Firstly, the distribution of these graves is not universal: they were mainly concentrated in the regions of Moesia Superior,

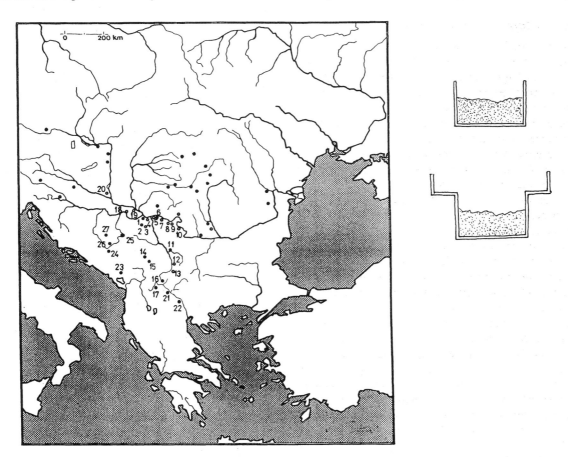

Fig. 21.2 *Cremation burials with burned walls and rectangular/stepped grave pit – the Mala-Kopašnica-Sase type (Balkan provinces)*

Pannonia, East Dalmatia, northern Macedonia and Dacia (Fig. 21.2). Secondly, if compared to other contemporaneous forms, these graves are very frequent in the cemeteries of Moesia and Pannonia Inferior, accounting for between 60%–90% of graves. This is in contrast to the general aspect of Roman cemeteries throughout the Empire, where the percentage of such graves (*busta*) was negligible. Regardless of various statements about the ethno-cultural affiliation of these graves (reviewed in Jovanović 1984: 100–110), we may leave this question open. I am inclined to believe that these graves should be related to the autochthonous people, and that they were not *busta* in the true sense of the term. This form of grave will also be discussed more extensively in the consideration of burials in Moesia Superior.

If an assumption of the autochthonous character of these graves is accepted, a corollary question about the evolution of Roman or Romanized forms of grave in the southern part of the province Pannonia Inferior can be addressed. Several forms of grave have appeared in the study region which can be interpreted as foreign intrusions within the autochthonous funerary milieu of Pannonia Inferior. These are stone receptacles for the ashes (ossuaries) and glass urns, as well as the tombstones of Aquileian type recorded in the Western cemetery at Sirmium and its surroundings (Milošević 1996: 39–48). These forms may undoubtedly be ascribed to Italic settlers or to a Romanized population. Specific grave constructions of stone and mortar (Milošević 1995: 198) – known from the western part of Pannonia Superior, particularly in the regions settled by Latobians (Knez 1968: 221–238) – may imply that Sirmium was settled by people coming from these regions as well. Burials in shafts, discovered in an isolated Sirmium cemetery (Jovanović 1984: 124–126; Milošević 1996: 40), could probably be related to settlers coming from Gallia where this peculiar form is known (e.g Fouet 1958; Schwarz 1963).

There is an impression that cremation burials marked by autochthonous funerary traits prevailed in the Early Empire cemeteries of the southern part of Pannonia, regardless of their location (in towns, villages or fortifications), and that foreign forms and Romanized elements did not surpass 10%. This indication is valid if one ascribes the graves of the Mala Kopašnica-Sase type to the indigenous population.

Apart from cremation graves, the cemeteries of large towns in Pannonia Inferior between the end of the first and the first half of the third centuries, particularly in Sirmium, contained inhumation graves which are marked by several common traits. In general, the deceased were placed in a burial pit lacking any evidence for a grave marker and without a coffin or sarcophagus. The orientation of graves was diverse, and the grave inventory was restricted and poor (Ercegović-Pavlović 1980: 12–18; Milošević 1995: 195–219). Inhumation did not have a significant share in the funerary practice of the indigenous population in the pre-Roman period. Therefore this form

of burial could be understood as reflecting the presence in the diverse ethnic structure of Sirmium of immigrant craftsmen, merchants, and soldiers from the eastern provinces, mainly Asia Minor (although Spanu, this volume, shows that the burial traditions of Asia Minor are likely to have been more complex than previously appreciated). However the remarkable poverty of these graves may reflect a certain social category unable to arrange the appropriate *funus*, perhaps slaves or the local poor. The appearance of decorated sarcophagi and rich inhumation graves was recorded only at the end of the second and in the third centuries at Sirmium, when a large number of immigrant merchants and craftsmen arrived from the East, in the context of the economic policy of the emperors from the Antonine and Severan dynasties (Cermanović-Kuzmanović 1965: 89–103; Dautova-Ruševljanin 1983: 93–112).

Generally, cremation graves and those with the funerary traits which could be ascribed to the indigenous population dominated in cemeteries of the southern part of Pannonia Inferior in the period between the first and the mid-third century. This situation was recorded in the metropolis of Sirmium, as well as in rural settlements, villas and fortifications. The conservatism of the population may also be illustrated by the persistence of cremation in urban and village cemeteries of the fourth century.

Moesia Superior

A significant level of similarity in burial practice may be established between the southern part of Pannonia Inferior and Moesia Superior. Particular forms of cremation graves are similar, and inhumation graves are also marked by a certain unanimity. However differences could be registered: the picture is somewhat more complex in the territory of Moesia Superior, witnessing a more heterogeneous ethnic composition in this area.

Graves with simple shallow burial pits containing a small quantity of unurned cremated human bone mixed with pyre remains have been excavated in the Danube valley. In most cases these graves were covered by a small stone mound, representing the grave marker. Traces of the deposition of red-hot pyre material were visible. Thus it seems that burial took place very soon after cremation – in contrast to Roman funerary practice. The grave inventory was very poor, consisting mainly of ceramic vessels, occasional jewellery, weapons and coins. Such graves are dated to the first and second centuries. They are recorded at Ram/Lederata, Boljetin/Smorna (Zotović 1969: 114–119), and at Ušće Slatinske reke (Jovanović and Korać 1986: 378; Fig. 21.3). The basic burial practice is similar to the pre-Roman, autochthonous form, attributable to the Celtic-Dacian population reported by Strabo (Strab. VII, 3,11). A small number of graves has been registered at several sites in the valleys of the Danube and Morava which have more direct analogues in Dacia, and might thus be attributed to a Dacian element or

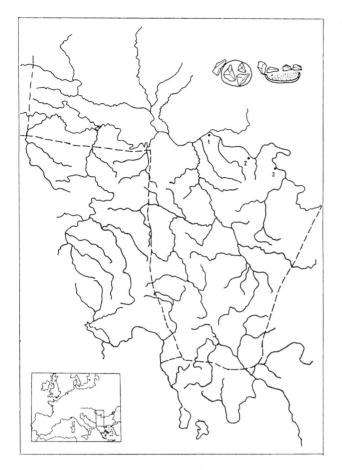

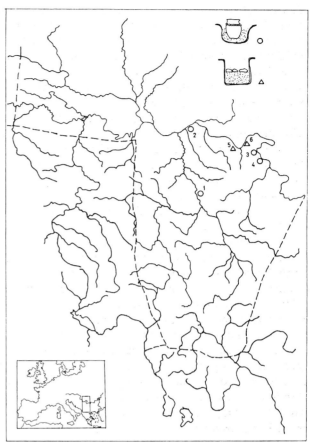

Fig. 21.3 *Simple cremation burials with stone markers (Moesia Superior)*

Fig. 21.4 *'Dacian' cremation burials (Moesia Superior)*

influence. These are those graves with urns, so called 'Dacian pots'. Grave goods, consisting of ceramic vessels, occasional jewellery, coins and weapons were placed in the urn. They are dated to the first and second centuries and have been recorded at Gloždar near Paraćin, Majur near Jagodina, Velesnica, Ušće Slatinske reke, and at the cemetery of 'Više grobalja' at Viminacium (Zotović and Jordović 1990: grave 91, 267, 268; Fig. 21.4). 'Barrel-shaped' graves, uncovered at Boljetin/Smorna/ and Hajdučka Vodenica, also belong to the Dacian cultural sphere. These graves are characterised by a deep cylindrical grave pit with the remnants of the cremated individual mixed with pyre remains, fragments of broken ceramics, and sometimes grinding stone fragments. The grave contents were covered by a layer of stones or pebbles. Such graves, considerably more frequent in Dacia (Protase 1971: 71–74) are dated to a period between the end of the first century BC, and the beginning of the second century AD. These burial forms with Dacian funerary attributes could be related to the deportation of the Dacian population to the area of Moesia Superior by Aelius Catus at the beginning of the first century AD and by Plautius Silvius Aelianus in the time of Nero (Mócsy 1959; Garašanin 1963).

In the eastern parts of the province of Moesia Superior appeared grave forms which could be related to a Thracian cultural sphere. Essentially these are graves under large mounds. Although insufficiently explored, these graves may point to a direct relation with a large number of analogues in the provinces of Thracia, Moesia Inferior and Scythia Minor (Getov 1970: 1–12), based on their basic characteristics (cremation and inhumation burial in the central part of the mound, a large grave pit and burial mound and the presence of chairs, bronze vessels, jewellery, boxes and nuts in grave inventories). Such graves are recorded mainly in the valleys of Nišava, South (Južna) Morava, and to the west in the vicinity of Ulpiana (Srejović 1986: 179–190; Fig. 21.5). A grave under a large mound with stone sarcophagus from Nozrena near Niš probably also belongs to this group. The deceased individual in this grave was accompanied by bronze trefoil oenochoe, a key for the box in the shape of a herm and a denarius of M. Aurelius (Jovanović 1981: 1–14). Such grave forms are characteristic for the northern Thracian zone, and are fairly numerous in Moesia Inferior and Scythia Minor (Fig. 21.6). Another grave form was registered in the eastern part of Moesia Superior, which could be compared to finds from the Thracian area. It is

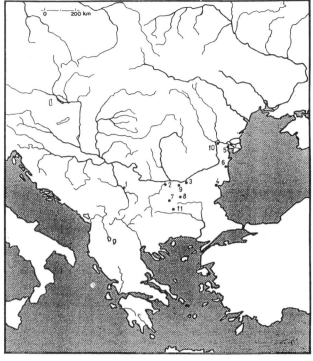

Fig. 21.5 (top left) *Barrow burials of 'Thracian' type (Balkan provinces)*

Fig. 21.6 (top right) *Barrow burials with stone sarcophagi (Balkan provinces)*

Fig. 21.7 (left) *Cremation burials with stone border and mound (Balkan provinces)*

represented by simple burial pits bordered and covered by stones, and the remains of pyres. Ceramic vessels, some of them manufactured on a slow wheel, predominate in the grave inventory. The date of these graves covers a period between the second and fourth centuries. They were registered in the eastern part of Moesia Superior in the vicinity of Vrace (Drašan), Zavoj near Pirot, and Nemanjica near Sveti Nikola (Fig. 21.7). These graves can be compared to similar examples observed at the western side of Rhodope, settled by Thracian tribes among which the Bessi were the largest.

Several dozen graves with simple, oval, shallow pits containing the remains of cremated individuals mixed with pyre remnants, were explored in the southern part of Moesia Superior. Such graves (Fig. 21.8) were registered in the cemeteries of small rural settlements (Karagač, Veleknice, Zaskok, Mala Kopašnica, Jašunja) as well as

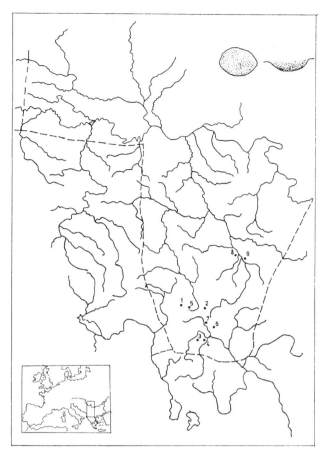

Fig. 21.8 *Simple cremation burials of the indigenous tradition (Moesia Superior)*

the towns (Skoplje/Scupi, Soćanica/Municipium DD, Glavnik /Vindenis) and in suburban cemeteries (Kamnik). Graves of this form appeared in a broad chronological horizon between the first and the fourth century; the latest examples from Mala Kopašnica and Kamnik were dated by coins of Constantine I. The inventory of early graves of this group consisted of weapons, and that of later graves ceramic vessels, occasional lamps, coins and simple jewellery. Luxury items are generally absent. These graves belong to a population of a low economic and social status. The similarity of these graves to pre-Roman burial forms in this region, such as those from the latest burial horizon at Romaja (Đurić, Glišić and Todorović 1975: 21, 26) or Karagač (Srejović 1973: 64) may indicate an auto-chthonous, probably Dardanian population.

The distribution of these graves partially coincides with the distribution of graves of the 'Mala Kopašnica – Sase' type. However, the distribution of the latter was considerably broader and represents the most numerous and most widely occurring burial form in Moesia Superior (more than 70% of the total number of graves). These graves are large and appear in two varieties, nearly rectangular grave pits measuring 120 × 60 × 30 cm and stepped graves with an upper step measuring ca. 200 × 100 × 30 cm, and

the lower step, i.e. the grave, similar in size to type 1. The lower step is often covered by tiles and these graves sometimes contained a ceramic libation pipe. The walls of this type of grave are burnt and fire-baked. A large quantity of cremated bone mixed with pyre remnants was scattered all over the grave pit. Urns are absent in such graves. The grave inventory is marked by a certain duality: coins and occasional specimens of jewellery were burnt, while ceramic vessels, lamps, glass vessels, and occasional weapons did not bear traces of contact with fire. It seems that they were placed into a grave after the remains of pyre had cooled.

Such graves were registered at the cemeteries of large towns in Moesia Superior (Viminacium (more than 200 graves), Margum, Singidunum, Scupi, Naissus, Ulpiana, Municipium DD) in small settlements (Pincum, Vindenis, Lamud), in rural settlements (Mala Kopašnica, Velika Grabovnica, Žuto Brdo, Orašje, Porećka reka) as well as in the mining zones (Guberevac at Kosmaj, and Sase near Srebrenica /Domavia/ in East Dalmatia (Srejović and Baum: 1959; 1960; Fig. II). The appearance of such graves in the mining zones of Dacia has actually been explained by immigration of the miners from East Dalmatia and Moesia Superior into the newly established province (see Daicoviciu 1961; Tudor and Vladescu 1972; Mrozek 1968).

The date of the graves of Mala Kopašnica- Sase type covers a period between the first and the third century, although a small number of fourth century examples are known. Two basic dilemmas are posed by graves of this type. The first concerns the question of whether these graves are *busta*, or whether the cremation took place at the pyre (*ustrinum*) and the remains were subsequently translocated into a burial pit. The second is the question of whether these graves represented an expression of Romanization, i.e. who was practising this burial mode? Opinions are opposed between those asserting that the graves were placed at the spot of cremation (i.e. were *busta*) (Mikulćić 1979: 254) and the thesis that cremation was performed at a separate pyre, such as for the graves discovered at Viminacium, Sase, Mala Kopašnica, Guberevac, etc. According to a large number of scholars, wall burning is a consequence of ritual cleansing of burial area by fire (purification). I also argue for this possibility. The dilemma of who practised this mode of burial is even more distinct. The presence of such graves in the large town cemeteries and their fairly broad area of distribution (compare Fig. 21.2), could imply that this grave form was that of a Romanized population (Zotović 1984: 165–170). However, the possible recognition of antecedent grave forms in pre-Roman funerary practice recorded on the territory of Serbia, as at Krševica (Mikulčić and Jovanović 1968, 357–375) or Skoplje (Mikulčić 1979: 245–255), the similarity of stepped forms of burial with Thracian graves under mounds and the relative poverty of grave goods would be more indicative of an indigenous population (Garašanin 1968; Jovanović 1984: 100–110).

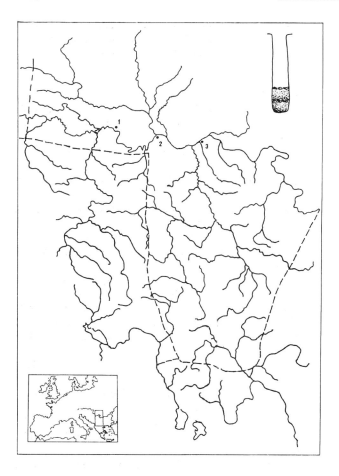

Fig. 21.9 *Cremation burials in shafts (Moesia Superior)*

If a Roman character of this grave form is accepted, it would announce a highly Romanized population in Moesia Superior. Other parameters, however, indicate that such assumptions could not conform to actual evidence (Mócsy 1970). I assume that this grave form could also be related to the indigenous population of Moesia Superior and Pannonia, which was partly Romanized. It is difficult to advance further from this general statement. The Moesian-Dardanian population predominated in the ethnic structure of Moesia Superior, and it was this population which is likely to have practised this common burial mode (see also Struck (1993) on the difficulty of determining the origins of the *bustum* rite).

'Foreign' forms of cremation also appeared in Moesia Superior, above all burials in shafts (Singidunum, Viminacium), which were also noted at Sirmium (Fig. 21.9). That they appear only in large urban centres with a heterogeneous ethnic composition, and the absence of a direct prototype for them in local funerary practice may imply that it was a foreign grave form. It was probably introduced from Gallia, where this grave form was frequent in the first and second centuries (see above). Grave forms related to areas of western Pannonia or Noricum were sporadically recorded, such as the circular

masonry grave from the vicinity of Vrnjačka Banja (Borović-Dimić 1995: 124–127). Grave forms which could certainly be taken as Roman and ascribed to a highly Romanized population or settlers are rare. Several ceramic and lead urns from Viminacium, Singidunum, and Scupi, as well as stone receptacles for ashes from Viminacium, Naissus, Scupi and Taskovići (Fig. 21.10), could indicate this segment of the population. Again as in the case of southern Pannonia Inferior the frequency of these graves is not high, and it more or less corresponded to the degree of Romanization in Moesia Superior.

The appearance of inhumation between the end of the first and the middle of the third century in Moesia Superior must also be noted. Two distinct types can be recognized. The first comprises graves with rich grave goods (precious metal jewellery, ceramic and glass vessels, lamps) placed in decorated sarcophagi of lead or the tile tombs, with prevalent south-north orientation. These graves were usually placed in the separate part of the town cemetery or were related to suburban villas. Examples were recorded at Scupi (Mikulčić 1975: 89–102), Ulpiana (Parović-Pešikan 1982: 57–72), Municipium DD (Fidanovski 1988: 11–47), Naissus (Ajdić 1972: 33–45), Viminacium (Tomović 1991: 69–80) and Vincea (Jovanović and Cunjak 1987: 139–147). This burial mode was practised by a rich class of settlers from the eastern provinces of the Roman Empire, Asia Minor in particular.

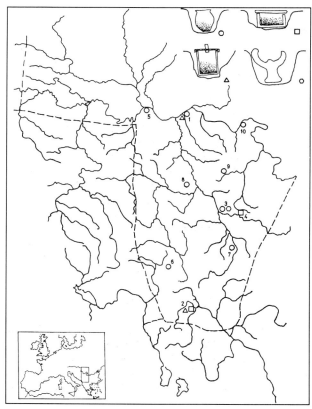

Fig. 21.10 *Cremation burials in various types of container (Moesia Superior)*

Another type comprises poor graves lacking grave architecture and with a diverse orientation. In some cases the deceased were laid upon or covered by a wooden plank. Generally these graves could be ascribed to the poor, mainly of oriental origin, and also perhaps to the lowest status local population. Children were inhumed, even those in the infans II age category (Zotović and Jordović 1990). Only in the second half of the third century did inhumation prevail as the burial mode in the cemeteries of Moesia Superior, although cremation continued to account for 30% of burials.

In summary, in the period between the first and the middle of the third century in Moesia Superior cremation burials predominated. They can be ascribed to the autochthonous population which was not significantly affected by Romanization, or at least not in the domain of burial. A close parallel may be established between circumstances in the southern part of Pannonia Inferior and Moesia Superior. The autochthonous element was strong and its conservatism in the domain of cult was reflected in the persistent tradition of its own local burial modes and grave forms. Immigrants from various regions, especially those from the provinces of Asia Minor and Gallia, introduced important novel practices but changes induced by Romanization are less conspicuous and their manifestations are sporadic.

Appendix

Sites located on figures 21.1 to 21.10

Figure 21.1

1. Sremska Mitrovica (SIRMIUM) – S. Ercegović-Pavlović 1980. Sirmium 12, 6–18; 34–37.
2. Zemun (TAURNUM) – S. Ercegović 1971. Vjesnik Arheološkog muzeja u Zagrebu, 3 ser. 2, 125–137; D. Dimitrijević 1958. Starinar, 7–8, 1956/57, 301.
3. Sotin (CORNACUM) – N. Majnarić-Panđić 1973. Vjesnik Arheološkog muzeja, 3 ser. 6–7, 1972/73, 55–71.
4. Banoštor (BONONIA) – J. Brunšmid 1901. Vjesnik Hrvatskog arheološkog društva, n.s. 5, 148.
5. Rakovac – O. Brukner, V. Dautova-Ruševljan, P. Milošević 1987. The Beginnings of Romanization in the southeastern part of Pannonia Province, Novi Sad, 40.
6. Novi Banovci (BURGENAE) – J.Brunšmid 1901. Vjesnik Hrvatskog arheološkog društva, n.s. 5, 157; D. Dimitrijević 1961. Limes u Jugoslaviji 1, Belgrade, 94.
7. Gomoglava – V. Dautova-Ruševljan, O. Brukner 1992. Gomoglava – The Roman Period, Novi Sad, 171.
8. Donji Tovarnik – D. Srejović 1965. Starinar 13–14, 58.
9. Beška – M. Marijanski-Manojlović 1987. A Roman Necropolis at Beška in Srem, Novi Sad, 9–17.
10. Sremski Karlovci – D.Srejović 1965. Starinar 13–14, 58.
11. Dalj (TEUTOBURGIUM) – J.Garbsch 1965. Die norisch-pannonische Frauentracht im 1. ind 2. Jahrhundert, Munich, 197.
12. Surčin – V. Hoffiller, 1907. Vjesnik Hrvatskog arheološkog drušva, n.s. 9, 199–200.
13. Vidovice – M. Babić 1979. Živa Antika, 29/2, 283–284.
14. Vinkovci (CIBALAE) – J. Brunšmid 1902. Vjesnik Hrvatskog arheološkog drušva, n.s. 6, 161.

Figure 21.2

1. Belgrade (SINGIDUNUM) – Z. Simić 1990. Arheološki pregled, 29, 123–128; S. Krunić 1995. Glasnik Srpskog arheološkog društva, 10, 192.
2. Banjica – M. Ružić, M.Valtrović 1889. Starinar, 6/3, 85–90
3. Gubarevac – M. Veličković 1964. Zbornik radova Narodnog muzeja, 4, 129–134.
4. Udovice (AUREUS MONS) – M. Cunjak 1996. Glasnik Društva konzervatora Srbije, 17, 38.
5. Dubravica (MARGUM) – A. Jovanović, M. Cunjak 1994. Saopštenja Republičkog zavoda za zaštitu spomenika, 26, 107–122.
6. Veliko Gradište (PINCUM) – M. Cunjak 1986. Glasnik Društva konzervatora Srbije, 10, 57–58.
7. Kostolac (VIMINACIUM) – Lj. Zotović, Č. Jordović 1990. Viminacium – Nekropole 'Više grobalja', Belgrade.
8. Žuto Brdo – M. Kosorić, D. Vučković-Todorović 1965. Starinar 13–14, 271–272.
9. Ušće Porečke reke – D. Vučković-Todorović 1968. Arheološki Pregled, 10, 71.
10. Prahovo (AQUIS) – D. Vučković-Todorović 1960. Limes u Jugoslaviji, 1, 139.
11. Niš (NAISSUS) – Lj. Zotović 1973. Niški zbornik , 1, 46.
12. Mala Kopašnica – Lj. Zotović 1968. Leskovački zbornik, 8, 19.
13. Velika Grabovnica – Lj. Zotović 1968. Leskovački zbornik, 8, 24.
14. Sočanica (MUNICIPIUM DD) – S. Fidanovski 1988. Glasnik Muzeja Kosova, 15–16, 13–49.
15. Gračanica (ULPIANA) – D. Srejović 1965. Starinar, 13–14, 71.
16. Lopate (LAMUD) – E. Petrova 1990. Macedoniae acta archaeologica, 11, 135–150.
17. Skopje (SCUPI) – I. Mikiličić 1970. Arheološki pregled, 12, 124–131; id. 1975. Godišen zbornik na Filozofski fakultet, 27, 127–151.
18. Sremska Mitrovica (SURMIUM) – S. Ercegović-Pavlović 1980. Sirmium, 12, 6–12; 34–37.
19. Beška – M. Marijanski-Manojlović 1987. A Roman Necropolis at Beška in Srem, Novi Sad, 10–17.
20. Osijek (MURSA) – M. Bulat 1977. Osiječki zbornik, 14, 79–87.
21. Gradsko (STOBI) – A.B. Wezolowsky 1973. Studies in the Antiquites of Stobi, 1, 97–143; I. Mikulčić 1973. Studies in the Antiquites of Stobi, 1, 61–95.
22. Demir Kapija (STENAI) – D. Vučković-Todorović 1961. Starinar, 12, 240–242; V. Sokolovska 1978. Macedoniae acta archaeologica, 4, 93.
23. Duklja (DOLCEA) – A. Cermanović-Kuzmanović, O. Žižić, D.Srejović 1975. The Roman Cemetery at Dolcea, Cetinje.
24. Komini (MUNICIPUM S...) – A. Cermanović-Kuzmanović 1981. Starinar, 31, 43–52.
25. Sase-Srebrenica (DOMAVIA) – D. Srejović, M. Baum 1975. Članci i građa za kulturnu istoriju istočne Bosne, 3, 23–54; 4 (1960), 3–31; 6 (1965), 7–49.

26. Rogatica – F. Fiala 1895. Glasnik Zemaljskog muzeja, 7, 199.
27. Stup – G. Čremošnik 1930. Glasnik Zemaljskog muzeja, 42, 211–225.

Figure 21.3

1. Ram (LEDERATA) – A. Jovanović 1996. Roman Limes of the Middle and Lower Danube, Belgrade, 72.
2. Boljetin (SMORNA) – Lj. Zotović 1967. Arheološki Pregled, 9, 70–71; id. 1968. Arheološki Pregled, 10, 84–85; id. Arheološki Pregled, 11, 114–119.
3. Ušće Slatinske reke – A. Jovanović, M. Korać 1986. Cahiers des Portes de Fer, 3, 378–380.

Figure 21.4

1. Paraćin – D. Garašanin 1964. Materijali Arheološkog društva Jugoslavije, 1, 78–89.
2. Kostolac (VIMINACIUM) – Lj. Zotović, Č. Jordović 1990. Viminacium – Nekropole 'Više Grobalja', Belgrade, 10.
3. Velesnica – A. Jovanović 1984. Forms of Burial in the Territory of Yugoslavia in the Time of the Roman Empire, Belgrade, 121.
4. Ušće Slatinske reke – A. Jovanović, M. Korać 1986. Cahiers des Portes de Fer, 3, 379.
5. Boljetin (SMORNA) – Lj. Zotović 1967. Arheološki pregled, 9, 69–71; id. 1969. Arheološki pregled, 11, 114–118.
6. Hajdučka Vodenica – A. Jovanović 1984. Starinar, 23–24, 321–322.

Figure 21.5

1. Gračanica (ULPIANA) – D. Srejović 1986. Starinar, 37, 179–189.
2. Ćićina – M. Vasić 1910. Godišnjak Srpske kraljevske Akademije, 24, 274–281.
3. Žitkovac – M. et D. Garašanin 1951. Sites archéologiques en Serbie, Belgrade, 167.
4. Orljani – A. Jovanović 1981. Starinar, 31, 11.
5. Knez Selo – M. et D. Garašanin 1951. Sites archéologiques en Serbie, Belgrade, 175.
6. Staničenje – M. et D. Garašanin 1951. Sites archéologiques en Serbie, Belgrade, 171.
7. Blato – M. et D. Garašanin 1951. Sites archéologiques en Serbie, Belgrade, 169.
8. Krupac – M. Vasić 1910. Godišnjak Srpske kraljevske Akademije, 24, 270.
9. Kalna – M. et D. Garašanin 1951. Sites archéologiques en Serbie, Belgrade, 205.
10. Negovanci – D. Džonova 1962. Arheologija, 1962/3, 33.
11. Vidin (BONONIA) – D. Džonova 1962. Arheologija, 1962/3, 31.
12. Butovo – L. Getov 1970. Arheologija, 1970/1, 10.
13. Lublen – D. Ovčarov 1979. Arheologija, 1979/3, 33.
14. Isakča (NOVIODUNUM) – E. Bužor 1960. Dacia n.s., 4, 533.
15. Histrija (HISTRIA) – P. Alexandrescu 1966. Histria, 2, 205
16. Konstanca (TOMIS) – V. Barbu. 1971. Studi si cercetari de istorie veche, 22, 49–56.
17. Mangalija (CALLATIS) – C. Preda 1965. Dacia n.s., 9, 233.
18. Ćustendil (PAUTALIA) – L. Ruseva-Slokoska 1965. Arheologija, 1965/4, 46.

19. Žilinci – I. Venedikov 1961. Izvestija na Arheologičeski institut, 24, 227.
20. Kadin most – J. Ivanov 1910. Izvestija na Blgarskoto arheologičesko družestvo, 1, 166.
21. Lileburgas – A. M. Mamsel 1941. Archaologischer Anzeiger, 1–2, 119.
22. Stralgža – D. Dimitrov 1933. Izvestia na Blgarskoto arheologičesko družestvo, 7, 386.
23. Meričleri – D. Aladžov 1965. Izvestija na Arheologičeski institut, 28, 77–122.
24. Ćatalka – D. Nikolov, H. Bujuklijev 1967. Arheologija 1967/1, 19; Arheologija 1967/3, 10.
25. Tulovo – G. Tabakova-Canova, 1961. Arhelogija 1961/3, 13.
26. Kirilometodijevo – T. Gerasimov 1946. Izvestia na Blgarskite arheologičeski institut, 15, 180.
27. Stara Zagora (AUGUSTA TRAIANA) – H. Bujuklijev 1973. Arheologija 1973/4, 39
28. Magliž – L. Getov 1969. Arheologija 1969/1, 42.
29. Brezovo – I. Velkov 1938. Izvestia na Blgarskite arheologičeski institut, 12, 269.
30. Belozem (PAREMBOLE) – A. Peev 1962. Godišnik na Narodna biblioteka, Plovdiv, 113.
31. Popovica – D. Gončev 1954. Godišnik na Muzejot ot Plovdiv, Plovdiv, 217.
32. Plovdiv (PHILIPOPOLIS) – D. Gončev 1960. Godišnik na Naroden arheologičeski muzej, 4, 21.
33. Džuljunica – A. Pisarev, P. Stanev 1987. Godišnik na muzejite ot Severnata Blgarija, 13, 15.
34. Nevrokopsko – I. Venedikov 1961. Izvestija na arheologičeski institut, 24, 227.
35. Stražica – A. Pisarev 1977. Godišnik na muzejite ot Severnata Blgarija, 3, 201–205.
36. Krušeto – A. Pisarev ibid.; A. Pisarev 1981. Godišnik na muzejite ot Severnata Blgarija, 6, 33–36.
37. Jambol (CABYLE) – L. Getov 1982. Kabile, 1, 40.
38. Smočin – L. Getov 1982. Kabile, 1, 57.
39. CAPIDAVA – N. Cheluta-Georgescu 1979. Materiale si cercetari arheologica, 13, 179–182.

Figure 21.6

1. Nozrina – D. Vučković-Todorović, J. Todorović 1959. Starinar, 9–10, 287.
2. Vardim – V. Velov 1965. Arheologija 1965/1, 30–34.
3. Belene – S. Stefanov 1933. Izvestia na Blgarski arheologičeski institut, 7, 396.
4. [tipsko – M. Mirčev 1968. Izvestija na Naroden muzej, 4 (19), 220.
5. Iskača (NOVIODUNUM) – E. Bužor 1960. Dacia n.s., 4, 525.
6. Konstanca (TOMIS) – V. Barbu 1971. Studii si cercetari de istoria veche, 11, 59.
7. Nikjup (NICOPOLIS AD ISTRUM) – L. Getov 1970. Arheologija 1970/1, 11.
8. Nadeždino – L. Getov 1970. Arheologija 1970/1, 11.
9. Somovit – T. Kovačeva 1977. Izvestija na muzeji ot Severozapadna Bulgarija, 1, 254.
10. Barboši – S. Sania 1981. Civilizatia romana la est de Carpati si romanitatea pe teritoriul Moldavei, Iaši, 81–84.
11. Hadžidimitrijevo – B. Sultov 1968. Izvestija na muzej V. Trnovo, 4, 220.

Figure 21.7

1. Zavoj – P. Pejić 1992. The Roman Cemeteries in the Surroundings of Pirot, Pirot, 50–79
2. Namanjci – S. Danev, M. Ivanovski 1986. Arheološki pregled, 26, 97–98.
3. Drašan – S. Mašov 1975. Arheologija 1975/1, 41–50.
4. Gela – V. Najdenova 1972. Thracia, 1, 145–152.
5. Rudnik – H. Džambov 1960. Arheologija 1960/1, 50–52.
6. Popovjane – D.Mitova-Džonova 1981. Kasnoantička keramika v Popovjane, Samokovsko, Samokov, 2–7.
7. Krdžali – C. Dremsizova-Neličnova 1988. Arheologija 1988/1, 36–43.

Figure 21.8

1. Sočanica (MUNICIPIUM DD) – S. Fidanovski 1988. Glasnik Muzeja Kosova, 15–16, 11–49.
2. Glavnik (VINDENIS) – S. Fidanovski 1985. Arheološki pregled, 24, 100–102.
3. Skopje (SCUPI) – I. Mikulčić 1974. Godišen Zbornik na Filozofski Fakultet, 26, 128–140.
4. Kamnik – G. Dimitrioska 1979. Macedoniae acta archaeologica, 5, 131.
5. Karadač – D. Srejović 1973. Balcanica, 4, 64–80.
6. Zaskok – S. Fidanovski 1995. The Age of the Tetrarchs, Belgrade, 102–110.
7. Veleknice – S. Fidanovski 1986. Arheološki pregled, 25, 47–48.
8. Mala Kopašnica – Lj. Zotović 1960. Arheološki pregled, 2, 123–125.
9. Jašunja – Lj. Zotović 1968. Leskovački zbornik, 8, 24.

Figure 21.9

1. Sremska Mitrovica (SIRMIUM) – P. Milošević 1996. Zbornik Muzeja Srema, 2, 39–46.
2. Belgrade (SINGIDUNUM) – M. Valtrović 1885. Starinar, 2, 33–45; J. Todorović, M. Birtašević 1955. Godišnjak Muzeja grada Beograda, 2, 32–33.
3. Kostolac (VIMINACIUM) – Lj.Zotović 1986. Viminacium, 1, 41–59.

Figure 21.10

1. Kostolac (VIMINACIUM) – Lj. Zotović, Č. Jordović 1990. Viminacium – Nekropole 'Više grobalja', Belgrade, 10–11; M. Pravilović 1981. Arheološki pregled, 21, 119.
2. Skopje (SCUPI) – D. Koračević 1977. Živa Antika, 27, 193–199; I. Mikulčić 1971. Živa Antika, 21, 476.
3. Niš (NAISSUS) – R.Ajdić 1972. Niški zbornik, 1, 38.
4. Taskovići-Kutina – R.Ajdić 1972. Niški zbornik, 1, 45.
5. Belgrade (SINGIDUNUM) – D. Garašanin 1948. Muzeji, 1, 122; id. 1954. Godišnjak Muzeja grada Beograda, 1, 67.
6. Glavnik (VINDENIS) – S.Fidanovski 1985. Arheološki pregled, 24, 100–103.
7. Žitora|a – M. et D. Garašanin 1951. Sites archéologiques en Serbie, Belgrade, 160.
8. Županjevac – M. et D. Garašanin 1951. Sites archéologiques en Serbie, Belgrade, 139.
9. Zorunovac – M. et D. Garašanin 1951. Sites archéologiques en Serbie, Belgrade, 175.
10. Karataš (DIANA) – I. Janković 1964. Arheološki pregled, 6, 55.

Bibliography

Ajdić, R. 1972. Antičke nekropole u Nišu. *Niški zbornik* 1: 33–45

Babes, M. 1970. Zu den Bestattungsarten im nördlichen Flachgräberfeld von Romula. *Dacia* n.s. 14: 167–206

Borović-Dimić, J. 1995. Grob sa spaljenim pokojnikom iz rimskog perioda sa Ladjarišta /Roman grave with incineration from Ladjarište/. *Glasnik Srpskog arheološkog društva* 10: 124–128.

Brukner, O. 1995. Domorodačka naselja /Native settlements/. *Archaeological investigations along the highway route in Srem*: 91–136

Buócz, T. P. 1961 Das frührömische Gräberfeld von Vasas. *Acta Archaeologica Academiae Scientarium Hungaricae* 9: 373–407.

Cermanović-Kuzmanović, A. 1965. Die dekorierten Sarkophage in der römischen Provinz von Jugoslawien. *Archaeologia Iugoslavica* 6: 89–103.

Daicoviciu, C. 1961. Les castella Dalmatarum de Dacie. *Apulum* 4: 51–58

Dautova-Ruševljan, V. 1983. *Rimska kamena plastika u jugoslovenskom delu provincije Donje Panonije /Römische Steindenkmäler aus dem jugoslawischen Gebiet der Provinz Pannonia Inferior*. Novi Sad: L'Association des Sociétés archéologiques de Yougoslavie.

Demo, Ž. 1982. Rezultati arheoloških iskopavanja ranocarske nekropole u Kunovec Bregu kraj Koprivnice / Ergebnisse der archäologischen Erforschung der frühkaiserzeitlichen Nekropole in Kunovec Breg bei Koprivnica. *Podravski zbornik* '82: 279–327.

Đurić, N., Glišić, J., Todorović, J. 1975. *Praistorijska Romaja / The prehistoric necropolis of Romaja*. Belgrade: L'Association des sociétés archéologiques de Yougoslavie.

Ercegović-Pavlović, S. 1980. Les nécropoles romaines et médiévales de Mačvanska Mitrovica. *Sirmijum* 12: 1–59.

Fidanovski, S. 1988. Nekropole Municipijuma DD u svetlu novih istraživanja /The necropolis of DD Municipality in the light of new discoveries/. *Glasnik Muzeja Kosova* 15–16: 11–49.

Fouet, G. 1958. Puit funéraires d'Aquitaine. *Gallia* 16.1: 115–186

Fülep, F. 1958. Das frühkaiserzeitliche Gräberfeld von Vasas. *Acta Archaeologica Academiae Scientarium Hungaricae* 9: 373–407.

Garašanin, D. 1964. Osvrt na problem kontinuiteta na dakogetskojnekropoli Glo'dar u Paraćinu / La probleme de la continuité géto-dace a la lumière des fouilles de la nécropole de Gložđar a Paraćin. *Materijali Arheološkog društva Jugoslavije* 1: 78–86.

Garašanin, M. 1963. Ein Beitrag zum Namen der Stadt Singidunum. *Recueil de Travaux de la Faculté de philosophie* 7–1: 45–53.

Garašanin, M. 1968. Razmatranja o nekropolama tipa Mala Kopašnica-Sase /Considérations sur les nécropoles du type Mala Kopašnica-Sase. *Godišnjak Centra za Balkanološka ispitivanja* 6: 5–34

Garašanin, M. and Garašanin, D. 1951. Arheološka nalazišta u Srbiji / Sites archéologiques en Serbie. Belgrade.

Getov, L. 1970. Pogrebalni običaji i grobni soroženije u Trakite prez rimskata epoha /Coûtumes et constructions funéraires chez les Thraces pendant l'époque romaine. *Arheologija* 12: 1–12.

Gregl, Z. 1981. La nécropole romaine a Zagreb-Stenjevac. *Inventaria Archeologica* 26: 1–14.

Horvath, J. 1972. Esztergom-Ovoda. *Archaeologiai Értesitö* 99: 257.

Jovanović, A. 1981. Tumuli iz antičkog perioda u jugoistočnoj Srbiji i na Kosovu / Tumuli de la période antique en Serbie du Sud-Est et au Kossovo. *Starinar* 31: 1–15.

Jovanović, A. 1984. *Rimske nekropole na teritoriji Jugoslavije / Form of Burial in the Territory of Yugoslavia in the time of the Roman Empire*. Belgrade: Centre for Archaeological Research.

Jovanović, A., and Cunjak, M. 1987. Novi nalazi kasnoantičkih grobova u Smederevu/ Récente mise au jour des tombes de la basse antiquité á Smederevo. *Saopštenje Republičkog zavoda za zaštitu spomenika kulture* 19: ¯39–146.

Jovanović, A. and Korać, M. 1986. L'embouchure de la rivière de la Slatinska reka. *Cahiers des Portes de Fer* 3: 378–401.

Knez, T. 1968. Oblike antičkih grobov na Dolenjskem / Antike Grabformen in Dolenjsko. *Arheološki Vestnik* 19: 221–238.

Marijanski-Manojlović, M. 1987. *Rimska nekropola kod Beške u Sremu / A Roman Necropolis at Beška in Srem*. Novi Sad: Museum of Voivodina.

Mikulčić, T. 1975. Ranirimski skeletni grobovi iz skupa / Tombes de haute époque romaine à inhumations de Scupi. *Starinar* 24–25: 89–102.

Mikulčić, T. 1979. Neilirski elementi medju skupskim nalazima na prelazu iz predrimskog u rimsko doba / Élements non-illyriens parmi les découvertes de Skoplje à la transition de la période préromaine à la période romaine. *Naučni skup Sahranjivanje kod Ilira*: 245–255.

Mikulčić, I. and Jovanović, M. 1968. Helenistički oppidum iz Krševica kod Vranja/ Oppidum hellénistique de Krševica près Vranje. *Vranjski glasnik* 4: 357–375.

Milošević, P. 1995. Rimska nekropola na izlaznici mitrovačke petlje / Roman cemetery at Mitrovica highway exit. *Archeological investigations along the highway route in Srem*: 195–218.

Milošević, P. 1996. Karakteristike nekropola i Sirmijumu / The Characteristics of the Necropolises from Sirmium. *Zbornik Muzeja Srema* 2: 39–48.

Mócsy, A. 1959. Untersuchungen zur Geschichte der römischen Provinz Moesia Superior. *Acta Archaeologica Academiae Scientarium Hungaricae* 11: 283–307

Mócsy, A. 1970. *Gesellschaft und Romanisation in der römischen Provinz Moesia Superior*. Budapest: Akadémiai Kiadó

Mrozek, S. 1968. Aspects sociaux et administratifs des mines d'or en Dacie. *Apulum* 7: 307–326.

Parović-Pešikan, M. 1982. Antička Ulpijana prema dosadašnjim istra'ivanjima / Ulpiana antique à la lumiere de l'état actuel des recherches. *Starinar* 32: 57–74.

Popović, I. and Borić-Brešković, B. 1994. *The Bela Reka Hoard*. Belgrade: National Museum

Protase, D. 1971. *Riturile funerare la Daci si Daco-Romani*. Bucharest: Academiei Republicii Romania

Schwarz, K. 1963. Zum Stand der Ausgrabungen in der spätkeltischen Viereckschanze von Holzhausen. *Bayerisches Landesamt für Denkmalpflege* 20/21: 136–191

Srejović, D. 1973. Karagač and the problem of the ethnogenesis of the Dardanians. *Balcanica* 4: 39–82.

Srejović, D. 1986 Grob ugledne Tračanke iz Ulpijane / La tombe d'une Thrace distinguée d'Ulpiana. *Starinar* 37: 179–190.

Srejović D. and Baum, M. 1959. Premiers résultats des recherches effectuées dans la nécropole romaine de Sase (*Domavia*). *Artikel und Materialien zur Kulturgeschichte Ostbosniens*, Tuzla 1959, 23–54.

Srejović, D. and Baum, M. 1960. Novi rezultati ispitivanja rimske nekropole i Sasama / Les nouveaux résultats des recherches de la nécropole romaine à Sase. *Čłanci i grada za kulturnu istoriju istočne Bosne* 4: 3–31.

Struck, M. 1993. *Busta* in Britannien und ihre Verbindungen zum Kontinent. Allgemeine Überlegungen zur Herleitung der Bestattungssitte. In Struck, M. ed, 1993. *Römerzeitliche Gräber als Quellen zu Religion, Bevölkerungsstruktur und Sozialgeschichte*, Mainz: Johannes Gutenberg-Universität Institut für Vor- und Frühgeschichte, 81–94

Szántó, I. 1953. Ein Urnenfriedhof in Cserszegtomaj aus der Früheneisenzeit und aus den Anfängen der Kaiserzeit. *Archaeologiai Értesitö* 80: 53–62

Todorović, J. 1974. *The Skordisci-History and Culture*. Belgrade: L'Association des archéologues de Yougoslavie.

Tomović, M. 1991. Prokoneski sarkofag sa girlandama iz Viminacijuma / Proconesian sarcophagus with wreaths from Viminacium. *Viminacium* 6: 69–82.

Tudor, D. and Vladescu, C. 1972. Dardanii la Romula-alva. *Apulum* 10: 183–190

Zotović, Lj. 1969. Boljetin- rimska nekropola spaljenih pokojnika. *Arheološki pregled* 11: 114–119.

Zotović, Lj. 1984. Prilog problemu etničke pripadnosti grobova tipa Mala Kopašnica-Sase / Contribution à l'interprétation ethnique des sépultures de type Mala Kopašnica-Sase. *Simpozijum Duhovna kultura Ilira*: 165–170.

Zotović, Lj. and Jordović, Č. 1990. *Viminacijum – Nekropole Više grobalja*. Belgrade: Archaeological Institute.

Society, religion and burial in late Roman Britain and Italy

These studies of Later Roman burial focus on two contrasting areas. Excavated evidence from Britain provides relatively fine-grained data. Aspects of these are explored by Quensel-von-Kalben and Davison. Quensel-von-Kalben provides a broad ranging comparative analysis using statistical methods, assessing the influence of date, age, gender, status/wealth, region, settlement type and religion. This brings out very clearly how significant variations in apparently homogenous data can be identified through systematic study. Davison explores in greater detail one of the 'notorious' features of the cemetery record of late Romano-British towns, the bias to males in the skeletal evidence. He reviews the methodology and interpretations, compares the urban samples to those from other types of settlement and attempts to relate patterning to more general social processes. The skeletal evidence discussed by Niblett from Verulamium suggests that larger samples of data from the late Iron Age and early Roman period will demand further nuances in these general models.

In contrast the burial record for the City of Rome is well known through the long-established exploration of its catacombs and basilicas but these provide relatively coarse grained data. These are being improved upon by new exploration and the detailed study of existing material. Del Moro presents a summary of welcome new data from the excavation of a sub-urban funerary basilica, discussing burial rites and the relative importance of grave goods and burial location as a means of differentiating individuals of different status. The three papers by Martorelli, Nuzzo and de Santis explore different aspects of the material from the catacombs, shedding new light on funerary traditions – the burial of the dead and the marking of the grave – and paying particular attention to the relationship of the archaeological material to the literary evidence. Together all four of these papers provide an impressive body of evidence to undermine the suite of features, in particular the absence of grave goods or of certain types of grave good, often deployed to identify Christian burial practices in the western provinces. In this context Martin-Kilcher's paper also shows that certain forms of burial practice, in this case the treatment of young women of high social status, transcends the pagan/Christian division. Finally, Meneghini and Santangeli Valenzani present the results of a chronological and locational study of burial within the walls of Rome in the fifth to seventh centuries. Their work demonstrates that far from being random, these graves show clear spatial and chronological trends which illuminate the social and institutional formation of the post-classical city.

22. Putting Late Roman burial practice in Britain in context

Lucas Quensel-von-Kalben

An Anglo-Saxon observing a late Romano-British burial would be very astonished by what he (or she) saw, the body of the deceased person being wrapped in a shroud, no worn dress items, no food and – in the case of a male person – no weapons are deposited as grave goods into the grave. Or the dead person gets a more 'decent' good-bye with pottery, coins and hob-nailed boots. Sometimes even jewellery is included, mainly bracelets which are deposited beside the dead. This kind of disposal of the dead is not self-evident and contrasts with burial customs in barbarian Europe and the later Germanic kingdoms in the Roman West as well as the earlier rites in Roman Britain.

This sketch of 'typical' Late Roman burials seems to indicate a fairly uniform mortuary behaviour. However this is oversimplified. Burial rituals of Late Roman Britain are not easy structured, and are probably determined by conflicting social roles as well as chronological fashions etc. To name only the most obvious, gender, age, religious beliefs, social status, wealth, ethnic identity, spheres of communication, i.e. regional fashions, urban or rural origin, occupational position and so on may all interfere in the mortuary ritual, and have been shown to do so in other contexts.

Traditional attempts to deal with this complex situation have compared the furnishing and the treatment of the individual graves or entire cemeteries in a rather intuitive way. Usually one group of artifact, e.g. pottery, coins or metalwork, or particular burial custom (decapitation, burial in chambers) of a cemetery is described in detail and then compared to the same group of artifacts or customs in other cemeteries. This procedure destroys exactly what processual and post-processual archaeologists tend to emphasise: contextual information. I suspect that this kind of analysis is a product of the specialist report, which tends to ignore everything beside its own field of study. In some cases skeletal data are published only in an already summarised manner and cannot be compared individually with grave furniture or the treatment of dead (e.g. Wenham 1968).

Another technique used for detecting regional and ethnic groupings is the distribution map (e.g. Philpott 1991). Not a burial pattern but one minute aspect of it is observed through space, usually ignoring questions of representativity and size: one spoon with a chi-rho monogram as evidence for the Christianity of a whole region.

I hope I will not be misunderstood. There are many valuable investigations of Late Roman burial practices, but a systematic exploration of the different social, economic and ideological factors is still missing, probably because of the lack of a workable methodology for dealing with such a complex subject matter.

Sample

For the kind of analysis I would like to do, the quality of the data has to be rather high. Only cemeteries with a complete record of grave goods, grave dimensions, burial layout and skeletal data can be included. Very few

Fig. 22.1 *Map of the Late Roman cemeteries in the sample*

Table 22.1a *Table of Late Roman cemeteries. Key data*

	Bradley Hill Somerset	Cirencester Bath Gate	Colchester Butt Rd. Period 1	Colchester Butt Rd. Period 2	Icklingham Suffolk
Graves:	56	471	60	669	45
Internal diff.:	Yes	Possible	No	No	No
Complete:	No	No	No	No	Possible
Dating:	IV	lt. III/IV	III/ea. IV	IV	lt. IV
Setting:	Villa	Urban	Urban	Urban	Vicus (?)
Disturbed gr.	20	76	0	0	0
Cremations:	0 (0)	2 (1)	1 (2)	1 (1)	0 (0)
Multiple bur.:	5 (9)	29 (6)	2 (3)	45 (7)	0 (0)
SIZE					
Grave length:	184	–	188	207	–
Grave width:	63	–	83	89	–
Grave depth:	24	86	–	–	–
ORIENTATION					
North:	3 (5)	108 (23)	0 (0)	0 (0)	0 (0)
East:	1 (2)	29 (6)	0 (0)	3 (1)	0 (0)
South:	0 (0)	190 (40)	21 (35)	0 (0)	0 (0)
West:	46 (82)	70 (15)	1 (2)	602 (90)	45 (100)
GRAVE					
Coffin:	1 (2)	129 (27)	37 (62)	532 (80)	18 (40)
Chamber:	0 (0)	1 (1)	5 (8)	66 (10)	0 (0)
Sarc./lead:	0 (0)	6 (1)	0 (0)	2 (1)	0 (0)
Stone packing:	44 (79)	28 (6)	0 (0)	5 (1)	1 (2)
Mausolea/encl.:	1 (2)	0 (0)	1 (2)	11 (2)	0 (0)
TREATMENT					
Supine:	42 (750)	337 (72)	31 52	429 (64)	45 (100)
Prone:	1 (2)	34 (7)	0 (0)	2 (1)	0 (0)
Crouched:	0 (0)	10 (2)	4 7	2 (1)	0 (0)
Decapitation:	0 (0)	6 (1)	0 (0)	0 (0)	0 (0)
Plaster:	0 (0)	0 (0)	1 2	7 (1)	0 (0)
GRAVEGOODS					
Min. of GG:	0	0	0	0	0
Max. of GG:	2	4	4	22	9
Average of GG:	0.14	0.29	0.8	0.29	0.24
Dress items:	0 (0)	17 (4)	6 (10)	26 (4)	2 4
Equipment:	0 (0)	6 (1)	1 (2)	9 (1)	0 (0)
Hobnails:	2 (4)	5 (1)	11 (18)	7 (1)	0 (0)
Coins:	3 (5)	60 (13)	0 (0)	6 (1)	1 (2)
Vessels:	1 (2)	5 (1)	20 (33)	15 (2)	0 (0)
SKELETAL DATA					
Female:	10	101	6	138	10
Male:	11	250	9	166	12
Children:	33	60	8	104	17
Male/Female:	1.1	2.48	1.5	1.20	1.2
Child./Adult:	1,41	0.15	0.15	0.18	0.67
Average age:	32. 6	34.82	35	34.21	44.18
Further observ.:	Infant burials in houses			Possible church	Possible church

Numbers in brackets represent the percentage of graves with this attribute.

Disturbed graves – as mentioned in the excavation report or easily recognisable.
Size – averages of adult single graves in cm
Average age – excludes the probably older infant burials in the houses at Bradley Hill. These included the average age at death is 18.34 y.

excavated cemeteries meet these requirements. A sample taking regions all over Britain and the different kinds of settlements (towns, small towns, villages, villas, non-villa rural settlements, temple sites) into account is difficult to obtain.

The cemeteries I am dealing with are dominated by inhumation. While a number of cremation cemeteries very probably of fourth century date exist, I will not explore these any further. Figure 22.1 shows the distribution of the cemeteries in southern and eastern Britain. Northern Britain and the Midlands are not represented. There are only few cemeteries excavated in this area and they often do not correspond to the above criteria. Trentholme Drive, for example, lacks the detailed anthropological data.

Table 22.1 summarises some of the data for these eight cemeteries. Nearly half the sample of burials is represented by Poundbury/Dorchester, while another quarter stems from the Colchester Butt Road cemetery. The four cemeteries with a more 'rural' background altogether have only about 200 graves. Beside the regional and urban

Table 22.1b *Table of Late Roman cemeteries. Key data*

	Ilchester	Lynch Farm	Poundbury (main)	Poundbury (periph.)	Lankhills
GRAVES	60	51	1117	273	459
Internal diff.:	Yes	probably not	No	Yes	possible
Complete:	No	probable	No	No	No
Dating:	lt. IV	III/IV	lt. III/IV	lt. III/IV	IV
Setting:	Small town	Rural	Urb. /rural	Urb./rural	Urban
Disturbed g. :	6	0	152	57	72
Cremations:	0 (0)	1 (2)	0 (0)	3 (1)	9 (2)
Multiple bur.:	9 (15)	15 (29)	28 (3)	19 (7)	13 3)
SIZE					
Grave length:	–	–	209	213	333
Grave width:	–	–	69	79	91
Grave depth:	–	–	87	94	85
ORIENTATION					
North:	53 (88)	6 (12)	1 (1)	23 (8)	9 (2)
East:	1 (17)	0 (0)	6 (1)	17 (6)	17 (4)
South:	0 (0)	5 (10)	3 (1)	45 (17)	6 (1)
West:	0 (0)	32 (63)	958 (86)	117 (43)	382 (83)
GRAVE					
Coffin:	33 (55)	15 (29)	889 (80)	176 (64)	360 (78)
Chamber:	0 (0)	0 (0)	0 (0)	0 (0)	0 (0)
Sarc. /lead:	0 (0)	0 (0)	34 (3)	3 (11)	0 (0)
Stone packing:	0 (0)	2 (4)	93 (8)	19 (7)	41 (9)
Mausolea/encl.:	0 (0)	0 (0)	23 (2)	3 (1)	9 (2)
TREATMENT					
Supine:	44 (73)	21 (41)	905 (81)	147 (54)	289 (63)
Prone:	4 (7)	1 (2)	1 (1)	6 (2)	14 (3)
Crouched:	6 (10)	1 (2)	3 (1)	17 (6)	25 (5)
Decapitation:	4 (7)	0 (0)	0 (0)	0 (0)	7 (2)
Plaster:	0 (0)	0 (0)	29 (3)	0 (0)	0 (0)
GRAVEGOODS					
Min. of GG:	0	0	0	0	0
Max. of GG:	4	3	10	4	31
Average of GG:	0.73	0.1	0.08	0.45	1.51
Dress items:	3 (5)	2 (4)	20 (2)	19 (7)	60 (13)
Equipment:	3 (5)	1 (2)	11 (1)	7 (3)	42 (9)
Hobnails:	20 (33)	0 (0)	1 (0)	46 (17)	150 (33)
Coins:	3 (5)	0 (0)	25 (2)	15 (5)	47 (10)
Vessels:	6 (10)	1 (2)	0 (0)	9 (3)	96 (21)
SKELETAL DATA					
Female:	19	15	382	55	74
Male:	30	21	321	59	111
Children:	9	5	268	97	132
Male/Female:	1.58	1.4	0.84	1.07	1.5
Child/Adult:	0.18	0.11	0.32	0.56	0.4
Average age:	33.27	29.64	30.7	22.72	24.18
Further observ.:	Graves at rear of houses				

Numbers in brackets represent the percentage of graves with this attribute.

Disturbed graves – as mentioned in the excavation report or easily recognisable.
Size – averages of adult single graves in cm

bias of the sample, very few cemeteries correspond to a demographically normal pattern for a pre-industrial population. Neither the proportion of men to women, nor the ratio of adult to sub-adults can be seen as a natural distribution. Women and infants are usually under-represented.

None of these cemeteries – all well known and often referred to in archaeological textbooks on Roman Britain – is completely excavated. And the problem even persists when looked at from an opposite perspective. Analysis of burial practice has shown that the excavated portions of cemeteries can be split up into different areas which are probably independent of each other. It is not always

possible to subdivide these as neatly as at Poundbury. In my sample I subdivided two cemeteries (Colchester Butt Rd. and Poundbury/Dorset) into two groups. In Colchester stratigraphic evidence supports this procedure. The cemetery at Poundbury has been claimed, on the basis of differences in grave treatment and furniture as well as ditches and other features, to consist of at least five different – mostly contemporary – cemeteries; my analysis however differentiates just two groups, the main cemetery and the peripheral ones. A third instance of internal subdivision may have been at Winchester Lankhills where again burials east of a large boundary ditch (feature 12 of the site report) differ from those in the west. This has

been argued by Clarke as a later chronological development within the cemetery.

But this is not another – German – cautionary tale, so
I will proceed.

Chronology

Late Roman burials are notoriously difficult to date. A
relative chronology can be established by stratigraphic
reasoning. Absolute dates are only available for very few
graves. This is easily explained by the low number of
grave goods in all the cemeteries. Glass, pottery, metalwork – usually dress items like brooches, rings etc. – and
sometimes coins give an approximate *terminus post quem*.
Horizontal stratigraphy, the successive spread of burials
starting from one point, has been claimed for Winchester
and other cemeteries, but cannot be substantiated. In some
cases the cemetery started well before 300 AD while most
begin in the first half of the fourth century. All excavators
have been very cautious in dating the end of their
cemeteries, so I will consider them as having been
abandoned at the end of the fourth or the beginning of the
fifth century.

Age

While there is an imbalance in the ratio between children
and adults, all cemeteries have at least some children (if
sometimes only of infans II (i.e. 8 to 14 years) or
adolescent age). At Lynch Farm the excavator suggests
that most infant burials have already been destroyed by
ploughing. A check of the depth of infant burials does
indeed show these to be shallower than their adult
counterparts. Are there any differences in the treatment

of children in comparison to older people? Several means
for the social differentiation of age do exist. Some are
fairly obvious: children can have more (or less) grave
goods than adults or they might get other types of grave
goods (amulets for example). Other means are more
subtle: the treatment of the corpse and the general layout
(orientation, grave furniture, size etc.) of the grave can
differ. And finally – at least in my analysis – the location
of child graves in respect to other graves and prominent
features of the landscape can be used by the burying
community to express a different status.

Most cemeteries but not all show some signs of
different treatment. In Ilchester/Somerset children tend
to have fewer grave goods than adults (Figs 22.2a and b).
The Colchester Butt Road cemetery in period 2 sees the
opposite pattern: children are furnished with a larger
amount of grave goods than average (Figs 22.3a and b).
In both cases most adults and most children are treated
the same way: usually they are not furnished with grave
goods at all, a point that holds true for nearly all of the
cemeteries in my sample and probably for most other
Late Roman burials in Britain as well.

On some cemeteries the distribution of specific
functional types is restricted to some age groups only. In
Colchester period 2 cemetery only children around the
age of 12 to 14 (with some minor exceptions) receive
bracelets. This has been explained as a form of dowry for
unmarried women. Be this as it may, this distribution can
be seen elsewhere too. In at least one instance bracelets
are not found with children but with adult women. The
same object seems to have different meanings in different
communities. Another example with an age distribution
of specific grave goods is Winchester-Lankhills where
beads are associated with infants and younger adults only,

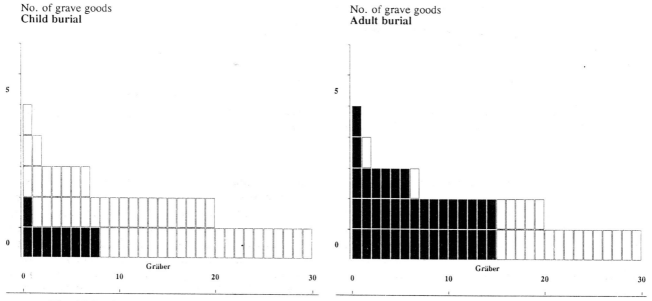

Fig. 22.2a–b *Ilchester/Somerset. Histograms of the number of grave goods in children and adult graves.*

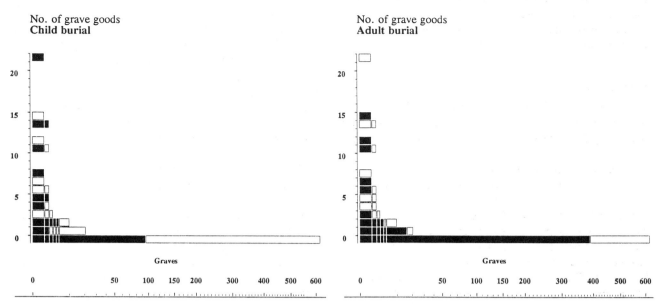

Fig. 22.3a–b *Colchester-Butt Road cemetery in period 2. Histograms of the number of grave goods in children and adult graves.*

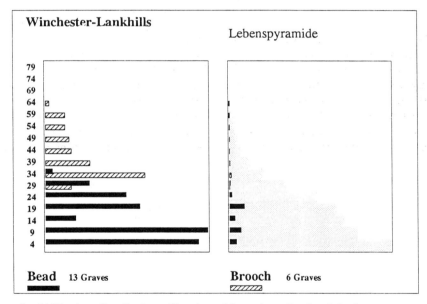

Fig. 22.4 *Winchester-Lankhills. Age distribution of beads and brooches. On the right the percentage of these grave goods plotted on a reconstructed age distribution of the living population.*

while brooches are found with adults aged 30 to 40 years and older (Fig. 22.4).

Different treatment of children to adults according to grave orientation or the position of body is not a common occurrence. Only slight indications exist that children are associated with plaster burials and are often part of a multiple burial (the other part not necessarily being the mother!).

A fourth dimension to explore is the location of child-

burials. In Bradley Hill/Somerset and Poundbury peripheral cemeteries (exactly the burials on site C) children cluster in compact groups. This is, I suspect, another explanation for the low number of infant burials on Late Romano-British cemeteries: They might have been clustered in unexcavated parts of a cemetery. However clustering is by no way typical of all the cemeteries I examined. Poundbury main cemetery, Colchester Butt Road cemetery in both periods and most of the smaller cemeteries include infant burials in a pattern that resembles family or kinship groups as one organising principle. I would argue that even Winchester which has been claimed to show an uneven distribution of age and gender groups shows a random pattern.

Sex and Gender

What applies to age is true for the sex distribution of the buried population as well, bearing in mind, that there is always the possibility of an anthropological misdetermination. Only two cemeteries (Bradley Hill and Poundbury periphery) are balanced in this respect, while only one (Poundbury main cemetery) is dominated by burials of women (Table 22.1).

Let us look at the different dimensions used for detecting differences in the treatment of age groups in respect to sex and gender.

The number of grave goods, which are generally notoriously low, is a seldom used attribute for the differentiation of men and women. In Winchester-Lankhills (Figs 22.5a and b), although a comparatively rich cemetery, where differences should be easy to detect, women and men have approximately the same number of grave goods. Only three cemeteries seem to have statistically significant differences in the average number of grave goods associated with sex. In Cirencester and the peripheral cemeteries of Poundbury women have fewer grave goods than men, while in Colchester Period 2 the opposite is true.

Table 22.2a-b *Table of inferred social differentiations in the Late Roman cemeteries.*

	Bradley Hill	Cirencester Bath Gate	Colchester Butt Rd Period 2	Colchester Butt Rd Period 2	Icklingham
Graves:	56	471	60	669	45
AGE					
AD in no. of GG	-2	0	-1	+2	9
AD in types of GG	0	0	1	1	9
AD in TM	0	0	0	1	0
AD in LOC	2	1	0	0	0
Age diff.	Yes	slight	slight	Yes	prob. no
GENDER					
GD in no. of GG	0	-1	+	0	9
GD in types of GG	0	0	1	0	9
GD in TM	0	0	0	0	0
GD in LOC	0	0	0	0	0
Gender diff.	No	No	slight	No	prob. no
STATUS					
SD in no. of GG	0	0	0	2	1
SD in types of GG	0	0	1	1	0
SD in TM	I	1	0	2	0
SD in LOC	0	0	0	1	0
Status diff.	slight	slight	slight	Yes	No
RELIGION					
No. of type I g.:	8	326	51	27	1
No of type 2 g.:	35	46	0	415	44
Christian / pagan:	C	P	P	C	C

	Ilchester	Lynch Farm	Poundbury Main Cemetery	Poundbury Peripheral cemetery	Lankhills
Graves:	60	51	1117	273	459
AGE					
AD in no. of GG	-2	0	0	-1	+1
AD in types of GG	1	0	0	0	2
AD in TM	1	0	0	1	0
AD in LOC	0	0	0	2	0
Age diff.	Yes	No	No	Yes	No
GENDER					
GD in no. of GG	0	0	0	-1	0
GD in types of GG	0	0	0	1	1
GD in TM	0	0	0	1	0
GD in LOC	0	0	0	0	0
Gender diff.	No	No	No	Yes	slight
STATUS					
SD in no. of GG	0	0	1	0	0
SD in types of GG	0	0	0	0	2
SD in TM	1	1	2	1	2
SD in LOC	0	0	1	0	1
Status diff.	No	No	Yes	No	Yes
RELIGION					
No. of type 1 g.:	42	13	32	112	257
No. of type 2 g.:	8	17	870	65	110
Christian / pagan:	P	P	C	P	P

Abbreviations: AD = Age differentiation; GG = Grave goods; TM = Grave treatment; LOC = Location;
GD = Gender differentiation; SD = Status differentiation

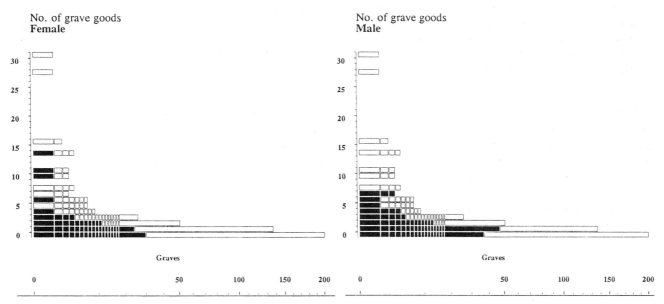

Fig. 22.5a–b *Winchester-Lankhills. Histograms of the number of grave goods in relation to sex.*

The use of different types of grave good for gender differentiation is more pronounced. In Winchester bracelets are only associated with but not worn by women (remember the dowry-argument for Colchester!) while buckles, belt-fittings and brooches are worn only by men. The development in Colchester is rather intriguing in this respect. While a different treatment can be observed in the period 1 cemetery (jewellery with women, hobnails with men) this does not hold true for the period 2 cemetery. The exclusive connection of hobnails with men in eastern England is very different from the southwest. Hobnails in Poundbury and Ilchester are equally distributed between both sexes.

Neither the treatment of the corpse, the layout of the grave nor its orientation can be shown to differ between the burials of women and men. The only exception might have been the peripheral cemeteries of Poundbury, where women are excluded from the mausolea. But this might be purely the product of chance.

There are also no differences in the location for the burial of men and women. Even where focal points are available, like possible churches (Icklingham, Colchester period 2), mausolea (Poundbury main and peripheral cemeteries), the distance to a road or the visibility from a habitation site (Ilchester), the sexes have not been treated differently (although see Davison this volume for a different view).

Status and Wealth

Status – as Manuela Struck has already shown – can be expressed in many ways. In the sample the number of grave goods does not seem to be important. We might deduce from some types of grave goods and the use of specific material that one person has a prominent place in his or her community. So styli (Colchester period 1) as a possible indicator of literacy and therefore special if not high status, silk garments (Colchester period 2) and crossbow brooches (Winchester-Lankhills) might indicate such status in society. Very few precious metals and other material have been deposited in my sample.

Mausolea and burial enclosures (Poundbury both cemeteries, Winchester), chambers (Colchester), stone lining, stone coffins (sarcophagi) and lead caskets in an environment that shows on average little investment in burial furniture are indicators for some kind of status differentiation in their local communities while not really comparable on a regional or even provincial level.

Sometimes these different strands of evidence coincide, but this need not always be the case. In the main cemetery of Poundbury (Figs 22.6a and b) the mausolea and enclosures are often associated with stone sarcophagi, but differ markedly from those graves with a high number of grave goods.

In Winchester another peculiar custom can be detected that might be of relevance to the question of social differentiation: a decapitated burial lay next to a richly furnished grave and has been interpreted as a possible sacrificial offering to an 'intrusive' burial (no. 443), possibly that of a Saxon mercenary – a strange kind of 'grave good' anyway (Clarke 1979:374) (see Esmonde Cleary this volume for further discussion).

To return to location, richly furnished graves tend at times to cluster in groups, which might again represent the above mentioned family groups.

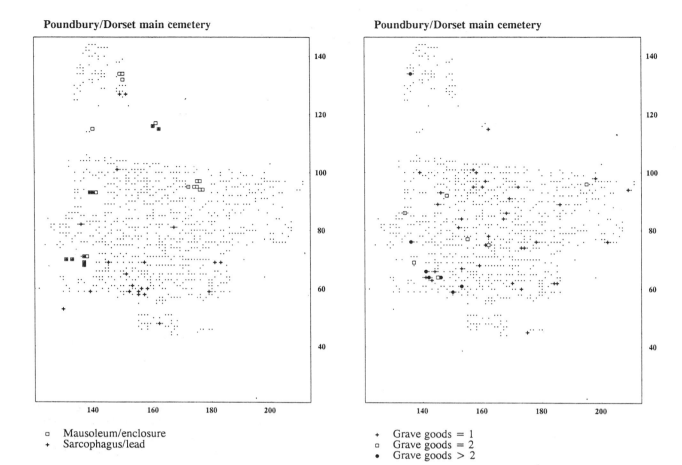

Poundbury/Dorset main cemetery   **Poundbury/Dorset main cemetery**

    □   Mausoleum/enclosure   +   Grave goods = 1
    +   Sarcophagus/lead   □   Grave goods = 2
                                             ●   Grave goods > 2

Fig. 22.6a–b *Poundbury/Dorset main cemetery. Distribution of mausolea, enclosures, stone sarcophagi and different numbers of grave goods.*

Cemeteries as a sphere of social interaction

These patterns are mentioned as examples of the work I have done, not a comprehensive overview of the subject. Based on a systematic survey along these lines I have summarised the results in another table (Table 22.2). The scoring is not entirely objective, but I could present at least some evidence for it.

Each of the three social dimensions (age, gender and social status (or wealth)) has been examined in relation to the number of grave goods, the attribution of artefact types, differences in treatment and the distribution in the cemetery. The last row in each category gives an overall impression of the existence or non-existence of differentiation.

Two codings have been used. The first applies only to the number of grave goods in relation to age and gender. Here a scale from '-2' to '+2' is used to express negative or positive discrimination against or towards depositing grave goods with women and children. A '-2' in the 'GD in no. of GG' (gender difference in number of grave goods) is for example saying, that there is a strong negative discrimination against women in the number of grave goods, while a '+2' means that women have significantly more grave goods than men. In all other

instances a simple scale from 0 (no differences) to 2 (strong differences) has been applied. A '9' simply means 'No data available'. The values are very sensitive to the low number of grave goods at Late Roman cemeteries. The same scale, applied to Anglo-Saxon cemeteries, would probably lead to very distinct results.

Only two cemeteries are similar in respect to the different treatment of social roles: Icklingham and Lynch Farm. Both do not treat any group different to another. The result of great heterogeneity is at odds with the once accepted view of a culturally homogenous population in Late Roman Britain and needs further exploration.

A systematic comparison of the cemeteries

A detailed comparison of more than two cemeteries at the same time has seldom been achieved. One main reason for this is the lack of an appropriate methodology which can deal with many variables at the same time. Two statistical multi-factorial approaches are well established in archaeology, mainly for the purpose of dating: cluster analysis and combination tables. Both try to order the data according to their similarity with each other. In the

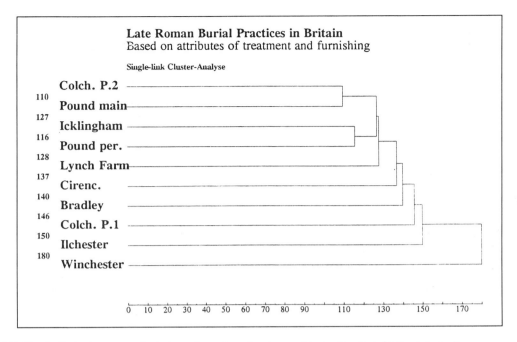

Fig. 22.7 *Single link cluster analysis based on directly observable traits of eight (ten) Late-Roman cemeteries.*

first step a cluster analysis is applied to different sets of criteria. The outcome of this analysis is then compared to chronological, regional (in terms of the *civitates* and the geographical setting of the cemetery), 'functional' (urban versus rural) and probable religious differentiations in Late Roman Britain. This last aspect of a possible structuring principle is explored by a different statistical technique, namely a combination table of supposed Christian and pagan attributes. The intention of this whole procedure is to detect patterns of social ordering in the cemeteries and give a glimpse of Late Roman Britain as a living society.

The first cluster analysis of the cemeteries (Fig. 22.7) is based on the criteria collected in Table 22.1. These can roughly be termed the 'pure evidence': orientation, number of grave goods, types of grave goods and so on. Not the absolute number of occurrences but their relative proportion has been used. The criteria have been weighted differently. Each apparently independent attribute (e.g. decapitations) got a weighting of 1, while dependent attributes have a combined weighting. Each of the four main orientations of the grave for example got a weighting of 0.25.

A further statistical 'trick' is the normalisation of the states of each attribute. The maximum number has been converted to 1, while all other are transformed to their ratio value. Hobnails for example (Table 22.1) are included in 33% of all graves in Winchester-Lankhills and Ilchester. This is converted to '1' (= maximum number). The 17% of graves with hobnails in the peripheral cemeteries at Poundbury are now expressed as '0.52' (ca. half the percentage of the graves with hobnails in Winchester and Ilchester). This procedure tries to eliminate differences in scale between attributes.

A matrix is set up, which shows the differences between any two cemeteries. From this matrix a dendrogram can be plotted: the two cemeteries with the lowest dissimilarity coefficient (= most similar) are united at the distance given by that number. In the case of a single link cluster analysis the next cemetery (or group of cemeteries) is included at the lowest distance to only one (the single link) of the cemeteries of another group. This is an apparent weakness of the technique. A cemetery which is fairly dissimilar to most other cemeteries in one group can be united at short distance because only one cemetery in the group has a close relationship to it.

At this point some results of the first cluster analysis shall be mentioned: Colchester period 2 and Poundbury main cemetery are most similar, while Winchester-Lankhills is most different to the others. This pattern still holds if an average link cluster analysis is used, but the special place of Winchester and Ilchester in this case is even more emphasised.

In a second cluster analysis (Fig. 22.8) the differentiations (in the number and types of grave goods, the treatment and the location of the deceased person) in age, gender and social status have been used as attributes. The overall impressions of each differentiation as given on Table 22.2 have been excluded. The resulting order is different to the first dendrogram. Cirencester and Lynch Farm are rather close to each other, while the peripheral cemeteries at Poundbury are very different to all others. The result for Icklingham cannot be taken at face value, because a '9' for an unknowable differentiation in the number and types of grave goods of gender and age distorts the picture (otherwise the closest link would be between Icklingham and Lynch Farm as mentioned above).

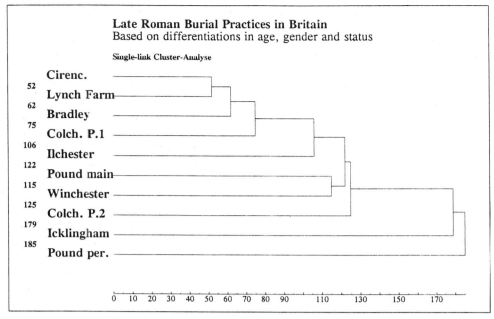

Fig. 22.8 *Single link cluster analysis based on inferred social differentiations of eight (ten) Late Roman cemeteries.*

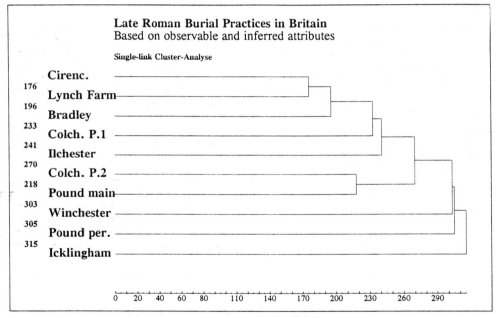

Fig. 22.9 *Single link cluster analysis based on directly observable and inferred traits of eight (ten) Late Roman cemeteries.*

The third cluster analysis (Fig. 22.9) includes directly observable and inferred attributes of the two other analyses. Both groups of attributes have been equally weighted. The resulting order is rather interesting: a group consisting of Cirencester, Lynch Farm and Bradley Hill (and probably Icklingham) is rather close to each other. A second group consists of Colchester period 2 and Poundbury main cemetery. Winchester and Poundbury peripheral cemeteries are furthest away from the main groups.

Are there any main factors involved which are respons-

ible for this order? Let us look for possible answers to this question.

Religion: Pagans and Christians in the Fourth Century

Dorothy Watts and Ann Woodward have tried to identify Christian burial customs in Late Roman Britain. Their starting point was a list of criteria which they believed to be either Christian or pagan. Some independent confirmation has been collected by Watts, direct or indirect statements from the Bible and the Church fathers, as well as pagan contemporaries concerning the correct performance of the burial ritual. Their examination of up to 29 (in Watts' sample) cemeteries across Britain established a list of likely Christian cemeteries. One problem of their lists is the gradual decrease of scores. It is very difficult to say where the Christian graveyards start and which have to be considered pagan. The reasons for this is threefold: first, both worked with purely presence/absence scales; second, an intermixing of Christian and pagan burials often seems to occur; and third, the criteria might not represent a Christian/pagan dichotomy as supposed.

In a slightly different approach I tried to check Watts' and Woodward's criteria and at the same time circumvent the other two problems of intermixing and scale. Therefore a combination table with the suggested criteria has been created, taking each grave into account. Table 22.3

shows the unordered matrix of entries. The diagonal represents the total amount of graves having this attribute.

But how strong are these associations? An attribute which is fairly common, such as west-east orientation of the body should be associated with most other attributes just by chance. One way of dealing with this problem is taking percentages, another and probably even more telling is using Yule-values, a measure that takes the numbers of both attributes, their common occurrences and the number of single occurrences for each attribute into account. Using Yule-values instead of absolute numbers decreases the influence of very large cemeteries in the sample. A Yule value usually falls between -100 and +100 (from complete dissociation to complete association). An '0' means that the occurrence of one attribute says nothing about the occurrence of the other. Table 22.4, a second combination table gives the Yule-values for the eight cemeteries and has at the same time shuffled the criteria in order to place the associated criteria close to each other.

Table 22.3 *Unordered combination table of supposed Christian and pagan mortuary rites and grave goods (absolute numbers of common occurrences)*

	1	2	3	4	5	6	7	8	9	10	11	12	13	14	15	16
1 W-E Orientation	1883		1828	55	334	8	31	94	31	79	20	165	72	30	159	352
2 N-S Orientation		136	107	29	37	3	1	11		20	6	36	9	4	6	61
3 Supine	1828	107	1936		354	10	32	88	30	91	23	184	76	32	156	381
4 Prone / crouched	55	29		84	17	1		17	1	8	3	17	5	2	9	32
5 Overlapping	334	37	354	17	371		5	32	5	3	6	27	17	5	41	62
6 Decapitation	8	3	10	1		11				1	1	4	1	1		7
7 Plaster	31	1	32		5		32		4	2					18	2
8 Neonatal / Infant	94	11	88	17	32			105		2		1	1		26	4
9 Maus. / Encl.	31		30	1	5		4		31	5	1	9	1		8	15
10 Vessels	79	20	91	8	3	1	2	2	5	99	6	35	9	2	2	98
11 Animal bones	20	6	23	3	6	1			1	6	26	12	1	1	1	26
12 Hobnails	165	36	184	17	27	4		1	9	35	12	201	19	9	17	199
13 Coins	72	9	76	5	17	1		1	1	9	1	19	81	34	10	81
14 Charon's fee	30	4	32	2	5	1				2	1	9	34	34	4	34
15 Grave protected	159	6	156	9	41		18	26	8	2	1	17	10	4	165	34
16 Gravegoods	352	61	381	32	6 2	7	2	4	15	98	26	199	81	34	34	413

Table 22.4 *Ordered combination table of supposed Christian and pagan mortuary rites and grave goods (Yule-values of the absolute numbers in Table 22.3).*

	6	14	11	12	2	16	13	4	10	5	9	15	3	1	8	7
6 Decapitation	11	71	77	68	68	74	41	39	32	-100	-100	-100	-4-	-68	-100	-100
14 Charon's fee	71	34	40	54	30	100	100	18	9	-14	-100	20	-19	-31	-100	-100
11 Animal bones	77	40	26	78	62	100	-3	50	71	14	44	-39	-51	-63	-100	-100
12 Hobnails	68	54	78	201	57	99	49	41	70	-21	58	2	-42	-58	-85	-100
2 N-S orientation	68	30	62	57	136	55	28	80	59	26	-100	-34	-81	-100	25	-39
16 Gravegoods	74	100	100	99	55	413	100	43	99	-15	57	0	-44	-56	-75	-60
13 Coins	41	100	-3	49	28	100	81	21	43	8	-12	23	-22	-28	-64	-100
4 Prone / crouched	39	18.	50	41	80	43	21	84	36	6	-14	15	-100	-80	68	-100
10 Vessels	32	9	71	70	59	99	43	36	99	-77	58	-64	-37	-60	-47	13
5 Overlapping	-100	-14	14	-21	26	-15	8	6	-77	371	-8	20	-7	-27	34	-10
9 Maus. / Encl.	-100	-100	44	58	-100	57	-12	-14	58	-8	31	60	13	100	-100	82
15 Grave protected	-100	20	-39	2	-34	0	23	15	-64	20	60	165	-16	33	61	88
3 Supine	-40	-19	-51	-42	-81	-44	-22	-100	-37	-7	13	-16	1936	79	-69	100
1 W-E orientation	-68	-31	-63	-58	-100	-56	-28	-80	-60	-27	100	33	79	1883	-25	38
8 Neonatal/Infant	-100	-100	-100	-85	25	-75	-64	68	-47	34		61	-69	-25	105	-100
7 Plaster	-100	-100	-100	-100	-39	-60	-100	-100	13	-10	82	88	100	38	-100	32

The outcome is probably a surprise for many. The differentiation is relatively clear cut and confirms the expectations of Watts and Woodward. It might even be clearer if some criteria (i.e. infant burials) could have been dropped. Comparing the number of graves falling in one of the two groups leaves no room for the ambiguous attributions of nine cemeteries as either Christian or pagan. In the final part of this paper the influence of belief for the similarities and differences in burying behaviour are checked.

The Urban – Rural divide

Another dimension which might structure Late Roman cemeteries (in death at least) is the connection to an urban or rural settlement site. This is not the place to argue whether towns exist in Late Roman Britain or not (Reece 1980). Here a simple division has been used, which takes size and walled settlement as indicator for an 'urban' community and a less structured settlement site (i.e. a small town, a vicus, a villa, a non-villa settlement or an isolated temple-site) as 'rural'.

The reason for different burying behaviour in urban and rural settings can be found in a difference in size, in degree of 'Romanization' (another highly controversial subject!), in economic role and relation to communications and other more subtle factors. Rural cemeteries have been described as much more conservative in character than urban ones. The normative pressure can be very different on both types of sites, relating to the cosmopolitan character of an urban community and the close connections of an often no more than a single family or kinship group on a rural site.

Cirencester, Colchester and Winchester have all been considered as urban burial grounds. The attribution of Poundbury is more complex (Farwell and Molleson 1993). Here the idea of a rural society burying its dead on a central cemetery has been put forward. Alternatively an attribution to the *civitas* capital of Durnovaria (Dorchester/Dorset) seems as least as likely, considering the very short distance between cemetery and town. Ilchester and Icklingham are at an intermediate level of conglomeration, i.e. at the level of a 'small town'. Bradley Hill and Lynch Farm represent rural settlements.

Regions and Civitates

The regional distribution of the cemeteries may have been responsible for differences in burying behaviour in two ways. Either the spheres of communication are strongest between neighbouring communities and rules of behaviour ('norms') are spread accordingly. Or groups use differences in burial customs as a conscious device for the display of group identity. i.e. two neighbouring groups are very different in their mortuary rites. To consider these two contradicting trends two measures are used, a purely

geographic label (southwest, west, south, east) and a attribution to one of the known *civitates*.

The sample – as already mentioned – is not distributed as evenly in Britain as one would wish for. However the cemeteries are at least spread over the territories of four to six *civitates*. One or possibly two of the cemeteries lie in the territory of the Trinovantes: Colchester and possibly Icklingham. The Iceni are represented by Lynch Farm (and also possibly Icklingham). Winchester-Lankhills is in the territory of the Atrebates (or the Roman creation of the *civitas Belgarum*). Cirencester falls in the territory of the Dobunni. In the Durotrigan area Ilchester, Poundbury and Bradley Hill can be found. There may be a further distinction (again created by Roman rule) of a northern (with a probable *civitas* capital at Ilchester) and a southern Durotrigan (around Dorchester/Dorset) *civitas*.

Final comparisons and conclusion

Each of the eight cemeteries explored in this paper and sometimes even parts of cemeteries has its own distinctive character. This is probably not a result of data quality and the partial excavation of most of the cemeteries, but represents a real difference in the behaviour of the burying communities. However there are also similarities.

Tables 22.5–22.7 try to organise the different strands discussed above. The cemeteries are listed in the order given by the different cluster analyses which includes formal and/or structuring attributes. The next columns give the approximate dating, the regional and functional setting of the cemetery and a tentative attribution to a Christian or pagan community. No clear correlation is apparent. At least some negative associations can be detected. The dating of the cemetery is of no relevance for the order. Regional customs are also widely absent. The functional setting, i.e. the association with a rural or an urban community, cannot be simply rejected as an ordering principle (vs. Esmonde Cleary 1992). The same holds true for the attribution of religious faith. A problem with the last aspect lies in the fact that the attribution of a religion is based on the presence and absence of some traits which are included in the cluster analysis as well. This seems to be a classic circular argument. A comparison between the cluster analysis which derives from the structured attributes alone (Fig. 22.9) and the religious attribution based on associations of furnishing and treatment of individual graves (Fig. 22.6) confirms the slight correlation between these aspects. The differentiation between rural and urban communities on the one hand and Christian and pagan groups on the other are probably the most promising explanation for the structuring of Late Roman cemeteries in Britain. These two principles are not entirely dependent on one another, i.e. Christian communities (according to the above mentioned attributes) can be urban as well as rural.

A formal statistical analysis like the one undertaken here, is a complementary, not a substitutional approach

Table 22.5 *Table of Late Roman cemeteries (ordered as in Fig. 22.7) compared with chronology, regional and functional attributes.*

	Relative distance to next group	Dating	Civitas	Region	Urban / Rural	Christian / Pagan
Colchester P2	110	IV	Trinovantes	East	Urban	Christian
Poundbury main	110	lt. III/ IV	Durotriges (S)	Southwest	Urban?	Christian
Icklingham	116	lt. IV	Iceni/Trinovantes?	East	Rural	Christian
Poundbury peri.	116	lt. III/IV	Durotriges (S)	Southwest	Urban?	Pagan
Lynch Farm	128	III/IV	Iceni	East	Rural	Pagan
Cirencester	137	lt. III/IV	Dobunni	West	Urban	Pagan
Bradley Hill	140	IV	Durotriges (N)	Southwest	Rural	Christian?
Colchester P 1	146	III/ea. IV	Trinovantes	East	Urban	Pagan
Ilchester	150	lt. IV	Durotriges (N)	Southwest	Rural	Pagan
Winchester	180	IV	Atrebates/Belgae	South	Urban	Pagan

Table 22.6 *Table of Late Roman cemeteries (ordered as in Fig. 22.8) compared with chronology, regional and functional attributes.*

	Relative distance to next group	Dating	Civitas	Region	Urban / Rural	Christian / Pagan
Cirencester	52	lt. III/IV	Dobunni	West	Urban	Pagan
Lynch Farm	52	III/IV	Iceni	East	Rural	Pagan
Bradley Hill	62	IV	Durotriges (N)	Southwest	Rural	Christian?
Colchester P 1	75	III/ea. IV	Trinovantes	East	Urban	Pagan
Ilchester	106	lt. IV	Durotriges (N)	Southwest	Rural	Pagan
Poundbury main	115	lt. III/IV	Durotriges (S)	Southwest	Urban?	Christian
Winchester	115	IV	Atrebates/Belgae	South	Urban	Pagan
Colchester P2	125	IV	Trinovantes	East	Urban	Christian
Poundbury peri.	185	lt. III/IV	Durotriges (S)	Southwest	Urban?	Pagan

Table 22.7 *Table of Late Roman cemeteries (ordered as in Fig. 22.9) compared with chronology, regional and functional attributes.*

	Relative distance to next group	Dating	Civitas	Region	Urban / Rural	Christian / Pagan
Cirencester	176	lt III/IV	Dobunni	West	Urban	Pagan
Lynch Farm	176	III/IV	Iceni	East	Rural	Pagan
Bradley Hill	196	IV	Durotriges (N)	Southwest	Rural	Christian?
Colchester P 1	233	III/ea. IV	Trinovantes	East	Urban	Pagan
Ilchester	241	lt. IV	Durotriges (N)	Southwest	Urban	Pagan
Colchester P2	218	IV	Trinovantes	East	Urban	Christian
Poundbury main	218	lt. III/IV	Durotriges (S)	Southwest	Urban?	Christian
Winchester	303	IV	Atrebates/Belgae	South	Urban	Pagan
Poundbury peri.	305	lt. III/IV	Durotriges (S)	Southwest	Urban?	Pagan

to the study of mortuary practice in Late Roman Britain. The relationship between settlement and cemetery has to be explored in more detail. Regions outside the scope of this paper (Midlands, the North) and trends on the continent should be included in the future. One main obstacle to a more detailed analysis and very probable point of criticism is the fact that most of the cemeteries run through a period of at least hundred years. Using the cemeteries in the above way as if they represent the ritual behaviour of a single moment in time certainly ignores their complex evolution The author does not see any way of dealing with this problem at the moment. Nevertheless some testable ideas and historically meaningful statements have been generated.

Being Christian or at least growing up in a Christian culture ourselves, we take the burial customs of Late Roman Britain for granted. But they are not self-evident. It is indeed a highly complex phenomenon and has its capacities for exploring social and ideological dimensions in the world of the once living. To phrase the purpose and results of this paper in a post-processual manner: the text is there, now let us start to read it. My deciphering of it is only the first beginning done by an illiterate.

Notes

1. Cemetery/Cirencester (McWhirr *et al.* 1982); Butt Road Cemetery/Colchester (Crummy et al. 1993); Bradley Hill/ Somerset (Leech 1981); Icklingham/Suffolk (West 1976); Ilchester/Somerset (Leach 1982); Lynch Farm/Peterborough (Jones 1975).
2. The age divisions of this graph are based only on provisional ageing. An individual aged as an 'adult' is spread proportionally all over the different age categories (*adultus* and *maturus*). The reconstruction of the living population is based on an algorithm developed by M. Gebühr (1994), which has found widespread acceptance by German physical anthropologists.
3. Instead of the nearest neighbour, the average distance to all members of a group is used.
4. Originally it is -1 and +1. To avoid real numbers these values have been multiplied by 100 and rounded.
5. The effect of Poundbury with its more than 1400 graves on the combination table has been criticised by Martin Millett. Besides using Yule-values, two tests for this effect have been carried out. First a combination table dropping the Poundbury data gives similar results, second the distinction in pagan and Christian burial customs is very clear cut, i.e. each cemetery is heavily dominated by one of these customs.
6. The number given in the last two rows of Figure 22.2 is based on a count of graves in a cemetery having at least one of the attributes (Table 22.4) from 6 (decapitation) to 10 (vessels) included in the grave as type 1 burial ('pagan'). The type 2 burials ('Christian') consist of those graves oriented west-east with a body in a supine position and which do not possess any of the attributes essential for a type 1 burial. The attribution to either Christian or pagan for a whole cemetery compares the two numbers. Only Bradley Hill presents some difficulties in this respect, because it seems to represent at least two different cemeteries which are separated by a short period of time.
7. Owslebury in Hampshire (Collis 1977), a rural cemetery which probably runs through the whole Roman period, is a good example of such conservatism. Here a very heterogeneous burying pattern (e.g. cremations and inhumations at the same time) developed.

Bibliography

Bassett, S. (ed.) 1992. *Death in Towns: urban responses to the living and the dead, 100–1600.* Leicester: Leicester University Press.

Clarke, G. 1979. *The Roman Cemetery at Lankhills.* (Winchester Studies 3: Pre-Roman and Roman Winchester). Oxford: Oxford University Press.

Collis, J. 1977. Owslebury (Hants) and the Problem of Burials on Rural Settlements. In: Reece, R. (ed.) *Burials in the Roman World* (CBA Research Report No. 22). London.

Crummy N., Crummy, P. and Crossan, C. 1993. *Excavations of Roman and Later Cemeteries, Churches and Monastic Sites in Colchester, 1971–88.* (Colchester Archaeological Report 9) Colchester.

Esmonde Cleary, S. 1992. *Town and Country.* In: Bassett 1992: 28–42.

Farwell, D.E. and Molleson, T.L. 1993. *Excavations at Poundbury 1966–80. Volume II: The Cemeteries.* (Dorset Natural History and Archaeology Society Monograph Series Number 11) Dorchester.

Foster, J. 1993. *The identification of male and female graves using grave goods.* In: Struck 1993: 207–213.

Gebühr, M. 1994. *Alter und Geschlecht. Aussagemöglichkeiten anhand des archäologischen und anthropologischen Befundes.* In: Stjernquist 1994: 73–86.

Jones, R. 1975. The Romano-British Farmstead and its Cemetery at Lynch Farm, near Peterborough. *Northamptonshire Archaeology* 10: 94–137.

Leach, P.J. 1982, *Ilchester Vol. 1 – Excavations 1974–1975.* (Western Archaeological Trust Excavation Monograph No. 3) Bristol.

Leech, R.H. 1981. The Excavation of a Romano-British Farmstead and Cemetery on Bradley Hill, Somerton, Somerset. *Britannia* 12: 177–252.

McWhirr, A., Viner, L. and Wells, C. 1982. *Romano-British Cemeteries at Cirencester.* Cirencester: Cirencester Excavation Committee.

Millett, M. 1992. Review of Christian and Pagans in Roman Britain by Dorothy Watts. *Archaeological Journal* 149, 426.

Philpott, R. 1991. *Burial Practices in Roman Britain* – A Survey of Grave Treatment and Furnishing A.D. 43–410 (BAR Brit. Ser. 219). Oxford.

Reece, R. 1980. Town and Country: the End of Roman Britain. *World Archaeology* 12: 77–92.

Stjernquist, B. (ed.) 1994.: *Prehistoric Graves as a Source of Information.* Symposium at Kastlösa, Öland, May 21–23, 1992. Kungl. Vitterhets Historie och Antikvitets Akademien Konferenser 29, Uppsala.

Struck, M. (ed.) 1993. *Römerzeitliche Gräber als Quellen zur Religion, Bevölkerungsstruktur und Sozialgeschichte.* Main: Johannes Gutenberg Institut für Vor- und Frühgeschichte.

Thomas, C. 1981. *Christianity in Roman Britain to AD 500.* London: Batsford.

Watts, D. 1991. *Christians and Pagans in Roman Britain.* London, Routledge.

Wenham, L.P. 1968. *The Romano-British Cemetery at Trentholme Drive, York.* (Ministry of Public Buildings and Works Archaeological Report 5).

West, S. 1976. The Romano-British Site at Icklingham. *East Anglian Archaeology* 3: 63–126.

Woodward, A.B. 1993. Discussion. In: Farwell and Molleson 1993: 215–39.

23. Gender imbalances in Romano-British cemetery populations: a re-evaluation of the evidence

Clive Davison

Introduction

Perhaps the most subtle, yet surely the most significant legacy of the post-processual era has been a growing awareness of the need to critically re-evaluate the basic assumptions of past researchers. In this paper I would like to consider one such assumption, the idea that the surplus of males in many Romano-British urban cemetery populations was due to an influx of military personnel, and to offer some alternative interpretations.

It is important to state from the outset that this study is *not* intended as a demographic analysis of Romano-British cemetery populations. Such an approach is difficult to justify given the highly fragmentary nature of burial data. The initial data analysis outlined in this paper attempts to define some generalised patterns and to provide a framework for a broader contextual interpretation of gender imbalances. For this reason and for the sake of brevity, I have avoided detailed discussions of specific sites and have instead concentrated on the broader discussions of sex and gender in cemetery reports. It is necessary to define what is meant here by 'sex' and 'gender'. I intend to use 'sex' with reference to the biological description of skeletal material. 'Gender' is socially constructed by individuals or groups, for example determining what are considered appropriate female/male attributes, roles or behaviour (e.g. the wearing of jewellery), which are unlikely to be universal but rather are formed within particular cultural contexts (Pader 1982; Allason-Jones 1995).

Methodology

25 Romano-British cemetery site reports were studied which had sufficient skeletal evidence to warrant further research into sex ratios (see appendix for list of sites). A total of 1,503 male and 973 female burials were incorporated into the database. Sites were subdivided into 3 categories: 'urban' (generally *civitas* capital, colony, or *municipium*), 'small urban' (military *vici* and small towns) and 'rural' (small settlements, homesteads and villas). These classifications are based primarily on the relationship of specific cemeteries with the *size* of their associated settlements; any conclusions are therefore highly generalised and do not take into account the socio-economic context of individual communities.

Sites were selected with a minimum of 30 sexed or possible sexed burials within 'urban' and 'small urban' contexts and a minimum of 18 sexed or possible sexed burials from 'rural' contexts. The lower threshold for rural sites stems from a relative shortage of suitable data (see below). The methods used to define sex from skeletal material vary according to the individual palaeopathologists and in some cases I am extremely sceptical of the apparently subjective assumptions on the basis of which sex has been determined (see below). Due to these reservations I decided to eliminate the 'possibles' from my data altogether and to only use interments where there was a high probability of biological sex being correctly determined.

Pre-Roman and Anglo-Saxon burials have been excluded from the totals, as have individual graves in clear isolation from the main cemetery area. Almost all of the burials used were of adults of various ages. An attempt to correlate sex/age distributions was abandoned as unworkable given the problems of combining partial skeletal evidence of sex with equally or even more partial evidence of age.

A further factor which distorts the over all picture is the fact that the vast majority of Roman period cemetery studies have been carried out on larger urban sites; rural contexts are comparatively under-represented. If one accepts that the majority of the population lived in the countryside then this imbalance may have a major effect on our perspective of sex ratios in the population as a whole. This problem of under-representation of rural burials is compounded by the fact that many interments in the countryside consist of single burials or small scattered groups (see Esmonde Cleary this volume) and often there is a shortage of grave goods to corroborate their dating to the Roman period.

Having selected appropriate data, histograms were produced to illustrate the male:female ratios at each site

(Davison 1997) and an attempt was made to relate any general patterns to geographical distribution, chronological variation and site type (as per the urban, small urban, rural classification).

Results

The geographical distribution of sites was disproportionately focused on southern England, partly as a result of variation in the survival of diagnostic skeletal material and, more specifically, because there has been a lack of Roman period cemetery analysis in the north and west of the country, an omission criticised by Clack and Gosling (1976) and Philpott (1991). In view of this uneven distribution I did not feel it was possible to draw any credible conclusions about any relationship between sex ratio and region.

The date of the samples used in this study spanned the entire period of Roman occupation but it should be stressed that the majority of material dates to the later 3rd and 4th centuries (see appendix). The primary reason for this is that cremation was still widely practised throughout most (but not all) of Britain up until the 3rd century (Whimster 1981; Black 1986). Cremated skeletal material is more limited in terms of its diagnostic potential. It is rare to find any detailed analysis of cremated bone in older site reports; it is only recently that the full analytical potential of cremated bone has been exploited (e.g. McKinley 1992; this volume). One wonders how much relevant information found its way onto past spoil-heaps. Interestingly, analysis of cremated bone from the St Stephens early Roman site at St Albans appears to show an excess of females (Niblett this volume); it would be extremely useful to have further contemporary samples.

Dating cemeteries is not always straightforward. In most cases date has been established by reference to grave goods. This may pose problems, as objects may have been in circulation for some time before deposition (e.g. Goings in Crummy *et al.* 1993: 149–51; Tuffreau-Libre this volume). Radiocarbon dating is usually less precise than artefact based dating in our period, save when it might

serve to distinguish unaccompanied late Roman inhumations from post-Roman burials, but very few cemetery sites have benefited from this or other absolute dating methods (see Rahtz 1977 for an exception).

Given all of these limitations the following pie-charts (Fig. 23.1) showing the male:female ratios according to site type should be regarded as highly generalised. Nevertheless, I felt that there was sufficient material evidence to suggest that sex ratios were distinctly biased to males within most urban cemetery populations, slightly less so in small urban cemeteries and evenly balanced at rural sites. In my analysis therefore site type emerged as the most distinct variable associated with sex differential.

Discussion

Clearly then, either the evidence is misleading or we are not looking at a 'typical' mixed sex society or burial rite in Romano-British towns. The traditional explanation of a surfeit of retired legionaries appears increasingly untenable in the light of modern research which emphasises the significance of civilian participation in urban development (see below). In the following discussion I would like to consider a number of scenarios which might provide a wider perspective on this subject, which are as follows:

1: The predominance of males reflects an influx of men into urban centres for military or economic reasons
2: The predominance of males reflects differential female infanticide
3: The predominance of males reflects flaws in sampling, analysis and interpretation of skeletal samples
4: The predominance of males reflects the cultural separation of males and females within cemeteries

1. The predominance of males was the result of an influx of men into urban centres for military/economic reasons

Reports on the human remains from Cirencester and York have both concluded that the predominance of males

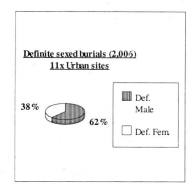

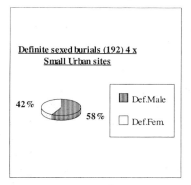

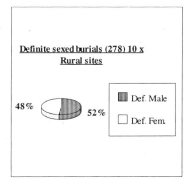

Fig. 23. 1 *Pie chart representation of sex ratios based on 2,476 definite sexed burials sampled in England. 'Urban' = civitas capital and colony, 'small urban' =* vici *or small towns, 'rural' = small settlements, homesteads or villas*

within Romano-British cemeteries was due to the presence of large numbers of retired legionaries within the garrison towns (McWhirr, Viner and Wells 1982; Wenham 1968). Such a view seems to be largely based on traditional preconceptions of Roman militarism and urbanisation in Britain. There are two key assumptions which need to be validated if we are to substantiate military populations as responsible for these unbalanced sex ratios, first that the Roman military presence was the main economic formative influence for urban development and second that the (male) military population formed the significant majority within these towns, hence their dominance within the cemetery samples.

The pre-Roman settlement pattern seems to have been more influential on the Roman military than vice versa. Archaeological evidence has shown that in some cases, Roman forts and *vici* were sited in conjunction with pre-existing British proto-urban centres (e.g. Colchester, Cirencester, St Albans). This suggests that a degree of socio-economic interdependence between civilian and military populations was considerable from the start (Millett 1984; 1990). Furthermore, the rapid expansion of the *vici* associated with Roman forts was primarily due to the immigration of civilian merchants and craftsmen along with their womenfolk (Sommer 1984), or of women traders and manufacturers in their own right. Even if a site can be linked to a military base we must therefore allow for the possibility of an unknown percentage of mixed sex civilian interments, particularly as it is virtually impossible to distinguish the individual graves by their material remains. A further factor to consider here is the fact that, following a dictate by Septimius Severus in AD 197, soldiers below the rank of centurion were allowed to marry, and most would very probably have had female attachments prior to that (Allason-Jones 1989). Inhabitants of towns would have included a substantial number of wives, daughters and consorts of serving soldiers. In general we must be wary of the influence of a Roman army estimated to comprise 50,000 men in 150 AD (Birley 1981) which probably represents a maximum of 5% of the population (Millett 1990).

Most importantly however, at many of the sites in question, the military phases of settlement precede the period of use of the cemetery, most of which relate to the 3rd to late 4th centuries (see appendix). One might question why serving or retired military personnel should have chosen to return to places which had had no military connections for many years or centuries? Admittedly in York the army would have been present throughout the Roman occupation: however in that particular case the bulk of the burial evidence comes from Trentholme Drive, for which the methodology of the bone report requires close scrutiny (see below).

The single factor from my research which might support the notion of a predominance of military males within urban cemetery populations is that the male to female ratio remains stable within *rural* contexts. This implies that civilian economic migrants to the *vici* must have moved in equal proportions of men and women. If, as has been suggested, cemeteries represent both military and civilian burials, then the surplus of males is more likely to be from the military sector. However the small size of the rural sample in comparison to the urban must be borne in mind.

2. The predominance of males reflects differential female infanticide

It has been argued from detailed analysis of skeletal evidence that infanticide was practised in Roman Britain (Mays 1993) and there are historical sources from elsewhere in the Empire to suggest that this might have been the case (Harris 1994; MacCary and Willcock 1976 etc.). There is a serious lack of archaeological evidence to support or refute any claim of differential female infanticide, given that skeletal remains of infants and children are notoriously difficult to sex.

Given the absence of corroborative evidence I did not feel justified in arguing that differential female infanticide was responsible for imbalances within cemetery populations. I also felt that many of the theories put forward on the extent of infanticide in Roman Britain were avoiding some key issues. Tales of infanticide have a certain tabloid fascination (see Scott 1992) but we should be careful before automatically assuming that infanticide would have been practised in Roman Britain. Anthropological studies of infanticide usually stress the desperate economic and physical circumstances which might impel people to kill their own offspring. There is definitely archaeological evidence for both strong social stratification and economic change over time in Roman Britain (Millett 1990). However Roman Britain was not, I would contend, an extreme environment where one's own survival would be dependent upon killing one's children. In my opinion the parent/child bond is a powerful, natural and instinctive one and I can see no valid reason to assume it was less so in Roman Britain. Even where children could not be supported there were alternatives to infanticide, for example slavery (Bradley 1984). If infanticide was practised in Roman Britain it would have been increasingly stigmatised by emergent Christianity and by an edict by Valentinian in AD 374 outlawing the practice (Harris 1984).

There does appear to be a relative shortage of infant graves in most cemeteries of this period. There are however one or two groups of burials with high proportions of children, for example at Hambledon Valley, Berks. (Cocks 1920) or Bradley Hill, Somerset (Leech 1981). At other sites isolated child burials have been found in or around the homestead, perhaps suggesting a symbolic placing of the body (Scott 1992). It could be argued that the cultural separation of the dead in age cohorts or in places of symbolic significance is indicative of a society which values its young enough to afford them distinctive burial rites rather than merely considering them expendable.

Given these arguments, differential female infanticide seems an unlikely candidate for explaining the surplus of males within Romano-British urban cemetery populations.

3. The predominance of males reflects flaws in sampling, analysis and interpretation of skeletal samples

Any discussion of gender imbalances within cemetery populations is, necessarily, defined by the quantity and quality of the palaeopathological evidence. Is it possible that the fragmentary nature of such material, combined with an innate systematic bias, may actually be creating a false picture of Romano-British sex ratios, thereby distorting our perception of gender structures?

The diverse techniques available for sexing skeletal material include *visual* (e.g. shape of pelvic features, skull, mandible etc.) and *metrical* indicators (e.g. comparative evidence of sexual dimorphism such as long bone or cranial measurements) (Brothwell 1981). Since much of this material is fragmentary owing to variable rates of decomposition, soil disturbance etc., the palaeopathologist is often required to assess sex on the largely subjective basis of his or her experience in recognising diagnostic features. In 1972 Kenneth Weiss was led to suspect that this subjectivity was creating 'an irresistible temptation in many cases to call doubtful specimens male' (Weiss 1972: 240), a suggestion supported by a world-wide series of 'blind-tests' on skeletal material of known sex which uncovered a 12% bias in favour of males.

I contend that the possibility of systematic bias is mainly restricted to older site reports such as at Trentholme Drive, York (Wenham 1968). In this case the anatomist Roger Warwick was content to assess possible sex on, in some cases, a single limb bone or a scattering of cranial fragments. In more recent studies analysis of skeletal data has become much more refined, and increasing emphasis is placed on the need to utilise *several* sexually diagnostic indicators (McKinley 1992). Nevertheless, Trentholme Drive and other older site reports continue to be used as comparative examples in modern publications. If, as I suspect, the fundamental data from these examples is, at best, flawed, then there is a real danger that our perception of sex ratio (and therefore gender) imbalances continues to be distorted.

Burials sexed on the basis of grave goods alone were not used in this survey because of the potential dangers of the approach. In a critique of the report on the Roman cemetery at Oudenburg in Belgium (Eisner 1991), the researchers (Mertens and Van Impe) were found to have imposed their own perceptions of the appropriate function of grave furnishings according to modern ideas of gender. For example, they assumed that 'all decorative or frivolous items' such as jewellery, combs, hairpins, gaming pieces etc. must be associated with female burials. Care is needed before stating that in the Roman period such items were not owned and used by males (see Allason-Jones 1995).

It was argued that these perceptions were: 'a reflection of 20th century behavioural ideas and patterns, and may have little relation to the Oudenburg reality' (Eisner 1991: 354). Similar criticisms could equally be applied to older Romano-British cemetery reports, although to what extent this has distorted our view can only be gauged by re-evaluating each of these studies in the light of recent archaeological thought. A study by Foster (1993) suggests that there may be some change over time in the gendered association of grave goods.

4. The predominance of males reflects the cultural separation of males and females within cemeteries

A further possibility is that some form of deliberate separation of males and females within individual or separate cemetery populations was practised, and that we have yet to find a representative sample of females. Very few archaeological reports have attempted to address this question, although occasional groupings have been identified. The great majority of sexed burials in Enclosure A at King Harry Lane were male (Millett 1993: 262). One notable attempt to analyse sex groupings can be found in Giles Clarke's study of the urban cemetery at Lankhills, Winchester (Clarke 1979). The author observed that, while there was no *absolute* pattern, there do appear to be quite clearly defined clusters of broadly contemporaneous single sex graves – as determined by combined grave goods and skeletal evidence. However Lankhills offered an unusually rich opportunity to explore gender-based patterning over time. A lack of corroborative dateable evidence makes it extremely difficult to place individual burials within any chronological sequence. The orderliness of Romano-British cemeteries is highly variable and stratigraphic sequencing is often complicated by reuse or over-cutting of graves.

Evidence of gender separation within cemeteries is therefore inconclusive at best. Nevertheless there is scope for greater research into this question and the dismissal of gender based burial separation on the grounds of a scattering of females in an otherwise male area requires revision. Given the diversity of contemporaneous burial practices within individual cemeteries (e.g. inhumation *and* cremation, decapitations, varied alignments, different body postures etc.), it is not necessarily surprising that the occasional female might be buried in an otherwise exclusively male area. We have yet to excavate a *complete* Romano-British cemetery in any urban or small urban context and it still remains a possibility that we are missing a representative sample of the female population.

It might also be possible that we are misinterpreting the symbolic and cultural structures that might promote these gender imbalances. For example, are we looking for evidence of *family units* as perceived from a modern day perspective? Clarke argued that at Lankhills 'the family as we understand it today was of no importance in the organisation of the cemetery'. He went on to speculate that 'It may be that the groupings of men represent male kinsfolk linked on a patrilineal basis, and that female burials represent related women, linked perhaps matrilineally or by marriage' (Clarke 1975).

The primary conclusion of my research was that male biased gender imbalance is an essentially urban phenomenon. I was unable to find evidence of sex groupings within any of the *rural* sites studied. Where possible however it would be interesting to apply Clarke's methodology to a wide range of cemetery sites because, if we are indeed looking at some form of cultural separation within urban areas, then this may well represent a shift in Romano-British burial tradition which is in some way linked to urbanisation.

Divergent models have been proposed for the impact of urbanisation on the role and status of women. In a study of women in Roman Britain, Allason-Jones (1989) has argued that the breakdown of tribal kin-structures and the loss of traditional working roles that must have accompanied migration to urban centres would have robbed women of their established position in society. According to Saller and Shaw however (1984) urbanisation in some parts of the Roman world would have given women a wider range of economic opportunities.

Assessing these arguments is beyond the scope of this paper. However if cultural separation of male and female burials is, as my own data suggests, an urban phenomenon, then perhaps we are seeing a manifestation of the disenfranchisement of women. Some (but not all) male-biased cemeteries tend to be in spatially dominant areas close to town walls and along roads etc.. If women were being buried elsewhere it must have been in less visible/central areas, perhaps further away from town. The symbolic value of the cemetery site *might* have been one way of emphasising male dominance in a new urban gender hierarchy (see Quensel-von-Kalben this volume for a different view).

Conclusion

My research has suggested that the association between towns and male-dominant cemeteries in Britain is valid. Discussion has tried to consider the possible reasons for this phenomenon in a broader contextual analysis. This involved consideration of a number of scenarios.

A surplus of retired military personnel is the most commonly cited reason for the preponderance of males within Romano-British cemeteries. This is not impossible but it is necessary to reconsider the demographic and socio-economic impact of the Roman army on the indigenous population before making such sweeping assumptions. Recent studies have stressed the significance of the indigenous settlement pattern and *civilian* migration as a catalyst for urban expansion and it is therefore necessary to consider the demographic influence of the female population. It has also been shown that the study of the human bone on one of the key sites for this

hypothesis, Trentholme Drive, requires close attention. The relatively even sex ratios within rural contexts might lend weight to the military male-bias hypothesis but the sample is small.

Differential female infanticide has been proposed as a possible explanation in some site reports. I consider this scenario unlikely for two key reasons. First there is no evidence of sex from most infant burials and second care is required in identifying the extreme circumstances which perpetuate the practice of infanticide in Roman Britain.

The cultural separation of the male and female dead offers a more credible explanation. Clarke's study of the cemetery at Lankhills, Winchester has raised strong suspicions that men and women might have been interred separately. Other samples need to be analysed to substantiate this pattern. However I tentatively suggest that the 'absence' of females might be related to a shift in the gender hierarchy within new urban communities, with the loss of traditional tribal roles and status. The location of male biased cemeteries in visually prominent areas could imply that women were being buried in more remote, less symbolically important areas. This suggestion too needs more research but it opens theoretical possibilities beyond the outdated picture of Roman Britain as a resort for retired soldiers.

Whatever the reasons for this male surplus, they are almost certainly more complex than traditional interpretation would have us believe, although it is possible that a combination of scenarios may have influenced sex ratios. With an ever increasing database of burial evidence and the freedom to challenge established ideas, I feel optimistic that archaeology can begin to explore *how* and *why* change occurred in Roman Britain rather than merely seeking to corroborate that which we have always assumed to be true.

Appendix – Sites used in this study with approximate date

Urban cemeteries

Alcester, Warwickshire., e. 2nd – m/l. 4th (Denston in Cracknell and Mahany 1994)
Bath Gate, Cirencester, Glos., 3rd – 4th (McWhirr *et al.* 1982)
Barton (Coll. of Art), Gloucester., l. 3rd – l. 4th (Heighway 1980)
Butt Road, Colchester, Essex, 3rd – l. 4th (Crummy *et al.* 1993)
Cranmer House, Canterbury, Kent., 2nd – 4th (Frere *et al.* 1987)
King Harry Lane, St Albans, Herts., 1st – 2nd (Stead and Rigby 1989)
Lankhills, Winchester, Hants., 4th (Clarke 1979)
Poundbury, Dorchester, Dorset., l. 2nd – l. 4th (Farwell *et al.* 1993)
Trentholme Drive, York., 2nd – l. 4th (Wenham 1968)
Westgate, Chichester, W. Sussex, 4th (Down and Magilton 1993)
West Tenter Street, London E1., e 2nd – l. 4th (Whytehead *et al.* 1986)

Small urban cemeteries

Bradley Hill, Somerset, l. 4th – 5th (Leech 1981)
Bletsoe, Beds., l. 3rd – m/l. 4th (Dawson 1994)
Cassington, Oxon., 4th (Harman *et al.* 1981)
Curbridge, Nr. Witney, Oxon., 4th (Chambers 1976)

Derby Racecourse, Derbs., l. 1st – 4th (Wheeler 1985)
Dunstable, Beds., l. 4th (Matthews 1981)
Icklingham, Suffolk, 3rd – l. 4th (West *et al.* 1976)
Skeleton Green, East Herts., l. 1st – e. 4th (Partridge 1981)

Rural cemeteries
The Grange, Welwyn, Herts., 1st – 4th (Rook 1973)
Lamyatt Beacon, Wilts., l. 4th – 6th (Leech 1986)
Lynch Farm, Peterborough, Cambs., 3rd – m. 4th (Jones 1975)
Radley, Berks., 4th (Atkinson 1952)
Stanton Harcourt, Oxon., m. 4th (McGavin *et al.* 1981)
Welwyn Hall, Welwyn, Herts., l. 4th (Herts. Arch. Trust 1995)

Bibliography

Allason-Jones, L. 1989. *Women in Roman Britain*. London: British Museum

Allason-Jones, L. 1995. Sexing Small Finds. In Rush, P. ed. *Theoretical Roman Archaeology – Second Conference Proceedings*, 22–32. Aldershot: Avebury

Atkinson, R.J.C. 1952. Excavations at Barrow Hills Field, Radley, Berks. *Oxoniensia* 17: 32–35

Barber, B. *et al.* 1990. Recent excavations of a cemetery of Londinium. *Britannia*, 21: 1–12

Birley, A.R. 1981. The economic effects of Roman frontier policy. In King, A. and Henig, M., eds, *The Roman West in the 3rd Century* B.A.R. (s) 109: 39–54

Black, E.W. 1986. Romano-British burial customs and religious beliefs in south-east England. *Archaeological Journal*, 143: 201–39

Bradley, K.R. 1984. *Slaves and Masters in the Roman Empire*. Brussels: Latomus – Revue d'Etudes Latines

Brothwell, D.R. 1981. *Digging up bones – the excavation, treatment and study of human skeletal remains*. London: British Museum

Chambers, R.A. 1987. The late and sub-Roman cemetery at Queensford Farm, Dorchester on Thames, Oxon.. *Oxoniensia*, 52: 35–69

Clarke, G. 1979. *The Roman cemetery at Lankhills*. Winchester Studies, 3. Oxford: Clarendon Press

Cocks, A.H. 1920. A Romano-British homestead in the Hambledon Valley, Bucks.. *Archaeologia*, 71: 141–198

Cox, P.W. 1988. A 7th century inhumation cemetery at Shepherds Farm, Ulwell, near Swanage, Dorset. *Proceedings of the Dorset Natural History and Archaeological Society*, 10: 36–47

Clack, P.A.G. and Gosling, P.F. 1976. *Archaeology in the North*. London: HMSO

Cracknell, S. and Mahany, C., eds, 1994. *Roman Alcester: Southern Extramural Area 1964–1966 Excavations. Pt. 2 Finds and Discussion*. CBA Research Reports, 97, York: CBA

Crummy, N., Crummy, P. and Crossan, C. 1993. *Excavations of Roman and Later Cemeteries, Churches and Monastic Sites in Colchester*. Colchester Archaeological Reports 9, Colchester: Colchester Archaeological Trust

Davison, C.M. 1997. *Gender imbalances in Romano-British cemetery populations – an evaluation of the material and literary evidence*. Durham: University of Durham (unpublished dissertation)

Dawson, M. 1994. *A Late Roman Cemetery at Bletsoe, Bedfordshire*. Bedfordshire Archaeology Monograph Series 1, Bedford: Bedfordshire County Council and Bedfordshire

Down, A. and Magilton, J. 1993. *Chichester Excavations 8*. Chichester: Chichester District Council

Eisner, W.R. 1991. The consequences of gender bias in mortuary analysis: a case study. In Walde, D. *et al.* eds, *The Archaeology of Gender*, 352–357. Calgary: University of Calgary

Farwell, D. and Molleson, T. 1993. *Excavations at Poundbury, Dorchester, Dorset, 1966–1980. Volume 2: the cemeteries*. Dorchester: Dorset Natural History and Archaeological Society

Foster, J. 1993. The identification of male and female graves using grave goods. In Struck, M. ed. *Römerzeitliche Gräber als Quellen zu Religion, Bevölkerungsstruktur und Sozialgeschichte*, 207–13. Mainz: Johannes Gutenburg-Universität

Frere, S.S. *et al.* 1987. *Canterbury excavations: intra and extramural sites 1949–55 and 1980–84*. Canterbury Archaeological Trust Report, VIII

Harman, M., Molleson, T.I. and Price, D.L. 1981. Burials, bodies and beheadings in Romano-British and Anglo-Saxon cemeteries. *Bulletin of the British Museum (Natural History). Geology*, 35: 145–89

Harris, W.V. 1994. Child exposure in the Roman Empire. *Journal of Roman Studies*, 84: 1–22

Heighway, C. 1980. Roman cemeteries in Gloucester District. *Transactions of the Bristol and Gloucester Archaeological Society*, 98: 57–72

Jones, R.F.J. 1975. The Romano-British farmstead and its cemetery at Lynch Farm, near Peterborough. *Northamptonshire Archaeology*, 10: 94–137

Leech, R. 1981. The excavation of a Romano-British farmstead and cemetery on Bradley Hill, Somerton, Somerset. *Britannia*, 12: 177–252

Leech, R. 1986. The excavation of a Romano-Celtic temple and later cemetery on Lamyatt Beacon, Somerset. *Britannia*, 17: 259–329

MacCary, W.T. and Willcock, M.M. (eds.) 1976. *Plautus – Casina*. Cambridge: Cambridge University Press

Matthews, C.L. 1981. A Romano-British inhumation cemetery at Dunstable, Durocobrivae. *Bedfordshire Archaeological Journal*, 15: 1–73

Mays, S.A. 1993. Infanticide in Roman Britain. *Antiquity* 67. 883–89

McGavin, N. 1980. A Roman cemetery and trackway at Stanton Harcourt. *Oxoniensia*, 45: 112–23

McKinley, J.I. 1992. *The Anglo-Saxon cemetery at Spong Hill, North Elmham, part VIII – the cremations*. East Anglian Archaeology, 69

McWhirr, A., Viner, L. and Wells, C. 1982. *Romano-British cemeteries at Cirencester*. Cirencester Excavation Committee Report, II.

Millett, M. 1984. Forts and the origins of towns: cause or effect? In Blagg, T.F.C. and King, A.C. eds, *Military and Civilian in Roman Britain*, B.A.R. (Brit. ser.), 136: 65–74

Millett, M. 1990. *The Romanization of Britain*. Cambridge: Cambridge University Press

Millett, M. 1993. A cemetery in an age of transition: King Harry Lane reconsidered. In Struck, M. ed. *Römerzeitliche Gräber als Quellen zu Religion, Bevölkerungsstruktur und Sozialgeschichte*, 255–282. Mainz: Johannes Gutenburg-Universität

Pader, E.J. 1982. *Symbolism, social relations and the interpretation of mortuary remains*. B.A.R. (Int. ser.), 130

Partridge, C. 1981. *Skeleton Green: a late Iron Age and Romano-British site*. London: Society for the Promotion of Roman Studies

Philpott, R. 1991. *Burial practices in Roman Britain – a survey of grave treatment and furnishing AD 43–410*. B.A.R. (Brit ser.), 219.

Rahtz, P.A. 1977. Late Roman cemeteries and beyond. In Reece, R. ed, *Burial in the Roman World*, CBA Research Reports, 22, 53–64. London: CBA

Rook, A.G. 1973. Excavations at the Grange Romano-British cemetery, Welwyn, 1967. *Hertfordshire Archaeology*, 3: 1–30

Saller, R. P. and Shaw, B. D. 1984. Tombstones and Roman family relations in the Principate: soldiers, civilians and slaves. *Journal of Roman Studies* 74. 124–156

Scott, E.. 1992. Images and contexts of infant burials: some thoughts on cross-cultural evidence. *Archaeological Revue from Cambridge,* II.I: 77–92

Sommer, C.S. 1984. *The military vici in Roman Britain.* B.A.R. (Brit. ser.), 129

Stead, I.M. and Rigby, V. 1989. *Verulamium: the King Harry Lane site.* London: English Heritage

Weiss, K.M. 1972. Bias in skeletal sexing. *American Journal of Physical Anthropology,* 37: 239–250

Wenham, L.P. *et al.* 1968. *The Romano-British cemetery at Trentholme Drive, York.* Ministry of Public Building and Works Archaeological Reports, 5. London: HMSO

West, S.C. and Plouviez, J. 1976. The Roman site at Icklingham. *East Anglian Archaeology,* 3, 63–126, Ipswich: Suffolk County Council

Wheeler, H. 1985. The Racecourse Cemetery. *Derbyshire Archaeological Journal,* 105, 222–80

Whimster, R. 1981. *Burial Practice in Iron Age Britain.* B.A.R. (Brit. Ser.), 90

Whytehead, R. *et al.* 1986. The excavation of an area within a Roman cemetery at West Tenter Street, London, E1. *Transactions of the London and Middlesex Archaeological Society,* 37: 23–124

24. Glass vessels as grave goods and grave ornament in the catacombs of Rome: some examples

Paola De Santis

Thanks to the distinctive character of Christian catacombs, we are now able to discuss the issue of grave furniture on the basis of new data. The form of the catacomb burials – *loculi* excavated in tufa, sealed with bricks or marble slabs – preserved objects fixed in the mortar which sealed the grave or were cemented into the small recesses excavated in tufa. Such funerary furniture, external to the grave, is still visible in cemeteries with intact *loculi* which escaped the systematic plundering that was carried out particularly during the seventeenth and eighteenth centuries.

The first catacomb explorers provided interesting evidence about the furniture inside the graves. In the first decade of the seventeenth century Antonio Bosio described the glass and pottery vessels that he had found in the burials examined during his reconnaissance of cemeteries on the via Appia and via Ardeatina: '*vi sono ancora trovati vasetti di vetro in diverse forme, alcuni lunghi di collo e di bocca stretta, e alcuni altri larghi e tondi come bicchieri...*' ('some small glass vessels occur as well, in different forms, some with long necks and narrow mouths, and others wide and round like beakers...'; Bosio 1632: 196–201 D).

According to Boldetti in 1720 the Christians, while depositing these '*vasi*', '*ebbero mira particolare al culto ed al contrassegno per farli conoscere a' posteri tali senza che non si prendessero la sollecitudine di doverne aprire ad uno per uno tutti i sepolcri, ma che questi rimanessero intatti... e giudicarono, anzichè collocare detti vasi entro a' sepolcri, di affiggerli fuor dei medesimi per contraddistinguerli con questo segno da quelli degli altri fedeli*' ('had a particular concern for cult, and aimed at letting posterity know that these were graves, so that future generations would not take the trouble to open them one by one, and they would remain intact ... and instead of depositing the aforementioned vessels inside, they thought it useful to affix them outside the grave in order to distinguish their graves from those of the other believers'; Boldetti 1720: 169, 180–181).

In 1877 Giovanni Battista De Rossi returned to Boldetti's idea about the position of these *ampolle* with respect to the grave: '*per lo più collocate presso il capo del defunto. Nei cimiteri cristiani quei vaselli sovente sono murati nella fronte esterna del loculo e sopra la mensa dell'arcosolio; d'ordinario presso l'angolo rispondente al capo del defunto*' ('they are generally placed near the head of the deceased person. In Christian cemeteries those small vessels are generally fixed outside, into the front wall of the *loculus* or above the corbel of the *arcosolium*, usually near the corner corresponding to the dead person's head'; De Rossi 1877: 616; De Santis 1998). These are general indications, but they remain useful pending a more systematic study of the interiors of the burial recesses.

Any interpretation should be based on the two concepts of ornament and furniture; in the catacombs, personal goods and those which were intended as an offering to the dead person coincide with the grave ornaments, as they too are placed outside the grave, sometimes with a specific decorative function. It is important to note that the glass artefacts placed outside the *loculus* are only partially visible; they are often covered with the mortar in which they are fixed, and in some cases it is only possible to examine the external surface. For this reason it is very difficult to identify glass vessel types so generic identification is sometimes proposed, mostly based on Isings' (1957) classification. Isings' catalogue, though insufficient, is referred to here as it is the most widely known. Morphological and typological analyses are essential in order to understand the role and function of glass artefacts in funerary contexts.

Two cemetery regions were chosen as suitable samples for this study because of their very good state of preservation and because they can be set against a sound and well defined chronological background. They are the lower floor of the catacomb of *Pamphilus*, along the via Salaria *vetus*, and a small gallery in the so-called 'regione delle cattedre' in the *Maius* cemetery on the via Nomentana.

The eastern area of the lower floor in the catacomb of *Pamphilus* consists of galleries, which are near to the entrance stairs, and can be dated to the first half of the fourth century (Josi 1926: 109–153). This group of galleries is typologically homogeneous: almost all *loculi* are closed by unstamped bricks, while marble slabs are rare. At present, glass objects are known from fourteen *loculi*.

Among the intact objects fixed in the mortar, glass unguent bottles are numerous. One of them was found intact, but cannot be easily identified, as it is completely covered by the mortar that fixed it to the tufa wall. Another intact unguent bottle, though only partially visible, can be ascribed to Isings form 82 a1, which was especially popular through the second and into the third century (Isings 1957: 97–98). Parts of a cylindrical unguent jar with indents were found; its form roughly corresponds to Isings form 68, a bulbous unguent jar that appeared in the first century although it survived throughout the third and fourth centuries (Isings 1957: 88–89). Two broken globular-bodied vessels lacking their necks can be considered as unguent containers of uncertain type. During the excavation of one of these galleries, an ointment vessel was recovered as a stray find. It was particularly interesting for its decoration which must signify that it was of some value (Josi 1926: 134; Salvetti 1978: 124–125).

Among the other closed forms it is possible to single out two spherical flasks; the first belongs to Isings form 103 (Josi 1926: 129) with a cylindrical neck which has a constriction at its base and becomes narrower towards the rim; this form appeared in the third century and was still popular throughout the fourth (Isings 1957: 121–122). Its long and narrow neck suggest that it may have functioned as an unguent vessel. Epigraphic evidence however attests beyond any doubt that it was used as a wine vessel; a specimen from the Museo Nazionale Romano bears the inscription *carpe atque bibe*. It is a rare form, possibly because it is a high quality artefact; one especially valuable set was engraved with views of Campanian towns (De Tommaso 1990: 112–113). The second spherical flask might be ascribed to Isings type 101 (Josi 1926: 144); its body is completely covered by the mortar that fixes it to the tufa and its cylindrical neck is bent outwards. This type appeared at the end of the third century, but became common during the fourth. It was particularly popular in the western provinces, and was used to serve wine and other liquids (Isings 1957: 119–120).

A hemispherical bowl – 12 cm in diameter- is the only intact example of an open form. It is difficult to identify as its hemispherical body is completely inserted in the recess excavated in the tufa.

Among the objects deliberately fixed in the mortar after being broken it was possible to identify the neck of a flask, placed horizontally on the tufa (possibly of Isings type 104 – Isings 1957: 122–125), three bases, probably of beakers, and one base – 8.5 cm in diameter – possibly from a plate. A goblet base of Isings type 111 also occurs, but although its form is more easily recognisable the chronology for this vessel type is disputed. According to Isings, it was manufactured from the fourth century in the

eastern empire and became especially popular through the fifth and sixth centuries, though it was apparently already present in Italy in the fourth century (Isings 1957: 139–140). More recent studies, reconsidering the chronology of the published stratigraphical contexts, have established that goblets appeared later, apparently not before the second half or the end of the fifth century (Saguì 1993: 127–129). The presence of goblet bases in fifth century catacombs may provide further chronological information although systematic analysis might show that reliable data is still lacking.

The excavation report of this cemetery area, published in 1926 by Enrico Josi, accurately enumerates all the objects found near *loculi*. However the terminology used makes it difficult to know what glass forms were present. The terms 'disco, piatto, cerchietto' (disk, dish, circle) may indicate bases, while diminutives such as 'ampollina, fialetta' (small bottle, small phial) highlight ill-defined differences in size. Nevertheless, it is clear that at the time of the excavation the number of glass finds in this cemetery area was greater than those that survive today (Josi 1926: 117–139; Felle *et al.* 1994: 131–132).

An interesting case to be noted is that of a *cubiculum* (Ib) on the lower floor of the catacomb of *Pamphilus* (Fig. 24.1): the exterior of the lower *arcosolium* was decorated with a set of more than 12 glass bowls of different sizes (diameters range from 15 to 20–21 cm) of which only traces remain today. They were fixed to the tufa by mortar (Josi 1926: 115).

The second area examined here is a small gallery dug into the southern wall of the main gallery from which the so-called 'regione delle cattedre' of the *Maius* cemetery extends; it was excavated at the end of the 1950s (Fasola 1961). Like the rest of the area, it can be dated to the first half of the fourth century thanks to an *in situ* inscription carrying a consular date of the year 364 (Fig. 24.2). Inside

Fig. 24.1 Cubiculum *Ib, catacomb of Pamphilus (from Josi 1926: fig. 35)*

Fig. 24.2 *Inscription of* Cepula *and hemispherical bowl Isings 96,* Maius *cemetery (from Fasola 1961: fig. 14)*

the gallery only nine children's *loculi* occur, three of which were provided with glass vessels.

A broken hemispherical bowl with cut rim and a wheel-incised line just under the rim can be ascribed to Isings form 96 (Isings 1957: 113–116); the form originated during the third century but became more common in the fourth when incised decoration became widespread. Another *loculus* has a hemispherical bowl of the same Isings type 96 on the right side, but with a slightly larger and rounder neck, evidence indicating a later date of production. The *loculus* also has a lamp and a bone bracelet, the latter no longer *in situ*. Finally, on the southern wall of the gallery, a *loculus* has a broken glass vessel on its left side. This was possibly an unguent jar of which only the lower part has been preserved; this object is associated with a small bronze bell (Fasola 1961: 255–256).

The fixing of intact objects, like flasks and bowls, to the mortar of the *loculus* is surely related to the rite of the *refrigerium*. According to this rite, food and drink had to be deposited into the grave on appointed days and a funeral feast had to be consumed. It was believed that a person was not nullified by death until his or her body had fallen into decay (Giuntella *et al.* 1985: 29–63; Giuntella 1990). Such a practice, inherited from pagan ritual, not only survived but long endured in Christian ritual; the use of glass furnishings is to be set against this background of beliefs and rituals which find different modes of expression. It is not possible absolutely to exclude a practical role for the glass vessels deposited near the *loculi*; they may have been filled with liquid related to the *refrigerium*. This is suggested by the flask of Isings form 101 in the cemetery of *Pamphilus* which is bent outward, possibly to make it easier to fill. Many written sources bear witness to drinking with *calices* near a dead relative's or martyr's grave. For example St Ambrose writes: *qui calices ad sepulcra martyrum deferunt, atque illic ire vesperam bibunt* (*De Elia et*

ieiunio 17, in *Patrologia Latina* 14: 719). In a famous passage from his Confessions, St Augustine described the *refrigerium* and in particular the drinking of wine, poured in a *pocillum*, near the burials (*Confessionum Libri tredecim,* VI, 2, in *Patrologia Latina* 32: 719–720; Hamman 1968: 213–215; Saxer 1980: 141–149).

Taking these pieces of evidence into account, a function evocative of a ritual seems most likely. For practical reasons like the shortage of space and light, or difficulty of access to the grave (which often became almost impossible due to the continual deepening of the galleries) funerary rites were carried out in more suitable places, such as the *cubicula* on the *sub divo* (Février 1978: 216; De Santis 1994: 48–51; Felle *et al.* 1994: 154–156).

In this regard we may note a series of inscriptions in which the written message is coupled with the symbolic power of figural representations. A lamp is depicted at the centre of an inscription in the cemetery of Callistus (ICVR, IV 9913) with a handled jug on one side and a short stemmed goblet on the other; the text reads: *Ianuaria bene refrigera et roga p/ro nos* (Fig. 24.3). On another slab in the cemetery of Domitilla (ICVR, III 6618) Cristor, the deceased woman's father, is portrayed drinking from a vessel that might be paralleled with the conical beaker of Isings form 106 (Fig. 24.4). The deceased Augurina, who is portrayed praying on a slab in a cemetery along the via Latina (ICVR VI 15867), seems to be holding the same kind of beaker (Fig. 24.5). All this bears witness to the importance of the rite of the *refrigerium* and to the fact that it was thought necessary to give it concrete form by means of either objects or images that could evoke its meaning. In the mentality of the period, funerary feasts offered the opportunity to express piety by means of collective rites when public and private funerary feasts marked the stages of social and family life, reproducing the characteristics of the living society in the grave context (Février 1978: 251–255, 261–263; Février 1977: 38–45).

Fig. 24.3 *Inscription, Callistus cemetery (ICVR, IV 9913)*

Fig. 24.4 *Inscription, Domitilla cemetery (ICVR, III 6618)*

Fig. 24.5 *Inscription, via Latina cemetery (ICUR, VI 15867)*

Unguent vessels might be related to the ritual of sprinkling perfumes near and inside the graves. The holes that were often made in the coverings or sealings of *loculi* or *arcosolia* apparently bear witness to this practice (Ferrua 1940: 13–14; Marrou 1968: 199; Saxer 1980: 53–55). A

famous poem by Prudentius offers remarkable evidence in this regard; it reads: *...et frigida saxa/ liquido spargemur odore* (*Cathemerinon X*, vv. 169–172, in *Patrologia Latina* 59: 888). It was thought to bring physical relief to the deceased person. Before being buried, people were washed and rubbed with scented ointments. It was a popular pagan funerary custom to burn ointments and perfumes at the moment of inhumation and survived in the Christian era although to a lesser extent (Philpott 1991: 118). Paulinus of Nola describes St Felix's tomb and the ritual of depositing perfumes, contained in '*vascula*', into the grave (*Poemata XXI*, vv. 590–615, in *Patrologia Latina* 61: 594–595: *Ista superficies tabulae gemino patet/ ore praebens infuso subiecta foramina nardi/ [...] haec subito infusos solito sibi more liquores vascula de tumulo terra subeunte biberunt,/ quique loco dederant nardum, exhaurire parantes,/ ut sibi iam ferrent*).

Ointment and perfume manufacture in Italy apparently ceased in the Severan period; at the end of the second century the centre of ointment manufacturing moved gradually from the core to the periphery of the empire, to

Syria, Egypt and the Rhineland cities. New types of unguent vessels were created within the established model for this vessel type. For example, the types attributed to Isings form 101 were first century unguent vessels in new versions and sizes. None of the new forms that appeared in Italy through the third century were apparently used as unguent vessels (De Tommaso 1990: 111–113). On the basis of recent research, it can be said that the number of unguent vessels occurring as grave furniture tends to decrease in comparison with that of either the open forms for the table or flasks. It is difficult to identify the reasons for this decline. It may have been the result of a production shortage or of a change in funerary custom with a decline in the burning of scents (Stiaffini 1990: 243–244; Stiaffini 1993: 179; Stiaffini 1995: 208). In the fourth century John Chrysostom condemned the excesses in funerary rites; in particular he stated that dressing up the dead person and strewing his or her body with perfumes could not prevent it from eventually decaying (Homilia LXXXV in Joannem, 5 in Patrologia Graeca 59: 465–468; Mathieu 1987: 317).

The available data from the areas of the Pamphilus and Maius cemeteries discussed here are insufficient to determine the relation between the use of unguent vessels and funerary rites. However, it should be noted that the fourth century marked a period of transition as far as both the circulation of unguent vessels and Christian funerary custom are concerned.

A further suggestion may be made with regard to the hemispherical bowls in the Maius cemetery. They may be linked to the refrigerium as discussed, but they may also have functioned as lamps. Thus, their practical function was coupled with the symbolic meaning of grave offerings and devotion to the deceased (De Santis 1994: 36–38, 46; Felle et al. 1994: 155).

To understand the significance of the glass vessels deliberately fixed into the mortar when already broken, it is important to consider the value of glass artefacts in Late Antiquity. From the beginning of the fourth century glass vessels began to be classed as prestige goods. A decrease can be noticed in the number of the forms produced, which were now basically intended as table wares. In Italy vitrarii certainly continued to work, as is proved by flasks of Isings form 103 which show views of Campanian towns, the Rome 'diatreti' vases, the rich series of incised plates and bowls which can be attributed to Rome, and the gold leaf glasses of Aquileia and Ravenna. However this is high value production, directed at high status groups (De Tommaso 1986: 115–116).

In this regard, a significant example may be the cubiculum in the cemetery of Pamphilus, of which the wall was decorated with twelve glass bowls. It displays the decorative intent of a wealthy family, who could afford a more monumental grave rather than a simple loculus. Such clients could choose to furnish and decorate their cubiculum with a group of artefacts, remarkable for both their quantity and quality (expressed through the large diameter of the bowls).

In antiquity a piece of broken glass was considered a catalyst in the melting process because it remelts at a lower temperature, hastening the melting of the mixture with which it comes into contact (Taborelli 1980: 144 note 21). For this reason there was a real trade in fragments of glass which may also be inferred from first century AD literary sources (Martial, De spectaculis liber, I, XLI, vv. 3–5, Walter C.A. Ker, M.A. ed., Harvard University Press 1968: 52–54: hoc quod transtiberinus ambulator,/ qui pallentia sulphurata fractis/ permutat vitreis. Juvenal, Saturarum I, V, 48, J.E.B. Mayor ed., Hildesheim 1966: 22: et rupto poscentem sulphura vitro. Statius, Silvae I, VI, 73–74 J.H.Mozley M.A. ed., Harvard University Press 1967: 68 mentions people who, during the emperor's party, comminutis/ permutant vitreis gregale sulphur). Evidence of collecting and selling broken glass is most clearly offered by the Serçe Limani wreck. The cargo of the ship, which was wrecked around 1025, consisted of about three tons of pieces of broken glass (Saguì 1993: 117; Price-Cool 1991: 23–24; Sternini 1995: 134). Glass fragments therefore had a commercial value, though very low (Sternini 1989: 59–64; Sternini 1995: 44).

Together these elements may contribute to an understanding of the significance of the glass fragment as both grave ornament and decoration, a status symbol based on the intrinsic value of glass. In the extreme poverty of the burial, affixing a piece of broken glass (or other kinds of material) may have expressed the will to free the grave from anonymity; the act of decorating becomes an important moment in the relationship with the dead person, a way to communicate beyond immediate temporal boundaries and to highlight the inviolability of the grave.

Bibliography

Boldetti, M. 1720. Osservazioni sopra i cimiteri de' santi martiri ed antichi cristiani di Roma. Rome.

Bosio, A. 1632. Roma sotterranea. Rome.

De Rossi, G.B. 1877. Roma sotterranea III. Rome.

De Santis, P. 1994. Elementi di corredo nei sepolcri delle catacombe romane: l'esempio della regione di Leone e della galleria Bb nella catacomba di Commodilla. Vetera Christianorum, 31: 23–51.

De Santis, P. 1998. La teoria dei 'segni mnemonici' negli scritti di G.B. de Rossi. Atti XIII Congresso Internazionale di Archeologia Cristiana (Split-Poreč 25.9.–1.10.1994), 339–350. Vatican City – Split.

De Tommaso, G. 1986. Ipotesi sulla produzione di vasellame vitreo in Italia tra III e IV secolo. Opus, 5: 111–125.

De Tommaso, G. 1990. Ampullae vitreae. Contenitori in vetro di unguenti e sostanze aromatiche dell'Italia romana (I sec. a.C.– III sec. d.C.). Rome.

Fasola, U.M. 1961. La regione delle cattedre nel cimitero maggiore. Rivista di Archeologia Cristiana, 37: 237–267.

Felle, A., Del Moro, M.P. and Nuzzo, D. 1994. Elementi di 'corredo-arredo' delle tombe del cimitero di S.Ippolito sulla via Tiburtina. Rivista di Archeologia Cristiana, 70: 89–158.

Ferrua, A. 1940. Sopra un'iscrizione del Museo Lateranese. Epigraphica, 17: 7–20.

Février, P.A. 1977. A propos du repas funéraire: culte et sociabilité. Cahiers Archéologiques, 26: 29–45.

Février, P.A. 1978. Le culte des morts dans les communautés chrétiennes durant le IIIe siècle. In *Atti del IX Congresso Internazionale di Archeologia Cristiana (Roma 21–27 settembre 1975)*: 211–274. Rome.

Giuntella, A.M. 1990. Sepoltura e rito. Consuetudini e innovazioni. In *Le sepolture in Sardegna dal IV al VII secolo*, Atti del IV Convegno su *L'Archeologia romana e altomedievale nell' Oristanese* (Cuglieri, 27–28 giugno 1987), 215–229. Oristano.

Giuntella, A.M., Borghetti, G. and Stiaffini, D. 1985. Mensae e riti funerari in Sardegna. La testimonianza di Cornus. In *Mediterraneo tardoantico e medievale. Scavi e ricerche 1.* Martina Franca.

Hamman, A. 1968. *Vie liturgique et vie sociale.* Paris.

ICVR – *Inscriptiones Christianae Urbis Romae septimo saeculo antiquiores. Nova Series* (eds. A. Silvagni, A. Ferrua, D. Mazzoleni, C. Carletti). Vols. I–X, Rome – Vatican City, 1922–1992.

Isings, C. 1957. *Roman Glass from Dated Finds.* Archaeologia Traiectina, II. Groningen-Djakarta.

Josi, E. 1924. Il cimitero di Panfilo I. *Rivista di Archeologia Cristiana*, 1: 15–119.

Josi, E. 1926. Il cimitero di Panfilo II. *Rivista di Archeologia Cristiana*, 2: 51–211.

Mathieu, J.M. 1987. Horreur du cadavre et philosophie dans le mond romain. Le cas de la patristique grecque du IVe siècle. In *La mort, les morts et l'au-delà* (ed. F. Hinard). Actes du colloque de Caen (Caen 20–22 novembre 1985): 311–320. Caen.

Marrou, H.I. 1968. Survivance païennes dans les rites funéraires des donatistes, in *Hommages à J. Bidez et Fr. Cumont*: 193–203. Brussels.

Philpott, R. 1991. *Burial practices in Roman Britain. A survey of grave treatment and furnishing A.D. 43–410.* Oxford.

Price J. and Cool, H.E.M. 1991. The evidence for the production of glass in Roman Britain. In *Ateliers de verriers de l'antiquité à la période préindustrielle* (eds. D. Foy and G. Sennequier). Association Française pour l'Archéologie du Verre, Actes des 4èmes rencontres (Rouen 1989): 23–30. Rouen.

Saguì, L. 1993. Produzioni vetrarie a Roma tra tardo-antico e alto medioevo. In *La storia economica di Roma nell'alto medioevo* (ed. L. Paroli): 113–136. Florence.

Salvetti, C. 1978. Il catalogo degli oggetti minuti conservati presso la Pontificia Commissione di Archeologia Sacra. *Rivista di Archeologia Cristiana*, 44: 103–130.

Saxer, V. 1980, *Morts, martyrs, reliques en Afrique chrétienne aux prémiers siècles.* Paris.

Sternini, M. 1989. *Una manifattura vetraria di V secolo a Roma.* Florence.

Sternini, M. 1995. *La fenice di sabbia. Storia e tecnologia del vetro antico.* Bari.

Stiaffini, D. 1990. La suppellettile vitrea nelle aree cimiteriali in Sardegna: IV-VII sec.. In *Le sepolture in Sardegna dal IV al VII secolo*, Atti del IV Convegno su *L'Archeologia romana e altomedievale nell'Oristanese* (Cuglieri, 27–28 giugno 1987): 243–256. Oristano.

Stiaffini, D. 1993. The Presence of Glass in Funerary Contexts in Italy (4th–7th Centuries). In *Annales du 12 Congrès de l'Associatione Internationale pour l'Histoire du Verre* (Wien 26–31 août 1991): 177–185. Amsterdam.

Stiaffini, D. 1995. La suppellettile in vetro. In *Ad mensam. Manufatti d'uso da contesti archeologici fra tarda antichità e medioevo* (ed. S.Lusuardi Siena): 189–228. Udine.

Taborelli, L. 1980, Elementi per l'individuazione di una officina vetraria e della sua produzione a Sentinum. *Archeologia Classica*, 32: 144–169.

25. Clothing in burial practice in Italy in the early Christian period[1]

Rossana Martorelli

'*Si enim, quia vestior (quoniam ille non potuit) ea veste quam fratri texueras, te aliquid consolatur; quanto debes amplius et certius consolari, quia cui fuerat praeparata, tunc incorruptibili indumento nullo egens, incorruptione, atque immortalitate vestietur*'.

So St Augustine writes to Sapida, in a letter written after 395, following her brother's death. If Augustine, bishop of Hippo, would like to wear the clothes that Sapida made for her brother, it was because Sapida's brother had left this world and would not need material possessions: his body would be clothed only by immortality.

At the beginning of the fifth century, theologians formulated the idea that the human body would rise again at the end of the world, as an angel and not as a human being (Janssens 1981: 272–273). According to this view material goods, clothing or ornaments in the afterlife were not required. 'What did you bring with you, when you were born? You cannot take anything with you when you die. Rich and poor men come into the world naked and in the same way they will pass away', preached St Augustine. He resumed the theme elsewhere: 'The rich are like the poor. The earth received both of them naked (at birth); death awaits them in the same way ... Their clothes are different, but their skin is the same. Even if a dead person is buried with fragrances he will rot, perhaps later, but he will rot all the same'. St Jerome was in agreement.

From the Early Christian period the Church Fathers fought against the enjoyment of wealth and bodily ornament. Tertullian blamed women for adorning themselves with jewels or using make up, as beauty lay on the inside. According to the *Constitutiones Apostolicae*, a sixth century liturgical text, the physical body was not important. At the same time St Ambrose, bishop of Milan, wrote in a letter: 'The most important goods are feelings, neither gold nor silver. These latter will be lost, because they remain in the world'.

So the Church taught that material goods are useful only in this world and that the rich should help the poor (Mara 1980: 11–25). In their burial practices early Christians should thus follow the example of Jesus Christ,

buried in a shroud by Joseph of Arimathaea. We may cite examples where this practice of burial in a shroud is followed or recommended. In the fourth century, the historian Eusebius of Caesarea praised the Christians of Alexandria, who – even when in danger from epidemic-were concerned that burial should be conducted properly and covered the bodies of the dead in linen grave clothes. In the Western Empire the poet Prudentius also recalled the white shroud whilst a few years later St Jerome wrote that the clergy had '*officium linteo cadaver obvolvere*', the duty of burying the dead in linen.

Records of the many sixteenth and seventeenth centuries explorations and excavations of the catacombs around the city of Rome, principally searching for martyrs' tombs, noted the frequent presence of items of clothing. In the early eighteenth century, M. A. Boldetti noted the tombs of martyrs everywhere and thought that the clothes were '*le bende che bendavano i martiri al momento del martirio*', i.e. those in which the martyrs were clad at the moment of their martyrdom (Boldetti 1720: 290, 293). It is more likely that these 'bende' were the remains of shrouds, attested in many of the Roman catacombs explored from the eighteenth century onwards (Leclercq 1923: 2707).

However a number of pieces of evidence suggests that dead were sometimes buried in more than a modest shroud. In the same antiquarian reports we also read of fine clothes interwoven with golden and silver thread, '*panni bianchi o colorati, vestimenti di varie sorti, corpi coi loro vestimenti tessuti a oro, e sebbene il panno era già consumato dal tempo, nondimeno erano rimaste ai suoi luoghi le strisce dell'oro medesimo, strisce di stoffe intessute d'oro pertinenti anche alle calze*'. In the latter case they reached so far because they were over the legs of a dead child. Boldetti's account suggests that these may not have been parts of shrouds but the remains of fine clothes worn when the deceased was alive (Boldetti 1720: 31, 287, 299, 300–303).

Other accounts are also suggestive. When Pope Paschalis I moved the body of St Caecilia in the ninth century, from the via Appia to the church of St Caecilia

Fig. 25.1

Fig. 25.2

Fig. 25.3

Fig. 25.4

Fig. 25.5

Figs. 25.1–25.5: 1. Rome. Hypogeum on the via Dino Compagni (Cubiculum O) (Photo: Pontificia Commissione di Archeologia Sacra). 2. Rome. Catacomb of Sts Peter and Marcellinus (Photo: Pontificia Commissione di Archeologia Sacra). 3. Rome. Catacomb of Sts Peter and Marcellinus (Photo: Pontificia Commissione di Archeologia Sacra). 4. Rome. Catacomb of Sts Peter and Marcellinus (Photo: Pontificia Commissione di Archeologia Sacra). 5. Rome. Hypogeum on the via Dino Compagni (Cubiculum O) (Photo: Pontificia Commissione di Archeologia Sacra)

Fig. 25.7

Fig. 25.6

Fig. 25.6–25.8: 6. Rome. Catacomb on the via Anapo (Photo: Pontificia Commissione di Archeologia Sacra). 7. Naples. Catacomb of St Gennarus. Cubiculum of Teotecnus (Photo: Pontificia Commissione di Archeologia Sacra). 8. Monza. Cathedral Treasury. Diptych of Stilicho and Severa (Milano tardoromana 1990)

Fig. 25.8

in Rome, he saw 'in cymiterio Praetextati, situm foris portam Appiam, aureis vestitum indumentis', the body clad in golden clothing (*Liber Pontificalis* II: 55–56; Boldetti 1720: 300–303). Again in 1599 Cardinal Sfondrati recognised the bones of the same martyr and near the body also noted blood-stained cloth and silk coverings with gold thread, '*madida sanguine vela et serica filo aureo obduata quae visebantur, iam vetustate solutae vestis illis aurotextae, cuius idem Paschalis meminit*' (Josi 1963: 1077).

Fifty years ago golden material, probably cloth was also found in tomb 'beta' in the Vatican cemetery beneath St Peter's, nearest to the tomb of St Peter and dated to the beginning of the fourth century (Apollonj Ghetti *et al* 1951: 111). We have evidence of similar practices elsewhere, for instance from Milan (excavations not yet fully published, see Milano tardoromana 1990: 126) and Aosta (Perinetti 1988: 84; 1990: 380–381) as well as more

widely in Italy (Milano tardoromana 1990: 331–332).

So recent archaeological evidence suggests a very different pattern to that traditionally assumed (Bosio 1632: 19; de Rossi 1864: 169, 334, 383; 1872: 66; Lanciani 1917: 24). We should not be put off by the relative scarcity of such archaeological finds that results from a variety of factors, especially environmental. In western Europe clothing is not generally preserved in damp soil conditions, in contrast to the better preservation of larger numbers of finds in Syria, Egypt and Middle East (e.g. Volbach 1942, Pl. I and III). So few pieces of cloth survive on or near the bones of the dead or with the objects in tombs that archaeologists are not generally able to identify clothing, although it may leave other evidence in the ground by chemical reaction. However earlier explorers did not understand such traces so much potentially useful information has probably been lost.

An important indication of the use of clothing in burial

comes from the discovery inside tombs of metal objects, for example belt and shoe buckles, brooches and iron hobnails (e.g. Giuntella *et al.* 1991: 283). However although in early medieval cemeteries, especially those related to Germanic groups, the proliferation of such finds provide information about the development of clothing, we generally lack comparable information from the Early Christian period.

We must turn to more general evidence for the clothes in which the dead may have been clad. Our evidence for the general dress of the period includes Diocletian's Price Edict (Giacchero 1974: 156–158; 174–206), the *Codex Theodosianus* (l. XIV, tit. 10,1, G. Haenel, Bonn 1842: 1400–1401) and catacomb frescoes of the third to the fifth century. Men seem to have worn a single tunic, short or full length, like the Roman 'toga', in linen, wool or cotton, sometimes silk, white or light yellow, decorated with two long stripes (*clavi*), circles (*orbiculi*), or embroidery (Fig. 25.1). Shepherds, fisherman, craftsmen and *fossores* (Fig. 25.2), whose work required freedom of movement, wore sleeveless tunics with a tied belt which lacked a buckle. Often over these tunics men wore either a *pallium*, a cloak that covered one shoulder and left the other free – like philosophers – or a short cloak with a hole for the head (*paenula*) (Fig. 25.3), or long cloak (*casula*), closed at the chin or at one of the shoulders (Fig. 25.4). Shoes were of leather, with a wooden sole – only the *campagi* had small iron or bronze nails (Levi Pisetzki 1964: 24–40). Soldiers wore short tunics, fastened with a belt with a metal buckle and a heavy cloak fastened by a metal *fibula* to protect against poor weather (Fig. 25.5) (Levi Pisetzki 1964: 29).

Women wore a white or yellowish *tunica intima*, large and with narrow sleeves, similar to those worn by men. Their equivalent to the man's *pallium* was the *palla*, but this covered the head like a veil. Instead of or together with this they also wore the *dalmatica*, a red or yellow coloured robe (*clavata*), with large sleeves, sometimes with a fine decoration (Fig. 25.6) (Levi Pisetzki 1964: 40–44).

Pope Stephen I in the mid third century decreed that clergy should not use their ordinary daily clothes during liturgical services (Mansi 1960: 887); but throughout the early Christian period priests wore the same clothes: tunic, *pallium* and *casula* (Levi Pisetzki 1964: 47–49). From the third to the fifth century typical clothing seem not to have differed substantially from that of the earlier period although the *pallium* came to be used by everyone, not only philosophers (Garcia Jurado 1996: *passim*).

The everyday clothing of Early Christians was simple, usually without metal decorations. However it is evident that they shared common tastes for more lavish clothing, even if the Church invited them to be modest. For example an image from the so-called *cubiculum* of Teotecnus and Proculus in the catacomb of St Gennarus in Naples provides very good evidence for fifth-century clothing. According to a painted inscription it shows Teotecnus with his wife Hilaritas and daughter Nonnosa. The women wear rich red coloured *tunicae*, with golden embroidery and with a belt closed by a round metal jewelled buckle (Fig. 25.7). This is a high status family and the picture pays particular attention to the details of their bodies and clothes (Fasola 1974: 96; 1982: 770).

We also have to consider developments in fashion when Germanic groups arrived in Italy at the end of the fourth century, in particular on the incorporation of soldiers of Germanic origin into the late Roman army (Milano tardoromana 1990: 78; Ducci and Ciampoltrini 1991: 54–57). Their clothing styles came to be generally adopted; men and women started to wear clothes with belts and metal buckles, brooches, and buckled shoes (Fig. 25.8) (Gelichi 1990: 134–137; I Goti 1994: 170–177, 194–202; Maioli 1988; Martorelli in press).

In conclusion, both literary sources and archaeological evidence suggest that in later Roman burial practice the dead were buried with the clothes that they wore when alive (Février 1987: 895). This practice, common after the fifth century, also seems to have been employed in an earlier period in a Christian context alongside the use of a simple shroud. Differences in the mode of burial probably depended on the social and economic status of the relatives of the dead, as Augustine recognised.

The following examples may demonstrate this connection between social status and early Christian mortuary ritual. St Iusta, a Roman noble woman, collected the body of the martyr Restitutus and having wrapped him in '*panni di lino*' buried him in a cemetery on the via Nomentana (Boldetti 1720: 51; Amore 1968: 137). During the sixteenth century building of St Peter's a marble sarcophagus was found in the tomb of St Petronilla containing bones and veils for the head and face. From the many objects and a chest bearing a name in Latin its discoverers thought that it was the tomb of Maria, wife of Emperor Honorius, who died at the beginning of the fifth century. These objects were sold to raise money to build the new church (Bosio 1632: 43). A few years later the body of Pope Leo I, buried under the porch in the Constantinian basilica of St. Peter, was brought within the church. He was still in his papal dress, *pianeta, casula, pallium*, and with a golden *fibula* (AA.SS. *Aprilis* II, Venezia 1738, p. 22; Bosio 1632: 35; Zannoni 1966: 1273–1275). We might have expected a Pope to have been buried in ordinary clothes, although according to the *Liber Pontificalis*, in the mid third century Pope Eutichianus ordered that each martyr should be buried with his own *dalmatica* as an important witness to Christianity (*Liber Pontificalis* I: 159; Boldetti 1720: 41).

The evidence assembled here therefore throws doubt on the hypothesis that early Christians were buried without ornament (Rebillard 1994: 68–69; Sannazaro 1990: 50). Literary sources and archaeological evidence show that the liking for material possessions and beautiful things yet persisted into the afterlife.

Notes

1. Please note that the early Christian period in the context of this article designates the third century to fifth century AD. Translations from the Church Fathers are the author's own.

2. Augustine, *Epistulae*, CCLXIII,4 = *Nuova Biblioteca Agostiniana*, XXIII (ed. L. Carrozzi, Rome 1974: 924–925).

3. Augustine, *De cura pro mortuis gerenda ad Paulinum episcopum*, II,4 = *Corpus scriptorum ecclesiasticorum latinorum*, XLI (ed. I. Zycha, Prague / Vienna / Leipzig 1900: 625); Augustine, *Epistulae*, CXLVIII, 5,16–17 = *Nuova Biblioteca Agostiniana*, XXII (ed. L. Carrozzi, Rome 1971: 450-455)

4. Tertullian, *De resurrectione mortuorum*, IV; XXVII, 3; XLII, 13 = *Corpus Christianorum*, II (ed. A. Gerlo, Turnhout 1954: 925–926; 956; 978); Lactantius, *Institutiones Divinae*, VII,6,1 = *Corpus scriptorum ecclesiasticorum latinorum*, XIX (ed. S.Brandt, Prague / Vienna / Leipzig, 1890: 604).

5. Augustine *Sermones*, CXXIII,5 = *Nuova Biblioteca Agostiniana*, XXXI,1 (ed. M. Recchia, Rome 1990: 68–69); Augustine *Sermones*, CLXXVII,7 = *Nuova Biblioteca Agostiniana*, XXXI,2 (ed. M. Recchia, Rome 1990: 886-889); Jerome, *Vita S.Pauli*, 17 = *Patrologia Latina*, 23 (ed. J. Migne, Paris 1845: 28).

6. Tertullian, *De cultu feminarum* (ed. S. Isetta = *Biblioteca Patristica*, 6, Florence 1986: 111); *Constitutiones Apostolicae*, I,3,8 = *Sources Chrétiennes*, 320 (ed. M. Metzger, Paris 1985: 113); Ambrose, *Epistulae*, IX,64,7 = *Biblioteca Ambrosiana*, 20 (ed. G. Banterle, Rome-Milan 1988: 177–179).

7. Matthew XXVII,59; Mark XV,46; Luke XXIII,53; John XIX,40.

8. Eusebius, *Historia Ecclesiastica*, VII,22,9 = *Sources Chrétiennes*, 41 (ed. G. Bardy, Paris 1955: 199); Prudentius, *Cathemerinon*, X,49-52 = *Corpus Christianorum*, CXXVI (ed. P. Cunningham, Turnhout 1966: 55); Jerome, *Epistulae*, I,12 = *Corpus scriptorum ecclesiasticorum latinorum*, 54 (ed. I. Hilberg, Prague / Vienna / Leipzig 1910: 7).

9. 'white and coloured cloths, clothes of various types, bodies of which the clothing was woven with gold thread, and even if the cloth had been consumed by time, nevertheless the stripes of gold itself remained in place, stripes of cloth woven with gold which reached down even to their shoes.'

10. Augustine, *Ennarationes in psalmos*, XXXIII, 25 = *Nuova Biblioteca Agostiniana*, XXV (ed. A. Corticelli, Rome 1947: 664–667)

Bibliography

Amore, A. 1968. Restituto. *Bibliotheca Sanctorum*, XI: 135–138

Apollonj Ghetti, B. M. *et alii* 1951. *Esplorazioni sotto la confessione di San Pietro in Vaticano*. Vatican City: Tipografia Poliglotta Vaticana

Boldetti, A. M. 1720. *Osservazione sopra i cimiteri de' santi martiri cristiani di Roma*. Rome: Stamperia Vaticana

Bosio, A. 1632. *Roma Sotterranea*. Rome: Stamperia Vaticana

de Rossi, G. B. 1864. *Roma Sotterranea*. I. Rome: Cromo-Litografia Pontificia

de Rossi, G. B. 1872. Le cripte storiche del cimitero. *Bollettino di Archeologia Cristiana*, 2nd Ser. III: 45–80

Ducci, S. Ciampoltrini, G. 1991. Capraia (Livorno). *Bollettino di Archeologia*, 7: 53–59

Fasola, U. M. 1974. *Le catacombe di S.Gennaro a Capodimonte*. Rome: Editalia

Fasola, U. M. 1982. Le raffigurazioni dei defunti e le scene bibliche negli affreschi delle catacombe di S. Gennaro. In *Parola e Spirito. Studi in onore di Settimo Cipriani*, 736–776. Brescia: Paideia

Février, P. A. 1987. La mort chrétienne. In *'Segni e riti nella chiesa altomedievale occidentale'. XXXIII Settimana di studio del Centro Italiano di Studi sull'Alto Medioevo (Spoleto, 11–17 aprile 1985)*, 881–942. Spoleto: Centro Italiano di Studi sull'Alto Medioevo di Spoleto

Garcia Jurado, F. 1996. La revolución indumentaria de la antigüedad tardìa. Su reflejo en la lengua latina. *Revue des Etudes Augustiniennes*, 42: 97–109

Gelichi, S. 1990. Imola (Bologna). Località Villa Clelia. *Bollettino di Archeologia*, 5–6: 134–137

Giacchero, M. 1974. *Edictum Diocletiani et Collegarum de pretiis rerum venalium*. Genoa: Istituto di Storia Antica e Scienze Ausiliarie

Giuntella, A. M. *et alii* 1991. Recenti indagini nella catacomba di Castelvecchio Subequo (AQ). *Rivista di Archeologia Cristiana*, LXVII: 249–321

I Goti, 1994. *I Goti. Catalogo della Mostra (Milano, Palazzo Reale, 28 gennaio-8 maggio 1994)*. Milan: Electa

Janssens, J. 1981. *Vita e morte del cristiano negli epitaffi di Roma anteriori al sec. VII*. Rome: Università Gregoriana

Josi, E. 1963. Cecilia. *Bibliotheca Sanctorum*, III: 1064–1081

Lanciani, R. 1917. Delle scoperte fatte nel 1838 e 1850 presso il sepolcro di Paolo Apostolo. *Nuovo Bullettino di Archeologia cristiana*, XXIII: 7–27

Leclercq, H. 1923. Funerailles. *Dictionnaire d'Archéologie et de Liturgie*, V, 2: 2705–2715

Levi Pisetzki, R. 1964. *Storia del costume in Italia*. Rome: Istituto Editoriale Italiano

Maioli, M. G. 1988. Caratteristiche e problematiche delle necropoli di epoca tarda a Ravenna e in Romagna. *Corsi di cultura sull'arte ravennate e bizantina*, XXXV: 315–350

Mansi, I. D 1960. *Sacrorum Conciliorum Nova et Amplissima Collectio*, I, Paris 1901; repr. Graz: Akademische Druck-Verlagsanstalt

Mara, M. G. 1980. Ricchezza e povertà nel cristianesimo primitivo. *Studi Patristici*, 1. Rome: Città Nuova editrice

Martorelli, R. in press. Aspetti di storia del costume in Europa dall'età giustinianea al VII secolo. *Atti del XIII Congresso Internazionale di Archeologia Cristiana (Split-Poreč, settembre 1994)*

Milano tardoromana, 1990. *'Milano capitale dell'impero romano'. Mostra (Milano – Palazzo Reale, 24 gennaio – 22 aprile 1990)*. Milan: Silvana Editoriale

Perinetti, R. 1988. Le necropoli e le tombe tardo-antiche di Augusta Praetoria. *Rivista di Studi Liguri*, LIV: 61–84

Perinetti, R. 1990. Le sepolture nella chiesa di San Lorenzo ad Aosta. In *'Le sepolture in Sardegna dal IV al VII secolo'. Atti del IV Convegno sull'archeologia tardoromana e medievale (Cuglieri, 27–28 giugno 1987)* = *Mediterraneo tardoantico e medievale. Scavi e ricerche*, 8, 881–942. Oristano: Editrice S'Alvure

Rebillard, E. 1994. In hora mortis. Evolution de la pastorale chrétienne de la mort aux IVe et Ve siècle dans l'occident latin. *Bibliothèque de l'école Française de Rome*, 283. Rome: Ecole Française de Rome

Sannazaro, M. 1990. *La cristianizzazione delle aree rurali della Lombardia (IV-VI secolo)*. Milan: Pubblicazioni dell'ISU. Università Cattolica

Volbach, W. F. 1942. *Catalogo del Museo Sacro della Biblioteca Apostolica Vaticana. I tessuti*. III,1. Vatican City: Biblioteca Apostolica Vaticana

Zannoni, G. 1966. Leone I. *Bibliotheca Sanctorum*, VII: 1232–1278

26. Amulet and grave in late antiquity: some examples from Roman cemeteries

Donatella Nuzzo

The presence of superstition and magical practices in Late Antiquity is widely attested alongside the spread of Christianity: several documents record the condemnation of such superstitions by both the imperial authorities and the Church (Barb 1963; Engemann 1975; Aune 1980). The emperor Constantine II repressed the use of amulets and condemned any person suspected of attempting communication with the dead (*Amm. Marc.* XIX, XII, 14) whilst under Valentinian I, the practice of magic became a capital offence (*Cod. Theod.* IX, XVII, 7). The Fathers of the Church were firmly opposed to the use of amulets and magical rites: their words were applied in specific decisions of the Church Councils. John Chrysostom condemned the use of amulets by women (*In epist. ad Colossenses*, III, VIII, 5 = PG, LXII 357–360); Augustine warned the Christians of superstitious practices (*In Io. evang. tr.*, VII, 6 = CChr. Series Latina, XXXVI 69–71). In the fourth century, Canon 36 of the Council of Laodikeia forbade ecclesiastics from practising magic or sorcery or making amulets; Canon 35 of the same Council tried to curtail the cult of angels, which seemed dangerously close to the practice of magic (Hefele and Leclercq 1973²: 1017–1019; cf. Ferrua 1947). As Manselli pointed out however, '*antimagico nella sua essenza il cristianesimo aveva, tuttavia, in sé un aspetto che apriva la porta alla magia, la presenza cioè e di angeli e di diavoli*'. Rome, as centre of the Empire and meeting-point of different cultures, was the place in which philosophical doctrines, religious conceptions and magical practices converged to give rise to syncretisms which spread from Rome over the Empire (Manselli 1976: 298).

The connection between superstition and burial practices is clearly documented by a funerary inscription, preserved in Rome, used to close a tomb in the year 398: *hic con<s>iste deus, hic [—]/ ne Bacus inqu<u>s temptet T[—] / depositus Sabin[—] / XVIII kal(endas d[ecembres] / d(omino) n(ostro) Honor[io IIII] et Fl(avio) Eutych[iano cons(ulibu)s]* (Ferrua 1940: 19–20). The text of the inscription is an invocation to God to defend the dead and his tomb from the dangers of the evil spirit *Bacus*. This is clear evidence of a belief in evil spirits and of the possibility that they could be of danger to the dead and their tombs. In defence of the tomb a magical element is used. This is added to or substituted for the provisions of Roman law, issued for the same purpose, to protect the *loci religiosi*. The inscription often records the extent of the area reserved for the burial, the names of the lawful owners and of the heirs, and the penalties for the violation of the tomb (De Visscher 1963: 103–127; 155–156). The funerary inscription could also accomplish a protective function, as demonstrated by other inscriptions in the Roman catacombs. The monogram composed of the letters *E, F, L* with the letter *P* (Fig. 26.1.1) – *p(alma) e(t) l(aurus)* – had a generic auspicious significance as witnessed by its frequent association with symbols connected to the Games. The same monogram is found in cemeteries after *c.* 350 both on stone inscriptions and engraved in the mortar sealing *loculi* (see for example *ICUR*, I 1426; VII 19931). In these funerary contexts it seems to have assumed value as an amulet, as recently pointed out (Carletti 1998).

On the mortar of a *loculus* in the catacomb of Sts Marco and Marcelliano on the Via Appia is engraved the name Ιαω, with letters *c.* 2.5 cm high (*ICUR*, IV 12090. Fig. 26.1.2). The name Ιαω also appears on some magical objects and amulets, particularly on requests for protection. On the reverse of some amulets, dating to the fourth century, is written the invocation Ιαω Σαβαωθ (Makhouly 1938, n. 9, 11; Bonner 1950: 302–305, figs. 298–300; 309–311). This name was believed to have had the power to drive away demons (Bonner 1950: 134–135; see also the gem-amulet found in a grave in the catacomb of St Gennarus in Naples: Miranda 1991) and thus had a prophylactic value in the funerary context: the magic name being engraved to protect the tomb.

In the lime sealing of a *loculus* in the catacomb of Commodilla is engraved a Greek cross with small circles at the extremities (*ICUR*, III 8713b. Fig. 26.1.3. See also Bagatti 1964–65: 122–123). Very similar signs (six-pointed stars with a small circle at the end of each arm) are engraved on two marble plates that closed two tombs of the catacombs of Ciriaca (*ICUR*, VII 19893b. Fig.

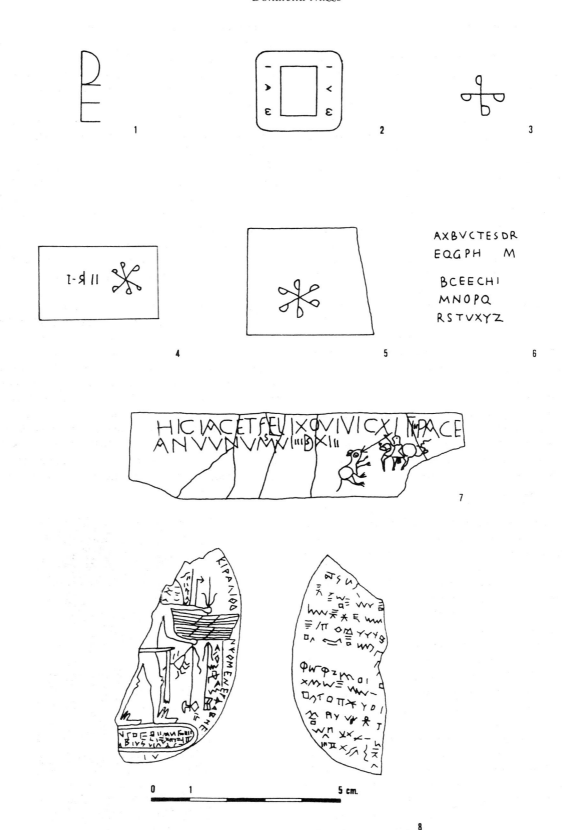

Fig. 26.1 1. P(alma) et l(aurus) *monogram (from Carletti 1998., type A); 2. ICUR, IV 12090; 3. ICUR, III 8713b; 4. ICUR,* VII 19839b; 5. ICUR, VII 20332b; 6. ICUR, VIII 23055c; 7. ICUR, II 6190; 8. oval plate of lapis-lazuli from the catacomb of St Hippolytus.

26.1.4) and St Hippolytus (*ICUR,* VII 20332b. Fig. 26.1.5) on the Via Tiburtina in Rome. They are the so-called 'ring signs', often used in the magical papyri and on the gem-amulets. To these signs was attributed the power to protect the bearer of the amulet (Bonner 1950: 194–196); in Late Antiquity their diffusion was very broad. They are found on the reverse of so-called 'Solomon the Rider' medals (see for example Bonner 1950: 304, fig. 306; 307, fig. 324 and Dauterman Maguire *et al.* 1989: 214–215) and in the amulets of Chnoubis (Vikan 1984: 76–77).

The presence of magical signs with evident apotropaic value on the outside of the tomb can be connected with the wish to defend the dead and the grave and to ward off tomb violation. The value of a widely recognised sign or symbol is greater than that of a written text because of its immediate intelligibility. The alphabet itself, on the other hand, assumes a magical significance when it is used as a simple sequence of signs, free from semantic connections, as occurs in some inscriptions engraved on various materials in the Roman catacombs (see *ICUR,* III 8030a, 8703–8704; VIII 22905b, 23055. Fig. 26.1.6). The writing itself rather than its contents assumes a magical value in such cases (Annequin 1973: 25–28; Cardona 1981: 174–183; Carletti 1984: 131–136).

An image with apotropaic character, distributed chiefly in the East, but also known in Rome (Calza 1917) is that of Solomon the Rider, occurring on a large number of amulets, gems, medals and armlets in Late Antiquity (Bagatti 1971; Nuzzo 1993). The scene engraved on a marble slab found in the catacomb of Commodilla seems to refer to the image of Solomon the Rider (*ICUR,* II 6190). It bears the epitaph of a child, Felix, who lived little more than one year (Fig. 26.1.7). On the lower right hand of the slab, is engraved an image of a horseman who kills a beast with a lance. A hunting scene (as in *ICUR, loc. cit.*) may seem unsuitable for a child's grave; but it is possible to recognise the iconographic scheme which recurs on amulets representing Solomon as he strikes the devil, clearly an allusion to the victory of good over evil. Amulets of Solomon were also found inside tombs in Sicily (tomb 12 of the Sofiana necropolis, fifth century: Bonomi 1964: 187–188; 216–218) and in Palestine (tombs 4, 14 in the cemetery of el-Gisc, fourth century: Makhouly 1938: 45–50; grave of Nahariya, sixth century: Reich 1985: 383–388).

During the archaeological excavations in the catacomb of St Hippolytus in 1990–91, a small oval plate of lapis-lazuli was found only, partially preserved, which would have been fixed in its metal setting and used as a pendant (Nuzzo 1994: 128–130. Fig. 26.1.8). On the stone is engraved the figure of a headless man with two pairs of wings and four arms, the figure of Bes Pantheos. The god holds a pole with two snakes with his upper right hand and a pole with a snake and a scorpion with the lower one. The figure is placed upon a cartouche, within which are engraved signs lacking any meaning. Similar signs

are also engraved around the image of Bes and on the reverse of the plate. The image of Bes, the war divinity with a strong apotropaic value, occurs not only in Egypt but also in many other regions of the Empire. This stone, which dates from the third century, was probably attached to the sealing mortar of a *loculus.*

This stone allows us to establish the meaning of a terracotta relief, reused to close a *loculus* in the cemetery of Praetextatus (Dolzani 1975). On this relief, dated to the first century AD, is represented the triad of the Egyptian divinities Isis, Serapis and Horus: the latter in the centre has the attributes of Bes. The deliberate choice of this slab is suggested by the placing of the carved face on the outside of the tomb. Rather than demonstrating the affiliation of the deceased to the cult of Isis before conversion to Christianity, as proposed by Dolzani – who consequently defined the piece as a '*semplice contrassegno distintivo*' (Dolzani 1975: 105), the object suggests a desire to protect the burial place by the deliberate reuse of an image reclaimed from a disused structure. The apotropaic value of the image of Horus-Bes was evidently still felt in Late Antiquity.

In the catacomb of Novatian there is still *in situ*, in the sealing mortar of a *loculus* a small porphyry slab with evident apotropaic value (Fig. 26.2): on the visible face, seen in profile, is engraved a male figure, wearing a short and narrow costume, with a snake-head (Josi 1934: 213, fig. 75; Lietzmann 1934: 359–362). The image is that of a monstrous god, half-human and half-animal and is still unidentified, although occurring in several amulets. It is

Fig. 26.2 *Porphyritic slab in the catacomb of Novatian (photo PCAS).*

also an Egyptian divinity and does not seem related to the Gnostic doctrine (Bonner 1950: 160–162). In the middle of the fourth century, Athanasius, bishop of Alexandria, strongly opposed the recourse by Christians to the Egyptian gods with heads of dogs, snakes or asses (*Contra Gentes*, 9 = PG XXV, 18–22). Among the pagan gods still respected by Christians, Athanasius mentions the triad Isis, Osiris and Horus (which partially corresponds to the figures on the terracotta slab found in the cemetery of Praetextatus). Also in a part of the catacomb of Commodilla was found a '*piastrina d'avorio... su cui era graffita... una figurazione di divinità egizia ritta in piedí*' (Ferrua 1957: 12), now lost.

A systematic examination of the objects fixed in the sealing mortar of the *loculi* in gallery 4 of the *coemeterium Maius* on the via Nomentana and of the lower levels in the catacomb of Pamphilus on the via Salaria has identified a set of objects with possible apotropaic value. They can be considered amulets of the dead and of the tombs, defenders of their integrity. Recent studies based on this systematic analysis have led to a new interpretation of the role of these objects, which were previously considered as having only a mnemonic role, differentiating tombs and allowing their recognition. As has been stressed the value to attribute to these items of furniture and ornament varies in relation to the type of object (De Santis 1994; Felle *et al.* 1994).

The most widely spread of the apotropaic objects examined in the galleries are the bronze bells (Fig. 26.3), which are only found in the lime that sealed children's tombs (see also Martin-Kilcher this volume). They are placed without apparent pattern on the right or left side of the tomb, usually with the clapper facing outwards, so that the object can be clearly identified. During the examination of the short gallery 4 of the *Coemeterium Maius* (containing only seven children's *loculi*; Fig. 26.4), I have found bronze bells in four tombs, one of which had two bells fixed in the sealing mortar. In this gallery, dated topographically to the first half of the fourth century (Fasola 1961: 254–256; 262), the percentage of this kind of object is particularly high. In the galleries of the catacomb of Pamphilus too the presence of bells is always connected with children's graves: for example in the intermediate level of the cemetery, dated to the first years of the fourth century, two bronze bells, not associated with other objects, were fixed in the mortar of two of the children's *loculi* (Josi 1926: 114, fig. 34).

The discoveries made in the two contexts examined are confirmed by similar findings made in the past in other underground cemeteries at Rome. In the seventeenth century Boldetti found bells that he attributes to children's tombs as toys (Boldetti 1720, tav. I 496, 7–9, 498–499). De Rossi mentions some bells found in the cemetery of St Callistus (De Rossi 1864–1877, III: 586, 616 note 4), interpreting them as objects which belonged to the dead in life and thus as grave identifiers. Armellini noted the occurrence of these bells in the sealing mortar of some

Fig. 26.3 Bronze bell fixed in the lime sealing a child's tomb in the catacomb of Pamphilus (photo PCAS).

Fig. 26.4 Gallery n° 4 of the Coemeterium Maius *(photo PCAS)*

loculi during his systematic analysis of the catacomb of St Agnes on the via Nomentana (Armellini 1880: 353). Similar discoveries in the Roman catacombs in recent investigations are numerous and the objects are generally alike: all the bells are small (with a diameter of 2.5–3 cm), they are almost always of bronze (rarely in copper), with the outside face when visible generally smooth but sometimes engraved with concentric circles (Salvetti 1978; Felle *et al.* 1994). Among finds in Rome particular attention should be drawn to a golden bell, discovered on the Esquiline in the last century, with an inscription (τοῖς ὄμμασι ὑποτέταγμαι). This demonstrates that the bell was used as an amulet: it was believed that the sound itself served to repulse and render powerless the effects of the evil eye (Bruzza 1875: 50–68). The opinion of John Chrysostom (*In ep. I ad Cor. homil.*, XII, 7 = PG, LXI 105–108) on this subject usefully confirms this indirect evidence for their apotropaic character: he condemned whoever entrusted the children to the protection of bells (cf. Russell 1995: 42–43).

Amongst the grave furniture from the burials of the middle level of the cemetery of Pamphilus in Rome Josi (1926: 148, fig. 60) identified the impression of a Gorgon's head, derived from an object fixed in the sealing mortar and now lost (Fig. 26.5); an *applique* in black glass paste with the image of Medusa's head was fixed in a *loculus* in the lower floor of the same catacomb. The apotropaic value of the image is connected above all with its monstrous appearance, believed capable of dispelling evil influences (Barb 1953: 208–212; cf. also the description of the demon Ὀβιζοὺθ in the *Testament of Solomon*: PG CXXII, 1333–1334). Besides a specific medical character, which is noted principally in objects of the Byzantine period (Bonner 1950: 90–91; Vikan 1990: 533), the Gorgon has a clear apotropaic function. This is confirmed, for example, in a Byzantine silver ring (Dalton 1901: 24), in the setting of which is represented a Medusa's head; on its edge is engraved the inscription κ(ύρι)ε βωήθι τὶ(ς) φοροῦοσι(ς), which mixes an invocation to God with faith in magic. The image of a Gorgon is frequently used in the funerary sphere, for example on some sarcophagi, with the purpose of protecting the tomb (Engemann 1975: 35–36, agreeing with the hypothesis of Cumont (1942: 339)). It is possible to attribute the same value to the objects fixed in the sealing mortar of the two *loculi* in the catacomb of Pamphilus, and to those showing the same image, discovered occasionally in other Roman cemeteries in the past (Buonarroti 1716: 14; Boldetti 1720: 513). This apotropaic function in burial places is also documented by the Gorgon's head on a fresco in the vault of the upper room in the mausoleum of *M. Clodius Hermes*, under the church of St Sebastian on the via Appia. Following a change of ownership of the mausoleum, or because of the owner's conversion to Christianity, between the end of the second century and the beginning of the third, a portion of the Gorgon's hair was whitewashed and, at the same time, the gospel scene of the possessed of Jerash (Luke 8, 26–39) was painted on the mausoleum attic. This strong contrast between the ancient superstitions and the elements of the new religion is particularly significant in this phase, when the choice in favour of Christianity corresponded to a deliberate detachment from pagan traditions (Carletti 1981: 295–296).

Fig. 26.5 *Impression of a Gorgon's head in the catacomb of Pamphilus (photo PCAS)*

Other materials connected with various forms of superstition have been found in the contexts examined but for the sake of brevity they are not considered at length here. Amongst these should be noted briefly masks, for example those recently discovered inside a tomb of an adult, in the catacomb of St Hippolytus (Felle *et al.* 1994: 136–138), nails, semi-precious stones (Février 1978: 262–263), and animal teeth (Engemann 1990: 529). There was an evident apotropaic function for the '*capsella (parimente) d'oro, composta di lastrine quadriforme saldata con quattro piccoli chiodi e sormontata da due appiccagnoli del medesimo metallo, per portarla appesa sul petto a guisa di encolpio e filatterio*', found in the grave of Maximus, *praepositus de via Flaminia*, in the cemetery *sub divo* of St Valentine, datable to between the end of the fourth and the beginning of the fifth century (De Rossi 1888: 262). Such a function can similarly be proposed for the small golden lamina found in the grave of Maria, wife of the Emperor Honorius in the Vatican basilica. On the lamina were scratched the names Michael, Gabriel, Raphael and Uriel (De Rossi 1863:54). These objects in precious material testify to the use of amulets in the burials of those of the highest social status.

This evidence demonstrates that condemnation by the ecclesiastical authorities was not sufficient to eliminate the more deep-rooted superstitions, those connected not to official religion but to a personal and ancestral piety. The Fathers of the Church tried to transform this phenomenon and to render it orthodox, '*di impadronirsene e di farla cristiana*' (Manselli 1976: 322). As early as the end of the second century Irenaeus of Lyon wrote: '*Nec invocationibus angelicis facit aliquid neque incantationibus neque aliqua prava curiositate; sed, munde et pure et manifeste orationes dirigens ad Dominum qui omnia fecit et nomen Domini nostri Iesu Christi invocans, virtutes ad utilitatem hominum sed non ad seductiones perficit. Si itaque et nunc nomen Domini nostri Iesu Christi beneficia praestat et curat firmissime et vere omnes ubique credentes in eum'* (*Adversus haereses* II, 32, 5 = SChr 294, 342). Two centuries later John Chrysostom asserted: πιστὴ εἶ; σφράγισον, εἰπέ, τοῦτο ἔχω τὸ ὅπλον μόνον, τοῦτο τὸ φάρμακον, ἄλλο δὲ οὐκ οἶδα (*In epist. ad Coloss.* III, VIII, 5 = PG, LXII 358). Only faith in Christ, in his name and in his cross can protect, heal and turn away the demons. The wish of the Fathers was granted in one way: by the period and in contexts where the affirmation of one's Christian faith had become unnecessary, the widespread distribution of the chi-rho monogram (used as a symbol, not as a *compendium scripturae*) in the cemeteries examined suggests that it too had also acquired an apotropaic value (Ferrua 1941: 79–80; cf. Russell 1995: 50). Different symbols, different traditions of pagan and Jewish origin coexisted with expression of the Christian faith in order to protect the dead and their tombs from evil forces and from whosoever would profane them. The mixture of different cultures and mentalities, and particularly the persistence of pagan symbols, seem to demonstrate that in Rome from the fourth century, to be Christian did not imply necessarily a radical rejection of tradition especially if it were connected with the magic sphere. The extraordinary power of tradition indicated *'la lentezza con la quale le coscienze religiose sono passate dal paganesimo al cristianesimo'* (Manselli 1976: 328).

Bibliography

Annequin, J. 1973. *Recherche sur l'action magique et ses représentations (I^e–IIe siècles après J.C.)*, Paris.

Armellini, M. 1880. *Il cimitero di S.Agnese*, Rome.

Aune, D.E. 1980. Magic in Early Christianity. In *Aufstieg und Niedergang der römischen Welt*, II, 23.2, 1507–1557. Berlin-New York.

Bagatti, B. 1964–65. Ricerche su alcuni segni delle catacombe romane. *Studii Biblici Franciscani. Liber Annuus*, 15: 98–123.

Bagatti, B. 1971. Altre medaglie di Salomone cavaliere e loro origine. *Rivista di archeologia cristiana*, 47: 331–342.

Barb, A.A. 1953. Diva matrix. *Journal of the Warburg and Courtauld Institutes*, 16: 208–212.

Barb, A.A. 1963. The Survival of Magic Arts. In *The conflict between Paganism and Christianity in the fourth century* (ed. by A. Momigliano), 100–125. Oxford.

Boldetti, M. 1720. *Osservazioni sopra i cimiteri de' santi martiri ed antichi cristiani di Roma*. Rome.

Bonner, C. 1950. *Studies in magical amulets chiefly Graeco-Egyptian*. Oxford.

Bonomi, L. 1964. Cimiteri paleocristiani di Sofiana. *Rivista di archeologia cristiana*, 40: 169–220.

Bruzza, L. 1875. Intorno ad un campanello d'oro trovato sull'Esquilino e all'uso del suono per respingere il fascino. *Annali dell'Istituto di Corrispondenza Archeologica*, 47: 50–68.

Buonarroti, F. 1716. *Osservazioni sopra alcuni frammenti di vasi antichi di vetro ornati di figure trovati ne' cimiteri di Roma*. Rome.

Calza, G. 1917. Un amuleto magico con l'effigie di Salomone rinvenuto in Ostia. *Notizie degli Scavi di Antichità*: 326–328.

Cardona, G.R. 1981. *Antropologia della scrittura*. Torino.

Carletti, C. 1981. Pagani e cristiani nel sepolcreto della 'piazzola'. *Vetera Christianorum*, 18: 287–307.

Carletti, C. 1984. Epigrafia cristiana a Bolsena. In *II Convegno 'Il Paleocristiano nella Tuscia' (Viterbo, 7–8 maggio 1983)*, 117–139. Rome.

Carletti, C. 1998. Un monogramma tardoantico nell'epigrafia funeraria dei cristiani. In *Domum tuam dilexi. Miscellanea A. Nestori*, 127–142. Vatican City

Cumont, F. 1942. *Recherches sur le symbolisme funéraire des romains*. Paris.

Dalton, O.M. 1901. *Catalogue of the Early Christian Antiquities*. London.

Dauterman Maguire, E., Maguire, H.P. and Duncan Flowers, M.J. 1989. *Art and Holy Powers in the Early Christian House*. Urbana and Chicago.

De Rossi, G.B. 1863. Disegni d'alquanti vasi del mondo muliebre sepolto con Maria moglie di Onorio imperatore. *Bullettino di Archeologia Cristiana*, 1: 53–56.

De Rossi, G.B. 1864–1877. *La Roma sotterranea cristiana*, I-III. Rome.

De Rossi, G.B. 1888. Del *praepositus de via Flaminia*. *Bullettino della Commissione Archeologica Comunale di Roma*, 17: pp. 257–262

De Santis, P. 1994. Elementi di corredo nei sepolcri delle catacombe romane: l'esempio della regione di Leone e della galleria Bb nella catacomba di Commodilla. *Vetera Christianorum*, 31: 23–51.

De Visscher, F. 1963. *Le droit des tombeaux romains*. Milan.

Dickie, M.W. 1995. The Fathers of the Church and the Evil Eye. In *Byzantine Magic* (ed. H. Maguire), 9–34. Washington.

Dolzani, C. 1975. Rilievo egittizzante nel cimitero di Pretestato (Roma). *Rivista di Archeologia Cristiana*, 51: 97–105.

Engemann, J. 1975. Zur Verbreitung magischer Übelabwehr in der nichtchristlichen und christlichen Spätantike. *Jahrbuch für Antike und Christentum*, 18: 22–48.

Engemann, J. 1990. Amuleto. In *Enciclopedia dell'Arte Medievale*, I, 527–530. Rome.

Fasola, U.M. 1961. La regione delle cattedre nel cimitero Maggiore. *Rivista di Archeologia Cristiana*, 37: 237–267.

Felle, A., Del Moro, M.P. and Nuzzo, D. 1994. Elementi di 'corredo-arredo' delle tombe del cimitero di s.Ippolito sulla via Tiburtina. *Rivista di Archeologia Cristiana*, 70: 89–158.

Ferrua, A. 1940. Sopra un'iscrizione del Museo Lateranense. *Epigraphica*, 2: 7–20.

Ferrua, A. 1941. Il refrigerio dentro la tomba. *La Civiltà Cattolica*, 92: 373–378/457–463.

Ferrua, A. 1947. Gli angeli di Tera. *Orientalia Christiana Periodica*, 13: 149–167.

Ferrua, A. 1956. Gli anatemi dei padri di Nicea. *La Civiltà Cattolica*, 107: 378–387.

Ferrua, A. 1957. Scoperta di una nuova regione della catacomba di Commodilla. I. *Rivista di Archeologia Cristiana*, 33: 7–43.

Ferrua, A. 1960. *Le pitture della nuova catacomba della via Latina*. Città del Vaticano.

Février, P.A. 1978. Le culte des morts dans les communautés chrétiennes durant le IIIe siècle. In *I monumenti precostantiniani*. Atti del IX Congresso Internazionale di Archeologia Cristiana (Roma 21–27 settembre 1975), I, 211–274. Città del Vaticano.

Giuntella, A.M. 1990. Sepoltura e rito: consuetudini e innovazioni. In *Le sepolture in Sardegna da IV al VII secolo*. IV Convegno sull'archeologia tardoromana e altomedievale (Cuglieri 27–28 giugno 1987) (= Mediterraneo tardoantico e altomedievale. Scavi e ricerche, 8), 231–244. Oristano.

Hefele, C.J. and Leclercq, H. 1973². *Histoire des conciles.* Hildesheim-New York.

ICUR.. Inscriptiones Christianae Urbis Romae VII saec. antiquiores, n.s., Rome 1922–

Josi, E. 1926. Il cimitero di Panfilo. *Rivista di Archeologia Cristiana,* 3: 51–211.

Josi, E. 1934. Cimitero alla sinistra della via Tiburtina al viale Regina Margherita. *Rivista di Archeologia Cristiana,* 11.

Lietzmann, H. 1934. Ein Gnostiker in der Novatianus Katakombe. *Rivista di Archeologia Cristiana,* 11: 359–362.

Makhouly, N. 1938. Rock-cut tombs at el Jisc. *The Quarterly of the Department of Antiquities in Palestine,* 8: 45–50.

Manselli, R. 1976. Simbolismo e magia nell'alto medioevo. In *Simboli e Simbologia nell'Alto Medioevo. XXIII Settimana di Studio del Centro italiano di Studi sull'alto medioevo,* 1, 293–329. Spoleto.

Miranda, E. 1991. Una gemma 'gnostica' dalle catacomba di s. Gennaro. *Rivista di Archeologia Cristiana,* 67: 115–124.

Mouterde, R. 1942–43. Objets magiques. *Mélanges de l'Université Saint-Joseph,* 25: 105–126.

Nuzzo, D. 1993. Immagini cristologiche negli amuleti di Salomone cavaliere. *Bessarione,* 10: 101–115.

Reich, R. 1985. A Samaritan Amulet from Nahariya. *Revue Biblique,* 92: 383–388.

Russell, J. 1995. The Archaeological Context of Magic in the Early Byzantine Period. In *Byzantine Magic* (ed. H. Maguire), 35–50. Washington.

Salvetti, C. 1978. Il catalogo degli oggetti minuti conservati presso la Pontificia Commissione di Archeologia Sacra. *Rivista di Archeologia Cristiana,* 54: 103–130.

Vikan, G. 1984. Art, Medicine and Magic in Early Byzantium. *Dumbarton Oaks Papers,* 38: 65–86.

Vikan, G. 1990. Amuleto. Area bizantina. In *Enciclopedia dell'Arte Medievale,* I, 531–533. Rome.

27. Funerary equipment from the *circiforme* basilica on the Via Ardeatina (Rome)

Maria Paola Del Moro

In September 1991 an early Christian basilica of the *circiforme* ('circus-shaped') type was located in the district of the Callistus catacomb, about 600 m. from the cross-roads between the Via Appia Antica and the Via Ardeatina, at a short distance from the latter (Fig. 27.1). The discovery occurred in farm land which had been sown with lucerne. A dry period had produced an abnormal degree of growth in the roots of this crop, seeking moisture. At a depth of 1.40 metres, some of these roots met with an obstacle which caused a lesser growth of the plants above. The differential plant growth on the surface revealed in negative the plan of a circus-shaped building, 66 m long and 28 m wide.

The remains which were found belong to a well identified type of basilica, of which the main characteristic is that the aisles extend around a U-shaped nave. Until now this type of building has been represented by five great churches located in the *suburbium* of Rome. They are the *Basilica Apostolorum* (to-day S. Sebastiano) on the Via Appia, the basilicas of SS. Pietro and Marcellino on the Via Labicana (to-day the Via Casilina), of S. Lorenzo on the Via Tiburtina, of S. Agnese on the Via Nomentana, and the so-called *anonima* on the Via Prenestina. These buildings all had a funerary function and were linked to imperial commission. Thanks to late Antique documentary sources we know that in the first four cases the Emperor Constantine or his relatives acted as donors. Therefore, the date of these basilicas falls between the Constantinian period and the mid-fourth century AD.

At the *XII Internationalen Kongresses für Christliche Archäologie* (Bonn, September 22nd–28th, 1991), V. Fiocchi Nicolai proposed the identification of the recently-located monument with the basilica that Pope Mark erected in the area (336 AD), and in which he was buried, as recorded in late-Antique and early-Mediaeval historical and topographical sources (Fiocchi Nicolai 1995: 776–786).

The archaeological excavations were carried out between 1993 and 1996. They were supported by the *Pontificia Commissione d'Archeologia Sacra*, and permitted by the *Ministero dei Beni Culturali*. The scientific

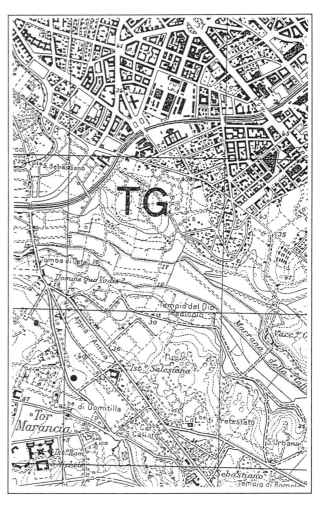

Fig. 27.1 *The location of the basilica* circiforme *by the via Ardeatina (basilica indicated by circle)*

direction of the excavations was under Professor Fiocchi Nicolai, while the different sectors were under the responsibility of D. Nuzzo, L. Spera and the writer of this paper. The data obtained from excavations seem to confirm that it was the basilica erected by Pope Mark (Fiocchi Nicolai *et al.* 1999).

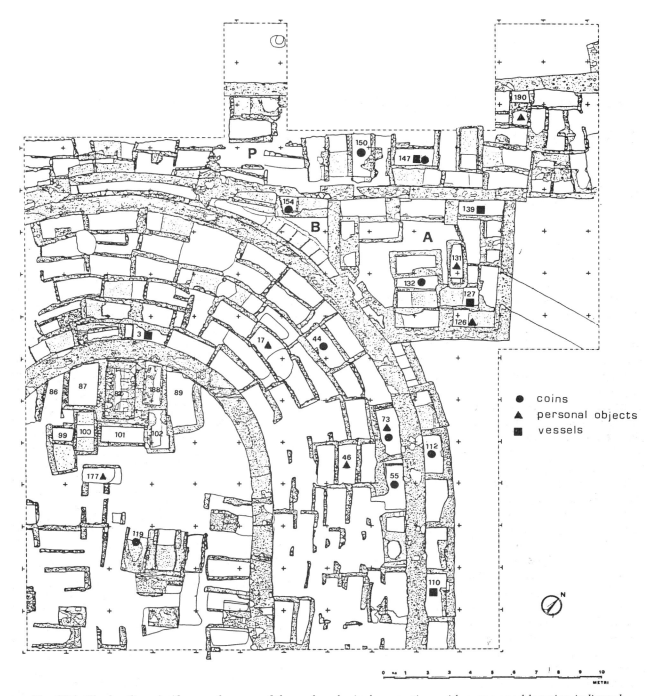

Fig. 27.2 *The basilica* circiforme: *the area of the archaeological excavation, with grave good location indicated*

The investigation was focused on the north-eastern end of the basilica, which was found almost entirely at foundation level (Fig. 27.2). The site was only excavated down to the tufa bank beneath the basilica in some areas, in order to reconstruct the history of the site in the period preceding the early Christian foundation. The analysis of the stratigraphy overlying the tufa and the material recovered seems to prove a widespread use of the site during the first two centuries of the imperial period. Its use was probably linked to a rural settlement of which the domestic and industrial areas were discovered in the same district during the course of this century. The area, which slopes down towards the Via Ardeatina, was modified by a deliberate levelling-up to prepare it for the early-Christian monumental complex. This levelling fill formed a layer into which the foundation pits of the walls belonging to the basilica and its associated buildings, as well as the pits of the floor-level graves, were cut.

The basilica is longitudinal in plan. Piers, which once supported the arcades, divide it in a nave and two aisles.

The aisles, which run all the way around the nave and envelop it, constituted the ambulatory. The terminal sector of the nave, or exedra, is delimited by a triforium. The altar has not been found but, as in the *Basilica Apostolorum*, it was probably located in the middle of the nave.

Two other buildings connected to the basilica were also discovered. They consist of a rear portico (P), at a tangent to the curve of the apse, which must have connected the basilica and the road (the Via Ardeatina or a branch running parallel) on which it is aligned, and a rectangular mausoleum (A), inserted to the east between the basilica and the portico. In the whole complex the floor level was occupied by burials which in general were laid out according to a rational scheme. The disposition of the graves is particularly regular in the ambulatory, where it follows what seems to be a planned scheme. The order in which the graves were constructed is, as a rule, recognisable by means of the successive walls pertaining to each grave: later graves re-employ the walls of earlier.

In the basilica the construction of graves spread from the facade toward the apse and from the foundations of the walls of the building (i.e. the external wall and the wall which supported the piers separating the nave from the ambulatory) inwards. A particular case is represented by a group of graves located in the northern sector of the exedra, placed against the foundations of the wall once supporting the partition piers between the nave and the ambulatory (Graves 82, 87, 88, 100, 101, 102). They were dug contemporaneously and are older than the adjoining burials placed against them (Graves 86, 89, 99). Furthermore, the position and monumentality of the central grave (Grave 82) seem to show a privileged status and an early role in the funeral use of the basilica: is it possible that the occupant of grave was Pope Mark? The lay-out of burials is generally ordered but there are a small number of exceptions. In the nave the graves lay in series at right angles to one another and therefore the *pozzetti* (i.e. the holes to admit the deceased) follow different orientations (only the *pozzetti* related to the graves placed against the foundation of the basilica wall keep a constant position, and open toward the nave). In the ambulatory, the graves are aligned in rows next to one another along the wall of the building, while the *pozzetti* are oriented to north-west or west.

As far as burials are concerned, the portico shows continuity from the terminal sector of the ambulatory. The construction of graves started from the foundations of the external walls and worked inwards. In the centre the burials are aligned on the structure of the portico, while in the eastern sector they are arranged in groups at right angles to one another. The mausoleum was the last area to be used for burial. Here, the earliest burials were those placed against the foundations of the external walls, and the central grave which has a vaulted ceiling. Further burials were made later, but the available space was not entirely exploited.

Almost all of the tombs which were excavated belong to the same type: earth-cut pits of which the sides are revetted with *tufelli* masonry, and which have one or more superimposed burial levels. Each level has a fixed covering made of clay tiles placed *a cappuccina* and a layer of mortar over the top of the tiles. In order to allow the deceased to be admitted, each grave had a *pozzetto* at one end. The occupation of the grave started from the bottom, and when a burial level had been completed, the *pozzetto* was closed by the same means. The upper covering of the grave was made of marble slabs which were sometimes engraved with a funerary inscription. These slabs constituted the floor of the building. The need for more burial spaces made some structural interventions necessary in a number of graves. The more common interventions consisted in digging pits at the bottom of the grave, or else, in building in the area of the *pozzetto*, at the lowest level, some small box-shaped masonry tombs. In both cases, the covering was made with clay tiles, which were laid either horizontally or *a semi-cappuccina* and covered with a layer of mortar.

Only the monumental grave in the middle of the exedra differs (Grave 82), along with some of the graves around it (Graves 87, 88, 89, 101). Grave 82, which had been robbed, had a vaulted ceiling and contained a saddle-roofed, uncarved marble sarcophagus. The other graves, which had been originally planned according to the ordinary *a pozzetto* type, were altered in a second stage in order to put sarcophagi inside. Only the marble sarcophagus from Grave 87, of which the front was carved with figures, was discovered still sealed with a thick layer of mortar, following a practice attested in Grave 82 and in some graves in the *Basilica Apostolorum* (Styger 1918: 11–16; Mancini 1923: 17).

On the basis of the architectural typology, it was assumed that the monument dated back to the fourth and the fifth decade of the fourth century (see above), and that it was used for burial from the mid-fourth to the mid-fifth century. The dating has been confirmed by archaeological data consisting of several elements, the stratigraphy preceding the basilica foundation, the particularities of the masonry, and dated artefacts in excavated contexts including burials. Among the latter the dated inscriptions, running from 368 to 445 AD, the coins and the grave goods, must be mentioned.

The basilica complex continued to be used for burial from the sixth until the mid-seventh century. Some pottery dated between the secnd half of the eighth and the ninth century show that the basilica was still frequented in the early Middle Ages (Zanotti 1998: 171–176). After it was abandoned, it became the object of grave robbing. Presumably in the seventeenth century the area was taken over for agricultural exploitation.

The identification of the monument with the basilica erected by Pope Mark was suggested by the analysis of the literary sources and the topographical observations. The *Liber Pontificalis* tells us that the basilica that Pope Mark erected was used for his burial and also records that it was endowed with the *fundus Rosarius* by the Emperor Constantine for its maintenance. The basilica of Pope Mark was restored in the early Middle Ages and was abandoned at about the end of the eleventh century, after the translation of his relics to the city church *in Via Lata*. The chronological and typological data provided by the building we excavated led to the same conclusions (Fiocchi Nicolai *et al.* 1999: 69–139).

The investigation produced a number of grave goods, some of them found out of context because of intensive and quite regular grave robbing. In order to provide a proper evaluation of the practices connected with the grave goods, only those found in sealed graves, or which at least derived from reliable stratified contexts, will be considered here. Given the chronological limits for this congress only the grave goods related to the burials of the period covering the fourth and fifth century will be considered, although it must be remembered that the re-use of the upper levels of the graves proves that the basilica continued to serve a funerary purpose during the sixth and the seventh century.

As noted, the graves were generally found to have already been disturbed when they were excavated. In most cases, they had lost the original upper burial level which was often filled with material deriving from the robbing of the same grave or those near to it. Nevertheless, sometimes the robbers did not reach the bottom of the grave pits so that the earliest graves in the lower levels remained sealed. The deceased was laid supine, with his arms stretched along the body and his legs extended and parallel. The head was generally in the area of the *pozzetto*. In some cases, one hand was laid on the pelvis or the legs were bent sideways. In one case, the single grave of an infant in the portico, the body was found lying on its left side.

Each burial layer housed one body or, more frequently, two bodies, one beside the other. Single burials were found mostly in the smaller graves, while the examples of multiple burials were connected to family groups or to a reoccupation of the same grave; in the latter case the reoccupation concerned the upper levels of the grave.

In comparison to the number of burials discovered still undamaged, only a few produced grave goods. In the basilica, grave goods were mostly ornaments and related to adult individuals. In Grave 73, a four level burial against the external wall of the ambulatory, the deceased in the lowest level had a bronze finger ring on the ring finger of his left hand, bearing the inscription: *R(—) I(—)*. The ring is of a late Antique type (Guiraud 1989: type 4a) similar to examples from fourth century contexts (Henkel 1913: nn. 968, 973, 1863; Drury Fortnum 1869: 145). Two coins were associated with the same grave: an unreadable AE3/4 and an AE4 with traces of the type *Victoria Aug, Augg,* or *Auggg*, with two Victories facing one another, each holding a wreath, a type issued from 382 AD. In the robbed Grave 17, in the northern sector of the ambulatory, a bronze bracelet was uncovered near the

Fig. 27.3 Bronze bracelet near left hand; Grave 17

left hand of the deceased (Fig. 27.3). In Grave 46, in the southern sector of the ambulatory, a gold ear-ring of a common late Roman type (Allason Jones 1989: 5–6, type 3) was found near the head of a female skeleton beneath the lower-level covering, which had been broken by robbers. In the still sealed double burial, the lowest of four superimposed burials in Grave 177 in the exedra, was a pierced coin which on the basis of the surviving legend can be ascribed to Valentinian I or II (364–392); it perhaps formed part of a necklace, or was fastened with a nail to a piece of wood or metal or stitched to a cloth (Arslan 1991: 125).

The practice of leaving single or small quantities of coins next to infant or adult burials is attested in the lowest levels of some still-sealed graves. Eight small bronze coins have been uncovered, generally poorly preserved AE4; only in Grave 73 were they associated with other finds. An AE4 with traces of a standing male figure in military uniform was found next to a child buried at the bottom of grave 44. Coins related to two different burials were found in Grave 55, a four level burial placed against the foundation of the external wall of the basilica. The lowest level underwent a series of structural alterations in order to allow intensive re-use of the grave. Three infant burials were excavated: a small box-shaped tomb, dug at the base of the north end, and two infant *loculi*, which were dug along the northern and the eastern walls. A double adult burial was added at the bottom of the grave and a further burial on a new surface, comprising tiles laid on the offsets on which the usual covering system *a cappuccina* had already been set. On this surface, one AE3 of Jovian was found, issued between 363 and 364 by the mint of Rome of the type *vot//v//mult//x* within wreath (Carson and Kent 1965: 61, n. 696; Kent 1981: 281, n. 333). A badly corroded AE4 and a AE3, the latter from the mint of Rome, can be ascribed to the lowest burial. They are of the *securitas reipublicae* type and date from 367 to 375 (Pearce 1951: 115, 121, n. 24; Carson and Kent 1965: 61, nn. 712–714, 718–720). In the three level Grave 119, in the exedra, an AE4 coin of the second half of the fourth century was found on the layer on which two burials had been laid.

The practice of putting pottery or glass vessels close to the deceased seems less common in this period. The only certain example is that from Grave 3 in the northern sector of the ambulatory. In a small box-shaped tomb excavated at the base of the grave, still sealed at the time of excavation, a clay money-box of a common late Roman type, broken in two, lay over the feet of the infant burial (Fig. 27.4) (Boldetti 1720: 498, tav. I,5; Ferrua 1978: 215–216). The context allows it to be dated to the second half of the fourth century.

Grave robbing affected few burials in the portico. These therefore often remained undamaged but few grave goods were found. A bronze finger ring, which had evidently slipped of the finger, was discovered near the left hand of one of the two individuals in Grave 190. The

***Fig. 27.4** The money-box; Grave 3*

ring, oval in section, and with a square, plain raised bezel, is similar to examples from fourth and fifth century contexts (Peroni 1967: tav. IX, nn. 53–54; Mawer 1995: 125–127, D3.Go.2, D3.Si5–6, D3.Si.9). In Grave 150 a single burial was furnished with a hoard of four AE4 coins. The oldest was issued by Valentinian I or II (364–392), one with traces of a Victory to left dates to the late fourth or to the early fifth century and the last two of the *Victoria Augg* type, holding wreath and palm, are identified by the monogrammed cross readable in the left field on one as Honorian issues, dating from the years 410–423 (Carson and Kent 1965: 63, n. 829; Kent 1994: 338, n. 1357). In the pit dug at the base of grave 147 to receive an infant burial was an unreadable AE4, datable to the second half of the fourth century. After the closing of the pit with horizontally-lain tiles, a further individual was laid to rest on the new surface, next to whom fragments of glass vessels were discovered. They are rim fragments from three vessels, a colourless cup with an folded outward rim, similar to an example from a late fourth or first half of the fifth century context in Luni (Roffia 1977: 285, n. 69, tav. 156.20), a greenish colourless conical beaker with vertical sides and two wheel-cut lines below the rim, similar to Isings type 106b (Sternini 1989: 29, fig. 4.18; Saguì 1993: 119, fig. 4.11) and a conical beaker with an out-turned fire-rounded rim, similar to Isings type 106c, both dated to the end of the fourth and the fifth century (Saguì 1993: 119, fig. 4.6).

Therefore, as stated grave goods found in reliable stratified contexts are not numerous, and only in one case comprise an object of personal ornament.

The investigation of undamaged burials in the lower levels of the mausoleum gave similar results. In Grave 126, a bronze finger ring was found next to the head of the deceased. The ring is similar to that found in Grave 190 and can therefore also be dated to the late fourth and fifth century. In a double burial in Grave 131 an ivory handle from a toilet utensil, decorated with an engraved double zig-zag pattern, is similar to others from fourth and fifth-century contexts (Lusuardi Siena 1973: 561, tav. 139, 4, 6). By the single burial in Grave 139 was a group of three clay oil-lamps, of which the shoulders are decorated with concentric rows of raised globules (Provoost 1970: 24–25, 43–44; Bailey 1980: 377–380), a type dated from the late-third to the early-fifth century (Paleani 1993: 10–20, 86–87). In the upper level of Grave 127, a fragmentary conical glass lamp associated with a triple burial can be dated from the fifth to the eighth century (Saguì 1993: 123, Fig. 7.51). The later of the two burials in the undamaged upper level of Grave 132 was accompanied by an AE3 coin with Victory to left, probably dating to the fourth or the early fifth century. This find is important as it is the only burial belonging to an upper level and consequently not related to the earliest burials.

Outside the basilica and its associated buildings additional burials were excavated. The two graves in the small space left unoccupied (B) when erecting the mausoleum, seem to be contemporary with it and its funerary occupation. In Grave 154, a small bronze coin was associated with the single still sealed burial belonging to the lowest level. The piece is an illegible AE4 dating from the late fourth or the first half of the fifth century.

Along the foundation of the external wall of the basilica, a row of graves was constructed in succession from south to north. In Grave 112, a badly corroded AE3 coin was the only grave good, datable to the second half of the fourth century. In the upper level of Grave 110, a fragmentary glass lamp was associated with the double burial. It is conical with three handles, and can be related to Isings type 134 (Isings 1957:162), dated from the end of the fourth to the eighth century (Saguì 1993: 123, Fig. 7.47).

The analysis of the grave goods found during the excavations allows some general remarks. The general similarity of the type and quality of grave goods gives the picture of a community homogenous from a social and cultural point of view. With the exception of the privileged group of tombs with sarcophagi, located in the exedra, a modest social status is also suggested by the ways in which the graves were constructed. In spite of the robbery and violation, giving only a partial impression of the quantity of grave goods, the relationship between the objects which were found and the still sealed burials is still significant. The absence of grave goods was usually noted, but this is not necessarily an index of poverty. As a matter of fact, there were no grave goods associated with the couple buried in the sarcophagus of Grave 87, nor with the individual buried in the lower layer of Grave 100, among the privileged graves. It would appear that there were no correspondence between the importance of the grave, and thus of the deceased, and the presence of funerary equipment. The same remark, however, was been made in relation to some pagan burial contexts, such as the necropolis of *Isola Sacra* (Taglietti 1990: 74). As for the objects constituting the grave goods, coins obviously occur much more frequently than personal ornaments or pottery and glass vessels (Fig. 27.5). The same relationship is documented in other Christian cemetery contexts dating from the late fourth and the fifth century; for example, in the graves of the basilica of *Pianabella* (Spagnoli 1993: 255). This situation is not however true of the sixth to the mid-seventh century, to which the upper levels of the graves belonging to the complex of the basilica *circiforme* can be related. In these levels pottery and glass vessels predominated.

The grave robbing frustrates a full analysis of the coin finds. To the finds mentioned above must be added a large quantity of bronze coins from the fourth and the fifth century, which belong to the disturbed layers. At the very least however it is evident that the presence of this kind of materials was frequent and bears witness to the persistent practice of offering coins in Christian contexts (Young 1977: 40–43; Martorelli 1992: 89–97; Spagnoli 1993: 256; Del Moro 1994: 107–109; Alföldi 1996: 33–

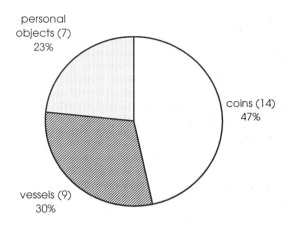

Fig. 27.5 *Numbers and proportion of different grave goods found in the basilica* circiforme

39). Moreover, the coins which were found in the undamaged burials, did not lie directly in contact with the bodies. This might have been caused by the bad state of preservation of the bodies but it can also be attributed to the deliberate deposition of the coin in the burial rather than with the deceased. 'Charon's obols', 'coins for the dead', must be distinguished from the 'burial coins' (Martini 1996: 231). The 'obol' consists of one or two coins laid on the body of the deceased according to a ritual pattern. In Christian funerary contexts of the fourth and fifth centuries, the coins were found inside the mouth, under the chin, or on the legs of the deceased, as in the basilica of *Pianabella* (Spagnoli 1993: 255) and in the cemetery of Kaiseraugst (Martin 1991: 62, 151–155). On the contrary, the coins generally found here in greater numbers, either spread out or collected in a hoard, belong to the second category.

As we have said, neither the lay-out of the furnished graves seems to follow a particular scheme, nor do the types of grave goods seem to show differences from the social point of view. If a 'hierarchy' exists among the funeral spaces of the monumental complex, and it does exist, this is not represented by the grave goods, but rather by the strategies adopted in the occupation of the funeral spaces. Notwithstanding the unified project of the basilica foundation, the portico represents a sort of continuation of the ambulatory, while the mausoleum, which has a private character, constitutes an additional and distinguished element.

Acknowledgements

I wish to thank Professor V. Fiocchi Nicolai both for the opportunity he extended to me to present here the results of the excavations led under his direction and for his encouragement. I also wish to make clear that the credit for what is presented must be shared with the whole excavation staff.

Bibliography

Alföldi, M.R. 1996. Münze im Grab, Münze am Grab. Ein ausgefallene Beispiel aus Rom. In *Coin Finds and Coin Use in the Roman World* (eds. C.E. King and D.G. Wigg), 33–39. Berlin: Mann

Allason Jones, L. 1989. *Ear-Rings in Roman Britain*. Oxford: British Archaeological Reports

Arslan, E.A. 1991. Monete. In *Archeologia a Monte Barro*, I, *Il grande edificio e le torri* (eds. G.P. Brogiolo and L. Castelletti), 125–135. Lecco: Editrice Stefanoni.

Bailey, D.M. 1980. *A Catalogue of the Lamps in the British Museum. II. Roman Lamps Made in Italy*. London: British Museum Publications

Boldetti, A. 1720. *Osservazioni sopra i cimiteri de' santi martiri ed antichi cristiani di Roma*. Rome

Carson, R.A.G. and Kent, J.P.C. 1965. *Late Roman Bronze Coinage A.D. 324–498*, II, *Bronze Roman Imperial Coinage of the Later Empire A.D. 346–498*. London: Spink and Son

Del Moro, M.P. 1994. Ambiti e metodi dell' analisi. In Felle, E.A., Del Moro, M.P. and Nuzzo, D. 1994. Elementi di «corredo-arredo» delle tombe del cimitero di S. Ippolito sulla via Tiburtina. *Rivista di Archeologia Cristiana*, 70: 107–114

Drury Fortnum, C. 1869. On some finger-rings of the early christian period. *Archaeological Journal*, 26: 137–148

Ferrua, A. 1978. Nuova regione catacombale presso S. Callisto. *Rivista di Archeologia Cristiana*, 54: 167–225

Fiocchi Nicolai, V. 1995. Una nuova basilica a deambulatorio nel comprensorio della catacomba di S. Callisto a Roma. In *Akten des XII Internationalen Kongresses für Christliche Archäologie* (Bonn. 22–28. September 1991), II, 776–786. Münster: Aschendorff

Fiocchi Nicolai, V. *et al.* 1995–1996 (1999). La nuova Basilica Circiforme della via Ardeatina. *Rendiconti della Pontificia Accademia Romana di Archeologia*, 68: 69–233

Guiraud, H. 1989. Bagues et anneaux à l'époque romaine en Gaule. *Gallia*, 46: 173–211

Henkel, F. 1913. *Die römischen Fingerringe der Rheinlande und der benachbarten Gebiete*. Berlin: Georg Reimer

Isings, C. 1957. *Roman Glass from Dated Finds, Archaeologica Traiectina 2*. Groningen-Djakarta: J.B. Wolters

Kent, J.P.C. 1981. *The Roman Imperial Coinage* (ed. C.H.V. Sutherland and R.A.G. Carson), VIII, *The family of Constantine I (A.D. 337–364)*. London: Spink and Son

Kent, J.P.C. 1994, *The Roman Imperial Coinage* (ed. R.A.G. Carson, J.P.C. Kent and A.M. Burnett), X, *The divided Empire and the Fall of the western parts. A.D. 395–491*. London: Spink and Son

Lusuardi Siena, S. 1973. Miscellanea (AE). In *Scavi di Luni. I. Relazione preliminare delle campagne di scavo 1970–1971* (ed. A. Frova) 548–567. Rome: L'Erma di Bretschneider

Mancini, G. 1923. Scavi sotto la basilica di S. Sebastiano sull'Appia Antica. *Notizie degli Scavi di Antichità*, 20: 3–79

Martin, M. 1991. *Das spätrömisch-frühmittelalterliche Gräberfeld von Kaiseraugst, Kt. Aargau.*, I. *Text*, Derendingen-Solothurn: Habegger

Martini, R. 1996. Le monete. In *Antichi Silenzi. La necropoli romana di San Lorenzo di Parabiago*, 231–236. Cassano Magnago: Comune di Legnano

Martorelli, R. 1992. Reperti numismatici. In Fiocchi Nicolai, V. *et al.* 1992. Scavi nella catacomba di S. Senatore ad Albano Laziale. *Rivista di Archeologia Cristiana*, 68: 89–97

Mawer, C.F. 1995. *Evidence for Christianity in Roman Britain. The small-finds*. Oxford: British Archaeological Reports

Paleani, M.T. 1993. *Le lucerne paleocristiane, Monumenti, Musei e Gallerie Pontificie. Antiquarium Romanum*. Rome: L'Erma di Bretschneider

Paroli, L. and Delogu, P. (eds.) 1992. *La storia economica di Roma nell' alto Medioevo alla luce dei recenti scavi archeologici*. Atti del seminario Roma 2–3 aprile 1992. Florence: All'Insegna del Giglio

Pearce, J. W.E. 1951. *The Roman Imperial Coinage* (eds. H. Mattingly, C.H.V. Sutherland and R.A.G. Carson), IX, *Valentinian I -Theodosius I*. London: Spink and Son

Peroni, A. 1967. *Oreficerie e metalli lavorati tardoantichi e altomedievali del territorio di Pavia. Catalogo*. Spoleto: Centro italiano di studi sull'alto medioevo

Provoost, A. 1970. Les lampes à récipient allongé trouvées dans les catacombes romaines. Essai de classification typologique. *Bulletin de l'Institut Historique Belge de Rome*, 41: 17–56

Roffia, E. 1977. Vetri. (Q). In *Scavi di Luni. II. Relazione delle campagne di scavo 1972–1973–1974* (ed. A. Frova) 270–290. Rome: Giorgio Bretschneider

Saguì, L. 1993. Produzioni vetrarie a Roma tra tardo-antico e alto medioevo. In L. Paroli and P. Delogu (eds.) 113–136

Spagnoli, E. 1993. Alcune riflessioni sulla circolazione monetaria in epoca tardoantica a Ostia (Pianabella) e a Porto: i rinvenimenti dagli scavi 1988–1991. In L. Paroli and P. Delogu (eds.) 247–266

Sternini, M. 1989. *Una manifattura vetraria di V secolo a Roma*. Florence: All'insegna del Giglio

Styger, P. 1918. Il monumento apostolico della via Appia. *Dissertazioni della Pontificia Accademia Romana d'Archeologia*, 13: 1–115

Taglietti, F. 1990. Il lato ovest. Le tombe non architettoniche: i modi di sepoltura. In AA.VV. Sepolture e riti nella necropoli dell'Isola Sacra. *Bollettino di Archeologia*, 5–6: 70–75

Young, B. 1977. Paganisme, christianisation et rites funéraires mérovingiens. *Archéologie Médievale*, 7: 5–81

Zanotti, M.G. 1998. Ceramica da fuoco ed acroma depurata. In Smiraglia, E. and Zanotti, M.G. Ceramiche medievali dallo scavo della nuova basilica circiforme della via Ardeatina. In *Le ceramiche di Roma e del Lazio in età medievale e moderna* (ed. E. De Minicis). Atti del III convegno di Studi Roma 19–20 aprile 1996, 171–176. Rome: Edizioni Kappa

28. Intra-mural burials at Rome between the fifth and seventh centuries AD

Roberto Meneghini and Riccardo Santangeli Valenzani[1]

One of the most obvious phenomena to signal the transition from classical antiquity to the early medieval period in Italian cities consists of the spread of burials inside town walls, a spread which seems to be located chronologically between the fifth and sixth centuries AD, in open contrast to the well-known prohibition of classical antiquity on burial within the *pomerium*.

At Rome this phenomenon has for some time aroused the interest of scholars. However in the absence of comprehensive investigations which might bring into focus the true quantitative extent and chronological limits of this problem, interpretations have only generalised from examples of a single aspect of burial practice, such as the connection with cult buildings of some privileged urban burials (Dyggve 1953), or in contrast the exceptional and expedient character of other burials related to the sieges of the Gothic war (Osborne 1984).

In the belief that only a comprehensive analysis could provide data useful for setting out this problem correctly, our research first of all concentrated on establishing an inventory of all the intra-mural burials found at Rome which could be assigned to the centuries between late antiquity and the early medieval period, located through archival and published documentation (Meneghini and Santangeli Valenzani 1993; 1994; 1995). This research resulted in the isolation of 74 sites, all located within the circuit of the Aurelianic wall, at which individual or groups of graves were identified (Fig. 28.1). This inventory puts at our disposal a statistical database sufficient to address some of the problems posed by these burials. The chronological problem is the first to be dealt with. Where these burial areas could be dated on a stratigraphic or epigraphic basis, only at four were burials datable to the fifth century, in contrast to thirty five where burials were datable to the sixth or seventh century. These data allow us to date the spread of the phenomenon of intra-mural burials to the years following the Gothic War. Moreover the few tombs of the fifth century present particular characteristics, occupying public thoroughfares or showing obvious indications of emergency circumstances. It is therefore probable that in the fifth century

the phenomenon was still exceptional, connected to particular crisis periods, such as sieges or outbreaks of plague. The other burial areas which have been identified, datable for the most part between the later sixth and seventh centuries, can be subdivided into at least three types, those connected topographically with cult buildings, large cemetery areas generally placed within public buildings, and small groups of tombs.

The practice of burial within or near churches is widely attested in the literary sources from the sixth century. The written sources reveal the widespread belief that burial in a church assisted the salvation of the soul (e.g. Gregory the Great. *Dialogues*, IV.52). It is therefore understandable that people were prepared to pay to obtain a church burial (Gregory the Great. *Dialogues*, IV.54). The archaeological data confirm conclusions which may be derived from the written sources. Burials placed inside or near cult buildings are often of a more elaborate type than other urban burials; from these burials the majority of funerary inscriptions and all the re-used sarcophagi have been found. All this provides a further demonstration of what was already obvious from an analysis of the written sources, that in the period in question burial within or close to church (like that in the extra-mural martyrial churches), was reserved for socially and economically privileged groups and ecclesiastics.

The majority of the burials recorded was related to cemeteries, sometimes of notable size. The tombs are almost all of a very poor type, generally simple pits enclosed *a cappuccina*, or more rarely, demarcated with and covered by fragments of marble or other re-used material. Burials in coffins are quite rare, with a pit lined with slabs of marble, covered by slabs laid flat or *a cappuccina*.

The choice of the areas in which to locate burials does not seem to be casual; rather public spaces and buildings were evidently preferred which had lost their original function in the new world of the early medieval city, in particular the baths (those of Caracalla, Decius and Diocletian), but also other types of building (the *porticus Liviae*, *castra Praetoria*, the warehouses of the river port,

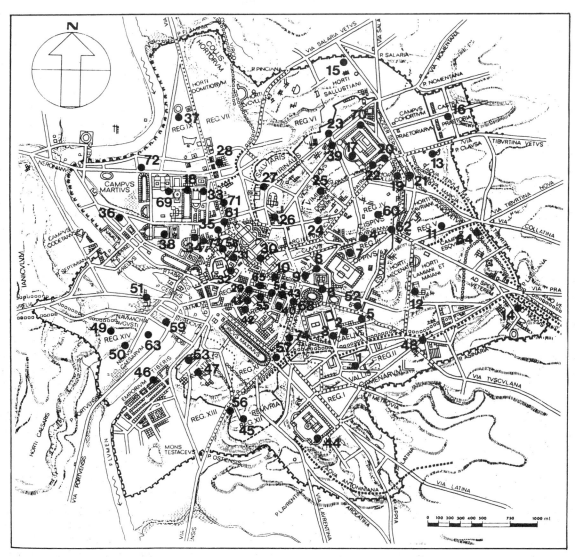

Fig. 28.1 *Individual burials and groups of graves within the Aurelianic walls, Rome, 5th–7th centuries AD*

the Mausoleum of Augustus). It is clear that this framework contrasts with the image of the emergence of intramural as a spontaneous and chaotic phenomenon, linked to a moment of disintegration in the urban fabric and a lack of centres of authority. On the contrary, the substantial continuity between public and private space, and the preference for buildings demarcated by enclosure walls, such as baths and *portici*, indicate the need to hypothesise the existence of authorities able to select the most suitable areas and to impose upon them a use related to changed circumstances.

The third type of burial area consists of small groups of tombs inserted within abandoned public or private buildings. However even in this case the restrictions on the location of burial conditioned by the existing urban structure are recognisable. Often, where it is possible to verify, burials are placed on the peripheries of *insulae* or

on the roadside, without however impinging on their course, thus demonstrating continuity of use and viability of the street network. The examples of tombs re-used on several occasions probably indicate a continuity in the use by family groups of spaces ordained for burial.

The distribution map of burials shows the extensive spread of the phenomenon, which affects the entire area enclosed by the 3rd century walled circuit. It therefore appears impossible to propose a clear distinction between inhabited areas and those converted to cemeteries. The presence of tombs on the edges of streets or public spaces frequented by the living, within buildings in areas for which continued occupation in the early medieval period is documented, just like the very practice of church burial, demonstrate that behind the phenomenon of intra-mural burial lies above all an ideological reason, linked to the radical change in the relationship of society to death. This change reveals itself from the fifth-sixth centuries onwards, a period at which cemeteries enter the cities, to paraphrase the chief student of the phenomenon, introducing the daily presence of the living amidst the dead (Ariès 1977). In the medieval period the cemetery area takes on the character of a public space, integrated into social life, which it maintains up to the 18th century. In the Carolingian period, people gathered in the cemetery to discuss business, fairs and markets developed there, and festivals and balls were held, as a later decree of the Council of Rouen of 1231 testifies (Ariès 1977: 69). The fundamental change in behaviour in the burial customs of the early medieval period with respect to classical antiquity seems obvious.

If the chronological evolution of the phenomenon of intra-mural burial now seems clear enough, it is more problematic to define the context of judicial and administrative practice in which it took place. Already by the third century the administration and religious responsibility of the Roman clergy for suburban cemeteries had been determined; the responsibility for conducting funerals fell to the deacons / *diaconi* placed in charge of the seven ecclesiastical regions, while the sale and purchase of tombs was managed by the *fossores*. From the end of the fifth century and in the sixth century *praepositi* and sometimes priests were in turn responsible for regulating the concessions to acquire burial plots in the extra-mural basilicas, as the epigraphic evidence of the period shows us, in which recurring formulae are cited which certainly repeat those used in charters (Guyon 1974). Taken together these data seem to outline a framework of funerary practice which allows little room for casual burial. If costly burial in connection with a sacred building was reserved for higher social classes and the clergy, even for the lower classes of the population a minimal burial rite and the excavation of a simple pit or tomb *a cappuccina* were anticipated, obliging the participation therefore of at least a priest and *fossores*, in a context of defined specialist roles and appropriate burial location in full legal regularity.

It remains to be verified. from these considerations, what were the circumstances of urban (intra-mural) burial with regard to the state of affairs described in the documentary sources. Until now, as has been seen, it has often been thought that these burials were directly linked to the confusion of the wars of the fifth and sixth centuries, and therefore to be interpreted essentially as evidence for irregular practice. However, as has been seen, the most recent analyses have shown that, if some fifth century intra-mural burials are the products of particular circumstances, the phenomenon increases enormously and is well-established from the second half of the sixth century. Moreover in this period, there appear among the burials, which are almost always *a cappuccina* or simple pits, coffins made from marble slabs, re-used imperial period sarcophagi and masonry *loculi*, all evidence which implies the existence of a trade in these materials and an organisation of specialists employed in their use. Practice does

not therefore differ from that of the suburbs, even if deep uncertainties persist with regard to the nature of the law which, if it existed, must have regulated the cemeteries within the city in a similar way to those outside it. A relevant piece of evidence derives from a single inscription found *in situ* on one of these tombs, a semi-cylindrical coffin excavated in 1895 in the cemetery which developed in the sixth century in the piazza of the Colosseum (Gatti 1895; Rea 1993). The text, cut on a marble tablet set into the side of the tomb, refers in the following terms to Gemmula who was buried there; + *hic est locus For/ tunati et Luciae in quo / iacet filia eorum Gem/mula qui visit an(nos) p(lus) m(inus) X et / qui hunc locum bio/ laberit abet parte cum Iuda* (Martorelli 1993: 657). The content is similar to that of many other contemporaneous inscriptions derived from Rome and the suburbs, but the indication of ownership of the tomb that the parents of Gemmula provide with the opening formula '*hic est locus*' plus genitive is of great interest. The formula recurs, in practically identical form, in other inscriptions of the fifth and sixth centuries, the fuller texts of which also contain explicit declarations of purchase (*comparavit se vivo, se vivi sibi emerunt* etc.), sometimes accompanied by the name of the seller, who is always the *praepositus* of a church. Therefore when their daughter died Fortunatus and Lucia bought the space necessary for the tomb, paid a stone-mason to cut the inscription and masons (*fossores* or *mansionarii*?) for the half-cylindrical coffin, the construction of which demanded a certain expertise, as well as the priest and the cortège. All this implies that the cemetery was organised and managed by whoever had the right to sell *loci*. As no evidence exists for activity of this sort by the civil authority, one is automatically led to conclude that the church hierarchy disposed of urban property intended for funerary use. If one extrapolates from this example to the whole city, allowing the hypothesis of formal organisation and planning of urban burials in the sixth and seventh centuries, a very impressive picture is offered of possible ecclesiastical properties which include, as well as churches proper, baths, public monuments, harbour installations, *insulae* and barracks, all abandoned and disused. The methods of donation which increased the original patrimony of the churches are well-known (Pietri 1976: 77–96), but the issue obviously needs further investigation.

Notwithstanding the slightness of the statistical sample, the analysis of these burials is also of interest for the study of funerary customs. In fact diachronic analysis demonstrates an obvious increase in the deposition of grave goods between the fifth and sixth century (in almost all cases a simple glass or ceramic flask placed near the head of the deceased) concomitant with the spread of intra-mural burial. The presence of this minimal grave furniture is attested in male, female, infant and adult graves, in those connected with cult buildings with which we have suggested the burials of privileged social groups to be associated, and in the graves scattered within

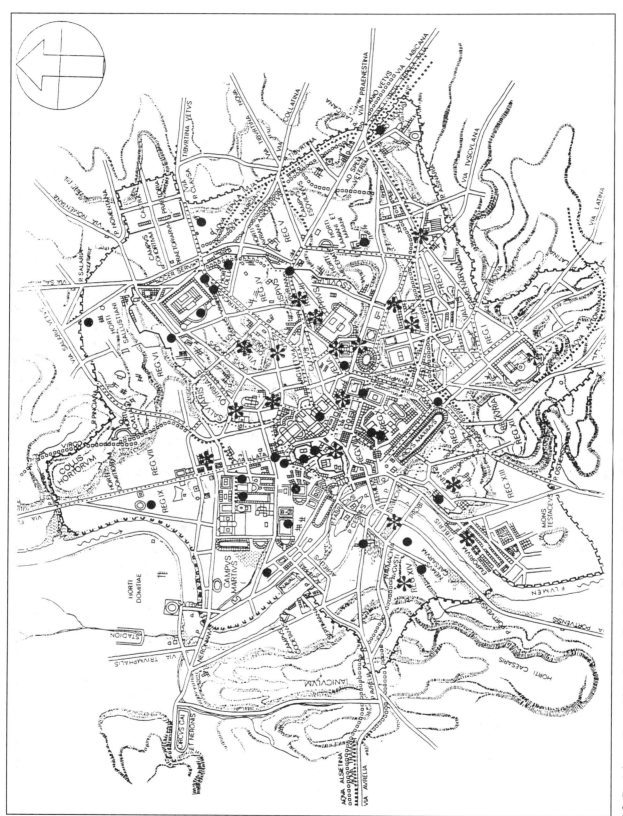

Fig. 28.2 *Burial practices within the Aurelianic walls, Rome, 5th–7th centuries AD (circles – tombs / groups of burials without grave furniture; asterisks – tombs / groups of burials of which at least some with grave furniture)*

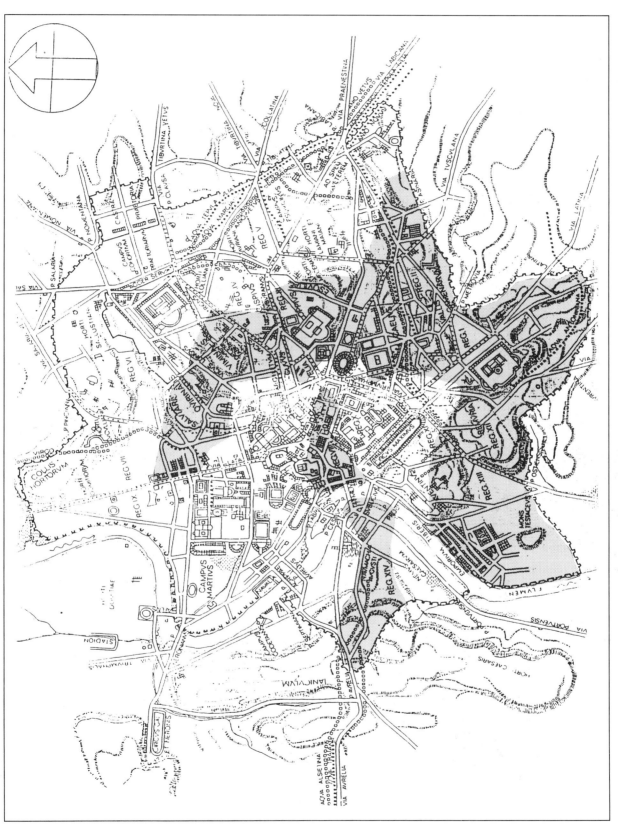

Fig. 28.3 Burial practices within the Aurelianic walls, Rome, 5th–7th centuries AD (areas without tombs with grave goods in white; areas with tombs with grave goods shaded)

abandoned buildings. The presence or absence of grave goods does not therefore indicate a distinction of some sort in the social sphere, but should be seen as evidence for the presence in early medieval Rome of diverse funerary customs (see also del Moro this volume). But did the choice between the different funerary practices depend only on the personal preferences of the family of the deceased, or was it instead conditioned by affiliations to groups with their own cultural traditions which lived together in the city? The comparison with data from other cemeteries in central Italy shows on the one hand the extreme variability of funerary practices, but on the other also a considerable homogeneity within individual groups (Meneghini and Santangeli Valenzani 1994: 326). It seems possible to deduce that in the period in question the deposition of grave furniture in the tomb did not depend on individual choice, but was rather the product of diverse but binding traditions. The incidence at Rome of both funerary customs (i.e. with or without grave goods) may therefore be a clue to the existence in the city of groups of people equipped with their own cultural identity. In this respect the distribution map of burial areas within the city seems quite significant (Fig. 28.2). It seems clear that the two types, tombs and groups of burials with and without grave furniture are not distributed uniformly. This fact emerges even more clearly from Figure 28.3, in which the areas without tombs with grave goods are left white while those areas with cemeteries with grave goods are indicated by shading. The boundaries between the two areas have been established using the method of Thiessen polygons. The results are extremely significant and the areas so homogenous that they cannot be considered the results of chance; cemeteries with grave furniture are limited to a restricted zone in the southern part of the city and to the central strip consisting of the summits of the Quirinal, Viminal, Oppian and Celian hills, plus part of the Forum and of Trastevere. In these areas more than one third of the burials have grave furniture, while in the rest of the city virtually not a single such burial is found. The zone of highest concentration comprises the area of the Celian and Oppian hills, in which the proportion of tombs with grave goods reaches 50%. The presence in both areas of burials or cemeteries dated on a stratigraphic or epigraphic basis to the sixth or beginning of the seventh century does not allow us to attribute the division of the city into zones without tombs with grave goods and others in which they are very well represented to a chronological difference into the use of different parts of the city for burial.

Following the hypothesis of a close connection between cemetery and inhabited areas, a settlement model for sixth century Rome can be proposed in which groups of people with particular cultural traditions occupied different zones of the city. This is a well-known model in studies in historical geography and anthropology in which these parts of cities, characterised by a strong internal economic, ethnic or cultural homogeneity are designated 'natural urban areas' (Park *et al.* 1925; Knox 1987; Ley 1983; Sobrero 1992). These studies have shown how in historically documented contexts the ethnically or culturally based 'natural urban areas' are generally the product of massive immigration movements following which the new arrivals, if not obstructed by excessive population density, tend to aggregate according to their ethnic or cultural affiliation. It seems plausible to hypothesise a similar process for sixth century Rome, given that the existence of immigration after the devastation of the Gothic War is explicitly attested in the literary sources (Procopius. *Bell. Goth.* VII, 24), and the very low population density assisted the formation of 'natural urban areas' based on ethnicity or culture. Among the dead buried with grave furniture one might therefore recognise immigrants derived from zones or groups in which the use of grave goods was still practised and which for two or three generations continued to follow their traditional custom. Thus they distinguished themselves both from the indigenous population which had almost completely abandoned such a practice, as well as possibly from other groups of immigrants which followed different traditions. The distressing scarcity of data from occupied areas and private buildings from early medieval Rome makes it currently impossible to recognise archaeologically other distinctive traits of the different cultural traditions of immigrant groups, and it is therefore a hopeless task to attempt to distinguish their geographical provenance. However, whatever the origin of the new arrivals, the uniformity of funerary practice documented at least from the mid-seventh century, with the disappearance of grave goods and the progressive aggregation of burials around cult places, is probably an index of their final integration with the indigenous population.

Notes

1. Translated by John Pearce, who would like to thank Daniela Colomo for her comments on the translation.

Bibliography

Ariès, P. 1977. *L'homme devant la mort.* Paris: Editions du Seuil

Dyggve, E. 1953. L'origine del cimitero entro la cinta della città. *Studi bizantini e neoellenici,* 8: 137–141

Gatti, G. 1895. Roma: nuove scoperte nella città e nel suburbio. Regione III. *Notizie Scavi,* 201–207

Guyon, J. 1974. La vente des tombes à travers l'épigraphie de la Rome chrétienne (III–VII siècles): le role des *fossores, mansionarii, praepositi* et prétres. *Mélanges de l'Ecole Française de Rome Archéologie,* 86: 549–596

Knox, P. 1987. *Urban Social Geography.* Burnt Mill: Longman

Ley, D. 1983. *A Social Geography of the City.* New York: Harper and Row

Martorelli, R. 1993. L'epigrafe di Gemmula, Appendice a Rea 1993: 657

Meneghini, R. and Santangeli Valenzani R. 1993. Sepolture intramuranee e paesaggio urbano a Roma tra V e VII secolo. In P. Delogu and L. Paroli (eds) *La storia economica di Roma nell'Altomedioevo alla luce dei recenti scavi archeologici*, 89–111. Florence: All'Insegna del Giglio

Meneghini, R. and Santangeli Valenzani R. 1994. Corredi funerari, produzioni e paesaggio sociale a Roma tra VI e VII secolo. *Rivista di Archeologia Cristiana*, 70: 321–337

Meneghini, R. and Santangeli Valenzani R. 1995. Sepolture intramuranee a Roma tra V e VII secolo d.C. – Aggiornamenti e considerazioni. *Archeologia Medievale*, 22: 283–290

Osborne, J. 1984. Death and burial in sixth-century Rome. *Echos du Monde Classique* (NS), 27: 291–299.

Park, R., Burgess, E.W. and McKenzie, R.D. 1925. *The City*. Chicago: University of Chicago

Pietri, C. 1976. *Roma Christiana. recherches sur l'Eglise de Rome, son organisation, sa politique, son idéologie de Miltiade a Sixte III (311–341)*, Rome: Ecole Française.

Rea, R. 1993. L'uso funerario della Valle del Colosseo tra tardo antico e altomedioevo. *Archeologia Medievale*, 20: 645–658

Sobrero, A.M. 1992. *Antropologia della Città*. Rome: La Nuova Italia Scientifica

Afterword

Richard Reece

In about 1980 I attended a conference on Roman Burial in Oxford and my contribution turned into the paper published in 1982 called Bones, Bodies and Dis-ease (Reece 1982). This was a cry of dissatisfaction at the state of Roman burial studies and a tribute to Calvin Wells the doctor and palaeopathologist who had died sometime earlier. I learned later, during the viva of a Ph D thesis, that it caused one participant to start the research for his thesis. Rob Philpott was disturbed by my statement that a study of Roman burial in Britain was an impossibly diverse subject for research, and set out to prove me wrong (Philpott 1991) By the time of the 1997 conference in Durham some aspects of the subject had moved on. I was unable to attend the conference for the most appropriate of reasons, a death in the family, but I have since read and thought about all the papers which make up this volume.

One difference between my earlier approach and the majority of these contributions is the difference between the inhumations of the later empire and the cremation burials of the early empire. This makes any repetition of my earlier remarks even more than irrelevant. Thus there is a lack of interest in bones in their own right in this volume, and the avoidance of what might be called Lankhills-type analyses of grave assemblages. Is there instead another suite of models or ideas which form the current mental set or fashion? I hope I am not being negative if I say that I cannot see one. Burial studies seem to be, if anything, more fragmented than in 1980 though they also seem to be more integrated into the good and bad aspects of national and regional archaeologies.

The volume demonstrates the diversity of modern archaeological approach with some contributors being happy with terms such as native and Roman, ethnic and racial while others veer away from what they see as the extreme complexities of such descriptions. Worries about accusations of political incorrectness have also taken their toll of usable words. Written sources have been given very different treatment in different papers and this also reflects national and regional backgrounds as well as trendiness and conservatism. For some, written sources

mean what they say, and ancient words can be translated into modern words. For others ancient sources need as much interpretation as ancient material, and ancient words can be no more than indicators of ancient opinions.

These trends mean that in many cases what is reported is not burial archaeology, but the use of information from the excavation of human remains in a multitude of different studies. In one sense this is good because human remains are taking their place in the acceptable repertoire of ancient material gathered through excavation and survey. Just as digging up coins is not considered a particular branch of archaeology, so the finding of human remains is being taken on board as part of the general work. But both coins and bodies need specialist comment and identification and it is at this point that opportunities can be lost.

Coins can be found by the excavators, recorded, and sent off to a specialist. The specialist, if divorced from archaeology, may identify the coins, make a list, and send them back. The coin list appears in the final report with perhaps a few dates quoted in the summary of phasing; if nothing more is done a lot of information may be lost, and many possible ideas may never be heard. There is always the need for comment from someone who is interested both in the coins themselves, their distribution on the site, and the comparison of the site in question with local and regional variation in coin loss.

Bodies from cemeteries pose even more opportunities and problems than coins. The human remains need expert comment to reveal evidence of disease, abnormality, pathology, and personal history. This is the equivalent to the identification of the coin, but is much more time-consuming, and needs much more knowledge and experience. If the details are sent back to the excavator at this stage and simply incorporated as a specialist report a whole range of potential information will not be found. The information on the inhumed or cremated bodies needs to be written in to the final report as thoroughly as the stratigraphy and the structures. Clearly, in any report the stratigraphy and the sequence are primary elements, but in a cemetery report the human remains should take the place of the walls and floors of the Roman villa, or the plan and decoration of a temple.

But an account of a cemetery is not just a sympathetic account of human remains – this would be total incompetence. What matters is the full discussion of burial archaeology. Once the accurate account of the human remains has been understood by the people writing the report they have to go forward to use this information in the light of local, regional and even empire-wide surveys. Some readers may regard this as obvious and hardly worth mentioning, others may regard it as impossible. But unless it happens to some extent total nonsense may result. Total isolation would produce without comment the report of a cemetery firmly dated to the early fourth century in the middle of France in which all the bodies had been cremated. This is of course impossible because there is a general knowledge that burial in the fourth century within the empire is generally inhumation. This is the point that I am making: publication must be informed by local, regional and wider comparison. The report that I think comes nearest to my ideals here is publication of the cemetery of Saint-Martin-de-Fontenay in Normandy in which all aspects of the bone study and the excavation have been sewn together in a single narrative (Pilet 1994, review Reece 1995).

This brings us on to my other remaining concerns which may have some potential for future study. I hope that the subjects are as applicable to cremation burials as to inhumations but I fear that the detail obtainable from burnt bone partially collected from the pyre will always be less than detail obtainable from a complete skeleton. In a sense my concerns are shared by archaeology in general – the characterisation of groups of people and the geographical description of human discontinuity. Both subjects are regarded as dangerous and both can be and have been misused in the present day, but this should not stop archaeologists following such research provided it is done thoroughly and written up sensitively.

The point that interests me about burial is that in a given society it is a focus for substantial ritual and fashion which needs major input to alter its inherent tendency to continuity. Change in the burial record is likely to record change in the society, and sudden change in the record, a major change in the society. None of the converse propositions is necessarily true. A grave, simply cut, with nothing more than a body set out in it makes no comment at all on the presence or absence of ritual at the time of burial; it may be the end product of weeks of intricate mourning. Continuity of burial record is no guarantee of continuity of social habit. There may be a total social revolution with complete continuity of burial practice. Slow changes which archaeologists find overwhelming can sometimes be shown from the burial record to include many aspects of continuity. The change from cremation burial to inhumation in the Roman empire often shows long-term elements of continuous ritual as in the suite of pots in both types of burial at Gerulata (Kraskovska 1976).

With such variation possible in the move from material observation to interpretation it is worrying that there has not been more effort put in to comparative Roman studies and the testing of hypotheses offered in interpretation.

This reaches the point which is the most dangerous but also has the greatest potential. Many papers in the volume are concerned with changes in the burial record, and these are harnessed at the wish of the excavators or writers to local problems of conquest, Romanization, invasion, de-Romanization, or religious change. Any change in the burial record can be seen, recorded and described with reasonable accuracy but interpretation immediately demands comparative information to be anything more than an exercise in fantasy. If it can be shown that change in custom is accompanied by discontinuity of skeletal characteristics then the way is open to propose invasion, war, conquest, or some other method of replacement of an earlier local population. Such interpretations are not proved, but they at least become possible. If the population, judged from its skeletal characteristics, is not seen to change, then it is more difficult to propose invasion, conquest or population replacement as the prime mover of change in burial rite, and some form of fashion change, from religious to commercial, seems more likely.

At Frénouville in Normandy (Pilet 1980) it was stated in the report that there was no reason to distinguish the people buried with objects in the Roman fashion from those buried with objects in the Merovingian fashion. The population showed no new characteristics in the fifth century AD and there seemed to have been little change in the area back as far as earlier prehistory. Pilet and Buchet continued their work at Saint-Martin-de-Fontenay, also in Normandy (Pilet 1994) but there some exotic objects do seem to be related to skeletal differences. The differences quoted are more to do with observation than with metrical analysis, but that aspect may receive more attention in the future. In Britain Heinrich Härke has shown that in Anglo-Saxon burials the people with weapons tend to be taller than the rest (Härke 1992: chapter 7) and, since physical height is characteristic of Germanic rather than British people, this observation seems to be consistent with a foreign military elite in post-Roman Britain. It could equally well be interpreted by those who fail to see a direct connection between cultural objects and national or ethnic groupings, as evidence that the Sub-Roman Securicor operated a firm set of recruitment criteria whether the applicant was Briton, Roman, Pict, or Saxon — whatever those labels might mean.[1] If, on the other hand, a majority of those weapon-bearing people had similarly unusual wormian bones in the skull, not otherwise known from Roman Britain, the case for population movement would have been advanced.

I hope the potential of such work is clear. I also described it as dangerous and that probably needs to be made explicit. We are in a time in which mental persecution and outright physical elimination of "others" is common whether in Britain, in the former Jugoslavia, or the Middle East. Perhaps for this reason a recent week-end conference in Oxford on Romanization failed to hear once the mention of immigrants, displacement, or replacement. I think this is to take sensitivity too far. Archaeological discussion of race, ethnicity, nationality, or culture has always had both a neutral and a bad side. To avoid such areas of enquiry for the present will fool no one. Those who want to justify their unpleasant claims will simply go back to earlier, and often less accurate, archaeological writing.

But this is not to object to the recent developments of use of words such as "ethnic". It has clearly been over-used, and in that over-use had lost much of any earlier meaning. What matters to me is the discovery during such use that judgements of ethnicity, or ethnic labels, mean very different things both to different users and to observers. They can be used to say something about others as well as to say something about ourselves, and both types of label may change substantially in a short time scale. This commonplace in prehistoric archaeology now needs to be applied rather more to interpretations of the Roman period so that the Roman-ness of some objects or customs is seen more as a statement by their users than a safe label of origin (from the City of Rome) for the use of archaeologists. At the other end of the Roman period the label Germanic should not be used unless it is qualified as geographical, art-historical, fashionable, or skeletal.

This leads to the last of my points of discomfort. If we work thoroughly on the skeletal material provided by burial archaeology we are still in uncharted territory so far as geographical distribution is concerned. This brings us back to the beginning. To make a valid interpretative statement from our repeatable observations of the material we need comparative information. There is no point in saying that a cranial index in this cemetery has a mean value of 10.4 if that value is the same in all known cemeteries. It is no more interesting or informative than a statement which says that human bodies were buried in the cemetery. Mummified ibises or cats would provide a point of difference and therefore of interest.

This is the problem with the Frénouville study of population. The skeletal characteristics are thought to be uniform in the area over the period which sees the end of the Roman empire and possibly for several centuries before. But how large is this area? If the characteristics changed slowly in cemeteries moving from the Seine eastwards to the Rhine so that people in cemeteries east of the Rhine were distinguishable as populations from those buried west of the Seine it would be possible to say that the people wearing Merovingian ornaments at Frénouville had probably not come from the area of modern Germany. We urgently need some idea of the geographical distributions of skeletal differences in the Roman period – or absences of difference over wide areas – so that population movements can be seen more easily and more reliably. In such an obscure area as coin studies we are beginning to see differences of coin use throughout the empire; skeletal study lags behind. I hope this does not mean that we now regard money as more important than people.

Note

1. I am very grateful to Dr Härke for gently pointing out that a greater mean height for Anglo-Saxon weapon-bearers, which is what he has established, does not mean that all weapon-bearers are tall. Since the range of heights is similar for weapon-bearers and the rest, my evidence for a Selective Securicor in post-Roman Britain crumbles.

Bibliography

Härke H. 1992. *Angelsächsische Waffengräber des 5 bis 7 Jahrhunderts*, Zeitschrift für Archäologie des Mittelalters Beiheft 6, Köln

Kraskovska L. 1976. *The Roman cemetery at Gerulata Rusovce*, BAR (Supplementary Series) 10, Oxford

Philpott R 1991. *Burial practices in Roman Britain*, BAR (British Series) 219, Oxford

Pilet, C. 1980. *La nécropole de Frénouville*. BAR (International Series) 83, Oxford

Pilet, C. 1994. *La nécropole de Saint-Martin-de-Fontenay, Calvados*. Gallia supplément 54, Paris

Reece R. 1982. Bones, bodies and dis-ease. *Oxford Journal of Archaeology* 1/3, 347–58

Reece R. 1995. Bones, bangles and barbarians: towards the perfect cemetery report. *Antiquity* 69/293, 414–7